ESSENTIALS

of Managed Health Care

Second Edition

Peter R. Kongstvedt, MD, FACP
Partner
Ernst & Young LLP
Washington, DC

AN ASPEN PUBLICATION®
Aspen Publishers, Inc.
Gatihersburg, Maryland
1997

Library of Congress Cataloging-in-Publication Data

Essentials of managed health care / [edited by] Peter R. Kongstvedt. -- 2nd ed.
p. cm.
Includes bibliographical references and index.
ISBN: 0-8342-0913-6
1. Managed care plans (Medical care)--Management.
I. Kongstvedt, Peter R. (Peter Reid)
[DNLM: 1. Managed Care Programs--organization & administration--United States. 2. Delivery of Health Care--economics--United States. W 130 AA1 E7 1997]
RA413.E87 1997
362.1'04258--dc21
DNLM/DLC
for Library of Congress
96-48815
CIP

For information, address Aspen Publishers, Inc., Permissions Department, 200 Orchard Ridge Drive, Suite 200, Gaithersburg, Maryland 20878.

Customer Service: (800) 234-1660
Orders: (800) 638-8437

Editorial Resources: Ruth Bloom

Library of Congress Catalog Card Number: 96-48815
ISBN: 0-8342-0913-6

Printed in the United States of America

2 3 4 5

This book is
dedicated to two of the finest
teachers that ever were, my parents:
my late father, Gerald Nicholas Kongstvedt and
my mother, Elizabeth Pearson Kongstvedt.

Table of Contents

Contributors

Frederick B. Abbey, MPA
National Director
Legislative and Regulatory Services
National Health Care Practice
Ernst & Young LLP
Washington, DC

Donald F. Anderson, PhD
Leader
National Behavioral Health Consulting Team
William M. Mercer, Incorporated
San Francisco, California

Jeffrey L. Berlant, MD, PhD
Senior Consultant
National Behavioral Health Unit
William M. Mercer, Incorporated
San Francisco, California

Thomas W. Bone, MCHA
Director
Products and Services
EDS State Health Care
Phoenix, Arizona

Garry Carneal, Esq.
President
Utilization Review Accreditation Commission (URAC)
Washington, DC

Stephen M. Cigich, FSA
Consulting Actuary
Milliman & Robertson, Inc.
Milwaukee, Wisconsin

Peter D. Fox, PhD
President
PDF Incorporated
Chevy Chase, Maryland

Dale F. Harding
Senior Manager
East/Great Lakes Healthcare Practice
Ernst & Young LLP
Iselin, New Jersey

Robert E. Hurley, PhD
Associate Professor
Department of Health Administration
Medical College of Virginia
Richmond, Virginia

Mark S. Joffe, Esq
Law Offices of Mark S. Joffe
Washington, DC

Leonard J. Kirschner, MD, MPH
Vice President
Health Care Initiatives
EDS State Health Care
Phoenix, Arizona

Peter R. Kongstvedt, MD, FACP
Partner
Ernst & Young LLP
Washington, DC

Glenn L. Laffel, MD, PhD
Executive Vice President for Medical Affairs
Preferred Health Systems LLC
Bethesda, Maryland

Jean D. LeMasurier
Director
Policy and Program Improvement
Office of Managed Care
Health Care Financing Administration
Baltimore, Maryland

William R. Maloney
Principal
Behavioral Healthcare Practice
William M. Mercer, Incorporated
San Francisco, California

Danna Mauch, PhD
President and Chief Operating Officer
Magellan Public Solutions, Inc.
Boston, Massachusetts

David B. Nash, MD, MBA
Director of Health Policy
Thomas Jefferson University
Philadelphia, Pennsylvania

Jerry R. Peters, Esq.
Partner
Health Care Practice Group
Latham & Watkins
San Francisco, California

David W. Plocher, MD
Partner
Health Care Consulting Practice
Ernst & Young LLP
Minneapolis, Minnesota

Robert Reese
Partner
Health Care Consulting Practice
Ernst & Young LLP
Detroit, Michigan

Pamela B. Siren, BSN
Director of Clinical Development
Lazo, Gertman & Associates
Waltham, Massachusetts

Richard L. Solit, MD
Fellow
Office of Health Policy and Clinical Outcomes
Resident
Department of Surgery
Thomas Jefferson University Hospital
Philadelphia, Pennsylvania

Eric R. Wagner, MBA
Vice President for Managed Care
Medlantic Healthcare Group
Washington Hospital Center
Executive Director
WHC Physician-Hospital Organization
Washington, DC

Carlos Zarabozo
Social Science Research Analyst
Special Analysis Staff
Office of the Associate Administrator for Policy
Health Care Financing Administration
Baltimore, Maryland

Preface

This text book has as its parent *The Managed Health Care Handbook, Third Edition.* When the first edition of that book was written and published, managed health care was still occasionally referred to as an "alternative delivery system." The alternative has now become mainstream. But as the American health care system has continued to evolve at an equally rapid pace. This evolution* means new approaches to managing cost, quality, and access will be created; some will fail, others will succeed and lead to still more changes in the near future.

The rate of the rise of health care costs has been variable. The shocking increases experienced in the early 1990's has slowed in the mid- and late 1990s, but there is no guarantee that they will continue to do so. Managed health care has been effective in holding down the rate of rise, but many of the fundamental reasons that lead to rises in health care costs are still with us today. These include:

- rapidly developing (and usually expensive) technology,
- cost shifting by providers to pay for care rendered to patients who either cannot pay or are covered by systems that do not pay the full cost of care,
- shifting demographics as our population ages,
- high (and not unreasonable) expectations for a long and healthy life,
- the current legal environment leading to defensive medicine,
- administrative costs related to the care that is delivered,
- wide variations in efficiencies and quality of care that is rendered by all types of providers (professional and institutional),
- serious inequities and variations in incomes among all types of providers (regardless of efficiency or quality),
- decreased levels of available public dollars to pay for health care in entitlement programs, and
- a myriad of other reasons.

In the three-year interval between the publication of the prior edition of this book and this edition, there have been enough changes in the health care system to warrant a considerable revision and expansion of this academic text. Many chapters have been entirely rewritten, some have been modified and added to, and some other topics are addressed for the first time.

Because this text is drawn from a much larger and more comprehensive book, the reader of this text will find that while the essentials of managed health care are indeed covered (especially medical and network management), there are a great many topics that are found only in the larger, parent publication. Such a reduction in comprehensiveness is required in order for this text to be affordable, accessible, and appropriate to most post-graduate academic programs. The reader who seeks more knowledge and information is referred to *The Managed Health Care Handbook, Third Edition* for discussions on the following topics:

- Acquisitions, Joint Ventures, and Partnerships between Providers and Managed Care Organizations

* Or in some cases, mutation.

- Compensation of Physicians in Medical Groups and Integrated Delivery Systems
- Specialty Networks from The Specialist's View
- Community Health Centers and Managed Care
- Case Management
- Clinical Paths
- Pharmaceutical Services in Managed Care
- Subacute Care and Managed Care
- Claims and Benefits Administration
- Other Party Liability and Coordination of Benefits
- Optimizing Health Plan Operations
- Assessing the Market for Managed Care
- Marketing Managed Health Care Plans
- The Employer's View of Managed Health Care
- External Accreditation of Managed Care Plans
- Risk Management in Managed Care
- Taxation of Managed Health Care Plans
- Actuarial Services in an Integrated Delivery System
- Operational Underwriting in Managed Care Organizations (although basic rating and underwriting are discussed in this text)
- The Federal Employees Health Benefit Program
- Medicare Risk Plans from the Health Plan's View
- CHAMPUS and the Department of Defense Managed Care Programs
- HMOs in Rural Markets
- Dental HMOs
- Workers' Compensation
- Federal Qualification
- Antitrust Implications of Provider Exclusion
- Medical Management and Legal Obligations to Members
- ERISA and Managed Care
- Effective Utilization of Legal Services

Although the chapters in *The Essentials of Managed Health Care, Second Edition* do not absolutely need to be read in order, they are presented in a logical order; the reader will gain better understanding by approaching the topics in the order presented. Chapters cross-reference each other when necessary. There is a glossary at the back of the book for those times when the acronyms run heavy or the terms become obtuse.

The book is intended to provide practical advice based on the experiences, both firsthand and observed, of managers and experienced consultants in the industry as it exists today. The book is also highly biased: my biases as well as those of the contributing authors. There is no shortage of impassioned opinions in this industry, and many of those opinions are held with nearly religious zeal. That means that there will be those who disagree with what they read here, and some of what will be presented in the following pages will become outdated, perhaps even as the book is published. Still, the information in this book has been created with a single focus: to enable the reader to succeed better in the world of managed health care.

Peter Reid Kongstvedt
McLean, Virginia

Acknowledgments

I wish to acknowledge and thank the following individuals for their help during the creation of this new edition of *The Essentials of Managed Health Care*. First, I want to thank Jack Bruggeman for getting things rolling, painful as that was. I also wish to thank Amy Martin and Bob Howard for their help in collecting research information and tracking and assisting the progress of the book in its protracted first stages. Ruth Bloom and Barbara Priest carried out the difficult task of copy editing the text and finding the errors and vagaries that I missed in compiling the manuscript; their efforts are much appreciated.

Lisa Shreve of the American Association of Health Plans (AAHP; formerly GHAA/AMCRA) provided some good referrals and advice while I was planning the content. I wish to express sincere thanks to Nina Lane and especially to Erin Carlson for their invaluable help in collecting research information from the AAHP library. Although I cannot name them all, since to do so would double the size of this book, I thank my many colleagues and friends in the managed care industry with whom I have had the pleasure both to work beside and to compete with over the years.

I can only express my appreciation and gratitude to my long-suffering and neglected wife and son for putting up with me during the many months I was an utter boor and bore during the creation of this text. Last, I want to give heartfelt thanks to the many readers of previous editions for the support and kind words that have fueled my ability to do it again.

Part I

Introduction to Managed Health Care

"Grasp the subject, the words will follow."

Marcus Porcius Cato [Cato the Elder]
(234–149 B.C.)
CAIUS JULIUS VICTOR,
Ars Rhetorica, I [4th century A.D.]

"You know more than you think you do."

Benjamin Spock, M.D. (b. 1903)
Baby and Child Care (1945)

Chapter 1

An Overview of Managed Care

Peter D. Fox

Study Objectives

- Understand the evolution of managed care, including the forces that have driven this evolution
- Understand current trends in managed care, including how market dynamics have changed over time
- Understand the public policy and market performance issues facing managed care

Managed care is rapidly dominating the health care financing and delivery system in the United States. To illustrate, health maintenance organization (HMO) enrollment reached 51 million in 1994. Although the estimates are less reliable, by all accounts the number of persons enrolled in preferred provider organizations (PPOs) and their variants rivals the number enrolled in HMOs.[1] Even traditional plans are adopting principles of managed care; for example, hospital precertification and large case management, daring innovations as recently as a decade ago, have become the norm in indemnity insurance. Public sector, notably Medicare and Medicaid, reliance on managed care is growing rapidly.

Managed care has also become a big business. Some 36.7 million HMO enrollees are in multistate firms, including nonprofits such as Kaiser and the HMOs owned by the various Blue Cross and Blue Shield plans (which operate largely autonomously).[2] Many of the large managed care companies are traded on the New York Stock Exchange and other stock exchanges, and the general business press regularly reports their profits along with the compensation of the chief executive officers, which can amount to millions of dollars annually.

When one thinks of managed care, one should distinguish between the techniques of managed care and the organization that performs the various functions. Managed care can embody a wide variety of techniques, which are discussed throughout this book. These include various forms of financial incentives for providers, promotion of wellness, early identification of disease, patient education, self-care, and all aspects of utilization management.

A wide variety of organizations can implement managed care techniques, of which the HMO has the potential to align financing and delivery most closely by virtue of enrollees' being (with some exceptions) required to use network providers. Managed care techniques can

---

Peter D. Fox, Ph.D., is an independent consultant, located in Chevy Chase, MD, specializing in managed care. His clients have included HMOs, PPOs, provider groups, employers, Taft-Hartley trust funds, government agencies, and foundations. He is the author of numerous articles and books.

The author is most grateful for the helpful comments of John Gabel (American Association of Health Plans), Peter Kongstvedt (Ernst & Young), Kenneth Linde (Principal Health Care), Robert Lurie (HealthCare Connections), Margaret O'Kane (National Committee for Quality Assurance), and George Strumpf (Health Insurance Plan of Greater New York).

also be employed directly by employers, insurers, union–management (Taft-Hartley) trust funds, and the Medicare and Medicaid programs. They can also be implemented by PPOs, organizations that allow enrollees to be reimbursed for care delivered by nonnetwork providers, although the enrollees face higher out-of-pocket payments (i.e., cost sharing) if they do. Finally, a variety of hybrid arrangements have evolved. One example is the point-of-service (POS) program, which operates as a PPO except that, to receive the highest level of benefits, the enrollee must obtain a referral from a primary care physician who is part of the contracted network. Increasingly, the arrangements are difficult to characterize, let alone profile statistically, in a meaningful manner.

MANAGED CARE: THE EARLY YEARS (BEFORE 1970)

Whatever its role today, managed care had humble origins and struggled to survive in its early years. To some extent it still struggles today, as evidenced by the controversies, mostly at the state level, surrounding "any willing provider" legislation and other legislative proposals that constrain the development of managed care (see Chapter 2). This section addresses the development of HMOs and other managed care organizations rather than focusing on techniques.

Sometimes cited as the first example of an HMO, or prepaid group practice as it was known until the early 1970s, is the Western Clinic in Tacoma, Washington.[3] Starting in 1910, the Western Clinic offered, exclusively through its own providers, a broad range of medical services in return for a premium payment of $0.50 per member per month. The program was available to lumber mill owners and their employees and served to assure the clinic a flow of patients and revenues. A similar program was developed by a Dr. Bridge, who started a clinic in Tacoma that later expanded to 20 sites in Oregon and Washington.

In 1929, Michael Shadid, M.D., established a rural farmers' cooperative health plan in Elk City, Oklahoma by forming a lay organization of leading farmers in the community. Participating farmers purchased shares for $50 each to raise capital for a new hospital in return for receiving medical care at a discount.[4] For his trouble, Dr. Shadid lost his membership in the county medical society and was threatened with having his license to practice suspended. Some 20 years later, however, he was vindicated through the out-of-court settlement in his favor of an antitrust suit against the county and state medical societies.[5] In 1934 the Farmers Union assumed control of both the hospital and the health plan.

Health insurance itself is of relatively recent origin. In 1929, Baylor Hospital in Texas agreed to provide some 1,500 teachers prepaid care at its hospital, an arrangement that represented the origins of Blue Cross. The program was subsequently expanded to include the participation of other employers and hospitals, initially as single hospital plans. Starting in 1939, state medical societies in California and elsewhere created, generally statewide, Blue Shield plans, which reimbursed for physician services. At the time, commercial health insurance was not a factor.[6]

The formation of the various Blue Cross and Blue Shield plans in the midst of the Great Depression, as well as that of many HMOs, reflected not consumers demanding coverage or nonphysician entrepreneurs seeking to establish a business but rather providers wanting to protect and enhance patient revenues. Many of these developments were threatening to organized medicine. In 1932, the American Medical Association (AMA) adopted a strong stance against prepaid group practices, favoring, instead, indemnity type insurance. The AMA's position was in response to both the small number of prepaid group practices in existence at the time and the findings in 1932 of the Committee on the Cost of Medical Care—a highly visible private group of leaders from medicine, dentistry, public health, consumers, and so forth—that recommended the expansion of group practice as an efficient delivery system. The AMA's stance at the national level set the tone for continued state and local medical society opposition to prepaid group practice.

The period immediately surrounding World War II saw the formation of several HMOs that are among the leaders today. They encountered varying degrees of opposition from local medical societies. They represent a diversity of origins with the initial impetus coming, variously, from employers, providers seeking patient revenues, consumers seeking access to improved and affordable health care, and even a housing lending agency seeking to reduce the number of foreclosures. The following are examples of other early HMOs:

- The Kaiser Foundation Health Plans were started in 1937 by Dr. Sidney Garfield at the behest of the Kaiser construction company, which sought to finance medical care, initially, for workers and families who were building an aqueduct in the southern California desert to transport water from the Colorado River to Los Angeles and, subsequently, for workers who were constructing the Grand Coulee Dam in Washington state. A similar program was established in 1942 at Kaiser shipbuilding plants in the San Francisco Bay area. Kaiser Foundation Health Plans now serve 16 states and the District of Columbia and, as of July 1, 1994, had 7.3 million members.
- In 1937, the Group Health Association (GHA) was started in Washington, D.C. at the behest of the Home Owner's Loan Corporation to reduce the number of mortgage defaults that resulted from large medical expenses. It was created as a nonprofit consumer cooperative, with the board being elected periodically by the enrollees. The District of Columbia Medical Society opposed the formation of GHA. It sought to restrict hospital admitting privileges for GHA physicians and threatened expulsion from the medical society. A bitter antitrust battle ensued that culminated in the U.S. Supreme Court's ruling in favor of GHA. In 1994, faced with insolvency despite an enrollment of some 128,000, GHA was acquired by Humana Health Plans, a for-profit, publicly traded corporation.[7]
- In 1944, at the behest of New York City, which was seeking coverage for its employees, the Health Insurance Plan (HIP) of Greater New York was formed. HIP is currently licensed in New York, New Jersey, and Florida and, as of July 1, 1994, had 1.1 million members.
- In 1947, consumers in Seattle organized 400 families, who contributed $100 each, to form the Group Health Cooperative of Puget Sound. Predictably, opposition was encountered from the Kings County Medical Society. Group Health Cooperative remains a consumer cooperative and had 588,000 members as of July 1, 1994.[8]

Only in later years did nonprovider entrepreneurs form for-profit HMOs in significant numbers.

The early individual practice association (IPA) type of HMOs, which contract with physicians in independent fee-for-service practice, was a competitive reaction to group practice-based HMOs. The basic structure was created in 1954, when the San Joaquin County Medical Society in California formed the San Joaquin Medical Foundation in response to competition from Kaiser. The foundation established a relative value fee schedule for paying physicians, heard grievances against physicians, and monitored quality of care. It became licensed by the state to accept capitation payment, making it the first IPA model HMO.

THE ADOLESCENT YEARS: 1970–1985

Through the 1960s and into the early 1970s, HMOs played only a modest role in the financing and delivery of health care, although they were a significant presence in a few communities, such as the Seattle area and parts of California. In 1970 the total number of HMOs was in the 30s, the exact number depending on one's definition.[9] The years since the early 1970s represent a period of vastly accelerated developments that are still unfolding.

The major boost to the HMO movement during this period was the enactment in 1973 of the federal HMO Act. That act, as described below, both authorized start-up funding and, more important, ensured access to the employer-based insurance market. It evolved from discussions that Paul Ellwood, M.D., had in 1970 with the political leadership of the U.S. Department of Health, Education, and Welfare (which later became the Department of Health and Human Services).[10] Ellwood had been personally close to Philip Lee, M.D., Assistant Secretary for Health during the presidency of Lyndon Johnson (and again in the Clinton administration), and participated in designing the Health Planning Act of 1966.

Ellwood, sometimes referred to as the father of the modern HMO movement, was asked in the early Nixon years to devise ways of constraining the rise in the Medicare budget. Out of those discussions evolved both a proposal to capitate HMOs for Medicare beneficiaries (which was not enacted until 1982) and the laying of the groundwork for what became the HMO Act of 1973. The desire to foster HMOs reflected the perspective that the fee-for-service system, by rewarding paying physicians based on their volume of services, incorporated the wrong incentives. Also, the term *health maintenance organization* was coined as a substitute for *prepaid group practice*, principally because it had greater public appeal.

The main features of the HMO Act were the following:

- Grants and loans were available for the planning and start-up phases of new HMOs as well as for service area expansions for existing HMOs.
- State laws that restricted the development of HMOs were overridden for HMOs that were federally qualified, as described below.
- Most important of all were the "dual choice" provisions, which required that employers with 25 or more employees that offered indemnity coverage also offer two federally qualified HMOs, one of each type—that is the closed panel or group or staff model, or the open panel or IPA/network model—if the plans made a formal request* (the different model types are discussed in Chapter 3). Most HMOs were reluctant to exercise the mandate, fearing that doing so would antagonize employers, who would in turn discourage employees from enrolling.

The statute also established a process under which HMOs could elect to be federally qualified. To do so, the plans had to satisfy a series of requirements, such as meeting minimum benefit package standards set forth in the act, demonstrating that their provider networks were adequate, having a quality assurance system, meeting standards of financial stability, and having an enrollee grievance system. Some states emulated these requirements and adopted them for all HMOs that were licensed in the state regardless of federal qualification status.

Obtaining federal qualification has always been at the discretion of the individual HMO, unlike state licensure, which is mandatory. Plans that requested federal qualification did so for four principal reasons. First, it represented a "Good Housekeeping Seal of Approval" that was helpful in marketing. Second, the dual choice requirements ensured access to the employer market. Third, the override of state laws—important in some states but not others—applied only to federally qualified HMOs. Fourth, federal qualification was required for the receipt of federal grants and loans that were available during the early years of the act. In 1994, 50.8 percent of HMOs nationally, accounting for 70.6 percent of all enrollment, were

* For workers under collective bargaining agreements, the union had to agree to the offering.

federally qualified.[11] Federal qualification is less important today than it was when managed care was in its infancy and HMOs were struggling for inclusion in employment-based health benefit programs, which account for most private insurance in the United States.

Ironically, in its early years the 1973 legislation may have retarded HMO development, earning it the nickname of the "Anti-HMO Act." This occurred for two reasons. The first stems from a compromise in Congress between members having differing objectives. One camp was principally interested in fostering competition in the health care marketplace by promoting plans that incorporated incentives for providers to constrain costs. The second camp, while perhaps sharing the first objective, principally saw the HMO Act as a precursor to health reform and sought a vehicle to expand access to coverage for individuals who were without insurance or who had limited benefits. Imposing requirements on HMOs but not on indemnity carriers, however, reduced the ability of HMOs to compete.

Of particular note were requirements with regard to the comprehensiveness of the benefit package as well as open enrollment and community rating. The open enrollment provision required that plans accept individuals and groups without regard to their health status. The community rating requirement limited the ability of plans to relate premium levels to the health status of the individual enrollee or employer group. Both provisions represented laudable public policy goals; the problem was that they had the potential for making federally qualified HMOs noncompetitive because the same requirements did not apply to the traditional insurance plans against which they competed. This situation was largely corrected in the late 1970s with the enactment of amendments to the HMO Act that reduced some of the more onerous requirements. The federal dual choice provisions were "sunsetted" in 1995 and are no longer in effect.

The second reason that HMO development was retarded was the slowness of the federal government in issuing the regulations implementing the act. Employers knew that they would have to contract with federally qualified plans. Even those who were supportive of the mandate, however, delayed until the government determined which plans would be qualified and established the processes for the implementation of the dual choice provisions.

The Carter administration, which assumed office in 1977, was supportive of HMOs. In particular, Hale Champion, as undersecretary of the U.S. Department of Health and Human Services, made issuance of the regulations a priority. As can be seen from Figure 1–1, rapid growth ensued, with enrollment rising from 6.3 million in 1977 to 29.3 million in 1987.

Politically, several aspects of this history are interesting. First, although differences arose on specifics, the congressional support for legislation promoting HMO development came from both political parties. Also, there was not widespread state opposition to the override of restrictive state laws. In addition, most employers did not actively oppose the dual choice requirements, although many disliked the federal government in effect telling them to contract with HMOs. Perhaps most interesting of all has been the generally positive interaction between the public sector and the private sector, with government fostering HMO development both through its regulatory processes and also as a purchaser under its employee benefits programs.

Other managed care developments also occurred during the 1970s and early 1980s. Of note was the evolution of PPOs. Although there is no widely accepted legal definition, PPOs are generally regarded as differing from HMOs in two respects. First, they do not accept capitation risk; rather, risk remains with the insurance company or self-insured employment-based entity (employer or Taft-Hartley employer–union trust fund). Second, enrollees may access providers that are not in the contracted network, but they face disincentives for doing so in the form of higher out-of-pocket liabilities. PPOs are generally regarded as originating in Denver, where in the early 1970s Samuel Jenkins, a vice president of the benefits consulting firm of The Martin E.

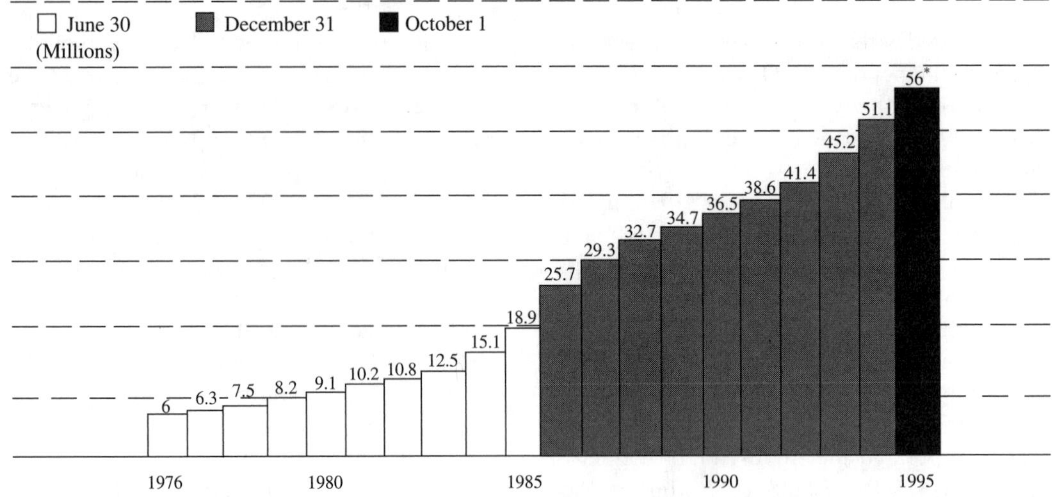

Figure 1–1 Number of people receiving their care in HMOs, 1976–1995. *1995 estimate based on Group Health Association of America's 1994 HMO performance report. *Source:* American Association of Health Plans (formerly GHAA/AMCRA). *Patterns in HMO Enrollment*, p. 3 (Washington, D.C., 1995).

Segal Company, negotiated discounts with hospitals on behalf of the company's Taft-Hartley trust fund clients. Starting in 1978, Jenkins negotiated discounts with physicians.[12] PPO enrollment is difficult to estimate accurately but now rivals that of HMOs.

Intermediate between the HMO and the PPO is the POS plan. It is sometimes referred to as a gatekeeper PPO. To avoid financial penalties under POS, the enrollee must designate a primary care physician, who in turn authorizes any referral services. Self-referral to a specialist, including one who participates in the network, generates higher out-of-pocket liabilities.

Utilization review evolved outside the HMO setting between 1970 and 1985, although it has earlier origins:

- In 1959, Blue Cross of Western Pennsylvania, the Allegheny County Medical Society Foundation, and the Hospital Council of Western Pennsylvania performed retrospective analyses of hospital claims to identify utilization that was significantly above the average.[13]
- Around 1970, California's Medicaid program initiated hospital precertification and concurrent review in conjunction with medical care foundations in that state, starting with the Sacramento Foundation for Medical Care.[14]
- The 1972 Social Security Amendments authorized the federal Professional Standards Review Organization (PSRO) program to review the appropriateness of care provided to Medicare and Medicaid beneficiaries. Although its effectiveness has been debated, the PSRO program established an organizational infrastructure and data capacity upon which both the public and private sectors could rely.
- In the 1970s, a handful of large corporations initiated precertification and concurrent review for inpatient care, much to the dismay of the provider community.

Developments in indemnity insurance, mostly during the 1980s, included encouraging persons with conventional insurance to obtain second opinions before undergoing elective surgery and widespread adoption of large case management—that is, the coordination of services for persons with expensive conditions, such as selected accident patients, cancer cases, and very low–birthweight infants. Also during the 1980s, worksite wellness programs became more prevalent as employers, in varying degrees and varying ways, instituted such programs as:

- screening (e.g., for hypertension and diabetes)
- health risk appraisal
- promotion of exercise (whether through having gyms, conveniently located showers, or running paths, or simply by providing information)
- stress reduction
- classes (e.g., smoking cessation, lifting of heavy weights, and the benefits of exercise)
- nutritional efforts, including serving healthy food in the cafeteria
- weight loss programs
- mental health counseling

For both employers and managed care organizations, wellness and prevention have become integral components of managed care (see Chapter 13).

MANAGED CARE COMES OF AGE: 1985 TO THE PRESENT

The last decade has seen a combination of innovation, maturation, and restructuring. These are briefly discussed below.

Innovation

Three areas of innovation are discussed. First, in many communities hospitals and physicians have collaborated to form physician–hospital organizations (PHOs), principally as vehicles for contracting with managed care organizations. PHOs are typically separately incorporated, with the hospital and the physicians each having the right to designate half the members of the board. Most PHOs seek to enter into fee-for-service arrangements with HMOs and PPOs, although an increasing number accept full capitation risk. Other variants on integrated delivery systems are described in Chapter 4.

Whether PHOs are an important development or little more than a transitional vehicle is hotly debated. Some have been successful as provider units of health care plans, particularly those that have accepted capitation risk from HMOs. The skeptics argue, however, that most PHOs are hospital and specialty dominated, whereas one of the success factors in managed care is a strong primary care orientation. Other reasons for skepticism are that most PHOs allow all physicians with admitting privileges at the hospital in question to participate rather than selecting the more efficient ones and that the physicians are commonly required to use the hospital for outpatient services (e.g., laboratory tests) that might be obtained at lower cost elsewhere, hence hurting the ability of the PHO to be price competitive. Finally, some PHOs suffer from organizational fragmentation, inadequate information systems, management that is inexperienced, and lack of capital.

A second innovation has been the development of carve-outs, which are organizations that have specialized provider networks and are paid on a capitation or other basis for a specific service, such as mental health, chiropractic, and dental. The carve-out companies market their services principally to HMOs and large self-insured employers. Similar in concept are groups of specialists, such as ophthalmologists and radiologists, that accept capitation risk for their services (sometimes referred to as subcapitation) through contracts with health plans and employer groups. One controversy surrounding carve-out arrangements is whether they result in fragmented care for the patient. Such specialty-based networks are also discussed in Chapter 10 as well as in greater detail in Chapter 13 of *The Managed Health Care Handbook*.[15]

A third set of innovations is those that have been made possible by advances in computer technology. Vastly improved computer programs, marketed by private firms or developed by managed care plans for internal use, have become available that generate statistical profiles of the use of services rendered by physicians. These profiles serve to assess efficiency and quality and may also serve to adjust payment levels to providers who are paid under capitation or risk-sharing arrangements to reflect patient severity. These topics are discussed in greater detail in Chapter 19.

Another example of the impact of computer technology is a virtual revolution in the processing of medical and drug claims, which is increasingly being performed electronically rather than by paper submission and manual entry. The result has been dramatically lower administrative costs—claims costs now are typically less than twice the price of a first-class postage stamp—and far superior information; an example of the latter is allowing the pharmacist at the time a prescription is dispensed to receive information about potential adverse effects. Management information systems can be expected to improve in the next few years as providers, almost universally, submit claims electronically. In addition, providers are likely to be assigned unique identification numbers, enabling profiling systems to combine data across multiple payers. Electronic data interchange and management information systems are discussed further in Chapter 20.

Maturation

Maturation can be seen from several vantage points. The first is the extent of HMO and PPO growth. Between 1992 and 1994, only a 2-year period, HMO enrollment rose 23 percent, reaching 51.1 million.[16] As mentioned earlier, PPO enrollment is difficult to estimate but approaches that of HMOs. Employers have come to rely on managed care at the expense of traditional indemnity insurance, as seen in Figure 1–2, with many no longer offering traditional insurance at all.

Medicare and Medicaid have also increasingly relied on managed care. Many HMOs regard Medicare risk contracting (i.e., capitation arrangements that HMOs enter into with the Medicare program) as an essential part of their business strategy, although the penetration is considerably below that of the working-age population. In April 1995, some 2,540,000 Medicare beneficiaries were enrolled in HMOs

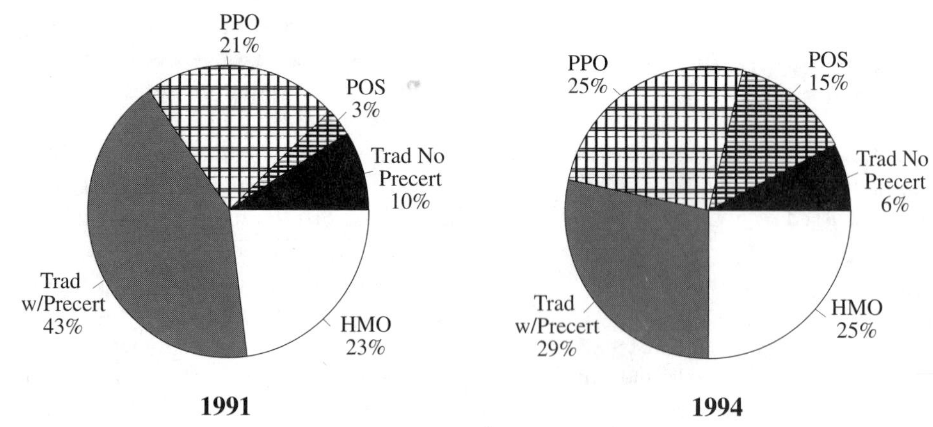

Figure 1–2 Market share by health plan type, 1991 and 1994. Trad, traditional; precert, precertification. *Source:* Courtesy of KPMG Peat Marwick, LLP, 1994, Washington, D.C.

having Medicare risk contracts, an increase of 31 percent in a single year.[17] (See Figure 1–3). Even more impressive, after several flat years the number of plans with Medicare risk contracting increased 75 percent in 2 years (Figure 1–4). The reasons include the realization that Medicare can be profitable; employer demands for HMO options for retirees; reluctance to ignore a major market at a time when HMOs are consolidating and, in some cases, fighting for survival; and the perspective that the plans that account for a high proportion of a provider's revenue will acquire competitive advantage because they have leverage in negotiating reimbursement arrangements. (Medicare and managed care is discussed further in Chapter 26.)

State Medicaid programs, too, have turned to managed care, and, like employers, many are removing the fee-for-service option. As of June 1994, 7.8 million beneficiaries were in managed care, representing 23.2 percent of the total Medicaid population, an increase from 11.8 percent just 2 years before.[18] Some 4.0 million of the 7.8 million beneficiaries were in HMOs, with the balance being under less restrictive arrangements, mostly so-called primary care case management (PCCM) programs, which entail beneficiaries electing a primary care physician, who must approve any referrals to specialists and other services. Under the PCCM programs, providers are generally paid a fee for service, except that the primary physician may receive a small (e.g., $2.00) monthly case management fee. (Medicaid and managed care are discussed further in Chapter 27.)

Another phenomenon is the maturation of external quality oversight activities. Starting in 1991, the National Committee for Quality Assurance (NCQA) began to accredit HMOs. The NCQA was launched by the HMO industry in 1979. It became independent in 1991, however, with the majority of board seats being held by

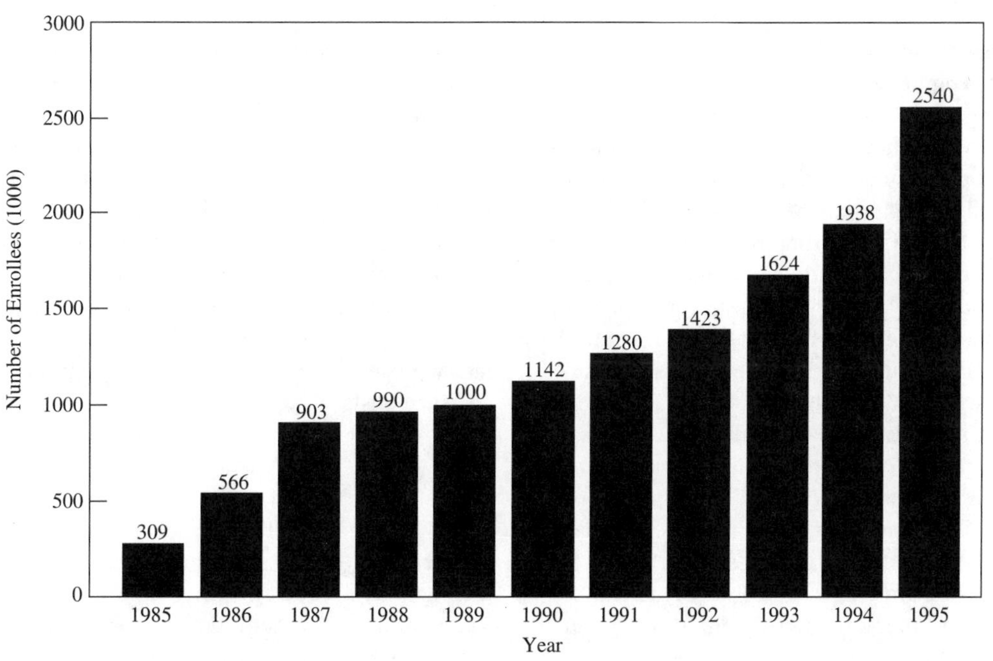

Figure 1–3 Medicare risk enrollees (month of April). *Source:* Data from *Managed Care Contract Reports*, Health Care Financing Administration, Baltimore, Maryland.

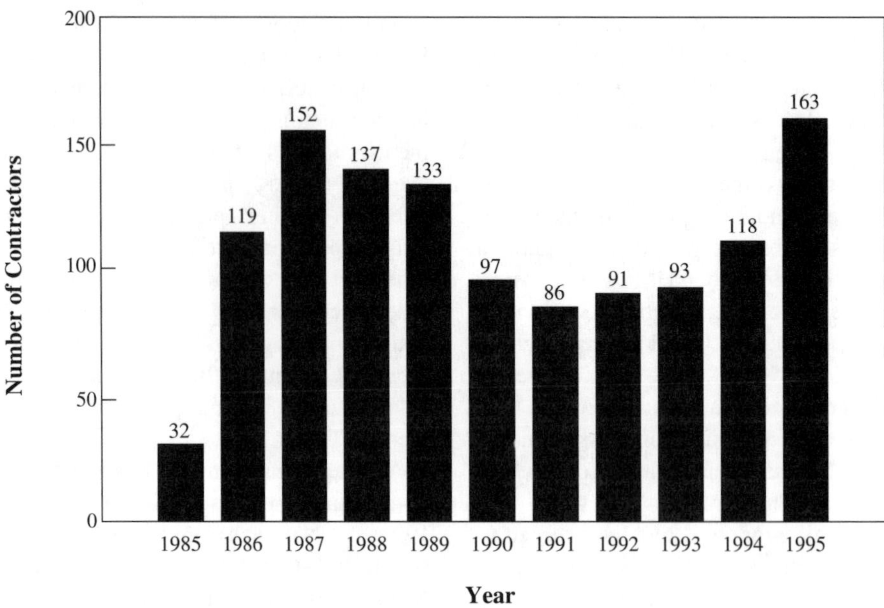

Figure 1–4 Medicare risk contractors (month of April). *Source:* Data from *Managed Care Contract Reports*, Health Care Financing Administration, Baltimore, Maryland.

employer, union, and consumer representatives. Many employers are demanding or strongly encouraging NCQA accreditation of the HMOs with which they contract, and accreditation is coming to replace federal qualification as the "Good Housekeeping Seal of Approval."

In addition, performance measurement systems (report cards) are evolving, although they are at an early stage. The most prominent is the Health Plan Employer Data and Information Set (HEDIS; see Chapter 20), which was developed by the NCQA at the behest of several large employers and health plans. The indices of quality that are part of the performance measurement system are incomplete but will be improved over time. Shortcomings include a focus on what is easily measurable and the lack of health outcome measures. In a related development, several consumer-oriented magazines regularly carry articles assessing HMOs in their respective communities. As more and more of the insured lose access to traditional indemnity plans, the issue of HMO performance will become more salient.

Another form of maturation is the focus of cost management efforts, which used to be almost exclusively inpatient hospital utilization. Practice patterns have changed dramatically in the last 20 years, however, and inpatient utilization has declined significantly. Although hospital utilization still receives considerable scrutiny, greater attention is being paid to ambulatory procedures such as the use of diagnostics and specialists.

Restructuring

Perhaps the most dramatic development is the restructuring that is occurring and that reflects the interplay between managed care and the delivery system. The definitional distinctions are blurring as managed care organizations undergo a process of hybridization. Staff and group model HMOs, faced with limited capital and a need to expand into new territories, are forming IPA components. Meanwhile, some IPAs have created staff model primary care centers while continuing to contract with physicians in independent practice for specialty services. HMOs are offering PPO and POS products, and some PPOs are obtaining HMO licenses. HMOs are also contracting with employers on a self-funded rather than a capitated basis, whereby the risk for medical costs remains with the employer, not to mention a variety of hybrid arrangements. In short, the managed care environment is becoming more complicated.

Another change, and a natural evolution of managed care, is the increasing dominance of the primary care physician, who assumes responsibility for overseeing the allocation of resources. Most managed care organizations regard gaining the loyalty of primary care physicians as critical to their success. The "food chain" analogy has become a popular one, with primary care physicians rising above specialists and hospitals in the "food chain" hierarchy. Contributing to this role reversal is the excess supply in many specialties, with primary care physicians being in tight supply, a phenomenon that varies geographically. The role reversal has been a mixed blessing for primary care physicians, who may feel caught between pressure to reduce costs on the one hand and, on the other hand, the need to satisfy the desires of consumers, who may question whether the physician has their best interests at heart in light of the financial incentives to limit resource consumption.

Finally, consolidation is notable among both health care plans and providers. The multistate managed care firms, including the Kaiser plans but excluding the Blue Cross and Blue Shield plans, which operate largely autonomously, accounted for 60 percent of all enrollment nationally in 1994.[19] Mergers are continuing to occur, as exemplified in 1995 by United Health Care, a publicly traded managed care company headquartered in Minnesota, purchasing MetraHealth, which in turn combined all the health insurance lives, managed care and indemnity, of the Travellers and Metropolitan insurance companies.

FUTURE ISSUES FACING MANAGED CARE

This chapter concludes with observations regarding managed care and how it has, and will, evolve with regard to the interplay between the public and private sectors; the role of quality in the new competitive, and managed care–dominated, environment; the locus of decision making on coverage of expensive and marginally effective technologies; and how the nation will address problems that managed care and competitive delivery mechanisms cannot solve and may exacerbate, notably access to coverage for the uninsured and the financing of graduate medical education.

Interplay between the Public and Private Sectors

One of the themes of this chapter is the generally positive interplay between the public and private sectors. HMOs, which are private entities, have proven themselves to be viable mechanisms for delivering care to Medicare and Medicaid beneficiaries. At the same time, government at all levels has contributed much to managed care growth. One of the earlier examples of a large employer contracting with HMOs on a dual choice basis was the agreement between the U.S. Office of Personnel Management and Kaiser Foundation Health Plans setting forth the terms under which Kaiser would be offered to federal employees. Today, federal, state, and local (including school district) government employees constitute the largest accounts of many HMOs. In addition, the HMO Act of 1973 provided a major impetus for HMO development. Even before then, the California Medicaid program represented one of the first examples of inpatient precertification and concurrent review. Also, many private plans have adopted diagnosis-related groups for hospital reimbursement and the resource-based relative value scale for physician reimbursement, both developed by Medicare for its fee-for-service program.

Ironically, many in the provider community, which is hardly unified, now look to the government for protection, such as by lobbying for laws that limit the ability of managed care plans to select the providers that are in their networks. A significant segment of the provider community appears to prefer government regulation to marketplace competition.

Role of Quality

The role of quality in employer contracting decisions as well as in consumer choice among plans is unclear. HMOs pay considerable attention to enrollee satisfaction and regularly conduct surveys of both enrollees and disenrollees. Satisfaction may not equate to technical quality, however. Managed care should have as its objective maximizing value, not minimizing cost. The degree and manner in which quality will enter into employer contracting decisions and consumer choice, thereby affecting financial performance and market share, are unclear.

Of particular concern to some is how the chronically ill, especially those with rare conditions requiring specialized care, will fare under capitated arrangements. By one estimate, chronic illness accounts for 80 percent of all medical costs.[20] HMOs focus considerable attention on the more prevalent conditions, such as diabetes and asthma (which are also the focus of HEDIS measures). How good is their performance in caring for persons with complex or rare chronic conditions? Unfortunately, the research literature has little to say on this question, which should be a matter of empirical study, not anecdotes or preconceived views. Also debated is the role of the specialist versus the primary care physician in caring for persons with certain chronic conditions, such as congestive heart failure and chronic obstructive pulmonary disease, both prevalent among the elderly in particular. Should the cardiologist or pulmonologist be allowed to serve as primary care physician for patients with these respective conditions?

Technology Assessment and the Coverage Determination Process

Another issue is the technology assessment or coverage determination process, that is, the process for making decisions about when new procedures or services are no longer experimental as well as when procedures in general, some in use for many years, are not effective. For example, when is a particular form of transplantation no longer experimental? Subscriber and employer contracts, indemnity or HMO, routinely exclude coverage of procedures that are investigational or experimental. There is not a uniform set of guidelines or a review process for determining when a procedure is no longer investigational or experimental, however. As a result, coverage denials are often litigated. Whether the courts are the best locus of decision making about what should be accepted medical practice is doubtful.

The extent to which such decisions should be within the province of the individual health care plan is debated among the HMOs themselves. Competition among health care plans based on the restrictiveness of their benefit interpretations is of questionable social merit. Segments of the HMO industry hold that such coverage decisions should be made by an external body, perhaps a public–private partnership, that establishes guidelines for all health care plans even while recognizing that such guidelines will always allow room for interpretation. Others oppose constraining individual plan latitude in coverage determinations.

This issue is not new with the advent of managed care. Under capitated systems, however, the plans have both more medical information about enrollees and greater incentive to scrutinize what is covered than is the case under conventional insurance.

Financing of Access for the Uninsured and for Graduate Medical Education

Finally, the growth of competitive delivery systems affects the nature of public policy debate for a broad gamut of issues. Even matters such as priorities for biomedical research are not immune. Managed care, however, places into particularly sharp relief the question of financing of access for the uninsured and graduate medical education. With regard to access, on the one hand managed care provides a vehicle for covering all populations efficiently; on the other hand it reduces the financial capacity of providers, operating in a more price competitive environment, to care for the uninsured.

Much of the cost of graduate medical education has traditionally been financed through higher fee-for-service billings. These costs are principally stipends to residents and interns along with the costs of supervision and those associated with services and procedures that are principally didactic in nature. Medicare reimburses hospitals for its share of these costs, which are incorporated into the county-specific rates at which Medicare pays HMOs. HMOs are not required to contract with teaching hospitals, however, which are often more expensive than their nonteaching peers. These hospitals need to be price competitive to survive, reducing their ability to support the teaching function.[21] The topic of academic health centers and managed care is also discussed in detail in Chapter 12.

CONCLUSION

Unmanaged care is no longer affordable, but several forces continue to fuel its growth. Purchasers of care, public and private, are unwilling to tolerate the growth in medical costs of the last several years. Purchasers also question the wide and unexplained variations in practice patterns among geographic areas and delivery systems, raising suspicions of widespread waste. Further fueling the growth of unmanaged care are the excesses in provider supply, such as in the numbers of specialists and hospital beds, leading to intense competition for limited health care dollars. Because medical care is such a personal matter, managed care will continue to generate anxiety among some consumers and to raise issues of societal values and public policy.

Study Questions

1. HMOs were initially formed in response to consumer demand—true or false?
2. In addition to contracting with HMOs, what are some of the managed care steps that employers can take to constrain health care costs and promote wellness?
3. How important to employers generally is it that HMOs demonstrate that they offer quality care?
4. What are PPOs and POS plans?

REFERENCES AND NOTES

1. Group Health Association of America (GHAA), *Patterns in HMO Enrollment.* (Washington, D.C.: GHAA, 1995). These figures include PPO and point-of-service products as well as pure HMO products. The principal sources of data on HMO enrollment are GHAA and InterStudy. They differ slightly in the data collected and the numbers reported. Both are regarded as generally reliable.
2. InterStudy, *Competitive Edge (Part II: Industry Report).* February 1995; 5, No. 1. Minnetonka, Minn.
3. T.R. Mayer and G.G. Mayer, HMOs: Origins and Development, *New England Journal of Medicine* 312 (1985): 590–94.
4. G.K. MacLeod, "An Overview of Managed Care" in *The Managed Health Care Handbook*, 2d ed., ed. P.R. Kongstvedt (Gaithersburg, Md.: Aspen, 1993), 3–11.
5. Mayer and Mayer, HMOs: Origins and Development.
6. P. Starr, *The Social Transformation of American Medicine* (New York, N.Y.: Basic Books, 1982), 295–310.
7. InterStudy, *Competitive Edge.*
8. InterStudy, *Competitive Edge.*
9. Mayer and Mayer, HMOs: Origins and Development.

10. G.B. Strumpf, "Historical Evolution and Political Process," in *Group and IPA HMOs*, ed. D.L. Mackie, D.K. Decker (Gaithersburg, Md.: Aspen, 1981), 17–36.
11. InterStudy, *Competitive Edge.*
12. J.J. Spies, et al., "Alternative Health Care Delivery Systems: HMOs and PPOs," in *Health Care Cost Management: Private Sector Initiatives*, ed. P.D. Fox, et al. (Ann Arbor, Mich.: Health Administration Press, 1984), 43–68.
13. J.E. Fielding, *Corporate Cost Management.* (Reading, Mass.: Addison-Wesley, 1984).
14. Fielding, *Corporate Cost Management.*
15. A. Fine, "Specialty Networks from the Specialist's View," in *The Managed Health Care Handbook*, 3d ed., ed. P.R. Kongstvedt. (Gaithersburg, Md.: Aspen, 1996), 191–201.
16. GHAA, *Patterns in HMO Enrollment.* These figures include PPO and POS products as well as pure HMO products.
17. U.S. Department of Health and Human Services (DHHS), *Medicare Care Contract Report* (Rockville, Md.: DHHS, 1995).
18. Health Care Financing Administration (HCFA), *National Summary of Medicaid Managed Care Programs and Enrollment* (HCFA, 1994).
19. InterStudy, *Competitive Edge.*
20. K.N. Lohr, et al., Chronic Disease in a General Adult Population: Findings from the Rand Health Insurance Experiment, *Western Journal of Medicine* 145 (1986): 537–545.
21. For a discussion of the managed care issues facing academic health centers, see P.D. Fox and J. Wasserman, Academic Medical Centers and Managed Care: Uneasy Partners. *Health Affairs* 12 (1993): 85–93.

SUGGESTED READING

Davis, K., Collins, K.S., and Morris, C. 1991. Managed Care: Promise and Concerns. *Health Affairs* 13 (4): 3–46.

Iglehart, J.K. 1993. The American Health Care System. *New England Journal of Medicine* 328 (12): 896–900.

Chapter 2

Health Care Reform: The Road Lies with Managed Care

Frederick B. Abbey

Study Objectives

- To understand the context of the enactment of the Health Insurance Portability and Accountability Act within federal and state health care reform efforts
- To understand the key policy drivers impacting health care and, in particular, managed care
- To gain insight into the use of managed care arrangements and their effect on Medicare and Medicaid
- To understand renewed federal efforts to combat health care fraud and abuse
- To understand the trend toward increased state regulation of managed care plans and its impact on Congress

With the coming enactment of the Health Insurance Portability and Accountability Act[1] in 1997, Congress and the Clinton administration have taken the first of many incremental steps in reforming the U.S. health care system. Indeed, the incremental nature of government-based health care reform is likely to continue in the foreseeable future. When any one industry represents fully one-seventh of a nation's economy—as the health care industry indeed does—it must be expected that there will be little or no consensus for wholesale changes to the health care marketplace. Accordingly, the federal government recognizes that meaningful health care reform must be done in a series of smaller legislative proposals and in a manner that involves *all* market players: patients, employers, providers, hospitals, insurance companies, health maintenance organizations (HMOs), and other similar health plans.

Any government-based reform of health care is not constructed in a vacuum. The federal budget deficit continues to confound lawmakers as they seek to restrain the rate of government growth while maintaining or expanding government services. National demographics offer little encouragement; beginning in 2010, the first of tens of millions of baby boomers will retire and become eligible for Medicare. Similarly, the number of Medicaid recipients and the cost of providing care to those recipients are also likely to increase greatly in the coming years. Public opinion, led by consumers and employers, may well clamor for the dual (and possibly contradictory) goals of increasing cost-containment in government health programs and the commercial market while also maintaining the government safety net. Faced with these competing challenges, the federal government will likely only accelerate the movement of govern-

---

Frederick B. Abbey is a Partner in the Washington, D.C., office of Ernst & Young LLP. For eight years, he served as a federal official in policy development at the U.S. Department of Health and Human Services and the Health Care Financing Administration.

Ernst & Young staff members Phil Blando, Peter Gunter, Mike Treash, Tracy Croft, and Sue Carrington also contributed to this chapter.

ment health programs into one proven cost containment mechanism—managed care.[2]

How should managed care organizations view these continuing reform efforts? This chapter describes the drivers of the federal health care policy and the four major areas of policy development. Each of these areas illustrates incremental policy steps Congress and the Clinton administration have taken and may continue to take to move more Americans toward a system of network-based care and away from traditional indemnity insurance.

FEDERAL HEALTH POLICY DRIVERS

Legislative proposals for health care reform have been floated since the early days of the Truman administration at the end of World War II. However, a relatively new pressure has been brought to bear on health care reform since the 1980s—the cost of the government health programs and their impact on the federal budget.

Beginning in the 1980s, Congress increased the scope and frequency of health-related legislative activity. A chief result of this activity was the reduction of federal payments to most providers of care. Consequently, the health care industry significantly increased its profile and impact on the legislative process. Recent estimates have indicated there are 763 health care–related associations and coalitions in Washington, D.C., that represent different points of view—more than triple the number a decade ago.[3] These various viewpoints, coupled with the American public's demand that the federal budget be balanced—and, by extension, that the Medicare and Medicaid programs be reformed—has led to an intense national debate both within and outside of the 104th Congress about the size and scope of government. The battles in the Congress during 1996 demonstrated that, in the legislative process, the concerns of all market players need to be addressed to achieve consensus on numerous health policy issues. The health care industry is enormously complex, and each impacted group—consumers, employers, providers, hospitals, insurance companies, and health plans—views itself as a potential winner or loser under any proposed incremental health care changes.

Massive in its structure, the health care system has multidimensional effects on federal, state, and private-sector spending, as well as on business innovation and competitiveness. Each of the following factors drives the formation and adoption of federal health care policy, including

- the U.S. budget and deficit
- Medicare trust funds
- state budget shortfalls
- business profits and growth
- the public demand and appetite for change

The federal budget comprises seven pieces, with more than one-half of spending devoted to entitlement and mandatory programs (Figure 2–1).[4] The federal deficit has long been and will continue to be a problem; recent estimates have projected the deficit to exceed $403 billion by 2006. Additionally, Medicare and Medicaid will continue to fuel federal spending at a steady rate of 9 percent to 10 percent each year at least until 2002.[5] Consequently, the government's ability to address other domestic issues is hindered. Because of their scope, health care entitlement programs continue to be the source of spending reductions to reduce the deficit and allow other concerns to be addressed.

The dire projections for the Medicare Hospital Insurance Trust Fund exemplify the need for congressional reform of entitlement programs. Unless measures are implemented quickly to reduce spending, the Medicare Part A Trust Fund, according to the most optimistic assessment, is expected to be depleted by 2001.[6] If the federal commitment to elderly Americans is to continue uninterrupted, a more efficient health care delivery system will be required. At the state level, many states have begun to realize there are limits to the services they can provide and have sought to restrain the growth of the Medicaid program. State funding provides the single largest source of Medicaid financing and currently takes, on average, more than 14 percent of a

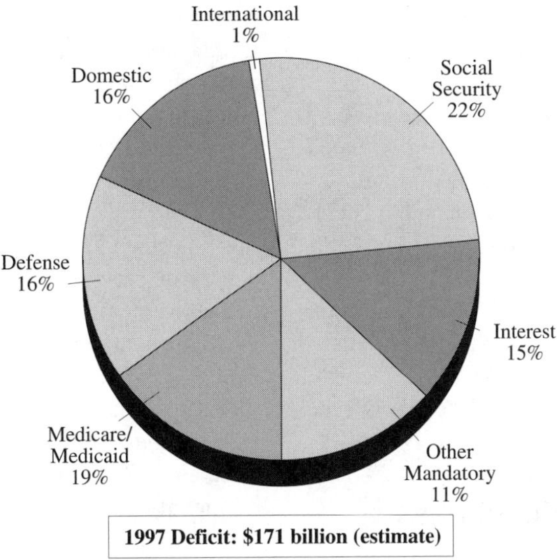

Figure 2–1 The Federal Budget. *Source:* Congressional Budget Office, *Reducing the Deficit: Spending and Revenue Options* (Washington, D.C.: U.S. Government Printing Office, 1996).

state's annual budget.[7] The increase in Medicaid financing has prohibited states from meeting other community needs such as education, road improvements, and crime prevention. With federal regulations limiting Medicaid fund-raising measures such as donations and provider taxes, states now support strongly increased efforts to move their Medicaid populations into managed care arrangements.

Rising health care costs also greatly impact employers in that they reduce profits and divert money from investments in business expansion. Many employers have taken steps to contain these costs, but the growing number of uninsured has forced health care organizations to shift the burden to the insured population. Many employers, however, have begun to balk at cost-shifting and are demanding more efficiency in their employee health benefit programs. Despite the reductions in the rate of increase in health care expenditures, a sustained efficient health care delivery system is still needed to provide more Americans access to health coverage and to abate the cost-shifting trend.

Further exacerbating attempts to resolve the many outstanding issues affecting the health care system are the views of the American public. Many Americans want to see the federal budget balanced, but, paradoxically, without significant changes to the Medicare and Medicaid programs. Typical are the responses to a July 1996 survey by the Kaiser-Harvard Program on Public and Health/Social Policy. When if asked if they would favor making major reductions in future spending on Medicare *to prevent the program from going bankrupt,* 54 percent of those Americans surveyed were opposed to major Medicare spending reductions. Similar views were found concerning the Medicaid program. Americans split in the Kaiser-Harvard study, 47 percent to 43 percent, when asked if they favored turning responsibility for Medicaid over to the states. However, when the survey noted that, under several proposals to turn Medicaid spending over to the states that each state would only be given a fixed amount of federal dollars along with the flexibility to decide how to spend those funds, 59 percent opposed efforts to turn

Medicaid over to the states. Just 29 percent were still in favor of exclusive state control over the Medicaid program.[8]

Any effort to change our nation's health care system involves literally dozens of interrelated elements. However, four key areas provide insight into how the federal government has accelerated the movement to a system of network-based health care systems. They are (1) Medicare payment policies; (2) Medicaid payment policies; (3) federal fraud and abuse regulation (discussed in Chapters 4 and 31); and (4) state regulation of managed care plans (see Chapter 29).

MEDICARE PAYMENT POLICIES

With fee-for-service spending threatening the financial solvency of the Medicare program, the federal government is pursuing risk-based payments as a cost-containment solution. Medicare has pursued risk-based payments through packaged pricing demonstration projects and its own managed care program. The transference of the risk of the Medicare program to health plans and providers has proceeded incrementally, yet has intensified as the program has continued to shift gradually from a traditional fee-for-service program to managed care and, possibly, other forms of network-based systems. In an era of budgetary limits and the impending bankruptcy of the Medicare trust funds, the movement to network-based systems of care will only accelerate (Figure 2–2).

Packaged Pricing

The effort of the Medicare program to pass the financial risk of the program to providers began with the hospital inpatient prospective payment system (PPS) implemented in 1983 (Figure 2–3). PPS is a case-rate methodology using the DRG system of patient classification. PPS pays hospitals by assuming patients will incur an average number of expenses and an average length-of-stay in the hospital. The financial incentive for hospitals is to increase admissions and reduce costs and length-of-stays by substituting inpatient care with less expensive post–acute care services; consequently, Congress is concerned that Medicare is paying twice for the same episode because the post–acute care services are billed to Medicare as well. Over time, the government will extend the definition of a hospital stay to incorporate more pre– and post–acute care services.

Taking its efforts to pass the risk related to an episode of care one step farther, the Health Care Financing Administration (HCFA) initiated a series of package pricing demonstrations. The first demonstration project was an effort to reduce costs and improve quality of care for two commonly performed open heart surgery procedures. Under the demonstration, hospitals and physicians are paid a single negotiated price to provide coronary artery bypass graft (CABG) surgeries to Medicare patients. About 145,000 CABG procedures are performed annually on Medicare beneficiaries. In the first two years, four of the seven participating hospitals developed cost-saving, quality-care protocols for the 2,552 surgeries, resulting in a savings of more than $13 million. Improved case management on each patient has reduced length-of-stay, increased hospital–physician communication, and permitted greater savings as well as improved quality of care. The participating hospitals reported no compromise in patient care; rather, patient satisfaction has been extremely positive.

HCFA followed up the CABG demonstration with a cataract surgery demonstration project. Although the CABG demonstration remains in place, HCFA has indicated its intent to terminate the cataract pilot project. CABG procedures are high priced and allow providers a lot of margin in which they can improve delivery and reduce costs. In contrast, annual Medicare payments for cataract procedures are high, mainly because of the volume of surgeries performed each year. The low margins in the cost of cataract surgeries (and subsequent savings) limit the provider and Medicare's incentive to pursue the demonstration project. Instead, Medicare is focusing its efforts on other high-cost–high-margin procedures

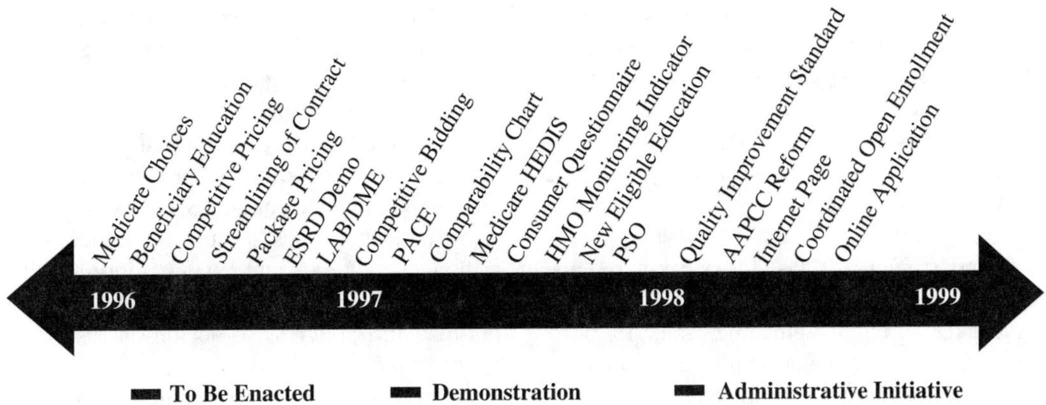

Figure 2–2 Medicare Managed Care Growth Initiatives. *Notes*: AAPCC: Adjusted Average per Capita Cost; DME: Durable Medical Equipment; ESRD Demo (End-Stage Renal Disease Demonstration); HEDIS: Health Plan Employer Data and Information Set; PACE: Program of All-Inclusive Care for the Elderly.

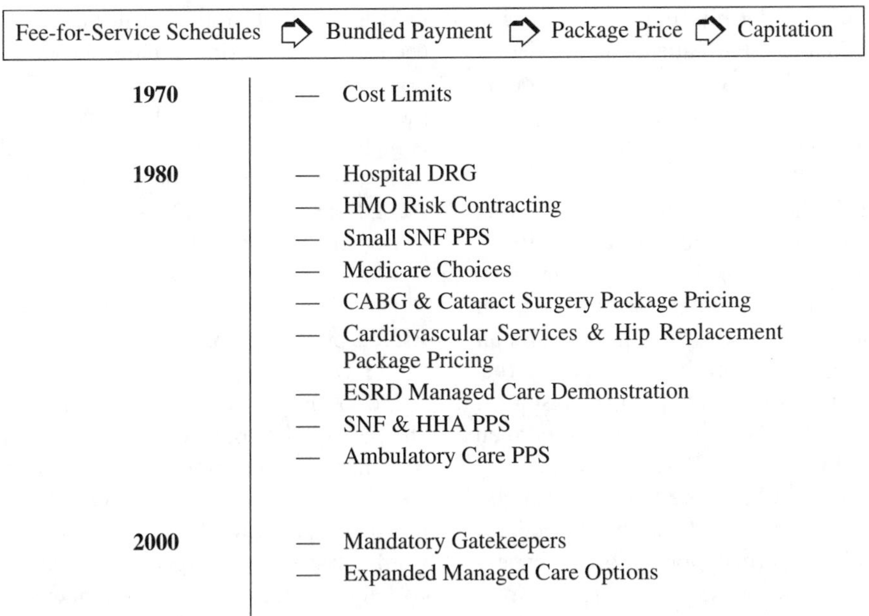

Figure 2–3 Medicare Payment Policy Development. *Notes:* CABG, coronary artery bypass graft; DRG, diagnosis-related group; HHA, home health agency; SNF, skilled nursing facility. *Source:* Ernst & Young LLP, 1994.

such as cardiovascular services and total hip replacement. Similar to the CABG demonstration, HCFA is negotiating packaged pricing products with providers in an effort to reduce its payments for these high-cost services.

In addition to DRGs and packaged pricing, the federal government is considering changing its reimbursement methods for other types of providers from a cost-based to a risk-based approach. Many legislated activities will likely be undertaken during the remainder of the 1990s to convert fee-for-service or cost-based reimbursement systems into risk-based sites. In this way, Medicare can limit its financial responsibility for paying for covered services by shifting the risk to the provider–practitioner community. Two likely providers that will be transitioned to risk-based sites are HHAs and SNFs.

In response to rising home health care expenditures, HCFA initiated the HHA Prospective Payment Demonstration project, which is designed to test the costs and benefits of prospective payment. The project compares the advantages and disadvantages of alternative approaches. It also permits the collection and analysis of data on HHA patient characteristics, service mix, and costs. The project is being implemented in two phases. Phase 1 tested a per-visit PPS on 26 HHAs in five states (California, Florida, Illinois, Massachusetts, and Texas). Initial findings indicated no significant change in either agency costs or program expenditures with implementation of this payment method. Phase 2 will institute a per-episode payment method that will involve a single payment for all Medicare-covered home health services furnished during the first 120 days of an episode of home health care. The rate will be subject to an annual adjustment in the HHA case mix.

Rapid growth in Medicare SNF program expenditures has prompted Congress to address payment policy reform options. Program expenditures have grown at an alarming rate, from $8.3 billion in 1994 to an estimated $10.3 billion in 1995.[9] Greater use due to changes in the benefit account for much of the increase since 1987. Several payment policy options have been proposed in an effort to control rising costs. Two such proposals are facility peer groups based on the type of facility or geographic location, or adjustments based on the SNF case mix. Another option would be payments combining acute hospital and post–acute care. Such bundling services would include not only SNF payments, but also payments for post–acute care services such as home health care and rehabilitation services. Details on the various choices have not yet been outlined for Congress to decide on a specific payment reform method.

Ambulatory services constitute the remaining large part of the delivery system under Medicare that will be transitioned to a risk-based reimbursement system. The Department of Health and Human Services (DHHS) recommended to Congress that Medicare should adopt a PPS for hospital outpatient care called ambulatory patient groups (APGs). This new patient classification system, which is similar to DRGs, forms the basis of payment for visit-based outpatient PPS. APGs serve as a patient classification scheme that reflects the amount and type of resources used in an ambulatory patient visit. Patients in each APG exhibit similar clinical characteristics regarding resource use and costs. Currently, there are roughly 300 APGs that describe the complete range of services provided in the outpatient setting. So far, Congress has yet to act on the DHHS recommendation. (APGs are discussed in Chapter 11.)

Effects of These Changes

Individually, these changes and proposed changes to the traditional Medicare program have had a modest impact on overall costs and use. However, collectively, they demonstrate that the future of Medicare is indeed moving toward a system that emphasizes greater use and cost controls. As Congress continues to explore reforming Medicare and bringing the federal budget into balance, it will reduce physician and hospital updates and pursue technical changes to stunt the growth of the traditional program and promote alternative systems of network-based care. Consequently, physicians and other providers in the Medicare program are likely to become accustomed to less autonomy in their practices and become more efficient providers of care to their patients. The result? These providers will become increasingly adept at managed care techniques and likely will pursue some form of a physician-based network contract with Medicare, including contracting with the program on a full-risk basis.

Medicare Risk-Based Contracting Program

Prospective payment and packaged pricing transfers the risk of a care episode to providers, but may fall short in achieving the substantial savings needed to restore solvency of the Part A Trust Fund and help balance the federal budget. Capitated Medicare payments transfer insurance risk of the program to the private sector, and giving the federal government better control over expenditure growth.

In 1985, Medicare began contracting with HMOs using full-risk–based payments. Medicare pays risk-contracting HMOs a fixed monthly amount set at 95 percent of the actuarial estimate of what it typically would have reimbursed health care providers and practitioners for covered services. (For a full discussion, see Chapter 17.) Initially, program growth was slow and sporadic, reaching 1.5 million enrollees in 1992. Spurred on by high penetration (and profits) in California, Florida, and Minnesota, interest and participation in Medicare managed care skyrocketed. As of August 1996, there were 229 risk-contracting health plans with 3.8 million Medicare members, in addition to approximately another 500,000 beneficiaries in cost-contracting plans and demonstration projects.[10] Despite the market popularity of the program, the public policy question is: Does Medicare managed care save the federal government money?

Developing an appropriate capitation rate-setting methodology is driving the current policy debate over the Medicare managed care program. One study has suggested that Medicare overpays HMOs 5 percent to 7 percent because the HMOs attract Medicare members who tend to be healthier than the average Medicare beneficiary.[11] Efforts to remedy the payment problem include Medicare Choices, a demonstration project to test risk adjusters, outlier pools, and rate-banding payment methodologies, and a proposed demonstration project to evaluate market-based competitive pricing. Congress recently proposed an administrative rate-setting methodology that would reduce the geographic disparity in rates. For 1997, monthly Medicare rates, which are county based, range from $140 in Puerto Rico to $760 in New York. The variation in payments has led to concentrations of high enrollment in markets with correspondingly high payment rates, whereas health plans avoid counties with low payment rates.

Within the Balanced Budget Act of 1995, Congress proposed a payment system that would have rewarded markets when overall provider practice patterns resulted in lower Medicare fee-for-service use.[12] However, for unrelated reasons, President Clinton vetoed the measure. As the 105th Congress (which had not convened at the time this chapter was written) considers health care reform legislation, it will be concerned about developing payment methods with rates that will attract health plan participation and achieve cost-containment goals.

Provider-Sponsored Organizations

The proposed Balanced Budget Act of 1995 also contained provisions allowing for the creation of a new type of Medicare managed care organization: the PSO. As proposed, the PSO would be a provider-based integrated delivery system that contracts with Medicare to accept full-risk payments to its Medicare members. Legislation allowing for the development of PSOs is virtually certain to be revisited in the coming 105th Congress. When enacted, PSOs will put providers in direct competition with health plans and greatly transform Medicare and the entire health care marketplace.

Because PSOs would accept risk solely under the Medicare program, Congress has proposed creating a regulatory framework different from that of other health plans. The PSO framework contained in the Balanced Budget Act may be illustrative for future legislative proposals. In the Balanced Budget Act, states would have been able to establish certification standards for PSOs. However, the secretary of the DHHS would have had to approve the state requirements. Together, the states and the secretary would have developed insolvency protection standards that are less stringent than the requirements for HMOs. Federal waivers would have been effective for 36 months and renewable in 6-month increments.

In the coming years, efforts to pass the financial risk of Medicare to the private sector will likely dominate public debate about the future of the program. Budgetary politics will force down fee-for-service payments and lead to incentives for the migration of health plans, providers, and beneficiaries to the managed care program (Figure 2–4). Congress will open the Medicare managed care program to other types of risk-bearing organizations, including provider-based integrated delivery systems and organizations. To ensure quality, it is likely that some form of Medicare HEDIS (see Chapter 20) or other quality yardsticks may be developed and implemented.

Wholesale expansion of the program will also depend on the development of an equitable payment system. Reform of the AAPCC will be a significant challenge in the coming years. Additionally, Congress or the administration may pursue a coordinated open enrollment process and, perhaps, even allow for enrollment by way of the Internet or other electronic means. In turn, it is the hope of federal legislators, regulators, and health care policymakers that these program changes will allow the government to retain more control over Medicare spending and reduce the financial risk of the program and the federal government.

MEDICAID PAYMENT POLICIES

Since its inception in 1965, Medicaid has improved access to medical services for many poor Americans. Despite its successes, the program presently has numerous limitations resulting from its basic design and financing. The recent debate over Medicaid reform has moved policymakers to review where Medicaid is, how it got there, and how it might be made more efficient. Already, many states have moved to managed care arrangements in an effort to maximize program efficiencies (Figure 2–5). (This topic is discussed more fully in Chapter 28.)

As with Medicare, the Medicaid program has its roots in a fragmented benefit and reimbursement structure. In the early days of the program, health care providers and practitioners were compensated through a variety of methods that differed by state. Before 1980, Medicaid generally reimbursed hospitals using the same cost-based principles adhered to by the Medicare program. Changes in the statute in 1980 and 1981 permitted states to develop their own methodologies for reimbursing hospital inpatient services, provided their rates were appropriate for an efficiently run hospital. Most states have now moved to a PPS in which a predetermined amount would compensate a hospital for a defined service. Many states use the DRG classification system used by Medicare to reimburse for hospital inpatient services. Other states contract directly with hospitals to provide for inpatient services. These payment systems place an organization at financial risk to provide all services incidental to a hospital stay, and thereby require more active management of the patient than did earlier reimbursement methods. Throughout the more than 30 years since the program was created, Medicaid payment rates have not kept up with hospital costs; presently they cover, on average, about 93 percent of inpatient hospital costs.[13]

Physicians and outpatient services have also experienced incremental payment policy

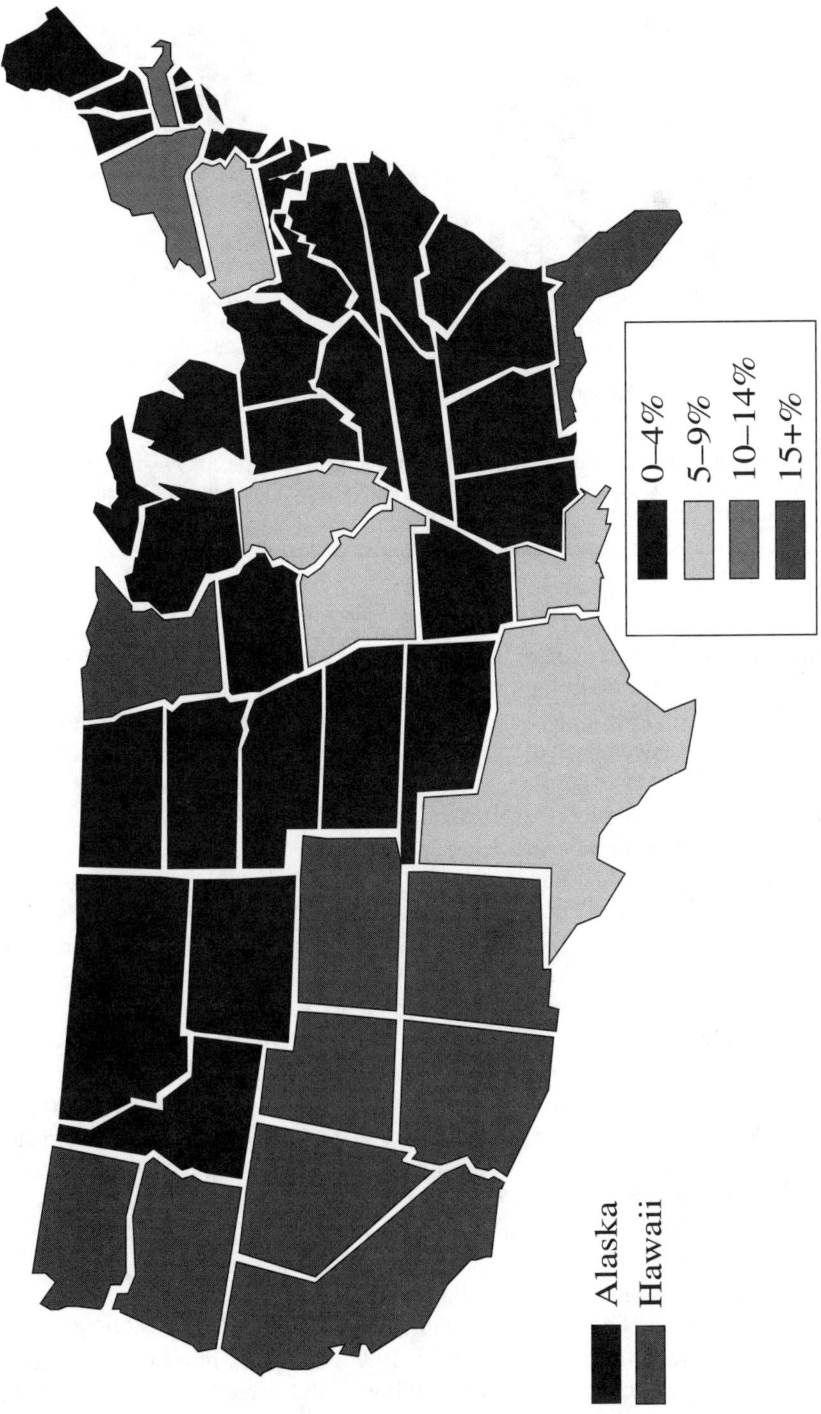

Figure 2–4 Medicare Managed Care Penetration (Percentage of Medicare Beneficiaries Enrolled in Managed Care in Each State). *Source:* U.S. Department of Health and Human Services, Health Care Financing Administration, 1996 Data Compendium (Baltimore, M.D.: Bureau of Data Management and Stratagy, 1996): 112–113.

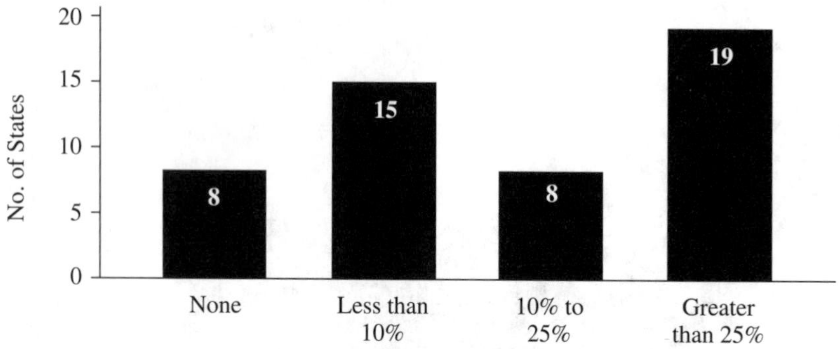

Figure 2–5 Percentage of Medicaid Beneficiaries Enrolled in Managed Care, by State, 1994. *Sources*: Health Care Financing Administration, *Data Compendium*, 1996; Kaiser Commission on the Future of Medicaid, "Medicaid and Managed Care," June 1995.

changes. States historically have established maximum allowable charges that provided the ceiling for physician and other individual practitioner payments. Over time, states have moved to adopt fixed fee-for-service schedules. Like hospital inpatient services, Medicaid payment rates for physician services now average about 73 percent of what would have been reimbursed using Medicare principles of reimbursement and only 47 percent of private insurance rates.[14]

Despite its poor payment rates and cumbersome eligibility and administrative processes, Medicaid is generally the single largest and fastest growing program in the budget of each state, averaging about 14 percent of a state's total expenditures.[15] At $140 billion in costs in 1995, state and federal Medicaid spending now accounts for 13 percent of the nation's health care spending.[16] Likewise, at the federal level, Medicaid spending is expected to grow rapidly. From 1996 to 2002, federal Medicaid spending is projected to grow at an annual rate of nearly 10 percent.[17] The absolute dollars involved, the growth rates, and the competing public policy demands have encouraged states to look for alternatives to contain costs and increase health care services and accessibility for the nation's poor population.

Managed Care Plans

Managed care has been tapped by numerous states to assist in their Medicaid access and cost-containment strategies. The Medicaid statute provides a number of options that allow states to pursue innovative methods of delivery and financing of Medicaid services. Figure 2–6 outlines Medicaid payment policy milestones. Since 1981, several freedom-of-choice waivers have been enacted, allowing states to lock Medicaid recipients into cost-effective alternative systems. A second type of waiver permits states to offer an enhanced home and community services benefit to a defined population. Both types of waivers share several characteristics: targeted enrollment of individual patients, defined formal contracts between the state Medicaid agency and provider–payer network, and a case manager or gatekeeping function. Beyond these general attributes, Medicaid managed care organizational structure varies by program and by state.

As of 1995, states have moved to enroll about 11.6 million, or 32 percent, of the 36.3 million Medicaid recipients into 403 Medicaid managed care plans. As of July 1996, 14 states had received comprehensive Section 1115 Medicaid

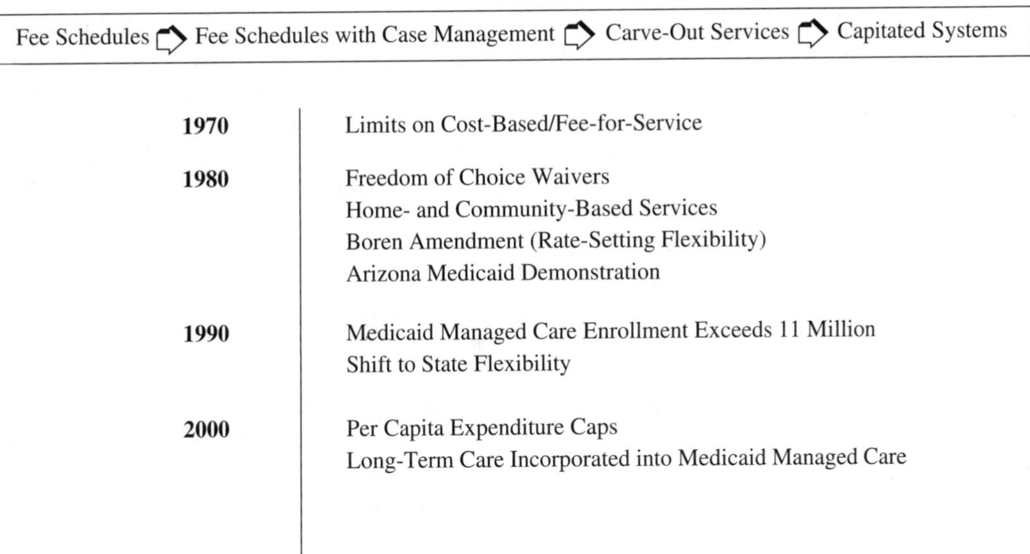

Figure 2–6 Medicaid Managed Care Payment Policies. *Source*: Ernst & Young LLP, 1994.

managed care waivers, with another 10 pending HCFA review.[18] Medicaid managed care recipients are concentrated in just a handful of states. As of 1994, Tennessee, California, Florida, Massachusetts, Washington, Michigan, and Pennsylvania accounted for approximately 53.5 percent of all Medicaid managed care recipients.[19]

The success of Medicaid managed care in containing costs and providing quality health care services has been under considerable scrutiny. As they examine the number of states pursuing managed care and the associated enrollment increase, policymakers are likely to disagree about the ability of state managed care programs to restrain the growth rate *and* provide quality health care. Nonetheless, federal policy will probably continue to allow Medicaid managed care programs to develop, but with increased legislative and regulatory oversight. Likely oversight bodies include the DHHS Office of the Inspector General, the Prospective Payment Assessment Commission; the Physician Payment Review Commission; the U.S. Government Accounting Office; the Office of Technology and Assessment; and, in Congress, the House Commerce Committee and the Senate Finance Committee.

As Congress continues to seek ways to rein in the explosive costs of the Medicaid program, the policy debate will undoubtedly examine the appropriateness of federal Medicaid waivers and their ability to meet—if not exceed—federal and state cost-containment goals. The focus of these policy discussions and ultimate legislation will include the need to standardize a benefit package, ascertain whether the federal or state standards will determine precisely the type of organizations that qualify to offer Medicaid managed care services, refine methods for calculating capitated payments, and develop greater measures of health care quality.

FRAUD AND ABUSE REGULATION

Managed care and the federal fraud and abuse regulatory process have evolve almost simultaneously (Table 2–1). Although many of the initial efforts to limit fraud and abuse were designed to protect the fiscal integrity of the public reimbursement programs—Medicare and Medicaid—more recent efforts have focused on defining appropriate provider relationships and referrals and have expanded to the private market.

Physician-directed or physician-owned vertically integrated systems (see Chapter 4) provide a good example. In these systems, a significant portion of revenue can come from ancillary providers in the form of referrals for certain services. Such services include diagnostic imaging, clinical laboratory, radiation therapy, physical and occupational therapy, ambulatory surgery, home infusion therapy and other home health services, durable medical equipment, parenteral and enteral nutrients and supplies, and outpatient prescription drugs. As a result of changes in Medicare and Medicaid law in 1993, physicians are prohibited from referring patients to such entities if an ownership relationship exists, unless such services are provided in the physician's office.[20] HMOs had previously been exempt from such limitations because an HMO maintains ownership of such services. Physicians typically have no ownership interest; they are employed either as staff of the HMO or are under contract as part of a medical group or as an independent practice association member. In physician-owned vertically integrated systems, however, such ownership interests must be structured to prevent violation. As providers position themselves for managed care contracting by developing other models (e.g., physician–hospital organizations), the federal government will continue to examine the extent to which such relationships are designed to generate referrals.

Efforts to combat fraud and abuse also extend to Medicare managed care. The DHHS Office of the Inspector General examines premium payments to risk-based HMOs. The current system, based on the AAPCC, is continuing to be evaluated to better understand the variables (i.e., de-

Table 2–1 A Fraud and Abuse Continuum

Federal Legislation	*Regulatory Guidance*	*Purpose*
1970s		
Medicare/Medicaid antifraud and abuse amendments	Correspondence	To protect fiscal integrity To protect beneficiaries
Office of the Inspector General created		
1980s		To limit financial gain
Medicare/Medicaid Patient, Program Protection Act	Safe harbors Fraud alert	
Medicare physician ownership restrictions		
1990s		
Physician ownership restrictions expanded, extended to Medicaid	Internal Revenue Service memoranda	To control use
Fraud and abuse control program	New statute	To prevent fraud and abuse
Medicare Integrity Program	New statute	To protect fiscal integrity
Intermediate sanctions for Medicare HMOs	New statute	To punish fraud and abuse violations
Future		
Managed Care Oversight	New statute	To evaluate quality effectiveness

Source: Courtesy of Ernst & Young LLP, 1996.

mographics, eligibility, and geography) used in calculation and whether those variables adequately reflect the risk of a given population. The financial solvency of all managed care plans is also being closely scrutinized by state and federal regulations. Plans lacking a solid financial base are considered a threat to both beneficiaries and providers.

Beginning with a focus on program fiscal integrity and beneficiary protection, government oversight in the late 1980s shifted to controlling use of services. As the federal government gained experience with capitation, it began to evaluate more closely the reasonableness of payment to plans. Another continuing government concern was that purely capitated systems might create incentives for health care providers to deny medically necessary services to enrollees of managed care plans. Consequently, plans and providers should be prepared for the government's continued close scrutiny of certain components of managed care relationships, including quality of care, patient access to providers and other use controls, and calculations for premium and payment amounts.

In addition to the increase in the scope and pace of its investigations, the government has increased the penalties it may impose against providers found guilty of fraudulent or abusive activities as the result of recently enacted federal legislation. The Health Insurance Portability and Accountability Act of 1996 dramatically increases the criminal and administrative penalties that may be imposed against providers who engage in fraudulent or abusive practices. These new penalties will apply not only to those providers who knowingly engage in improper practices, but also to those entities or individuals who deliberately ignore, or recklessly disregard, their legal obligations. The new law also provides millions of dollars for new programs designed to detect fraud and abuse in the delivery of health care and improve recoupment of government monies.

In response to the increased scrutiny and accountability expected of providers, many health care organizations are developing and implementing corporate compliance programs. These enterprisewide programs are designed to detect and prevent violations, identify areas of vulnerability that may place the organization at risk of noncompliance, and reduce an organization's vulnerability to government investigations and other potential liabilities (e.g., whistle-blower actions). An effective program comprises monitoring and auditing systems, reporting or feedback mechanisms, employee training and education, and policies that ensure consistent responses and disciplinary actions to confirmed violations. In addition, if a provider with an effective compliance program is convicted of a violation, the government may reduce the amount of fines and penalties imposed against the provider.

An effective compliance program, at a minimum, should meet the following three objectives: (1) decrease the risk of culpable action by the organization's employees and agents; (2) reaffirm key organizational themes, such as quality and superior service; and (3) meet legal regulatory requirements and those of the U.S. Sentencing Commission Guidelines for Organizations. According to these federal guidelines, the seven key steps to creating an effective compliance program are as follows:

1. Establish compliance standards and procedures.
2. Appoint a "high-level" corporate compliance officer.
3. Delegate discretionary authority to the appropriate individuals within the organization.
4. Implement monitoring, auditing, and reporting systems, including an employee hotline, and publicize the availability of such a mechanism to achieve compliance with standards.
5. Communicate standards and procedures to all employees through effective employee training and dissemination of written information.

6. Establish consistent and appropriate disciplinary mechanisms for employees who are found to be in violation.
7. Establish consistent and appropriate responses to detected violations, including any necessary modifications to the program.[21]

The formality of the compliance plan should reflect the size of the organization; larger organizations generally will have more formalized plans, which tend to include more frequent auditing and more elaborate employee communication programs. Similarly, the compliance plan of smaller organizations will tend to rely more heavily on outside consultants, for example, accountants and coding experts to perform the auditing and educational components of the plan.

Moreover, the board and management must be committed to the written principles and code of conduct developed and must convince employees that they must adhere to these principles. Without achieving enterprisewide commitment and an understanding of the program, the code is worthless. Even worse, the Department of Justice considers a program without substance or commitment a *sham*, that is, worse than no program at all, which will result in the full wrath of the justice system on organizations found out of compliance.

Indeed, the regulatory agencies have begun recently to back their words with actions. In winter 1996, one medium-sized Medicare HMO was found in violation of the HCFA Medicare enrollment guidelines.[22] Continued Medicare enrollment in the plan was suspended and the plan was required to devise and implement corrective actions. Correcting its enrollment problems was not the plan's only problem; the media attention and congressional scrutiny that accompanied these developments was far from flattering.

In the future, health care providers can expect government scrutiny and investigations to continue, if not increase. In the light of this more punitive environment, the risk of not having an effective compliance program in place to detect and prevent violations of the legal requirements that apply to health care providers may ultimately be a risk too great—and too costly—for providers to take.

STATE REGULATION OF MANAGED CARE

The federal government has often enacted national reforms that mirrored legislative trends at the state level. Certainly, the passage of the Health Insurance Portability and Accountability Act reflects that trend. The new law contains provisions providing for portability of coverage, restrictions on the use of preexisting condition limitations, and the establishment (on a demonstration basis) of medical savings accounts. These provisions reflect laws already in place in many states:

- 14 states have enacted legislation providing for guaranteed issue and renewal in the individual market
- 37 states have enacted guaranteed issue and renewal in the small group market
- 33 states have enacted restrictions on the use of preexisting condition limitations that are equal to or greater than the new law
- 20 states have enacted some form of legislation providing for the establishment of medical savings accounts[23]

Washington does not innovate—it replicates, using consensus achieved at the state level as a blueprint for federal activity.

If the U.S. government does indeed replicate state actions, it may then also be moving toward managed care reform. The issue of maternity length-of-stay provides a telling example. As a response, in part, to intense public demand and media scrutiny, 29 states as of August 1996 had enacted some form of mandatory coverage for a minimum hospital maternity length-of-stay for mothers and their newborns (Figure 2–7).[24] Additionally, at this writing, President Clinton has

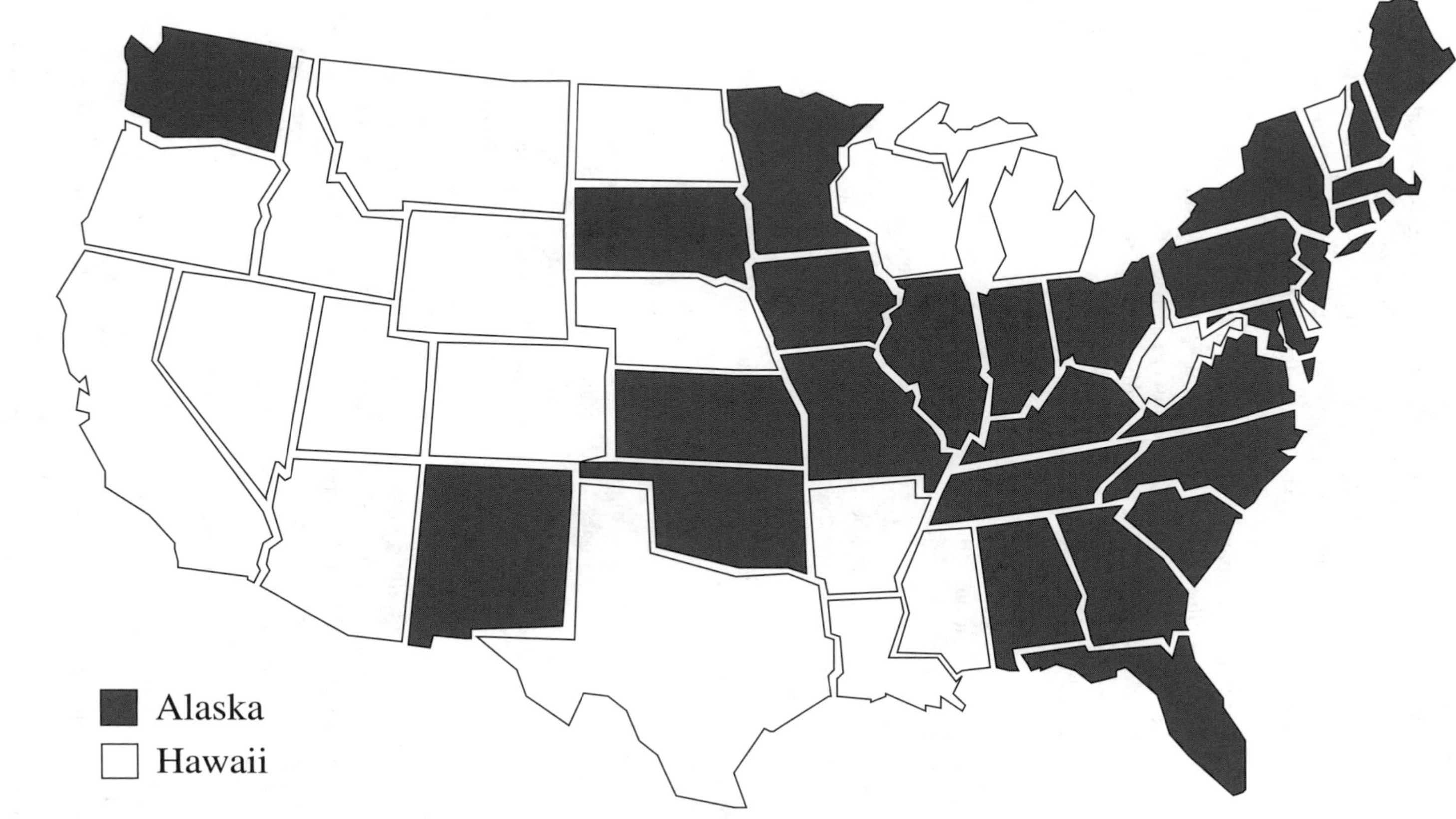

Figure 2–7 States with Mandated Maternity Length-of-Stay, as of August 1996. *Source:* American Association of Health Plans, 1996.

signed federal legislation establishing a similar national standard. These initiatives—due in no small part to anecdotal reports—have resulted despite evidence indicating that HMOs, on average, are already providing a little more than two-day maternity length-of-stay for normal deliveries.[26]

Furthermore, consider that, in a span of 18 months (January 1995 to July 1996),

- 10 states passed laws providing for increased consumer access to and coverage of emergency services by managed care plans
- 13 states now require managed care plans to provide a range of additional information to enrollees and prospective enrollees
- 15 states have prohibited so-called *gag rules*, which restrict the ability of a health plan to limit the discussion of treatment options with the patients
- 17 states now require HMOs to provide direct access to obstetricians and gynecologists (Figure 2–8)[27]

In part, because states have traditionally regulated insurance products, their approach to policy contains far greater detail, clarity, and regulation than that of the federal government. Historically, some states concentrated on regulating Blue Cross/Blue Shield and commercial health plans and, in some cases, allowed managed care plans to operate in an environment relatively free of regulation. In contrast, other states for many years have heavily regulated the managed health care industry. In recent years, the increasing penetration of various managed care plans has prompted a greater need for more market oversight in most parts of the country.

Nonetheless, other forces may also be at work. It is apparent that a backlash has arisen in some quarters against managed care. Although managed care has been proven to reduce the rates of increase in medical costs, its record on improving or maintaining the quality of care has been more difficult to ascertain. Consequently, elements critical of managed care have succeeded in enacting legislation at the state level that they believe will make health plans more accountable to both patients and purchasers.

The trend toward increased regulation of managed care plans only accelerated state activity during the early 1990s. Indeed, as of 1993, 38 states had passed more than 100 laws regulating the operations of managed care plans.[28] Typically, such legislation was a response to an evolving managed care product portfolio. A 1993 survey found that at least 15 states had enacted one or more "any willing provider" laws. An any willing provider law requires a network-based health plan to contract with any and all providers willing to meet their contracting, payment, and credentialing criteria, regardless of whether the network has reached capacity. An additional 20 states were maintaining various other open-panel requirements.[29]

Regulation of New Arrangements

As the health care market matures and new types of risk-sharing arrangements between health care organizations and managed care plans emerge, some states have taken to devising a new regulatory framework.[30] As of this writing, the National Association of Insurance Commissioners is trying to determine whether the risk integrated delivery and financing systems (IDFSs) are assuming is insurance risk or business risk. State regulators have reached consensus on one topic: An IDFS should not be considered to be in the business of insurance if it accepts risk from a licensed insurance carrier (e.g., a percentage of premium arrangements). This carve-out may by revisited, however, if regulators determine that a regulatory gap is developing and consumers are not being protected from insolvencies and incentives for providers to withhold care.

States such as Colorado, Maryland, and Minnesota are leading players in developing new managed care regulations. Colorado requires that an IDFS that accepts risk from a licensed

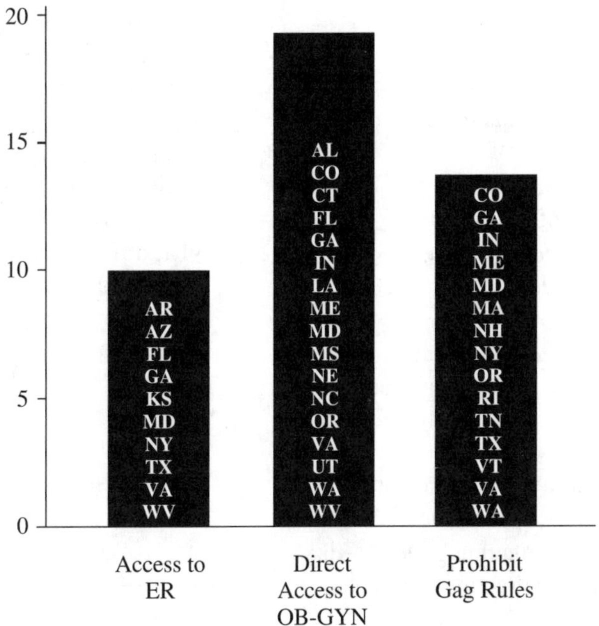

Figure 2–8 States Seek To Reform Managed Care. *Source*: Reprinted with permission from "HMO Consumers at Risk: States to the Rescue," *Families USA* (July 1996).

entity must certify that it is not engaging in the business of insurance. Maryland is developing solvency standards for community health networks that will vary with the level of risk they assume. Minnesota appears to have decided to establish a threshold enrollment level. That state has instituted a different threshold for deposit, reserve, and solvency requirements for community integrated services networks. These networks are essentially IDFSs with 50,000 or fewer lives. Other states that have addressed the IDFS issue include Iowa, Pennsylvania, North Dakota, Texas, and Virginia.[31]

CONCLUSION

As incremental reform of the private and public health care markets continues to be debated and enacted during the remainder of the 1990s and beyond, consumers, employers, lawmakers, regulators, and health policymakers will only increase their reliance on network-based health care systems. At the heart of the debate is the struggle to accept that an integrated delivery system has greater benefit than a system that relies on sole practitioners and traditional fee-for-service. In the coming years, the debate both on and off Capitol Hill is expected to focus on restructuring the Medicare and Medicaid programs to reduce the federal deficit and provide program beneficiaries the same options as those offered to Americans who are younger than age 65 years. Additional activities are likely to center on ensuring that health plans are providing *accountable* health care that maintains or improves the health of its members, as well as making efforts to combat health care fraud and abuse.

To allow continuation of these incremental changes, Congress and the administration will need to address the following areas, among others:

- the regulation and licensure of evolving risk-sharing arrangements
- a renewed focus on the outcomes, quality, and accountability of health plans
- the increased trend toward state-mandated and, potentially, federally mandated benefits
- the increased reliance by federal and state governments on the use of managed care arrangements to meet budgetary spending targets
- standards for health plan participation in the Medicare and Medicaid programs
- a revised payment methodology for Medicare and Medicaid contracting health plans

Each of these areas will have an independent and a collective impact on the development of managed care organizations.

Government-based health care reform will not be accomplished with one grandiose legislative proposal, but, rather, through a series of targeted reforms on which all market players agree. Managed care is already firmly established in the commercial market and is increasing its presence in government programs. Passage of the Health Insurance Portability and Accountability Act may well be the final "nail in the coffin" of traditional indemnity insurance. The future challenge for managed care will not be to increase market presence, but to rebuff legislative attempts to change significantly the manner in which managed care systems operate. The private sector is already engaging in reform of the marketplace. It remains to be seen whether legislative reform efforts will complement the direction of the private market or contradict its movement and evolution.

Study Questions

1. Explain the apparent contradiction between the public's desire for reduced government expenditures and its preferences for maintaining the federal health care safety net.
2. What primary factors are accelerating the movement of Medicare and Medicaid beneficiaries into managed care arrangements?
3. What differentiates previous federal efforts to combat health care fraud and abuse from current efforts?
4. Why does Congress typically follow state-enacted health care reforms when crafting legislation? Based on recent state activity, what reforms might Congress pursue in the coming years?

NOTES

1. Public Law 104-191 (Washington, D.C.: U.S. Government Printing Office, 1996).
2. Congressional Budget Office, *CBO Memorandum: Effects of Managed Care: An Update* (Washington, D.C.: U.S. Government Printing Office, 1994). David C. Stapleton; Lewin-VHI, Inc., *New Evidence of Savings from Network Models of Managed Care* (May 5, 1994).
3. National Health Council, Inc. Health Groups in Washington, Directory, 13th edition (Washington, D.C.: National Health Council 1995).
4. Congressional Budget Office, *Reducing the Deficit: Spending and Revenue Options* (Washington, D.C.: U.S. Government Printing Office, 1996), 2.
5. *Ibid.*
6. Board of Trustees, Federal Hospital Insurance Trust Fund, *1996 Annual Report* (Washington, D.C.: U.S. Government Printing Office), 11.
7. Congressional Budget Office, *Reducing the Deficit,* 433.
8. Kaiser-Harvard Program on the Public and Health/Social Policy, *Survey of Americans on Health Policy* (Menlo Park, C.A., Boston, M.A.: a joint program of the Henry J. Kaiser Foundation and Harvard University) July 30, 1996, 13.
9. HCFA, Office of the Actuary, *Financing Review* (Washington, D.C.: U.S. Government Printing Office, 1996), 234.
10. Health Care Financing Administration, *Monthly Report: Medicare Prepaid Health Plans* (Washington, D.C.: U.S. Government Printing Office, 1996).

11. Mathematica Policy Research, Inc., *Does Managed Care Work for Medicare? An Evaluation of the Medicare Risk Program for HMOs* (1993).
12. U.S. House of Representatives, Committee on the Budget, *Balanced Budget Act of 1995,* conference report to accompany H.R. 2491, 104th Congress. Report 104-350, First Session.
13. Alliance for Health Reform, *A Medicare and Medicaid Sourcebook* (Washington, D.C.: Alliance for Health Reform, 1995).
14. *Ibid.*
15. Congressional Budget Office, *Reducing the Deficit,* 433.
16. Faulkner & Gray, Inc., *Medicaid Managed Care Sourcebook: A Progress Report and Resource Guide on Managed Care Programs in the States* (New York, N.Y.: Faulkner & Gray, Inc., 1996, A).
17. Congressional Budget Office, *Reducing the Deficit,* 433.
18. Health Care Financing Administration, press release, "State Medicaid Demonstrations" (Washington, D.C.: U.S. Government Printing Office, July 1996).
19. Alliance for Health Reform, *A Medicare and Medicaid Sourcebook,* B-15.
20. U.S. House of Representatives, Committee on the Budget, *Omnibus Budget Reconciliation Act of 1993,* conference report to accompany H.R. 2264, 103rd Congress. Report 103-213, First Session; 807.
21. U.S. Sentencing Commission Guidelines for Organizations (1991), Title 18, Chapter 8, Part A, Section 8A1.2.
22. News and Strategies for Managed Medicare & Medicaid, "Massachusetts Blue Cross Medicare HMO Gets Slapped with Federal Sanctions" (Washington, D.C.: Atlantic Information Services, Inc.), 2 (5):1.
23. National Association of Insurance Commissioners (NAIC), telephone conversation with Mary Beth Senkewicz, Counsel for Health Policy, NAIC. August 1996.
24. American Association of Health Plans, August 1996.
25. Public Law 104-204 (Washington, D.C.: U.S. Government Printing Office).
26. National Committee for Quality Assurance, press release, "NCQA Launches Quality Compass: Reports Provide Wealth of Data on Health Plan Quality," August 21, 1996.
27. "HMO Consumers at Risk: States to the Rescue;" Washington, D.C.: Families USA, July 1996. Reprinted with permission.
28. The George Washington University, Intergovernmental Health Policy Project, *Managed Care: An Overview of 1993 State Legislative Activity* (Washington, D.C.: The George Washington University, 1993).
29. Group Health Association of America (GHAA). Open-Panel Survey, December 15, 1993: 2.
30. National Association of Insurance Commissioners, 1996.
31. Ernst & Young LLP, *Navigating the Changing Currents: IDFS Profile 1996* (Washington, D.C.: Ernst & Young), 5.

Chapter 3

Types of Managed Care Organizations

Eric R. Wagner

Study Objectives

- Understand the different types of managed care organizations
- Understand key differences between these types of organizations
- Understand the inherent strengths and weaknesses of each model type

The various types of managed health care organizations were reasonably distinct as recently as 1988. Since then, the differences between traditional forms of health insurance and managed care organizations have narrowed substantially. More recently, the distinctions between health care providers and health care insurers have blurred substantially. In contrast to the situation 10 years ago, when managed care organizations were often referred to as *alternative delivery systems*, managed care is now the dominant form of health insurance coverage in the United States.

Originally, health maintenance organizations (HMOs), preferred provider organizations (PPOs), and traditional forms of indemnity health insurance were distinct, mutually exclusive products and mechanisms for providing health care coverage. Today, an observer may be hard pressed to uncover the differences among products that bill themselves as HMOs, PPOs, or managed care overlays to health insurance. For example, many HMOs, which traditionally limited their members to a designated set of participating providers, now allow their members to use nonparticipating providers at a reduced coverage level. Such point-of-service (POS) plans combine HMO-like systems with indemnity systems, allowing individual members to choose which systems they wish to access at the time they need the medical service. Similarly, some PPOs, which historically provided unrestricted access to physicians and other health care providers (albeit at different coverage levels), have implemented primary care case management or gatekeeper systems and have added elements of financial risk to their reimbursement systems. Finally, most indemnity insurance (or self-insurance) plans now include utilization management features in their plans that were once found only in HMOs or PPOs.

As a result of these recent changes, the descriptions of the different types of managed care systems that follow provide only a guideline for determining the form of managed care organization that is observed. In many cases (or in most

Eric R. Wagner is Vice President for Managed Care at Medlantic Healthcare Group and Washington Hospital Center where he is responsible for the development of managed care strategy, negotiation of participation agreements, and maintenance of relationships with managed care plans. In addition, he serves as Executive Director of and has operational responsibility for the WHC Physician-Hospital Organization. Previously, Mr. Wagner was with the health care strategy and managed care practice of an international professional services firm. He has more than 14 years of experience in the health care industry specializing in managed care strategy, development, operation, and finance and has published several books, chapters, and articles on managed care evaluation, development, negotiations, and provider compensation.

cases in some markets), the managed health care organization will be a hybrid of several specific types.

Some controversy exists about whether the term *managed care* accurately describes the new generation of health care delivery and financing mechanisms. Those commentators who object to the term raise questions about what it is that is managed by a managed care organization. These commentators ask: Is the individual patient's medical care being managed, or is the organization simply managing the composition and reimbursement of the provider delivery system?

Observers who favor the term *managed care* believe that managing the provider delivery system can be equivalent in its outcomes to managing the medical care delivered to the patient. In contrast to historical methods of financing health care delivery in the United States, the current generation of financing mechanisms includes far more active management of both the delivery system through which care is provided and the medical care that is actually delivered to individual patients. Although the term *managed care* may not perfectly describe this current generation of financing vehicles, it provides a convenient shorthand description for the range of alternatives to traditional indemnity health insurance.

A simplistic but useful concept regarding managed care is the continuum. On one end of the continuum is managed indemnity with simple precertification of elective admissions and large case management of catastrophic cases, superimposed on a traditional indemnity insurance plan. Similar to indemnity is the service plan, which has contractual relationships with providers addressing maximum fee allowances, prohibiting balance billing, and using the same utilization management techniques as managed indemnity (the nearly universal, although not exclusive, examples of service plans are Blue Cross/Blue Shield plans). Further along the continuum are PPOs, POSs, open-panel [individual practice association (IPA) type] HMOs, and closed-panel (group and staff model) HMOs. As you progress from one end of the continuum to the other, you add new and greater elements of control and accountability, you tend to increase both the complexity and the overhead required to operate the plan, and you achieve greater potential control of cost and quality. This continuum is illustrated in Figure 3–1.

This chapter provides a description of the different types of managed health care organizations and the common acronyms used to represent them. A brief explanation is provided for each type of organization. In addition, this chapter includes descriptions of the five most common forms of HMOs—the original managed care organizations—and their relationships with physicians.

TYPES OF MANAGED CARE ORGANIZATIONS AND COMMON ACRONYMS

The managed care and health care industries have spawned a large number of acronyms to describe their distinctive organizations; many people have described these acronyms as a confusing alphabet soup of initials. Nevertheless, knowledge of a few key acronyms makes an understanding of the managed care environment easier.

HMOs

HMOs are organized health care systems that are responsible for both the financing and the delivery of a broad range of comprehensive health services to an enrolled population. The original definition of an HMO also included the aspect of financing health care for a prepaid fixed fee (hence the term *prepaid health plan*), but that portion of the definition is no longer absolute, although it is still common.

In many ways, an HMO can be viewed as a combination of a health insurer and a health care delivery system. Whereas traditional health care insurance companies are responsible for reimbursing covered individuals for the cost of their health care, HMOs are responsible for providing health care services to their covered members

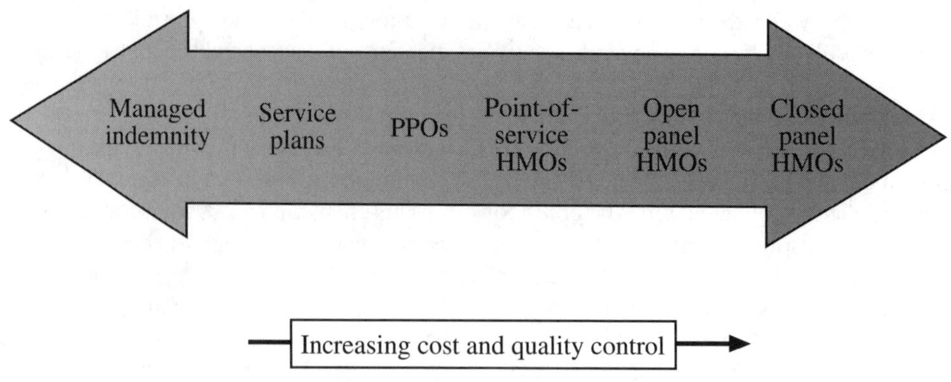

Figure 3–1 Continuum of managed care.

through affiliated providers, who are reimbursed under various methods (see Chapters 6, 8, 9, and 10).

As a result of their responsibility for providing covered health services to their members, HMOs must ensure that their members have access to covered health care services. In addition, HMOs generally are responsible for ensuring the quality and appropriateness of the health services they provide to their members.

The five common models of HMOs are (1) staff, (2) group practice, (3) network, (4) IPA, and (5) direct contract. The primary differences among these models are based on how the HMO relates to its participating physicians. These relationships are described in more detail later in this chapter.

PPOs

PPOs are entities through which employer health benefit plans and health insurance carriers contract to purchase health care services for covered beneficiaries from a selected group of participating providers. Typically, participating providers in PPOs agree to abide by utilization management and other procedures implemented by the PPO and agree to accept the PPO's reimbursement structure and payment levels. In return, PPOs often limit the size of their participating provider panels and provide incentives for their covered individuals to use participating providers instead of other providers. In contrast to individuals with traditional HMO coverage, individuals with PPO coverage are permitted to use non-PPO providers, although higher levels of coinsurance or deductibles routinely apply to services provided by these nonparticipating providers.

PPOs sometimes are described *as preferred provider arrangements (PPAs)*. The definition of a PPA is usually the same as the definition of a PPO. Some observers, however, use the term *PPA* to describe a less formal relationship than would be described by *PPO*. The term *PPO* implies that an organization exists, whereas a PPA may achieve the same goals as a PPO through an informal arrangement among providers and payers.

The key common characteristics of PPOs include the following:

- *Select provider panel.* PPOs typically contract with selected providers in a community to provide health services for covered individuals. Most PPOs contract directly with hospitals, physicians, and other diagnostic facilities. Providers are selected to participate on the basis of their cost efficiency, community reputation, and scope of services. Some PPOs assemble massive databases of information about potential providers, including costs by diagnostic category, before they make their contracting decisions.

- *Negotiated payment rates.* Most PPO participation agreements require participating providers to accept the PPO's payments as payment in full for covered services (except for applicable coinsurance or deductibles). PPOs attempt to negotiate payment rates that provide them with a competitive cost advantage relative to charge-based payment systems. These negotiated payment rates usually take the form of discounts from charges, all-inclusive per-diem rates, or payments based on diagnosis-related groups. Some PPOs have established bundled pricing arrangements for certain services, including normal delivery, open heart surgery, and some types of oncology.
- *Rapid payment terms.* Some PPOs are willing to include prompt payment features in their contracts with participating providers in return for favorable payment rates. For example, a PPO may commit to pay all clean claims submitted by its providers within 15 days of submittal in return for a larger discount from charges.
- *Utilization management.* Many PPOs implement utilization management programs to control the utilization and cost of health services provided to their covered beneficiaries. In the more sophisticated PPOs, these utilization management programs resemble the programs operated by HMOs. Unlike indemnity plans where failure to comply with utilization management precertification programs increases the financial liability to the member (or covered insured), many PPOs impose the financial penalty for noncompliance on the participating provider, who may not balance bill the penalty to the member. (Of course, if the member uses a nonparticipating or out-of-network provider, the financial penalty for noncompliance falls back to the member.)
- *Consumer choice.* Unlike traditional HMOs, PPOs generally allow covered beneficiaries to use non-PPO providers instead of PPO providers when they need health services. Higher levels of beneficiary cost sharing, often in the form of higher copayments, typically are imposed when PPO beneficiaries use non-PPO providers.

Exclusive Provider Organizations

Exclusive provider organizations (EPOs) are similar to PPOs in their organization and purpose. Unlike PPOs, however, EPOs limit their beneficiaries to participating providers for any health care services. In other words, beneficiaries covered by an EPO are required to receive all their covered health care services from providers who participate with the EPO. The EPO generally does not cover services received from other providers, although there may be exceptions.

Some EPOs parallel HMOs in that they not only require exclusive use of the EPO provider network but also use a gatekeeper approach to authorizing nonprimary care services. In these cases, the primary difference between an HMO and an EPO is that the former is regulated under HMO laws and regulations, whereas the latter is regulated under insurance laws and regulations or the Employee Retirement Income Security Act of 1974 (ERISA; this topic is discussed in detail in *The Managed Health Care Handbook, Third Edition*), which governs self-insured health plans.

EPOs usually are implemented by employers whose primary motivation is cost saving. These employers are less concerned about the reaction of their employees to severe restrictions on the choice of health care provider and offer the EPO as a replacement for traditional indemnity health insurance coverage. Because of the severe restrictions on provider choice, only a few large employers have been willing to convert their entire health benefits programs to an EPO format.

POS Plans

Capitated and Primary Care PPOs

These are hybrids of more traditional HMO and PPO models. The following are characteristics of these types of plans:

- Primary care physicians are reimbursed through capitation payments (i.e., a fixed payment per member per month) or other performance-based reimbursement methods. (See Chapter 8.)
- Often, an amount is withheld from physician compensation that is paid contingent upon achievement of utilization or cost targets.
- The primary care physician acts as a gatekeeper for referral and institutional medical services.
- The member retains some coverage for services rendered that either are not authorized by the primary care physician or are delivered by nonparticipating providers. Such coverage is typically significantly lower than coverage for authorized services delivered by participating providers (e.g., 100 percent compared with 60 percent).

Traditional HMOs may offer similar benefit options through an out-of-plan benefits rider or POS option.

Open Access or POS HMOs

Many HMOs have recognized that the major impediment to enrolling additional members and expanding market share has been the reluctance of individuals to forfeit completely their ability to receive reimbursement for using nonparticipating providers. These individuals consider the possibility that they would need the services of a renowned specialist for a rare (and expensive to treat) disorder and believe that the HMO would not refer them for care or reimburse their expenses. This possibility, no matter how unlikely, overshadows all the other benefits of HMO coverage in the minds of many individuals.

An expanding number of HMOs (and insurance carriers with both HMOs and indemnity operations) have adopted a solution to this problem: They provide some level of indemnity-type coverage for their members. HMO members covered under these types of benefit plans may decide whether to use HMO benefits or indemnity-style benefits for each instance of care. In other words, the member is allowed to make a coverage choice at the point of service when medical care is needed.

The indemnity coverage available under POS options from HMOs typically incorporates high deductibles and coinsurance to encourage members to use HMO services instead of out-of-plan services. Members who use the non-HMO benefit portion of the benefit plan may also be subject to utilization management (e.g., preadmission certification and continued stay review). Despite the availability of out-of-network benefits, studies have found that most POS plans experience between 65 percent and 85 percent in-network usage, thus retaining considerable cost control compared to indemnity-type plans.

There are two primary ways for an HMO to offer a POS option: (1) via a single HMO license or (2) via a dual-license approach. The single-license approach means that the HMO provides the out-of-network benefit using its HMO license. In many states, this restricts the total dollar amount of out-of-network care to 10 percent or less. The dual-license approach is more flexible in that the health plan uses an HMO license to provide the in-network care and an indemnity license to provide the out-of-network coverage. Dual license obviously requires either that a single company possess both licenses (e.g., a commercial insurance carrier with a subsidiary HMO) or the HMO to partner with a licensed insurance carrier. In a few cases, an HMO has contracted with an indemnity carrier to front the indemnity portion but has retained the bulk of the risk for medical expenses through the funding arrangement with the carrier.

This hybrid form of health benefit coverage represents an attractive managed care option for many employers and their covered employees, particularly when the employer is looking toward POS as a consolidation of existing indemnity coverage and multiple HMOs in the group (i.e., total replacement coverage). Coverage under HMO POS plans recently has been the fastest growing segment of health insurance.

Self-insured and Experience-Rated HMOs

Historically, HMOs offered community-rated premiums to all employers and individuals who enrolled for HMO coverage. The federal HMO Act originally mandated community rating for all HMOs that decided to pursue federal qualification. Community rating was eventually expanded to include rating by class, where premium rates for an individual employer group could be adjusted prospectively on the basis of demographic characteristics that were associated with utilization differences. Such characteristics often included the age and sex distributions of the employer's work force and the standard industrial classification of the employer.

Although community rating by class provided HMOs with some flexibility to offer more attractive rates to selected employer groups, many employers continued to believe that their group-specific experience would be better than the rates offered by HMOs. Some HMOs developed self-insured or experience-rated options in response to the needs expressed by these employers.

Under a typical self-insured benefit option, an HMO receives a fixed monthly payment to cover administrative services (and profit) and variable payments that are based on the actual payments made by the HMO for health services. There is usually a settlement process at the end of a specified period, during which a final payment is calculated (either to the HMO by the group or to the group by the HMO). Variations in the payment arrangement exist and are similar in structure to the different forms of self-funded insurance programs.

Under experience-rated benefit options, an HMO receives monthly premium payments much as it would under traditional premium-based plans. There typically is a settlement process where the employer is credited with some portion (or all) of the actual utilization and cost of its group to arrive at a final premium rate. Refunds or additional payments are then calculated and made to the appropriate party.

The HMO regulations of some states and federal HMO qualification regulations preclude HMOs from offering self-insured or experience-rated benefit plans. HMOs avoid these prohibitions by incorporating related corporate entities that use the HMO's negotiated provider agreements, management systems, utilization protocols, and personnel to service the self-insured line of business.

Rating and underwriting methodologies are discussed in detail in Chapter 23.

Specialty HMOs

Specialty HMOs have developed in some states to provide the benefits of the HMO model to limited components of health care coverage. Dental HMOs have become common as an option to indemnity dental insurance coverage. (This topic is discussed in detail in *The Managed Health Care Handbook, Third Edition.*) Specialty HMOs serving other health care needs (e.g., mental health) have also developed in certain states where they are permitted under the insurance or HMO laws and regulations. One challenge to the formation of such HMOs is that state laws often define a broad range of health services that are required to be offered by licensed HMOs; other states, however, have regulations to allow so-called "single specialty HMOs."

Managed Care Overlays to Indemnity Insurance

The perceived success of HMOs and other types of managed care organizations in controlling the utilization and cost of health services has prompted entrepreneurs to develop managed care overlays that can be combined with traditional indemnity insurance, service plan insurance, or self-insurance. (The term *indemnity insurance* is used to refer to all three forms of coverage in this context.) These managed care overlays are intended to provide cost control for insured plans while retaining the individual's freedom of choice of provider and coverage for out-of-plan services.

The following types of managed care overlays currently exist:

- *General utilization management.* These companies offer a complete menu of utilization management activities that can be selected by individual employers or insurers. Some offer or can develop panels of participating providers within individual markets and bear a strong resemblance to PPOs.
- *Specialty utilization management.* Firms that focus on utilization review for specialty services have become common. Mental health and dental care are two common types of specialty utilization management overlays.
- *Catastrophic or large case management.* Some firms have developed to assist employers and insurers with managing catastrophic cases regardless of the specialty involved. This service includes screening to identify cases that will become catastrophic, negotiation of services and reimbursement with providers who can treat the patient's condition, development of a treatment protocol for the patient, and ongoing monitoring of the treatment. See Chapter 16 for further discussion of this topic.
- *Workers' compensation utilization management.* In response to the rapid increases in the cost of workers' compensation insurance, firms have developed managed care overlays to address what they claim are the unique needs of patients covered under workers' compensation benefits. Managed care and workers' compensation programs are discussed in detail in *The Managed Health Care Handbook, Third Edition.*

Physician–Hospital Organizations

As their name implies, *physician–hospital organizations (PHOs)* are organizations that generally are jointly owned and operated by hospitals and their affiliated physicians. These organizations typically are developed to provide a vehicle for hospitals and physicians to contract together with other managed care organizations to provide both physician and hospital services. They represent one approach taken by providers who are implementing integrated delivery systems.

In their simplest form, PHOs are separately incorporated entities in which physicians and one or more hospitals are shareholders or members. These members execute provider agreements with the PHO under which they delegate responsibility for negotiating agreements with managed care organizations (or, in some cases, employers) to the PHO and agree to accept as reimbursement the PHO's payment schedules.

PHOs can offer several advantages for providers who develop them:

- They may increase the negotiating clout of their individual members with managed care organizations.
- They provide a vehicle for physicians and hospitals to establish reimbursement and risk-sharing approaches that align incentives among all providers.
- They can serve as a clearinghouse for certain administrative activities, including

credentialing and utilization management, thereby reducing the administrative burden on their individual physician and hospital members.

- They provide an organized approach for physicians and hospitals to work together on managed care issues, including utilization management and quality improvement.

PHOs may also offer advantages to some managed care organizations:

- For organizations that are new to a market, PHOs can provide a means of rapidly establishing a panel of participating physicians and hospitals.
- If the managed care organization delegates claim processing responsibility to it, the PHO can provide a means of reducing operating costs.

Despite their potential for benefits to health care providers and managed care organizations, many observers believe that PHOs have fallen far short of their promise. Recent surveys suggest that PHOs have achieved only limited success in contracting with managed care plans and generally have not implemented medical management programs. (For example, see Ernst & Young's *Survey of PHOs*.[1]) Among the reasons for the lack of success for PHOs are the following:

- Managed care organizations in many markets have achieved great success in enrolling large panels of participating physicians and hospitals. For these organizations, PHOs may offer little or no benefit.
- Although many PHOs have professed strong interest in assuming financial risk for delivering health services by accepting capitation-based payments, many managed care organizations have been reluctant to cede global capitation payments because they continue to earn margins by managing the utilization and cost of health services. These margins would be reduced or eliminated if they passed capitated risk along to PHOs.

PHOs and other forms of integrated delivery systems are discussed in detail in Chapter 4.

HMO MODELS

The five commonly recognized models of HMOs are (1) staff, (2) group, (3) network, (4) IPA, and (5) direct contract. The major differences among these models pertain to the relationship between the HMO and its participating physicians. Until recently, individual HMOs usually could be neatly categorized into a single model type for descriptive purposes. Currently, many (if not most) HMOs have different relationships with different groups of physicians. As a result, many HMOs cannot easily be classified as a single model type, although such plans are occasionally referred to as *mixed models*. The HMO model type descriptions now may be more appropriately used to describe an HMO's relationship with certain segments of its physicians. The following sections provide brief descriptions of the five common HMO model types. Further discussion can be found in Chapters 1, 6, and 7.

Staff Model

In a staff model HMO, the physicians who serve the HMO's covered beneficiaries are employed by the HMO. These physicians typically are paid on a salary basis and may also receive bonus or incentive payments that are based on their performance and productivity. Staff model HMOs must employ physicians in all the common specialties to provide for the health care needs of their members. These HMOs often contract with selected subspecialists in the community for infrequently needed health services.

Staff model HMOs are also known as *closed panel HMOs* because most participating physicians are employees of the HMO, and community physicians are unable to participate. A well-known example of staff model HMOs is Group Health Cooperative of Puget Sound in Seattle, Washington. Many staff model HMOs are incorporating other types of physician relationships into their delivery system.

Physicians in staff model HMOs usually practice in one or more centralized ambulatory care facilities. These facilities, which often resemble outpatient clinics, contain physician offices and ancillary support facilities (e.g., laboratory and radiology) to support the health care needs of the HMO's beneficiaries. Staff model HMOs usually contract with hospitals and other inpatient facilities in the community to provide nonphysician services for their members.

Staff model HMOs can have an advantage relative to other HMO models in managing health care delivery because they have a greater degree of control over the practice patterns of their physicians. As a result, it can be easier for staff model HMOs to manage and control the utilization of health services. They also offer the convenience of one-stop shopping for their members because the HMO's facilities tend to be full service (i.e., they have laboratory, radiology, and other departments).

Offsetting this advantage are several disadvantages for staff model HMOs. First, staff model HMOs are usually more costly to develop and implement because of the small membership and the large fixed salary expenses that the HMO must incur for staff physicians and support staff. Second, staff model HMOs provide a limited choice of participating physicians for potential HMO members. Many potential members are reluctant to change from their current physician and find the idea of a clinic setting uncomfortable. Third, some staff model HMOs have experienced productivity problems with their staff physicians, which have raised their costs for providing care. Finally, it is expensive for staff model HMOs to expand their services into new areas because of the need to construct new ambulatory care facilities.

Group Model

In pure group model HMOs, the HMO contracts with a multispecialty physician group practice to provide all physician services to the HMO's members. The physicians in the group practice are employed by the group practice and not by the HMO. In some cases, these physicians may be allowed to see both HMO patients and other patients, although their primary function may be to treat HMO members.

Physicians in a group practice share facilities, equipment, medical records, and support staff. The group may contract with the HMO on an all-inclusive capitation basis to provide physician services to HMO members. Alternatively, the group may contract on a cost basis to provide its services.

There are two broad categories of group model HMOs, as described below.

Captive Group

In the captive group model, the physician group practice exists solely to provide services to the HMO's beneficiaries. In most cases, the HMO formed the group practice to serve its members, recruited physicians, and now provides administrative services to the group. The most prominent example of this type of HMO is the Kaiser Foundation Health Plan, where the Permanente Medical Groups provide all physician services for Kaiser's members. The Kaiser Foundation Health Plan, as the licensed HMO, is responsible for marketing the benefit plans, enrolling members, collecting premium payments, and performing other HMO functions. The Permanente Medical Groups are responsible for rendering physician services to Kaiser's members under an exclusive contractual relationship with Kaiser. Kaiser is sometimes mistakenly thought to be a staff model HMO because of the close relationship between itself and the Permanente Medical Groups.

Independent Group

In the independent group model HMO, the HMO contracts with an existing, independent, multispecialty physician group to provide physician services to its members. In some cases, the independent physician group is the sponsor or owner of the HMO. An example of the independent group model HMO is Geisinger Health Plan of Danville, Pennsylvania. The Geisinger Clinic, which is a large, multispecialty physician group practice, is the independent group associated with the Geisinger Health Plan.

Typically, the physician group in an independent group model HMO continues to provide services to non-HMO patients while it participates in the HMO. Although the group may have an exclusive relationship with the HMO, this relationship usually does not prevent the group from engaging in non-HMO business.

Common Features of Group Models

Both types of group model HMOs are also referred to as *closed-panel HMOs* because physicians must be members of the group practice to participate in the HMO; as a result, the HMO is considered closed to physicians who are not part of the group. Both types of group model HMOs share the advantages of staff model HMOs: making it somewhat easier to conduct utilization management because of the integration of physician practices and providing broad services at their facilities. In addition, group practice HMOs may have lower capital needs than staff model HMOs because the HMO does not have to support the large fixed-salary costs associated with staff physicians.

Group model HMOs have several disadvantages in common with staff model HMOs. Like staff model HMOs, group model HMOs provide a limited choice of participating physicians from which potential HMO members can select. The limited physician panel can be a disadvantage in marketing the HMO. The limited number of office locations for the participating medical groups may also restrict the geographic accessibility of physicians for the HMO's members. The lack of accessibility can make it difficult for the HMO to market its coverage to a wide geographic area. Finally, certain group practices may be perceived by some potential HMO members as offering an undesirable clinic setting. Offsetting this disadvantage may be the perception of high quality associated with many of the physician group practices that are affiliated with HMOs.

Network Model

In network model HMOs, the HMO contracts with more than one group practice to provide physician services to the HMO's members. These group practices may be broad-based, multispecialty groups, in which case, the HMO resembles the group practice model described above. An example of this type of HMO is Health Insurance Plan of Greater New York, which contracts with many multispecialty physician group practices in the New York area.

Alternatively, the HMO may contract with several small groups of primary care physicians (i.e., family practice, internal medicine, pediatrics, and obstetrics/gynecology), in which case, the HMO can be classified as a primary care network model. In the primary care network model, the HMO contracts with several groups consisting of 7 to 15 primary care physicians representing the specialties of family practice and/or internal medicine, pediatrics, and obstetrics/gynecology to provide physician services to its members. Typically, the HMO compensates these groups on an all-inclusive physician capitation basis. The group is responsible for providing all physician services to the HMO's members assigned to the group and may refer to other physicians as necessary. The group is financially responsible for reimbursing other physicians for any referrals it makes. In some cases, the HMO may negotiate participation arrangements with specialist physicians to make it easier for its primary care groups to manage their referrals.

In contrast to the staff and group model HMOs described previously, network models may be either closed- or open-panel plans. If the network model HMO is a closed-panel plan, it will only contract with a limited number of existing group practices. If it is an open-panel plan, participation in the group practices will be open to any physician who meets the HMO's and group's credentials criteria. In some cases, network model HMOs will assist independent primary care physicians with the formation of primary care groups for the sole purpose of participating in the HMO's network.

Network model HMOs address many of the disadvantages associated with staff and group model HMOs. In particular, the broader physician participation that is usually identified with network model HMOs helps overcome the marketing disadvantage associated with the closed-panel staff and group model plans. Nevertheless, network model HMOs usually have more limited physician participation than either IPA model or direct contract model plans.

IPA Model

IPA model HMOs contract with an association of physicians—the IPA—to provide physician services to their members. The physicians are members of the IPA, which is a separate legal entity, but they remain individual practitioners and retain their separate offices and identities. IPA physicians continue to see their non-HMO patients and maintain their own offices, medical records, and support staff. IPA model HMOs are open-panel plans because participation is open to all community physicians who meet the HMO's and IPA's selection criteria.

Generally, IPAs attempt to recruit physicians from all specialties to participate in their plans. Broad participation of physicians allows the IPA to provide all necessary physician services through participating physicians and minimizes the need for IPA physicians to refer HMO members to nonparticipating physicians to obtain services. In addition, broad physician participation can help make the IPA model HMO more attractive to potential HMO members.

IPA model HMOs usually follow one of two different methods of establishing relationships with their IPAs. In the first method, the HMO contracts with an IPA that has been independently established by community physicians. These types of IPAs often have contracts with more than one HMO on a nonexclusive basis. In the second method, the HMO works with community physicians to create an IPA and to recruit physicians to participate in it. The HMO's contract with these types of IPAs is usually on an exclusive basis because of the HMO's leading role in forming the IPA.

IPAs may be formed as large, community-wide entities where physicians can participate without regard to the hospital with which they are affiliated. Alternatively, IPAs may be hospital-based and formed so that only physicians from one or two hospitals are eligible to participate in the IPA.

Hospital-based IPAs are sometimes preferred by HMOs over larger, community-based IPAs for at least two reasons. First, hospital-based IPAs can restrict the panel of the IPA to physicians who are familiar with each other's practice patterns. This familiarity can make the utilization management process easier. Second, by using several hospital-based IPAs, an HMO can limit the impact of a termination of one of its IPA agreements to a smaller group of physicians.

Most HMOs compensate their IPAs on an all-inclusive physician capitation basis to provide services to the HMO's members. The IPA then compensates its participating physicians on either a fee-for-service basis or a combination of fee-for-service and primary care capitation. In the fee-for-service variation, IPAs pay all their participating physicians on the basis of a fee schedule or a usual, customary, or reasonable (UCR) charge approach and withhold a portion of each payment for incentive and risk-sharing purposes.

Under the primary care capitation approach, IPAs pay their participating primary care physicians on a capitation basis and pay their specialist physicians on the basis of a fee schedule or UCR approach. The primary care capitation payments are based on fixed amounts per member per month and usually vary depending on the HMO member's age and sex. The IPA typically withholds a portion of both the capitation and fee-for-service payments for risk-sharing and incentive purposes. Compensation for primary care is discussed in Chapter 8.

IPA model HMOs overcome all the disadvantages associated with staff, group, and network model HMOs. They require less capital to establish and operate. In addition, they can provide a broad choice of participating physicians who practice in their private offices. As a result, IPA model HMOs offer marketing advantages in comparison to the staff and group model plans.

There are two major disadvantages of IPA model HMOs from the HMO's perspective. First, the development of an IPA creates an organized forum for physicians to negotiate as a group with the HMO. The organized forum of an IPA can help its physician members achieve some of the negotiating benefits of belonging to a group practice. Unlike the situation with a group practice, however, individual members of an IPA retain their ability to negotiate and contract directly with managed care plans. Because of their acceptance of combined risk through capitation payments, IPAs are generally immune from antitrust restrictions on group activities by physicians as long as they do not prevent or prohibit their member physicians from participating directly with an HMO. Second, the process of utilization management generally is more difficult in an IPA model HMO than it is in staff and group model plans because physicians remain individual practitioners with little sense of being a part of the HMO. As a result, IPA model HMOs may devote more administrative resources to managing inpatient and outpatient utilization than their staff and group model counterparts. Notwithstanding this historical disadvantage, recent analyses suggest that some IPA model HMOs have overcome the challenge and have succeeded in managing utilization at least as well as their closed-panel counterparts.

Direct Contract Model

As the name implies, direct contract model HMOs contract directly with individual physicians to provide physician services to their members. With the exception of their direct contractual relationship with participating physicians, direct contract model HMOs are similar to IPA model plans. A well-known example of a direct contract model HMO is US Healthcare and its subsidiary HMOs.

Direct contract model HMOs attempt to recruit broad panels of community physicians to provide physician services as participating providers. These HMOs usually recruit both primary care and specialist physicians and typically use a primary care case management approach (also known as a *gatekeeper system*).

Like IPA model plans, direct contract model HMOs compensate their physicians on either a fee-for-service basis or a primary care capitation basis. Primary care capitation is somewhat more commonly used by direct contract model HMOs because it helps limit the financial risk assumed by the HMO. Unlike IPA model HMOs, direct contract model HMOs retain most of the financial risk for providing physician services; IPA model plans transfer this risk to their IPAs.

Direct contract model HMOs have most of the same advantages as IPA model HMOs. In addition, direct model HMOs eliminate the potential of a physician bargaining unit by contracting directly with individual physicians. This contracting model reduces the possibility of mass termination of physician participation agreements.

Direct contract model HMOs have several disadvantages. First, the HMO may assume additional financial risk for physician services relative to an IPA model HMO, as noted above. This additional risk exposure can be expensive if primary care physicians generate excessive referrals to specialist physicians. Second, it can be more difficult and time consuming for a direct contract model HMO to recruit physicians because it lacks the physician leadership inherent in an IPA model plan. It is more difficult for nonphysicians to recruit physicians, as several direct contract model HMOs discovered in their attempts to expand into new markets. Finally, utilization management may be more difficult in direct contract model HMOs because all contact with physicians is on an individual basis, and there may be little incentive for physicians to participate in the utilization management programs.

CONCLUSION

Managed care is on a continuum, with a number of plan types offering an array of features that vary in their abilities to balance access to care, cost, quality control, benefit design, and flexibility. Managed care plans continue to evolve, with features from one type of plan appearing in others and new features continually being developed. There is no single definition of the term *managed care* that has endured in the past or will survive into the future.

Study Questions

1. Describe the continuum of managed health care plans and key differences for each. Give examples of each.
2. What are the principal elements of control found in each type of managed care plan? In which plans do these elements appear?
3. Describe the primary strengths and advantages, and weaknesses and disadvantages, of each type of managed care plan.
4. In what type of market situations might each type of managed care plan be the preferred model?
5. Describe how a managed care plan of one type might evolve into another type of plan over time.

REFERENCE AND NOTE

1. Ernst & Young LLP, *Physician–Hospital Organizations: Profile 1995* (Washington, D.C.: Ernst & Young LLP, 1995).

SUGGESTED READING

Boland, P. 1993. *Making Managed Healthcare Work: A Practical Guide to Strategies and Solutions.* Gaithersburg, Md.: Aspen.

Dasco, S.T. and Dasco, C.C. 1996. *Managed Care Answer Book.* New York: Panel Publishers.

Ernst & Young LLP. 1995. *Physician–Hospital Organizations: Profile 1995.* Washington, D.C.: Ernst & Young LLP.

Hale, J.A. 1988. *From HMO Movement to Managed Care Industry: The Future of HMOs in a Volatile Healthcare Market.* Minneapolis, Minn.: InterStudy.

Rahn, G.J. 1987. *Hospital-Sponsored Health Maintenance Organizations.* Chicago, Ill.: American Hospital Publishing.

Shouldice, R.G. 1991. *Introduction to Managed Care.* Arlington, Va.: Information Resources Press.

Traska, M.R. 1996. *Managed Care Strategies 1996.* New York: Faulkner & Gray.

Wagner, E.R. 1987. *A Practical Guide to Evaluating Physician Capitation Payments.* Washington, D.C.: American Society of Internal Medicine.

Wagner, E.R, and Hackenberg, V.J. 1986. *A Practical Guide to Physician-Sponsored HMO Development.* Washington, D.C.: American Society of Internal Medicine.

Chapter 4

Integrated Health Care Delivery Systems

Peter R. Kongstvedt and David W. Plocher

Study Objectives

- Understand the basic forms of Integrated Delivery Systems (IDSs)
- Understand the major strengths and weaknesses of each type of IDS
- Understand the roles of physicians and hospitals in each type of IDS
- Understand when each type of IDS can succeed in managed care, and when it is not likely to succeed
- Understand the concept of virtual integration
- Understand the legal pitfalls facing IDSs

The concept of integrated health care delivery systems (IDSs) is neither new nor novel. Kaiser Permanente Health Plans, Group Health of Puget Sound, the Henry Ford Health System, and others have operated as IDSs [though as health maintenance organizations (HMOs) rather than as providers] for many years, in some cases for more than half a century. Even before managed care came to play as dominant a role as it does today, an increase in vertical integration was predicted by Paul Starr in 1982 in his book *The Social Transformation of American Medicine*, albeit in a form somewhat different from what is currently occurring.[1]

Managed care has placed increasing pressures on providers of health care both to reduce costs and to maintain or improve quality as well as find ways to protect their market share. The prospect of impending reform of the American health care system, whether through regulatory reform or marketplace-driven reform, provides even greater impetus for change. This has led to the still-evolving desire on the part of health care providers to become aligned. Such alignment provides, at least theoretically, greater economies of scale, the ability to deploy clinical resources most cost effectively, a greater ability to influence provider behavior, and greater negotiating strength. Whether these and other goals can be met through integration is not always clear at the outset, and certain types of integration models appear to have greater potential than others. It must also be borne in mind that effective control of medical utilization by any model of managed care organization (MCO) will achieve greater and longer-lasting savings than will any economies of scale.

This chapter provides an overview of the more common forms of IDSs. The taxonomy is that in general use at the time of this writing. It is expected that, because this is an area in continual evolution (as is managed care in general), these terms and definitions will not remain constant. Even if the nomenclature changes, however, many of the concepts discussed here will remain valid. The closely related topic of joint ventures, mergers, and acquisition between payers and

David W. Plocher, M.D., is a partner in the Minneapolis office of Ernst & Young LLP, an international accounting and consulting firm.

providers is discussed in Chapter 5 of *The Managed Health Care Handbook*.[2]

IDSs may be described as falling into three broad categories: systems in which only the physicians are integrated, systems in which the physicians are integrated with facilities (hospitals and ancillary sites), and systems that include the insurance functions. Within the context of the first two categories, IDSs fall along a rough continuum. Figure 4–1 illustrates the common names used for such organizations. As one proceeds from one end of the continuum to the other, the degree of integration increases, as does the potential ability of the organization to operate effectively in a managed care environment. Also, the complexity of formation and operation, required capital investment, and political difficulties increases from one end of the continuum to the other. The primary political difficulty encountered in the development of these systems, or at least the systems that are tightly managed, is that not all providers can participate. This can present a significant challenge for both hospital and physician leadership that, if not addressed deftly, can result in a career limiting move by the responsible executive.

As this chapter is written, comprehensive health reform has not been enacted at the federal level and has been carried out only erratically in a few states. It is safe to assume, however, that the regulatory framework will continue to evolve (see Chapters 28 and 30), which will alter the form and methods used in alignment but not the need for IDSs.

INDIVIDUAL PRACTICE ASSOCIATIONS

The first type of IDS to be described is the individual practice association (IPA), a form that has been in existence for several decades and was even codified to some degree by the original HMO Act of 1973. The IPA is a legal entity, the members of which are independent physicians who contract with the IPA for the sole purpose of having the IPA contract with one or more HMOs. IPAs are usually not for profit, although that is not an absolute requirement. The term *IPA* is often used synonymously (and inaccurately) with terms for any type of open panel HMO (see Chapter 3); although the use of the term in this fashion is now widespread, it is not technically accurate. The true IPA is discussed here.

In its common incarnation, the IPA negotiates with the HMO for a capitation rate inclusive of

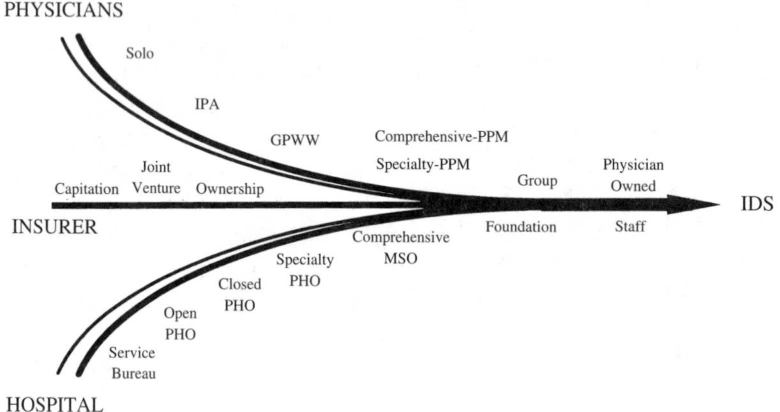

Figure 4–1 Types of integrated health care organizations. IPA, independent practice association; GPWW, group practice without walls; PPM, physician practice management; PHO, physician–hospital organization; MSO, management services organization.

all physician services (for a detailed discussion of such forms of reimbursement systems, see Chapter 8). The IPA in turn reimburses the member physicians, although not necessarily using capitation. The IPA and its member physicians are at risk for at least some portion of medical costs in that, if the capitation payment is lower than the required reimbursement to the physicians, the member physicians must accept lower income. It is the presence of this risk sharing that stands the IPA apart from a negotiating vehicle that does not bear risk. It is also the reason that true IPAs generally are not subject to antitrust problems (unless the IPA was formed solely or primarily to keep out competition). The usual form of an IPA is as an umbrella organization for physicians in all specialties to participate in managed care. Recently, however, IPAs that only represent a single specialty have emerged; specialty IPAs are discussed in Chapter 10.

The IPA may operate simply as a negotiating organization, with the HMO providing all administrative support, or it may take on some of the duties of the HMO, such as utilization management (UM), network development, and so forth. The IPA generally has stop-loss reinsurance, or the HMO provides such stop-loss coverage, to prevent the IPA from going bankrupt (see Chapter 8). The history of IPAs in the early years of HMOs was variable, and a number of IPAs did indeed go out of business. Recently, IPAs have been enjoying considerable success, especially in the western part of the country. The hospital usually has no role in a traditional IPA, although some hospitals have begun sponsoring IPA development as an alternative to a physician–hospital organization (PHO) structure, which is discussed later.

Advantages of an IPA

There is a current, although undocumented, resurgence of interest in IPAs as a vehicle for private physicians to contract with managed care plans. It stops well short of full integration but has more ability to share risk and obtain HMO contracts than many PHOs. It is also a model that is more easily understood and accepted by many managed care executives, who may cast a wary eye on less traditional models. The newly dominating IPAs are those that allow more convenient geographic access, have succeeded in bearing risk, and have limited specialist membership. They may be the only model available in nonurban areas, where one to two physician offices are the norm. Finally, in contrast to staff models, IPAs require much less capital to start up and operate, and some managers feel that IPAs motivate their physicians more successfully than models that depend on salary.

Disadvantages of an IPA

The IPA is inherently unwieldy because it is usually made up of a large number of independent physicians whose only commonality is the contracting vehicle of the IPA (well, perhaps they have other loci of commonality, but not for the purposes of this discussion). The IPA's ability to preserve private practice also means its inability to leverage resources, achieve economies of scale, or change behavior to the greatest degree possible. An IPA that accepts a high degree of risk for medical costs may be found by the state insurance commissioner to be an HMO and be required to become licensed, with all the issues that go along with being a licensed health plan (see Chapter 28). Finally, many IPAs contain a surplus of specialists, resulting in upward pressure on characteristic resource consumption (although see Chapters 10 and 13 of *The Managed Health Care Handbook*[3] for a discussion of specialty IPAs).

PHYSICIAN PRACTICE MANAGEMENT ORGANIZATIONS

Physician practice management (PPM) organizations are recent arrivals in the integration scene. PPMs may in some ways be viewed as variants in management services organizations (MSOs), but unlike the MSO described below (in the discussion of physician–hospital vertical integration), PPMs are physician only. In other words, there is no involvement by the hospital. Some managed care taxonomists refer to these organizations as physician-only MSOs, but that convention is not the predominant one as this chapter is being written.* The operations of a full MSO are described in a later section of this chapter.

Recently, some large PPMs have been branching into more activities than physician-only management. These activities include joint ventures in PHO development and even the purchase of insurance licenses. Thus PPMs, like everything else in managed care, continue to make classification a high challenge indeed.

For-Profit, Comprehensive PPMs

In a melding of Wall Street and the physician's office, entrepreneurs have capitalized for-profit PPMs operating independent of hospitals. These have most often purchased physician practices, beginning with primary care groups but including certain large specialty groups as well, and have signed multiyear contracts with those physicians. The physicians may be given varying degrees of equity participation in the PPM (the equity model PPM) and a voice in governance. In some cases, the PPM may not necessarily offer equity to all physicians. The PPM may offer equity only to those physicians who are early participants, or it may offer equity in exchange for the value of the acquired practice but not offer equity if it pays cash for the practice.

These entities may be attractive to some practitioners who, exasperated by the business pressures of practice, would prefer selling to an entity specializing in managing physician practices as opposed to a possibly distrusted hospital or may simply feel that a PPM has more capability to manage a practice than a hospital. As these entities become publicly traded, a further attraction to physicians is based on seeing their equity grow. Recent successes in such PPMs have been complicated by changes in identity as noted earlier, for example through the purchase of an HMO or small insurance company (thus producing taxonomist cognitive dissonance).

In general, the PPM provides management for all support functions (e.g., billing and collections, purchasing, negotiating contracts, and so forth) but remains relatively uninvolved with the clinical aspects of the practice. In many cases, the physician remains an independent practitioner, although the PPM owns all the tangible assets of the practice. The PPM usually takes a percentage of the practice revenue, often at a rate equal to or slightly below what the physician was already experiencing for overhead. The physician agrees to a long-term commitment as well as noncompetition covenants.

Although the early track record appears promising, it is far too soon to articulate clear advantages and disadvantages. Compared with hospitals' and insurers' acquiring practices, the PPM is theoretically able to be more nimble and is better able to give physicians an investment return. All practice acquisitions make the physician an employee (or employeelike) for many years, however, with all the attendant motivational concerns. The guiding principle behind the early success of PPMs may be the virtue of an IDS that is physician driven as opposed to hospital or insurer driven. This advantage derives in part from the fact that physicians control or direct between 75 percent and 90 percent of health resources consumed.

Specialty PPMs

A variation on the comprehensive PPM theme, the specialty PPM has taken most of the comprehensive PPM features into consideration for a single specialty's market share preservation or expansion. The most common specialties involved are oncology and cardiology, and multistate networks are now in place. Other specialties involved include ophthalmology, radiol-

* Not that there is much stability in the naming of new types of organizations in managed care. As the field evolves, or perhaps mutates is more accurate, terms and labels will mutate as well.

ogy, anesthesiology, and occupational medicine. The specialty PPM is a variant of a specialty network.

The early experience with this PPM variant is at least as promising as the experience with the comprehensive PPM. Promises will probably be fulfilled only if two conditions are met, however: the ability to bear financial risk, and willingness on the part of the PPM's customers to deal with another carve-out vendor. Although the first point is an obvious managed care fundamental, the second requirement may need clarification. We can consider the emergence of disease management vendors a valuable model (see Chapter 14). The vendors that are concentrating narrowly on rare, expensive diseases, such as hemophilia, have made some inroads. The typical HMO medical director may be willing to carve that out and devote internal case manager skill to more common conditions. The field of oncology may be viewed as too common, however, and therefore intrinsically embedded in the HMO's operations (note that disease management vendors, for example those specializing in hemophilia, usually do not employ their own hemophilia experts but rather contract with them *and* provide more customized care management).

The potential ability of an oncologist PPM to survive this caveat is enhanced by the presence of a less aggressive buyer, such as a preferred provider organization. Alternatively, if the oncologist PPM happens to have its oncologist network in place in a given city before the HMO provider relations manager begins recruiting specialists, this oncologist PPM could become the dedicated oncologist network for the HMO. Finally, an HMO may choose to use such a specialty PPM because it allows the HMO to improve quality and lower cost compared with using a less organized network of private specialists.

Advantages of PPMs

The primary advantage of a PPM is that its sole purpose in business is to manage physicians' practices. This means that it will either have or obtain expertise that is not usually resident in either a hospital or a payer (other than a group or staff model HMO). Also, the PPM has the ability to bring substantial purchasing power to bear though combining the purchasing needs of several hundred (or potentially more) physicians. The PPM can also provide a greater sense of ownership to the participating physicians in an equity model, thus helping align incentives and goals.

Disadvantages of the PPMs

The primary disadvantage is that the PPM may not achieve sufficient mass in the market to influence events substantially, or negotiate favorable terms. Also, the physicians may chafe under the long terms usually required and may not change their practice habits sufficiently to be truly effective in managed care; this last issue becomes especially critical if the PPM is seen more as a vehicle to negotiate fees than as a system to lower costs and improve quality. These PPMs often lack strong physician leadership; business leadership comes from nonphysicians. Finally, investor-owned PPMs are businesses that are expected to return a substantial profit; they are not philanthropic institutions. If that profit is not forthcoming, it may be anticipated that the investors will begin to demand action, some of which may not be palatable to the participating physicians.

GROUP PRACTICE WITHOUT WALLS

The group practice without walls (GPWW), also known as the clinic without walls, is a significant step toward greater integration of physician services. The GPWW does not require the participation of a hospital and, indeed, is often formed as a vehicle for physicians to organize without being dependent on a hospital for services or support. In some cases, GPWW formation has occurred to leverage negotiating strength not only with MCOs but with hospitals as well.

The GPWW is composed of private practice physicians who agree to aggregate their practices into a single legal entity, but the physicians continue to practice medicine in their independent locations. In other words, the physicians appear to be independent from the view of their patients, but from the view of a contracting entity (usually an MCO) they are a single group. This is differentiated from the for-profit, physician-only MSOs described earlier by two salient features: First, the GPWW is owned solely by the member physicians and not by any outside investors, and second, the GPWW is a legal merging of all assets of the physicians' practices rather than the acquisition of only the tangible assets (as is often the case in an MSO).

To be considered a medical group, the physicians must have their personal income affected by the performance of the group as a whole. Although an IPA will place a defined portion of a physician's income at risk (that portion related to the managed care contract held by the IPA), the group's income from any source has an effect on the physician's income and on profit sharing in the group; that being said, it is common in this model for an individual physician's income to be affected most by individual productivity.

The GPWW is owned by the member physicians, and governance is by the physicians. The GPWW may contract with an outside organization to provide business support services. Office support services are generally provided through the group, although as a practical matter the practicing physicians may notice little difference in what they are used to receiving.

Advantages of the GPWW

The GPWW enjoys an advantage over some other models in that it has the legal ability to negotiate and commit on behalf of all the members of the group. Unlike a PHO, where the physicians remain independent private practitioners, the GPWW *is* a legal group and can legitimately bargain with MCOs or other organizations. The GPWW also has the ability to achieve some modest economies of scale, similar to those found in MSOs. The most common subset of these services includes centralized billing, centralized scheduling, group purchasing, and data sharing. Less often, the GPWW centralizes recruiting and can help with employee leasing. The GPWW is free of hospital influence (at least theoretically) and therefore is able to have greater flexibility.

Perhaps the key advantage of the GPWW is that income is affected by the performance of the group as a whole. Therefore, the GPWW has some ability to influence practice behavior. If a member physician is practicing in such a manner as to affect adversely the group as a whole, considerable peer pressure can be brought to bear. The group can even proceed to expel a physician member if the problems are serious and are not rectified.

Disadvantages of the GPWW

The primary disadvantage of the GPWW is that the physicians essentially remain in independent practice. Except for obvious practice behavior, the physicians continue to practice in the manner to which they have become accustomed. The ability of the group actually to manage practice behavior is thus seriously limited to only those elements that are gross outliers (e.g., exceptionally long lengths of stay). Thus optimal efficiencies are not achieved. Although there is some alignment of incentives, disparate goals still exist.

The ability of a GPWW to accept risk-based reimbursement (e.g., capitation) is enhanced but is not optimal. The GPWW is potentially capable of negotiating with MCOs for such contracts, but distribution of income and risk usually defaults to those methods used by IPAs (see Chapter 8).

The very feature that attracts many physicians, independence from a distrusted hospital, is also a source of GPWW weakness. That is, new sources of capital, information systems, and management expertise must be explored (such as an insurance partner).

Finally, the GPWW structure generally does not have as strong a leadership as is seen in a true medical group. This, along with the other disadvantages noted, may lead to a relative instability in the structure. Some managers in the industry believe that the GPWW concept is transitional to a more traditional medical group. Furthermore, although sharing of certain administrative services represents an improvement in overhead, there are many more economies of scale to be found in a true, or consolidated, medical group practice.

CONSOLIDATED MEDICAL GROUP

The term *consolidated medical group*, or *medical group practice*, refers to a traditional structure in which physicians have combined their resources to be a true medical group practice. Unlike the GPWW, in which the physicians combine certain assets and risks but remain in their own offices, practicing medicine as they always have, the true medical group is located in a few sites and functions in a group setting; in other words, the physicians occupy the same facility or facilities. This means a great deal of interaction among members of the group and common goals and objectives for group success.

Traditional medical groups are totally independent of the hospital. Even so, it is common for the group to identify strongly with one or more hospitals. Although this is good for the hospital as long as relations are good, it can be devastating to a hospital if relations sour or if the group is motivated to change hospitals for any reason. Some hospitals sponsor medical groups, but those operate more like other models discussed later in this chapter.

The group is usually a partnership or professional corporation, although other forms are possible. Usually the more senior members of the group enjoy more fruits of the group's success (e.g., higher income, better on-call schedules, and so forth), although one hopes not to an abusive degree. New members of an existing group who pass a probationary period often are required to pay a substantial contribution to the group's capital to join, which can create an entry barrier to growth. Other groups employ new physicians for a lengthy period to control the finances of the group as well as to give all parties the opportunity to see whether it is a good fit. In any event, it is common for the group to require physicians to agree to a noncompetition clause in their contract to protect the group from a physician defecting and taking patients away from the group. A discussion of the general management of medical groups is beyond the scope of this chapter. Physician compensation in such groups is discussed in Chapter 10 of *The Managed Health Care Handbook*.[4]

Advantages of Medical Groups

Medical groups have the ability to achieve substantial economies of scale, have strong negotiating leverage, and have the ability to influence physician behavior. Groups are usually attractive to MCOs because they not only deliver a large block of physicians with one contract but also have the ability to manage their own resources. The group can also decide to make a change in resource use (e.g., change hospitals) that can have a rapid and substantial positive effect on managed care.

Although the capital investment required of partners or group shareholders can be an entry barrier, it is also an exit barrier, promoting greater stability. An additional exit barrier is seen in the form of a noncompetition clause required of member physicians, again promoting stability, which is desirable in the eyes of a managed care plan. Medical groups are often able to recruit new physicians more easily because they offer an improved lifestyle compared with that of solo practice, which allows them to grow along with a managed care plan. On the whole, medical groups are in a superior position to benefit from managed care compared with many other models, and certainly compared with independent private physicians.

Disadvantages of Medical Groups

Medical groups can certainly have serious problems, such as uncontrolled overhead or poor utilization patterns. If these problems are not rectified, the impact of failure is felt to a far higher degree than is the case if a single physician or small group fails. If the group has markedly disproportionate compensation or lifestyle differences between the senior members and the new physicians, the turnover of new members can be unacceptably high. Medical groups can also inflate their own opinions of their worth, impeding effective contracting.

Medical groups can become calcified in their ways and be less able to change than individual physicians. This is a serious problem if compounded by the group being top heavy with subspecialists and, in turn, treating primary care physicians (PCPs) as second-class members. If the group is unwilling to consider redistributing the rewards to the PCPs, it may suffer defections of those physicians, which will make the group less desirable from a managed care standpoint.

PHOs

The PHO is an entity that, at a minimum, allows a hospital and its physicians to negotiate with third party payers. PHOs may do little more than provide for such a negotiating vehicle, although this could raise the risk of antitrust. PHOs may actively manage the relationship between the providers and MCOs, or they may provide more services, to the point where they may more aptly be considered MSOs (see below).

In its weakest form, the PHO is considered a messenger model. This means that the PHO analyzes the terms and conditions offered by an MCO and transmits its analysis and the contract to each physician, who then decides on an individual basis whether to participate.

In its simplest and more common version, the participating physicians and the hospital develop model contract terms and reimbursement levels and use those terms to negotiate with MCOs. The PHO usually has a limited amount of time to negotiate the contract successfully (e.g., 90 days). If that time limit passes, then the participating physicians are free to contract directly with the MCO; if the PHO successfully reaches an agreement with the MCO, then the physicians agree to be bound by those terms. The contract is still between the physician and the MCO and between the hospital and the MCO. In some cases, the contract between the physicians and the MCO is relatively brief and may reference a contract between the PHO and the MCO.

PHOs are generally considered the first step on the evolutionary ladder in vertical integration with respect to practitioners and facilities. They often form as a reaction to market forces from managed care. PHOs are considered the easiest type of vertically integrated system to develop (although they are not actually that easy, at least if done well). They also are a vehicle to provide some integration while preserving the independence and autonomy of the physicians.

By definition, a PHO requires the participation of a hospital and at least some portion of the admitting physicians. Often, the formation of the PHO is initiated by the hospital, but unless the leadership of the medical staff is also on board it is unlikely to get far. It is not uncommon for a PHO to be formed primarily as a defensive mechanism to deal with an increase in managed care contracting activity. It is also not uncommon for the same physicians who join the PHO already to be under contract with one or more managed care plans.

The PHO is usually a separate business entity, such as a for-profit corporation. This requires thorough legal analysis for the participating not-for-profit, tax exempt [Internal Revenue Code 501c (3)] hospital because the hospital could lose its tax exempt status if access to tax exempt financing confers an advantage to the PHO's balance sheet (see Chapter 30).

Initial capitalization and ownership occur with varying formulas, but most strive toward equal ownership between the physicians and the hospital. The hospital may put up the majority of the cash, however. For the sake of practitioner motivation, physician equity is considered a desired feature.

Ongoing revenue to the simplest form of PHO may be a nonitem because the entity could serve only as a cost center for the hospital. As the PHO takes on various MSO functions, however, participating providers pay a fee for those services. Third party payers also may pay an access fee.

Governance can evolve similarly. That is, in its simplest form hospital administrators may run the entity. Most PHOs are establishing formal governing boards, however. Board composition is usually equally divided between hospital administrators and physicians, with attention being given to primary care representation within the physician component.

PHOs fall into two broad categories: open and closed. These are described separately because MCOs often view them that way.

Open PHOs

The open PHO is one that is open to virtually any member of the medical staff of the hospital. There will often be minimum credentialing requirements (see Chapter 7), but not necessarily even that. Open PHOs are almost universally specialty dominated; in other words, there are disproportionately more specialists in the PHO than there are PCPs. The creators of the open PHO are often the specialists themselves, who become concerned that MCOs are selectively contracting, thereby reducing the amount of business that the specialists (as a group) are doing. The medical staff then approach the hospital administration to form the PHO primarily to allow all the members of the medical staff to participate with MCOs. In this situation, PCPs are usually courted but may still be relegated to secondary citizenship, even if unconsciously.

Some open PHOs claim that, although their genesis is an open format, the ultimate goal will be to manage the membership and remove those physicians who are unable to practice cost effectively. MCOs view such claims with skepticism, although it is certainly possible. The political reality of an open PHO is that it is quite difficult to bring sufficient discipline to bear on medical staff members who wield a high level of influence. This is currently complicated by the continued dichotomy of payment mechanisms, in which a certain portion of reimbursement to the hospital rewards cost effectiveness (e.g., prospective payment, capitation, and package or bundled pricing), whereas other forms of reimbursement reward the opposite (e.g., fee for service and simple discounts on charges). Finally, one must never underestimate the influence of the medical staff, particularly when they are united; failure to attend to the needs of the medical staff may be a serious career limiting move on the part of the hospital chief executive officer (CEO). In light of this, some PHOs have featured hospital CEOs permitting more than half the board seats to be occupied by physicians, although some are hospital-based physicians; in the case of not-for-profit PHOs, however, physicians may not represent more than 20 percent of the governance, regardless of the hospital's desire (see Chapter 30 for a discussion of this issue).

One last note regarding PHOs: The "PO" portion of a PHO may be a different model entirely. As an example, a GPWW or an IPA could represent the physician portion of the PHO. Although the most common model at the time of this writing is one in which the physicians remain independent and contract individually with the PHO, it is by no means the only method of organization.

Closed PHOs

The primary difference between a closed PHO and an open one is the proactive decision to limit physician membership in the PHO. This is clearly more difficult politically than an open model, but it carries greater potential for success. The two general approaches to limiting membership are by specialty type and by practice profiling.

Limitations by specialty type are most common and most easily done. The most common limitation is the number of specialists, to address the imbalance of PCPs and specialists found in an open PHO. In fact, it is not uncommon to find closed PHOs having a disproportionate number of PCPs on the governance board as well as in the membership of the PHO. Although an extreme demonstration of this concept is the primary care–only PHO that simply subcontracts with certain specialists, the PHO usually places limits on the number of specialists of any given specialty type beyond primary care for equity sharing and/or membership status. This limitation on the number of specialists is most often accomplished by projecting the enrollment (or covered lives) that the PHO is expected to cover over the next several years and then recruiting specialists according to predetermined ratios of specialists needed for that enrollment.

The second type of limitation involves practice profiling and is more difficult to carry out for technical reasons. This type of limitation requires the PHO to examine some objective form of practice analysis (it could be a subjective analysis, but that would probably raise a restraint of trade issue). Based on that analysis, physicians are invited to join the PHO or not. This is difficult to accomplish unless the PHO has access to adequate data, which is most uncommon. The closed PHO may be impeded in its quest to demonstrate selectivity by those states enacting any willing provider legislation and needs to be aware of any possible antitrust issues (see Chapter 57 of *The Managed Health Care Handbook*[5] for a discussion of both issues).

As part of ongoing recredentialing, the PHO also regularly reevaluates the number of physicians required in each specialty. If the PHO has the ability to capture and analyze data regarding practice behavior and clinical quality (see Chapters 17 and 19), those data may be used in managing the physician membership and, ultimately, in ending the participation agreement with any physicians who repeatedly depart from the PHO's practice guidelines. Such analyses are difficult to perform properly. It is important for the PHO (or for any type of IDS, for that matter) that accepts full risk to negotiate the right to receive claims data on all members for whom the PHO has the full capitated risk because otherwise the PHO will not have sufficient data to analyze all medical costs.

Advantages of a PHO

The primary advantage of a PHO is its ability to negotiate on behalf of a large group of physicians allied with a hospital. This advantage can be ephemeral if no MCO wishes to negotiate (see below), but it may be very real if the hospital and key members of the medical staff are attractive to MCOs and are not already under contract. Closed PHOs are more attractive to MCOs than open ones. Of course, if the providers have already contracted with the MCO and threaten to pull out (i.e., boycott the MCO) unless the MCO uses the PHO, a serious antitrust problem may arise. If the MCO has not already contracted with the providers, the PHO may be an expeditious route to developing a delivery system capability. Even in those situations where a contract already exists, contracting through the PHO may represent a sufficient improvement in terms such that an MCO will be willing to switch from direct contracting to using the PHO; for example, the PHO may be willing to provide performance guarantees. Finally, physicians may view the PHO as a facilitator in landing direct contracts with self-insured employers, with the Health Care Financing Administration for Medicare risk contracts, and with the state for managed Medicaid contracts.

A second advantage of a PHO is its theoretical ability to track and use data and to manage the delivery system, at least from the standpoints of UM and quality management. Once again, this advantage is more likely to be found in a closed PHO than in an open one, primarily because a closed PHO has a greater concentration of events over fewer physicians.

The third advantage of a PHO is that it is the first step to greater integration between a hospital and its medical staff. Although a PHO by itself may result in improved relations, those relations can quickly sour if the PHO consumes time, energy, and money but fails to yield results. If the PHO does result in a better ability to contract or yields economic rewards, then its mission is successful, at least for the near term. If the PHO does not succeed, or if success appears to be short lived, then the PHO may be the base from which a more integrated model may be built.

Disadvantages of a PHO

The chief disadvantage of a typical PHO is that it often fails to result in any meaningful improvement in contracting ability. In many cases, MCOs already have provider contracts in place and see little value in going through the PHO. Even worse, an MCO may see the PHO as little more than a vehicle for providers to keep their reimbursement high.

Open PHOs are at a significant disadvantage if the MCO (or employer, in the event that the PHO chooses to contract directly with employers) does not want all the physicians in the PHO to be participating with the health plan. MCOs often want the right to select the providers and are unlikely to give up that ability. Even closed PHOs may suffer from this problem if the MCOs specifically wish to avoid contracting with certain physicians who are members of the PHO.

MCOs may view the PHO as a barrier to effective communication with the physicians and a hindrance to fully effective UM. Unless the PHO has a compelling story to tell regarding its ability to manage utilization, the MCO may believe that it can do a better job without the PHO's interference. Alternatively, if the health plan has relatively unsophisticated UM capabilities, or if the plan is too small to be able to devote adequate resources to UM, the PHO may represent an attractive alternative.

Because PHOs are relatively loose in their structure, and because the physicians may still be completely independent, the PHO's ability to affect provider behavior is rather limited. This can have an impact not only on UM but also on getting the entire organization to make necessary changes.

In a 1995 study performed by Ernst & Young LLP, the majority of PHOs were young, had little enrolled membership, had little systems support, and did not have full time management, especially medical management.[6] It is possible, and even likely, that by the time this book is published that PHOs in the aggregate may have improved their performance and infrastructure. If not, then it is probable that PHOs will not be long-term entities.

Regrettably, there have been a few cases where a hospital and medical staff with existing managed care contracts formed a PHO with the intent of using the PHO to improve their negotiating strength, only to lose the existing managed care contract and be unable to replace it with anything better. In other words, the PHO actually harmed them because it was considered undesirable by the MCO. Because PHOs do allow the participating physicians to contract directly with the MCO in the event that the MCO does not offer terms agreeable to the PHO, this risk is usually minimal.

Specialist PHOs

A recent variant of the PHO has emerged over the past few years. The specialist PHO has taken the general closed PHO concepts down to the level of a single specialty. Common specialties involved are cardiology and pediatrics; psychiatric PHOs also have existed for many years. Their track record is too brief in most cases for definitive observations, but the value placed on them by the market should follow the logic described above under specialist PPMs, except that this entity brings with it an expensive facility.

MSOs

An MSO represents the evolution of the PHO into an entity that provides more services to the physician. Not only does the MSO provide a vehicle for negotiating with MCOs, but it also provides additional services to support the physician's practice. The physician, however, usually remains an independent private practitioner. The MSO is based around one or more hospitals. The reasons for the MSO's formation are generally the same as for the PHO, and ownership and governance issues are similar to those discussed earlier.

In its simplest form, the MSO operates as a service bureau, providing basic practice support services to member physicians. These services include such activities as billing and collection, administrative support in certain areas, electronic data interchange (such as electronic billing), and other services.

The physician can remain an independent practitioner, under no legal obligation to use the services of the hospital on an exclusive basis. The MSO must receive compensation from the physician at fair market value, or the hospital and physician could incur legal problems (discussed in Chapter 30 as well as below). The MSO should, through economies of scale as well as good management, be able to provide those services at a reasonable rate.

The MSO may be considerably broader in scope. In addition to providing all the services described above, the MSO may actually purchase many of the assets of the physician's practice; for example, the MSO may purchase the physician's office space or office equipment (at fair market value). The MSO can employ the office support staff of the physician as well. MSOs can further incorporate functions such as quality management, UM, provider relations, member services, and even claims processing. This form of MSO is usually constructed as a unique business entity, separate from the PHO. Because they are their own corporations, legal advisors are finding advantages in characterizing these as limited liability corporations, but alternatives exist.

The MSO does not always have direct contracts with MCOs for two reasons: Many MCOs insist on having the provider be the contracting agent, and many states will not allow MCOs (especially HMOs) to have contracts with any entity that does not have the power to bind the provider. The physician may remain an independent private practitioner under no contractual obligation to use the hospital on an exclusive basis. It should be noted here that there are IDSs that operate under the label of MSO that actually do purchase the physician's entire practice (possibly including intangible values such as goodwill) and function much like a more fully integrated system, as discussed later in this chapter.

Advantages of an MSO

The primary advantage of an MSO over a PHO is the ability of the MSO to bind the physician closer to the hospital, although not as a contractual obligation to use the hospital on an exclusive basis. The MSO certainly has the ability to bring economies of scale and professional management to the physician's office services, thus potentially reducing overhead costs. The MSO may have the potential ability to capture data regarding practice behavior, which may be used to help the physicians practice more cost effectively. This develops when the MSO contains more advanced functions, such as UM and claims processing.

Disadvantages of an MSO

The disadvantages of an MSO are similar to those of a PHO in that the physician may remain an independent practitioner with the ability to change allegiances with relative ease. Also, when the MSO does not employ the physician, it has somewhat limited ability to effect change or to redeploy resources in response to changing market needs.

Special problems arise with MSOs, problems that can be compounded by MSOs that purchase assets from a physician's practice. These are the problems of the transaction being perceived as inuring to the benefit of the physician in an illegal manner and of fraud and abuse for federally funded patients. These issues are briefly discussed later in this chapter and in detail in Chapter 30.

FOUNDATION MODEL

A foundation model IDS is one in which a hospital creates a not-for-profit foundation and actually purchases physicians' practices (both tangible and intangible assets) and puts those practices into the foundation. This model usually occurs when, for some legal reason (e.g., the hospital is a not-for-profit entity that cannot own a for-profit subsidiary, or there is a state law against the corporate practice of medicine), the hospital cannot employ the physicians directly or use hospital funds to purchase the practices directly. It must be noted that, to qualify for and maintain its not-for-profit status, the foundation must prove that it provides substantial community benefit.

A second form of foundation model does not involve a hospital. In that model, the foundation is an entity that exists on its own and contracts for services with a medical group and a hospital. On a historical note, in the early days of HMOs many open panel types of plans that were not formed as IPAs were formed as foundations; the foundation held the HMO license and contracted with one or more IPAs and hospitals for services.

The foundation itself is governed by a board that is not dominated by either the hospital or the physicians (in fact, physicians may represent no more than 20 percent of the board) and includes lay members. The foundation owns and manages the practices, but the physicians become members of a medical group that, in turn, has an exclusive contract for services with the foundation; in other words, the foundation is the only source of revenue to the medical group. The physicians have contracts with the medical group that are long term and contain noncompetition clauses.

Although the physicians are in an independent group, and the foundation is also independent from the hospital, the relationship in fact is close among all members of the triad. The medical group, however, retains a significant measure of autonomy regarding its own business affairs, and the foundation has no control over certain aspects, such as individual physician compensation.

Advantages of the Foundation Model

The primary advantages of this model pertain to legal constraints that require the foundation's creation in the first place. Because the construction of this entity is rather unwieldy, it is best suited to those states in which it is required (e.g., California, at the time this chapter is being written) so that a not-for-profit hospital can proceed with a fully integrated model. That said, the foundation model provides for a greater level of structural integration than any other model discussed to this point. A not-for-profit foundation may also be better able to access the bond market for capital in an advantageous manner.

Because the foundation clearly controls the revenue that the medical group will get, it has considerable influence over that group. The foundation also has the ability to rationalize the clinical and administrative resources required to meet obligations under managed care contracts (and fee for service, of course) and can achieve greater economies of scale. If the foundation consolidates medical office locations, these economies are improved, as is the foundation's ability to provide more comprehensive services to enrolled members. A foundation also has the ability to invest required capital to expand services, recruit PCPs, and so forth. For these reasons, a foundation model may be viewed quite favorably by a contracting MCO.

Disadvantages of the Foundation Model

The primary disadvantage of a foundation model is that the physicians in the medical group are linked only indirectly to the foundation and the business goals of that foundation. Although that indirect link is quite strong, the medical group remains an intermediate organization (vaguely analogous to an IPA) that can operate in ways that are potentially inconsistent with the overall goals of managed care. One example of this becoming a problem would be a medical group that is seriously top heavy with specialists and in which PCPs are treated as second-class members. Another example would be a group that compensated member physicians based on fee for service or other measures that are easily gamed, leading to less than optimal control of utilization and quality.

Related to this issue is a built-in potential for conflicts between the governance boards of the hospital and the medical group. If the goals and priorities of those two organizations are not completely aligned (and they rarely are), then it is possible for serious disputes to arise, which impede success.

The last main disadvantage is the not-for-profit status of the hospital and foundation. Because of that status, the foundation must continually prove that it provides a community benefit to maintain its status. The risk of private inurement (discussed below) is also heightened. As this book is being written, several not-for-profit hospitals, to compete against foundation models, have formed PHOs and MSOs (both for-profit and not-for-profit entities) allowing well over 20 percent board representation by physicians. These developments have been permitted by a favorable interpretation of regulatory requirements, although their ultimate corporate stability is still undetermined (see Chapter 30).

STAFF MODEL

Not to be confused with the staff model HMO (see Chapter 3), a staff model in the context of this chapter refers to an IDS owned by a health system rather than by an HMO. The distinction is whether the primary business organization is a licensed entity (e.g., an HMO) or primarily a provider. This distinction is not always easy to observe, and in some cases the only way to make any distinction is to look at the genesis of the parent organization: Was it founded to be a health plan or founded to be a provider? If the distinction rests on history only, then it is meaningless.

The staff model is a health system that employs the physicians directly. Physicians are integrated into the system either through the purchase of their practices or by being hired directly. The system is often more than a hospital, being rather a larger, more comprehensive organization for the delivery of health care. Because the physicians are employees, the legal issues that attach to IDSs using private physicians are attenuated.

Advantages of Staff Models

Staff model IDSs are theoretically in a good position to be able to rationalize resources and to align goals of all the components of the delivery system. Physicians are almost always paid based on a salary, and incentive programs can be designed to reward the physicians in parallel with the goals and objectives of the system (see Chapters 6 and 9). Far greater economies of scale are achievable, and capital resources can be applied in a businesslike manner. Staff models also have a greater ability to recruit new physicians because there is no cost to the new physician and the income stream to the new physician begins immediately. The ability to manage the physicians in the system is also at least theoretically enhanced. The problems of taxable status, private inurement, and fraud and abuse are greatly diminished. MCOs generally consider staff model IDSs as desirable business partners, assuming that cost, quality, and access are acceptable; the exception would be if the staff model chooses to pursue obtaining its own HMO license, thus becoming a direct competitor and threat to a contracting MCO.

Disadvantages of Staff Models

One key problem with staff models is when management assumes that, simply because the physicians are employees, they can be managed in a manner similar to that of other employees of the system; that is a false and unproductive assumption. Physicians are highly intelligent and highly trained professionals who must operate clinically with considerable autonomy. Any health system that does not recognize these qualities is bound to have difficulties with its medical staff.

Despite the previous statement, staff models often run into problems with physician productivity. Salaried physicians are obviously no longer motivated to see high volumes of patients, as they are under fee for service. Staff models may be most attractive to physicians who do not wish to practice full time or who wish to limit their hours. Some staff model HMOs have had such problems with low productivity that they have at least partially eroded the economies of scale that are available in tightly integrated systems. Staff models, although having a somewhat easier time recruiting than a medical group, suffer from the dopplegänger of easy entry, easy exit. Physicians in staff models often feel little loyalty and are more easily recruited away than physicians who have an investment in a group.

The last disadvantage is the high capital requirement to build and operate the system. Once adequate patient volume is coming through, staff models can have excellent financial performance. Until then, however, they are heavily leveraged. Expansion of an existing system likewise requires a great deal of capital investment.

PHYSICIAN OWNERSHIP MODEL

The physician ownership model refers to a vertically integrated system in which the physicians hold a significant portion of ownership (i.e., equity) interest. In some cases, the physicians own the entire system; in other cases, the physicians own less than 100 percent, but more than 51 percent. The physicians' equity interest is through their medical group(s). Physicians holding equity as simple shareholders could raise problems with Medicare fraud and abuse (see below and Chapter 30). It is theoretically possible for physicians to own equity through a limited partnership, although that format would require serious legal review. It is also possible to craft a model in which physicians own less than 50 percent as a group, but it is not clear whether that model would survive legal scrutiny (see below) or whether it would confer the same advantages as the model described here.

The physician ownership model operates with features combining those of the staff model and MSO. Unlike the situation with the staff model, the medical groups have a strong role in the overall management of the system, and the physicians (at least those physicians who are partners in the group) have a clear vested interest in the system's success.

Advantages of the Physician Ownership Model

The advantages of the physician ownership model are similar to those enumerated for the staff model above. In contrast to the staff model, this model enjoys a powerful advantage by virtue of the physician ownership: total alignment of goals of the medical group and the health system. Because the physician owners' success is tied directly to the overall success of the entire organization, there is far less of a problem with conflicting goals and objectives (within the boundaries of human nature). Because of this alignment, strong physician leadership is present, which is more effective in managing the medical groups. Finally, this model can choose either to contract with or to own the hospital rather than be dominated by the hospital.

Disadvantages of the Physician Ownership Model

The primary disadvantage of the physician ownership model is the high level of resources required to build and operate it. Large capital resources are required to acquire the personnel, facilities, and practices necessary to provide comprehensive medical services, an adequate level of managerial support, and the required infrastructure. The source of this capital is primarily the physicians' practices, although outside access to capital is certainly possible. Related to that issue is the generally high buy-in cost to new physician partners, which may be a barrier to some physicians joining the group as other than employees.

As this chapter is being written, it is unknown whether models in which physicians are significant equity holders will face problems with the fraud and abuse provisions discussed below and in Chapter 30, but it is possible. This is because the physicians receive an economic reward for patient services that is unrelated to their own services.

VIRTUAL INTEGRATION

Goldsmith argues that it is possible, and even likely, that many of the structurally rigid vertical integration models are not going to succeed.[7] He argues that success will be more probable with models of virtual integration, in which more or less independent parties come together for the purpose of behaving like an IDS under managed care but retain their own identities and mission. This virtual integration requires an alignment of the financial incentives among the parties as well as an alignment of business purpose.

In a virtual integration, each of the major segments of the health care system—the physicians, the institutional providers, the payers/MCOs, and the ancillary providers (e.g., pharmacy)—act in concert for a common cause, but none is an employee or subdivision of another. This allows each party to manage its own affairs and meet its own financial goals without being managed by another segment of the industry. In this model, there is greater horizontal integration (e.g., between hospitals, between physicians, and so forth), with each of those horizontally integrated systems then forming relationships with other parts of the health care system.

GLOBAL CAPITATION

Global capitation applies to IDSs that are capable of accepting full or nearly full risk for medical expenses, including all professional, institutional, and many ancillary services as well. This differs from the full capitation described in Chapter 8, which applies to primary care groups accepting full risk for all professional services but not for institutional or ancillary services. Global capitation includes institutional as well as professional services, and the party accepting the capitation payment is a large, vertically integrated organization with presumably greater resources. Even though the IDS has accepted global capitation, it often purchases reinsurance to protect it against catastrophic cases; that reinsurance is either provided by the HMO or purchased by the IDS from a reinsurer.

Many IDSs accept a percentage of premium revenue from an HMO rather than a fixed capitation. Although these forms of revenue are similar, they are not the same. A percentage of premium may be affected by underwriting and marketing issues (primarily in commercial enrollment; in Medicare and Medicaid, percentage of revenue and capitation are nearly the same). As discussed in Chapter 23, if underwriting is poor and there is a revenue shortfall from the standpoint of covered lives, the percentage of that shortfall passed on to the IDS will mirror the percentage of revenue it is receiving from the MCO.

Although the HMO may have capitated the IDS, the IDS still faces the issue of how to divide up the revenue and risk among the parties. In a sense, global capitation simply transfers the burden of payment and management from the HMO to the IDS, but the fundamental issues remain. If the IDS employs the physicians, then it is relatively easier to distribute income.

Many IDSs, however, are combinations of private and employed physicians. Even hospitals that employ physicians usually still rely on private physicians for at least some services, and often the genesis of the IDS was to allow the hospital and private physicians to remain competitive in a managed care environment. Therefore, the IDS that accepts global capitation must still figure out how to allocate risk and reward. The managers of the IDS must be realistic and recognize that individual physicians will be unable and unwilling to bear a high level of financial risk (e.g., how many individual physicians could afford to pay $200,000 as their share of overutilization?) but will usually demand a disproportionate share of financial reward. Although risk and reward are always related, the IDS management must be careful to incent the physicians properly as well as to avoid the legal problems of private inurement and fraud and abuse regulations. Reimbursement of physicians is discussed in Chapters 6 and 7.

The last major issue in global capitation is who is actually the licensed health plan. If an IDS accepts global capitation, then a state's insurance department may require the IDS to become licensed as an HMO. This issue is discussed below and in detail in Chapter 28. Regulation of IDSs accepting full-risk capitation is an area undergoing considerable change, and the reader will need to keep aware of applicable regulations and laws.

PROVIDING THE INSURANCE FUNCTION

Until this point, this chapter has concentrated on vertical integration of practitioners and facilities. The MSO and PHO models are examples of delivery systems that can expand horizontally (by finding other PHO partners and forming a regional network—the super PHO—with convenient geographic access) and then become independently capable of direct contracting with self-insured purchasers. This capability requires incorporating most of the typical insurance functions. These usually begin with claims processing but may extend to ownership of the insurance license itself.

Options for an IDS to converge with insurance functions include the following: The insurer buys the hospital and physician groups, an integrated provider network buys or builds the insurance function, or the insurer and the integrated provider network form a joint venture with shared ownership (or perhaps a looser relationship). All these options, and more, are discussed in greater detail in Chapter 5 of *The Managed Health Care Handbook*.[8] An integrated provider network may also rent an insurance function; for example, it may pay several dollars per subscriber per month for third party administrator (TPA) functions and possible insurance licensure fronting services.

Clearly, when dealing with purchasers that are not self-insured, the IDS or MSO needs to incorporate all the classic insurance functions, including underwriting and actuarial rate development, as it takes on risk. The IDS also needs to have an insurance license. Many small insurance companies and TPAs are willing to price their role in this scheme competitively and are capable of avoiding the double digit overhead associated with the largest insurance companies. One must be cognizant, however, that many of these TPAs are not capable of carrying out sophisticated managed care functions. It is also possible for an IDS to contract with an insurer to front the license, that is, to use the insurer's license to back up the IDS's activities.

Advantages

A joint venture between an IDS and an insurer or MCO has several advantages. Both parties bring assets to the venture (at least theoretically): The IDS brings a network, some medical management, the ability to accept some level of risk for medical expenses, and a framework for contracting, and the insurer or MCO brings a license (and its ability to meet the attendant capital and regulatory needs), possibly an enrolled subscriber base, and expertise in functions such as claims processing, member services, and the like.

Disadvantages

The main disadvantage of an IDS assuming the insurance functions is that it may fail to carry them out competently, and failure would have far-reaching effects. The activities of an insurance company or MCO go well beyond medical management, and it would be naive for the management of an IDS to believe that those functions do not require expertise or that they are not fraught with complexities.

The pursuit of the insurance partner requires great caution. Too many insurance entities are configured as indemnity claims processors, incapable of understanding the subtleties associated with managing care. Significant capital may be required to structure the new entity. A large organization perceived to have deep pockets that has gotten closer to the provision of care will also need to evidence due diligence in credentialing providers to minimize the risk associated with negligent credentialing.

Governance and control of a joint venture may be a sensitive area. Although joint representation on the board is likely to be required, controlling representation may become a contentious issue. Control is generally subject to the Golden Rule (whoever has the gold makes the rules), but supermajority rights may help address control concerns by the minority partner.

Finally, these relationships often begin as nonexclusive. When the stakeholders have multiple alliances, true allegiance and true alignment of motivation are difficult to achieve. Gradually, consolidation will require a deliberate "choosing up sides" evolution. As noted earlier, for more detailed discussion see Chapter 5 of *The Managed Health Care Handbook.*[9]

LEGAL PITFALLS

There are many legal pitfalls in the development and operation of IDSs, and this chapter cannot possibly address them all. A few particular legal problems are especially worthy of note. Two related issues are the problems of private inurement and fraud and abuse; the other two especially noteworthy issues are problems of antitrust and licensure requirements. Readers are urged to review these and other legal issues in Chapters 28 and 30, and in the numerous other sources of material available in the literature. More important, competent legal counsel should be obtained before and during any operational activities involving these types of IDSs or any other integration activity not discussed here.

Private Inurement

This issue is one raised primarily by the Internal Revenue Service (IRS), which has set rules against the inurement of private benefits from activities of a tax exempt organization. The tax exempt organization pertinent to these discussions is usually a hospital but could be any tax exempt vehicle. The issue at hand is that a tax exempt organization cannot do any business that provides more than incidental monetary benefit to private individuals. Specifically, if a hospital provides services to a physician at less than fair market value, provides a below-market (or forgiven) loan to a physician, or purchases a practice at greater than fair market value, then the physician has benefited in a manner not allowed by the IRS. As this chapter is being written, there is also the possibility that a PHO that has majority or even parity board representation by physicians would be considered an organization created for the private inurement of the physicians; it is not known whether that position will be held.

Fraud and Abuse

The federal government, through Medicare and Medicaid, has developed regulations regarding what it considers fraud and abuse in the provision of services to federally funded patients. These regulations are extensive, and this chapter will not be able to review them. One pertinent portion of these regulations is similar to the issue discussed above, that of hospitals providing a financial benefit to physicians over what would be considered fair market value. In this case, the federal government views such an offense as fraudulent payments in return for referrals of federally funded patients to the hospital, in other words, kickbacks. This problem would apply to any hospital or provider that serves Medicare or Medicaid patients, regardless of the taxable status of the provider.

A key to avoiding this problem (including the problem of private inurement), in addition to competent legal counsel, is to pay or charge only fair market value. If a hospital purchases a physician's practice, it must have that practice valuated by an independent firm that is competent to conduct valuation studies. If a hospital provides services to a physician (e.g., facilities, billing and collection, and so forth), it must charge fair market value and manage those services in a businesslike fashion. The exact same caveat applies to a hospital system infusing capital into physicians' practices or into an IDS: The capital infusion must be based on reasonable business terms and must be recovered over time, just as any investment. It must be stressed that even strict adherence to these guidelines may not guarantee that there will be no problem with charges of fraud and abuse; the federal government is likely to examine each individual situation on its merits.

A special problem under the fraud and abuse regulations of the federal government relates to prohibitions against self-referral by physicians, the so-called Stark amendments.* Although this is easily avoided for some situations (e.g., a private physician cannot refer a Medicare or Medicaid patient to a radiology facility that the physician owns), the application of these regulations is not necessarily as clear as it might be to a physician-owned IDS. There are safe harbor provisions for some licensed HMOs and for certain clinical activities that are an integral part of a physician's practice, but whether these provisions would apply to certain forms of IDSs that are owned or controlled (even partially controlled) by physicians is unclear. As an example, GPWWs and fee-for-service MSOs may have an exposure. This is a new area of law that has not been fully clarified; competent legal counsel is critical here because the penalties for noncompliance with these federal regulations can be severe. At the time of writing, there appears to be a bit of loosening of these restrictions, but it is unclear as to how this issue will be resolved (if it ever is), and there is debate in Congress that could affect how this problem manifests.

Antitrust

It is well beyond the scope of this chapter to discuss antitrust in any depth, but a general point may be made. If an IDS is perceived to have been formed primarily to stifle competition, then it may be found in violation of antitrust provisions. Examples of so-called per se violations of antitrust law would include competitors agreeing to fix prices (either minimums or maximums!), sharing pricing information, agreeing to divide the market among themselves, and so forth. Although per se violations refer to actions that are clearly wrong, other activities may be subject to the rule of reason, in which there are good procompetitive reasons for the activity even though there may be some elements that could be perceived as antitrust. For example, an IDS may encompass greater than 20 percent to 30 percent of the total number of providers in a community but can clearly demonstrate that resources are rationalized and competition has increased. Again, competent counsel is required to review this issue. Antitrust issues are also discussed in Chapter 57 of *The Managed Health Care Handbook*.[10]

Licensure Provisions

Except in situations where the IDS is part of a joint venture with a licensed insurer or MCO, if

---

* Named after California Representative Fortney "Pete" Stark; the actual provisions are included as amendments to the Omnibus Reconciliation Act of 1993.

an IDS takes on too much risk for medical expenses, the state insurance department may conclude that the delivery system should be the licensed entity, not the HMO or insurance company that contracted with the delivery system. This problem has occurred in some states in which well-organized IPAs or PHOs took full capitated risk, and the insurance department forced the IPA or PHO to cede back a portion of that risk to the HMO or else obtain an HMO license of its own. As of the time of this writing, the National Association of Insurance Commissioners had issued a policy statement that IDSs that accept risk will require licensure as HMOs. Alternatively, if a licensed HMO provides adequate financial strength and protection from failure, the provider system may accept high levels of risk as long as a licensed HMO is involved. Although this policy statement does not have the force of law, it carries considerable stature. See Chapter 28 for more discussion of this topic.

The costs associated with becoming a licensed entity are not trivial and can easily exceed several million dollars, including capital necessary to meet statutory reserve requirements. Furthermore, compliance with licensure regulations is a resource- and capital-consuming task that many provider organizations will not be willing to take on. An interesting variation sometimes occurs: An IDS becomes a licensed HMO but only sells services to other HMOs (in other words, it does not market directly to enrollees). How much risk is too much in the eyes of a state insurance department? That issue is not at all clear as this chapter is being written.

CONCLUSION

IDSs have existed for quite some time, but under current pressures they are evolving rapidly. The more a system is truly integrated, and the more the goals and objectives of all stakeholders can be aligned, the greater the likelihood of success. IDSs may provide a viable vehicle for managed care plans to deliver services to their members, but no one should assume that the presence of an IDS does not also bring a large set of challenges, both managerial and legal. If those challenges cannot be overcome or managed, the downside of failure in an IDS is potentially more severe than if smaller, unintegrated medical groups fail. When designed and implemented well, however, the IDS can show advantages over many conventional managed care models.

Study Questions

1. Describe the key elements of the different types of integrated delivery systems.
2. For each type of integrated delivery system, describe conditions that would make that model preferable over all others.
3. Describe the conditions under which an HMO would desire to contract with an integrated delivery system; describe these conditions for each model type.
4. Describe the conditions under which an HMO would actively avoid contracting with an integrated delivery system; describe these conditions for each model type.
5. How can an advanced model integrated delivery system improve its chances of success under managed care?

REFERENCES AND NOTES

1. P. Starr, *The Social Transformation of American Medicine* (New York, N.Y.: Basic Books, 1982).
2. P.R. Konstvedt and D.W. Plocher, "Acquisitions, Joint Ventures, and Partnerships between Providers and Managed Care Organizations," in *The Managed Health Care Handbook*, 3d ed., ed. P.R. Kongstvedt (Gaithersburg, Md.: Aspen, 1996), 66–77.
3. A. Fine, "Specialty Networks from the Specialist's View," in *The Managed Health Care Handbook*, 3d ed., ed. P.R. Kongstvedt (Gaithersburg, Md.: Aspen, 1996), 191–201.
4. J.A. Rodeghero, "Physician Compensation in Groups and Integrated Delivery Systems," in *The Managed*

Health Care Handbook, 3d ed., ed. P.R. Kongstvedt (Gaithersburg, Md.: Aspen, 1996), 147–165.

5. W.G. Kopit and A.B. Bouton, "Antitrust Implications of Provider Exclusion," in *The Managed Health Care Handbook*, 3d ed., ed. P.R. Kongstvedt (Gaithersburg, Md.: Aspen, 1996), 906–929.
6. Ernst & Young LLP, *Physician–Hospital Organizations: Profile 1995* (Washington, D.C.: Ernst & Young LLP, 1995).
7. J.C. Goldsmith, The Illusive Logic of Integration, *Healthcare Forum Journal* (September/October 1994): 26–31.
8. Kongstvedt and Plocher, "Acquisitions, Joint Ventures, and Partnerships."
9. Kongstvedt and Plocher, "Acquisitions, Joint Ventures, and Partnerships."
10. Kopit and Bouton, "Antitrust Implications of Provider Exclusion."

SUGGESTED READING

Beckham, J.D. 1995. Redefining Work in the Integrated Delivery System. *Healthcare Forum Journal* May/June: 76–82.

Boland, P. 1994. Organized Delivery Systems. *Managed Care Quarterly*, 2 (4).

Burns, L.R., and Thorpe D.P. 1993. Trends and Models in Physician–Hospital Organizations. *Health Care Management Review* 18:7–20.

Coddington, D.C., Moore, K.D., and Fisher, E.A. 1994. *Integrated Health Care: Reorganizing the Physician, Hospital, and Health Plan Relationship*. Englewood, Colo.: Center for Research in Ambulatory Health Care Administration/MGMA.

Coile, R.C. 1994. Year 2000 Scenario for Physician-Hospital Organizations. *Topics in Health Care Financing* 20 (4): 75–83.

Conrad, D. and Hoare, G. (eds.). 1994. *Strategic Alignment: Managing Integrated Health Systems*. Ann Arbor, Mich.: Health Administration Press/AUPHA.

Dasco, S.T. and Dasco, C.C. 1996. *Managed Care Answer Book*. New York, N.Y.: Panel Publishers.

DeMuro, P.R. 1994. Integrated Delivery Systems. *Topics in Health Care Financing* 20 (3).

Ernst & Young LLP. 1995. *Physician–Hospital Organizations: Profile 1995*. Washington, D.C.: Ernst & Young LLP.

Fine, A. 1993. *The Integrated Health Care Delivery Systems Manual*. New York, N.Y.: Thompson Publishing Group.

Fine, A. (ed.). 1995. *Integrated Health Care Delivery Systems: A Guide to Successful Strategies for Hospital and Physician Collaboration*. New York, N.Y.: Thompson Publishing Group.

Korenchuk, K.M. 1994. *Transforming the Delivery of Health Care: The Integration Process* (2nd ed.). Englewood, Colo.: Center for Research in Ambulatory Health Care Administration/MGMA.

Traska, M.R. 1996. *Managed Care Strategies 1996*. New York, N.Y.: Faulkner & Gray.

Chapter 5

Elements of the Management Control and Governance Structure

Peter R. Kongstvedt

Study Objectives

- Understand the basic elements of governance and control of a managed care organization
- Understand the typical key executive roles in an MCO
- Understand risk management at the board level

It is not really possible to deal comprehensively with the topic of the elements of management control structure in one chapter of a book. There are myriad courses, texts, and other learning resources available to the reader that deal with the basic elements of management. For the purposes of this chapter, it is assumed that the reader has a working knowledge of business and management, so that certain fundamental aspects of management are not discussed here (e.g., how to read a balance sheet, write a job description, or construct an organizational chart). What follows in this chapter is a brief overview of certain management control elements as they pertain specifically to managed care. Detailed discussions of these activities are the topics of much of this book.

Ironically, there is no standardization of management governance or control structure in managed care; for example, the function, or even the very presence, of a board of directors will vary from plan to plan. The function of key officers or managers, as well as of committees, will likewise vary depending on the type of organization, the ownership, and the motivations and skills of the individuals involved. Because each plan will construct its own management control structure to suit its needs, only a few of the most common elements are described in this chapter.

BOARD OF DIRECTORS

Many, although not all, types of managed care plans will have a board of directors. The make-up and function of the board will be influenced by many factors (discussed below), but the board has the final responsibility for governance of the operation. Examples of plans or managed care operations that would not necessarily have their own boards include the following:

- preadmission certification and medical case management operations of insurance companies
- preferred provider organizations (PPOs) developed by large insurance companies
- PPOs developed for single employers by an insurance company
- employer-sponsored/developed plans (PPOs and precertification operations)
- health maintenance organizations (HMOs) or exclusive provider organizations set up as a line of business of an insurance company

These operations or plans are subsidiaries of larger companies; those companies do have boards of directors, but their boards are involved with oversight of the entire company, not the subsidiary operation. PPOs or HMOs that are divisions of insurance companies may be required to list a board on their licensure forms, but that board may have little real operational role.

Board Make-Up

All HMOs have boards, although not all those boards are particularly functional. This is especially true for HMOs that are part of large national companies. Each local HMO is incorporated and required to have a board, but it is not uncommon for the chains to use the same two corporate officers (perhaps with one local representative; see below) as the board for every HMO. Again, the board fulfills its legal function and obligation, but the actual operation of the HMO is controlled through the management structure of the company rather than through a direct relationship between the plan director and the board.

There are legal requirements for boards, particularly for HMOs. Those requirements are spelled out in each state's laws and regulations; for federally qualified HMOs, there are federal regulations as well. A common (although recently less so) requirement for HMOs is the necessity for member representation; new start-up operations may be exempt from that requirement for a period of time. Many state regulations require that at least one third of the board be members of the plan. In the case of the national HMO companies, that often translates into one individual who meets periodically with two corporate officers for brief board meetings. In the case of community-based HMOs, that may mean that multiple board seats (up to one third) are held by members.

Board make-up will also vary depending on whether the plan is for profit, in which case the owners' or shareholders' representatives may hold the majority of seats, or not for profit, in which case there will be broader community representation. Some not-for-profit health plans are organized as cooperatives, in which case the board members are all members of the plan. Not-for-profit plans that are not cooperatives are generally best served by board members who are truly independent and have no potential conflicts of interest; provider-sponsored not-for-profit plans may be restricted to no more than 20 percent of board seats being held by providers. The use of outside directors rather than plan officers as directors in any case will be dictated by local events, company bylaws, and laws and regulations (including the tax code for not-for-profit health plans). Provider-sponsored for-profit plans may have majority representation by providers and so must take special precautions to avoid antitrust problems.

Function of the Board

As stated earlier, the function of the board is governance: overseeing and maintaining final responsibility for the plan. In a real sense, the buck stops with the board. Final approval authority of corporate bylaws rests with the board. It is the bylaws that govern the basic structure of power and control not only of the plan officers but of the board itself.

The fiduciary responsibility of the board in an operating plan is of paramount importance. General oversight of the profitability or reserve status rests with the board, as do oversight and approval of significant fiscal events, such as a major acquisition or a significant expenditure. In a for-profit plan, the board has fiduciary responsibility to protect the interests of the stockholders.

Legal responsibilities of the board also may include review of reports and document signing. For example, a board officer may be required to sign the quarterly financial report to the state regulatory agency, the board chairperson may be required to sign any acquisition documents, and the board is responsible for the veracity of financial statements to stockholders.

Setting and approving policy represent another common function of an active board. This function may be as broad as determining the overall policy of using a gatekeeper system, or it may be as detailed as approving organizational charts and reporting structures. Although most policies and procedures will be the responsibility of the plan officers, an active board may set a policy regarding what operational policies must be brought to the board for approval or change.

In HMOs and many other types of managed care plans, the board has a special responsibility for oversight of the quality management (QM) program and for the quality of care delivered to members. Usually this responsibility is discharged through board (or board subcommittee) review of the QM documentation (including the overall QM plan and regular reports on findings and activities) and through feedback to the medical director and plan QM committee.

In free-standing plans, the board also has responsibility for hiring the chief executive officer (CEO) of the plan and for reviewing that officer's performance. The board in such plans often sets the CEO's compensation package, and the CEO reports to the board.

Active boards generally have committees to take up certain functions. Common board committees may include an executive committee (for rapid access to decision making and confidential discussions), a compensation committee (to set general compensation guidelines for the plan, set the CEO's compensation, and approve and issue stock options), a finance committee (to review financial results, approve budgets, set and approve spending authorities, review the annual audit, review and approve outside funding sources, and so forth), and a QM committee (as noted above).

Board Liability Issues

Any board faces the problem of liability for its actions. This is especially so in a board made up of outside directors and in the board of a not-for-profit organization. This is not to say that a board must always make correct decisions (it may make an incorrect decision, but it must do so in good faith), although being right is usually better than being wrong. Rather, a board should act in ways to reduce its own liability, and such actions will also be consistent with good governance. It is beyond the scope of this chapter to discuss fully board liability and prevention, but a few general comments may be made. Examples given in this section do not constitute legal opinions but are simply provided to help illustrate possible issues. The reader is urged to consult competent legal counsel as needed to understand board liability fully.

It is of paramount importance that board members exercise their duties to the benefit of the plan and not in their own self-interest. Conflict of interest is a difficult problem and can surface more readily than one might suppose. Examples of such conflicts would include actions that preferentially profit the board members, actions that are more in the interest of the board members than the plan (e.g., influencing how services are purchased by the plan), taking advantage of proprietary information to profit, and so forth. It is certainly possible for an action to benefit both the plan and the board members, but extra care must be taken to ensure that the action is first in the interest of the plan. In many cases, a board member with an obvious conflict of interest will abstain from voting on an issue or may even absent himself or herself from discussing the issue at all.

The board must also take care that it operates within the confines of the plan bylaws. In other words, the board cannot take any action that is not allowed in the bylaws of the organization. Examples of such actions might include paying an individual beyond the normal reimbursement policies, entering into an unrelated line of business, and so forth.

Board members must also perform their duties with some measure of diligence. For example, if plan management provides board members with information they need to decide properly on a course of action or a policy, it is incumbent on the board members to understand what is being provided and to ask however many questions are necessary to gain an adequate understanding to make an informed decision. Related to this is a duty actually to attend board meetings; although this would seem obvious, some board members may be so lax in their attendance as to provide virtually no governance or oversight. In any event, thorough documentation of the decision-making process is valuable, and those records should be maintained for an appropriate length of time.

As mentioned earlier, the board's primary responsibility is to the plan or organization and to the shareholders in the event that the plan is for profit. The board may also have some measure of responsibility to other individuals or organizations if the plan acts in such a way as to harm another party illegally. For example, if a health plan knowingly sets a policy not to perform credentialing of physicians and a panel physician commits malpractice, it is possible that the board (which either agreed to the policy or failed to change it) may have some liability. Corporate compliance programs as discussed in Chapter 2 are good examples of approach, plan management and the board should adopt.

Regardless of how the board is made up, it is important for there to be adequate director and officer liability insurance as well as insurance for errors and omissions. The need for such insurance may be attenuated by certain provisions in the company's or plan's bylaws holding the board members and officers harmless from liability. This issue requires review by legal counsel. The reader is referred to Chapter 38 of *The Managed Health Care Handbook* for an in-depth discussion of risk management.[1]

KEY MANAGEMENT POSITIONS

The roles and titles of the key managers in any plan will vary depending on the type of plan, its legal organization, its line of business, its complexity, whether it is free-standing or a satellite of another operation, and the local needs and talent. There is little consistency in this area from plan to plan. How each key role is defined (or even whether it will be present at all) is strictly up to the management of each plan. What follows, then, is a general overview of certain key roles.

Executive Director/CEO

Most plans have at least one key manager. Whether that individual is called a CEO, an executive director, a general manager, or a plan manager is a function of the items mentioned earlier in this chapter (e.g., scope of authority, reporting structure of the company, and the like). For purposes of discussion, this key manager will be referred to as an executive director.

The executive director is usually responsible for all the operational aspects of the plan, although that is not always the case. For example, some large companies (e.g., insurance companies or national HMO chains) have marketing reporting vertically to a regional marketing director rather than through the plan manager. A few companies take that to the extreme of having each functional area reporting vertically to regional managers rather than having all operations coordinated at the local level by a single manager; thus reporting is a function of the overall environment, and there is little standardization in the industry.

In free-standing plans and traditional HMOs, the executive director is responsible for all areas. The other officers and key managers report to the executive director, who in turn reports to the board (or to a regional manager in the case of national companies). The executive director also has responsibility for general administrative operations and public affairs.

Medical Director

Almost by definition, managed care plans will have a medical director. Whether that position is a full-time manager or a community physician who comes in a few hours per week is determined by the needs of the plan. The medical director usually has responsibility for provider relations, provider recruiting, QM, utilization management, and medical policy.

Some plans (e.g., simple PPOs) may only use the medical director, or a medical consultant, to review claims, perhaps to approve physician applications, and to review patterns of utilization.

The spectrum of medical director involvement parallels the intensity of medical management activities. Usually the medical director reports to the executive director.

As a plan grows in size, particularly if it is a complex plan such as an HMO, the need for the medical director to leverage time becomes crucial. If the medical director gets bogged down in day-to-day minutiae, his or her ability to provide leadership in the critical areas of utilization, quality, network management, and medical policy becomes dramatically reduced.

There are two approaches commonly employed to deal with this problem. The most common is bringing in an associate medical director. An associate medical director usually starts as a part-time position, but as the plan grows in size and complexity the position may evolve into a full-time function, and in fact there may be many associate medical directors in large plans. The role of the associate medical director is often defined as a subset of the overall duties of the medical director; for example, this person may focus primarily on utilization management or QM. This concept of adding qualified staff is not different from basic management practices for any specialized activity, but health plan managers are occasionally slow to realize the value of adding physician managers when they may be quick to realize the value of adding multiple layers of management in other operational areas.

The second approach to the issue of dealing with medical management in a large plan is to decentralize certain functions. For example, in a closed panel plan (e.g., a staff model HMO or a multisite group practice) it is common practice to assign management responsibilities to a physician at each geographic site. This on-site physician manager may have responsibility for utilization and staffing at the site or other duties as necessary. In an open panel setting (e.g., an open panel HMO), the network may be divided up into regions, and associate medical directors may be assigned responsibilities for designated regions. In either case, management must be realistic about the time and resources required for these associate medical directors to do their jobs. The skills, motivations, and compensation for decentralized or delegated medical management must be carefully thought through, and of course the medical director retains ultimate accountability.

Finance Director

In free-standing plans or large operations, it is common to have a finance director or chief financial officer. That individual is generally responsible for oversight of all financial and accounting operations. In some plans, that may include functions such as billing, management information services, enrollment, and underwriting as well as accounting, fiscal reporting, and budget preparation. This position usually reports to the executive director, although once again some national companies use vertical reporting.

Marketing Director

This person is responsible for marketing the plan. Responsibility generally includes oversight of marketing representatives, advertising, client relations, and enrollment forecasting. A few plans have marketing generating initial premium rates, which are then sent to finance or underwriting for review, but that is uncommon. This position reports to the executive director or vertically, depending on the company.

Operations Director

In larger plans, it is not uncommon to have an operations director. This position usually oversees claims, management information services, enrollment, underwriting (unless finance is doing so), member services, office management, and any other traditional backroom functions. This position usually reports to the executive director.

COMMITTEES

Again, there is little consistency from plan to plan regarding committees. Nonmedical committees may be limited to the member grievance committee (see Chapter 24). Other nonmedical committees are often ad hoc, convened to meet a specific need and then dissolved. Most plans tend to have standing committees to address management issues in defined areas, but that is idiosyncratic from plan to plan.

In the medical management area, committees serve to diffuse some elements of responsibility (which can be beneficial for medical–legal reasons) and allow important input from the field into procedure and policy or even into case-specific interpretation of existing policy. These aspects are discussed in greater detail in Chapter 58 of *The Managed Health Care Handbook.*[2]

Some examples of common medical management committees are given below. The actual formation, role, responsibility, and activity of any committee are local calls. More information about each of these areas can be found in the pertinent chapters of this book.

QM Committee

This topic is discussed in Chapter 17. This is one area where a committee is essential for oversight of the QM activity, setting of standards, review of data, feedback to providers, follow-up, and approval of sanctions. A peer review committee may be a subset of the QM committee, or it may be separate.

Credentialing Committee

This important topic is discussed in Chapter 7. This committee may also be a subset of the QM committee, or it may be separate. In new plans with heavy credentialing needs, it is probably best for the committee to be separate.

Medical Advisory Committee

Many plans have a medical advisory committee, whose purpose is to review general medical management issues brought to it by the medical director. Such issues may include changes in the contract with providers, compensation, changes in authorization procedures, and so on. This committee serves as a sounding board for the medical director. Occasionally it has voting authority, but that is rare because such authority is really vested with the board.

Utilization Review Committee

This committee reviews utilization issues brought to it by the medical director. Often this committee approves or reviews policy regarding coverage. This committee is also the one that reviews utilization patterns of providers and approves or reviews the sanctioning process (for utilization reasons) against providers.

Sometimes this committee gets involved in resolving disputes between the plan and a provider regarding utilization approval and may be involved in reviewing cases for medical necessity. In large plans, this function may be further subdivided into various specialty panels for review of consultant utilization. This committee may be a subset of the medical advisory committee, or it may be free-standing.

Pharmacy and Therapeutics Committee

Plans with significant pharmacy benefits often have a pharmacy and therapeutics committee. (Pharmacy is discussed in detail in Chapter 23 of *The Managed Health Care Handbook.*[3]) This committee is usually charged with developing a formulary, reviewing changes to that formulary, and reviewing abnormal prescription utilization patterns by providers. This committee is usually free-standing.

MANAGEMENT CONTROL STRUCTURE

Control structure refers to issues such as reporting responsibility, spending (and other commitment) authority, hiring and firing, the conduct of performance evaluations of employees, and so forth. Each plan will set these up to fit its situation and needs. Although these issues are too diverse to be addressed in this chapter, a wealth of material on all these functions can be found in the general management literature.

One item that is of special significance is the monthly operating report (MOR). Most tightly run managed care plans develop an MOR to use as the basic management tool. The typical MOR reports the month- and year-to-date financial status of the plan. Those data are backed up with details regarding membership, premium revenue, other revenue, medical costs (usually total and broken out into categories such as hospital, primary care, referral care, ancillary services, and so forth), marketing costs, administrative costs, other expenses, taxes (if appropriate), and the bottom line. Results are generally reported in terms of whole dollars and per member per month. This issue is discussed in detail in Chapter 22.

How much detail is reported routinely or on an ad hoc basis is a local call. The point here is that managed care, especially in tightly run plans, is so dynamic that managers cannot wait for quarterly results. Managers must have current and reliable data from which to manage. Sutton's law dictates that you must "go where the money is," and that can only be done if the MOR tells you where to look. In the case of hospital utilization, one cannot even wait for the MOR but must have daily reporting (see Chapter 13).

Various other types of reports are described throughout this book. What reports and routine reviews a manager needs to run the business is a decision each plan must make. If the plan is not producing an MOR, however, it is probably not managing optimally.

CONCLUSION

The basic functions of governance and control in HMOs are similar to those in any business, although the specifics regarding the board of directors, plan officers, and responsibilities of key managers vary tremendously from plan to plan.

Study Questions

1. Describe the most important functions of a board of directors.
2. Describe how a typical board can lower its risk profile.
3. Describe the key executive positions and their functions.
4. Describe typical operating committees of the board and their functions.

REFERENCES AND NOTES

1. B.J. Youngberg, "Risk Management in Managed Care," in *The Managed Health Care Handbook*, 3d ed., ed. P.R. Kongstvedt (Gaithersburg, Md.: Aspen, 1996), 608–621.
2. J.L. Touse, "Medical Management and Legal Obligations to Members," in *The Managed Health Care Handbook*, 3d ed., ed. P.R. Kongstvedt (Gaithersburg, Md.: Aspen, 1996), 930–943.
3. H.F. Blissenbach and P.M. Penna, "Pharmaceutical Services in Managed Care," in *The Managed Health Care Handbook*, 3d ed., ed. P.R. Kongstvedt (Gaithersburg, Md.: Aspen, 1996), 367–387.

SUGGESTED READING

Bader, B.S. 1994. Governance of Community-Based Integrated Healthcare Delivery Systems. *Health System Leader* 1 (9): 4–12.

Coile, R.C. 1994. *The New Governance: Strategies for an Era of Health Reform.* Ann Arbor, Mich.: Health Administration Press/American College of Healthcare Executives.

Part II

The Health Care Delivery System

"When one's all right, he's prone to spite
The doctor's peaceful mission.
But when he's sick, it's loud and quick
He bawls for a physician."

Eugene Field (1850–1895)
Doctors, st. 2 [1890]

Chapter 6

Primary Care in Closed Panel Plans

Peter R. Kongstvedt

Study Objectives

- Understand the basic types of closed panel HMOs
- Understand staffing issues in closed panels
- Understand basic compensation of physicians in closed panels
- Understand the recruiting process in closed panels
- Understand the role of nonphysician providers
- Understand productivity issues
- Understand physician retention issues

This chapter deals with issues involving primary care physicians (PCPs) in closed panel health plans, that is, group and staff model health maintenance organizations (HMOs) or large group practices in which managed care provides the majority of practice income. Although primary medical care can and is delivered by consultants, this chapter restricts its scope to PCPs.

Conventional definitions of primary care encompass internal medicine, family practice, and pediatrics. Obstetrics/gynecology (OB/GYN) is generally considered specialty care, although it is not uncommon for HMOs to allow self-referral by members to OB/GYN physicians for certain services (e.g., Pap smears). In that context, many of the comments regarding PCPs will hold equally well for OB/GYN physicians in closed panels because issues of recruiting, compensation, and so forth will be similar.

Many of the issues discussed in this chapter will also apply to large integrated delivery systems (IDSs), at least those IDSs that either employ physicians or have a tight relationship with a large medical group (see Chapter 4 for a discussion of different IDS models). Last, issues germane to primary care in closed panels may also hold relevance in open panels, particularly for private medical groups of ten or more physicians that have a significant level of managed care participation.

NEEDS ASSESSMENT

To assess a closed panel's needs for PCPs, you must look at realistic staffing ratios, availability, scope of practice, and acceptance.

Staffing Ratios

In closed panel HMOs, staffing ratios look at the number of PCPs relative to the number of members. There are significant differences in staffing ratios depending on the size of the health plan and whether there is a considerable Medicare and/or Medicaid population being served. Staffing ratios are also occasionally addressed in state regulations; for example, in Pennsylvania a minimum staffing ratio of 1 physician per 1,600 members is required. Staffing ratios will be discussed in terms of full-time equivalents (FTEs), although most closed panel plans in fact use part-time providers on their staff. There are two common units of measurement for staffing: physicians per members (e.g., 1:1,300), and physicians per 1,000 members (e.g., 0.8:1,000). This chapter will use the latter convention.

Based on research published in 1995, there appear to be some differences in staffing ratios between large and small closed panel HMOs, with the difference occurring at approximately 80,000 members. In plans with less than 80,000 members, the weighted mean PCP staffing ratio (rounded) was 0.89:1,000, with a standard deviation of 0.68; for plans with more than 80,000 members, the weighted mean PCP staffing ratio (rounded) was 0.66:1,000, with a standard deviation of 0.51. The weighted mean staffing ratio for all physicians (not just PCPs) was 2.8:1,000 for small plans and 1.2:1,000 for large plans.[1]

These data compare with data published in 1992 obtained at an earlier point in time from essentially the same sources, in which large, closed panel plans that served a primarily commercial population had an average PCP staffing ratio of 0.8:1,000 and an average physician staffing ratio of 1.3:1,000. Plans that were smaller had more than twice those ratios. In the 1992 data, the ratios per 1,000 members, by specialty type, were 0.3 for full-time general/family practice, 0.3 for internal medicine, 0.2 for pediatrics, and 0.1 for OB/GYN.[2] When one is looking solely at general pediatricians for *pediatric* enrollees (as opposed to all enrollees, which is what the other ratios look at), recent data report 0.54:1,000 for large plans and 0.79:1,000 for small plans.[3]

These figures may vary considerably from plan to plan. Some private, for-profit, closed panel plans have used primary care staffing ratios of 0.6:1,000, and some large, well-known, closed panel plans use ratios closer to 1.2:1,000.

As noted in the data, the size of a health plan has a clear impact on staffing ratios. Economies of scale are achievable in large plans. Plans that have a large medical staff also have the ability to cover clinic sites more easily, so that there is less need for overstaffing simply to ensure the presence of a provider at a site. Smaller plans not only need to ensure site coverage (assuming that they have more than one site to cover) but must staff for growth as well.

The scope of clinical practice by the PCPs has an effect on staffing. If PCPs are performing many procedures that might otherwise go out to referral specialists, there will be a need for more generous staffing. For example, if family practitioners are performing obstetrical services, some of their time will be taken up with prenatal care and deliveries, so that greater staffing will be required to meet the primary care needs of the members.

Medicare members utilize more services, including office visits, than commercial members. Commercial enrollees younger than 65 have an average of 3.6 to 3.8 physician encounters per year, of which 2.5 are primary care visits. Medicare members average 7.0 encounters per year for Medicare risk enrollees and 6.4 encounters per year for Medicare cost enrollees[4]; these data refer to total physician encounters, not necessarily those for primary care only, and do not include encounters with nonphysicians. Nevertheless, the implications for staffing are clear: Staffing needs are greatly increased when a substantial Medicare population is served. In the previously cited study, the majority of closed panel HMOs increased their staffing ratios for Medicare members to a mean of 1.6 per 1,000 Medicare enrollees.[5]

The effect of Medicaid members is less clear. In one set of data, Medicaid HMO members received approximately 13 percent more ambulatory care and were hospitalized 52 percent more frequently than commercial members.[6] This has led at least one researcher to conclude that a Medicaid member requires 21 percent more physician time than a commercial member.[7] In one study examining actual staffing patterns in HMOs, however, plans with Medicaid members did indeed show a higher median physician-to-member ratio than plans without Medicaid members, but there was no statistical correlation with the number of physicians per 100,000 members.[8] Therefore, the need for increased staffing for HMOs with Medicaid members is likely to be higher than in a commercial population, but the degree of increase is not obvious.

Staffing ratios are useful guides for management to use when addressing recruiting needs, but they are also useful when addressing issues of efficiency and productivity. Ratios that are lean may, over time, erode the level of service and cost-effectiveness of a plan. For example, if you run at 0.5:1,000 or tighter for an extended period, the stress level of the PCPs may rise as they try to meet the demand for services by members. When that happens, the harried PCPs will have less time and patience for evaluating problems and will be inclined to refer the member to a consultant to deal with any but the most routine care. Furthermore, the attitude of the PCPs will degenerate and be reflected back to members during office visits.

Ratios that are significantly richer may over time become an insupportable overhead cost. If overstaffing continues for too long, productivity could take a nose dive, and efforts to improve it will be met with resistance. Once low productivity levels become institutionalized, it is often quite difficult to improve them because you are demanding more work for no increase in compensation, and the usual result is the retort that plan management's demands for greater productivity will have a serious negative impact on patient care quality. A more detailed discussion of productivity is presented later in this chapter.

Availability

The availability of high-quality physicians may have an impact on staffing ratios. Although there are many things that may affect physician availability, two important elements are the cycle of physician training and the desirability of your practice situation.

Virtually all residency programs begin and end in midsummer. Usually a resident fresh out of training will want to decompress for a few weeks or more, so that physicians from training programs often are not available to start until August or September. Even for physicians a few years out of training, it is not uncommon for them to have signed 1-year contracts, so that they also may not be available until the late summer. If a physician has been out of training for a number of years and is in private practice or is coming out of the military, there is much more variability in availability.

If you are in a situation where there is sufficient variation in physician availability to make recruiting difficult, you may have to overstaff in the summer and fall to be able to serve projected increases in membership in January and February because many open enrollments occur in the fall.

Scope of Practice

The scope of clinical skills that the physicians in your group have will also affect your staffing needs. If the PCPs perform a large variety of procedures or if supervision of midlevel practitioners is required (e.g., family practitioners performing routine obstetric procedures, internists performing stress tests and reading electrocardiograms, or PCPs supervising physician assistants), there will be an incremental decrease in the amount of time available for regular office care.

You may wish to recruit a PCP with special skills rather than recruit a consultant, and this too may have an effect on your staffing ratios. For example, your PCPs may be sending all the routine flexible proctosigmoidoscopies out to a gastroenterologist. If your plan is large enough, you may consider recruiting specifically for an internist skilled in that procedure, even though it would alter your staffing ratios slightly downward. The same argument may exist for stress testing or a number of other high-volume procedures that a well-trained PCP can perform as well as a consultant.

One concern with this idea, which applies equally to adding consultants (see Chapter 10), is that once such a resource becomes easily available, utilization tends to rise. The service is often seen as free, and other PCPs will tend to request it more readily. Furthermore, if a physician truly enjoys doing the procedure, he or she may tend to recommend it more often as an unconscious means of displacing other less enjoyable clinical activities (e.g., routine health assessments).

Acceptance

Your needs may be affected by the acceptability of your current PCPs by your target markets, the medical community as a whole, and your membership. For example, you may require the addition of only one PCP according to the staffing ratios, but your plan is located in a community where family physicians are not generally accepted. To provide adequate coverage, you may have to consider adding an internist and a pediatrician, even though it ostensibly makes your staffing ratios too high for half the year.

NONPHYSICIAN PROVIDERS

Closed panel plans are more likely to use nonphysician providers (i.e., physician assistants, advanced practice nurses, nurse practitioners, clinical nurse specialists, or certified nurse-midwives) to deliver some medical care to their members. In a previously cited study, 65 percent of closed panel plans reported the use of nonphysician providers, with a mean ratio of 0.08:1,000.[9] In a 1992 report, fully 86 percent of closed panel plans reported using nonphysician providers (compared with 48 percent of open panel plans), 52 percent of plans used physician assistants, 52 percent of plans used nurse practitioners, and 28 percent of plans used certified nurse-midwives.[10]

Well-qualified nonphysician practitioners are generally found to be a great asset to a plan in that they are able to deliver excellent primary care, provide more health maintenance and health promotion services, tend to spend more time with patients, and receive generally good acceptance from most members. In many states, nurse practitioners (and, in a smaller number of states, physician assistants) have the authority to write prescriptions.

Nonphysician providers may also play an important role in the management of chronically ill patients. They may provide the primary locus of coordination of care or case management for patients with diseases such as chronic asthma, diabetes, and the like. In a similar vein, nonphysician providers may take a key role in managing high-risk patients, using practice protocols for prevention and health maintenance in this population. Certified nurse-midwives not only may provide services for routine deliveries but may in fact provide primary gynecological care using practice guidelines and protocols.

Most plan managers use slightly different staffing ratios for nonphysician providers than for PCPs. For example, a nonphysician provider may be considered between 0.5 and 0.8 FTE for PCP staffing purposes. The primary reasons for this are the tendency for nonphysician providers to spend more time with their patients (which often accounts for their popularity with their patients), the fact that nonphysician providers generally do not make hospital rounds and are less likely to perform procedures, and the need for the nonphysician provider to staff cases with a physician. The physician who staffs such cases may also have a slightly diminished productivity strictly from the point of view of personally seeing patients.

The availability of nonphysician providers varies widely from state to state and correlates strongly with a favorable state practice environment.[11] The practice environment includes such variables as the ability to write prescriptions, the ability to practice in a (relatively) autonomous manner for certain situations, and the ability to receive direct reimbursement. Many elements of the practice environment will also have an impact on a nonphysician provider's efficiency.

RECRUITING

Practice Attributes

The desirability of your practice opportunity clearly affects the availability of physicians. Geographic location, climate, plan size and history, reputation, and lifestyle potential will all have an impact. The presence of other well-qualified and congenial physicians on your staff will also improve your recruiting potential because a collegial atmosphere with support from fellow physicians is an important element in making your plan desirable from the PCP's standpoint.

Table 6–1 lists attributes deemed desirable in a study of physicians at the Lovelace Clinic in New Mexico. It is likely that any HMO or medical group would find a slightly different constellation of attributes considered desirable by physicians, but in general these attributes would still be considered.

Timing

New managers who are recruiting physicians for the first time often underestimate how long it takes to recruit well-qualified PCPs. Although physicians coming out of training programs are usually not available until middle to late summer, they frequently have decided where they are going by the preceding fall or winter. There are always exceptions, and there are certainly excellent physicians who have not decided by the time they are done with their residency programs, but that is not the norm. According to one large study, the average time it takes to recruit a physician for a closed panel HMO is 9 months.[12]

Even for PCPs who have been in practice and desire to make a change, the process is a long one. Physicians, like other people, do not wish to contemplate another change, so they will take their time in choosing their next location. If they are well qualified, they can afford to be choosy and explore many opportunities.

In general, the window for recruiting is most open between November and April, although opportunities do exist all year long. As a rule of thumb, it is best to plan on beginning the recruiting process at least 5 to 9 months before new physicians are required to be on board. This gestation period may be cut short if you are lucky, in which case you may have to decide whether you are willing to add the new PCP(s) to your staff early.

Table 6–1 Practice Attribute Rating by Physicians Employed at Lovelace Clinic, New Mexico ($N = 76$)

Practice Attribute	*Mean**	*Standard Deviation*	*Rating as Very or Extremely Important (%)*
Quality of care provided	4.66	0.58	95
Amount of clinical time spent on patients	4.19	0.68	84
Number of hours worked per week	4.18	0.78	80
Interaction with colleagues	4.14	0.69	80
Professional autonomy	4.00	0.79	77
Salary	4.01	0.77	76
Geographic location	4.04	0.84	75
Call schedule	4.08	0.87	74
Nonsalary fringe benefits	3.87	0.75	71
Input into managerial decisions	3.70	0.87	55
Amount of administrative time	3.07	1.04	32

* Scoring: 1 = least important, 5 = most important. *Source:* Reprinted from N.B. Fisher, H.L. Smith, and D.P. Pasternok, "Critical Factors in Recruiting Health Maintenance Organization Physicians," *Health Care Management Review*, Vol. 18, No. 1, pp. 51–61, © 1993, Aspen Publishers, Inc.

Sources

Two of the most effective methods of finding candidates for recruiting are word of mouth and professional relationships. Clinical chairpersons as well as the medical staff often have frequent contact with other physicians. Such contact may be collegial (e.g., at the hospital, in a specialty society, and so forth), through a teaching program, through personal friendships, and through friends of friends. Some HMOs and medical groups pay staff physicians a recruiting bonus for initiating contacts with physicians who are later successfully recruited.

Spontaneous inquiries occur randomly. If your plan is in a desirable location, you can count on frequent inquiries. If a physician is already in your community or once lived there and wishes to return, he or she may contact you directly.

Advertisements in professional journals are another common method of making contact with PCPs interested in making a change. The lead time for getting the ad in the periodical can be quite long, so plan ahead. Some managers hold that it is enough to run the ads every other issue rather than every issue. State medical societies also have journals, which are good places to run ads, especially in your home state and the states surrounding your plan. Examples of national medical journals that routinely run advertisements include the following:

- *American Journal of Obstetrics and Gynecology*
- *Annals of Internal Medicine*
- *Journal of the American Medical Association*
- *Journal of Family Practice*
- *Pediatrics*
- *New England Journal of Medicine*

Newspaper advertisements are less useful, although some widely circulated newspapers, such as the *New York Times*, do run ads for physicians in their areas. Military publications, such as *Military Press* and *Stars and Stripes*, may reach physicians who will be completing their service and are looking for civilian practice opportunities.

Letters to cooperative residency programs may be useful, especially if the program director is willing to post your letter on a common bulletin board where residents can see it. Recruiting physicians on site at a training program is not often allowed, so some large plans host informal off-site gatherings for residents of area programs. If your plan participates as a training site for a residency program, you will have a reasonably good chance of recruiting some of the residents who rotated through.

Direct mail can be quite effective. Mailing labels may be obtained from a number of sources, such as the American Medical Association and Business Mailers, Inc. Preparing a professional-looking brochure is important, although a well-written letter will still have an impact. Because preparing a direct mailing can be labor intensive, you may wish to contract with an outside agency to collate the material, stuff the envelopes, and so on. Your brochure or letter should contain, at a minimum, the following elements:

- a description of the health plan in terms of its size, the number of medical facilities (or clinics, if you use that term), medical services available, current physicians on staff, and any unique points about the plan
- a description of the hospitals, their location, their size, their services, and so forth
- a description of the community and its positive points, such as colleges or universities, special cultural and recreational offerings, religious and social organizations, shopping and dining, and the weather

Professional Recruiting Agencies

A carefully selected professional agency can be a resource in locating and recruiting physicians. When you do your own recruiting, you will be dismayed at the number of responses you get from poorly qualified candidates. Separating out the well-qualified candidates from the unqualified, as well as weeding out the tire kickers, can be an exhausting chore for someone not trained in it. Even worse, you may inadvertently pass over an important piece of information about a candidate, or not look for it at all, and have a disastrous outcome. For those plans or medical groups that do not have a professional physician recruiting department, the use of an external recruiting agency may be worthwhile.

Professional recruiters will not be able to guarantee a placement, nor can they guarantee that a candidate who does get placed with you will ultimately work out. They can, however, remove a great deal of the burden from you in the recruiting process. They may also have access to candidates who are looking to change but who do not wish to contact anyone directly for fear of compromising their current position.

Such help does not come cheap, although fees for placements are quite variable. The most you might see is 30 percent of the physician's first-year salary, but lesser fees are more common. For example, a recruiter may charge a straight fee of $15,000 or $20,000 for a placement. Some recruiters require a retainer to be paid at the beginning with the balance contingent on placement, whereas others work strictly on contingency. It is common for a recruiter to give you a discount for multiple placements in a year. Fees are sometimes negotiable, although if you negotiate the fee down too low the recruiter may be less motivated to help you.

In selecting a recruiting agency, be sure to check the agency's references. Try to get an idea of how many physicians it has placed, whether it has successfully placed PCPs in groups similar to your own, how long it took on average, and whether the physicians are still there. If you are unfamiliar with contracts, be sure to have the agency's contract reviewed by an attorney before signing.

Initial Selection of Candidates To Consider

After you have responses from candidates, you need to select whom you will consider asking in for an interview. Although this process will be easier if you have been using a professional recruiter, it cannot be eliminated entirely. It is important to evaluate inquiries and respond promptly to initiate contact while the candidate is still available and interested.

The curriculum vitae is the first source of data for you to use and should describe the physicians' credentials and current situation, their training, where they went to medical school, where their postgraduate training took place, and specialty board certification or eligibility (some specialties, such as OB/GYN, require a certain amount of practice experience before certification is given). Most board certifications are now time limited; although physicians who received their board certification before that board's setting a time limitation may have their certification status unaffected, physicians who receive their certification after that may have to renew their certification every 10 years.

From either the cover letter or a phone call, try to ascertain the professional goals and needs of the PCP. For example, a physician may simply be looking for someplace to park for a year while a spouse finishes training. In that case, you need to decide whether that is acceptable.

The process of checking the credentials of a candidate should be thorough; shortcuts must not be taken, even if your group is suffering from understaffing. Failure to perform credentials checking properly not only opens the group up to a serious legal liability but may compromise care to the members, cause a serious embarrassment to the group, and result in the need to recruit again under even more stress, especially because it was found in one well-known study that up to 5 percent of physicians applying for positions in ambulatory care clinics misrepresented their credentials in their applications.[13] A more thorough discussion of physician credentials checking is found in Chapter 7; the process in closed panels should contain all the elements found in open panels plus those items discussed specifically in this chapter.

Finding out the malpractice history is an important exercise. Usually it is enough simply to ask the candidates to list any malpractice claims that were judged against them or settled with an award. It is not uncommon for a physician to have been sued or even to have settled a case to avoid costly and lengthy litigation, even though the physician may have been perfectly innocent. Do not allow the presence of a malpractice history alone to deter you from considering a candidate, but look closely at that history for evidence of a pattern or of a truly malfeasant act.

You should find out what type of malpractice insurance the potential candidate currently has. You want to know who the carrier is, whether the insurance is on a claims-made or occurrence basis, and whether the candidate has or will purchase tail coverage if necessary. In other words, if candidates have the occurrence type of malpractice insurance (which is becoming uncommon), they are covered for any claim arising against them in the future for events that occurred during the time they had the policy. If they have the claims-made type of coverage (the most common type), their coverage ends as soon as the premiums stop. To continue coverage for future claims arising from events that occurred during the policy period, they must buy tail coverage. Tail coverage can be quite expensive (for example, an OB/GYN in practice for 10 years may have to pay well over $75,000 for tail coverage), and you need to determine whether your plan would have to provide it to attract the candidate. If you do provide it, you may want to consider a 3-year forgiveness of the cost. In other words, you will pay for the coverage, but its cost is considered a loan to the new physician. For each year the physician practices with your group, you forgive a third of the original loan. If the physician leaves before 3 years are up, he or she has to repay whatever portion of the loan remains.

Under no circumstances may you refuse to consider a candidate for reasons of age, sex, religious beliefs, race, or any other elements considered under the Equal Employment Opportunity Act.

Before inviting a physician to your plan for an interview, conduct a telephone interview. This may reveal, for example, that the candidate has little or no communication skills, is unable to speak the same language as your members, or has unreasonable demands. This will also give you an opportunity to explore further reasons why the candidate wants to be considered for your group.

Reference checks are usually done at this point but are occasionally done after the candidate has come in for an interview. There are two types of reference checks: formal letters of reference, and telephone reference checks. Ask your candidates to submit three letters of reference from physicians who have known them professionally in their current position. If that is not possible for reasons of confidentiality, reserve the right to check those references after a job offer has been made, and ask for references from the next most recent position. It is unusual in this litigious era for reference letters to do anything except either state what percentage of time the candidate spends walking on water or simply confirm employment, revealing no information whatsoever except that the candidate was employed.

Telephone reference checks are more useful because they are confidential, and you may sometimes be able to read between the lines. The most useful telephone conversations occur between physicians. When nonphysicians question physicians about the competence of another physician, negative responses are likely to be muted. Again, it is unusual for a reference to say negative things for fear of a lawsuit, even after you have assured him or her of complete confidentiality.

You may wish to telephone references who have not been provided by the candidate (only after the candidate has given permission for you to do reference checks; it could be devastating if the current employer or medical group does not know that the candidate is looking to leave). Such references could include the president of the candidate's local medical society, the chief of staff where the candidate currently has active privileges, or, in the case of physicians just completing training, the director of the residency program.

The National Practitioner Data Bank

A special type of reference check was created by the Health Care Quality Improvement Act of 1986: the National Practitioner Data Bank (NPDB). In addition to providing immunity from antitrust lawsuits, the act requires hospitals, health plans, malpractice carriers, and state licensure boards to report settled or lost malpractice suits and adverse acts, sanctions, or restrictions against the practice privileges of a physician. In the first full year of operation, the NPDB reported that the annual rate of licensure actions was 2.7 per 1,000 physicians (0.0 to 9.7 per 1,000), that the annual rate of clinical privileges actions was 1.4 per 1,000 physicians (0.0 to 3.6 per 1,000), and that there were an average of 21.1 medical malpractice payments per 1,000 physicians.[14] By the end of 1994, the NPDB reported the following statistics: The data bank contained more than 97,500 reports, of which 82 percent were related to malpractice payments, with licensure reports making up most of the rest; it had processed more than 4.5 million requests for information; and 8 percent of queries were matched with a report.[15] The act is further discussed in Chapter 18.

The act also states that any hospital or HMO may contact the NPDB to obtain information about a physician and that, if the hospital or health plan fails to do so, it will be assumed that it did so anyway. In other words, there is a potential for liability on the part of the plan if it fails to check with the NPDB and hires a physician who has a poor record as reported in the data bank, and there is a malpractice problem later on. Information about the NPDB may be obtained by writing to:

National Practitioner Data Bank
P.O. Box 10832
Chantilly, VA 22021
1-800-767-6732

Interview Process

After candidates to interview are selected, the plan needs to send the candidates adequate information about the plan, the practice environment, and so forth. The next step is to invite them to the plan. The trip should be arranged so that as little work as possible is required of the candidates. You should prepay the air fare, arrange to have someone meet them at the airport, have the hotel arranged, and so forth. It is good form to invite spouses as well, but that may be delayed until a second interview.

The interview should be scheduled carefully. Plan for the candidate to meet with other PCPs in the plan, the chief of staff of the appropriate medical department, and other plan executives as necessary (e.g., the marketing director, the nursing or operations director, the executive director, and so forth).

A visit to the main hospital that the PCP would be using is also important. Hospitals are usually quite accommodating about giving tours to prospective new physicians. If there is time, an informal tour of the community is helpful, with an emphasis on the types of neighborhoods that are available to live in. If the candidate and spouse have both come, you may wish to arrange for a real estate agent to give the spouse a tour while the candidate is interviewing.

Try not to leave large blocks of time where the candidate has nothing to do and feels adrift. The same goes for the spouse (unless the spouse wants to be left alone; inquire first). This carries over to the evening if the candidate is staying overnight. A dinner invitation is appropriate, although the candidate may feel too tired and may wish to decline, in which case you should graciously accept the refusal.

It is important to schedule an exit interview with the candidate. This meeting allows the medical director to find out how the candidate views the situation and to ascertain a level of interest (although it is unusual to hear an outright rejection at this point, even if the candidate is no longer interested). Likewise, this final meeting allows the candidate to ask any last minute questions or clarify any information that may have been obtained during the visit.

After the initial interview is complete, be sure to follow up promptly within 7 to 14 days. If you are no longer interested, it is still good form to send a letter thanking the candidates and indicating that the final selection did not include them but that you appreciate their interest and wish them luck. If you are still interested, arrange for a second visit, this time for the candidate and spouse to see the community. Assuming that you have satisfactorily completed the reference check, you will want to make an offer of employment at that time. The candidate may wish to think it over and review the contract. If that is the case, ask for an answer within a fixed time frame, such as 3 weeks.

When offering a contract, you will wish to include a provision that, if the candidate has falsified any information or has failed to provide complete information, you have the right to terminate the contract. If you have not been able to complete the reference check because of confidentiality issues, you will wish to be able to contact references at the candidate's current location upon the candidate's acceptance of your offer, and final acceptance by you is contingent upon that last reference check.

COMPENSATION

The issue of compensation of physicians in medical groups and IDSs is a complicated topic and is discussed in full in Chapter 10 of *The Managed Health Care Handbook*.[16] An overview of some of the issues is provided here. The basic tenet of compensation for PCPs in closed panels is that they should be on approximate parity with their fee-for-service colleagues. This does not refer to gross income but includes benefits (e.g., malpractice insurance, health and life insurance, retirement, and so forth), duty requirements (e.g., frequency of being on call, hours worked, and so forth), bonus pay, and net take-home pay. Because physicians do not look at gross dollars alone when assessing a practice opportunity, neither should you. Further discussion about factors leading to physician retention is found later in this chapter.

Straight Salary

A straight salary is the most common payment mechanism in staff model HMOs and is often found in group models as well, where the group's salary costs are passed back directly to the plan. Some private group practice groups use straight salary, although usually as a base, after which productivity, medical costs, or other modifiers are applied. Although it is rare for a staff model to use some form of risk, group models may use withholds on salary. Bonus arrangements are commonly attached to salary plans as well.

Capitation

Some group model closed panel plans capitate a medical group (or groups) that makes up the physician panel. In that case, the plan negotiates the overall capitation rate with the group, and the group then decides how to compensate the physicians. Again, salary with a bonus plan is the most common arrangement within the group (with or without a withhold), although some groups use fee for service, and a few capitate individual providers. A more thorough discussion of both capitation and fee for service in managed care is found in Chapter 8.

Benefits

Benefits are a vital part of the total compensation package. Whether the plan pays straight salary and provides the benefits directly to the physicians or the group is capitated and provides the benefits itself, benefits are an integral part of compensation.

The following are benefits that are almost universally provided to physicians as part of their compensation:

- malpractice insurance
- life insurance

- health insurance
- continuing medical education time and funds
- professional licensure fees
- vacation and sick leave

Benefits that are quite commonly provided as well, but perhaps not in every case, include:

- dental insurance
- disability insurance
- auto allowance and parking fees at hospitals
- professional society dues
- retirement plan
    1. 401(k)
    2. simplified employee pension plan individual retirement account
    3. tax deferred annuity

Finally, the following are benefits that are not routinely provided but that you may wish to consider for special circumstances:

- book and journal allowance (separate from continuing medical education funds)
- paid time off for nonplan activities
    1. research
    2. jury duty
    3. military leave
    4. volunteer work
- compensation time
- extended leave without pay
- in-plan moonlighting
    1. extended hours
    2. urgent care
- sabbatical program
- paternity leave (maternity leave is assumed to be provided)
- deferred compensation
- profit sharing
- low-interest unsecured loans

Risk and Bonus Arrangements

Bonus plans are common in closed panels, whereas risk arrangements are less so. In capitated groups, there is the inherent risk that the capitation payment represents all the money there is; in a sense, that is a clear risk. Again, the reader is referred to Chapter 10 of *The Managed Health Care Handbook* for an in-depth discussion of compensation of physicians in medical groups and IDSs.[17]

The most common mechanism to deal with risk in a closed panel is a withhold. In a withhold, part of the capitation payment (e.g., 20 percent) or salary (e.g., 10 percent) is withheld until the end of the year. That withhold is used to cover excess medical expenses. If there is still money in the withhold, the physicians receive it. For a more complete discussion of risk arrangements, refer to Chapter 7.

Bonus plans are most often based either on total plan performance or on medical cost alone. When bonus is based on total plan performance, it may be affected by things outside the physician's control, such as membership growth, underwriting criteria, premium yield, and so forth. This will be perceived as unfair in the event that no bonus is paid. On the other hand, it clearly points out that everyone is in it together.

Bonus based on medical expense only is more closely related to actions under the control of the physicians. For example, if the plan outperforms budget on per member cost for medical services, 10 percent of the total base salary is paid as a bonus. When medical expense is measured on a per member per month or per member per year basis rather than on whole dollars, there can be no charge that the bonus is based on anything outside the physician's control.

Bonus plans may pay straight bonus to every physician, or they may be tied to performance evaluations. It is unwise to pay bonus on the basis of a few single criteria for individual PCPs because any single criterion can be manipulated to the benefit of the PCP but to the detriment of the plan. If bonus is to be paid to PCPs on a differential basis, you are better off using a broader performance evaluation system. Such performance evaluation systems are discussed in Chapter 9.

The amount of bonus available may be calculated as a percentage of the total base salary paid during the year or as a percentage of savings over budget. If a percentage of savings is used, you need to determine whether there will be an upper limit on the bonus. For example, you may wish to share savings of per member per month medical expenses on a 50:50 basis with the physician group, but only to a maximum of 20 percent of the total base salary paid.

If you intend to pay a bonus on the basis of making the budget targets (e.g., paying 10 percent of base salary if the per member per month medical expense targets are met), be sure to include the amount of the bonus payment in your overall accruals for physician salary and benefits. If you are going to pay on the basis of exceeding budget only, then you will not have to face an unexpected expense.

CREDENTIALING

The process of credentialing new physicians in closed panels is basically one of making sure that they have the necessary documents to allow them to practice with your group. This use of the term *credentialing* differs from its use in open panels. In the open panel setting, credentialing refers primarily to checking references and documentation (e.g., licensure verification, malpractice insurance, and so forth); this activity is discussed in an earlier section of this chapter.

In open panels, it is the physician's responsibility to have the necessary documentation to practice; in closed panels, it is the plan's responsibility to obtain it for the physician so that the physician can practice in the group. Because some of the documents require a lengthy lead time, you should plan to begin as soon as the physician has signed an employment contract.

Obtaining a state license to practice medicine takes the longest amount of time. If the physician has licenses in many other states, it lengthens the process because the state must check with each other state to determine whether the PCP's license is valid.

The Drug Enforcement Agency (DEA) number allows a physician to prescribe scheduled narcotics. Although it is a federally issued permit, the number is good only for one state location. Therefore, even if the physician has a DEA number from another state, he or she must reapply for a new number. Some states also issue narcotics numbers.

After state licensure has been obtained, the physician must obtain malpractice insurance. If your plan has a group policy, it is a simple matter to add the newcomer. If candidates had claims made through malpractice insurance, they will need a tail coverage policy to cover against suits that may haunt them from the past. Your carrier may insist on seeing evidence of such coverage before issuing a new policy, and you should as well.

Once state licensure and malpractice coverage have been obtained, the physician must apply for hospital privileges at your participating hospitals. An application for membership in the county and state medical societies may also be made at that time.

ORIENTATION

Time invested in proper orientation will be time well spent. If your plan has been understaffed for some time, there will be pressure to get the new PCP seeing patients as soon as possible, or perhaps after half a day of brief overview. The new PCP will learn the ropes eventually, but if you want to foster a good attitude and help the new PCP learn his or her way around more efficiently, spend the time with a good orientation program.

Plan the orientation to expose new PCPs to all the personnel with whom they will be interacting in the future. Have those individuals review the important elements of their areas. When new PCPs understand what is expected of them and what to expect from others in the plan as well as the technical components of practicing in your group, they will be more comfortable. Consider orientation administrative preventive medicine. Exhibit 6–1 lists some topics that may be appropriate for an orientation program.

Although you may spend 3 or 4 days going over orientation material, there is no way a new PCP will be able to absorb all the information about your plan in that short time. Therefore, for the first few weeks it is best to schedule a reduced patient load. For example, you may want to schedule only half the normal number of appointments for the new PCP to see. It is also helpful to assign an experienced nurse to the new PCP to help explain the forms, assist in getting laboratory and radiology studies, help with preadmission requirements, and so forth. After 2 or 3 weeks, the new PCP may be assigned a permanent nurse or aide if such a change is necessary.

Many groups use a buddy system for the first few weeks as well. This means that an experienced plan physician in the same specialty as the new PCP is designated to help the new PCP acclimate to the system. This extends to the new PCP taking phone calls with the experienced PCP (the first call, actually; the new PCP takes the call, and then, if more than advice is needed, the new PCP in turn calls the experienced PCP to review procedure). By designating another physician to help out the new PCP, there is less chance of the new PCP feeling reluctant to ask for help.

In a few large group and staff model HMOs and medical groups, the orientation program is highly formal. These HMOs or groups may dedicate numerous days to training, either in a large block or, more often, spread out over a longer period, such as a year. For example, the program may have formal, didactic classes to teach the fundamentals of managed care, how capitation and financing work, how utilization and quality are managed, and so forth. The group may also develop formal training in standards of care and treatment protocols, methods of improving communications with members, risk management, the treatment of common conditions, and other medical topics. The reader is referred to the literature for further discussion of these interesting approaches to formal training of physicians in managed care.[18]

Exhibit 6–1 Suggested Topics for Orientation of Closed Panel Physicians

- Plan mission, values, and strategic plan
- Physician leadership roles
- Expectations
  - —Of the plan for the physician
  - —Of the physician for the plan
- Productivity
- Plan practice manual or principles of practice
- Scheduling and appointments
  - —Appointment system, including control of the schedule
  - —Scheduling of procedures
  - —Schedule of regular hours and on-call hours
- Patient responsibilities and clinical duties
- Utilization management policies and procedures
  - —Authorization policies and procedures
  - —Forms and paperwork
  - —Consultants
  - —Institutions
  - —Case management and clinical pathways
  - —Ancillary services
  - —Affiliated providers
- Nonclinical duties
- Meetings and committees
- Continuing medical education
- Quality management program and peer review
- Administrative forms and paperwork
- Plan subscription agreement and plan schedule of benefits
- Plan member grievance procedures

PRODUCTIVITY

Measuring outpatient productivity in closed panel managed care plans is far more complicated than measuring it in a standard fee-for-service setting. Because the economic incentives in fee for service are so straightforward, productivity is a simple product of how much a physician bills and collects. In managed care, one is trying to practice cost effectively and yet provide high-quality care. Therefore, the measures must be modified.

One common unit of measurement involves looking at the number of patient visits per unit time (e.g., visits per day). Other common measures are visits per hour, per session (usually half a day, but that can be subtly altered), per week, per month, and per year. The larger the time scale, the less the influence of minor factors. For example, if you measure visits per session but fail to define a session rigidly, you will not know whether all the visits are occurring in the space of 2 hours, 3 hours, and so on. The problem with larger time scales is that they are slow to respond to changes and will be less sensitive indicators of current productivity. A reasonable combination is to look at visits per day or per week on average for a month and then have a rolling 12-month average for the year to date.

In the fee-for-service setting in 1993, the mean outpatient productivity by PCPs was 76.1 office visits per week, with the breakdown by specialty going from 62.0 visits per week for internal medicine (including Medicare visits), 99.6 visits per week for pediatrics, 109.5 visits per week for family practice, and 86.9 visits per week for OB/GYN. Hospital rounds add to these numbers as follows: The mean number of hospital visits per week in 1993 was 20.7, with the breakdown by specialty going from 31.5 rounds per week for internal medicine (including Medicare visits), 19.0 rounds per week for pediatrics, 14.4 rounds per week for family practice, and 17.4 visits per week for OB/GYN.[19]

Comparing productivity in closed panel HMOs with that found in private practice is not always easily done. Although it is perfectly reasonable to expect somewhere around the private practice level of productivity from PCPs on your staff, productivity in staff and group model HMOs is estimated to be approximately 83 percent of that found in fee-for-service practice.[20] In addition, recently there has been an increase in the number of female physicians: In 1992, women accounted for 16 percent of practicing physicians; in 1994, more than 40 percent of medical students were women.[21] Although two studies have reported that, in private practice, on average female physicians work approximately 85 percent as many hours as male physicians (primarily because of increased family responsibilities), most experienced medical directors find that lifestyle issues are present with a large number of physicians who are recruited into group or staff model HMOs regardless of gender.[22] In one large study, reasonable and regular work hours and salary were the most important reasons for staff model HMO physicians to join.[23] These issues must be clearly understood and accounted for not only during the recruiting process but also during the management of productivity.

Using productivity as an absolute measure can cause problems. Just as in an uncontrolled fee-for-service setting, if you pressure the PCPs too heavily to get productivity up, the easiest thing for them to do is start churning the patients (e.g., refer sick patients out and schedule 35 blood pressure checks per day). This is obviously counterproductive in a managed health care plan. The point is to have a reasonable expectation of PCP productivity and stick to it but not rely inappropriately on productivity in measuring how well the plan is doing. If studies of appointment availability show reasonable accessibility to care, and if the medical expenses are well controlled (including salary and benefits for the medical staff), you may feel little need to apply pressure to improve productivity.

RETENTION OF QUALITY PHYSICIANS

Physician turnover in group and staff model HMOs, once a chronic problem, is now relatively modest. A review of young HMO physicians reported more than 82 percent are satisfied with their practice.[24] One recent study of 27 group and staff model HMOs reported that the mean turnover rate of physicians who left or were dropped from the staff was 5 percent; and the two most common reasons were departure from practice due to retirement, death, or change in career (61 percent) and departure from the service area (66 percent).[25] These data are supported by data from the Lovelace Clinic study cited earlier, which also reported a turnover rate of 5 percent.[26] Interestingly, in the earlier cited study the percentage of physicians who reported that they would be likely to leave was more than 16 percent, with a higher level of self-reported intention of leaving being found among non-Hispanic minority physicians.[27] No plan or group wants to lose quality physicians. Therefore, the medical leadership and plan management (if they are not one and the same) need to be attentive to some issues that may lead a physician to choose to leave for other than the two reasons cited above.

Issues of physician autonomy tend to rise quickly to the surface in tightly managed closed panels, and perceived lack of autonomy is the leading reason for dissatisfaction in physicians in closed panels.[28–30] Because tight medical management equates with frequent physician management, some physicians grow uncomfortable with practicing in a fishbowl environment. Closely related to this is the heavy use of practice protocols; although such protocols may be necessary for the efficient and effective practice of medicine, they extract a price in perception of autonomy.[31] Physicians generally would prefer a practice where there is no retrospective secondary evaluation of their decisions and where they are the unquestioned authority. Situations such as this are becoming more rare with increasing intervention by third party payers, but the image of the autonomous, hard-working, well-compensated physician is one that is placed in front of physicians as the ideal throughout training and beyond. This issue becomes especially critical in the recruiting and retention of physicians right out of residency training, who have little knowledge of how difficult the real world of private practice can be.

Other reasons that a physician may feel stress or choose to leave include a narrow range of problems seen in practice, the stress of dealing with demanding patients, high demands for productivity with little or no financial incentive, and lack of control over workload.[32] One large study reported that workload and scheduling were actually the leading causes of burnout in staff model HMO physicians, with lack of influence and autonomy issues being second.[33] It is not possible to create practice Nirvana for a physician, but recognition of these issues may help address them, presumably at an affordable cost. In the earlier cited report, it is important to note that the onset of burnout and dissatisfaction occurred in the first 2 to 5 years of employment, arguing for the fact that attention to this issue must take place early in a physician's career with the plan.[34]

Another problem in closed panels is that there is no real entry or exit barrier. Few closed panels require new physicians to ante up $50,000 for a partnership or place physicians in the position of trying to sell their equity stake if they leave. Because of that, group and staff model HMOs are convenient places for physicians to practice for a few years while trying to figure out what they ultimately want to do.

Although one can argue that new physicians cost less than experienced ones (thus reducing overhead), the cost to the plan of high physician turnover is large. When one factors in recruiting costs, such as recruiters' fees, advertising, time spent interviewing candidates, travel costs, and so forth, the costs are considerable. New physicians also do not know the system as well, which reduces efficiency in medical management. Last, problems of member satisfaction and plan reputation are markedly exacerbated by high physician turnover.

Exhibit 6–2 presents some ideas that could be incorporated into a closed panel to promote retention of high-quality physicians; a plan may choose to incorporate some of these ideas but could not possibly use them all. One key caution is not to develop a system that entrenches a few senior physicians with all the longevity benefits and allows new physicians little hope of attaining those benefits, thereby continuing the turnover problem.

Exhibit 6–2 Items To Consider for Physician Retention in Closed Panels

Longevity-related benefits, within limits (must use great care so as not to make physicians with less longevity into second-class citizens, or attrition will occur from below)

- Cafeteria style
- Flex time of some sort
- On-call responsibilities
    1. Amount
    2. When
- Participation in profit sharing
- Vesting schedule for tail malpractice insurance and relocation expenses
- Sabbatical time
- Tuition aid for dependents
- Increasing vacation time
- Stock options
- Preferential opportunity for investment in plan
- Personal financial counseling
- Retirement plan with vesting schedule on plan-matching contributions

On-call responsibilities for all physicians

- Outside backup
- After-hours telephone triage system

Physician input into support staff

Staff development for physicians beyond continuing medical education

- Telephone skills
- Stress management
- Coping skills
- Handling difficult patients
    1. Entitled demanders
    2. Other hateful patients
- Communications skills
- Time management skills

Formal recognition programs

Career path development

Encouragement of academic affiliation

Social events with professionals

Utilization of group or staff physicians for larger task force objectives

Participation in and encouragement of research

Professional newsletter

Development of survey instruments

- Structured exit interviews
- Profile of high-quality physicians who are likely to remain with the group

Training programs for ancillary and support staff

- Telephone skills
- Stress management
- Coping skills
- Handling difficult patients (as above)
- Communications skills
- Time management skills

CONCLUSION

The development and maintenance of a high-quality medical staff in a closed panel health plan take a great deal of thoughtful attention and work, but the reward is high. Ensuring that compensation (both monetary and nonmonetary) is comparable with the community norms, properly orienting new physicians, paying considerable attention to proper incentive programs and performance requirements, and keeping in touch with the short- and long-term needs of the medical staff are necessary management tasks.

Study Questions

1. How many primary care physicians (PCPs) would a staff model HMO require to cover 70,000 members distributed over seven clinic sites? What possible combinations of specialties might accomplish this? How might this change if physician extenders are used? How many and what type of support staff would be required to support those PCPs?

2. What reasons would a new PCP have to join a group model HMO? What reasons might a PCP have to not want to join? How might those reasons change over time? Present these same issues for a PCP already in private practice. How would a staff model HMO use this knowledge in its recruiting needs?
3. Devise a work plan for recruiting new physicians into a staff model HMO under the following assumption: The plan currently has 55,000 members in five sites, plans to open a new site in 2 months, and plans to add 9,000 new members over the next 9 months.
4. Develop a reimbursement system for physicians in a large staff model HMO.

REFERENCES AND NOTES

1. T.H. Dial, et al., Clinical Staffing in Staff- and Group-Model HMOs, *Health Affairs* (Summer 1995): 168–180.
2. Group Health Association of America (GHAA), *HMO Industry Profile, Vol. 2: Physician Staffing and Utilization Patterns* (Washington, D.C.: GHAA, 1992).
3. Dial, et al., Clinical Staffing.
4. Group Health Association of America (GHAA), *HMO Industry Profile* (Washington, D.C.: GHAA, 1994).
5. Dial, et al., Clinical Staffing.
6. Group Health Association of America (GHAA), *HMO Industry Profile* (Washington, D.C.: GHAA, 1992).
7. J.P. Weiner, Forecasting the Effects of Health Reform on U.S. Physician Workforce Requirement, Evidence from HMO Staffing Patterns, *Journal of the American Medical Association* 272 (1994): 222–230.
8. Dial, et al., Clinical Staffing.
9. Dial, et al., Clinical Staffing.
10. J. Packer-Thursman, The Role of Midlevel Practitioners, *HMO Magazine* (March/April 1992): 28–34.
11. E.S. Sekscenski, et al., State Practice Environments and the Supply of Physician Assistants, Nurse Practitioners, and Certified Nurse-Midwives, *New England Journal of Medicine* 331 (1994): 1266–1271.
12. S.E. Palsbo and K.B. Sullivan, *The Recruitment Experience of Health Maintenance Organization for Primary Care: Final Summary Report* (Washington, D.C.: Group Health Association of America, 1993).
13. W.A. Schaffer, et al., Falsification of Clinical Credentials by Physicians Applying for Ambulatory Staff Privileges, *New England Journal of Medicine* 318 (1988): 356–357.
14. F. Mullan, et al., The National Practitioner Data Bank—Report from the First Year, *Journal of the American Medical Association* 268 (1) (1992): 73–79.
15. R.E. Oshel, et al., The National Practitioner Data Bank: The First Four Years, *Public Health Reports* 110 (4) (July/August 1995): 383–394.
16. J. Rodeghero, "Physician Compensation in Groups and Integrated Delivery Systems," in *The Managed Health Care Handbook*, 3d ed., ed. P.R. Kongstvedt (Gaithersburg, Md.: Aspen, 1996), 147–165.
17. J. Rodeghero, "Physician Compensation."
18. T. Defino, Educating Physicians in Managed Care, *Health System Leader* (May 1995): 4–12.
19. American Medical Association (AMA), *Socioeconomic Characteristics of Medical Practice 1994* (Chicago, Ill.: AMA, 1994).
20. Weiner, Forecasting the Effects of Health Reform.
21. R.A. Cooper, Seeking a Balanced Physician Workforce for the 21st Century, *Journal of the American Medical Association* 272 (1994): 680–687.
22. Cooper, Seeking a Balanced Physician Workforce.
23. D. Murray, Doctors Rate the Big HMOs, *Medical Economics* (January 1995): 114–120.
24. L.C. Baker, et al., What Makes Young HMO Physicians Satisfied?, *HMO Practice* 8 (1994): 53–57.
25. M. Gold, *Arrangements between Managed Care Plans and Physicians, Results from a 1994 Survey of Managed Care Plans, Mathematica Policy Research and the Medical College of Virginia* (report submitted to the Physician Payment Review Committee, 7 February 1995).
26. N.B. Fisher, et al., Critical Factors in Recruiting Health Maintenance Organization Physicians, *Health Care Management Review* 18 (1993): 51–61.
27. Baker, et al., What Makes Young HMO Physicians Satisfied.
28. Fisher, et al., Critical Factors.
29. R.A. Schmoldt, et al., Physician Burnout: Recommendations for HMO Managers, *HMO Practice* 8 (1994): 58–63.
30. Baker, et al., What Makes Young HMO Physicians Satisfied?
31. Baker, et al., What Makes Young HMO Physicians Satisfied?

32. E. Freidson, Prepaid Group Practice and the New "Demanding Patient," *Milbank Memorial Fund Quarterly* 51 (1973): 473–488.
33. G. Deckard, et al., Physician Burnout: An Examination of Personal, Professional, and Organizational Relationships, *Medical Care* 37 (1994): 745–754.
34. Deckard, et al., Physician Burnout.

SUGGESTED READING

American Medical Association (AMA). 1995. *Socioeconomic Characteristics of Medical Practice 1994/1995.* Chicago, Ill.: AMA.

Felt, S., Frazer, H., and Gold, M. 1994. *HMO Primary Care Staffing Patterns and Processes: A Cross-Site Analysis of 23 HMOs.* Washington, D.C.: Mathematica Policy Research, Inc.

Fisher, N.B., Smith, H.L., and Pasternok, D.P. 1993. Critical Success Factors in Recruiting Health Maintenance Organization Physicians. *Health Care Management Review* 18 (1): 51–61.

Hammon, J.L. 1993. *Fundamentals of Medical Management.* Tampa, Fla.: American College of Physician Executives.

Konrad, T.R., et al. 1989. *The Salaried Physician: Medical Practice in Transition.* Chapel Hill, N.C.: University of North Carolina at Chapel Hill.

Nash, D.B. (ed.). 1994. *The Physician's Guide to Managed Care.* Gaithersburg, Md.: Aspen Publishers.

Palsbo, S.E., and Sullivan, C.B. 1993. *The Recruitment Experience of Health Maintenance Organizations for Primary Care Physicians: Final Report.* Washington, D.C.: Health Resources and Services Administration.

Shouldice, R.G. 1991. *Introduction to Managed Care.* Arlington, Va.: Information Resources Press.

Chapter 7

Primary Care in Open Panel Plans

Peter R. Kongstvedt

Study Objectives

- Understand what is meant by primary care in open panel plans
- Understand the role of the primary care physician (PCP) in the plan
- Understand recruiting issues
- Understand basic credentialing
- Understand different methods of contracting with PCPs
- Understand how physicians may view the health plan
- Understand issues of network maintenance
- Understand issues of sanctioning and removal of physicians from the network

DEFINITIONS

One must begin with definitions of what will be considered primary care. In virtually all systems, care rendered by physicians in the specialties of family practice, internal medicine, and pediatrics is considered primary care. Many obstetrics/gynecology (OB/GYN) specialists feel that they, too, deliver primary care to their patients. They argue that they are often the only physician a young woman sees for many years. This is true in the case of generally healthy young women, but it is not always so when medical problems not involving the female reproductive tract occur. In at least one program designed to retrain OB/GYN physicians to provide a broader range of primary care, the results were quite disappointing, with a high dropout rate and a high level of dissatisfaction with broad primary care being seen among the OB/GYNs.[1] It is worth noting that in at least two western states, OB/GYNs are allowed, by law, to be considered primary care physicians for purposes of managed care.

Still, a number of plans that capitate primary care or otherwise use primary care physicians (PCPs) as case managers (i.e., use a gatekeeper system) also include OB/GYN as primary care for OB/GYN services and split the care (and often the capitation) between the OB/GYN and an internist or family practitioner. Plans that use this method must define what services are to be delivered by each. For example, the OB/GYN may be seen without referral for Pap smears and pelvic examinations, for pregnancy, and for sterilization procedures; in fact, more than 71 percent of surveyed health maintenance organizations (HMOs) in one study allowed self-referral to OB/GYN.[2] For any other problems, the member must see the PCP for either treatment by or referral to another specialist and perhaps even for referral back to the OB/GYN whom she has chosen for services beyond those defined as being allowed under the self-referral option.

In general, it is probably easier to define OB/GYN as a specialty service and treat it as any other specialty. For marketing reasons as well as medical acceptability in the community, however, most plans make special arrangements for direct access to OB/GYNs for routine gynecologic and obstetric services while still requiring coordination with the PCP for all other care.

NETWORK DEVELOPMENT

Young or newly forming plans will concentrate primarily on network development. Mature plans will concentrate more on network maintenance (discussed later in this chapter), although recruiting to fill in areas with suboptimal access will always be an ongoing process, particularly during periods of high growth or expansion into a new service area. The initial section of this chapter discusses recruiting in an environment in which physicians contract directly with the plan; similar issues would apply in the case of an integrated delivery system (IDS) or management services organization (MSO) that needs to recruit physicians (see Chapter 4 for a discussion of IDSs).

The ease of developing a network is influenced by many factors. Markets that are heavily saturated with managed care plans may have difficulty recruiting PCPs (or consultants) if those providers see no need to sign up with yet another plan. Conversely, competition may be so fierce, or there may be so many (underutilized) providers, that recruiting will be easier. In any event, recruiting PCPs for open panels is best done by means of an orderly approach. Without proper planning, the timeline will be substantially drawn out, and the physician panel may not complement hospital choices or market needs.

Setting Priorities

If you are beginning from scratch, you are likely to start with a few easy recruits (often friends of the medical director or physicians with whom contact has already been made). That will rarely be sufficient by itself, so that there is a need to recruit systematically to achieve an acceptable panel size and configuration.

Consider geographic needs first. This generally breaks down into two main considerations: the need to target potential new members, and the need to use certain hospitals (discussed in Chapter 11). In the first case, you should already have identified your primary target markets (e.g., a large and growing suburban–industrial community). In the second case, you may have selected a high-quality hospital and need to recruit physicians from that medical staff in preference to physicians who practice only at a noncontracting hospital, even if it is in the targeted area.

Priorities will also be affected by the availability, acceptability (to you, to your potential members, and to the rest of the medical panel), scope of practice, and practice capacities of physicians in target areas. If you have more than one geographic high priority for recruiting but there is a major difference in the ease with which you will be able to recruit qualified and acceptable physicians, you will want to give early attention to the area from which it will be the easiest to recruit. This is for two reasons. First, the success of your physician recruiters will be enhanced with the amount of successful experience they have, and second, there is often a chain reaction when your panel reaches critical mass. In other words, when there are enough physicians already on your panel, it becomes more acceptable or even competitively necessary for physicians to join.

Access Needs

In addition to the broad geographic needs and hospital-related needs, it is important to assess accessibility in general. There are a number of ways to do this. One method is to look at the number of physicians per 1,000 members. One large survey, now dated, reported the mean total physicians per 1,000 members in mature open panel plans to be 36.92, and the mean total PCPs per 1,000 members was reported as 14.43.[3] This last ratio equates to 71 members per physician, which may represent an average enrollment but does not at all predict capacity.

It is more useful to look at the number of members whom each physician must accept (on the basis of contractual terms, see Chapter 29), such as 200 members per PCP. The ratios of physicians to members in open panels can vary tremendously depending on the age of the plan, geographic access needs, the product lines being sold (e.g., a Medicare risk product may require a higher number of physicians than a commercial product), maturity of the marketplace in general, the number of open practices, and marketing needs.

Another useful measure is geographic accessibility. This is generally calculated through one of two methods: drive time, and number of PCPs by geographic availability. Drive time refers to how long members in the plan's service area have to drive to reach a PCP (or a PCP with an open practice, that is, one still accepting new patients). In general, drive time should be no more than 15 minutes, although 30 minutes may be appropriate for certain rural areas. A drive time of 20 minutes may be acceptable for access from a purely medical viewpoint, but it may not be as acceptable in a heavily urbanized market.

Analyzing the number of PCPs by geographic availability is also useful. Generally, you want to be able to provide at least two PCPs within 2 or 3 miles of each ZIP code from which your plan will be drawing members (the density is usually greater in urban areas and less in rural areas). Another measure of geographic availability is the radius from where the members live (e.g., two PCPs within an 8-mile radius for urban areas and two PCPs within a 20-mile radius for rural areas). Again, these ratios may represent a minimum configuration and will not necessarily be acceptable in your marketplace.

Identification of Candidates

Selection of candidates to recruit is based on a number of sources. First is the personal acquaintances of the medical director. These are often the easiest physicians to recruit, but they are relatively few in number.

Second, the list of physicians with privileges at the hospitals with which you are contracting should be used. The hospital administrator will frequently be able to guide you toward those physicians you should approach early and those you should avoid. The hospital executive staff is often helpful in enhancing the environment for recruiting because in many situations the physicians will value highly the judgment of the hospital administration. An important caveat is in order here: Sometimes the reason a physician is considered desirable from the hospital's point of view is the fact that the physician admits a lot of patients, and a heavy user of hospital services is not always the most desirable from the point of view of a managed care plan. It is therefore crucial that the plan retain independent judgment about whom to recruit and why.

A third source for identification of candidates is the physician list of your competitors. In general, unless your competition has signed the physicians to an exclusive agreement, you will have an easier time signing up these physicians because they have already made the commitment to join a managed health care plan panel.

Fourth, the local county or state medical society may be a good source for obtaining mailing labels. You can rent the list for a single label run, or the society may actually provide the labels for a reasonable fee. If possible, you want this broken down by primary care and by ZIP code.

Last, if all else fails (or simply as a backup), there are the Yellow Pages. Although the phone book provides the most complete list, it is absolutely unselective and must be used only with extreme caution.

One special method of identifying candidates is available only to large insurance carriers, and that is claims data. A large carrier may already have sufficient data on hand from indemnity business to be able to make an initial evaluation of which physicians practice cost effectively and which physicians have been pillaging the system for years. Claims data may also provide a crude method of assessing quality, for example by identifying physicians with abnormally high rates of certain procedures (e.g., hysterectomies) or those who frequently use outmoded treatments (e.g., routine tonsillectomies). Although interpretation of indemnity claims history is not as easy as it first appears, clear outliers are not difficult to identify if there are sufficient data to draw statistically valid conclusions. In other words, a large database is of no value if there are insufficient transactions at the level of individual providers in an area. The subject of provider profiling is addressed in greater detail in Chapter 19.

Timing

You need to develop a realistic time frame within which to work. You also need to give the physician recruiters a reference to use in recruiting so as not to let one step of the recruiting process overshadow the others. Each aspect of physician recruiting should have set goals for both number and duration. Begin the time frame with first contact and continue through successful completion, which occurs when both the physician and your plan sign the contract. In a new start-up, you may want to begin the time frame with the start of the enterprise and include physician identification as the first step.

Each plan and community will have its own special characteristics, but in general the time between the first letter to the physician and the first telephone contact should be no more than 7 to 10 days. If it is longer than that, the physician will have forgotten you.

The time between the first telephone contact and the first visit should likewise be no more than 7 to 10 days, although a busy physician's schedule may necessitate a slightly longer lead time. Try to avoid scheduling the first visit during normal office hours because the physician, who is under pressure to see patients, will be unable to give enough time and thought to the discussion. A lunch meeting (you bring the deli tray) or a meeting on an afternoon off or just after office hours is best. This first visit should last about 1 hour and involve explaining the concept and the contract, determining the level of interest, and obtaining initial information about the physician and the practice. This is also the time for the recruiter to obtain an initial impression of the ambiance of the physician's office for marketing purposes.

If possible, you wish to obtain closure (actually, contingent closure) on the second visit. Generally, allow 1 or 2 weeks between the first and second visits, and make the appointment for the second visit during the first one. In some cases, physicians will want to have their attorney look at the contract, and you will need to allow sufficient time for that. In any event, have a definite time for follow-up and potential closure.

In general, it is best to keep the pressure on. If you allow too much time to elapse between contacts or steps, your ease in getting a signed contract will be diminished. It is preferable to keep the entire time from first letter to signed contract or signed letter of intent to 2 months or less.

As discussed below under credentialing, the contract or letter of intent is contingent on the credentialing process. If a physician does not meet the standards of your plan, you reserve the right not to add that physician to your panel.

Role of the Recruiter

The key personnel in this process are the physician recruiters. In some plans, recruiters are drawn from the marketing department; in others, they are part of the provider relations department. The use of marketing representatives for physician recruiting may be necessary during the first few months of a new start-up plan, but the function is really best carried out by people who have more understanding and empathy with physicians and who will be responsible for maintaining the relationship after a physician has joined the panel. The recruiters are supervised by a director or manager of provider relations.

The recruiters make the telephone calls and do the leg work. They must be able to explain to the physician and the physician's support staff any necessary details to facilitate an informed decision. This includes all the aspects of physician compensation, best and worst case scenarios, the scope of covered services, covered benefits to members, benefits to the physician for joining, operational policies such as authorization systems and preadmission requirements, and any other pertinent information. A detailed understanding of the reimbursement system is, of course, critical (compensation models are discussed in Chapter 8).

The number of recruiters will depend on the number of physicians you hope to add to the panel and the geographic area you want to cover. In the early phases of a start-up, when there is an intense need for physician recruiting, you may need three to five individuals. Later, during a controlled growth phase, recruiting is handled by the regular provider relations staff.

Role of the Medical Director

In addition to making the personal contacts in the recruiting process, the medical director has at least two other primary responsibilities in recruiting (besides credentialing, as discussed below).

First, the medical director adds prestige and legitimacy to the endeavor. The medical director endorses the plan, both explicitly and implicitly, by being the medical director. If the medical director has been in the area for some time, this local endorsement may be the deciding factor in new plans looking to recruit physicians.

It is important for the medical director to understand the plan and its policies. This seems obvious, but there have been cases where medical directors have been recruited solely to add prestige and have been unaware of how the plan actually operated. This poses two serious problems. The medical director may promise things that are not possible, and he or she may quit in an embarrassing huff after finding out how things really work. Fortunately, over the past few years, the level of management expertise found in medical directors of open panels has increased significantly, and the medical director is much more likely to be able to manage the process than have to be managed.

The second primary recruiting responsibility of the medical director is closing certain difficult cases. There will be times when the physician recruiter has done all the preparatory work but a sought-after physician will be hesitant about signing. In these cases, the medical director's personal contact may be the deciding factor.

TYPES OF CONTRACTING SITUATIONS

There are a number of possible types of contracting situations with which an open panel may have to deal in developing a network. The subject of the contract itself is addressed in Chapter 29, and reimbursement is discussed in Chapter 8. This discussion focuses on the types of situations that may present themselves regardless of specific contracting and reimbursement issues.

Individual Physicians

This is the most common category of contracting in open panels, which is not surprising given the large number of solo practitioners in many parts of the country. In this model, the physician contracts directly with the health plan and not through any third party or intermediary. The advantage to the plan is that there is a direct relationship with the physician, which makes it cleaner and simpler to interact. The disadvantage is that it is only one physician, and therefore the effort to obtain and maintain that relationship is disproportionately great.

Small Groups

Not substantially different from individual physicians, small groups usually operate relatively cohesively. The advantage to the plan is that the same amount of effort to obtain and maintain a small group yields a higher number of physicians. Plans generally prefer to contract with small groups for that reason. The disadvantage is that, if the relationship with the group needs to be terminated (for whatever reason, theirs or yours), there is greater disruption in patient care.

Multispecialty Groups

Multispecialty groups represent a special category. Relatively uncommon in certain parts of the country, they are occasionally the dominant practices in certain areas. The advantage of contracting with multispecialty groups is that you obtain not only PCPs but specialty consultants as well. This provides for broader access (including specialists to whom other PCPs may refer) and allows for existing referral patterns to continue.

One disadvantage is that multispecialty groups sometimes are dominated by the specialty or referral physicians in the group, which may lead to inappropriate utilization of referral services. Another potential disadvantage is the case where, by accepting the group, you are forced to accept a specialist whose cost or quality is not what you desire (although not so bad as to prevent contracting with the group). Again, as a general rule, if relations with large groups founder, there is a greater likelihood that there will be disruptions in patient care.

Individual Practice Associations

The individual practice association (IPA) is the original form of open panel plan. In the early 1970s, it was envisioned that open panel plans would all be IPA model plans. In this situation, there is actually a legal entity of an IPA, which contracts with physicians and in turn with the health plan. The advantage to the plan is that a large number of providers come along with the contract. Furthermore, if relations between the IPA and the health plan are close, there may be a confluence of goals, which benefits all parties.

There are two primary disadvantages to contracting with IPAs. The first is that an IPA can function somewhat as a union. If relations between the IPA and the health plan are arm's length or problematic, the IPA can hold a considerable portion (or perhaps all) of the delivery system hostage to negotiations. This fact has not been lost on the Justice Department of the federal government. IPAs that function as anticompetitive forces may encounter difficulties with the law.

The second disadvantage is that the plan's ability to select and deselect individual physicians is much more limited when contracting through an IPA than when contracting directly with the providers. If the IPA is at risk for medical expenses, there may be a confluence of objectives between the plan and the IPA to bring in cost-effective and high-quality providers and to remove those providers whose cost or quality is not acceptable. Unfortunately, the IPA has its own internal political structure, so that defining who is cost effective or high quality, as well as dealing with outliers, may not match exactly between the plan and the IPA. If the plan has the contractual right to refuse to accept or to departicipate individual providers in the IPA, that obstacle may be avoided, although the purely political obstacles remain.

IDSs

Many hospitals have been exploring methods of developing organizations that will legally and structurally bind the physicians to the hospital. Sometimes these are referred to as physician–hospital organizations (PHOs) or MSOs. In addition to hospital-based IDSs, there are physician practice management companies (PPMs) and physician-only MSOs. These and other forms of IDSs are discussed in further detail in Chapter 4. The positive and negative ramifications that apply to IPAs are similar to those for IDSs (including their antitrust risk) and have been discussed above. In addition to those issues, there are two other broad issues that relate specifically to hospital-based organizations.

First is the link between a hospital's own willingness to do business with a plan and the plan's willingness to do business with the PHO or MSO. In other words, the hospital may refuse to contract with the plan or may not provide favorable terms unless the plan brings in the PHO, perhaps even on an exclusive basis. That obviously removes control of that entire portion of the delivery system (physicians and hospital), leaving the plan at the mercy (or abilities) of the PHO or MSO to achieve the goals of the plan. If the PHO or MSO is at significant risk for medical expenses, there may be confluence of goals.

The second issue relates to the reasons that the PHO formed in the first place. If the hospital has the goals of keeping beds filled and keeping the medical staff happy (and busy), the selection process for choosing which providers are in the PHO may be weighted toward those physicians who admit a lot of patients to the hospital, a criterion that may not be ideal from the plan's perspective. Another reason that the PHO may have formed was to circle the wagons, that is, to resist aggressive managed care. In that event, there may be a real mismatch between how the plan wants to perform medical management and how the PHO will allow it to occur. Issues of control of utilization management, quality management, and provider selection become difficult to resolve.

Nonetheless, IDSs can function effectively. If the organization is formed with a genuine understanding of the goals of managed care, a genuine willingness to deal with difficult issues of utilization, quality, and provider selection, and a willingness to share control with the health plan, it is possible to work together.

PPMs are similar to IPAs in some regards, except that the bond between the physician and the PPM is generally quite tighter than that found in a typical IPA. PPMs often desire to contract with a plan with the specific intent of not including the hospital in any risk sharing. This is done to allow the PPM to buy hospital services on the medical spot market through per diem reimbursement (see Chapter 11) and keep the savings (and profit) from lower utilization.

The primary advantage to a health plan in contracting with an IDS is the ability to have a network in rapid order. This may be a primary driver in the case of a plan entering into a new market or one that is already competitive, and it may in fact be the only way an HMO can get a network. This last issue will be especially true if a large number of physicians have sold their practices to hospitals or PPMs. A plan that needs to expand its medical service area quickly or is expanding into entirely new geographic areas may find that contracting through IDSs allows it to achieve its expansion goals and be first to market.

An additional advantage may occur if the IDS is willing to provide a substantial savings to the plan, better than what would be available on a direct contract basis. If the plan is entering into a new product line (e.g., Medicare risk or Medicaid), the plan may desire to share the risk for medical costs through aggressive capitation with the IDS.

The last broad condition that may make contracting with an IDS the most desirable option is when an insurer with little or no managed care experience desires to enter into the managed care arena (such a strategy may be the only alternative to death by attrition for some insurers in markets with heavy or growing managed care penetration). In this case, the non–managed care health insurer plans to capitalize on the IDS's (hoped for) ability to manage utilization and quality.

It should be noted that, in certain states, HMOs are not allowed to contract solely with the IDS but must have contracts directly with the physicians. The contract may be brief and encompass no more than standard hold harmless language (see Chapter 29) and then reference the contract between the IDS and the physician and the contract between the IDS and the plan. This requirement is meant to ensure that each and every individual physician understands and agrees to certain provisions required under state law, such as the prohibition on balance billing. See Chapter 30 for more discussion of legal issues in IDSs.

Faculty Practice Plans

Faculty practice plans (FPPs) are medical groups that are organized around teaching programs, primarily at university hospitals. An FPP may be a single entity or may encompass multiple entities defined along specialty lines (e.g., cardiology or anesthesiology). Plans generally contract with the legal group representing the FPP rather than with individual physicians within the FPP, although that varies from plan to plan.

FPPs represent special challenges for various reasons. First, many teaching institutions and FPPs tend to be less cost effective in their practice styles than private physicians. This probably relates to the primary missions of the teaching program: to teach and to perform research. Cost effectiveness is a secondary goal only (if a goal at all).

A second challenge is that an FPP, like a medical group, comes all together or not at all. This again means that the plan has little ability to select or deselect the individual physicians within the FPP. Related to that is the lack of detail regarding claims and encounter data. Many FPPs simply bill the plan, accept capitation, or collect encounter data in the name of the FPP rather than in the name of the individual provider who performed the service. This means that the plan has little ability to analyze data to the same level of detail that is afforded in the rest of the network.

A third major challenge is the use of house officers (interns and residents in training) and medical students to deliver care. In teaching hospitals, the day-to-day care is actually delivered by house officers rather than by the attending faculty physician, who functions as a teacher and supervisor. House officers and medical students, because they are learning how to practice medicine, tend to be profligate in their use of medical resources; they are there to learn medicine, not simply to perform direct service to patients. Furthermore, experience does allow physicians to learn what is cost effective, and house officers and medical students have yet to gain such experience. Nevertheless, there is some evidence that intensive attention to utilization management by faculty can have a highly beneficial effect on house staff.[4]

The last major issue with teaching programs and FPPs is the nature of how they deliver services. Most teaching programs are not really set up for case management. It is far more common to have multiple specialty clinics (e.g., pulmonology, cardiology, or vascular surgery) to which patients are referred for each specific problem. Such a system takes on characteristics of a medical pinball machine, where the members ricochet from clinic to clinic, having each organ system attended to with little regard for the totality of care. This leads to enormous runups in cost as well as continuity problems and a clear lack of control or accountability.

Despite these difficulties, there are good reasons for health plans to contract with teaching programs and FPPs other than the societal good derived from the training of medical practitioners. Teaching programs and FPPs provide not only routine care but tertiary and highly specialized care as well, care that the plan will have to find means to provide in any event. Teaching programs also add prestige to the plan by virtue of their reputation for providing high-quality care, although that can be a two-edged sword in that the participation of a teaching program may draw adverse selection in membership.*

Most teaching programs and FPPs recognize the problems cited above and are willing to work with plans to ameliorate them. For example, they may be willing to extend a deep discount to a managed care plan in the recognition that the plan's ability to control utilization is limited and therefore must be made up on price. Teaching programs may occasionally be willing to accept

* In other words, if there is more than one health plan competing in a single group account (e.g., an employer group) for membership, members with serious illnesses may choose the health plan affiliated with a teaching program to ensure access to high-quality tertiary care. That means that sicker members join that health plan and less sick members join the health plan that does not have such an affiliation. This issue does not come up if the plan is the sole carrier in an account or if all the competing plans use the teaching program, but it is a clear problem if there are multiple plans competing freely for members in a single account.

a high level of risk for medical expenses, but that can be a problem for them because of the risk of adverse selection mentioned above. Risk for defined services (e.g., laboratory or radiology) may be more acceptable.

See Chapter 12 for a detailed discussion of academic medical centers and managed care.

CREDENTIALING

It is not enough to get physicians to sign contracts. Without performing proper credentialing, you will have no knowledge of the quality or acceptability of physicians, nor will you have any idea whether they will actually be an asset to your plan. Furthermore, in the event of a legal action against a physician, the plan may expose itself to some liability by having failed to carry out proper credentialing. In one well-known study, up to 5 percent of physicians applying for positions in ambulatory care clinics misrepresented their credentials in their applications; how that might translate for an HMO or other managed care organization (MCO) where physicians are likely to be more stable in their community is unknown.[5] In most plans, the medical director bears ultimate responsibility for credentialing along with a credentialing committee, although the activities of credentialing are usually carried out by the provider relations department.

The credentialing process is a critical one and should be carried out during the recruiting process and, if necessary, after the contract or letter of intent is signed. Periodic recredentialing (usually every 2 years) should also take place. Recredentialing may be less extensive than primary credentialing, but more sophisticated plans are adding new elements to the recredentialing process, including looking at measures of quality of care, member satisfaction, compliance with plan policies and procedures, and utilization management.

As this book is being written, a new organization has come into existence: the third-party credentialing verification organization (CVO). The CVO performs primary credentialing on a physician, and then the HMO or PPO relies on the CVO for that credentialing verification. The purpose of this is to reduce the need for an individual physician to be required to provide identical credentialing data to numerous MCOs; in addition, the MCO can obtain the data in a more timely fashion, and the data will be complete on the first pass. The chief problem with this approach is the requirement by many regulators and outside accreditation agencies that the HMO conduct primary source verification (i.e., obtain the information directly rather than relying on another party to obtain it). The National Committee for Quality Assurance (NCQA) has created a CVO certification program to allow third party CVOs to meet NCQA standards in credentialing to perform credentialing for MCOs.[6]

If the credentialing process is incomplete at the time the physician is ready to sign, then a provision must be included in the signed document (either the contract or the letter of intent) indicating that the final contract is contingent upon the plan's completing the credentialing process. If the predetermined standards are not met, then the plan will be unable to accept that physician in its panel. A word of warning: It is more difficult than one might imagine to tell physicians that the plan is not going to accept them after they have signed a contract.

The elements illustrated in Exhibit 7–1 are some examples of data that should be captured in the credentialing process.

Verification of Credentialing Data

Primary verification of the elements in Exhibit 7–1 should also be performed as appropriate. Verification of data may be obtained from a number of sources, including the National Practitioner Data Bank (NPDB; see below) and those noted in Exhibit 7–2.

NPDB

A special type of credentialing requirement and reference check was created by the Health

Exhibit 7–1 Elements of Credentialing

Basic elements

- Training (copy of certificates)
  1. Location
  2. Type
- Specialty board eligibility or certification (copy of certificate)
- Current state medical license (copy of certificate)
  1. Restrictions
  2. History of loss of license in any state
- Drug Enforcement Agency (DEA) number (copy of certificate)
- Hospital privileges
  1. Name of hospitals
  2. Scope of practice privileges
- Malpractice insurance
  1. Carrier name
  2. Currency of coverage (copy of face sheet)
  3. Scope of coverage (financial limits and procedures covered)
- Malpractice history
  1. Pending claims
  2. Successful claims against the physician, either judged or settled
- National Practitioner Data Bank status
- Medicare, Medicaid, and federal tax identification numbers
- Social Security number
- Location and telephone numbers of all offices
- Yes/no questions regarding:
  1. Limitations or suspensions of privileges
  2. Suspension from government programs
  3. Suspension or restriction of DEA license
  4. Malpractice cancellation
  5. Felony conviction
  6. Drug or alcohol abuse
  7. Chronic or debilitating illnesses

Additional elements

- Hours of operation
- Provisions for emergency care and backup
- Use of nonphysician (i.e., midlevel) practitioners
- In-office surgery capabilities
- In-office testing capabilities
- Languages spoken
- Work history, past 5 years
- Areas of special medical interest
- Record of continuing medical education

Care Quality Improvement Act of 1986. This act, an important law for managed care plans, is discussed in Chapter 6 and in detail in Chapter 57 of *The Managed Health Care Handbook*.[7] The reader is urged to refer to those chapters and to become familiar with the credentialing aspects of this act. An early report from the NPDB stated that the annual rate of licensure actions was 2.7 per 1,000 physicians (0.0 to 9.7 per 1,000), that the annual rate of clinical privileges actions was 1.4 per 1,000 physicians (0.0 to 3.6 per 1,000), and that there were an average of 21.1 medical malpractice payments per 1,000 physicians.[8] By the end of 1994, the NPDB reported the following statistics: The data bank contained more than 97,500 reports, of which 82 percent were related to malpractice payments, with licensure reports making up most of the rest; it had processed more than 4.5 million requests for information; and 8 percent of queries were matched with a report.[9]

Office Evaluation

If the plan is contracting directly with physicians, it will probably desire to perform a direct evaluation of the physician's office. If the plan has contracted through an IDS, it is more likely to forgo such a review if the IDS has already performed the review to the satisfaction of the plan. In some cases, the plan may choose not to perform an office review because of the associated cost or the need to get the network up quickly or for fear of offending physicians; these are inadequate reasons.

There are two main items to evaluate in a physician's office: capacity to accept new members, and office ambiance. In addition, the plan or IDS may review the office from the standpoint of a quality management process, compliance with Occupational Safety and Health Administration guidelines, presence of certain types of equipment (e.g., a defibrillator), and so forth. If capacity and ambiance are the only review areas, the evaluation is best accomplished by having the recruiter visit the office and may be performed in one fairly short visit. A more

Exhibit 7–2 Credentialing Data Verification Sources

Note: **Standards 5.0 through 8.0 apply to the initial credentialing process. Surveyors will consider both delegated and nondelegated activity. Surveyors should indicate any findings that are different for delegated entities. Surveyors will also consider whether credentialing activities are ongoing and up-to-date as well as the percent of eligible practitioners that have been credentialed. When reviewing files, DCs, DDSs, or DPMs surveyors should use NCQA's monitoring standards.**

CR 5.0 The initial credentialing process is ongoing and up-to-date. At a minimum, the MCO obtains and reviews verification of the following from primary sources:

The MCO should review and verify all the items listed in CR 5.1 through CR 5.7, from primary and/or NCQA-approved sources as specified below. Verification can be either written or oral. Oral verification requires a dated, signed note in the credentialing file stating who verified the practitioner's status and how it was verified. Written verification may take the form of documented review of cumulative reports released by the primary sources of credentialing data. For example, some state medical boards release bulletins that list all practitioners holding a valid, current license to practice in that state. The MCO should use the latest cumulative report released by the primary source and the date on which the report was queried should be noted in file. If the MCO uses an automated system to track credentialing queries, collection, and reporting, there should be a mechanism to identify the individual verifying the information and the date of verification, the source, and report date, if applicable.

For Standards CR 5.1 through 5.7, the MCO should collect and verify all credentials prior to review and assessment by the Credentialing Committee. Information should be no more than 180 days old at the time of Committee review, unless otherwise noted in the Standard.

CR 5.1 A current valid license to practice;

The MCO should confirm that the practitioner holds a valid, current license

CR 5.2 Clinical privileges in good standing at the hospital designated by the practitioner as the primary admitting facility; applicable;

The MCO obtains oral or written confirmation from the practitioner's primary admitting facility that the practitioner has clinical privileges in good standing. The confirmation should include the date of the appointment, and restrictions on the scope of privileges. If the practitioner does not have hospital clinical privileges, the MCO should have a written statement delineating the inpatient coverage arrangement if appropriate and should credential and recredential the practitioner(s) providing such coverage.

CR 5.3 A Valid DEA or CDS certificate, as applicable;

The MCO can verify the Drug Enforcement Agency (DEA) certificate or Controlled Dangerous Substances (CDS) certificate through one of the following means:

- copy of the DEA or CDS certificate;
- visual inspection of the original certificate;
- confirmation with CDS
- entry in the National Technical Information Service (NTIS) database;
- confirmation with the state pharmaceutical licensing agency, where applicable.

CR 5.4 Graduation from medical school and completion of a residency, or board certification, as applicable;

Verification of board certification fully meets this requirement. However, NCQA does not mandate board certification. For individuals who are not board certified, verification of completion of residency fully meets this requirement. For those individuals who have not completed a residency program, verification of graduation from medical school meets this

Exhibit 7–2 continued

requirement. Any one element of the following list is an acceptable method of verification for the levels shown.

Board certification
- entry in the ABMS Compendium;
- entry in the AOA Directory of Osteopathic Physicians;
- confirmation from the appropriate specialty board;
- entry in the AMA Physician Master File;
- confirmation from the state licensing agency, if the agency conducts primary verification of board status.

Completion of residency training:
- confirmation from the residency training program;
- entry in the AMA Physician Master File;
- confirmation from the state licensing agency, if the agency conducts primary verification of residency training, according to the NCQA definition (recent proof of this should be available).

Gradution from medical school:
- confirmation from the medical school;
- entry in the AMA Physician Master file;
- confirmation from the Education Commission for Foreign Medical Graduates, for international medical graduates licensed after 1986;
- confirmation from the state licensing agency, if the agency conducts primary verification of medical school graduation. The MCO should be able to demonstrate recent validation from the state licensing agency.

CR 5.5 Work history;
At a minimum, five years of work history should be included on the application or the curriculum vitae. The MCO is not required to verify work history from primary sources.

CR 5.6 Current, adequate malpractice insurance according to the managed care organization's policy; and
The MCO should obtain a copy of the current malpractice coverage that shows dates and amount of coverage. The copy may be obtained from the malpractice insurance carrier or the practitioner.

CR 5.7 History of the professional liability claims which result in settlements or judgments paid by or on behalf of the practitioner.
The MCO should obtain written confirmation of the last five years of history of malpractice settlements from the malpractice carrier or query the National Practitioner Data Bank (NPDB). These years may include reidency years.

Source: National Committee for Quality Assurance, 1996 NCQA Reviewer Guidelines for the Standards for Accreditation.

detailed review will require a trained health professional, usually a nurse, and may take an hour or two.

In addition to asking physicians directly how many new members they will accept (and usually including that in the contract), the recruiter should ask to examine the appointment book. In this way, the recruiter can get a reasonably good idea of how much appointment availability the physician has. For example, if there are no available appointment slots for a physical examination for 6 weeks or more, the physician may be overestimating his or her ability to accept more work.

The recruiter can also get an idea of how easy it is for a patient with an acute problem to be put on the schedule. This may be examined by looking at the number of acute slots left open each day and by looking at the number of double-booked appointments that were put in at the end of each day.

In addition, the recruiter can assess less tangible items, such as cleanliness of the office, friendliness of the staff toward patients, and general atmosphere. Hours of operation can be verified, as can provisions for emergency care and in-office equipment capabilities.

MEDICAL RECORD REVIEW

Many plans require a review of sample medical records by the medical director. The purpose of this is to assure the medical director that physicians do indeed practice high-quality medicine and that their practice is already cost effective. Some physicians object to submitting to this review, but if it is required for participation, and if the physician is assured that it is strictly confidential and not a witch hunt, there should be fewer problems. Because the physician presumably has no plan members whose charts can be reviewed, care will need to be taken to protect the identity of the patients because the plan has no legal right to access confidential medical records.

If the plan already has a quality assurance program that involves chart review, a physician should agree to the initial review as a matter of course. Sometimes it is not objections by the physicians that form the impediment to this review but rather the embarrassment of the medical director in having to perform it.

COMPENSATION

Compensation of PCPs in open panels is discussed in detail in Chapter 8.

ORIENTATION

In all enterprises, time invested in the beginning to ensure real understanding is time well spent. Therefore, a planned approach to orientation of a newly added PCP will pay off in improved compliance with your plan's procedures and policies, in increased professional satisfaction on the part of the PCP, and in increased member satisfaction. Orientation is aimed at two audiences: the PCP and the PCP's office staff. Exhibit 7–3 lists some topics to consider in orienting physicians, and Exhibit 7–4 lists some topics for orienting their office staff.

NETWORK MANAGEMENT

Maintenance of the professional relationship with physicians in the network recently has assumed a far greater role in managed care than at any previous time in the industry's history. The saturation of managed care plans in some communities, coupled with increasing interventions by third party payers (commercial, Medicare, and Medicaid) limiting providers' ability to cost shift to other fee-for-service payers, has placed increasing strain on physicians and has clearly colored how they view participation with managed care plans. Failure to service the network properly can lead to defections or closure of practices to your plan, difficulty with new recruiting, and a slow downward spiral. Even for those plans that have not properly maintained their networks, however, it is never too late to put in the effort because it is certainly possible to recover from a poor history.

If the plan contracts with an IDS for its network, that does not mean that obligations to maintain the network cease. Many of the issues discussed here remain under the control of the plan and will continue to exert a strong influence over the physicians in the contracted network. The IDS will have the burden of responsibility for network maintenance and must therefore also pay attention to these issues. It is imperative that *both* the plan and the IDS pay close attention

Exhibit 7–3 Suggested Topics for Orientation of Open Panel Physicians

- Plan subscription agreement and schedule of benefits
- Authorization policies and procedures
- Forms and paperwork
- Utilization and financial data supplied by plan
- Committees and meetings
- Quality management program and peer review
- Recredentialing requirements
- Member transfer in or out of practice
  - —Member initiated
  - —Physician initiated
- Plan member grievance procedure
- Schedule of compensation from plan
- Contact persons in plan
- Affiliated providers
  - —Primary care
  - —Consultants
  - —Institutions
  - —Ancillary services

Exhibit 7–4 Suggested Topics for Orientation of Office Staff

- Plan subscription agreement and schedule of benefits
- Authorization policies and procedures
- Forms and paperwork
- Member transfer in or out of practice
  - —Member initiated
  - —Physician initiated
- Plan member grievance procedure
- Member eligibility verification
- Member identification card
- Current member list and eligibility verification
- Affiliated providers
  - —Primary care
  - —Consultants
  - —Institutions
  - —Ancillary services
- Contact persons in plan
  - —Names
  - —Telephone numbers
- Hours of operation

to network maintenance and not rely solely on one party for this vital function. If both parties are not actively involved, there is the strong possibility of network problems degenerating into finger-pointing, in which case both parties lose.

The Physician's View of Managed Care

To maintain the network, it is first important to understand how physicians view managed care. These issues are discussed at length in Chapter 18 but are mentioned briefly here. An understanding of these elements allows provider relations staff to key in on those items that are important to physicians.

In general, physicians see managed care as a general threat and pain in the neck. The issue of loss of or impingement on autonomy is perhaps the most emotionally charged issue there is. There are organizational demands on physicians as well: compliance with a restricted referral and hospital panel, increased bureaucratic overhead, multiple plans that use different forms and procedures, and an inability to rid themselves easily of difficult patients (so-called entitled demanders[10,11]).

Managed care often places the physician in an adversarial relationship with a patient (actually less often than one would think, but it only takes a few). This is uncomfortable because physicians are not trained for it.[12] This most often comes up in the guise of clearly unnecessary or medically marginal care that is demanded by the patient, but it may also occur when something is medically necessary but not a covered benefit; this issue most often appears under the term *patient advocacy*.

Some physicians have a real fear that managed care can lead to decreased quality of care. This has never really been proven, and there are now some data specific to open panel plans that show good quality of care along with lower utilization.[13–16] Nevertheless, the fear remains, and coupled with this is a fear of increased malpractice liability. The Wickline case, combined with threats of legal action by members demanding certain services, has increased the anxiety level of practicing physicians.

Managed care often results in a demand to discount fees or, more important, restricts the ability of a physician to cost shift into the plan as other payers (especially government programs) squeeze down. In plans with capitation or withhold mechanisms, some income is placed at risk, a situation generally not greeted with enthusiasm.

Last, most managed care plans are quite poor at providing appropriate feedback to physicians. Feedback is often sporadic, usually coinciding with annual payouts (or lack thereof) of risk pools. Routine useful information, such as the status of risk pools and utilization data, is often inadequate. In fact, in some plans the physicians hear from the plan only when there is a problem, such as overutilization, and never at all when performance is good.

In the face of all these issues, many physicians in fact are quite satisfied with their participation in managed care. Their incomes are maintained or enhanced, their patients are able to receive medical care without economic barriers to access, and they enjoy participating in a more structured delivery system that has the ability to deal with issues of cost and quality.[17] In general, physicians who are satisfied with their participation have been able to make an attitudinal adjustment more successfully than their colleagues who are not satisfied.[18]

Maintaining the Network

This topic is so important that most of the key elements are discussed in a separate chapter. The reader is referred to Chapter 18, which examines changing provider behavior, because changing behavior involves many issues that are important to network maintenance. The issues of data and feedback, the use of positive feedback, translation of goals and objectives, autonomy needs, quality of care, role conflict, understanding the insurance functions of the plan, plan differentiation in the marketplace, and discipline and sanctioning will not be repeated here.

In most plans, there are individuals who are solely responsible for maintaining communications with the physician panel, both PCPs and consultants, and with the physicians and their office staff. The roles of these provider relations representatives are to elicit feedback from the physicians and office staff, to update them on changes, to troubleshoot, and generally to keep things running smoothly.

The importance of this function cannot be overstated. Some care must be taken in selecting the individuals who will fill this role. Unless provider relations staff are mature and experienced, they may fall into the trap of forgetting for whom they are actually working. It is appropriate and necessary for them to represent the PCPs' point of view to plan management, but it is inappropriate if they find themselves siding against the health plan in the event of a dispute unless the plan is egregiously at fault. The provider relations staff must seek to prevent rifts, not foster them.

Provider relations are similar to customer relations, but an even better metaphor is that of a business partner. In a customer relation, the customer is always right; in a health plan, neither the plan nor the physician is always right. It is perhaps more useful to strive to be seen as a reliable and desirable business partner to the providers with whom you do business under contracts and agreements. Provider relations must therefore be proactive rather than simply reactive.

In addition to the items discussed in Chapter 18, the plan should have a well-developed early warning system for troubleshooting. Such a system could include regular on-site visits by provider relations staff (and occasionally by the medical director) and regular two-way communications vehicles. Changes in patterns, particularly patterns in utilization and compliance with plan policy and procedure, will often be a sign that the relationship is going awry. Last, close monitoring of the member services complaints report can yield crucial information; physicians will often tell their patients what they think and what they intend to do long before they tell the plan.

Removing Physicians from the Network

Beyond the elements referred to above, another function of network maintenance is the determination of whom not to keep in the plan. In any managed care plan, there will be physicians who simply cannot or will not work within the system and whose practice style is clearly cost ineffective or of poor quality. Quality is discussed in Chapter 17, and sanctions for reasons of poor quality are discussed in Chapter 18; quality-related actions will not be repeated here. The point of this section is not whether those physicians practice poor medicine (that judgment need not be made) but whether their practice style is one that the plan can afford.

A plan may also choose to terminate physicians because the physician panel is too large. This is rarely an issue for PCPs because most plans can always use wider access to primary care for both medical delivery and marketing reasons. Specialty networks (see Chapter 12) are a different matter, and plans may reduce the size of the specialty network to concentrate business or achieve better discounts and more control. The exception in primary care is likely to occur when a plan makes a wholesale commitment to an IDS and, as part of that commitment, agrees to terminate any PCPs who are not part of the IDS. In this situation, plans will usually resist terminating existing PCP relationships but may agree no longer to recruit new PCPs who are not part of the IDS (unless the IDS cannot provide sufficient PCPs in a geographic region).

Regarding the issue of unacceptably costly practice style, the plan must develop a mechanism for identification of such practitioners that uses a combination of claims and utilization data (see Chapter 19) and some type of formal performance evaluation system. If identified providers are reluctant to change, even after the medical director has worked closely with them, then serious consideration should be given to terminating them from the panel. In fact, if a plan is in serious financial difficulties stemming from the behavior of the network providers, management may decide to act unilaterally (assuming that the contract between the plan and the providers allows either party to terminate without cause upon adequate notice) and to departicipate those (presumably few) providers whose practice behavior is so far out of line that there will be an immediate positive impact on plan performance.

There are any number of objections to removing a physician from the panel. Asking the members to change physicians is not easy or pleasant, benefits managers get upset, and invariably the physician in question is in a strategic location. The decision often comes down to whether you want to continue to subsidize that physician's poor practice behavior from the earnings of the other physicians (in capitated or risk/bonus types of reimbursement systems) and from the plan's earnings or drive the rates up to uncompetitive levels. If those are unacceptable alternatives, then the separation must occur.

In some states, organized medicine has succeeded in persuading the state legislatures to pass due process laws, putting the plan in a position of having to follow potentially cumbersome and bureaucratic procedures to terminate a physician for any reason (without requiring the physician to follow those same procedures in the event that he or she wants to quit the plan). In these situations, the plan has no choice but to conform; the cost of such conformance is generally minimal compared with the economic consequences of failing to take action. The primary problem with these types of laws (other than the long period of time it requires to go through the process) is the possibility that a physician whose practice style is truly not a match for managed care may prevail, through utterly procedural measures, and continue to practice in the plan, with negative consequences for the rest of the network.

Once the decision has been made to departicipate a provider from the network, it is best to act promptly. Some HMOs, however, contractually require a physician to participate until the entire membership has had a chance to change plans (which may take a year unless the physician's member panel is small), but that option can be quite costly because the physician will have no incentive to control cost once he or she has been notified of termination. In those cases, the contract usually also allows the plan to increase the amount of withhold (e.g., from 20 percent up to 50 percent) to cover excess costs. In preferred provider organizations there is usually no need for such arrangements because the member may still see that physician, albeit at a higher level of coinsurance.

CONCLUSION

Network development requires an orderly project management approach, whether such development is undertaken by a health plan or by an IDS. It is equally important to invest in proper orientation of new physicians and their office staff. Maintenance of the relationship between the physicians and the plan is a key element of success that is gaining increasing importance as plans become ever more competitive in the marketplace. The plan or IDS must be willing to departicipate a provider in certain circumstances to deliver the proper combination of quality and cost effectiveness that is a requirement of managed care.

Study Questions

1. Develop a work plan for an open panel, direct contract model HMO to recruit new PCPs into its network under the following assumptions: The plan currently has 35,000 members and 211 PCPs in 139 groups, 27 physicians in 14 practices now have closed their practices to new patients, and the plan will add 7,000 new members over the next 9 months.
2. Describe a typical credentialing process, indicating which steps are required and for which reasons. Describe possible problems that may arise for any steps that are not completed.
3. Describe the pros and cons of contracting with faculty practice plans, and how a managed care plan addresses those issues.
4. Develop policies and procedures for network maintenance in an open panel HMO.
5. What proactive steps can an open panel HMO take to improve provider relations?

REFERENCES AND NOTES

1. T. Defina, Educating Physicians in Managed Care, *Health System Leader* (May 1995): 4–12.
2. Group Health Association of America (GHAA), *HMO Performance Survey* (Washington, D.C.: GHAA, 1994).
3. Group Health Association of America (GHAA), *HMO Industry Profile, Vol. 2: Physician Staffing and Utilization Patterns* (Washington, D.C.: GHAA, 1991).
4. J.R. Woodside, et al., Intensive, Focused Utilization Management in a Teaching Hospital: An Exploratory Study, *Quality Assurance and Utilization Review* 6 (1991): 47–50.
5. W.A. Schaffer, et al., Falsification of Clinical Credentials by Physicians Applying for Ambulatory Staff Privileges, *New England Journal of Medicine* 318 (1988): 356–357.
6. National Committee for Quality Assurance (NCQA), *CVO Certification Program 1995–1996* (Washington, D.C.: NCQA, 1995).
7. W.G. Kopit and A.B. Bouton, "Antitrust Implications of Provider Exclusion," in *The Managed Health Care Handbook*, 3d ed., P.R. Kongstvedt (Gaithersburg, Md.: Aspen, 1996), 906–929.
8. F. Mullan, et al., The National Practitioner Data Bank—Report from the First Year, *Journal of the American Medical Association* 28 (1992): 73–79.
9. R.E. Oshel, et al., The National Practitioner Data Bank: The First Four Years, *Public Health Reports* (July/August 1995): 383–394.
10. E. Friedson, Prepaid Group Practice and the New "Demanding Patient," *Milbank Memorial Fund Quarterly* 51 (1973): 407–411.

11. J.E. Groves, Taking Care of the Hateful Patient, *New England Journal of Medicine* 298 (1978): 883–887.
12. N. Daniels, Why Saying No to Patients in the United States Is So Hard, *New England Journal of Medicine* 314 (1986): 1380–1383.
13. J.E. Ware, et al., Comparison of Health Outcomes at a Health Maintenance Organization with Those of Fee-for-Service Care, *Lancet* 1 (1986): 1017–1022.
14. I.S. Udvarhelyi, et al., Comparison of the Quality of Ambulatory Care for Fee-for-Service and Prepaid Patients, *Annals of Internal Medicine* 115 (1991): 394–400.
15. E.M. Sloss, et al., Effect of a Health Maintenance Organization on Physiologic Health, *Annals of Internal Medicine* 106 (1987): 130–138.
16. C.M. Clancy and B.E. Hillner, Physicians as Gatekeepers—The Impact of Financial Incentives, *Archives of Internal Medicine* 149 (1989): 917–920.
17. R. Schultz, et al., Physician Adaptation to Health Maintenance Organizations and Implications for Management, *Health Services Research* 25 (1990): 43–64.
18. H.R. Reames and D.C. Dunstone, Professional Satisfaction of Physicians, *Archives of Internal Medicine* 149 (1989): 1951–1956.

SUGGESTED READING

Felt, S., Frazer, H., and Gold, M. 1994. *HMO Primary Care Staffing Patterns and Processes: A Cross-Site Analysis of 23 HMOs*. Washington, D.C.: Mathematica Policy Research, Inc.

Fisher, N.B., Smith, H.L., and Pasternok, D.P. 1993. Critical Success Factors in Recruiting Health Maintenance Organization Physicians. *Health Care Management Review* 18 (1): 51–61.

Greeley, H.P. and Woods, K.A. 1994. *Credentialing in the Managed Care Environment: A Guide for Managed Care Organizations and Health Care Networks*. Marblehead, Mass.: Opus Communications.

Nash, D.B. (ed.). 1994. *The Physician's Guide to Managed Care*. Gaithersburg, Md.: Aspen.

Palsbo, S.E. and Sullivan, C.B. 1993. *The Recruitment Experience of Health Maintenance Organizations for Primary Care Physicians: Final Report*. Washington, D.C.: Health Resources and Services Administration.

Chapter 8

Compensation of Primary Care Physicians in Open Panel Plans

Peter R. Kongstvedt

Study Objectives

- Understand the different methods of compensating primary care physicians (PCPs) in health plans
- Understand the variations of the most common forms of each method
- Understand the strengths and weaknesses of each method and each variation
- Understand under what circumstances a health plan would desire to use each method over the others
- Understand under what circumstances a PCP would prefer each method over the others
- Be able to create financial models of each major type of reimbursement method under differing scenarios

Managed care organizations (MCOs), primarily health maintenance organizations (HMOs), frequently use some form of risk-based reimbursement to pay physicians, especially primary care physicians (PCPs).* Specialty care physicians may also be paid under some form of risk-based reimbursement, although with less frequency than occurs with PCPs; reimbursement of specialty care physicians is discussed in Chapter 10. This chapter provides an overview of the most common risk-based methods to reimburse PCPs.

All risk-based reimbursement systems require a change in attitude from unmanaged fee for service (FFS). Economic reward comes from lowering *total* health care costs. Depending on the design of the reimbursement system, the financial reward may be directly or indirectly related to total health care costs. Financial reward may be only partially related to utilization and may also be affected by member satisfaction and quality (see Chapter 9). Reimbursement systems may be perceived as primarily punitive, as primarily reward based, or as a system that shares with providers the savings achieved from good management of medical utilization. Those perceptions are driven partially by the design of the reimbursement system and partially by the HMO's attitude to the management of that system.

A reimbursement system is simply one of the many tools available in managed care and has limited ability to achieve desired goals in the absence of other tools, such as competent management of utilization and quality. Neither the divisions by provider type nor the reimbursement mechanisms described here are found often in a pure state. Managed care is marked by a high degree of continual change and variation.

* PCPs are assumed to be in the specialties of family practice, internal medicine, and pediatrics; general practice (i.e., non–board certified general practitioners) is also considered primary care in those plans that contract with general practitioners. Obstetrics and gynecology, while sharing some attributes of primary care, are generally treated as specialties by HMOs. Physician extenders, such as physician assistants and clinical nurse practitioners, are generally treated as being associated with PCPs and so are not discussed separately.

BASIC MODELS OF REIMBURSEMENT

This chapter addresses reimbursement of PCPs in open panels. This is distinct from the compensation of individual physicians in organized groups or integrated delivery systems (IDSs); that topic is discussed in detail in Chapter 10 of *The Managed Health Care Handbook*.[1] It is possible (and even likely in the case of IDSs) that these methods of reimbursement will be used on an individual physician basis in such groups, but not necessarily. In the case of organized groups, this chapter discusses only the reimbursement of the group, rather than any one physician in that group by the MCO. In the case of IDSs, if the IDS accepts risk for primary care services, it will still need to apply these methods to compensate the physicians within the IDS, even if that method is different from how the IDS is compensated by the MCO.

There are two basic ways to compensate open panel PCPs for services: capitation and FFS. Large surveys have reported that approximately 60 percent of open panel plans use capitation and that the remainder use FFS (with a rare and puzzling small percentage of salary), as illustrated in Figure 8–1.[2] Another study reports that 69 percent of HMOs use capitation to reimburse PCPs; the difference between these two reports is probably due to sampling techniques but is not terribly important.[3] This distribution of reimbursement methods has been relatively stable for the past several years, although there is no guarantee that it will remain so.[4,5]

CAPITATION

Capitation is prepayment for services on a per member per month (PMPM) basis. In other words, a PCP is paid the same amount of money every month for a member regardless of whether that member receives services and regardless of how expensive those services are.

Scope of Covered Services

To determine an appropriate capitation, you must first define what will be covered in the

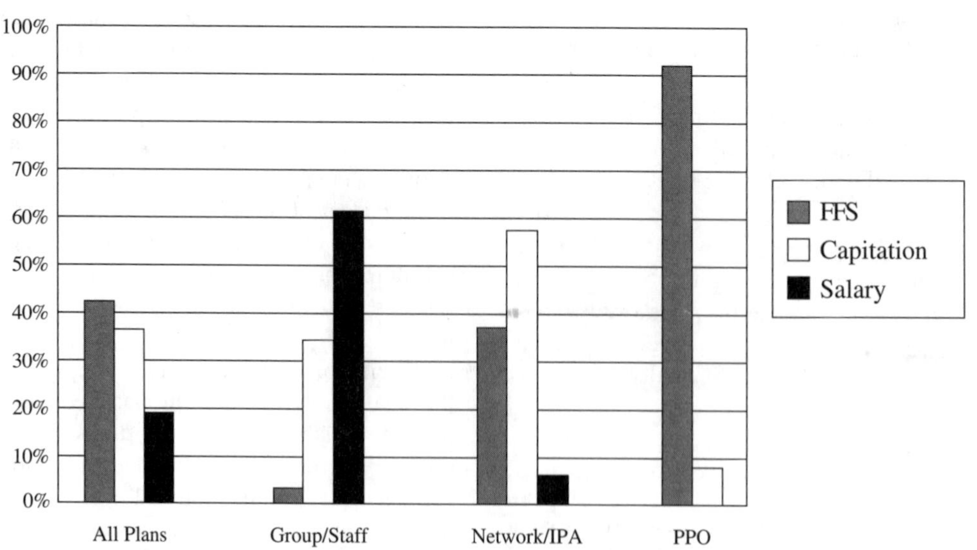

Figure 8–1 Primary care reimbursement. IPA, individual practice association; PPO, preferred provider organization. *Source:* Reprinted from *Arrangements between Managed Care Plans and Physicians: Results from a 1994 Survey of Managed Care Plans*, 1995, Physician Payment Review Commission.

scope of primary care services. Include all services that the PCP will be expected to deliver, including preventive services, outpatient care, and hospital visits. Certain areas are difficult to define, for example diagnostic testing, prescriptions, surgical procedures (what if the same procedure is performed by the PCP and by a referral physician?), and so forth. Other services, such as immunizations, office care, and so forth, are easier to define. If a plan is unable to define primary care services easily, a good reference is published by Milliman & Robertson, a national actuarial firm.[6] Defining the scope of covered services forms the basis for estimating the total costs of primary care.

Many performance-based compensation systems also hold the PCP accountable for non–primary care services through either risk programs or positive incentive programs, both of which are discussed later in this chapter. For such programs, the same exercise of categorizing what and how services are defined should be carried out for specialty or referral services, institutional care, and ancillary services. Essentially, you need to be able to estimate costs for each of the categories you will capitate or track for capitated or at-risk PCPs.

Calculation of Capitation Payments

The issue of expected costs in defined categories is beyond the scope of this chapter; greater discussion can be found in Chapter 23. Most plans use an actuary to set these cost categories initially, but if you have been in operation for some time and have a data system capable of tracking the detail, estimating costs in categories is simply a matter of collating the existing data. If you do not have that experience or cannot draw upon it, you will have a more difficult time. In those cases, it is frequently necessary to have an actuary develop the data on the basis of your geographic area, the benefits you will offer, and the controls you will put in place. In fact, it may be best to consult an actuary in any case, even though it is not inexpensive.

A plan wishing to convert from an FFS system to capitation will have to calculate the capitation equivalent of average FFS revenues for the physicians. In other words, calculate what physicians would receive from FFS for that membership base, assuming appropriate utilization.* This figure may then be discounted or not, depending on your situation. In plans where you fully expect the PCPs to receive a substantial bonus from control of utilization, a discount may be appropriate. In most cases, however, you will not wish to discount PCP services heavily.

As a rough example, if a physician receives approximately $45.00 per visit (collected, not just billed), and you can reasonably estimate a visitation rate of three primary care visits per member per year (PMPY),† then multiplying 3 × $45.00 and dividing the result by 12 (to get the revenue per month) yields $11.25 PMPM. That could approximate the capitation rate. This example is crude and does not take into account any particular definition of scope of covered services, actual visitation rates for an area, visit rate differences by age and sex, average collections by a physician, effect of copays, or differences in mean fees among different specialties, so that it should not be used in capitating primary care services.

If your plan uses a risk/bonus arrangement, it is useful to be able to demonstrate to physicians that if utilization is controlled they will receive more than they would have under FFS. For example, if your plan uses a blended capitation rate of $11.25 PMPM and there are in fact three visits PMPY, and if good utilization control yields a bonus of $2.25 PMPM from the risk pools, then the physician receives a year-end reconciliation that blends out to $13.50 PMPM, or $54.00 per visit.

---

* In other words, if high utilization is one of the primary reasons to convert from FFS, it would not be appropriate simply to memorialize the high utilization rates when one is calculating a capitation equivalent; it is more appropriate to calculate the capitation on the basis of what utilization should be.

† The actual rate is closer to 3.3 to 3.6 (see Chapter 6), but it is easier to use 3.0 for the purposes of illustration.

Variations by Age and Gender

Most capitation systems vary payments by the age and gender of the enrolled member to take into account the differences in average utilization of medical services in those categories. For example, the capitation rate for a member younger than 18 months of age might be $34.00 PMPM to reflect the high utilization of services by newborns.* The capitation rate may then fall to $12.00 PMPM for members 1 to 2 years of age, $7.00 PMPM for members 2 to 18 years of age, $10.00 PMPM for male members 18 to 45 years of age, and $14.00 PMPM for female members 18 to 45 years of age (reflecting the higher costs for women in their childbearing years), and so forth.

Those plans without the capability of capitating by age and gender must take special care in developing capitation rates. This is a particular problem when one is recruiting pediatricians because utilization of services by members in the first 18 months of life is quite high. In plans that capitate an independent practice association (IPA) or an IDS with a single payment, the issue will remain. Unless the IPA or IDS has worked out an equitable method of distributing funds, the plan may need to provide support in this area.

Variations by Other Factors

It is possible, although not common, to vary capitation by factors other than age and sex. One example would be to vary capitation on the basis of experience, either expected or real. In this case, the capitation calculations would need to factor in the experience of each account group. In other words, if an account had an unusually healthy population of enrollees (e.g., all healthy, young nonsmokers who use seat belts and advocate nonviolence), the capitation would be factored downward; the reverse would be true for a group with high expected utilization (e.g., all hypertensive, overweight asbestos workers who smoke and drink heavily before racing on their motorcycles, without helmets, to buy illegal drugs). On a prospective basis, this could be done with standard industry codes in a manner similar to that used in developing premium rates under some forms of community rating (see Chapter 23). In the case of actual experience, a commercial account's retrospective experience could be used to adjust capitation payments up or down on a prospective basis. It is also possible to adjust capitation based on current health status, through the use of health status questionnaires and physical examinations, but that is cumbersome to administer and is not likely to reflect the actual premium collected from the account from which the members came. The reader is referred to the literature for further discussion of methods of risk adjustment.[7] In all cases, the calculation of capitation would be highly complex compared with simple age and sex adjustments.

Another, more easily analyzed factor is geography. Even in the same statistical metropolitan area, there may be considerable differences in utilization. For example, in the Washington, D.C. metropolitan area there are highly significant differences in utilization among some counties in Maryland, northern Virginia, and the District of Columbia (Blue Cross/Blue Shield of the National Capitol Area, unpublished data, 1989–1992). In such situations, it may be appropriate to factor in geographic location when capitation payments are calculated.

Practice type may occasionally be a legitimate capitation factor. As an example, internists argue that the case mix they get is different from the case mix family practitioners get. This has not been borne out in any research, but there is some evidence that, even in the same stratum of age and sex, specialty internists (e.g., cardiologists) have sicker patients than general internists[8] (it must also be pointed out that the same investigators noted that, after adjustment for patient mix, there was a whopping 41 percent higher level of utilization in unmanaged FFS

---

* This includes immunizations unless the plan carves out immunization costs from the capitation rate; this is discussed later in the chapter.

systems compared with HMOs[9]). The actual mix of services delivered in the office may also differ by specialty type (Blue Cross/Blue Shield of the National Capitol Area, unpublished data, 1989–1992). University teaching programs tend to attract adverse selection from the membership base and may have a legitimate claim in that regard (see Chapter 12).

There may be straightforward business adjustments to capitation as well. One example that occurs in certain plans is an adjustment for exclusivity. In this case, the plan pays a higher capitation rate to those providers who do not sign up with any other managed care plans (there are usually no restrictions against participating with government programs or indemnity carriers). Such arrangements may raise the potential for antitrust actions, but that is dependent on the particular situation.

In any event, if factors other than age and sex are to be used to adjust capitation, the calculations become highly complex, and communicating these factors to the participating providers becomes far more difficult. The plan must also guard against an imbalance in factors that lead to a higher than expected (or rated for) capitation payout over the entire network. In other words, adjustments lead not only to increases in capitation but to decreases as well.

Carve-Outs

Occasionally, capitation systems allow for certain services normally considered covered to be carved out of the capitation payment. For example, immunizations may not be paid under capitation but may be reimbursed on a fee schedule. As a general rule, carve-outs should only be used for those services that are not subject to discretionary utilization. In the case of immunizations, the medical guidelines for administering them are clear-cut but subject to change (e.g., there may be an increase in the number of immunizations that are to be given in the first years of life), and there is little question about their use. That would not be the case, for example, for office-based laboratory testing. If your plan reimburses capitation for all services but pays fees for office-based laboratory work, you may see a rise in routine testing.

Risk

There are two broad categories of risk for capitated PCPs: service risk and financial risk. Service risk refers to the PCP receiving a fixed payment but not being at risk in the sense of having potentially to pay money out or not receive money as a result of risk. Service risk is essentially the fact that, if service volume is high, then the PCP receives relatively lower income per encounter, and vice versa. Although the PCP may not be at obvious financial risk, the PCP does lose the ability to sell services to someone else for additional income in the event that his or her schedule fills up with capitated patients at a rate that is higher than that used to calculate the capitation. This issue is irrelevant if the PCP has slack time in his or her appointment book but can be an issue if the PCP is extremely busy. It is common for PCPs to feel that their capitation patients are abusing the service by coming in too frequently, but the perception often is more grievous than the reality.

Financial risk refers to actual income placed at risk regardless of whether the PCP has a service risk as well. There are two common forms of financial risk: withholds and capitated pools for non–primary care services. Figure 8–2 illustrates relative percentages of MCOs that use withholds and incentives as part of their capitation of PCPs.

Of special note, a plan with a Medicare Risk Contract (see Chapters 26 and 27) should be aware of proposed regulations that limit the amount of risk a physician may be at for a Medicare member. These proposed regulations (which have not been finalized at the time this book was written, despite existing for many years) limit a physician's risk to 25 percent of total income if adjusted annually, and 15 percent if adjusted more frequently than annually; the plan is also required to provide stop loss (see below). If a plan places the physician at risk for

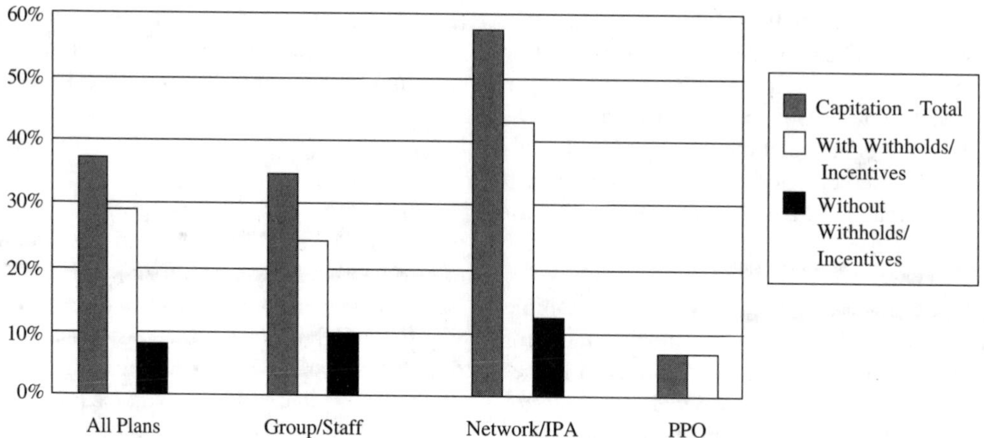

Figure 8–2 Primary care capitation and risk. IPA, individual practice association; PPO, preferred provider organization. *Source:* Reprinted from *Arrangements between Managed Care Plans and Physicians: Results from a 1994 Survey of Managed Care Plans*, 1995, Physician Payment Review Commission.

more than 25 percent of total income for the year, then the plan is required to perform surveys of its members in a statistically valid sample to determine satisfaction with quality and access.[10]

WITHHOLDS AND RISK/BONUS ARRANGEMENTS

One common risk arrangement is the withhold. A withhold is simply a percentage, for example, 20 percent, of the primary care capitation that is withheld every month and used to pay for cost overruns in referral or institutional services. In the earlier example of $11.25 PMPM, a 20 percent withhold would be $2.25. The PCP would actually receive a check each month for the difference between the capitation rate and the withhold, in this case $9.00; the remainder, in this case $2.25, is held by the plan and used at year end (or whenever) for reconciliation of cost overruns. The amount of payment withheld varied from 5 percent to 20 percent in one survey, with few plans reporting routine withholds greater than 20 percent (in fact, concern was registered that withholds greater than 20 percent could have a risk of incenting inappropriate underutilization).[11]

Many plans also have a clause in their physicians' contract that states that the plan may increase the amount of withhold in the event of cost excesses beyond what is already being withheld. For example, the withhold can be increased from 20 percent to 30 percent if referral costs are out of control. The general guideline is to cover the actual and accrued expenses through the capitated pools and the withhold.

Although there are a few plans that have attempted to put the entire PCP capitation payment at risk for cost overruns, this is unwise. If a PCP's entire capitation payment is withheld, that is tantamount to indentured servitude and may lead to serious service problems. It is better to limit the maximum risk at which the primary care capitation may be placed (e.g., 50 percent, although even that level of withhold cannot be sustained for long).

CAPITATION POOLS FOR REFERRAL AND INSTITUTIONAL SERVICES

When capitation exists for primary care services, payment for referral services and institutional services is often made from capitation funds or pools as well. The services themselves may be paid for under a number of mechanisms (FFS, per diem, capitation, and the like), but the expense is drawn against a capitated fund or pool. There are a variety of ways that HMOs handle these types of risk pools, and some common methods will be described. It must be stressed that the illustration that follows probably does not exist in the real world exactly as it appears here. In those HMOs that use this approach, there is usually considerable variation; the illustration also reflects models that were more prevalent roughly a decade ago; mature HMOs have undergone considerable changes since then.[12] Nevertheless, the illustration provides a common basis for understanding this type of model. Figure 8–3 illustrates schematically how some of these risk pools operate.

There are three broad classes of non–primary care risk pools: referral (or specialty care), hospital (or institutional care, regardless of whether it is inpatient, outpatient, or emergency department), and ancillary services (e.g., laboratory, radiology, pharmacy, and so forth). Many HMOs also have a fourth pool, usually called "other," in which they accrue liabilities for such things as stop-loss or malpractice and in which the physicians have no stake (see below). Some HMOs combine the ancillary services into the "other" pool, which is the model illustrated in Figure 8–3. It is not uncommon for these risk pools to be handled in different ways regarding the flow of funds and levels of risk and reward for the physicians and the plan.

As an example, the PCP receives an $11.25 PMPM blended capitation rate for primary care services (in other words, the blend of all the age and sex capitation rates for that physician's membership base comes out to $11.25 PMPM). For each member, $22.00 PMPM is added to a capitated pool for referral services, and $40.00 PMPM is added to a capitated pool for hospital or institutional inpatient and outpatient services. The PCP does not actually receive the money in those pools; the plan holds onto it. Any medical expenses incurred by members in that PCP's panel will be counted against the appropriate pool of funds. At the end of the year, a reconciliation of the various pools is made (see below).

As with primary care, the scope of covered services must first be defined. For example, will home health be covered under institutional or referral (probably institutional because it reduces institutional costs), and will hospital-based professionals (radiology, pathology, and anesthesia) be covered under institutional or referral? The same exercise is carried out with any category for which capitated funds will be accrued.

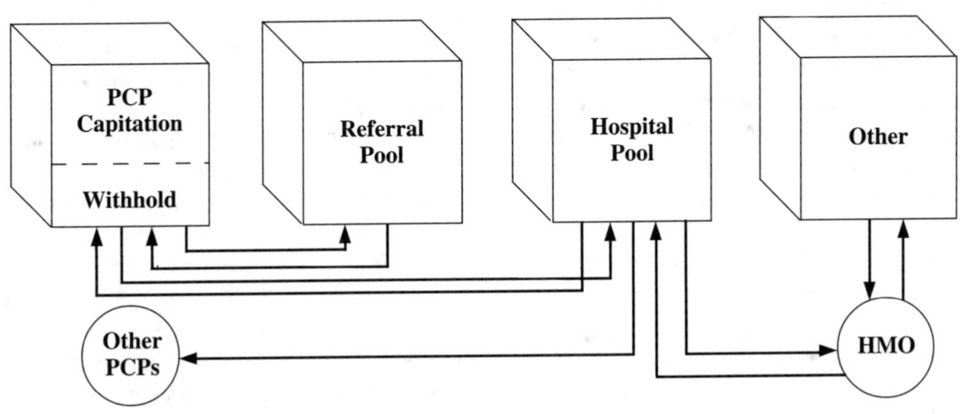

Figure 8–3 Capitation risk pools.

What if not all the withhold is used (if the plan employs a withhold system) or there is a surplus in either the referral pool or the institutional services pool? First, any surplus in one pool is generally first used to pay for any excess expenses in the other pool. For example, if there is money left in the referral pool but the institutional pool has cost overruns, the extra funds in the referral pool are first applied against the excessive expenses in the hospital pool, and vice versa.

After both funds are covered, any excess money is shared with or paid to the physicians. In general, only those physicians with positive balances in their own risk pools receive any money. For example, a PCP has referral services funds tracked for his or her own patients. If the cost of services for those members leaves a positive balance in the referral pool, and if there is money left in the institutional services pool on a planwide basis, the PCP receives a pro rata share of the money. In other words, risk is shared with all physicians in the plan, but reward may be tracked individually. In another example, some plans have decided to disburse positive balances in referral and institutional funds on the basis of both utilization and measures of quality and member satisfaction; a discussion of such incentive programs is found in Chapter 9.

The degree to which an individual PCP's pools will have an impact on year-end bonus disbursements may vary. If the decision is to minimize risk to individual PCPs, then you will want to set low threshold protection or stop-loss (see below) and minimize or even stop tracking expenses against an individual PCP's pools while those expenses are still low. For example, if a PCP has a member with acquired immune deficiency syndrome (AIDS), the referral expenses will be paid either out of the planwide referral capitation pool or out of a separate stop-loss fund and will not count against the individual PCP's referral risk fund after referral expenses have reached $2,500. In this way, high-cost cases, which could wipe out an individual PCP's risk pool, will have less effect than that PCP's ability to control overall referral expenses in the rest of the member panel.

It is common, although not absolute, for a plan to pay out all extra funds in the referral pool but only half the funds in the hospital pool. In some cases, there is an upper limit on the amount of bonus a PCP can receive from the hospital pool. The justification for this is that the plan stands a considerably greater degree of risk for hospital services and therefore deserves a greater degree of reward. Furthermore, it is often a combination of utilization controls and effective negotiating that yields a positive result, and the plan does most of the negotiating.

Medical Expenses for Which the PCP Is Not at Risk

Even in plans that use withholds and risk/bonus arrangements, there are sometimes certain medical expenses for which PCPs will not be at risk. For example, a plan may negotiate a capitated laboratory contract; laboratory capitation is then backed out of the referral and primary care capitation amounts and accounted for separately. If the PCP orders laboratory services from another vendor, that cost is deducted from his or her referral pool; otherwise, laboratory cost and use have no effect on the PCP's compensation.

Other examples of such nonrisk services might include any type of rider benefit (e.g., vision or dental) or services over which PCPs have little control, such as obstetrics. Another example would be defined catastrophic conditions (e.g., persistent vegetative state), where the PCP is taken out of the case management function by the plan and the plan's case management system takes over the coordination of care. The danger here is that there will be pressure to include too much in this category, thereby gutting the entire concept of capitation. Once a service has been taken out of the at-risk category, it is exceedingly difficult to put it back in.

Reinsurance and Stop-Loss or Threshold Protection

The degree of risk to which any physician is exposed needs to be defined. As mentioned earlier, it is common for a plan to stop deducting expenses against an individual PCP's pool after a certain threshold is reached for purposes of the year-end reconciliation. There are two forms of stop-loss or threshold protection: costs for individual members, and aggregate protection.

As an example of individual case cost protection, if a PCP has a member with leukemia, after the referral expenses reach $2,500 they will no longer be counted against the PCP's referral pool, or, more commonly, only 20 percent of expenses in excess of $2,500 will be counted against the referral pool. The uncounted expenses will be paid either from an aggregate pool or from a specially allocated stop-loss fund.

It is possible to vary the amount of threshold protection by the size of a PCP's member base to reduce the element of chance. For example, if a PCP has fewer than 300 members, the threshold is $2,000; if the PCP has more than 800 members, the threshold is $4,000. It is equally common for a threshold to exist for hospital services, although the level is much higher, for example $30,000. As alluded to earlier, the lower the threshold, the less the effect of high-cost cases on individual capitation funds and the greater the effect of overall medical management. On the other hand, if the threshold is too low there may be a perverse incentive to run up expenses to get them past the threshold. Multitiered thresholds also create an artificial barrier to the PCP's acceptance of new members. For example, if the threshold for 300 members or fewer is less than that for 301 members or more, PCPs may resist adding members above the 300 limit so as to protect the lower threshold level. Tiered thresholds can be time limited to prevent this problem.

Aggregate protection is not as common. As an example of aggregate protection, the plan may reduce deductions to 20 percent or even stop deducting referral expenses after total expenses for an individual PCP reach 150 percent of the capitation amount. Providing aggregate stop-loss protection on the basis of a percentage of total capitation allows such protection to be tied to the membership base of the PCP. This is another way of ensuring that a PCP's capitation will not be totally at risk.

The combination of threshold protection and risk sharing across the physician panel serves to reduce any individual PCP's exposure to events outside his or her control. It is frustrating to manage all your cases properly but receive no reward because one seriously ill patient had high expenses.

In any case, providing threshold protection to an individual physician is important, and you need to remember to budget for its cost. Although such stop-loss protection can be paid from the aggregate of all the physician's referral funds, that ensures that there will be a draw on the withhold (if there is one). Because positive referral balances will be paid back to PCPs, negative balances will need to be funded through the withhold, so that there can never be a full return of the withhold. Therefore, it is preferable to budget a line item for stop-loss expense and to reduce the referral allocations by that amount.

It is likewise important for there to exist a mechanism for peer review of excess expenses to determine whether they were due to bad luck or poor case management. In the latter situation, the plan must have recourse to recovering all or part (up to the contractually agreed-upon maximum individual physician risk) of the excess costs from a physician who failed to provide proper case management.

Individual versus Pooled Risk

All forms of financial risk are affected by how the HMO handles the issue of individual risk versus pooled risk. In other words, to what degree is an individual physician at risk for his or her performance compared with the degree to which that risk is shared with some or all other PCPs? It is human nature to wish to share the downside risk (and pain) with others but to keep the upside (profit) for oneself.

In one large survey, 25 percent of plans reported using individual risk pools, 12 percent reported using risk pools of 2 to 50 physicians, and 63 percent used risk pools of more than 50 physicians.[13] In those plans that do track risk pools individually, it is more common for only one pool (usually referral), if any, to be tracked on an individual basis while the withhold, if any, and hospital pool are aggregate.

Although many HMOs contract directly with PCPs, there are many that contract through the vehicle of the IPA,* physician–hospital organization (PHO), management services organization (MSO), or other form of IDS (see Chapter 4 for discussions of these organizations). The HMO capitates the IPA or IDS, but that organization may or may not capitate the PCPs. In fact, many of these organizations pay the PCPs on a FFS basis, using one or more of the performance-based FFS reimbursement methods described below.

Even when there is no intervening organization, the issue of who actually is being capitated, and for what, still remains. Is it the individual PCP, a subset of the total network of PCPs (i.e., pools of doctors or PODs), or the entire network of PCPs? The answer may not be the same for each category or risk. For example, a plan may wish to capitate PCPs individually for their own services, combine them into PODs for purposes of referral services, and use the performance of the entire network for purposes of hospital services.

A plan can also choose to use different categories for risk and for reward. For example, a plan may spread risk across the entire network but only reward a subset of PCPs. An example was given earlier in which positive balances in withholds or referral pools were used to offset deficits in the hospital pool; any remaining surplus balance would only be paid to those PCPs with a positive balance.

There are common and predictable problems with individual risk. The majority of those problems relate to the issue of small numbers. As noted earlier, luck can have as much or more of an impact on utilization as good management, at least in small member panels. As a PCP's panel grows to more than 500 members, this problem starts to lessen, but it persists. This is one of the most important reasons that an HMO will contractually require a PCP not to close his or her practice to the HMO until that PCP has 250 or more members (see Chapter 29); it is the identical reason that a PCP should desire to have a large panel enrolled. When PCPs have good utilization results, they generally desire to keep the reward for their hard labor; when results are poor, they frequently feel that they have been dealt an abnormally sick population of members and should not be held accountable for the high medical costs.

The larger the number of dollars at stake, the more dangerous the problem of small numbers becomes to an individual PCP. Although stop-loss and reinsurance somewhat ameliorate the problem, the problem remains. This is the very reason that plans may be willing to use individual pools for referral services but will not do so for hospital services, where the dollars are substantially higher.

The other major problem with individual risk is the ability of some PCPs to game the system. In other words, to enhance income the PCP manages to get his or her sickest patients to transfer out of the practice, with a resulting improvement in that individual PCP's medical costs. Although all plans prohibit PCPs from kicking a member out of their practice because of medical condition, a wily and unethical PCP can find a way to do so and remain undetected. Related to this issue is the concern that individual risk incents a PCP to withhold necessary medical care (discussed below). Although this charge has been leveled at the HMO industry for many years, it has never been proven.

* The term *IPA* is often used to describe any HMO that uses private physicians practicing in their own offices (as opposed to a group or staff model HMO), but in fact the term technically refers to an actual legal entity. See Chapter 3.

Last, there have been cases of HMOs requiring an individual PCP (or small group) actually to write a check to the plan to cover cost overruns in medical expenses (as opposed to simple reconciliation of accidental overpayments). This has usually occurred when the plan agreed not to keep the withhold (in response to the PCP's plea to improve cash flow) but to track it nonetheless. Whenever a PCP is required to pay money back to the plan, a severe problem in provider relations is likely to occur.

If the plan chooses to pool risk across the entire network, then the flip side of individual risk occurs: The impact of any individual PCP's actions are diluted so much as to be undetectable. If a PCP is having good results, then he or she may resent having to cover for the problems of colleagues with poor results (of course, no one objects to being helped out when one's own results are poor). If the plan does not track individual results, then it will have little capability of providing meaningful data to individual physicians to help them better manage medical resources.

Because of these two extremes, many plans have chosen to use PODs for at least some financial risk management. PODs are a subset of the entire network, although there is no standard size. A pool may be a large medical group, an aggregation of 10 to 15 physicians, or made up of all participating PCPs in an entire geographic area. A POD could also be made up of the physicians in a PHO or MSO that accepts risk. The common denominator is that the number of members enrolled in practices in the POD will be sufficient to allow for statistical integrity but small enough to allow the pool to make changes that will be seen in utilization results. The chief risk is that PODs require support from the plan in the form of data and utilization management.

It should not be assumed that PODs are a panacea; they are not. If a POD fails, the repercussions are greater than if an individual physician fails because far more members are affected and the dollars are higher. There are times when using individual risk and reward is best, times when the entire network should be treated as a single entity, and times when PODs will make sense. Medical managers should be aware that there is evidence that individual risk/bonus arrangements elicit strong changes in behavior whereas aggregated risk/bonus arrangements do not.[14]

FULL-RISK CAPITATION

Full-risk capitation refers to the PCP receiving money for all professional services, primary and specialty, but not hospital services (although the group may still be on an incentive program regarding hospital utilization management). The PCP not only authorizes the referral but actually has to write a check to the referral specialist. This was once marginally popular but is currently uncommon because there were a number of problems in the past with such systems when the PCPs did not have sufficient funds to cover specialty costs and members were exposed to balance billing. There has been a recent resurgence of interest in this form of capitation as PCPs band together into large groups or other forms of collective activity such as IPAs, PHOs, and MSOs.

Full-risk capitation is generally not supportable by other than a large group or organized system of PCPs. The more the primary care group can capitate specialists for services, the less the danger of having insufficient funds. Many state insurance departments, however, will not allow a provider to subcapitate; that is, the insurance department believes that only a licensed HMO, not another provider, may capitate a provider (see Chapter 28).

Any group accepting full-risk capitation needs strong financial management skills and good computer systems support. Of considerable interest is one substantial study that looked at how physicians at such a form of financial risk managed their own utilization. The physicians employed techniques identical to traditional HMO utilization management, including the use of a PCP gatekeeper, an authorization system, practice profiling, clinical guidelines, and managed care education (see Chapter 13, for discussion of these techniques).[15] It should be noted that many HMOs are reluctant to enter into such arrangements, unless they are convinced that the physicians will be able to manage utilization because they do not wish to be exposed to the risk of failure.

REASONS TO CAPITATE

The first and most powerful reason for an HMO to capitate providers is that capitation puts the provider at some level of risk for medical expenses and utilization. Capitation eliminates the FFS incentive to overutilize and brings the financial incentives of the capitated provider in line with the financial incentives of the HMO. Under capitation, costs are more easily predicted by the health plan (although not absolutely predictably because of problems of out-of-network care). Capitation is also easier and less costly to administer than FFS, thus resulting in lower administrative costs in the HMO and potentially lower premium rates to the member.

The most powerful reasons for a provider to accept capitation from an HMO are financial. Capitation ensures good cash flow: The capitation money comes in at a predictable rate, regardless of services rendered, and comes in as prepayment, thus providing positive cash flow. Also, for physicians who are effective medical case managers as well as cost-effective providers of direct patient care, the profit margins under capitation can exceed those found in FFS, especially as FFS fees come under continued pressure. The main nonfinancial reason for a provider to accept capitation is that it eliminates any disagreements over the level of fees that the provider may charge a patient, thus providing some level of insulation regarding finances and the provision of health care.

PROBLEMS WITH CAPITATION SYSTEMS

The most common problem with capitation is chance. As mentioned earlier, a significant element of chance is involved when there are too few members in an enrolled base to make up for bad luck (or good luck, but nobody ever complains about that). Physicians with fewer than 100 members may find that the dice simply roll against them, and they will have members who need bypass surgery or have cancer, AIDS, or a host of other expensive medical problems. The only way to ameliorate that is to spread the risk for expensive cases through common risk-sharing pools for referral and institutional expenses and to provide stop-loss or threshold protection for expensive cases.

The problem of small numbers is especially acute in the early period of a PCP's participation with the MCO unless the MCO is failing to grow. To deal with this, and to entice PCPs to participate, some HMOs have offered to pay the PCP on a FFS basis for the first 6 months or until the PCP has more than 50 enrollees, whichever comes first. A few HMOs have offered to pay capitation but have guaranteed that the PCP would receive the higher of capitation or FFS in that first 6 months. A few HMOs have even agreed to pay FFS until the PCP has more than 50 members without any time limit, but that is unwise because it may disincent the PCP to enroll an adequate number of members.

Another frequent problem is the perception of the physicians and their office staff of capitation. Although many practices have now acclimated to capitation, there is a feeling that capitation is really "funny money." When PCPs are receiving a capitation payment of \$11.25, this is sometimes unconsciously (or consciously) confused with the office charge. In their minds, it appears as though everyone is coming in for service and demanding the most expensive care possible, all for an office charge of \$11.25. It is easy to forget that many of the members who have signed up with that physician are not even coming in at all. It only takes 10 percent of the members to come in once per month to make it seem as if there is a never-ending stream of entitled demanders in the waiting room. The best approach to this is to make sure that the plan collects data on encounters so that the actual reimbursement per visit can be calculated.

The last major perceived problem is inappropriate underutilization. An argument made against capitation in general, and against risk/bonus arrangements in particular, is that you are paying physicians not to do something, and that is dangerous.[16–20] Although there was one spectacular case of fraud in south Florida in the mid-1980s where providers were placed on individual risk arrangements and serious quality problems were noted, that was a failure of management and regulation. In fact, not only is there no real evidence that capitation or risk/bonus systems have led to poor quality (a fact that the sources noted earlier in this paragraph have themselves all conceded), but there is some evidence that managed care systems have provided equal or better care to members than uncontrolled FFS systems even while lowering costs.[21–28]

Under a well-crafted capitation program, you are not paying physicians to underutilize services; you are sharing the savings of cost-effective care. In an unmanaged FFS system, there is a direct relationship between doing something and getting paid for it; under capitation, the reward is removed from the action. In other words, the capitation check does not change each month depending on services. Furthermore, by carefully constructing a stop-loss or threshold protection program, you can attenuate the effect of high-cost cases on capitation funds. Spreading the risk over more than one physician can lower the effect of single cases on a physician's reimbursement, but at the cost of not recognizing individual performance. In addition, it must be kept in mind that HMOs, with their lack of deductibles and high levels of coinsurance, lower economic barriers to care, thus improving access to care.

In the final analysis, it is the obligation of plan management to monitor the quality of services and to ensure that there is no inappropriate underutilization of services. One can argue that in a well-managed plan identification of poor quality is easier because there is more access to data and a tighter quality assurance system, and that is exactly how the plan must approach this issue.

One last issue should be raised, although it is not a problem per se but something to be aware of. In a capitated system, savings from decreased utilization may not always result in direct savings to the plan. In other words, if primary care services undergo a reduction in utilization, the capitation payments will not go down, just as they will not go up when there is increased utilization. If a system uses capitation extensively for primary care, specialty care, and hospitalization, there may be no reduction in expenses even if controls result in a dramatic lowering of utilization rates. On the other hand, such reductions will result in less pressure to increase capitation and premium rates the next year.

EFFECT OF BENEFITS DESIGN ON REIMBURSEMENT

Benefits design may have a great effect on reimbursement to PCPs in capitated programs, although the effect may be felt in any reimbursement system that relies on performance. The three major categories of benefits design that have such an impact are reductions in benefits, copayment levels, and point-of-service (POS) plans.

Benefits Reductions

Because many managed care plans have adopted greater flexibility in benefits design in response to marketplace demands, the underpinnings of actuarial assumptions that were used to build capitation rates have become less reliable. If a plan has adopted exclusions for preexisting conditions, has imposed waiting periods, or does not offer benefits that have usually been covered, the related expenses for those conditions are no longer applicable to the reimbursement rate. In other words, the capitation rate may now be higher than actually required. The impact of benefits reductions on primary care services is usually not so great as to warrant changing previously acceptable capitation rates, but that is not an absolute.

Benefits changes have a greater impact on risk pools. For example, if mental health and chemical dependency coverage is carved out of the PCP managing system and turned over to a dedicated management function (a common occurrence in managed care; see Chapter 16), then concomitant reductions in the referral and hospital risk pools are warranted. The same is true if an account wanted to carve out pharmacy services to another vendor (e.g., a national company that administers a card and mail-order program).

Copayment Levels

Copayment levels can have an immediate impact on capitation rates, both for PCP capitation and for risk pool allocations. The amount of capitation due a PCP will be different with a \$3.00 copay compared with a \$10.00 copay. For example, if a capitation rate were calculated to be \$11.25 on the basis of three visits PMPY at \$45.00 per visit, then application of a \$10.00 copay would reduce the capitation amount to \$8.75 (\$45.00 – \$10.00 = \$35.00; three visits × \$35.00 = \$105.00; \$105.00 ÷ 12 months = \$8.75 PMPM). The same issue applies for calculating contributions to referral risk pools and hospital risk pools. For example, if consultant care has a \$10.00 copay, then estimated consultant visit costs would have to take the copay into account. The same is true for hospital care if copays of \$100.00 or \$200.00 are applied.

The effect of copays and cost sharing on utilization is real, although it differs with respect to the amount of out-of-pocket expense to which the member is exposed.[29–31] It should be noted, however, that cost sharing does not necessarily selectively reduce inappropriate hospitalization (in other words, although total utilization may be reduced with cost sharing, the change in utilization may not reflect a change in whether the utilization was appropriate in the first place).[32] Deciding whether to adjust capitation rates on the basis of expected utilization differences from copays is difficult. Explaining such adjustments to PCPs is no easy task either because changes in utilization are population based, and any individual member may or may not change his or her behavior.

Adjusting capitation rates for copays is not easily done if there are widespread differences in copay amounts among different accounts. For example, if 50 percent of the members have a \$3.00 copay, 35 percent have a \$5.00 copay, and 15 percent have a \$10.00 copay for primary care services (not to mention different copays for referral services), calculating the appropriate capitation can be difficult. Even so, it is worth doing unless the variations are minor or infrequent.

POS Plans

For the purposes of this discussion, POS plans are those that allow members to obtain a high level of benefits by using the HMO or gatekeeper system while still having insurance type benefits available if they choose to use providers without going through the managed care system. For a discussion of POS, see Chapter 3.

Because members with POS benefits are not totally locked into the managed care plan, utilization occurs both in network and out of network. Although the plan can actuarially determine the level of in-network and out-of-network use for the entire enrolled group, that cannot be said for an individual physician's member panel. This has an obvious impact on capitation rates.

Some plans attempt to adjust capitation rates on the basis of prospective in-network utilization. That usually means a reduction in the capitation rate. Other plans attempt to make adjustments on a retrospective basis, although this is a terribly difficult exercise in provider relations when a PCP is asked to refund a percentage of the capitation payment he or she had received all year. In either event, it is no easy task to explain to a PCP who feels underpaid anyway that you are going to pay even less. An alternative is not to reduce the capitation rate, but that can result in a windfall for the PCP whose POS members never come in for services (or, on a more pernicious note, for the PCP who does not provide adequate access for POS members, thereby driving them out of network for services). This has become so difficult that many plans capitate PCPs for pure HMO (i.e., not POS) members and pay FFS for POS members. This creates problems due to the schizophrenic reimbursement systems and results in what psychologists refer to as cognitive dissonance. Many HMOs with high levels of POS membership simply do not capitate all and use FFS exclusively. Figure 8–4 illustrates relative percentages of MCOs that use different reimbursement systems for different product types.

POS makes it difficult to measure the performance of PCPs as well. For example, if performance is based only on in-network utilization, one good way to look like a stellar performer is subtly to encourage POS members to seek services out of network. If PCPs are held accountable for all services, both in network and out of network, then they may argue that it is not fair that they are held accountable for utilization that is completely out of their control. Although this issue is not easily resolved, many plans with extensive experience in POS have chosen to fold out-of-network utilization into the performance-based reimbursement system, whether capitation or FFS. To attenuate the problem of lack of control by an individual PCP, the risk or reward system is spread out among groups of PCPs or the entire network, thereby maintaining actuarial integrity.

Although capitating individual PCPs is a challenge with POS, it is certainly possible to capitate a large group or an IDS. In most cases, a prospective adjustment is made to the capitation rate based on the actuary's best estimate of in-network versus out-of-network utilization. Out-of-network claims are paid by the plan from the funds that had been backed out of the capitation rate. Surpluses (or a percentage of surpluses) in that pool of funds may be returned to the group or IDS to encourage it to find ways of getting its enrolled members to seek care in network, thus reducing out-of-network utilization.

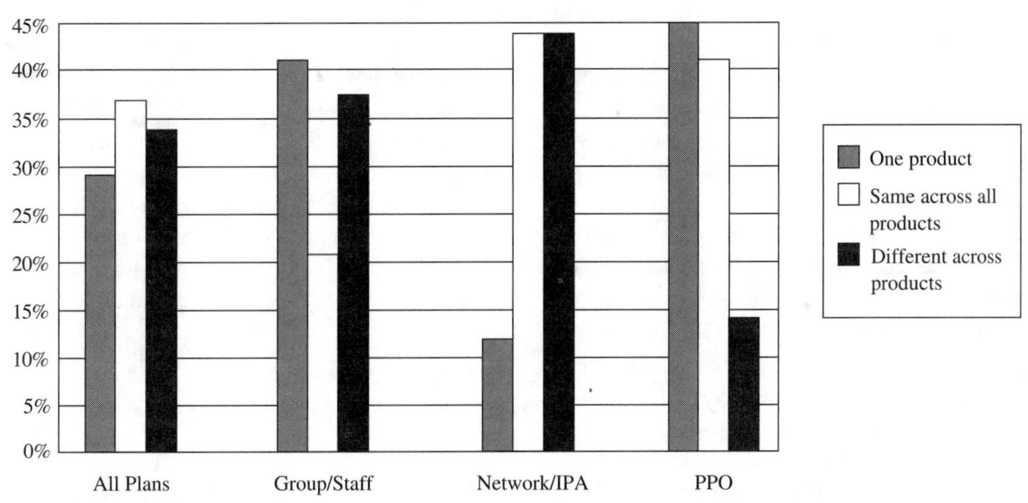

Figure 8–4 Variation in reimbursement models by product. *Source:* Reprinted from *Arrangements between Managed Care Plans and Physicians: Results from a 1994 Survey of Managed Care Plans*, 1995, Physician Payment Review Commission.

FFS

There are some veterans of managed health care who hold that the FFS system of American medicine is the root of all the problems we face with high costs. Although that is simplistic, there is some truth to it, particularly when there are no controls in place. In a system where economic reward is predicated on how much one does, particularly if procedural services pay more than cognitive ones, it is only human nature to do more, especially when it pays more. The reward is immediate and tangible: A large bill is made out, and it usually gets paid. Doing less results in getting paid less. On the other side of the argument, FFS results in distribution of payment on the basis of expenditure of resources. In other words, a physician who is caring for sicker patients will be paid more, reflecting that physician's greater investment of time, energy, and skills.

In a managed health care plan, FFS may be used to compensate physicians and may be the method of choice in certain situations. For example, in a simple preferred provider organization (PPO), FFS will be virtually the only option available (except in the rare and oxymoronic capitated PPO). The reasons for an HMO to use FFS reimbursement are varied and have not been systematically studied. One dynamic is that FFS is frequently more acceptable to physicians, so that many HMOs use FFS to get more physicians to sign up, at least in an HMO's initial period of development. This is especially true in markets where managed care penetration is low; where managed care penetration is high, PCPs often prefer capitation. As noted earlier, HMOs may also capitate IPAs or PHOs, but those organizations actually pay FFS to the physicians. Also as noted earlier, certain products, such as POS, also are difficult to capitate, leading many HMOs with a large POS enrollment to use FFS. Last, some HMOs simply believe that FFS is a good way to reimburse PCPs and have operated that way for more than 20 years.

There are two broad categories of FFS: straight FFS and performance-based FFS. The first category is less common in HMOs but nearly universal in PPOs and Blue Cross/Blue Shield service plans. In some cases, an HMO may not even be allowed to use straight FFS because the PCPs are required to be at some level of financial risk for the HMO to qualify for licensure.

Performance-based FFS simply refers to the fact that the fees that the PCPs ultimately receive will be influenced to some degree by performance. Whether performance refers to overall plan performance, performance of only one segment of medical costs (professional costs, for example), or performance of the individual PCP is quite variable. How performance affects the fees is likewise variable. Figure 8–5 illustrates the relative percentages of MCOs using straight FFS versus performance-based FFS. Both these forms of FFS are described in the following sections.

Standing Risk

In an FFS plan, determining who will stand risk for services is a major issue. This may run from a situation where the plan stands virtually all the risk, such as in a simple PPO or indemnity plan, to a system where the risk is shared fully with the providers, such as in an HMO. The no balance billing clause (see Chapter 29) is highly important to a tightly managed FFS plan. This clause states that the physician will only look to the plan for payment of services and will accept payment by the plan as payment in full. In other words, if the plan has to reduce or otherwise alter the amount of payment, the physician will not look to the member for any additional fees.

Determination of Fees

Usual, Customary, or Reasonable

The historical method of fee determination is the usual, customary, or reasonable (UCR) fee. In some cases, this is really a euphemism for the physician sending a bill and the plan paying it. There is little uniformity to UCR because it rep-

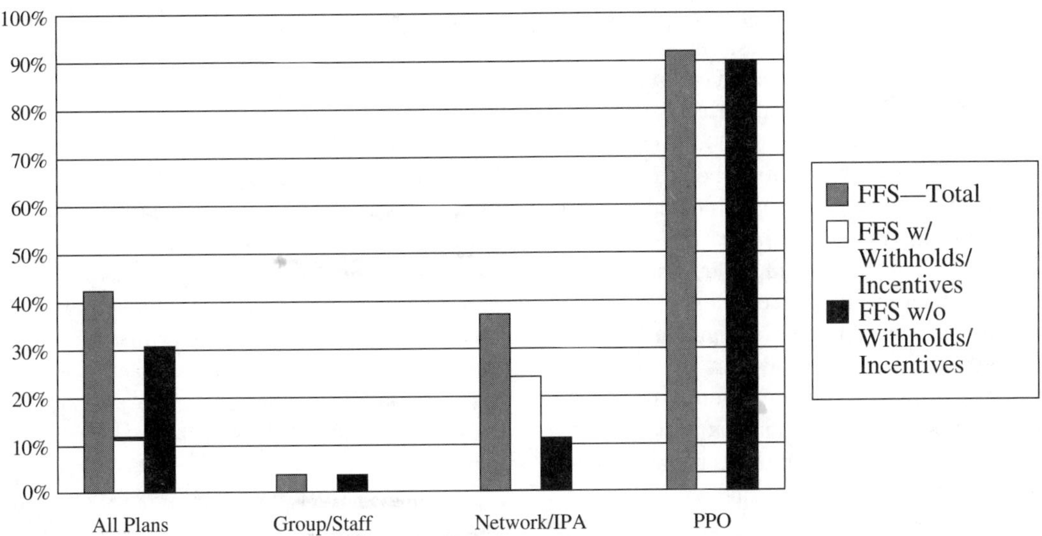

Figure 8–5 FFS and risk/incentives for PCPs. PPO, preferred provider organization. *Source:* Reprinted from *Arrangements between Managed Care Plans and Physicians: Results from a 1994 Survey of Managed Care Plans*, 1995, Physician Payment Review Commission.

resents what the physician usually bills for that service, and there can be tremendous discrepancies among physicians' fees for the same service. One common methodology for determining UCR is to collect data for charges by current procedural terminology (CPT) code, calculate the charge that represents the 90th percentile, and call that the UCR maximum. When a claim is submitted, it is paid in full if it is lower than the 90th percentile; if it is higher than the 90th percentile, it is paid at the UCR maximum. Some plans use different technologies to determine what is reasonable and arrive at allowances different from the 90th percentile. Still other plans negotiate a further percentage discount of the UCR (e.g., 20 percent) and use that to pay claims.

The advantage to using a percentage of UCR is that it is extremely easy to obtain. Most physicians will gladly accept a discount on fees if it ensures rapid and guaranteed payment. The problem is that there is nothing to prevent the physician from increasing the fees by the same percentage as the discount, although excessive fee hikes will bump into the fee maximum. Some plans require the physician to notify the plan of a fee hike, but in truth there is little that the plan can or will do if it has no real clout.

Relative Value Scales

The use of a relative value scale (RVS) has gained popularity in FFS plans. In this system, each procedure, as defined in CPT, has a relative value associated with it. The plan pays the physician on the basis of a monetary multiplier for the RVS value. For example, if a procedure has a value of 4 and the multiplier is $12, the payment is $48.

A classic problem in using an RVS and negotiating the value of the multiplier has been the imbalance between procedural and cognitive services. Until recently, in most available RVS systems, as in FFS in general, procedures have more monetary value than cognitive services. In other words, there is less payment to a physician for performing a careful history and physical examination and thinking about the patient's problem than for doing a procedure involving needles, scalpels, or machines. This has changed with the adoption of the resource-based relative value scale (RBRVS) by the Health Care Financing Administration (HCFA) for Medicare.

RBRVS has addressed to some extent the imbalance between cognitive and procedural services, lowering the value of invasive procedures (e.g., cardiac surgery) and raising the value of cognitive ones (e.g., office visits). The HCFA has imposed this on all physicians for Medicare recipients. Many large insurers are following suit in setting their determination of reasonable fees, although they lack the statutory ability to require acceptance of that fee as payment in full unless there is a contractual agreement to do so by the provider.

Negotiated Fee Schedule, Fee Maximum, or Fee Allowance

Fee allowance schedules are quite useful and common. In this case, the plan determines what it considers the correct FFS, usually on the basis of CPT codes, and the physician agrees to accept those fees as payment in full. This has the advantage of allowing the plan to control determination of payment for services on a uniform basis. In essence, this is an RVS that has already been multiplied. It is common practice to pay a percentage discount off charges subject to the fee schedule maximum. As mentioned above, the use of RBRVS is becoming a common method of building the fee allowance schedule.

Of special concern in the use of a fee schedule or RVS is the possibility of an antitrust violation. This is of particular concern in physician-sponsored plans. You do not really want a group of competing physicians to get together and set fees. It is preferable to use nonphysicians or an outside agency to perform this task.

Global Fees

A variation on FFS is the global fee. A global fee is a single fee that encompasses all services delivered in an episode. Common examples of global fees include obstetrics, in which a single fee is supposed to cover all prenatal visits, the delivery itself, and at least one postnatal visit, and certain surgical procedures, in which a single surgical fee pays for preoperative care, the surgery itself, and postoperative care.

Some plans are using global fees to cover primary care as well. In this case, the plan must statistically analyze what goes into primary care to calculate the global fee. That analysis must include the range of visit codes as well as all covered services that occur during primary care visits (e.g., electrocardiography, simple laboratory tests, spirometry, and so forth). The analysis will vary by specialty type (i.e., internal medicine, family practice, and pediatrics).

The analysis then builds by specialty a composite type of visit. The average type of visit for internal medicine, for example, may be an intermediate visit, and 20 percent of the time an electrocardiogram is performed, 30 percent of the time a urinalysis is performed, and so forth (these figures are fictitious and should not be used for actual fee calculations). The plan then builds up the global fee by putting together the pieces, for example \$42 for the office visit, \$7 for the electrocardiogram (\$35 × 0.2), and so forth.

The chief value of a global fee is that it protects against problems of unbundling and upcoding. With unbundling, the physician now bills separate charges for services once included in a single fee; for example, the office visit is \$45, the bandage is \$10, starch in the nurse's uniform is \$3, and so forth. Upcoding refers to billing for a procedure that yields greater revenue than the procedure actually performed; an example is coding for an office visit that is longer than the time actually spent with the patient. Global fees offer no protection against churning, which is the practice of seeing patients more often than is medically necessary to generate more bills; in fact, global fees, if not managed correctly, may exacerbate a problem with churning.

Plans that use global fees often tie them to performance. For example, utilization targets may be set for some or all medical services. How a PCP or group of PCPs performs against these targets may be used to set the global fees. For example, PMPM targets are set for primary care, referral care, institutional care, and ancillary services. Performance of a group of PCPs is measured against those targets on a rolling 12-month basis, and performance against those targets is used to adjust prospectively the next quarter's global fee up or down. Targets are modified by age, sex, product type (e.g., pure HMO versus POS), or any other variables that are appropriate. Targets are also modified for the effect of stop-loss against catastrophic cases. In other words, measurement of performance is similar to that used in capitated systems.

A performance-based global fee system is a hybrid of capitation and FFS. Unlike capitation, there are generally no payouts from capitated risk pools (e.g., referral pools), so that there is no dollar-for-dollar relationship between utilization and reimbursement. Like capitation, PMPM targets in all categories of medical expense are monitored, and reimbursement is still associated with good performance. Also like capitation, there is a statistical build-up to determine reimbursement. Like FFS, payment is only made if services are rendered, and no payments are made if there are no services.

This last feature makes such systems attractive to employer groups that have much lower than normal utilization (i.e., those that have healthy employees and dependents who require fewer services than a typical capitation calculation assumes) and to POS plans where the plan desires to reward performance but needs to address both in-network and out-of-network utilization. As discussed earlier, under capitation you run the risk of paying twice for services under POS, once through capitation, and again through out-of-network claims.

Withholds

As with capitation, many plans that use FFS withhold a certain percentage of the fee to cover medical cost overruns. For example, the plan may be using a negotiated fee schedule that amounts to a 20 percent discount for most physician fees. The plan then withholds an additional 20 percent in a risk pool until the end of the year. In effect, physicians receive what amounts to 60 percent of their usual fee but may receive an additional 20 percent at the end of the year if there were no excess medical costs that year.

It is possible to try to create profiles of physicians' utilization patterns to distribute more equitably the withhold funds in the event that some, but not all, of the withhold is used to cover extra medical costs. Unfortunately, this is difficult in an FFS system if there is no gatekeeper model in place. Most plans simply return remaining withhold funds on a straight pro rata basis, although some plans return withhold on a preferential basis to PCPs as opposed to specialty care physicians.

Mandatory Reductions in All Fees

In a plan where risk for medical cost is shared with all the physicians and where straight CPT codes are used to reimburse on an FFS basis, there must exist a mechanism whereby fees may be reduced unilaterally by the plan in the event of cost overruns. This is the usual method in an HMO and may be employed in a strongly controlled PPO as well.

For example, the plan may be using a fee schedule that is equivalent to a 20 percent discount on the most common fees in the area. In the event that medical expenses are over budget and there is not enough money in the risk withhold fund to cover them, all physicians' fees are reduced by a further percentage, say an additional 10 percent, to cover the expenses. At this point, the effective discount is 30 percent, although this would really be 50 percent in the event that a withhold system was in place, all the withhold funds had been used, and there were still excess medical liabilities.

Budgeted FFS

Related to mandatory fee reductions, budgeted FFS is used in a few plans. In this variation, the plan budgets a maximum amount of money that may be spent in each specialty category. This maximum may be expressed either as a PMPM amount (e.g., $7.50 PMPM) or as a percentage of revenue (e.g., 5.6 percent of premium revenue). As costs in that specialty category approach or exceed the budgeted amount, the withhold in that specialty, not across all specialties, is increased.

This approach has the advantage of focusing the reimbursement changes on those specialties in which excess costs occur rather than on all specialties in the network. The disadvantage is that this may not be provider specific; in other words, all specialists are treated the same, and there is no specific focus on individual outliers. Plans that do not use gatekeepers to manage care may find this type of approach useful, and one model uses this form of reimbursement in lieu of any type of precertification requirements on the physicians.[33] This type of system usually only works when there are regular reports and practice profiles provided to the physicians (see Chapters 18 and 19), and when the enrolled membership is very large in order to ensure statistical integrity.

Sliding Scale Individual Fee Allowances

Related to budgeted FFS is the sliding scale individual fee allowance. In this model, PCP performance is again measured against benchmark targets in all categories of medical expense with appropriate protection for expensive outlier cases. On the basis of performance, the PCP's reimbursement may vary from 70 percent of allowable charges up to 110 percent if performance exceeds targets.[34] Although this system still allows for upcoding and unbundling, it does vary by individual on the basis of performance and could be applied to groups of physicians as well as to individuals.

POS and Performance-Based FFS

As discussed earlier, a central issue facing plan management in applying performance-based FFS under POS is determining whether to include out-of-network costs in the performance evaluation of PCPs. At first blush, it does not seem fair to do so because such expenses are not under the control of the PCP. The best way to make one's performance profile look good, however, is to force members to seek care out of network (through poor service), thereby subverting the ultimate goal of cost control. Therefore, most plans are now including out-of-network expenses in performance evaluations and are working with PCPs to encourage in-network use by members. Related to that, it is important for plans to set performance parameters accurately that vary by product type; in other words, if you expect 30 percent out-of-network use by members under POS, that assumption must find its way into the PMPM standards against which you measure a PCP's performance.

PROBLEMS WITH FFS IN MANAGED HEALTH CARE PLANS

There are two significant problems with using FFS in managed health care plans. These problems can become markedly exacerbated if the plan starts to get into financial trouble.

The first problem is churning. This simply means that physicians perform more procedures than are really necessary and schedule patient revisits at frequent intervals. Because most patients depend on the physician to recommend when they should come back and what tests should be done, it is easy to have a patient come back for a blood pressure check in 2 weeks instead of a month and to have serum electrolytes measured (unless laboratory services are capitated) in the physician's office at the same time. Few patients will argue, and the physician collects for the work.

Few physicians consciously churn, but it does happen, even if unconsciously. The more serious problem comes when the plan reduces the fees because of medical expense overruns. When this happens, a "feeding frenzy" can occur. In effect, physicians start to feel that they have to get theirs first. If the fees are lowered 10 percent this month, what might happen next month? Better to get in as many visits as possible this month because next month may bring a 20 percent fee reduction. This creates a self-fulfilling prophecy, and the inevitable downward spiral begins.

The only effective approach to churning is tight management (or switching to capitation). Some plans develop physician peer review committees to review utilization. These committees have the authority to sanction physicians who abuse the system. This has some slowing effect if there are enough reviewers and not too many physicians to review. The actions of such committees should follow a process that includes warnings and a probationary period in which expectations for improvement are clearly outlined. Other plans apply differential withholds selectively on those providers whose utilization is clearly out of line, although defining that takes some care.

Better still, manage the plan so that few sanctions are necessary. This means controlling referrals, controlling hospital and institutional utilization, and negotiating effective discounts with providers and hospitals. It also means closely monitoring utilization and billing patterns by PCPs and acting when necessary. Performance-based programs such as those described earlier can also be applied to lessen the impact of churning, but this problem still remains in any FFS plan.

On the other hand, if cost overruns bring fees down to grossly unacceptably low levels, utilization may decrease simply because the plan does not pay enough to get providers to do the work. That is a potentially problematic situation that can lead to inappropriate underutilization.

The second major problem is upcoding (sometimes referred to as CPT creep) and unbundling. As mentioned earlier, upcoding refers to a slow upward creeping of CPT codes that pay more; for example, a routine office visit becomes an extended one, a Pap smear and pelvic examination become a full physical examination, or a cholecystectomy becomes a laparotomy. Unbundling refers to charging for services that were previously included in a single fee without lowering (or lowering sufficiently) the original fee.

These problems are best monitored by the claims department in coordination with whichever department is responsible for data analysis. There are two useful approaches. The first is to look for trends by providers. Individuals who are trying to game the system will usually stand out. If there is one physician who has 40 percent extended visits compared with 20 percent for all the other physicians in the panel, it may be worth further review (this topic is addressed in Chapter 19). The second approach is to automate the claims system to rebundle unbundled claims and to separate for review any claims that appear to have a gross mismatch between services rendered and the clinical reason for the visit. The problems of upcoding and unbundling may also addressed through the use of global fees, as discussed earlier in this chapter.

CONCLUSION

To be effective, an MCO, whether it is an HMO or an IDS, must align the financial incentives and goals of all the parties: the health plan and the providers who deliver the care. Capitation, and to a somewhat lesser extent performance-based FFS, do that in ways that traditional FFS does not.

In a tightly managed plan, such as an HMO, capitation will be more consistent with the overall goal of controlling costs. Although capitation is initially harder to calculate, and although it is sometimes harder to gain acceptance for it from physicians, this system has less likelihood of leading to overutilization than FFS. Problems of inappropriate underutilization must be guarded against with effective monitoring and an effective quality assurance system.

FFS can be used as well but requires a different set of management skills. It is easier to install and is often more acceptable to physicians, but it can quickly get out of control unless it is watched carefully. New products such as POS require new approaches to reimbursement because classic approaches are not ideally suited. As managed care evolves, reimbursement may be expected to evolve further.

The reimbursement system is a tool, and like any tool it has limitations. A hammer is the correct tool for pounding and removing nails, but it is poor for cutting wood and drilling holes. In the same way, a reimbursement system is a powerful and effective tool, but it can only be effective in conjunction with other managed care functions: utilization management, quality management, provider relations, and the many other activities of a well-run MCO.

Study Questions

1. Describe the key elements in most capitation programs in open panel HMOs.
2. Describe a performance-based FFS reimbursement system in open panel HMOs.
3. Describe the difference between service risk and financial risk in capitation.
4. Describe how an IPA might accept capitation, but reimburse its member physicians on a FFS basis, and still be considered as a risk-bearing entity. How might the IPA operate to lower its risk profile?
5. How would a capitated direct contract model open panel HMO change or not change its reimbursement methodologies as its POS product grows to be over 30 percent of enrolled membership?

REFERENCES AND NOTES

1. J.A. Rodeghero, "Physician Compensation in Groups and Integrated Delivery Systems," in *The Managed Health Care Handbook*, 3d ed., ed. P.R. Kongstvedt (Gaithersburg, Md.: Aspen, 1996), 147–165.
2. M. Gold, et al., *Arrangements between Managed Care Plans and Physicians: Results from a 1994 Survey of Managed Care Plans* (Washington, D.C.: Physician Payment Review Commission, 1995).
3. InterStudy, *The InterStudy Competitive Edge* (St. Paul, Minn.: InterStudy, 1994).
4. Group Health Association of America (GHAA), *HMO Industry Profile, Vol. 2: Physician Staffing and Utilization Patterns* (Washington, D.C.: GHAA, 1991).
5. Gold, et al., *Arrangements between Managed Care Plans and Physicians.*
6. R.L. Doyle and A.P. Feren, *Healthcare Management Guidelines, Vol. 3: Ambulatory Care Guidelines* (Milliman & Robertson, updated periodically).
7. N. Goldfeld, Risk Adjustment, Reinsurance, and Health Reform, *Managed Care Quarterly* 2 (1994): 82–94.
8. R.L. Kravitz, et al., Differences in the Mix of Patients among Medical Specialties and Systems of Care: Results from the Medical Outcomes Study, *Journal of the American Medical Association* 267 (1992): 1617–1623.
9. S. Greenfield, et al., Variations in Resource Utilization among Medical Specialties and Systems of Care: Results from the Medical Outcomes Study, *Journal of the American Medical Association* 267 (1992): 1624–1630.
10. *Federal Register* 57 (14 December 1992): 59024–59040.
11. A.L. Hillman, et al., HMO Managers' Views on Financial Incentives and Quality, *Health Affairs* (Winter 1991): 207–219.
12. N. Schlackman, Evolution of a Quality-Based Compensation Model: The Third Generation, *American Journal of Medical Quality* 8 (1993): 103–110.
13. Hillman, et al., HMO Managers' Views on Financial Incentives and Quality.
14. L. Debrock and R.J. Arnould, Utilization Control in HMOs, *Quarterly Review of Economics and Finance* 32 (1992): 31–53.
15. E.A. Kerr, et al., Managed Care and Capitation in California: How Do Physicians at Financial Risk Control Their Own Utilization?, *Annals of Internal Medicine* 123 (1995): 500–504.
16. A.L. Hillman, Health Maintenance Organizations, Financial Incentives, and Physicians' Judgments, *Annals of Internal Medicine* 112 (1990): 891–893.
17. A.L. Hillman, Financial Incentives for Physicians in HMOs—Is There a Conflict of Interest?, *New England Journal of Medicine* 317 (1987): 1743–1748.
18. A.L. Hillman, et al., How Do Financial Incentives Affect Physicians' Clinical Decisions and the Financial Performance of Health Maintenance Organizations?, *New England Journal of Medicine* 321 (1989): 86–92.
19. M.D. Reagan, Toward Full Disclosure of Referral Restrictions and Financial Incentives by Prepaid Health Plans, *New England Journal of Medicine* 317 (1987): 1729–1734.
20. General Accounting Office (GAO), *Medicare: Physician Incentive Payments by Prepaid Health Plans Could*

Lower Quality of Care (Washington, D.C.: GAO, 1988), GAO Publication GAO/HRD-89-29.

21. J.E. Ware, et al., Comparison of Health Outcomes at a Health Maintenance Organization with Those of Fee-for-Service Care, *Lancet* 1 (1986): 1017–1022.
22. I.S. Udvarhelyi, et al., Comparison of the Quality of Ambulatory Care for Fee-for-Service and Prepaid Patients, *Annals of Internal Medicine* 115 (1991): 394–400.
23. E.M. Sloss, et al., Effect of a Health Maintenance Organization of Physiologic Health, *Annals of Internal Medicine* 106 (1987): 130–138.
24. C.M. Clancy and B.E. Hillner, Physicians as Gatekeepers—The Impact of Financial Incentives, *Archives of Internal Medicine* 149 (1989): 917–920.
25. N. Lurie, et al., The Effects of Capitation on Health and Functional Status of the Medicaid Elderly: A Randomized Trial, *Annals of Internal Medicine* 120 (1994): 506–511.
26. P. Braveman, et al., Insurance-Related Differences in the Risk of Ruptured Appendix, *New England Journal of Medicine* 331 (1994): 444–449.
27. A. Relman, Medical Insurance and Health: What about Managed Care? *New England Journal of Medicine* 331 (1994): 471–472.
28. J.P. Murray, et al., Ambulatory Testing for Capitation and Fee-For Service Patients in the Same Practice Setting: Relationship to Outcomes, *Medical Care* 30 (1992): 252–261.
29. M.F. Shapiro, et al., Out-of-Pocket Payments and Use of Care for Serious and Minor Symptoms, *Archives of Internal Medicine* 149 (1989): 1645–1648.
30. J.P. Newhouse, et al., Some Interim Results from a Controlled Trial of Cost Sharing in Health Insurance, *New England Journal of Medicine* 305 (1981): 1501–1507.
31. K.F. O'Grady, et al., The Impact of Cost Sharing on Emergency Department Use, *New England Journal of Medicine* 313 (1985): 484–490.
32. A.L. Siu, et al., Inappropriate Use of Hospitals in a Randomized Trial of Health Insurance Plans, *New England Journal of Medicine* 315 (1986): 1259–1266.
33. Cleveland MCO QualChoice Is Using Risks and Incentives To Determine Provider Fees, *Managed Healthcare* (June 1994).
34. D.E. Church, et al., An Alternative to Primary Care Capitation in an IPA-Model HMO, *Medical Interface* (November 1989): 37–42.

SUGGESTED READING

Pauly, M.V., et al. 1992. *Paying Physicians: Options for Controlling Cost, Volume, and Intensity of Services.* Ann Arbor, Mich.: Health Administration Press.

Wozniak, G.D. 1995. *Evaluating Capitation Payments: A Guide to Calculating Benchmark Capitation Rates.* Chicago, Ill.: American Medical Association.

Chapter 9

Non–Utilization-Based Incentive Compensation for Physicians

Peter R. Kongstvedt

Study Objectives

- Understand the key differences between incentive compensation based on medical utilization and that based on non-utilization measures
- Understand the differences in approaches between open panels and closed panels
- Understand possible categories for non-utilization performance measurements
- Understand how such programs may be used in practice

Physician compensation is an area with a great deal of variation. In managed care it is difficult to use any single criterion or small set of criteria for judging performance. As discussed below, it is relatively easy to game a system that has only a few elements, and that can lead to problems. Basic methods of compensation of primary care physicians (PCPs) is addressed in Chapter 6 (for closed panels) and Chapter 8 (for open panels), compensation of specialty care physicians (SCPs) is addressed in Chapter 10, and compensation of physicians in medical groups and integrated delivery systems is addressed in Chapter 10 of *The Managed Health Care Handbook*.[1] Although those chapters do give the reader a sense of the complexity of reimbursement issues, it is often believed by many that physician compensation in managed care focuses solely on issues of utilization and cost. It is accurate to state that the alignment of financial incentives between the managed care organization (MCO) and the physicians is highly important in managed care, but it is inaccurate to state that there is no interest in aligning physician incentives with goals that are not based on utilization. Therefore, although many MCOs combine utilization and nonutilization financial incentives, this chapter focuses on incentive compensation programs that rely on standards of performance outside utilization management.

CLOSED PANELS COMPARED WITH OPEN PANELS

Obviously, there are significant differences between closed and open panels that affect formal physician performance evaluations. In closed panels it is easier to observe behavior, and a greater reliance on subjective evaluations is possible. Closed panels also frequently include both PCPs and SCPs, both of whom may authorize services and may care for a regular panel of patients. Formal performance evaluations in closed panel managed care plans similar to what is discussed in this chapter have been in use for many years.[2]

In open panels, the issues may be confused by existing risk/bonus systems in the private practice setting that often reward physicians strictly on the basis of utilization or productivity. Such systems generally place a greater reliance on objective measures. Furthermore, open panels tend to focus more on PCPs than on both PCPs and SCPs. It is certainly possible to construct an open panel performance evaluation program for SCPs as well as PCPs, and the principles will be the same. This chapter focuses on PCPs, looks at both types of systems, and makes suggestions for methods that may work in one or the other. Although most performance evaluation systems have been applied to PCP managing plans (i.e., gatekeeper plans), it is also possible to apply them to preferred provider organizations.[3]

THE VALUE OF FORMAL PERFORMANCE EVALUATIONS

Beyond the intellectual challenge, there are some practical uses for formal performance evaluations. What follows are examples for closed panels, open panels, or both.

Annual Compensation Adjustments in Closed Panels

Formal performance evaluations are quite useful in groups that use merit raises to adjust annual compensation. If a group uses strict percentage raises, or perhaps tails off the percentage after time but still handles raises in an across-the-board manner, adding an element of merit to the process of getting a raise can help reward the types of behavior one wishes to encourage.

Few physicians will argue that there are various levels of contributions from the closed panel medical staff. In a private fee-for-service practice, the less you collect, the less money you get. In a managed care setting, the criteria are not all that clear, and there may be no built-in reward structure for superior performance. Formal evaluations provide that structure.

In prepaid groups, where the idea of performance-based compensation may be too volatile to implement fully, it is possible to combine an element of across-the-board raise with a performance-based raise. For example, if a plan has budgeted a 6 percent increase in physicians' base salary, one could allocate 3 percent for an across-the-board (or cost of living) raise, and the remaining 3 percent would be based on performance.

Bonus Distribution in Open or Closed Panels

In open panels, year-end payouts from withhold or risk-sharing pools are frequently based strictly on utilization, either individual or aggregate. It is possible for a plan to budget for a bonus or to use some profit or withhold for incentive compensation payments based on performance evaluations.[4–7] This allows the plan to reward individual performance by some physicians beyond low utilization.

Behavior Modification

Certainly the purpose of any system that has an impact on compensation is geared toward modifying behavior. Even if you have chosen not to use a formal evaluation process for adjusting compensation or bonus distribution, or in those years when there is no bonus to distribute, there remains merit in its use. Most professionals are motivated to do a good job simply for its own sake but often lack sufficient feedback. A formal system for performance evaluations is designed to provide such feedback. In addition, systems that collect and disseminate data will produce what is referred to as the sentinel effect: The very fact that the organization is observing behavior will cause that behavior to change, usually in the direction the organization wants it to.

Feedback of information to physicians will allow them to examine and perhaps modify their performance based on available data. Because frequent feedback about performance has a more significant impact than an annual review, it is generally desirable to provide such feedback on a quarterly or semiannual basis unless constraints in data processing, personnel, or money require that feedback be given only annually.

Documentation of Substandard Performance

Documenting and tracking substandard performance also represents one of the elements of formal performance evaluation. Beyond the issues of discipline and sanctions (see Chapter 18), there will certainly be instances where performance is not so poor as to warrant immediate termination or probation but where improvement is clearly required. A system that provides information about utilization and nonutilization performance is an excellent vehicle for documenting needed improvements. This allows the plan to indicate clearly the need for improvement and provides the necessary documentation in the event that the plan or group feels compelled to terminate the relationship with the individual physician.

PROBLEMS WITH EVALUATION SYSTEMS

Evaluating physician performance is unique in managed health care. As mentioned earlier, traditional fee-for-service has a straightforward reward system: The more you collect, the more you are rewarded. Because that often works in opposition to the goals of managed care, different criteria are necessary.

At first, it would appear that simply reversing the economic reward would work. In other words, the less physicians utilize services, the more money they get. Unfortunately, not only does that method fail to take into account certain behaviors that have no direct impact on utilization [such as member satisfaction, participation with the quality management (QM) program, or compliance with administrative procedures], but it may also be subject to inappropriate manipulation or, worse yet, inappropriate underutilization.

Objective Criteria

The use of strictly objective criteria has recognized drawbacks. Examples of strictly objective criteria include utilization rates (e.g., hospital rates, referral rates, and ancillary testing), overall medical cost [e.g., per member per month (PMPM) cost], productivity (e.g., visits per day), and so forth. The major problem with strictly objective criteria is that they can be gamed. The two major games played with objective criteria are churning and "buffing and turfing."

Churning is the major complaint against fee-for-service medicine but can be equally prevalent in some managed care environments that rely heavily on productivity measures. Churning is simply increasing the revisit rate of existing patients more than is medically necessary. For example, it is just as easy to schedule a hypertension recheck in 4 weeks as in 8 weeks. Furthermore, a revisit is a lot easier than a new patient, so that the temptation can arise to see many revisits rather than allow the time for lengthy visits from new patients. Of course, if productivity is *not* tracked and rewarded in a closed panel system or medical group, overhead and costs will rise while access declines.

Buffing and turfing can occur in any plan with an undue emphasis on low utilization and when the compensation and reward structure for physicians is heavily weighted toward individual physicians having low utilization profiles. Buffing and turfing refers to a physician's culling sick patients out of the practice to make the utilization profiles look better. Buffing refers to a physician's making this practice appear (to the plan) to be justifiable, and turfing refers to transferring the sickest patients to other physicians for care to look like a low-utilizing provider.

This problem is not to be confused with the common excuse for failing to control utilization: "But I've got all the sick patients!" It is up to the medical director to determine whether there is validity to that. Buffing and turfing refer specifically to physicians trying to dump their high-cost patients on other physicians.

Subjective Criteria

Strictly subjective criteria are just as problematic as strictly objective criteria. Examples of strictly subjective criteria can include judgments about attitude, professionalism, demeanor, and the like. The principal problems with subjective criteria are the variability of interpretation and charges of favoritism and bias.

The very nature of subjective criteria demands variability in interpretation. Although a subjective category may be defined, performance in that category will be judged on the basis of the evaluator's opinion rather than on a set of numbers. This is certainly legitimate because presumably the manager making the judgment has a reasonably good idea of what he or she wants to see. It is still true, however, that different managers may judge the same behavior in different ways.

Charges of favoritism and bias are much more serious. If strictly subjective criteria are used, and if a negative evaluation is given to a physician, the manager may find that the physician does not accept the results, and charges of favoritism or bias may ensue. This can be of great concern if disciplinary actions are necessary and could theoretically lead to legal action against a plan.

CATEGORIES FOR EVALUATION OF PHYSICIAN PERFORMANCE

As we have seen, the use of strictly objective or subjective criteria can cause problems. It is therefore often useful to use both types of evaluation criteria in assessing physician performance. There are clearly objective items that can be measured and evaluated, items that a medical manager will consider important, such as utilization or productivity. The same is true for subjective measures, such as participation, attitude, and so forth. The real issue is to combine objective with subjective in such a way as to avoid as much as possible the disincentive aspects of concentrating too heavily on any one category. It is unlikely that any plan will use all categories discussed; rather, plan management will choose what is important to the plan's particular situation.

Categories for Evaluation in Closed Panels

This section discusses suggested categories for evaluation of physician performance in closed panels. These categories are listed in Exhibit 9–1 and are discussed below. In any individual plan, certain categories will have more or less importance, and there are surely categories that are not even mentioned here. Unlike the situation in open panels, where utilization results may have a direct economic impact on a physician, in many closed panels a physician's utilization-based performance will require increased attention during this process.

It is important that the physicians in the group buy in to the process and not feel that it is being forced upon them. It is up to medical management to decide what behavior it wishes to motivate and then to present the concept to the practicing physicians. Allowing the physicians to have input into developing the criteria against which their performance will be judged is crucial to gaining acceptance and cooperation with the program.

What follows are areas that one may wish to consider for evaluation of closed panel physician performance. A general idea of how the category is defined is also given, although before using these categories one would want to define more specifically just what aspects of behavior would be evaluated.

Exhibit 9–1 Possible Categories for Evaluation in Closed Panels

- Productivity
- Medical charting
- Dependability and efficiency
- After-hours call duty
- Medical knowledge
- Management of patient care
- Management of outside resources
- Patient relations
- Staff relations
- Attitude and leadership
- Participation

Productivity

This category looks at volume of work and efficiency. Whatever standard a plan sets, such as number of visits per week, hours worked, and so forth, would be used as the judgment criterion. One could add an element of time management as well. Productivity is discussed in Chapter 6.

Medical Charting

This would evaluate a physician's outpatient charts for legibility, timeliness, thoroughness, and compliance with whatever system is being used (e.g., chart format, face sheets, medication sheets, and so forth).

Dependability and Efficiency

This category would include arriving on time for work, sticking to the schedule, and complying with administrative aspects of the plan, such as properly using the forms.

After-Hours Call Duty

This category looks at responsiveness, appropriate use of emergency medical resources, proper documentation, ensuring continuity of care through follow-ups or transfer of care to the appropriate primary physician, and any other aspects of care delivered through the after-hours on-call mechanism.

Medical Knowledge

This evaluates the level of medical knowledge, amount of technical skill, evidence of proper medical judgment, awareness of limitations in skills and knowledge, and appropriate use of continuing medical education opportunities.

Management of Patient Care

Closely related to the category of medical knowledge, this category looks at how the basic medical skills are translated into action and how that relates to cost-effectiveness. This category would include both outpatient and inpatient care. Examples include logical and efficient plans for diagnosis and treatment, proper discharge planning, appropriate follow-up intervals, and so forth. The common thread is how patient care is handled by the physician being evaluated rather than by a consultant.

Management of Outside Resources

This category looks at a physician's use of outside resources, including consultants and ancillary services, both diagnostic and therapeutic. Evaluations of appropriateness, cost-effective use, and maintenance of continuity would be made.

Patient Relations

This category looks at a physician's ability to communicate effectively with patients, the quality of patient relations, and any concerns regarding member satisfaction. Member surveys may be conducted to obtain the opinions of members after their encounter; telephone surveys generally yield more data than mail-based surveys.

Staff Relations

This looks at a physician's ability to communicate and cooperate with other members of the medical staff, including a physician's working relationship with support staff.

Attitude and Leadership

Attitude looks at a physician's enthusiasm, interest, commitment, flexibility, responsiveness, and so forth. Although essentially this is a measure of positive attitude, one may wish to add specifics about what is considered most important in judging attitude. Leadership refers to a physician's ability to train others and to motivate and lead as well as to his or her decision and communication skills in nonmedical matters.

Participation

Closely related to attitude, participation refers specifically to participation in plan committees and meetings. This looks at attendance, contribution, and initiative in taking responsibility.

Categories for Evaluation in Open Panels

This section discusses possible categories for formal performance evaluation in open panels; again, this list is not exhaustive, and a plan would not necessarily use all the categories. These categories are much more objective than subjective, in keeping with the management structure of open panels. They are listed in Exhibit 9–2 and are discussed below.

Exhibit 9–2 Possible Categories for Evaluation in Open Panels

- Utilization
  —Hospital utilization
  —Referral utilization
  —Ancillary utilization
- Productivity and access
  —Productivity
  —Access
  —Panel size and status
- Compliance with administrative procedures
  —Cooperation with precertification and authorization requirements
  —Compliance with use of the plan network
  —Use of electronic data interchange
  —Cooperation with other plan policies and procedures
- QM
  —Participation with and results of the QM program
  —Continuing medical education
- Patient relations and member satisfaction

Utilization

Utilization is included in this section, but not in any detail. It is included only because many open panel plans that have incentive programs include utilization data as part of the total program and do not necessarily separate these data from the final incentive result. Issues such as adjustments for case mix and severity are important, and data used in medical management and practice profiling are discussed in greater detail in Chapters 18 and 19.

Hospital utilization. This could measure days per 1,000 (annualized) or could be subdivided to look at the admission rate and the average length of stay. Cost on a PMPM basis may also be tracked. The plan may include ambulatory surgery as well. Values that are either too high or too low could require additional review.

Referral utilization. One could look at referrals per member per year (PMPY), total referral costs PMPM, both, or other common measures of referral utilization, such as referrals per 100 primary encounters. Values that are either too low (e.g., fewer than 0.5 referral PMPY or less than $30 PMPY) or too high (e.g., more than 3 referrals PMPY or more than $100 PMPY) could require additional review.

Ancillary utilization. This category would measure the physician's use of laboratory, radiology, pharmacy, or whatever ancillary service the plan wished to observe. Members' use of the emergency department is often measured as well, although that may be part of hospital utilization.

Productivity and Access

Productivity. Productivity is generally measured as office visits PMPY. Too low a number (e.g., fewer than 1.5 visits PMPY) could indicate either good luck or denied access. Too high a number (e.g., more than 5) could indicate either bad luck or inefficient case management.

Access. Accessibility can be measured in several ways. One easy measure is the total number of office hours available, and the plan may wish to reward the availability of increased office hours, especially nights and weekend hours. The plan may also perform on-site office reviews and examine the appointment book of the physician to determine how long it takes to get an appointment.

Panel size and status. Some plans want to incent large panels and will therefore provide incrementally higher incentives to larger panels (up to a limit; the plan does not want to incent such large panels that access is hampered). The plan may also want to encourage physicians to keep their panels open to new members of the plan and will provide incentives for the PCPs to keep their panels in an open status. Because most plans require PCPs to keep their panels open to a set number of members (e.g., 250 members), this incentive may be used only for panels with more than the minimum required number of members.

Compliance with Administrative Policies and Procedures

In addition to clinical behavior, the plan benefits from high compliance with administrative policies and procedures.

Cooperation with precertification and authorization requirements. This measures the physician's compliance with the plan's requirements for precertification and authorization of services and is measured as a percentage. For example, 88 percent of admissions for a physician are precertified, and 95 percent of referrals are prospectively authorized. There is no value that can be too low; the scale is linear rather than bell shaped.

Compliance with use of the plan network. This measures a physician's use of the plan network, both consultant and hospital. The more a physician uses nonparticipating providers, the worse the compliance. A certain amount of background noise (e.g., from out-of-area emergencies) is to be expected, especially with point-of-service plans.

Use of electronic data interchanges. Electronic communications between the plan and the physicians improve efficiencies and timeliness. Therefore, the plan may wish to provide an incentive to practices that are linked electronically to the plan's computers for defined activities such as encounters, authorizations, claims, and reimbursement.

Cooperation with other plan policies and procedures. Beyond the policies and procedures for precertification and authorization, this measures compliance with encounter tracking, participation in meetings and committees, fee structures, and so forth. This measure may be somewhat subjective.

QM

Participation with and results of QM program. This would look at a physician's cooperation with the QM program and the results of actual audits and focused chart reviews. Failure to cooperate would result in either no points or a negative score or evaluation. Standards of care for such things as health maintenance or common problems (e.g., hypertension) would be evaluated, and a cumulative score would be developed. For example, 85 percent compliance with standards for a particular audit would yield a result equal to 85 percent of the maximum possible score.

Continuing medical education. The plan may wish to provide incentives for physicians to comply with enhanced continuing medical education programs. Although such compliance is often required for state licensure or for recredentialing (see Chapter 7), the plan may wish to incent particular forms of continuing education or may even wish to provide the programs directly to the physicians. For example, additional training in preventive care may be desired, or the plan may want to focus on defined clinical conditions.

Patient Relations and Member Satisfaction

These data are obtained from member services reports (see Chapter 24). Evaluations could include the rate at which members transfer out of the practice, the rate at which the physician asks to remove members from the practice, and complaints or grievances about the physician.

Another source for member satisfaction data is member surveys. Periodic mail or telephone surveys with a well-designed survey instrument can yield valuable information about patient satisfaction and perceived quality of service.

MEASURING THE CATEGORIES AND PRODUCING A RESULT

Although you may wish to use the above categories simply for discussion, there is utility in quantifying the results of the evaluation. For example, if you are using a formal evaluation system for allocating bonus or incentive payments, it is extremely useful to have the results of the evaluation tie directly to the amount of money that is paid out.

To facilitate measurement, it is sometimes helpful, although not required, to assign relative weights to each category. These weights would reflect the importance of that category in the overall scheme of things. For example, you may decide that medical charting is less important than cost-effective use of resources. Regardless of whether you use a weighting factor, it is quite helpful to translate the evaluation of performance in each category into a numeric value or score. For example, you may use a scale of 1 to 5 or 1 to 10. The better the performance in that category, the higher the number.

For categories in which the result depends on achieving a norm, a bell-shaped curve could be used. For example, if PCP encounters are expected to be 3.5 visits PMPY, then 5 points could be awarded for visits of 3.0 to 4.0 visits PMPY, 3 points for 1.5 to 2.9 or 4.1 to 5.0 visits PMPY, 2 points for 0.5 to 1.4 or 5.1 to 6.0 visits PMPY, and so forth. If you are using weighting factors, you would then multiply the score by the weight to achieve a numeric result. For example, if a score of 5 is given and the weight is also 5, the score would be 25. The last step is to tabulate the results. For example, if you were using an evaluation system with 11 categories, a scale of 1 to 5, and no weighting factor, the highest possible result or score would be 55.

If you are using an evaluation system for allocating bonus or adjusting annual base compensation, the numeric result would be used to calculate the amount of payout as described in the examples provided below.

Closed Panel Example

The following example illustrates the use of a formal evaluation system for allocation of bonuses in a group or closed panel plan. Assume that there are 50 physicians eligible to participate in a year-end incentive equal to $500,000. Assume also that the medical leadership has chosen to focus on the following areas of concern and with the following weights: productivity (weight, 5), utilization management and resource use (weight, 3), member satisfaction (weight, 3), and attitude and participation (weight, 2). Each category is evaluated on a scale of 1 to 5, so that the highest possible score would be 65 for any single physician [$(5 \times 5) + (5 \times 3) + (5 \times 3) + (5 \times 2) = 65$]. After all the physicians are evaluated, the total points for each physician are added together to yield a maximum number of points. In this case, assume that the grand total equals 1,250 (an average score of 25 for the 50 eligible physicians). Therefore, each point is worth $400 ($500,000 ÷ 1,250). Multiplying each physician's score by $400 results in the incentive payment; for example, a score of 50 would result in an incentive payment of $20,000. The medical leadership may also choose to pay no incentive to any physician with a score less than a certain number (e.g., lower than 15), thus slightly increasing the amount available to those who remain eligible.

Open Panel Example

How complex one makes an incentive program will be dependent on the plan's goals for the program, the level of sophistication in the physician panel, the size of the panel to be covered under the program, and the amount of money available for incentive compensation. Some plans pay incentive compensation from utilization-based risk pools (such as referral or institutional; see Chapter 8); other plans budget incentive compensation as a separate line item independent of utilization. In open panels, it is also quite useful to look at both behavior and the size of the membership base for which a physician is responsible, with greater potential rewards going not only to those physicians who demonstrate desired behavior but also to those whose panel size is large.

In a small, stable, and sophisticated individual practice association, one may use all the abovementioned categories for evaluation. In a large and heterogeneous direct contract model open panel, the focus may be more narrow. The following examples illustrate some different ways to approach an open panel.

Many physicians in private fee-for-service practice complain about the administrative burden placed on them by managed care. That complaint is partially legitimate, although if utilization is controlled the economic reward should offset the hassle factor. Nevertheless, one may agree to compensate through incentive compensation for those items that are important to the plan but do not necessarily result in a direct utilization-based economic reward (e.g., QM, compliance with administrative procedures, and member satisfaction). In this example, payment of performance-based incentive compensation is not influenced by utilization results or the status of any utilization-based risk/bonus pool. The incentive compensation is funded on a PMPM basis and as a distinct line item. Points are assigned for each category, and a minimum score (say, 50 percent of the total possible points) must be achieved for the physician to participate in the incentive compensation program.

In this example, assume that there are 180 PCPs in a direct contract open panel health maintenance organization (HMO). Because of problems with member satisfaction, it is decided to pay out incentive compensation based 40 percent on member satisfaction and 30 percent each on compliance with administrative procedures and QM. For simplicity's sake, assume that translates to 40 possible points for member satisfaction and 30 possible points each for compliance and QM. Funding is at $0.30 PMPM, and there are 60,000 members in the HMO, so there is $216,000 potentially available (60,000 × 12 × $0.30) at year end.

Member satisfaction is measured by telephone surveys of members who have seen the PCP in the past 6 months, transfer rates out of the practice, and member complaints and concerns. Compliance with administrative procedures is measured by looking at compliance with precertification requirements (measured as a percentage of hospital admissions and outpatient surgeries that are precertified), encounter form submission (measured against a statistical average, 3.2 visits PMPY for example), and compliance with the referral authorization system (measured by timeliness and completion of the referral authorization form and use of participating providers). QM is measured by compliance with standards of care set by the QM committee for both routine health maintenance and disease-specific process audits. For example, a set number of charts are audited for a fixed set of criteria; if the PCP meets the criteria 90 percent of the time, then the score would be 90 percent of the maximum number of possible points. If a PCP refuses to participate in the QM program, or if the PCP has been sanctioned by the QM committee, no participation in the incentive program is allowed.

The plan may choose to pay out only on the basis of the PMPM allocation to any individual PCP, or it may choose to pay out the entire incentive pool but only to those PCPs who are eligible to participate. In other words, if half the network qualifies, the plan must choose whether to pay out only half the incentive pool (based on the assumption that PCPs who fail to qualify increase the overhead cost to the plan because of their poor habits) or to pay out the entire incentive pool but only to half the network.

In the case of only paying out an individual PCP's allocation, the plan simply pays out the individual PCP's PMPM allocation times the total member months for a qualifying physician times the percentage of the maximum score received. For example, assume that a single PCP has 700 members and has achieved a rating of 85 percent on member satisfaction, 75 percent on compliance, and 80 percent on QM. The calculation would then be ($0.30 × 700 × 12) × [(0.4 × 0.85) + (0.3 × 0.75) + (0.3 × 0.8)] = $2,028.60.

In the situation where the entire fund is to be paid out to qualifying PCPs, the following calculations illustrate disbursement of incentive compensation. First, membership must be factored into the score. One simple method is to multiply the score by the membership base that the PCP covers; for example, if a PCP has achieved results as noted above, the total score would be (700 × 12) × [(0.4 × 0.85) + (0.3 × 0.75) + (0.3 × 0.8)] = 6,762. Next, the entire incentive fund must be divided by the total number of available points to assign a value to each point; for example, if 70 PCPs qualify to participate and the aggregate point value of those 70 PCPs is 444,500, then each point is worth ($216,000 ÷ 444,500) = $0.486. Last, each PCP has his or her individual total points multiplied by the point value; in our example that would be (6,762 × $0.486) = $3,286.33.

Some managers feel that, if a PCP has already received a substantial bonus from the utilization risk/bonus pools (in a capitated system), then incentive compensation should be reduced, and they therefore include a negative factor for bonus already received. In that way, the incentive program preferentially rewards PCPs who were good case managers but who experienced more than their share of bad luck in terms of adverse selection. This method of adjustment is not common.

CONCLUSION

Most managed care products have similar benefit designs. As the industry matures, the plans that survive will no doubt be those that motivate health care providers to provide cost-efficient service. As efficiencies standardize across plans, price competition intensifies and creates a marketplace where plans can only distinguish themselves on service. Performance evaluation in health care therefore should reward cost efficiency and high-quality service.

Formal evaluations of physician performance can and should be made in a managed care plan, and appropriate incentives can be provided. Professional behavior may be evaluated with a combination of objective and subjective criteria. Excessive emphasis on any one area must be avoided to prevent inappropriate manipulation of the system. Even in the absence of monetary rewards associated with an evaluation system, feedback regarding behavior is still a useful tool for a medical director.

Study Questions

1. Of what value are non–utilization-based incentive compensation programs for physicians in managed care?
2. Describe examples of non-utilization performance measures in open panels, and why they are important for a plan to measure.
3. Describe examples of non-utilization performance measures in closed panels, and why they are important for a plan to measure.
4. Construct a non–utilization-based incentive compensation program for a hypothetical health plan. Explain the reasons for using the selected measures, and the possible difficulties the plan may encounter in trying to administer the program.

REFERENCES AND NOTES

1. J.A. Rodeghero, "Physician Compensation in Groups and Integrated Delivery Systems," in *The Managed Health Care Handbook*, 3d ed., ed. P.R. Kongstvedt (Gaithersburg, Md.: Aspen, 1996), 147–165.
2. C.M. Cooper, Formal Physician Performance Evaluations, *Journal of Ambulatory Care Management* 13 (1980): 19–33.
3. M. McGuirk-Porell, et al., A Performance-Based Quality Evaluation System for Preferred Provider Organizations, *Quality Review Bulletin* (November 1991): 365–373.
4. N. Schlackman, Integrating Quality Assessment and Physician Incentive Payment, *Quality Review Bulletin* (August 1989): 234–237.
5. N. Schlackman, Evolution of a Quality-Based Compensation Model: The Third Generation, *American Journal of Medical Quality* (1993): 103–110.
6. J. Beloff, "AV-Med Health Plan of Florida: The Physician Incentive Bonus Plan Based on Quality of Care," in *Making Managed Healthcare Work: A Practical Guide to Strategies and Solutions*, ed. P. Boland (Gaithersburg, Md.: Aspen, 1993): 322–330.
7. C. Morain, HMOs Try To Measure (and Reward) "Doctor Quality," *Medical Economics* (6 April 1992): 206–215.

Chapter 10

Contracting and Reimbursement of Specialty Physicians

Peter R. Kongstvedt

Study Objectives

- Understand the different methods of compensating specialty care physicians (SCPs) in health plans
- Understand the variations of the most common forms of each method
- Understand the strengths and weaknesses of each method and each variation
- Understand under what circumstances a health plan would desire to use each method over the others
- Understand under what circumstances an SCP would prefer each method over the others
- Be able to create financial models of each major type of reimbursement method under differing scenarios

In previous years, some health maintenance organizations (HMOs) had difficulties contracting with specialty care physicians (SCPs).* In more recent years, the oversupply of SCPs in some markets, along with the increasing penetration of managed care organizations (MCOs), has led SCPs in those markets actively to pursue contracts with MCOs. Concomitant with that shift in attitude, many HMOs and other forms of MCOs, such as preferred provider organizations (PPOs) and even some integrated delivery systems (IDSs; see Chapter 4), have closed their panels to new SCPs and have even departicipated some SCPs with existing contracts. In that environment, MCOs find contracting for specialty services to be relatively easier than in the past. In a number of such markets, some plans have also required that any participating SCPs agree to follow established practice guidelines in addition to accepting the other terms and conditions of participation.[1]

In other markets, SCPs remain in strong financial positions or may not be overrepresented (at least not by desirable candidates), or managed care may not yet be in a strong market position. In those cases, an MCO, especially an HMO, will need to be aware of the reasons that contracting for specialty services is of high priority and of the reasons that an SCP may wish to contract with the MCO.

This chapter discusses common issues involved in SCP network development and contracting and in the reimbursement of SCPs. The reader is also referred to Chapter 13 of *The Managed Health Care Handbook*[2] for a discussion of specialty networks as organizations in their own right.

Perhaps the most obvious reason for a plan to contract with SCPs is to save money by having a financially advantageous agreement, such as a discounted fee schedule, or to lower risk for medical costs through capitation. There are other reasons in addition to obtaining financial terms. For an HMO, the issue of subordinated funds for

* For purposes of this discussion, SCPs refer not only to physician SCPs but to nonphysicians as well, such as psychologists, physical therapists, and the like. The chapter is most germane, however, to physician specialists.

uncovered liabilities is very real. Regulatory reserve requirements include calculations that are based on the number of real or expected visits to outside providers who have not signed a contract containing the National Association of Insurance Commissioners' (NAIC) no balance billing clause (see Chapter 29 for a discussion of this issue). Just as important, contractual arrangements will aid in getting and holding an SCP's attention, will help in the administration of an authorization system, will allow the plan to forecast and budget medical expenses more accurately, and will help ensure access to care for the members of the health plan.

An SCP will be acutely interested in the total volume of referrals. If the plan intends to restrict the size of the referral panel significantly (or has already done so), and if the plan has a reasonable membership base, then one can easily calculate the expected number of referrals. In addition, time really is money. Most SCPs will value a plan's ability to turn around a claim quickly. If SCPs do not understand the value of rapid claim turnaround, their office manager will. Of course, if the plan cannot turn the claim around in a reasonable amount of time (e.g., 30 days or sooner), it will have considerable difficulty in negotiating and maintaining contracts.

In tightly managed plans with well-functioning prospective authorization systems, being able to guarantee payment for authorized services for covered benefits is valuable. Elimination of uncertainty will be worth a measure of peace of mind to most SCPs. If a plan depends heavily on retrospective review and claims adjudication, however, it may not be able to guarantee payment.

Some contracts will provide a regular revenue stream for the SCP. This is most valuable in capitated arrangements but holds for other arrangements as well. Depending on the payment mechanism agreed on and the volume of work that the SCP will do, this can be a powerful incentive, especially in an overcrowded medical market or to an SCP just getting started.

An SCP may also hope to see an increase in fee-for-service (FFS) referrals. This is important only in open panel arrangements or in those closed panels that do a significant amount of FFS work. Because most physicians prefer to work with those SCPs whom they know and trust, a contractual arrangement that leads to that type of relationship will be valuable. The reverse is also true: An SCP may contract with your plan to prevent the disruption of FFS referrals or as a favor to a valued primary care physician (PCP) who has been a good source of referrals. Last, an SCP may contract simply to prevent a competitor from getting there first. There is often fierce competition among SCPs, although most physicians are reluctant to admit it.

HOW MANY SCPs?

The number of SCPs of each type with which a plan needs to contract is not an easy calculation. Many plans have between two and three times as many SCPs as PCPs, whereas some aggressive systems in the western United States have equal numbers of SCPs and PCPs. Certain specialties, such as general surgery, orthopedics, and obstetrics and gynecology, and some of the medical subspecialties (e.g., cardiology and gastroenterology) need to be adequately represented at each major hospital with which a plan contracts. Other specialties, such as neurosurgery or cardiothoracic surgery, need only be represented at those hospitals to which the plan refers members for appropriate treatment.

In one widely read article, the number of SCPs required was estimated to be between 80 and 110 per 100,000 population depending on the type of MCO, as illustrated in Table 10–1 (adjustments for Medicare and Medicaid were noted in the article).[3] There was, however, considerable variation in staffing ratios for all types of plans and all specialties. In another study, group model HMOs were used to project the number of covered lives needed for each of a variety of specialists in nonrural areas, as illustrated in Table 10–2.[4] In both these cases, the projections were based on maximum efficient use of SCPs and not on other considerations, as discussed below; therefore, they probably repre-

Table 10–1 Physician Requirements per 100,000 Population

Sector	*Overall*	*Primary Care*	*Specialty Care*
Staff/group HMO	146.4	65.9	80.5
IDS and IPA	124.4	55.9	68.5
Managed FFS	171.0	61.6	109.4
Open FFS	180.1	64.8	115.3

Source: Weiner JP. Forecasting the Effects of Health Reform on US Physician Workforce Requirements: Evidence from HMO Staffing Patterns. *JAMA*. 1994;272(3):222–230.

Table 10–2 Group Model HMO Covered Lives per Physician

Type of Practice	*Number of Enrollees*
Family practice and general internal medicine	2,250
Pediatrics	6,000
Obstetrics/Gynecology	7,000
General surgery	15,000
Anesthesiology	17,000
Radiology	20,000
Orthopedics	20,000
Mental health	20,000
Ophthalmology	25,000
Otolaryngology	35,000
Cardiology	35,000
Dermatology	35,000
Cardiovascular surgery	35,000
Gastroenterology	50,000
Neurosurgery	150,000

Source: Reprinted with permission of *The New England Journal of Medicine*, The Marketplace in Health Care Reform: The Demographic Limitations of Managed Competition, *The New England Journal of Medicine SPECIAL REPORT*, Vol. 328, p. 150, © 1993, Massachusetts Medical Society.

sent a far more draconian reduction in the need for SCPs than actually exists or is likely to exist in the United States, even in nonurban markets.

An MCO or IDS must balance between the lowest possible number of SCPs required for the purposes of medical management and a somewhat higher number of SCPs required for the purposes of access and marketing. In other words, an MCO or IDS may have a higher number of SCPs than would be required to provide specialty services in the most efficient manner to provide good access to services by members and PCPs, thus improving satisfaction and retention of both members and PCPs.

PRIMARY VERSUS SPECIALTY CARE DESIGNATION

It is not uncommon, especially in open panel HMOs and in IDSs, for the same physician to desire to be designated as both a PCP and an SCP. The usual argument is that the SCP, almost always a medical subspecialist, performs a significant amount of primary care, perhaps as much as half their practice time. In some cases, the same physician also wishes to be able to see a member for primary care and then to refer that member back to himself or herself at a later time for specialty services (i.e., get paid first to see the member as a PCP and then get paid a second time to see the same member as an SCP). It is uncommon and foolish to allow physicians to be able to authorize referrals back to themselves and get paid twice to provide care for the same member.

In some cases, a plan will make the decision based on criteria such as an objective review of a physician's practice and thereby designate the physician as a PCP or an SCP. In other cases, the plan may allow a medical subspecialist to self-designate but will prohibit that physician from being both a PCP and an SCP. It is also possible for a physician to be a PCP for his or her own panel of members but to take referrals as an SCP from other PCPs who are not associated with that physician in some way, such as in the same multispecialty group.

There is conflicting evidence on how costly SCPs are versus PCPs in overall use of medical resources to deliver similar episodes of care. Several studies support the notion that SCPs are far more costly than PCPs in managing care.[5,6] It is likely that some of this variation is caused by a different mix of cases and severity because SCPs do get sicker patients on average than PCPs.[7] There is also some evidence that, for certain chronic conditions, medical specialists are more efficient in their use of resources than PCPs.[8]

As a plan takes on a sizeable Medicare or elderly population, there may be many instances where a specialty-trained physician will function more efficiently than a PCP who does not have the same depth of training in a particular clinical area. This is especially true for certain complex conditions, such as acquired immune deficiency syndrome (AIDS), and it may be true for other chronic and complex medical conditions.

It is not at all unreasonable for a specialty-trained internist to function as a PCP, especially in an open panel type of MCO or in an IDS. As managed care increases its penetration in the health care market, and as the supply of physicians who are trained specifically as PCPs is strained, this issue will take on even greater importance.

CLOSED PANELS: IN-HOUSE AND OUTSIDE CONTRACTS

Closed panel plans, such as staff or group model HMOs (or large primary care group practices with a significant managed care practice), must carefully weigh the advantages and disadvantages of bringing an SCP in house to join the medical staff rather than contracting out for services. The need to bring an SCP in house may arise if the volume of referrals is high, if the plan is unable to obtain satisfactory contracts outside, if there are questions about the quality of care being delivered by outside SCPs and there are no good alternatives, if there is patient dissatisfaction, or if there are problems with proper utilization control.

Balanced against this are issues that may militate against the decision to bring an SCP in house. Providing adequate on-call coverage could be a problem. If there is only one of that type of SCP and cross-coverage with another in-house SCP is not possible, the SCP could burn out; if coverage previously had been provided by outside SCPs who now no longer receive referrals, they may be less than cooperative about sharing calls.

Another potential problem can arise if there is a large geographic area to cover. If the plan uses multiple hospitals covering a wide territory or if there are multiple medical centers, the SCP may not be able to provide sufficient coverage, and the volume of referrals coming back inside may decrease. Even if referrals can be tightened up on an outpatient basis, attention must be paid to emergency care, especially for surgery, obstetrics, orthopedics, and cardiology.

CREDENTIALING

Credentialing of SCPs is performed the same way as it is for PCPs. It should be noted that many MCOs require SCPs to be fully board certified or board eligible and make no exceptions. (See Chapter 7 for a discussion on credentialing.)

TYPES OF REIMBURSEMENT ARRANGEMENTS

This section discusses reimbursement of SCPs on the basis of the financial relationship between the plan and the SCPs as a whole. It is possible that a contracting entity, such as a group or a management services organization, may accept reimbursement from the plan but compensate individual physicians in a separate manner. The compensation of physicians in groups and

IDSs is discussed in Chapter 10 of *The Managed Health Care Handbook*.[9]

As illustrated in Figure 10–1, approximately 20 percent to 30 percent of HMO specialists are paid through capitation as the predominant form of reimbursement.[10,11] The majority of SCPs are paid through FFS, the rest through other mechanisms, such as salary, retainer, hourly, and so forth. Exhibit 10–1 lists some of the common (and less common) methods. The most appropriate method for use in any given situation will be predicated on the goals of the plan, the SCP, and each party's ability actually to manage within the terms of the agreement.

Charges and Discounts

The simplest arrangement to understand, although a highly unsatisfactory one, is straight FFS. The SCP sends a claim, and the plan pays it. Then why bother to contract at all? The answer is to get the SCP to agree to the NAIC sole source of payment clause (see Chapter 29). Although certainly not a preferred arrangement, occasionally it is all an MCO can get, particularly in high-cost specialties (e.g., neurosurgery) when there are no good alternatives or in small start-up plans without a significant enrollment. Paying straight charges is uncommon.

Another simple arrangement is discounted FFS. There are two variations here: a straight discount on charges, such as 20 percent; and a discount based on volume or a sliding scale. In the latter type, the degree of discount is based on an agreed-upon set of figures. For example, for an obstetrician who performs 0 to 5 deliveries per month there is a 10 percent discount, for 6 to 10 per month there is a 15 percent discount, and so forth. Many plans combine a discount arrangement with a fee maximum. The fee maximum is a fee allowance schedule (see below); the plan pays the lesser of the SCP's discounted charges or the maximum allowance.

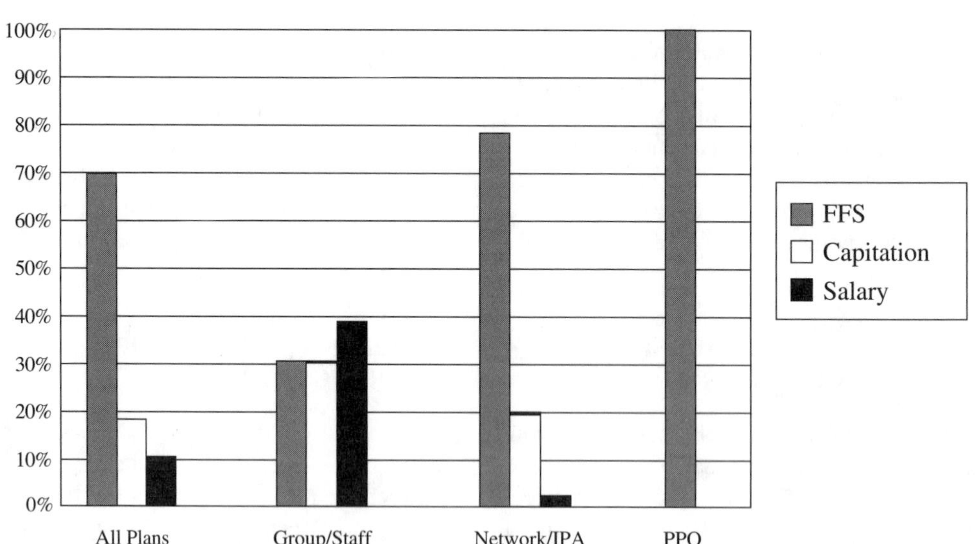

Figure 10–1 Predominant form of reimbursement for SCPs. IPA, individual practice association. *Source:* Reprinted from *Arrangements between Managed Care Plans and Physicians: Results from a 1994 Survey of Managed Care Plans*, 1995, Physician Payment Review Commission.

Exhibit 10–1 Models for Reimbursing SCPs

- Charges
- Discounts
- Fee allowances
- Global fees
- Changing schedules based on performance
- Capitation (with or without carve-outs)
- Retainer
- Hourly and salary
- Outpatient and professional diagnosis-related groups or ambulatory patient groups
- Withholds
- Penalties
- Periodic interim payments or cash advances

Relative Value Scale or Fee Allowance Schedule

The most common form of FFS is the relative value scale, such as the resource-based relative value scale (RBRVS), or a fee allowance schedule. The RBRVS is discussed in Chapter 8. The difference between a relative value scale and a fee allowance schedule is that in the former each procedure is assigned a relative value, usually on the basis of current procedural terminology revision 4 (CPT-4). That value is then multiplied by another figure (the conversion factor) to arrive at a payment. Rather than negotiate separate fees, one negotiates the conversion factor. In a fee allowance schedule, the fees for procedures (again, usually on the basis of CPT-4) are explicitly laid out, and the SCP agrees to accept those fees as full payment unless the discounted charges are less than the fee schedule, in which case the plan pays the lesser of the two. The majority of MCOs that use FFS use the RBRVS, and the majority of those set the conversion factor somewhat higher than that used by Medicare.[12]

The real utility of RBRVS or a fee allowance schedule is the avoidance of unanticipated fee hikes. If you have simply negotiated a discount on charges, the discount can easily be made up by raising fees. This may be partially offset by contractually requiring notice for any fee increases, assuming that you can and will actually spot the stray fee hike, but that still leaves you with the problem of administering a jumble of different agreements. It is far preferable to have one uniform method of handling claims.

Performance-Based FFS

Performance-based FFS for SCPs is similar to that discussed for PCPs in Chapter 8. The most common examples are through withholds and fee adjustments in an individual practice association (IPA), in which all physicians are treated the same regardless of whether they are PCPs or SCPs. A few IPAs have attempted to adjust fees based on each specialty, so-called budgeted FFS. In this approach, each specialty has a per member per month (PMPM) budget (e.g., $2.50 PMPM for cardiology), and actual costs are measured against that budget. If costs exceed budget, then fees are lowered, but only for that specialty, and vice versa if costs are better than budget. Although this is an interesting variation, it takes a highly sophisticated tracking system, sound actuarial analysis, and a large membership base to ensure with statistical integrity that utilization patterns are based on provider behavior rather than on random chance. A variation on FFS is the global fee, flat rate, or case rate. These are discussed later in this chapter.

Capitation

Although only 20 percent to 30 percent of HMOs use capitation as the predominant form of reimbursement to SCPs, a much higher percentage of plans do use capitation to reimburse individual specialties (in other words, FFS is the predominant method, but capitation is still used for some SCPs), and there may be some level of risk sharing as well. This is illustrated in Figure 10–2. It is important to note that, in the same study that produced these numbers, fully 79 per-

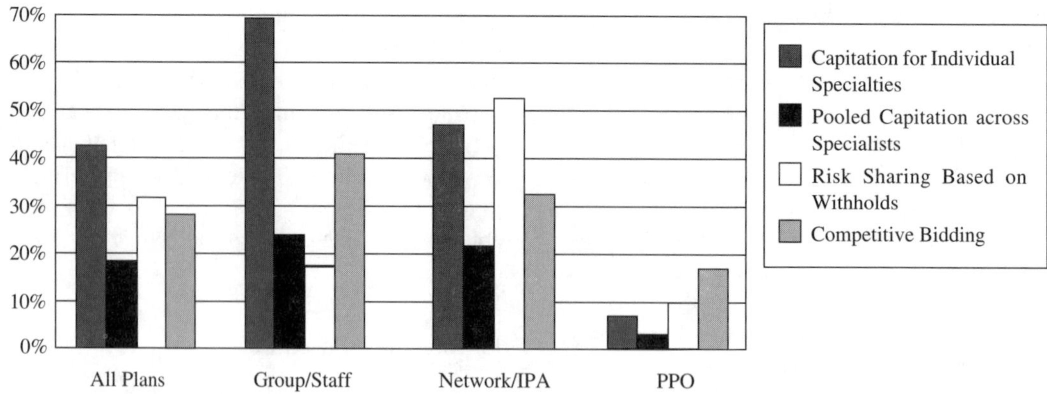

Figure 10–2 Capitation to individual specialists. *Source:* Reprinted from *Arrangements between Managed Care Plans and Physicians: Results from a 1994 Survey of Managed Care Plans*, 1995, Physician Payment Review Commission.

cent of all HMOs planned to increase the use of SCP capitation.[13]

SCP capitation is in general simpler than PCP capitation, as discussed in Chapter 8. Again, capitation refers to a fixed payment PMPM for services. The capitation payment may be adjusted for age, sex, and product type, but not as universally as is found in PCP capitation. You first must calculate the expected volume of referrals, the average cost, your ability to control utilization, and your relative negotiating strength. Your plan may have past data to guide you, or you may need to depend on an actuary or your best assumptions to derive the correct capitation amount. Please refer to Chapter 42 of *The Managed Health Care Handbook* for more discussion of capitation and utilization rates.[14]

Although theoretically the same utilization issues apply to specialty care as to primary care, the numbers involved in SCP capitation are often significantly smaller for any given specialty (even though specialty PMPM costs as a whole are usually 1.5 to 2 times higher than those for primary care). For example, PCP capitation may average $14.00 PMPM, and the capitation for neurology may be $0.55. Thus adjustments based on demographic variables become very small indeed and may not be worth the effort. Because the numbers can be smaller, an SCP requires a much larger number of members for capitation to have meaning. Where a PCP may achieve relative stability in capitation at a membership level of 400 to 600, an SCP may require triple that number or more to avoid the problem of random chance having more effect than medical management on utilization. Capitation of SCPs can be challenging, particularly if you have a lot of point-of-service (POS) benefits in your plan (see Chapter 3 for a discussion of POS).

Capitation clearly has the advantages of allowing you to budget for expected medical costs and to place a degree of risk and reward on the SCP, and the financial incentives encourage the SCP to be a more active participant in controlling utilization. If done properly, capitation can be valuable both to the SCP and to your plan, a genuine win–win situation. If done poorly, it can be a chronic headache. Figure 10–3 illustrates the current relative percentages of the various specialties that are capitated.

In FFS plans, it is probably not a good idea to capitate SCPs before capitating PCPs. If you do so to any great degree, you may find that you have obligated more money than you intended to

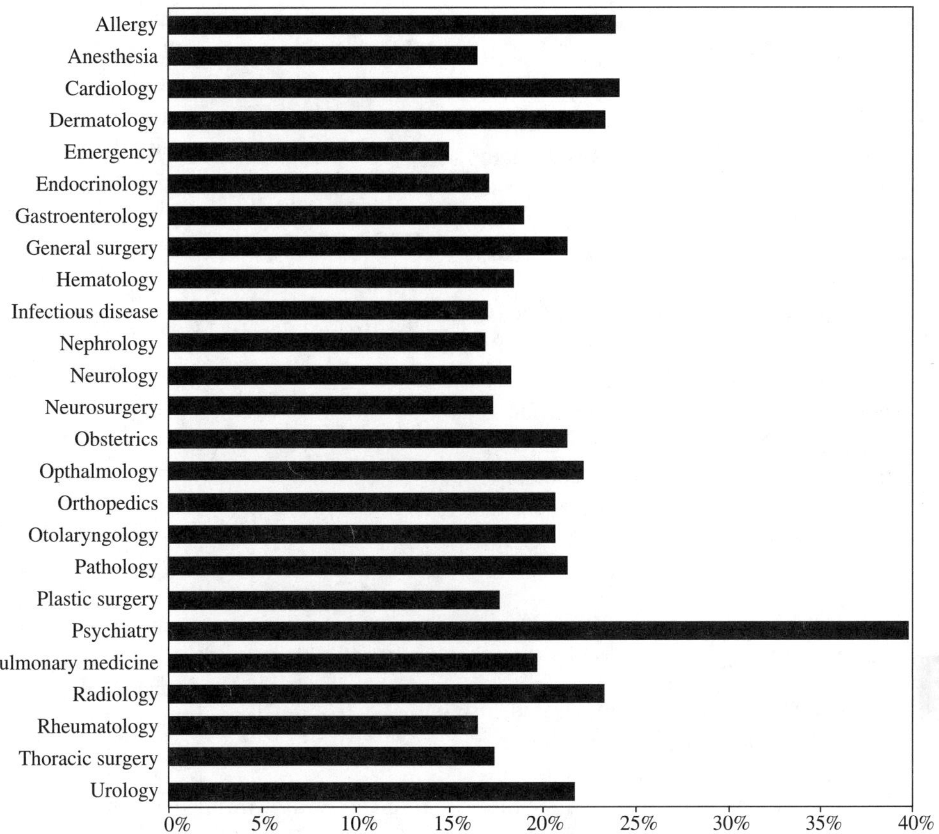

Figure 10–3 Percentage of SCPs capitated as of 1994. *Source:* Reprinted with permission from Industry Report Data as of January 1, 1994, *The InterStudy Competitive Edge*, Vol. 4, No. 1, p. 49, © 1994, InterStudy Publications.

SCP capitations, to the detriment of primary care and hospital funds. There may be exceptions to this, such as physical therapy or mental health and chemical dependency, but those are infrequent.

Organizational Models for Capitating Specialty Services

Capitating for specialty services has some complexities compared with PCP capitation. When PCPs are capitated, a member must choose a PCP and it becomes a straightforward issue of tracking that membership. Specialty capitation is different in that any given SCP will provide care to patients of multiple PCPs, and there is no requirement on the part of a member to choose an SCP.* Because of these issues, HMOs must use alternative methods to deter-

* The common exception to this last point is obstetrics and gynecology (OB/GYN). More than 71 percent of HMOs allow members to self-refer to OB/GYNs, although those OB/GYNs generally do not have the authority to refer the member to another specialist.[15] Many of those plans require all female members over the age of 12 to choose an OB/GYN, and the plan in turn capitates that OB/GYN in a fashion similar to that used for PCPs (although the capitation rate is less frequently varied by age and, of course, sex).

mine how to capitate SCPs. Some of these methods are described as follows.

Organized Groups

The easiest form of SCP capitation is through organized medical groups. In some cases, the group is a multispecialty group, inclusive of primary and specialty care. In that case, it is assumed that any member assigned to a PCP in that group will likewise be assigned to the SCPs in the group.

Organized single-specialty groups are also good candidates for capitation. If the group is large enough, then the group may be capitated for the entire network. If it is not large enough to cover the entire medical service area, then the group may be capitated for that portion of the geographic medical service area that it can cover.

Geographic Distribution

Geographic distribution is closely related to the way an organized medical group is capitated. The reason to discuss it separately is that it involves the same principle applied to a smaller group. In essence, a small (e.g., two or three) physician specialty group accepts capitation for all relevant specialty services in a defined portion of the medical service area but not the entire service area. For example, a group of general surgeons might be capitated to cover all services rendered at a single hospital. In an urban area, a capitated SCP might cover all PCP practices located in a particular set of ZIP codes. Because it is not uncommon for PCP practices (or SCP practices, for that matter) to have multiple locations, assignment is based on whatever office is considered the physician's principal office.

Specialty IPAs

Specialty-specific IPAs are not common, but the recent increase in vertical integration activities (such as physician–hospital organizations) has led to an increase in interest in this form of specialty capitation. The specialty IPA operates like a standard IPA, as described in Chapter 8. The specialty IPA accepts capitation from the HMO but usually pays FFS to the participating specialists. Capitation of individual SCPs within the specialty IPA is certainly possible but is rarely seen because specialty IPAs are often created to preserve the opportunity for multiple, unrelated SCPs to participate with aggressive HMOs. Whether specialty IPAs will remain viable is unknown.

Disease Management Companies

A new variation on single group capitation is capitation for single specialty services to a specialty corporation (e.g., a vendor that specializes in cancer services or cardiac care). The corporation employs physicians and support staff and provides facilities and ancillary services. The corporation is then responsible for providing all specialty services within the HMO's medical service area. This approach is best suited to specialty care that is not usually associated with emergencies, unless the vendor's employed physicians are on staff at all the HMO's participating hospitals.

Single Specialty Management or Specialty Network Manager

This method is uncommon but may increase as managed care experiments with different methods of capitating specialty services. It involves the HMO contracting with one single entity to provide all services within a single specialty, but that entity does not actually provide all the services. There are two basic approaches.

In one approach, an HMO capitates a single specialist (i.e., an individual physician) to manage all services in that specialty for all HMO members, even though the SCP cannot personally provide the services. This contracted SCP, the specialty network manager, must then subcontract with other specialists to provide services throughout the medical service area. The specialty network manager either makes or loses money, depending on how efficiently specialty services are managed. The specialty network manager may subcapitate with other SCPs if that is allowed by the state insurance department (many states will not allow a provider to capitate another provider; see Chapter 28), or may pay FFS. In any event, the primary SCP acts like a second gatekeeper in that PCPs need to work through the primary SCP to access specialty care for members. Sometimes the primary SCP receives the full capitation payment and must pay the other SCPs directly, or the HMO may administer the claims payments and provide the accounting and reporting for the primary contract holder. In fact, the HMO may wish to do so to track performance on a real-time basis as well as to protect members from possible nonpayment of claims by the primary contract holder.

In the other approach, an HMO contracts with a single institution for single specialty services (e.g., the HMO contracts with a local university faculty practice plan for all cardiology services). The contracted institution is then responsible to arrange for specialty services that it cannot provide itself. The primary specialty contract holder receives the capitation payment and must then administer payment to subcontractors. In some cases, the administrative cost to the primary contractor may be greater than the total capitation payment because it is often a manual process.

By PCP Choice

A theoretically interesting (although seldom used) method of capitating SCPs is through the mechanism of PCP choice. This model requires each PCP to choose which SCP from the applicable specialties will be used on an exclusive basis. The presence of choice means that multiple SCPs have agreed to a capitation rate but that no single SCP has exclusive rights. The plan is then required to track the members assigned to those SCPs by virtue of being on the PCP's panels and to pay the SCP capitation based on that. Although this is interesting and has great logic and appeal, most HMO management information systems are not capable of handling it, and the administrative headache would be great.

COMMON PROBLEMS WITH SPECIALTY CAPITATION

There are some common problems that need to be addressed before you capitate SCPs. If you fail to explore these issues, you may find yourself in the position of having to live with a yearlong arrangement that is to your disadvantage.

The pressure to capitate frequently comes as a result of uncontrolled utilization. Referrals are high, expenses are out of control, and there is high negative variance to budget. The pressure to capitate is to prevent costs from going even higher and to bring some predictability to medical expenses. This is usually the wrong time to capitate. Be assured that the SCP knows exactly how much you have been paying and will not eagerly agree to a capitation rate that amounts to a substantial discount, unless the plan (and the PCPs) is willing to change SCPs. It is far preferable to control utilization before negotiating a capitation rate. If you do not, you may be locked into the higher rate for at least a year. Of course, if the SCP, not the PCP, is the cause of inappropriately high utilization, then you really should look for a new SCP.

Another common problem is being able to control the flow of referrals. It is easy to assume that, once you cut a deal with an SCP, all you need to do is notify the PCPs and/or members and your problems are solved. This is not so. Disrupting old referral patterns is tough, and you may find that you do not have the system capabilities to respond proactively to referrals outside the capitated system. Furthermore, your capitated SCP may not be able to provide adequate geographic or emergency coverage. When referrals go outside your capitated system, you are essentially paying for them twice. This problem virtually defines a POS plan, which is why capitating SCPs in a POS plan is problematic.

One possible approach to the geographic coverage problem is to capitate only for an appropriate geographic primary care base. This balkanization of the specialty base frequently is more acceptable, unless the capitating specialty group has wide coverage.

Capitation may actually serve to increase utilization. If the PCPs who are controlling the referrals, and perhaps even the medical director of the plan, see capitation as putting a lid on expenses, there is far less pressure to control utilization because it appears that the service costs the same regardless of use; you could almost say that it is free! If you fail to control utilization of capitated services, you will have a most unpleasant surprise when the contract comes up for renegotiation. Most SCPs will keep track of what they would have made in FFS equivalents. If you have failed to control utilization, the capitation rate may be equivalent to an unacceptable discount on charges. You will either have to give in, find a new SCP, or hang tough. In each of those cases, someone loses.

The other problem with high levels of SCP utilization is the increase in other forms of utilization as well. As noted earlier, there is evidence that at least for many routine types of conditions SCPs use more resources than PCPs. Increases in institutional and ancillary services may follow increases in SCP referrals.

The last major problem encountered in capitation is the issue of carve-outs. A carve-out is a particular service that the SCP does not include in the capitation rate. For example, ophthalmologists may capitate for all services except cataract extractions, for which they will give you a 25 percent discount on charges. The problem here is that you may find yourself with an unexplainably high rate of cataract extractions. If the service is one for which only the SCP can reasonably judge the need, and that service is a carve-out, you have a potential problem. In all fairness, it is unlikely that you will be the victim of outright fraud, but it still makes for some uneasiness.

A variation of the carve-out problem arises when the SCP cannot or will not handle all the services. If you capitate for all services but the SCP refers out for the delivery of some of those services, you may wish to consider deducting those costs from the capitation payment. There are no consistent guidelines here. If the service is one that the SCP truly cannot perform (e.g., an ophthalmologist who does not do retinal surgery), then you can probably budget properly and not roll that expense into the capitation rate, thereby avoiding having to adjust the rate frequently and pressuring the SCP (perhaps inappropriately) not to refer cases. On the other hand, if the SCP can perform the service but simply does not (e.g., an ophthalmologist who is never available on Wednesday afternoons), then it is appropriate to deduct those expenses from the capitation payment. If you intend to do so, you must be clear about your intentions from the start and place appropriate language in the contract.

OTHER FORMS OF SPECIALTY PHYSICIAN REIMBURSEMENT

Retainer

A retainer is identical to what is commonly used with law firms. You simply pay a set amount to an SCP every month and reconcile at periodic intervals on the basis of actual utilization, either as a prenegotiated fee schedule or on some other objective measure. This ensures availability of the SCP to members and provides for the steady income desired by the SCP while still allowing payment on the basis of actual utilization. One issue to address early is whether the reconciliation goes both ways or whether it only goes up. That issue surfaces more often than one would expect.

Hourly and Salary

Just as it sounds, with hourly and salary arrangements the plan pays an SCP an hourly rate or salary for performing services. In essence, you are buying block time. This works to your advantage if you contract with an already busy SCP because there will be little incentive for him or her to stretch out sessions. This type of arrangement is common in emergency departments or other settings when a physician needs to be available for a defined time period. This also works if you need to buy on-call coverage to back up an in-house SCP. Hourly and salary arrangements lend themselves more to closed panel than open panel plans.

Case Rate, Global Fee, or Flat Rate for Procedures

Case rates, global fees, or flat rates are single fees that are paid for a procedure, and the fee is the same regardless of how much or how little time and effort are spent. For example, many plans use the same flat rate for either a vaginal delivery or a cesarean section, thereby eliminating any financial incentive to perform one or the other; this has been associated with a decrease in the cesarean section rate, although there may be other factors affecting this rate as well.[16]

Related to the flat rate is the global fee. A global fee is a flat rate that encompasses more than a single type of service. For example, a global fee for surgery may include all preoperative and postoperative care as well as one or two follow-up office visits. A global fee for obstetrics may include all prenatal and postnatal care.

Global fees must be carefully defined as to what they include and what may be billed outside them. For example, if ultrasound is billed outside the global fee for a delivery, you will need to monitor its use to determine whether any providers are using (and billing for) an abnormally high number of ultrasounds per case.

Bundled Case Rates or Package Pricing

Bundled case rates refer to a reimbursement that combines both the institutional and the professional charges into a single payment. For example, a plan may negotiate a bundled case rate of $20,000 for cardiac bypass surgery. That fee covers the charges from the hospital, the surgeon, the pump technician, and the anesthesiologist as well as all preoperative and postoperative care. Bundled case rates sometimes have outlier provisions for cases that become catastrophic and grossly exceed expected utilization.

Diagnosis-Related Groups and Ambulatory Patient Groups

These are important topics for hospital reimbursement but currently have limited utility in SCP reimbursement other than through bundled case rates, as discussed above. Further discussion of these two methods is found in Chapter 11.

Periodic Interim Payments and Cash Advances

Occasionally, a plan may use periodic interim payments (PIPs) or cash advances with SCPs. In the case of PIPs, the plan advances the provider a set amount of cash equivalent to a defined time period's expected reimbursable charges. As claims come in from that SCP, the claims are taken against the PIP, but the PIP is routinely replenished. In this way, the SCP gets a positive cash flow as well as the use of the plan's money interest free. Cash advances are simply that: The plan advances the provider a set amount of cash and then carries it as a receivable on the books. In the event that the relationship between the SCP and the plan terminates, the final claims are taken against the cash advance.

Neither of these techniques can be recommended for routine use. In either case, the advanced cash may not be treated as a liability by the SCP but rather simply as a payment, which makes it difficult to recover the funds. Capitation will accomplish much of what a PIP is intended to accomplish and is a preferred method. It is possible that in a plan with a heavy POS enrollment this method may be employed, but even then it is probably not necessary.

RISK/BONUS ARRANGEMENTS

In addition to whatever reimbursement arrangement you make with an SCP, there are times when it is mutually advantageous to add an element of risk and reward. This is almost always done in the context of utilization but could conceivably be tied to other objectives as well.

These types of arrangements are best suited to those specialties in which the SCPs themselves control a major aspect of utilization and in which there is a sufficient volume of referrals to rule out random chance playing too large a role in the results. Risk and reward arrangements are far easier to do in a pure HMO environment than in a PPO (where they may not be allowed by state regulations) or a POS plan.

In setting risk and reward levels, keep in mind that you do not want to make the risk or reward so great that it has the potential of having a serious negative impact on clinical decision making. It is better policy to devise a reimbursement mechanism that fairly compensates an SCP up front for appropriate and judicious use of clinical resources and then sets a risk or bonus level that, while still being attention getting, is not potentially seriously injurious to the fiscal health of the SCP. You do not want to put the SCP, the plan member, or yourself in the position of having economics override proper medical care. What you do want is a risk or bonus arrangement that will help focus the attention of the SCP on controlling unnecessary utilization. Also, as noted in Chapter 8 regarding PCP risk/bonus arrangements, a plan with a Medicare risk contract must be aware of the possible limitations on the total amount of risk to which a physician may be subject without requiring the plan to undertake detailed member surveys.[17]

Set Targets

There are a number of objective criteria that one can use in setting targets for risk/bonus arrangements. A frequent one is average length of stay; a variation would be total bed days per 1,000 members (e.g., all surgical bed days per 1,000 members for the total plan membership, or whatever geographic base you choose).

Another possibility is PMPM cost. You need to define carefully the cost area, such as professional, hospital, all inclusive, and so on. If you have the systems capabilities to track accurately, this method has the advantage of being tied more directly to the bottom line of your plan.

Another method is to look at a particular medical expense as a percentage of premium revenue. This is less useful because, although it ties directly to your plan's margin, it can lead to disputes that are based on your premium rates and yield.

Avoid setting targets for productivity. If you set a risk or bonus on the basis of seeing a certain number of patients per hour or any of the other usual FFS incentives, you could have the problem of churning.

Define the Risk or Bonus

You must define the amount of payment that will be at risk or the amount that will potentially be available for bonus. For example, in a capitation situation it may be 10 percent or 20 percent of the total capitation payments for the year (in whole dollars). Next you must choose between a straight bonus arrangement for exceeding goals or a risk/bonus band in which the SCP is at risk for failing to meet goals and may achieve a bonus for exceeding them (in other words, a withhold on payment, possibly combined with a bonus plan).

After you have set the goals and amount of risk and reward, determine the spread of bonus payments. For example, achieving a 2 percent reduction in length of stay yields a 1 percent bonus up to a maximum of 10 percent of the total payments for the year. Be as specific as possible to avoid disputes later, and be absolutely sure that you can accurately track whatever objectives you set.

A simple warning here: Be sure that you have done a financial model of the possible outcomes of a bonus arrangement. You do not want to set up an arrangement where the bonus negates any savings achieved from meeting the goals. If the bonus will be paid simply for meeting goals and you have included those goals in your budget, be sure to include the bonus in your budget and reported medical benefit expenses as well. This should be obvious, but occasionally it is overlooked.

A frequently encountered criticism of bonus arrangements is that you are paying a provider to deliver reduced (i.e., inferior) care. This should simply not be the case. You are sharing the savings that high-quality, cost-effective medical care produces; furthermore, any providers caught trying to line their pockets by delivering inferior care will be terminated from participation in your plan. It is the SCP's responsibility to provide high-quality care. It is your responsibility to make sure that the SCP is properly reimbursed and to monitor the quality of care delivered.

NON–UTILIZATION-BASED INCENTIVE COMPENSATION

Some MCOs may wish to consider non–utilization-based incentive compensation. Described in detail in Chapter 9, this is an incentive program that rewards SCPs based on factors other than utilization, although it is certainly possible to combine a utilization-based and non–utilization-based program. Typical factors would include adherence to practice protocols or clinical pathways (see *The Managed Health Care Handbook*, Chapter 19), member satisfaction (see Chapters 9 and 24), PCP satisfaction, and other forms of outcomes measures.

PROHIBITION OF SUBAUTHORIZATIONS

Of all the contractual terms (see Chapter 30), in a tightly controlled managed care plan with a primary care authorization system there must be a clear understanding that the SCP is not allowed to authorize services for a member but must obtain authorization from the PCP or the health plan. This includes hospitalizations, ancillary testing, and referrals to other SCPs.

There are some common occurrences of this problem. One example is the SCP who owns an expensive piece of diagnostic equipment; although there may be no genuine plan to do unnecessary testing, there is still a subtle pressure to use the machine and generate some revenue from it. If such self-authorizations are prohibited contractually, either the SCP will be forced to contact the PCP and discuss the need for the test, or the SCP will not be allowed to bill for the test (remember the sole source of payment clause).

Another common occurrence is the SCP choosing to hospitalize the member. Although hospitalization may be appropriate, your ability to manage the case is severely hampered if you do not know about it until it is all over. In most managed health care plans, hospitalization requires either preadmission review by the plan's utilization management department or authorization from the PCP and health plan. It is crucial to ensure that you will be able to manage hospital cases concurrently, and that means preadmission notification and authorization. See Chapter 13 for further discussion about utilization management.

The last common occurrence is the problem of referrals to other SCPs. If the plan allows an SCP to refer to another SCP without obtaining authorization, the member can start getting shunted from one SCP to another like a game of medical air hockey. Not only is that an inefficient and expensive way to deliver medical care, but the lack of continuity has implications for the quality of care as well.

How tightly you enforce this will vary in certain circumstances. For example, an obstetrician may only need to notify the plan when a member is admitted for a delivery and would not require PCP preauthorization at all. If an SCP is capitated for all office services, that capitation may include office procedures and tests as well (e.g., office radiology for an orthopedist). Even without capitation, you may decide to allow selected SCPs to perform certain studies because it is simply necessary for the delivery of care (e.g., allowing neurologists to order magnetic resonance imaging). These exceptions must be carefully thought through, and reimbursement for them should not encourage overutilization.

The point of this is not to make a system so rigid that it becomes impossible to deliver proper care but to have a system that allows you to manage the health care that is delivered by timely intervention when it is appropriate and to direct the care in the most cost-effective way possible. It is certainly possible that a tightly run plan could allow SCPs to function as managing physicians in certain circumstances (e.g., for active AIDS cases), but that is an analysis that each plan must make for itself.

CONCLUSION

Medical care delivered by SCPs is a crucial element in the cost and quality of health care. The roles of the SCP are continuing to evolve in managed care, as are the organizational structures that SCPs are using to contract for services. Reimbursement arrangements and contracts are tools that codify and clarify the responsibilities of each party to the other. They will not solve your problems and will not take the place of good management. Remember: A 20 percent discount will not make up for poor utilization control, and nothing will make up for poor quality of care.

Study Questions

1. Describe the key advantages and disadvantages of capitation and FFS when contracting for specialty services in an open panel HMO.
2. Describe key differences between open panel and closed panel HMOs when contracting for specialty services.
3. Which specialties are relatively easier than others to capitate? Why?
4. How might an open panel HMO capitate specialty services when the specialists are not organized into large groups?
5. When would a closed panel HMO choose to bring a specialty in-house? When would it choose to capitate with private specialists? When would it choose to pay FFS?

REFERENCES AND NOTES

1. Atlantic Information Services, Inc., *Provider Contracting and Capitation* (Washington, D.C.: Atlantic Information Services, 1993).
2. A. Fine, "Specialty Networks from the Specialist's View," in *The Managed Health Care Handbook*, 3d ed., ed. P.R. Kongstvedt (Gaithersburg, Md.: Aspen, 1996), 191–201.
3. J.P. Weiner, Forecasting the Effects of Health Reform on U.S. Physician Workforce Requirements: Evidence from HMO Staffing Patterns, *Journal of the American Medical Association* 272 (1994): 222–230.
4. R. Kronick, et al., The Marketplace in Health Care Reform: The Demographic Limitations of Managed Competition, *New England Journal of Medicine* 328 (1993): 148–152.
5. S. Schroeder and L. Sandy, Specialty Distribution of U.S. Physicians—The Invisible Driver of Health Care Costs, *New England Journal of Medicine* 328 (1993): 928–933.
6. S. Greenfield, et al., Variations in Resource Utilization among Medical Specialties and Systems of Care: Results from the Medical Outcomes Study, *Journal of the American Medical Association* 267 (1992): 1624–1632.
7. R. Kravitz, Differences in the Mix of Patients among Medical Specialties and Systems of Care: Results from the Medical Outcomes Study, *Journal of the American Medical Association* 267 (1992): 1617–1623.
8. M. May, Resource Utilization in Treatment of Diabetic Ketoacidosis in Adults, *American Journal of Medical Sciences* 306 (1993): 287–294.
9. J.A. Rodeghero, "Physician Compensation in Groups and Integrated Delivery Systems," in *The Managed Health Care Handbook*, 3d ed., ed. P.R. Kongstvedt (Gaithersburg, Md.: Aspen, 1996), 147–165.
10. M. Gold, et al., *Arrangements between Managed Care Plans and Physicians: Results from a 1994 Survey of Managed Care Plans* (Washington, D.C.: Physician Payment Review Commission, 1995).
11. InterStudy, *The Interstudy Competitive Edge* (St. Paul, Minn.: InterStudy, 1994).
12. Gold, et al., *Arrangements between Managed Care Plans and Physicians.*
13. Gold, et al., *Arrangements between Managed Care Plans and Physicians.*

14. S.M. Cigich, "Actuarial Services in an Integrated Delivery System," in *The Managed Health Care Handbook*, 3d ed., ed. P.R. Kongstvedt (Gaithersburg, Md.: Aspen, 1996), 659–666.
15. Group Health Association of America (GHAA), *HMO Performance Survey* (Washington, D.C.: GHAA, 1994).
16. E.B. Keeler and M. Brodie, Economic Incentives in the Choice between Vaginal Delivery and Cesarean Section, *Milbank Memorial Fund Quarterly* 71 (1993): 365–404.
17. *Federal Register* 57 (14 December 1992): 59024–59040.

SUGGESTED READING

Palsbo, S.E. and Sullivan, C.B. 1993. *The Recruitment Experience of Health Maintenance Organizations for Primary Care Physicians: Final Report.* Washington, D.C.: Health Resources and Services Administration.

Pauly, M.V., Eisenberg, J.M., and Radany, M.H. 1992. *Paying Physicians: Options for Controlling Cost, Volume, and Intensity of Services.* Ann Arbor, Mich.: Health Administration Press.

Chapter 11

Negotiating and Contracting with Hospitals and Institutions

Peter R. Kongstvedt

Study Objectives

- Understand the basic approaches to contracting for hospital services
- Understand the basic forms of reimbursement for hospital services
- Understand what circumstances make certain forms of reimbursement more favorable than other forms
- Understand critical differences between inpatient and outpatient services and how that relates to contracting

INTRODUCTION

Hospital contracting is one of the most important tasks that an executive director and other appropriate plan managers face. Hospital executives likewise need a thorough understanding of the issues involved in contracting with managed care organizations (MCOs). Although there are a few states (e.g., Maryland) that are so heavily regulated that there is little or no latitude allowed in reimbursing hospitals, in general this represents an area of tremendous potential for creativity.

REASONS TO CONTRACT

The reasons for a plan to contract with hospitals are obvious and much the same as those for contracting with consultants; this is discussed in Chapter 10 and will not be repeated here. It should be noted that, because of the amount of money involved with hospital care, the issues take on greater importance for any given contract. This is particularly true for both required reserves for uncovered liabilities (see Chapter 22) and the impact of favorable pricing. In some cases, failure to have adequate contracts with hospitals will lead to a rejection of state licensure for an MCO or federal qualification for health maintenance organizations (HMOs) and competitive medical plans (see Chapter 54 of *The Managed Health Care Handbook* for a discussion of federal qualification).[1]

The reasons for a hospital to agree to a contractual arrangement are likewise similar to those of a consultant. The hospital will be acutely interested in improving, or in some cases holding onto, a volume of inpatient days and outpatient procedures. This becomes crucial if the hospital is suffering from a low occupancy rate. A hospital will also be interested in a plan's ability to turn around a claim; the time value of money is even more important to a hospital than to a consultant because the amount of money is so much greater and because the public sector (i.e., fee-for-service Medicare and Medicaid) is a notoriously slow payer.

Guaranteed payments for authorized services for covered benefits will also be valuable, especially if the hospital has been absorbing losses as a result of denial of payments from a retrospective review process. As with consultants in an open panel, a hospital may hope to see an increase in regular fee-for-service patients; because physicians prefer not to perform rounds in multiple hospitals, this is a genuine possibility.

Last, a hospital will contract to shut out a competitor. Competition among hospitals is usually much more open than competition among physicians and is usually a regional issue; a hospital will have a reasonably defined service area from which most of its admissions come. If an MCO is willing to limit the number of participating hospitals in each service area, this becomes a strong negotiating point.

HOSPITAL NETWORK DEVELOPMENT

Selecting Hospitals

Selecting which hospitals for an MCO to approach is done by balancing a number of variables. In a small or rural market there may be a limited choice. In most cases, though, there will be some latitude. Before beginning the selection process, plan managers must first decide how much they are willing to limit the choices in the plan.

Generally, the more the MCO is willing to limit the number of participating hospitals, the greater its leverage in negotiating. Limiting the number has potential disadvantages as well. If the MCO strictly limits itself to just a few hospitals, it may have a competitive disadvantage in the marketplace because prospective members and accounts often use hospitals as a means of judging whether to join an MCO; therefore, if the plan fails to include a sufficient selection of hospitals, it may see disappointing marketing results. On the other hand, if the MCO refuses to limit the number of hospitals, it will have considerable difficulty in extracting favorable agreements and in managing utilization.

A certain number of hospitals will be required to cover a medical service area effectively. In some small communities, a single hospital may be able to serve the entire population, but that is rare. It is important to map out the hospital locations relative to the defined service area and to look for overlap among competing hospitals.

Selecting which hospitals to approach first in a service area is a combination of hard data—such as occupancy, cost, and services offered—and judgment about the hospital's willingness to negotiate and the perception of the public and physician community about the hospital's quality. It does little good for an MCO to make an agreement with a hospital that is perceived as inferior. Likewise, it is less than optimal to contract with a hospital that does not do high-volume obstetrics if there is a regional competitor that does because the plan will be less attractive to young families.

In some instances, the presence of a well-run integrated delivery system (IDS; see Chapter 4) will make a particular hospital attractive. This is most likely to be the case if a plan is a new entrant to the market, is introducing a new service line, or has been unable to create an attractive network from a marketing standpoint. The IDS may be in a position to accept considerable financial risk, such as total capitation, which may be desirable to an HMO that wishes to limit financial risk.

If the hospital is a sponsor or joint venture partner in an MCO, the choice factors become rather clear. If a hospital is an enthusiastic supporter of the MCO, or if there is a long history of a good working relationship, that should also be taken into consideration.

Finally, consolidation in the hospital industry has been occurring at a rapid pace. In many cases, this leads to the creation of a system with multiple hospitals. The MCO is then in a position of negotiating a broader contract with the system for services at multiple sites. The system may also demand a higher level of preference or even exclusivity in exchange for favorable terms. Although consolidation does not always bring value, the potential of cost reduction and rationalization of clinical services may allow the new system to provide care far more efficiently than individual hospitals, thus allowing for a considerable price advantage.

General Negotiating Strategy

An MCO's ability to negotiate successfully with the hospitals in its area will depend on a number of things. Chief among them are the personal abilities of the negotiator, the size of the plan, the MCO's ability actually to shift patient care, and the track record of the MCO in being able to deliver what was promised. A new start-up operation has considerably less clout than an existing large plan. If the new start-up can demonstrate genuine potential for significant growth, that may help offset the weakness of having little to offer but promises.

Setting an overall strategy is important to the ultimate success of an MCO's hospital network. It is certainly possible to approach the project of hospital negotiations by using the managerial equivalent of Brownian motion, but the end results could be disappointing.

The strategic plan should address both regional and planwide issues. There may be one set of criteria for primary care services in a service area and a different set for tertiary services. After plan managers have selected the hospital they wish to approach first, they must then select the hospitals to approach next if the initial hospital either is unwilling to come to agreement or offers too little to make the agreement worth the risk. The plan managers may find that they will want to approach some hospitals for tertiary services on a much wider regional basis than for primary care. If the MCO does not intend significantly to restrict its hospital panel, then it should first select those hospitals with the most marketing value.

Data Development

After selecting individual hospitals to approach, make a worksheet for each and one for the entire service area as well. Estimate the hospital's occupancy rate (these data may be available from the local or state health department or the American Hospital Association[2]) and operating margin (this, too, may be available at the health department or may be published in the hospital's annual report).

Estimate the total number of bed days the plan currently has in the hospital. If the plan is a new start-up, estimate the total number of bed days the medical director believes can be controlled and over what time span (be honest here). Estimate as well the number of bed days the plan can realistically shift into the hospital or, if necessary, away from the hospital. This estimate will be affected by geographic accessibility and acceptability of such case shifting by members and physicians. It is helpful to both parties if the bed days are categorized at least into broad categories such as medical–surgical, obstetrics, intensive care, mental health, and so forth.

Last, calculate the whole dollars associated with all the above estimations or facts. Plan management will want to know what whole dollar amount the plan represents to the hospital now and in the future. Calculate what happens if utilization shifts into and out of the hospital and what percentage of the hospital's gross income that would represent.

Goal Setting

Markets with Low Managed Care Penetration

In markets that do not have high levels of managed care penetration (e.g., where managed care, primarily HMOs, accounts for less than 30 percent of *total* health care), it is axiomatic that medical services are bought at the margin. As with purchasing an automobile or furniture, it is unusual to pay the sticker price. This goes for primary care, consultant care, and, most important, hospital services. If a hospital ward is fully staffed but running at less than full occupancy, the marginal cost of filling another bed on that ward is minor compared with the revenue. It is unlikely that the hospital will call in extra nurses, hire extra support staff, buy new equipment, or take out more insurance to care for a 10 percent increase in bed days; those costs are relatively fixed. The marginal costs (such as laundry, food, drugs and supplies, and the like) are less than the fixed overhead.

Because of this, a hospital has room to maneuver in negotiating. This does not mean that you can expect a hospital to reduce its charges by half (unless its charges are grossly inflated to begin with), but you can reasonably expect effective discounts of 20 percent to 30 percent if you are able to deliver sufficient volume. Certain for-profit hospitals are actually managed to show a profit at less than 50 percent occupancy. In those cases, even greater discounts may sometimes be obtained because much of the added revenue to the hospital goes right to the bottom line. Conversely, such high-margin hospitals may feel little pressure to increase their occupancy if they have a decent market share and may be difficult to deal with because they hope to freeze you out.

After you have developed the worksheet referred to above, take your assumptions regarding how much you can shift into the hospital and apply the desired discount. If a hospital has a low occupancy rate, or if it has less than a full occupancy rate but is enjoying healthy profit margins (or reserves if it is not for profit), and you can deliver or remove a significant volume of patients, you may be able to achieve a good discount. If the hospital is running above 90 percent occupancy, your prospects of substantial savings are not as good.

Include outpatient procedures in the calculations. It is increasingly common to find that outpatient procedures, if paid on a discounted charges basis, are actually more expensive than identical procedures done in an inpatient setting. Hospital managers have not been idly watching utilization shift to the outpatient department; they have adjusted charges to enhance revenues.

Markets with High Managed Care Penetration

In markets with high levels of managed care penetration, the dynamics may look considerably different. In those markets the margin has been reduced, and few payers are paying full charges. Public sector fee-for-service reimbursement (i.e., Medicare and Medicaid) certainly does not pay full charges, and if managed care accounts for most of the rest, as well as a considerable portion of the public sector, then charges become relatively meaningless, and a hospital's ability to absorb payment differentials is diminished. In such markets, MCOs, especially HMOs, are most likely to use a reimbursement system that is unrelated to charges (see below). The MCO and the hospital must then balance the actual cost to provide the service (if the hospital has a cost accounting system, which is not always the case), the ability to provide volume to offset fixed costs, the market power and desirability of the parties, and the cost of not doing business together.

Markets with high managed care penetration also tend to have high levels of hospital consolidation. This changes the dynamic as noted earlier. In addition, the levels of sophistication increase on all sides. More creativity comes into play, and the MCOs and hospitals find themselves operating more as business partners (or at least close acquaintances) and less as arm's length contracting entities. Although price and clinical services are still the most important factors, the ability of the parties to operate together becomes of greater importance. The ability to interface administratively, the ability to resolve operating problems, and similar factors play heavily in the negotiating strategy.

Last, in such markets there is often a desire on the part of the hospitals, through their IDS, to accept greater amounts of risk for medical expenses because there is the perception that there is greater margin in that form of reimbursement. Paradoxically, large and successful HMOs may have little incentive to do so because it could erode their margin as well as increase the possibility of failure if the IDS is unable to manage the risk. These issues often become key negotiating points in crafting a long-term relationship between MCOs and hospitals.

Responsibilities and Timing

Plan Management

The key players in hospital negotiations from the health plan side are the executive director, the medical director, and the finance director. It is the responsibility of the executive director to initiate the contact, set the stage or tone, and be sure that the executive director of the hospital feels comfortable with the plan's commitment to proceed fairly, openly, and honestly. It is not always necessarily the role of the executive director actually to negotiate the details of the agreement, because it is unlikely that the executive director of the hospital will be doing so. Nevertheless, a relationship between the chief executive of the MCO and the chief executive of the hospital is important to establish. Large HMOs may have an officer who is responsible for managing relations with hospitals, and that individual may also be the most senior person in the plan who will manage the process. In small plans or in early start-ups, or sometimes for political reasons, the executive director may end up carrying the ball all the way through.

The role of the finance director is to work closely with the plan's executive director (or the officer responsible for hospital contracting) and the hospital's finance director or controller. In many cases, the actual negotiation takes place at this level. The finance director should not have the authority actually to sign off on the agreement because the controller of the hospital will surely not have this authority, and it further serves a useful purpose to be able to break the negotiations to confer with the executive director back at the plan. Because the hospital may not believe the numbers produced by the plan, it falls to the finance director of the plan to present those numbers in a credible and understandable way (not only the numbers now but the numbers the plan expects).

In addition to evaluating the quality of the institution and helping elucidate the political climate, the medical director needs to be able to convince the hospital administrator that the plan will genuinely shift the patient caseload as necessary. If the medical director cannot persuade the hospital that the plan is able to move patients in or out, the plan will have lost a key advantage in the negotiations. This need not be done in a heavy-handed way or as a naked threat. It suffices for this issue to be brought out in a businesslike and unemotional way.

It is important to set a realistic time schedule. The degree to which plan management achieves success in its hospital negotiations will be reflected in the amount of effort put into the negotiating process. It is not realistic to think that one can obtain favorable pricing and contracts with a number of hospitals in less than 2 or 3 months (and perhaps considerably longer). It will take time to do the preplanning work, for the hospital to digest what is being proposed, for the hospital to make a counteroffer and for the plan to counter that, and so on. After that, each side's lawyers will want to review the contract language.

Conversely, try not to let too much dust collect on the proposal before either following up or approaching another hospital as an alternative. There is no reason for the hospital to hurry the process unless it believes that delaying will mean losing the contract. If the plan has proposed a reduction in what it is currently paying, the hospital will obviously prefer to keep collecting revenue under the existing terms as long as possible unless the plan is promising a sizeable increase in volume that it is not now getting.

Hospital Management

The chief executive officer (CEO) or executive director of the hospital must set the overall strategy for managed care contracting. Managed care is now far too important to delegate to a lower level individual in the organization. Many hospital CEOs may not be comfortable with this role because their training and experience are in the operations of the clinical facility, and they may choose to delegate the development of managed care strategy to another officer or director. This is perfectly acceptable and may even be necessary, but the CEO should be fully knowledgeable about the terms and strategies and accept ultimate responsibility for them. In many cases, it is important for the hospital CEO to establish a good working relationship with the CEO of the MCO to indicate the level of importance that the hospital holds for the MCO and to work through any obstacles in the negotiating process. It also allows the CEO to understand better the goals and strategies of the MCO.

As noted above, it is common for a hospital to appoint a high level individual to be the primary source of managed care relations. It is a serious mistake to use an individual who is not sufficiently senior in the system or one who cannot make any decisions. The MCO will become frustrated in dealing with a lower level functionary, and this will impede success. This individual may have primary responsibility for all aspects of the negotiation, including financial analysis, operational issues, and reimbursement terms.

The hospital's finance director must be closely involved in the process as well. Unless the MCO is of trivial size, managed care revenues need to be carefully analyzed as described above (and if the MCO is of trivial size, there better be a pretty compelling reason if the hospital is to provide it with favorable terms). Of special concern is the ability of the hospital to meet its direct costs for providing care; if the MCO's reimbursement terms do not even cover direct cost, then the hospital is in trouble. How much the MCO's terms contribute to the hospital's indirect costs and margin is at the core of the negotiation, along with the usual issues of market strength, services offered, and ability to shift volume.

The hospital should have a medical director involved as well. In the past, hospital medical directors were primarily involved with issues of credentialing and privileges, clinical services, recruiting, and so forth. In a market with high levels of managed care penetration, the medical director needs to be heavily involved in clinical aspects of the relationship with the MCO, including clinical efficiency, utilization management, quality management, and member satisfaction. The hospital must be able to provide quality services efficiently and to manage its costs to prosper under managed care reimbursement terms.

Last, it is now common for hospitals to have some form of IDS, and the MCO may or may not be willing to contract with it. In the event that the IDS does indeed accept a significant level of risk for medical expenses, then the IDS and hospital will need to apply managed care utilization management techniques or face a negative financial result.

TYPES OF REIMBURSEMENT ARRANGEMENTS

There are a number of reimbursement methodologies available in contracting with hospitals, except in those states where regulations prohibit creativity. Exhibit 11–1 lists a number of methods that have been used by plans. Lack of imagination is the only real impediment to negotiating, although many plans have found that their inability to handle administratively what is otherwise a bright idea has led to problems such as high administrative cost, frequent errors, and disputes over reconciliations. Figure 11–1 provides a snapshot of the four most common forms of hospital reimbursement as of the

Exhibit 11–1 Models for Reimbursing Hospitals

- Charges
- Discounts
- Per diems
- Sliding scales for discounts and per diems
- Differential by day in hospital
- Diagnosis-related groups
- Differential by service type
- Case rates
  - Institutional only
  - Package pricing or bundled rates
- Capitation
- Percentage of premium revenue
- Bed leasing
- Periodic interim payments or cash advances
- Performance-based incentives
  - Penalties and withholds
  - Quality and service incentives
- Outpatient procedures
  - Discounts
  - Package pricing or bundled rates
  - Ambulatory patient groups

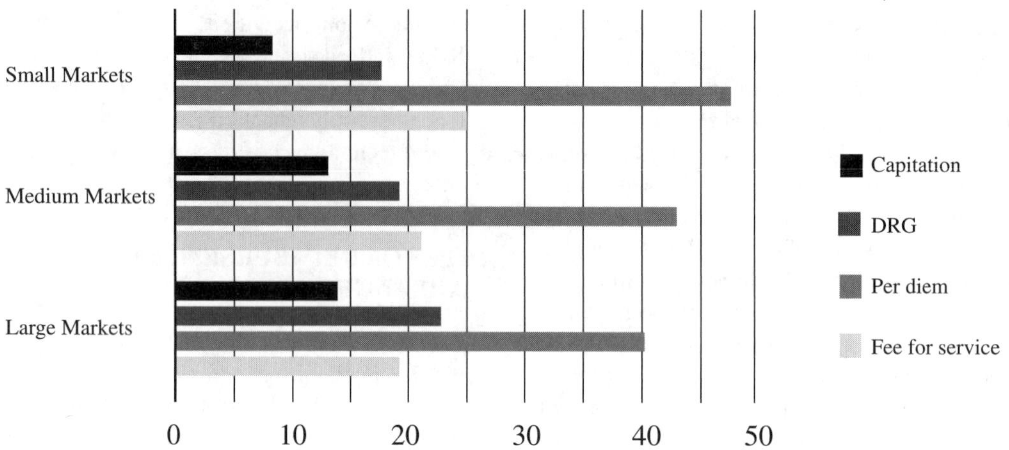

Figure 11–1 HMO reimbursements to hospitals. DRG, diagnosis-related group. *Source:* Reprinted with permission from Regional Market Analysis Reporting Data as of July 1, 1994, *The InterStudy Competitive Edge*, Vol. 5, No. 1, p. 46, © 1995, InterStudy Publications.

time this book was written. It is possible, and even likely, that the percentage distribution of these methods will change, and perhaps change rapidly. A brief discussion of these reimbursement methodologies follows.

Straight Charges

The simplest (albeit least desirable) payment mechanism in health care is straight charges. It is also obviously the most expensive, after the option of no contract at all. This is a fallback position to be agreed to only in the event that you are unable to obtain any form of discount at all, but it is still desirable to have a contract with a no balance billing clause in it (see Chapter 29) for purposes of reserve requirements and licensure.

Straight Discount on Charges

Another possible arrangement with hospitals is a straight percentage discount on charges. In this case, the hospital submits its claim in full, and the plan discounts it by the agreed-to percentage and then pays it. The hospital accepts this payment as payment in full. The amount of discount that can be obtained will depend on the factors discussed above. This type of arrangement is not infrequent in markets with low levels of managed care penetration but is uncommon in markets with high levels of managed care.

Sliding Scale Discount on Charges

Sliding scale discounts are an option, particularly in markets with low managed care penetration but some level of competitiveness among hospitals. With a sliding scale, the percentage discount is reflective of the total volume of admissions and outpatient procedures. Deciding whether to lump the two categories together or deal with them separately is not as important as making sure that the parties deal with them both. With the rapidly climbing cost of outpatient procedures, savings from reduction of inpatient utilization could be negated by an unanticipated overrun in outpatient charges.

An example of a sliding scale is a 20 percent reduction in charges for 0 to 200 total bed days per year with incremental increases in the discount up to a maximum percentage. An interim percentage discount is usually negotiated, and the parties reconcile at the end of the year based on the final total volume.

How the plan tracks the discount is also negotiable. You may wish to vary the discount on a month-to-month basis rather than yearly. You may wish to track total bed days, number of admissions, or whole dollars spent. Whatever you finally agree to, be sure that it is a clearly defined and measurable objective.

The last issue to look at in a sliding scale is timeliness of payment. It is likely that the hospital will demand a clause in the contract spelling out the plan's requirement to process claims in a timely manner, usually 30 days or sooner. In some cases you may wish to negotiate a sliding scale, or a modifier to your main sliding scale, that applies a further reduction based on the plan's ability to turn a clean claim around quickly. For example, you may negotiate an additional 4 percent discount for paying a clean claim within 14 days of receipt. Conversely, the hospital may demand a penalty for clean claims that are not processed within 30 days.

Straight Per Diem Charges

Unlike straight charges, a negotiated per diem is a single charge for a day in the hospital regardless of any actual charges or costs incurred. In this most common type of arrangement, the plan negotiates a per diem rate with the hospital and pays that rate without adjustments. For example, the plan will pay $800 for each day regardless of the actual cost of the service.

Hospital administrators are sometimes reluctant to add days in the intensive care unit or obstetrics to the base per diem unless there is a sufficient volume of regular medical–surgical cases to make the ultimate cost predictable. In a small plan, or in one that is not limiting the number of participating hospitals, the hospital administrator is concerned that the hospital will be used for expensive cases at a low per diem while competitors are used for less costly cases. In such cases, a good option is to negotiate multiple sets of per diem charges based on service type (e.g., medical–surgical, obstetrics, intensive care, neonatal intensive care, rehabilitation, and so forth) or a combination of per diems and a flat case rate (see below) for obstetrics.

The key to making a per diem work is predictability. If the plan and hospital can accurately predict the number and mix of cases, then they can accurately calculate a per diem. The per diem is simply an estimate of the charges or costs for an average day in that hospital minus the level of discount.

A theoretical disadvantage of the per diem approach, however, is that the per diem must be paid even if the billed charges are less than the per diem rate. For example, if the plan has a per diem arrangement that pays $800 per day for medical admissions, and the total allowable charges (billed charges less charges for noncovered items provided during the admission) for a 5-day admission are $3,300, the hospital is reimbursed $4,000 for the admission ($800 per day × 5 days). This is acceptable as long as the average per diem represents an acceptable discount, but it has been anecdotally reported that some large, self-insured accounts have demanded the lesser of the charges or the per diems for each case (i.e., laying off the upper end of the risk but harvesting the reward). Such demands are to be avoided because they corrupt the integrity of the per diem calculation.

A plan may also negotiate to reimburse the hospital for expensive surgical implants provided at the hospital's actual cost of the implant. Such reimbursement would be limited to a defined list of implants (e.g., cochlear implants) where the cost to the hospital for the implant is far greater than is recoverable under the per diem or outpatient arrangement.

Sliding Scale Per Diem

Like the sliding scale discount on charges discussed above, the sliding scale per diem is also based on total volume. In this case, the plan negotiates an interim per diem that it will pay for each day in the hospital. Depending on the total number of bed days in the year, the plan will either pay a lump sum settlement at the end of the year or withhold an amount from the final payment for the year to adjust for an additional reduction in the per diem from an increase in total bed days. It may be preferable to make an arrangement whereby on a quarterly or semiannual basis the plan will adjust the interim per diem so as to reduce any disparities caused by unexpected changes in utilization patterns.

Differential by Day in Hospital

This simply refers to the fact that most hospitalizations are more expensive on the first day. For example, the first day for surgical cases includes operating suite costs, the operating surgical team costs (nurses and recovery), and so forth. This type of reimbursement method is generally combined with a per diem approach, but the first day is paid at a higher rate. For example, the first day may be $1,000 and each subsequent day is $600.

Diagnosis-Related Groups

As with Medicare, a common reimbursement methodology is by diagnosis-related groups (DRGs). There are publications of DRG categories, criteria, outliers, and trim points (i.e., the cost or length of stay that causes the DRG payment to be supplemented or supplanted by another payment mechanism) to enable the plan to negotiate a payment mechanism for DRGs based on Medicare rates or, in some cases, state regulated rates. First, though, the plan needs to assess whether it will be to its benefit.

If it is the plan's intention to reduce unnecessary utilization, there will not necessarily be concomitant savings if it uses straight DRGs. If the payment is fixed on the basis of diagnosis, any reduction in days will go to the hospital and not to the plan. Furthermore, unless the plan is prepared to perform careful audits of the hospital's DRG coding, it may experience code creep. On the other hand, DRGs do serve to share risk with the hospital, thus making the hospital an active partner in controlling utilization and making plan expenses more manageable. DRGs are perhaps better suited to plans with loose controls than plans that tightly manage utilization.

Service-Related Case Rates

Similar to DRGs, service-related case rates are a cruder cut. In this reimbursement mechanism, various service types are defined (e.g., medicine, surgery, intensive care, neonatal intensive care, psychiatry, obstetrics, and the like), and the hospital receives a flat per admission reimbursement for whatever type of service to which the patient is admitted (e.g., all surgical admissions cost $6,100). If services are mixed, a prorated payment may be made (e.g., 50 percent of surgical and 50 percent of intensive care).

Case Rates and Package Pricing

Whatever mechanism a plan uses for hospital reimbursement, it may still need to address certain categories of procedures and negotiate special rates. The most common of these is obstetrics. It is common to negotiate a flat rate for a normal vaginal delivery and a flat rate for a cesarean section or a blended rate for both. In the case of blended case rates, the expected reimbursement for each type of delivery is multiplied by the expected (or desired) percentage of utilization. For example, a case rate for vaginal delivery is $2,000, and for cesarean section it is $2,600. Utilization is expected to be 80 percent vaginal and 20 percent cesarean section, and therefore the case rate is $2,120 ($2,000 × 0.8 = $1,600; $2,600 × 0.2 = $520; $1,600 + $520 = $2,120). With the recent legislative activity regarding minimum length of stay for obstetrics, flat case rates (regardless of either length of stay or cesarean section versus vaginal delivery) are clearly the preferred method of reimbursement other than capitation.

Although common, case rates are certainly not necessary if the per diem is all inclusive, but a plan will want to use them if it has negotiated a discount on charges. This is because the delivery suite or operating room is substantially more costly to operate than a regular hospital room. For example, you may negotiate a flat rate of $2,100 per delivery. The downside of this arrangement is that you achieve no added savings from decreased length of stay. The upside is that it makes the hospital a much more active partner in controlling utilization.

Another area for which a plan would typically want to negotiate flat rates is specialty procedures at tertiary hospitals, for example coronary artery bypass surgery or heart transplants. These procedures, although relatively infrequent, are tremendously costly.

A broader variation is package pricing or bundled case rates. As discussed in Chapter 10, the package price or bundled case rate refers to an all-inclusive rate paid for both institutional and professional services. The plan negotiates a flat rate for a procedure (e.g., coronary artery bypass surgery), and that rate is used to pay all parties who provide services connected with that procedure, including preadmission and postdischarge care. Bundled case rates are not uncommon in teaching facilities where there is a faculty practice plan that works closely with the hospital.

Capitation or Percentage of Revenue

Capitation refers to reimbursing the hospital on a per member per month (PMPM) basis to cover all institutional costs for a defined population of members. The payment may be varied by age and sex but does not fluctuate with premium revenue. Percentage of revenue refers to a fixed percentage of premium revenue (i.e., a percentage of the collected premium rate) being paid to the hospital, again to cover all institutional services. The difference between percentage of revenue and capitation is that percentage of revenue may vary with the premium rate charged and the actual revenue yielded. Although capitation and percentage of premium revenue are essentially the same for public sector programs (i.e., risk contracts for Medicare and Medicaid), that is not the case for the commercial sector. In the event that the plan fails to develop rates properly or perform underwriting (or gets caught up in a price war), a proportionate percentage of that shortfall will be passed directly to the hospital. In both cases, the hospital stands the entire risk for institutional services for the defined membership base; if the hospital cannot provide the services itself, the cost for such care is deducted from the capitation payment.

For this type of arrangement to work, a hospital must know that it will serve a clearly defined segment of a plan's enrollment and that it can provide most of the necessary services to those members. In these cases, the primary care physician is clearly associated with just one hospital. Alternatively, if the plan is dealing with a multihospital system with multiple facilities in the plan's service area, it may be reasonable to expect that the hospitals in the system can care for the plan's members on an exclusive basis. It is possible for capitation to be tied to the percentage of admissions to a hospital. For example, the capitation rate is $35 PMPM. The plan has 10,000 members, and 50 percent of admissions go to that hospital that month. The payment therefore is $\$35 \times (10{,}000 \times 0.5) = \$175{,}000$. This is quite uncommon, however.

The hospital must also perform aggressive utilization management to see any margin from capitation; if utilization management is carried out so as to ruffle the least number of feathers of attending staff, the hospital will pay a stiff price. There needs to be a clear definition of what is covered under the capitation and what is not. For example, the capitation may include outpatient procedures, but the plan and hospital need to account for outpatient procedures that are being performed outside the hospital's domain. Will home health be part of the capitation, and, if so, what agency? It is preferable not to place the hospital at risk for services it cannot control. The hospital also needs to be provided with stop-loss insurance to protect it against catastrophic cases;

for example, the plan may reimburse the hospital at a low per diem for all days of a case after it has been in the hospital for a number of days (e.g., beyond 30 days in a year). Alternatively, the plan may pay a percentage of charges after a certain charge level has been reached, and the plan's own reinsurance comes into play.

The advantage of capitation is that it is not only budgetable but succeeds in laying off all or most of the risk for institutional expenses. The hospital becomes a full partner in controlling utilization, and the plan has less need to control. The problem is that the plan will see none of the savings for improved utilization control. Another problem can arise if the hospital refuses to share any of the savings (calculated as though there were a per diem or discounted charges model) with the physicians who are controlling the cases; if you pursue such an arrangement, the HMO may want to include provisions for a bonus plan between the hospital and the physicians.

Point-of-service (POS) plans with an out-of-network benefit make capitation methods difficult to use. As discussed in Chapter 8, capitation in POS may mean having to pay twice for a service: once under capitation and again if the member seeks service outside the network. In areas where there are no real alternatives to a certain hospital (e.g., a rural area or an area where a hospital enjoys a monopoly), this problem may not be material, but that is the exception. Capitation tied to the percentage of admissions to that hospital, as mentioned earlier in this chapter, may also attenuate this problem. The alternative is to deduct out-of-area costs from the capitation payment. Closely related to this is the idea of global capitation, in which an IDS accepts capitation or percentage of premium revenue in exchange for total risk for medical services. This is discussed in Chapter 4.

The last issue of which you need to be aware in this arrangement is that some state insurance departments may consider this degree of risk transfer too much. It may be reasoned that, if the health plan is not actually assuming the risk for services, then it is not really a health plan at all but only a marketing organization. In such a case, there may be a question as to who should really hold the certificate of authority or license to operate the health plan. This issue is discussed in Chapter 28.

Bed Leasing

A relatively uncommon reimbursement mechanism is bed leasing. This refers to a plan actually leasing beds from an institution, for example paying the hospital $350 per bed for 10 beds regardless of whether those beds are used. This ensures revenue flow to the hospital, ensures access to beds (at least some beds) for the plan, and is budgetable. It is perhaps best used in those situations where a plan is assured of a steady number of bed days with little or no seasonality. The problem with bed leasing is that there is no real savings from reducing utilization unless contract terms allow the plan to lease back the beds to the hospital if they are not being used.

Periodic Interim Payments and Cash Advances

Once common but now rare, periodic interim payments (PIPs) and cash advances are methods whereby the plan advances a hospital cash to cover expected claims. This cash advance is periodically replenished if it gets below a certain amount. Claims may be applied directly against the cash advance or may be paid outside it, in which case the cash advance serves as an advance deposit. The value of this to a hospital is obvious: positive cash flow. PIPs and cash advances are quite valuable to a hospital and will generate a discount in and of themselves.

Performance-Based Reimbursement

The largest portion of reimbursement to hospitals is likely to be done under one or more of the methods described above. Capitation is clearly an example of performance-based reimbursement, in that the hospital only profits if it can provide services at a low cost and a high level of quality. Beyond that, there are other forms of performance-based reimbursement, although they are not common at this time.

Penalties and Withholds

As with physician services (see Chapters 6 and 8), occasionally penalties or withholds are used in hospital reimbursement methods. As an example, a plan may negotiate with a hospital to allow the hospital's own utilization management department to perform all the utilization management functions (see Chapter 13). As part of that negotiation, goals are set for average length of stay and average admission rate. Part of the payment to the hospital may be withheld, or, conversely, the plan may set aside a bonus pool. In any event, if the goals are met or exceeded, the hospital receives its withhold or bonus, and vice versa. One complication with this is the possibility that a hospital can make its statistics look good by simply sending patients to other hospitals; this is similar to problems encountered with physician capitation. If a service area is clearly defined, or if the hospital is capitated, then it may be easier to apply a risk or reward program. The reader should be aware, however, that there is evidence that financial penalty models applied to hospitals have little or no effect on utilization or physician performance.[3]

Service and Quality Incentives

An alternative approach to financial penalties associated with utilization levels is to provide the hospital incentives for improving its quality and service as well as its business operations. In one model, hospitals receive an incentive payment that is affected by three broad variables: satisfaction with services (measured by surveys of patients and physicians), clinical care (measured by looking at complication rates, average length of stay, and other measures), and business structural support for managed care (e.g., electronic data interchange, case management support, and other aspects).[4] In another model, hospitals receive modest incentives based on outcomes for certain clinical procedures (Blue Cross/Blue Shield of Minnesota, unpublished data, 1993).

Outpatient Procedures

As mentioned earlier, the shift from inpatient to outpatient care has not gone unnoticed by hospital administrators. As care has shifted, so have charges. It is not uncommon to see outpatient charges exceeding the cost of an inpatient day unless steps are taken to address that imbalance.

Discounts on Charges

Either straight discounts or sliding scale discounts may be applied to outpatient charges. Some hospitals argue that the cost to deliver highly technical outpatient procedures actually is greater than an average per diem, primarily because the per diem assumes more than a single day in the hospital, thereby spreading the costs over a greater number of reimbursable days. Some plans have responded by simply admitting patients for their outpatient surgery, paying the per diem, and sending the patient home. Many plans negotiate the costs of outpatient surgery so that they never exceed the cost of an inpatient day, whereas other plans concede the problem of front-loading surgical services and agree to cap outpatient charges at a fixed percentage of the per diem (e.g., 125 percent of the average per diem).

Package Pricing or Bundled Charges

Plans may negotiate package pricing or bundled charges for outpatient procedures. In this method of reimbursement, all the various charges are bundled into one single charge, thereby reducing the problem of unbundling and exploding (i.e., charging for multiple codes or brand new codes where previously only one code was used). Plans may use their own data to develop the bundled charges, or they may use outside data (one such source is published by Milliman & Robertson, a national actuarial firm[5]). Bundled charges are generally tied to the principal procedure code used by the facility. Bundled charges may also be added together in the event that more than one procedure is performed, although the second procedure is discounted because the patient was already in the facility and using services.

Related to this approach are tiered rates. In this case, the outpatient department categorizes all procedures into several different categories. The plan then pays a different rate for each category, but that rate covers all services performed in the outpatient department, and only one category is used at a time (i.e., the hospital cannot add several categories together for a single patient encounter).

Ambulatory Patient Groups

Ambulatory patient groups (APGs) were developed by 3M Health Systems under a contract with the Health Care Financing Administration (HCFA), primarily for use with Medicare.[6] As this book is being written, APGs have not been put into use, although the HCFA has recommended that they be phased in over several years. The commercial market, however, has begun actively to use APGs.[7]

APGs are to outpatient services what DRGs are to inpatient ones, although APGs are based on procedures rather than simply on diagnoses and are considerably more complex. As with bundled charges (discussed above), under APGs all the services associated with a given procedure or visit are bundled into the APG reimbursement. More than one APG may be billed if more than one procedure is performed, but there is significant discounting for additional APGs.

CONCLUSION

Reimbursement mechanisms and contracts with hospitals, as with consultants, are tools. The importance of these tools cannot be overestimated, and an MCO must craft these tools with all the skills it has available. It is possible and desirable to develop win–win situations with hospitals, and that can be a pivotal issue in the ultimate success of a plan.

Study Questions

1. Develop a work plan for a new start-up open panel HMO to contract with hospitals.
2. Describe the key advantages and disadvantages of the various reimbursement systems for hospitals from the point of view of a managed care plan, by type of plan. Perform the same exercise, but from the point of view of the hospital.
3. When would an HMO choose to use DRGs? Per diems? Capitation?
4. Devise a reimbursement system for a hospital that allows it to be paid based on total utilization, quality, and member satisfaction.
5. What management tools would a hospital need to be able to operate effectively in a heavily capitated environment?

REFERENCES AND NOTES

1. C.C. Boesz, "Federal Qualification: A Foundation for the Future," in *The Managed Health Care Handbook*, 3d ed., ed. P.R. Kongstvedt (Gaithersburg, Md.: Aspen, 1996), 835–848.
2. American Hospital Association (AHA), *American Hospital Association Guide to the Health Care Field* (Chicago, Ill.: AHA, 1995).
3. L. Debrock and R.J. Arnould, Utilization Control in HMOs, *Quarterly Review of Economics and Finance* 32 (1992): 31–53.
4. C. Sennett, et al., Performance-Based Hospital Contracting for Quality Improvement, *Journal of Quality Improvement* 19 (1993): 374–383.
5. R.L. Doyle and A.P. Feren, *Healthcare Management Guidelines, Vol. 3: Ambulatory Care Guidelines* (Milliman & Robertson, updated periodically).

6. R.F. Averill, et al., *Design and Evaluation of a Prospective Payment System for Ambulatory Care, Final Report* (Health Care Financing Administration Cooperative Agreement 17-C-99369/1-02, Health Care Financing Administration, 1995).
7. S. Larose, Preparing for Ambulatory Patient Groups, *Capitation and Medical Practice* 1 (1995): 1, 4–6.

SUGGESTED READING

Profiles of U.S. Hospitals. 1995. Baltimore, Md.: HCIA, Inc.

Pyenson, B.S. (ed.). 1995. *Calculated Risk: A Provider's Guide to Controlling the Financial Risk of Managed Care*. Chicago, Ill.: American Hospital Publishers.

Chapter 12

Academic Health Centers and Managed Care

Richard L. Solit and David B. Nash

Study Objectives

- Be able to define the challenges to academic medicine in terms of a changing marketplace
- Be able to describe potential strategies that must integrate primary and specialty care with network formation
- Appreciate how academic health centers must create and cultivate stakeholders in their mission to support nonprofitable research and educational activities
- Describe how these internal changes to academic medical centers require innovation and new types of leadership

Academic health centers (AHCs) have symbolized the great technological advancements and specialization in patient care that have occurred in this century. They have been successful in their classic mission to train health professionals, foster basic and clinical research, and provide the highest quality of patient care. As a result, applications to medical schools, clinical revenues, and research discoveries are at record highs.

Richard L. Solit, M.D., is a fellow in the Office of Health Policy and Clinical Outcomes and a resident in the Department of Surgery at Thomas Jefferson University, Philadelphia, Pennsylvania.

David B. Nash, M.B.A., M.D., is the director of the Office of Health Policy and Clinical Outcomes and Associate Professor of Medicine at Thomas Jefferson University, Philadelphia, Pennsylvania.

These traditional ways face an uncertain future in today's rapidly changing health care environment, however. Public generosity toward research and education is tempered by a strong deficit-lowering sentiment in the nation. Furthermore, with the failure of comprehensive health reform, medical educators have lost confidence in the certainty of future public support for education, research, and patient care in the academic setting. This would not present an insurmountable problem if the historical subsidization of education and research by profitable clinical activities continued indefinitely. It is clear, however, that this cannot continue as the purchasers of health care seek continued cost containment through managed care. As a result, the AHC is forced to compete in the marketplace on cost and quality. This may leave little support for less profitable activities and requires a transformation of the current structure.

An understanding of the complex interaction among patients, physicians, hospitals, insurers, employers, and government agencies is necessary before one develops a strategy for the managed care market. The traditional role played by each party is in a state of flux. Definitions of a few of the terms used in this discussion therefore may be helpful. Providers deliver care to patients and include hospitals and physicians. Insurers provide various financing arrangements as defined by a specified benefits plan for purchasers and beneficiaries (or patients). The purchasers of health care include patients, employers, and government agencies, such as Medicare and Medicaid, who pay premiums to insurers or pay providers directly for services. Managed care is defined as the integration of financing with the delivery of health care services. Therefore, managed care organizations (MCOs) provide plans or products that integrate the health care financing activities of insurers with the delivery of care by providers for purchasers. Insurers are increasingly becoming MCOs as they go beyond simply paying for services rendered in a fee-for-service (FFS) system to managing provider activity and in turn arranging the delivery of care. Providers are also becoming MCOs by providing financing and delivery of health care services when they contract directly with purchasers. Some MCOs, such as staff model health maintenance organizations (HMOs), provide financing and delivery within one system and assume both the provider and insurer role. Stemming from the rapid changes in the industry, this terminology is somewhat artificial. Further discussions of the evolving taxonomy of MCOs and integrated provider systems are found in Chapters 3 and 4.

This chapter defines the challenges to academic medicine in terms of changing market mechanisms and financial support for AHCs and demonstrates how the unique organizational and cultural environment within the AHC contributes to the problem and obstructs potential solutions. Potential strategies must integrate primary and specialty care with network formation to secure a solid patient base. Furthermore, the AHC must create and cultivate stakeholders in its mission to support necessary but nonprofitable activities. Internal changes to meet these new demands require innovation and leadership in realigning incentives, managing information and outcomes, and reinventing education and research. Finally, anticipating change to improve market position and profitability will prove valuable as rapid change continues.

DIMENSIONS OF THE PROBLEM

With the rapid growth of managed care, AHCs face multiple financial challenges that threaten their ability to perform their traditional academic mission. The potential loss of public funds that directly and indirectly support medical education, research, charity, and complex care take on new implications in the context of the challenges presented by managed care. It is important to recognize that managed care is a reflection of the change in societal values and attitudes. It is the response of the free market to two decades of runaway medical inflation caused by a cost-plus system that encouraged unlimited use of medical services. Although the AHCs benefited immensely in this environment, continued reliance on the structure and culture of the past is the real threat to their viability. Salvation lies in recognizing that "they can no longer operate as specialty-driven institutions largely divorced from the trends that favor lower costs, less hospitalization, and more primary care."[1(p.407)] The dimensions of the problem will be examined here in terms of the interaction between the barriers to organizational change and the changes in market mechanisms and financial support for academic medicine. The reader is also referred to Chapter 1 for an overview of the broad forces at play in managed care.

Change in Market Mechanisms

Many feel that the multiple roles of AHCs make them noncompetitive in this changing environment. Excluding the direct cost of teaching, a 1991 study places the average cost of care per admission at $6,000 in AHCs compared with $4,400 in nonteaching hospitals.[2] Because clinical activities under capitation become cost centers, like the programs they support, managed care plans avoid contracting with teaching hospitals. According to predictions by the University HealthSystem Consortium (an organization of 70 AHCs that helps its members with the business of medicine), the movement toward managed care has created a clear trend toward markedly lower utilization of secondary and tertiary services with fewer admissions and shorter lengths of stay. These data suggest that hospital admissions and revenues would decline by 25 percent and 50 percent, respectively, in aggressively managed markets. Similarly, contributions to revenues by specialists would decline by approximately 30 percent. Given that an average of 40 percent of medical school revenues are derived from professional and hospital services, academic funding will suffer considerably under these conditions.[3]

To respond to the threat of declining revenues, academic leaders must focus on the market mechanisms that create the environment in which they will operate. The paradigm shift in health care toward cost containment occurred in 1982, when prospective payment was introduced for Medicare. Although this did not control the growth of medical expenditures, a clear message was sent that the 20-year era of cost-plus medicine was over. Real changes, however, occurred only with an increasing role of the purchasers of health care and the subsequent shift in financial risk allocation from these purchasers to insurers, providers, and patients.

Increasing Role of Purchasers

The importance of the purchasers, who bear the burden of health insurance premiums, cannot be overstated. The separation of the consumer (patient) from the provider by third party payers (insurers) has removed the normal economic mechanism that controls utilization, namely cost to the consumer. The vast majority of Americans are sheltered from the direct cost of rising premiums because health care is a benefit funded either by their employer through pretax payroll deductions (37 percent of insured Americans) or by the taxpayer through Medicare and Medicaid (42 percent of insured Americans).[4] Rampant medical inflation increased this responsibility immensely and forced these purchasers to be the most significant catalyst for the movement toward managed care.

Because the consumer is sheltered from the rising cost of health care premiums in addition to the direct cost of care, there is no market mechanism to control demand for health services and, in turn, total costs. Simply stated, total medical expenditures depend on the product of the volume of services and the price for these services. Although discounted FFS and price controls in the form of diagnosis-related groups (DRGs) for hospitals slowed the rate of medical inflation for Medicare, true cost reduction in the absence of demand control requires a reduction in the volume of services provided. For years after DRGs were introduced, AHC revenues were not drastically threatened because physicians still controlled the flow of patients into the system and could therefore continue to generate volume in an atmosphere of price control. Intense use of services continued along with a shift toward FFS outpatient services.

Private industry, and now Medicare and Medicaid, are increasingly attracted to managed care.[5–7] Approximately 65 percent of employees of large firms were enrolled in managed care plans by 1994. This had grown from 47 percent in 1991. Only 6 percent remain in traditional indemnity plans that use no utilization control.[8] Even though this is an employer decision rather than a beneficiary preference, reports indicate a high level of patient satisfaction.[9] Many states have followed the example set by employers and now encourage managed care for Medicaid beneficiaries. Since 1987, the Medicaid population in managed care has doubled to 12 percent. See Chapter 27 for a discussion of Medicaid and managed care. The Health Care Financing Administration has also encouraged HMOs for Medicare beneficiaries since the early 1980s. Although enrollment is growing at an annual rate of 12 percent, projected growth by 1994 was only 6 percent of the estimated 36 million beneficiaries.[10] See Chapter 26 for a discussion of Medicare and managed care.

Utilization control is the undeniable result of increasing purchaser involvement in cost containment. Purchasers have long noted regional variation in practice patterns as well as lower levels of spending per capita in other industrialized countries. As the level of medical inflation has continued, they have turned to managed care as a mechanism for removing "fat" from the current system. The government considered regulatory mechanisms and forms of universal health care used in other nations to control total expenditures. Instead, the private market concentrated on changing incentives from FFS that produced independent profit centers to managed care with annually capitated cost centers.[11] The result was minimal premium increases and some reductions by 1995.[12]

This distinct about face from the previous culture of overutilization is the fundamental threat to the AHC. The decline in the utilization of high technology and other AHC services directly reduces revenues that have traditionally subsidized "unprofitable" activities such as education, research, and unreimbursed patient care. Academic leaders must also recognize that economics is not the only factor promoting managed care. Although health spending decreased by 1 percent for American industry in 1994, employers are not yet satisfied.[13] They want further information about quality and experience to improve their purchasing decisions. Purchasers and their beneficiaries are concerned with determining quality and appropriateness of care based on definable outcomes and physician accountability. MCOs are responsive to these needs, and the managed care culture supports deliberate evaluation of outcomes, accountability, utilization control, primary care, disease management, and integration of care for defined populations.[14] If viewed broadly as the integration of financing with the delivery of services, whether through capitation or a combination of financial mechanisms, managed care is seen by purchasers as essential for transforming medicine into an efficient, high-quality industry for the 21st century.

Shift in Financial Risk Allocation

The most important factor in the proper allocation of resources is the proper allocation of financial risk among patients, purchasers, insurers, and providers. When patients assume risk, they gain in the form of savings through demand control. When risk is assumed by insurers and providers, profit is achieved by more efficient delivery of fewer services. Insurers are in the best position to assume risk for catastrophic conditions, whereas providers are in the best position to control utilization on a case-by-case basis.

Purchaser involvement led to utilization control by shifting financial risk to insurers and providers. The ideal strategy is to allocate financial risk to the party that is most able to manage utilization and outcomes effectively. Even though purchasers are the least able party to manage processes and outcomes, they assumed the greatest risk under a cost-plus FFS system in the form of ever-increasing insurance premiums or direct costs for self-insured businesses. (This topic is discussed in detail in Chapter 59 of *The Managed Health Care Handbook*.[15]) The patient has had no motivation to constrain utilization. Additionally, AHCs, like all providers, could profit from overutilization while passing along all costs resulting from inefficiencies. Under managed care, capitation allows for a fixed budget and transfers financial risk to insurers and providers. Future attempts to distribute more risk to employees through increased deductibles and copayments are likely.[16,17]

Change in Financial Support

Three interrelated factors directly decrease support for the academic mission. First, employers are selecting health plans largely on the basis of cost because there is little information available about differences in quality.[18,19] The perceived superiority of care in AHCs no longer guarantees continued utilization or funding of their services. In effect, the focus on price by purchasers has transformed medicine into a commodity market. Second, the failure of legislative health care reform in late 1993 (see Chapter 2) means that academic centers must face the threat of diminishing revenues under managed care with no likelihood of greater government support. Third, the loss of federal support, in the context of the purchaser shift toward a commodity view of health care, may lead to elimination of the financial support derived from the clinical revenues of academic providers.

Medicine as a Commodity

Most types of insurance have traditionally acted as commodities in the market. Because commodities are usually indistinguishable, commodity businesses compete solely on price and cannot keep market share at prices above others in the marketplace. Conversely, health insurers, and especially Blue Cross/Blue Shield and indemnity plans (see Chapter 3) as well as providers such as AHCs, have enjoyed a noncommodity identity. In the past, they could increase prices without losing market share. Profitable organizations were high-cost producers. The shift toward competition based solely on price suggests that medical care has transformed into a commodity in which the products offered are virtually indistinguishable. Reports indicate that patients are willing to change plans for a price differential as low as $5.00.[20] Unless services can be distinguished through measures of quality or overcapacity decreases dramatically, AHCs must become low-cost producers.

Studies comparing the quality and satisfaction of managed care patients demonstrate equal quality.[21] Reports also indicate that HMOs consistently perform better in preventive care with a greater proportion of mammography, general physical, pelvic, and rectal examinations.[22,23] Even more important, these results are disseminated in the financial papers and general media, exposing purchasers to data suggesting that care provided to managed care enrollees is indistinguishable from that provided through traditional indemnity insurance.[24] Therefore, academic pursuits are not immune to economic forces, and the feeling of superior quality of care at AHCs cannot be taken for granted. Private insurers, and now Medicare and Medicaid, will not pay higher prices to support increased costs incurred by AHCs for teaching, research, and indigent care because they no longer perceive greater quality of services in AHCs.[25]

Graduate Medical Education

The academic mission has been subsidized by a process with no logic and no basis in proper allocation of society's resources. Public support for education, indigent care, and research has traditionally been hidden in Medicare payments as adjustments for graduate medical education (GME). The indirect cost of GME as well as uncompensated care was factored into DRG payments to hospitals with resident training. There were two unanticipated results from these hidden payments. First, there was a dramatic rise in accredited programs for GME, which increased by 21 percent from 1983 to 1991.[26] Second, these hidden payments supported managed care profits. When the Health Care Financing Administration targeted payments to managed care organizations at 95 percent of projected FFS levels as defined by geographic area, it included direct and indirect support for GME in these capitated payments. There was no obligation for MCOs to pass along these funds for educational activities. In addition, enrollment of healthier patients may have increased expenses for the remaining FFS population, raising the measured FFS levels the following year and in turn further increasing payments to MCOs.[27,28] Many would argue that the federal subsidy for GME does not properly allocate the nation's limited capital resources.

The federal government has never supported undergraduate medical education, and the failure of health care reform eliminated assurances of continued support for GME. As Medicare increasingly turns toward managed care, GME funding no longer reaches academic institutions. In conjunction with diminishing federal support, an avoidance of AHC services by purchasers and insurers resulting from the shift toward a commodity view of health care leads to a divergence of medical center and medical school goals.

Historically, medical schools and their associated teaching hospitals have prospered by supporting each other. The linkage of GME support to Medicare payments resulted in a mutual financial dependence between the medical school and academic providers. The academic hospital and its physicians gained surplus revenues for the teaching they provided in two ways. First, they benefited directly from inflated Medicare payments. Second, higher prices and volume were achieved from the perception that the professor is the expert and delivers the highest-quality care. In return, physicians and hospitals provided the medical school with financial support and a large, comprehensive patient base for students and residents.

With the introduction of managed care, divergent needs exist between academic providers and medical schools. Association with the medical school may no longer provide the hospital and faculty the benefit of increased payments through Medicare and increased referrals through reputation. As described earlier, lack of outcome measures showing better quality converts medicine to a commodity market based on price. Therefore, academic providers can no longer maintain higher prices. Conversely, the medical school benefits less from association with the hospital. The health care system of the future will not revolve around the hospital, and the inpatient environment does not provide fully the education needed for managed care. Instead of handling all aspects of care, hospitals will only care for those patients who cannot be cared for in other settings. Furthermore, separation of GME payments from Medicare along with declining revenues means that medical schools cannot count on hospitals for continued financial support. Association with the hospital and faculty plans may also present a conflict of interest in attempts to align with other providers or MCOs that are able to add to the teaching patient base or act as new sources of support.

As hospitals and medical schools realign their goals for survival, common areas will present for continued collaboration, but the paradigm shift suggests that the two need not remain inextricably linked.[29] Acting independently, they will be free to pursue alliances with other competing organizations. Unless the teaching hospital and academic faculty pursue a strategy that addresses proper training for managed care, the medical school will need to look elsewhere for an appropriate teaching environment. Even with successful adaptation to managed care, hospitals alone cannot support the academic mission. The cost of education and research will require funding by the federal government or comprehensive support from the managed care industry. Funding for medical schools must be separated from the revenues of the medical centers.

Barriers to Organizational Change

The unique organizational and cultural structure of the traditional AHC is an impediment to adaptation to a competitive environment. Although the AHC has been tremendously successful under the FFS system, its present structure appears ill suited to enable it to adapt to the rapid changes affecting the industry. The changes in market mechanisms and financial support provide an incredible challenge for the AHC. How can the AHC create a cultural and organizational structure that improves competitiveness, fosters education and research, contributes to efficient use of resources, and maintains a high level of technical quality? The traditional culture, based in physician autonomy, presents the strongest barrier to collaboration. A market in transition further prevents changes by providing conflicting incentives to providers. Finally, the current information structure, based in a billing function, does not allow for accurate determination of cost bases, processes, and outcomes for services and education.

Traditional Culture

The structure of the AHC is the product of a culture that fostered great clinical and technical advances over the last half century. This structure is based in a culture or system in which the physician is the main focus. The hospital is the physician's workshop; the medical school is the physician's classroom. Autonomy of the individual physician results from revenue generation. In an FFS, the individual physician controls access and therefore generates revenues for the AHC. Within the hospital, specialists who can generate a large volume of services through procedures and hospital admissions have developed a great deal of power. This system defines the physician as the knowledgeable decision maker. The autonomy of the individual is so important, however, that bias and habits often replace true outcomes-based decision making (see Chapter 18 for a discussion of this issue).

Because the culture of the AHC is centered on the individual physician, it revolves around the needs of the departments of various specialties. Stemming from the frustration that many feel in dealing with the divergent needs of different departments, these departments have often been described in a derogatory manner as fiefdoms. This political entrenchment prevents beneficial change, and individual power struggles destroy the ability of the AHC to act in a rational, cohesive manner. Given that purchasers increasingly insist on cost-effectiveness, a culture that obstructs fundamental change will increasingly weigh on the AHC. The present structure forms a bias against primary care, population focus, outcomes-based decision making, and sound business principles.

The Transition Market

The profits of today are a barrier to the profits of tomorrow. Continued revenues for individuals and autonomous departments, as a result of incomplete capitation and utilization control, obstruct attempts at changing the traditional culture of the AHC. With this dichotomy in place, the AHC remains a revenue center, while increasing capitation and its resulting shift in financial risk transform it into a cost center. The AHC still needs the individual physicians, in particular the specialists, to generate revenues in the current hybrid environment. Therefore, the needs for future viability of the AHC do not coincide with the needs for today's profitability. A transition market dictates that the timing of strategic actions takes on great importance. Additionally, change that precedes the arrival of fierce competition requires leadership that will alter the traditional culture by creating a common vision for those with a stake in the AHC.

Information Structure

The absence of information regarding clinical processes and cost structures is a significant barrier to effective competition. For the majority of physicians, current information systems perform a billing function and do not provide information about clinical processes and their underlying cost structures. A few hospitals have internal cost accounting systems that can be used to evaluate physician practice patterns and overall institutional averages by diagnosis. These hospitals, however, do not usually have this information available in a timely manner for immediate clinical use and feedback.

As AHCs assume increased financial risk and the economics begins to resemble a commodity market, internal cost and process accounting becomes necessary for success. Profit under capitation can only occur at the margin between revenues and costs of services provided, and only the low-cost provider in a commodity market can profit because there is little price flexibility. This involves creating higher margins that result from cost controls and aggressive cost analysis. Information systems of the future must combine clinical resources such as guidelines and protocols with accurate cost data to manage process and outcome effectively.[30]

With improved information management, medical centers can withstand poor economic environments and strengthen their market positions by driving weaker competitors from the market. Problems in operations can be identified more easily as well. Furthermore, improved profit margin allows growth without debt and accumulation of funds for the academic mission. Management information systems and the use of data for medical management are discussed in Chapters 19 and 20.

STRATEGIES FOR SUCCESS

Attempts at uniformity and standardization aimed at reducing variability in treatment are a first step toward lowering costs within academic health centers. As purchasers shift their focus from cost to value, however, an information-based industry such as health care requires a new system or culture that promotes decentralized decision making and accountability to purchasers. Impediments to cooperation are especially strong from the physician perspective. Hospital administration has always depended on physicians to provide care for patients. Physicians, however, have not relied on outside parties for strategy, marketing, capital allocation, and cost structure, to name a few. Success with cultural change in the AHC will depend more on effective leadership than traditional corporate management to create a clear mission and vision, foster cooperation and collaboration, and promote appropriate physician education.

Because managed care will ultimately limit the number and types of specialists and reduce hospital overcapacity, AHCs must alter their training and culture. Success will depend largely on leadership and its ability to find innovative ways of maintaining a patient base, transforming the traditional culture, and creating new stakeholders in the academic mission. In addition, the AHC must reinvent education and research in the context of these strategies. Because the literature on this subject is largely anecdotal, a framework for potential solutions must be based on common trends in the industry. As a result of rapid changes in the industry, current information often comes from non–peer reviewed journals and news sources.

Innovation and Leadership

Given the speed with which the market is evolving, successful strategies will not be known until they are tried and tested. Projects attempting to delineate strategies for dealing with educational funding have begun. The Council on Graduate Medical Education is expected to release its sixth report specifically dealing with the effect of managed care on the physician workforce and medical education. The University HealthSystem Consortium commissioned two task forces that conducted research in an attempt to identify effective organizational structures and models for the delivery of care in the evolving managed care environment. They determined that a quick and radical response to the eventual dominance of managed care and integrated delivery systems (IDSs; see Chapter 4) is needed to maintain the clinical income required to support the academic mission.[31] Although a complete review and analysis of this work are beyond the scope of this chapter, it is apparent that survival for the AHC will ultimately depend on innovation and a responsiveness to change.

Managed care is rooted in the notion that health care can be managed. Who will be management in an AHC, however, and how do you manage highly skilled people in an information-oriented industry? Traditional management evolved from the industrialization of manufacturing. Before industrialization, craftsmen produced goods while educating apprentices, a process similar to medical education today. By simplifying production processes into small, definable tasks, less skilled workers could produce similar goods more efficiently. Labor became more interchangeable, but the new system needed managers to supervise and control the process. Simplification of the processes meant skilled labor was no longer required, and apprentices disappeared. Unfortunately, innovation and creativity were effectively removed from the labor force. In the end, thinking resided with management, and anything but obedience by workers led to chaos in production.

The industrialization of medicine parallels that of manufacturing in certain ways. There is a drive toward standardization through the use of guidelines, protocols, and benchmarking. Standardization implies simplification and the need for less skilled labor. In addition, the lure of standardization is that the generalist will be able to replace the specialist without needing the same knowledge or experience. Medicine, however, is a complex, knowledge-dependent process. Although improved information capabilities foster the industrialization of medicine, they also require a different form of management.

Systems play an important role in defining management and producing outcomes. Although traditional corporate culture has defined the manager as the knowledgeable decision maker, traditional medical culture has given the physician this role. Knowledgeable people, however, tend to lack an understanding of the complexity of skills they do not possess. Without experience or training in financial and managerial skills, physicians could "manage" medicine successfully, albeit inefficiently, because price and ultimately cost were unimportant. In a commodity business, where aggressive cost control and differentiation are essential, management takes on greater importance. Similarly, managed care executives who have successfully capitalized on overcapacity, negotiating substantial price discounts, believe that they can "deskill," simplify, and in effect control processes they cannot fully understand.

As with any imperative, the outcome is inevitable regardless of individual or group opposition. The market imperative for change created by the purchasers of health care leads to the inevitability of the industrialization of medicine. Network formation is clearly necessary in the evolution of medical organizations. Network formation does not automatically lead to system improvement, however, and a primary care strategy for negotiating capitated contracts does not intrinsically lead to greater physician productivity and competitiveness (see Chapter 4). The ultimate challenge for the AHC will be what to do with networks once they are formed. Furthermore, what role will the primary care physician hold within a newly created system?

Innovative ways of maintaining the AHC patient base, and in turn clinical revenues, are a top priority. Strategies for integrating hospital, generalist, and specialist services into functional networks are essential for successful positioning in the marketplace. Concurrently, the creation and cultivation of stakeholders in the academic mission are of paramount importance to supplement revenues that cannot be maintained as a result of the changes in support for GME. Collaboration with new stakeholders can reinvent education and research in the academic environment. Although innovation is necessary for survival in the short run, anticipating change is essential for prosperity in the long run.

Maintaining a Patient Base

Maintaining a patient base is fundamental for the financial survival of academic physicians and hospitals. For the university, it is mandatory for maintaining quality educational and training programs. As a result of the market forces discussed earlier, total inpatient and specialty service volume will decline as care shifts away from AHCs and toward less expensive settings. To remain viable, AHCs must focus on gaining covered lives through risk sharing and capitated contracts as well as on maintaining their share of the remaining FFS market. In addition, as discussed elsewhere in this book, in an environment of capitation providers want and need more members than patients because most of the money in a capitated system comes from members of health plans who use few or inexpensive medical services. This issue is especially important for AHCs, which stand a greater than normal risk of adverse selection in an enrolled population (see Chapters 42 through 44 of *The Managed Health Care Handbook* for detailed discussions of risk selection).[32–34]

Consolidation between academic and nonacademic hospitals is expected and will leave the remaining institutions in a stronger financial position. Furthermore, declining support for AHCs may lead to a contraction in the number of medical schools and residency programs, which, one hopes, will leave the remaining institutions with more adequate funding. Current strategies for maintaining a patient base by an AHC rest upon network formation in combination with primary and specialty care strategies.

Network Formation

Maintaining clinical revenues requires satisfying the demands of purchasers of health care for access, low cost, appropriate care, ease of contracting, and patient satisfaction. The marketplace response has been the formation of networks that can eventually serve as the backbone for IDSs. Positioning by insurers, hospitals, and AHCs to create service networks of primary care physicians and specialists has reached a rapid pace.[35,36] Networks provide access to geographic areas, reduce the cost of capital, and foster information systems development. As a result, network formation is expected to increase market share and reduce operating costs. Networks are useful to AHCs in preserving the academic mission by educating primary care physicians and retraining specialists in a managed care environment.[37] Additionally, an IDS allows the creation of insurance products that can be marketed directly to purchasers such as employers, Medicare, and Medicaid. By integrating the financing and delivery of care with networks, AHCs can become MCOs in their own right and can profit from greater risk sharing.

Large networks do not always equate with purchaser satisfaction, however. After encouraging market consolidation into three large HMOs, employers in Minnesota decided to negotiate contracts directly with smaller groups of physicians and hospitals. This move occurred for two simple reasons. First, the health plans were engaging in price wars instead of focusing on medical care. Second, they wanted to get employers and health plans "out of the middle" between patients and their physicians.[38] This will give providers such as AHCs an opportunity to develop networks that eliminate the "middleman." Yet, within any delivery system, care will continue to be influenced, if not managed, by parties other than individual physicians. Therefore, elimination of MCOs that have provided value through innovative management of care in combination with the creation of delivery systems may be shortsighted. Ultimately, though, this example reinforces for everyone involved that networks must satisfy purchasers by providing measurable quality care to patients.

AHCs can form primary care networks, hospital networks, or a combination. Primary care networks often require significant capital compared with hospital networks. Positioning in the marketplace can range from forming networks providing a full range of services for a capitated population to providing services to other networks, employers, and insurers in the form of niche, secondary, and tertiary focused services. These strategies are not mutually exclusive and will probably coexist in the future. A network can be created by acquisition of hospitals or physician practices, partnering with established MCOs, and joint ventures with local physician groups and community hospitals.[39]

Primary Care Strategy

Current thinking stresses the importance of a primary care strategy for success in a market dominated by managed care. Whether loosely associated or acquired, physicians who will accept capitated payments for defined populations are the prerequisite for negotiating broader arrangements. The adoption of a primary care strategy by the AHC has other important benefits. Besides revenue generation through capitated payments, an environment is created within the academic setting for education and research in managed care.

Some options for gaining covered lives through primary care include purchasing existing practices, affiliating with existing practices or MCOs, or forming a teaching staff model HMO. Each has different risks and rewards. Purchasing practices and building staff model systems require large capital expenditures. The University of Pennsylvania is pursuing a strategy of purchasing physician practices in Philadelphia and the surrounding metropolitan area. It anticipates needing 150 primary care physicians who will form the backbone of an integrated network capable of caring for defined populations. This capital-intensive strategy will probably cost $100 million.[40] The university does not expect to compete directly with insurers but instead will provide a full range of services to MCOs in the area. Across the river in Philadelphia, Thomas Jefferson University has formed the Jefferson Health System through an agreement with several suburban hospitals.[41] This is a less expensive strategy for affiliating with generalists who can eventually assume risk for defined populations. Another approach might consist of partnering with a strong MCO and taking a role as its sole provider. By reducing the fixed cost per covered life and avoiding the complexity of managing primary care, the risk created by building the infrastructure needed for primary care is avoided.

There are a few caveats that must be noted in forming a primary care strategy, however. First, it cannot be used as mechanism to provide patients for continued specialty and tertiary care. This will continue to encourage overutilization, raising premiums for insurers and purchasers and resulting in poor competitiveness. Second, the AHC must attract healthy members to profit on capitated contracts. Converting the present patient population to a risk contract will be financially dangerous if the patients are an older or sicker group. Excellence in well baby care, sports injuries, and general obstetrics and gynecology may attract younger and healthier enrollees.[42] A focus on the ability to treat complex cases may be a disadvantage, leading to adverse risk selection by patients requiring access to costly tertiary care.

Third, the AHC must recognize that the immediate importance of primary care physicians in network formation is gaining covered lives. Competitiveness based on expected reductions in specialist use or improved population health through preventive care will depend on primary care physicians of the future.[43] Although health care expenditures for American industry decreased in 1994, it is unclear whether managed care as it exists today lowers overall costs or just allows a selection bias, reducing the proportion of sick and elderly in these plans.[44] There is no doubt that fierce competition leads to lower prices. Continued price reductions based on real changes in the delivery of health services, however, will depend on increased physician productivity created with a combination of system improvements and innovative physician training.

Specialty Strategy

The role of the specialist in managed care and network formation is a more challenging issue. FFS, global packaging, and capitation arrangements will probably remain in varying combinations. Further growth of managed care is expected to lead to continued decreases in the use of specialty and tertiary services. To maintain current levels of specialist revenue, AHCs would need to serve larger populations. The number of managed care enrollees needed to support current levels within any particular AHC would differ depending on whether the AHC provides all the specialty services needed by a defined HMO population or only a portion of referral services for the members of various managed care plans. Furthermore, the number of enrollees needed to support revenues varies widely among specialties.[45] Examples of such numbers can be found in Chapter 10.

Options include broader than normal geographical linkages with community providers and insurers as well as increased referrals within their primary service areas. A reliance on referrals from community physicians to teaching hospitals is not viable, however, as the market moves increasingly toward managed care.[46] As stated earlier, primary care cannot be viewed as a means to support specialist and tertiary services. The corollary is that a specialty strategy should be structured to support market needs for such services. AHCs must recognize that, although the current goal of MCOs is to reduce specialty use, elimination is impossible. In the ideal, the goal is the elimination of inappropriate utilization. Although fewer high-priced specialists will be needed, this area can continue to provide a large portion of revenue for the AHC. It is possible that AHCs will have a long-run competitive advantage in situations requiring complex care or the use of new technology for chronic, difficult to manage conditions. Real differences would allow lower per member per month premiums for covered lives within AHC integrated networks. Also, consolidation among AHCs may parallel consolidation of specialty services. The remaining providers will be a combination of low-cost providers and providers of excellence who can demonstrate superior results at a reasonable premium. This may allow the expansion of local and broader referral bases. Arbitrary designations as "centers of excellence" in the absence of superior results, however, will require aggressive marketing in an attempt to differentiate services from the competition.

The battle between producing services within the organization or network versus subcontracting to more efficient providers is a fundamental challenge to all organizations within managed care. Therefore, centers of excellence and integrated networks are not mutually exclusive. Outsourcing often allows more efficiency and less risk for organizations. If the AHC can package specialty and tertiary care for a price below the marginal cost for other networks and managed care organizations, it can create revenues outside of its own capitated contracts. This requires aggressive tertiary marketing that segments and satisfies different customer needs. Unfortunately, adverse risk selection to plans offering these services may eliminate AHC competitive advantage and make these services unappealing to other organizations. Therefore centers of excellence may exist only for a minority of complex cases or procedures such as transplantation.[47]

Transforming the Traditional Culture

AHCs must compete with service-oriented community providers to survive. Clearly, the clinical faculty must offer price-competitive and user-friendly services. Clinical training needs to focus on more relevant and emerging practice situations. Finally, the AHC must delineate funding streams and identify cross-subsidies taking place among teaching, research, and patient care enterprises. This can strengthen clinical training and the financial positions of the AHC and faculty.[48]

Leadership is essential for overcoming the barriers to such organizational changes. By stressing the inevitability of managed care, academic leaders can use market imperatives to begin the process toward transforming the traditional culture. The system must encourage centralized capital allocation and information management in the context of flexible, decentralized delivery of care. Focusing attention on accountability to purchasers for the cost and quality of care is an important first mechanism for fostering cooperation within the AHC. Next, managing outcomes through information and aligning incentives can promote a common vision within the AHC. New organizational structures will depend on functional production rather than departmental orientation, and the traditional risk-averse culture must evolve to take financial risk. Ultimately, though, the challenge for academic leaders may be to prepare for the inevitable external jolt of fierce competition that can unite powerful internal interest groups and successfully guide their institutions to a competitive position.[49]

Accountability

Although the traditional academic culture based in physician autonomy presents a barrier to collaboration, the threat of extinction will be the ultimate catalyst forcing cooperation. The need for provider accountability to purchasers is one market imperative for change within the AHC. Normal market mechanisms always make the seller accountable to the buyer, but the presence of third party payers and purchasers has altered these normal market forces and eliminated provider accountability. By altering the physician's ability to control the stream of revenues, managed care has taken the once autonomous physician and made him or her accountable to the market. Interference in autonomy through imposed practice guidelines and utilization review is a function of providers' past unwillingness to be accountable for the resources they use. Physician accountability assumes that individual physicians determine outcomes, and the question of whether provider accountability and autonomy are mutually exclusive is left to be determined.

Providers assume that, by engaging in risk contracts, they may retain their autonomy while becoming accountable to the consumer. Problems defined in terms of individual physicians, however, often lead to inappropriate solutions. As a result, defining the challenges faced by AHCs as a function of systems as opposed to individuals implicitly alters the culture. Essentially, good people can have bad results depending on the system in which they operate. This was clearly demonstrated in the 1994 cardiac surgery report cards released in New York state.[50] As a result of a poor report card, a system flaw was found and corrected at one hospital in the study. Yet ranking this particular surgeon last implied that the problem was with the individual physician.

As the New York report card indicates, defining the problem in terms of individuals is too simplistic. The assumption of financial risk under capitation by individuals creates accountability for outcomes that may depend on institutional structures or societal issues, such as violence, pollution, lifestyle, diet, alcohol, tobacco, and illicit drug use. By emphasizing the need for group accountability, a common goal is created, and a cultural shift that embraces managed care can begin.

Information Sharing and Outcomes

Response to external pressure for proof of value by purchasers is another market imperative for cooperation within the AHC. Employers want information about value based on measures of cost and quality. AHCs have always claimed superior results. Now they must be able to document these results to justify higher fees for their services. Current information systems perform a billing function and do not provide information about clinical processes and their underlying cost structures. As AHCs assume increased financial risk and the economics of the health care system more resemble those of a commodity market, information about internal cost and process becomes necessary for success. Information systems of the future must combine clinical and financial data to manage process and outcome effectively.[51]

The 1994 report cards released for cardiac surgery in New York once again provide insight into the motivation for cooperation. Because the results suggested problems with individual physicians, purchasers may view report cards as a mechanism to improve care by eliminating poorly performing physicians. The usual argument against the use of such information is that it is not statistically significant for the individual physician and low-volume providers. This fact will not end requests for better outcomes measurements. Although providers will continue to block the release of outcomes data because they fear that the results may be misleading to the public, the marketplace will prevail. Successful integration provides statistically significant samples from which outcomes can be measured. Good results will promote increased market share for providers who are willing to cooperate.

Besides creating valid report cards, linking process to outcomes improves quality and controls costs. There is tremendous variation in the clinical and economic performance of individual providers.[52] Continuous internal evaluation involves separating practice bias and habits from truly effective clinical principles. Ideally, there is a method to promote the best health possible for each individual patient. Medicine, once impervious to standardization because of its complexity, can benefit from application of newer information techniques. The process of identifying best practices is a result of normal industrialization. Although clinical intuition cannot be ignored, a database that knows how 100,000 patients responded to a particular treatment compares favorably with a physician who has seen 100 patients. The initial step toward coordinating efforts at creating clinical pathways and practice protocols depends on elucidation of unexplained clinical variability that increases costs without improving outcomes (see Chapter 19 of *The Managed Health Care Handbook*). Information management using clinical pathways can determine the best of a multitude of alternatives. Using these breakthroughs in information technology and statistics, "complex calculations incorporating the clinical variability that physicians have struggled with for centuries" may provide the ability to determine best practices.[53(p.A8)] In the ideal, one clinical approach will be better, more cost effective, and less risky than another. When raw data are transformed into comparative clinical information, the decision process, management structure, and processes of the institution transform as well.

Many MCOs are using information with traditional management techniques that control, instead of improve, processes. Although the technology to examine complex variables in care exists, the information gained is only as good as the data used and the people who interpret them. Real gains in productivity will result from greater provider use of information in managing processes and outcomes rather than standardization and managerial control.[54] Protocols should be viewed as a way of gaining feedback to improve quality. By evaluating the current processes and adjusting practice patterns to align with cost containment and quality goals, overall value can be optimized. Information transforms opinion and clinical bias into the rational weighing of alternatives. Information also shifts control of process to the point of service.

AHCs cannot rely on MCOs for information. Controlling data is strategically important and operationally essential. Fundamentally, it is an important core competence regardless of strategy. There is evidence to show that, as MCOs become more sophisticated with information management, they are less likely to share financial risks and rewards with providers. Since they profit from retaining financial risk and controlling utilization, decapitation occurs because MCOs often choose discounted FFS options over global packaging and capitation.[55,56] Aggressive utilization management with a per diem fee schedule in lieu of capitation allows an MCO to retain the financial benefits of lowered utilization. MCOs may also fear that shifting financial risk to providers eliminates their major function as insurers. Once at risk, providers can obtain their own licenses, bypass MCOs, and contract directly with purchasers. With or without capitation, information management using efficient systems and meticulous records is vital for continuous internal evaluation within the AHC. Academic leaders must stress that technological and information demands have become too complex and require a collaborative framework between the medical staff and hospital administration.

Reinventing Education and Research with New Stakeholders

Because hospitals and medical schools cannot determine the true cost structure for the activities in which they engage, there is vast disagreement as to whether residents are a burden that promotes inefficiency and noncompetitive care or an inexpensive source of highly trained labor that creates a competitive advantage. Clearly, residents enhance productivity after an initial learning period. Residents are less effective as substitutes for primary care, and there is pressure to keep them in the hospital, where low cost and high skill allow a competitive advantage.[57] But is it ethical to train people for jobs that will not exist?

Education must parallel, and prepare students for, the workforce as it is, not as it has been. Because the current trend is toward ambulatory and primary care, physicians must be trained in this way and in these settings. Effective management should lead to improved education. Controlling the desire to use all available technology requires more oversight and teaching on the part of faculty. Although current educational efforts are based on advancement of medical knowledge, future education will include a focus on efficient and effective delivery of quality care.

The introduction of managed care has created divergent needs between academic providers and medical schools. Although alterations in the culture of the AHC may lead to improved financial strength and an improved patient base, the real cost of education and research may place an insurmountable burden on clinical support for these activities. For example, Tulane University sold 80 percent of its hospital to Columbia/HCA Hospital Corporation while continuing to channel its 20 percent share of the profits to support the academic mission.[58] Meeting the challenges created by managed care involves reconciling the academic mission with the demands of the marketplace. In addition, communication of the importance of the academic mission by academic leaders can foster the creation and cultivation of new stakeholders with an interest in the educational and research value provided by the AHC.

The traditional sources for support, namely the clinical activities of the medical center and the federal government, will remain important. Support for medical education has always been provided by the federal government, and in all likelihood this will continue in some form. Although there may be heavy political negotiation regarding the necessary funding of education and research, the focus must shift toward proper allocation of resources. AHCs can gain public support for endeavors that promote the public good, but not as a proxy to continue inefficiencies. Separation of federal subsidies from Medicare payments is in the best interest of the university. As discussed earlier, the current system of indirect and disguised support is inefficient and unreliable. Restructuring funding for education would markedly diminish reliance on indirect GME funding provided through clinical revenues and eliminate unintended subsidies to local MCOs. Ultimately, educational funding should flow directly to the medical school. Continued federal subsidies in any form will require lobbying to promote the true value of the AHC.

Federal action will also be extremely important to help with adverse patient selection, ensuring that hospitals and physicians in the academic setting are properly reimbursed for more complex cases. AHCs, however, must be able to prove that their patient population has greater needs that require additional support. Pressure by AHCs can promote discussions of public policy issues, such as undergraduate and graduate education, research funding, and care for the indigent.[59] Support will come with increased political involvement concerning the use of these funds, however.

Support from clinical operations will also continue, possibly for different reasons than today. Systems that remain fully integrated with the university can only profit from and support the academic mission if education is also fully integrated and adds value to the system. This may be the crux of reinventing education. Academic providers may find that association with the medical school helps recruit and retain top physicians.[60] As a result, the institution will have an opportunity to select and recruit the best and brightest before its competition.

Consolidated tertiary care hospitals will still need and support training of qualified specialists, but the classic tertiary hospital of today will not control the majority of physician training. In response, Harvard Medical School is attempting to bring the academic and managed care cultures together by forming a partnership with the Harvard Community Health Plan. This is the first medical school department to be based in a free-standing HMO, turning the teaching hospital structure into a "teaching HMO" that creates a practice setting for education and research in a managed care environment.[61,62]

Aside from government and clinical subsidies, the most likely stakeholders in the academic mission are MCOs, pharmaceutical manufacturers, and medical device companies. By providing new avenues for income and investment, new stakeholders reduce university reliance on clinical and federal funds. By way of complex joint ventures, universities are already forming relationships with other stakeholders in the academic mission, such as pharmaceutical companies and medical device manufacturers. Collaboration with these new organizations gives industry access to academic experience and resources. For example, Duke University has formed a business unit called the Duke Clinical Research Center. It will compete directly with private companies that perform clinical trials for drug and medical device companies. Other ventures will promote the development of information tools that improve the quality and cost-effectiveness of care.[63]

A NEW ROLE FOR MCOs

Few MCOs have formal relationships with AHCs other than through contracts for tertiary services. First, MCOs find that it is difficult to provide the cost-effective care needed to survive under the influence of the needs and culture of teaching hospitals.[64] This is especially true because MCOs seek to limit specialist use while the traditional academic culture encourages its use. Second, university medical centers in urban areas offer few services that are not available in community hospitals and from specialists in private practice.[65] A change in the AHC culture is important to overcome barriers to collaboration with outside MCOs. It is also clear, however, that MCOs will need to embrace the advantages of supporting academic endeavors. As the chief executive officer of a major insurer commented, "We recognize that AHCs have educational costs. We just aren't going to pay for them."[66]

Nevertheless, there are powerful reasons for MCOs to collaborate with AHCs. Simply put, education and research will become more critical in transforming managed care and medicine in the future. The major benefits from managed care have come through macro-management, which has reinvented the financing of health services. The resulting change in financial incentives has promoted a population-based, cost-effective perspective that rests with defining appropriate care. In response, provider organizations are adopting management techniques that were previously only used by insurers.[67] Innovation in the future, however, will increasingly depend on micro-management of the delivery of care. Reports of increasing physician management of care at the clinical level represent a fundamental transformation in the practice of medicine.

Undoubtedly, MCOs and providers will struggle in defining their respective roles in decision making. This is a fundamental conflict between management and labor in highly technical, specialized service industries. Given the importance of knowledge in today's information society, however, the power of implementation ultimately lies with the service provider.[68] The role of capital assets in the delivery of services will continue to diminish. At the same time, labor's inexorable transformation from an expense to an asset requires a dedicated investment.[69]

Consequently, provider education and training are important in creating value for managed care. The quality of primary care graduates is already a concern to MCOs that employ them, and shortages of primary care physicians have been reported as a limiting factor in the growth rates of staff and group models, HMOs in particular.[70] An unwillingness to support education could have deleterious long-term effects for MCOs. Without new financial supporters, current educators could dramatically decrease the training of their competition, ultimately raising expenses for MCOs. Partnerships with medical centers will allow greater input into the training needs of an MCO and ensure an adequate supply of well-trained physicians. This is not an abstract concept; as private practices affiliate or merge, the ability of an MCO to purchase practices or to contract with existing groups becomes more difficult. If an MCO has an established and good relationship with an AHC that is training the types of physicians most attractive to the MCO, then recruiting becomes at least a bit easier.

Next, the growth of managed care has highlighted the need for outcomes research while diminishing the funds available. The philosophy of managed care emphasizes appropriate care based on outcomes analysis. Yet (with some exceptions) MCOs do not support research in this area.[71] The fight for survival may provide the impetus for innovative management techniques within successful AHCs. Through association with medical centers, MCOs can benefit from continued improvements that result from systematic research on best practices and outcomes measurements. Furthermore, as MCOs have increasing responsibility for older and sicker populations, they will require further advances in basic and clinical resources.[72,73] Many AHCs have extensive experience with complex cases, Medicare populations, and indigent populations, which are becoming a greater source of revenue for MCOs. The AHC provides a legitimate source for research into health service delivery, with dissemination of literature that influences the definition of medically acceptable and appropriate care.

Examples of support for the academic mission by MCOs appear regularly in many of the rapidly changing local markets. In the area of direct support for education and research, US Healthcare (an open panel or independent practice association model HMO operating primarily in the northeast) has a managed care fellowship at Thomas Jefferson University in Philadelphia. This unique collaboration, one of the few in the country, is designed to train physicians for influential roles in MCOs. In addition, US Healthcare has joined the Jefferson Cancer Center to promote clinical research in health services.

Despite long-term benefits for the support of AHCs by MCOs, fierce price competition may leave little excess revenue for such direct support. The collaboration between Sanus Health Systems, a subsidiary of New York Life Insurance, and Duke University Medical Center goes beyond direct support for the academic mission and transforms the relationship between MCOs and AHCs from contractor and contracted to equal partners. The new health management and benefits company, WellPath Community Health Plans Holdings, splits ownership and decision making between the two organizations. Sanus sees this partnership as an opportunity to take advantage of the excellent relationships already established between the academic medical center and hospitals and physicians in the community. The success of the venture, however, focuses on effective community-based care and is not a mechanism for steering patients to Duke for specialized care. Contracts will be created with other hospitals, including other tertiary care centers.[74] MCOs interested in creative approaches to contracting with AHCs must recognize the importance of shared ownership and decision making with academic centers and providers.

In addition to the above, many MCOs have developed attractive primary care networks and affiliations with community hospitals. An MCO that is newly entering the market or is entering into a new line of business, such as Medicare or Medicaid, may find contracting with the AHC and its network to be an efficient way to get into the market and that negotiating a global capitation (with stop-loss protection) is an equally efficient way to attenuate the risk for health care costs. As AHCs learn more about the management of health care resources, they are ever more willing to accept that level of risk, especially in partnership with an MCO that can provide the kind of data and support necessary for the AHC to succeed.

CONCLUSION

The threat to the traditional financing of the academic mission by the spread of managed care presents many challenges for academic health centers. Still, opportunities exist for improved patient care amid physician doom and gloom. Surely, bright individuals with a stake in this mission can respond to the challenges outlined in this chapter. Physicians appreciate and foster the scientific model. AHCs are positioned to create the "new" science of medical practice, promoting the industrial revolution in medicine. Although altered, the AHC will remain the centerpiece of American medicine.

Study Questions

1. Briefly compare and contrast the role of the purchaser relative to academic medical centers prior to 1983 and after.
2. What are the significant barriers to organizational change within academic health centers?
3. Broadly outline some current strategies for success for academic health centers.

4. How do academic health centers maintain an adequate patient base in the face of intensified managed competition?
5. What are some new roles that managed care organizations are taking on in the current environment relative to academic health centers?

REFERENCES AND NOTES

1. J.K. Iglehart, Rapid Changes for Academic Medical Centers: Second of Two Parts. *New England Journal of Medicine* 332 (1995): 407–411.
2. J.K. Iglehart, Rapid Changes for Academic Medical Centers: First of Two Parts. *New England Journal of Medicine* 331 (1994): 1391–1395.
3. University Hospital Consortium, Responding to a Dynamic Health Care Marketplace: Implementation Strategies for Academic Health Centers (presented at the University Hospital Consortium 1995 Research Conference, St. Petersburg, Fla., 2–3 February 1995).
4. Office of National Cost Estimates, Health Care Financing Administration, *1991–1992 Hospital Fact Book* (Sacramento, Calif.: California Association of Hospitals and Health Systems, 1992).
5. R.S. Brown, et al., *Does Managed Care Work for Medicare? An Evaluation of the Medicare Risk Program for HMOs* (Princeton, N.J.: Mathematica Policy Research, Inc., 1993).
6. D.G. Clement, et al., Access and Outcomes of Elderly Patients Enrolled in Managed Care, *Journal of the American Medical Association* 271 (1994): 1487–1492.
7. Managing Medicaid, *American Medical News* (19 December 1994): 11.
8. University Hospital Consortium, Responding to a Dynamic Health Care Marketplace.
9. J.P. Kassirer, Academic Medical Centers under Siege, *New England Journal of Medicine* 331 (1995): 1370–1371.
10. HMOs Are Changing the Face of Medicine, *New York Times* (11 January 1995): A1.
11. U.E. Reinhardt, The Bounty Hunters, *Imaging Economics* (July/August 1995): 9–10.
12. A.J. Slomski, Employers to Doctors: It's Time for REAL Savings, *Medical Economics* (August 1995): 34–48.
13. Reinhardt, The Bounty Hunters.
14. University Hospital Consortium, Responding to a Dynamic Health Care Marketplace.
15. J.M. Saue and G.H. Dooge, "ERISA and Managed Care," in *The Managed Health Care Handbook*, 3d ed., ed. P.R. Kongstvedt (Gaithersburg, Md.: Aspen, 1996), 944–966.
16. Slomski, Employers to Doctors.
17. Demand Management: A "New" Strategy To Solve Our Health Care Ills, *Managed Care Update* (July 1995): 3–10.
18. Reinhardt, The Bounty Hunters.
19. Managed Care Maelstrom, *American Medical News* (25 July 1994): 1.
20. University Hospital Consortium, Responding to a Dynamic Health Care Marketplace.
21. S. Greenfield, et al., Outcomes of Patients with Hypertension and non–Insulin-Dependent Diabetes Mellitus Treated by Different Systems and Specialties: Results from the Medical Outcomes Study, *Journal of the American Medical Association* 274 (1995): 1436–1474.
22. D.J. Shulkin and A.H. Rosenstein, "Towards Cost-Effective Care," in *The Physicians Guide to Managed Care*, ed. D.B. Nash (Gaithersburg, Md.: Aspen, 1994), 119–159.
23. Clement et al., Access and Outcomes of Elderly Patients Enrolled in Managed Care.
24. Large Study Finds Certain Patients Fare as Well in HMOs as in Insurance Plans, *Wall Street Journal* (8 November 1995): B13.
25. University Hospital Consortium, Responding to a Dynamic Health Care Marketplace.
26. University Hospital Consortium, Responding to a Dynamic Health Care Marketplace.
27. J.K. Iglehart, Academic Medical Centers Enter the Market: The Case of Philadelphia, *New England Journal of Medicine* 333 (1995): 1019–1023.
28. P. Fox and J. Wasserman, Academic Medical Centers and Managed Care: Uneasy Partners, *Health Affairs* 272 (1993): 85–93.
29. K. Pallarito, New York's Academic Medicine Goes Ape, *Modern Healthcare* (28 August 1995): 34–41.
30. S.R. Craig, Practicing Medicine under Capitation: One Group's Experience, *Internist* (May 1995): 8–9.
31. University Hospital Consortium, Responding to a Dynamic Health Care Marketplace.
32. S.M. Cigich, "Actuarial Services in an Integrated Delivery System," in *The Managed Health Care Handbook*, 3d ed., ed. P.R. Kongstvedt (Gaithersburg, Md.: Aspen, 1996), 659–666.
33. S.M. Cigich, "Rating and Underwriting," in *The Managed Health Care Handbook*, 3d ed., ed. P.R. Kongstvedt (Gaithersburg, Md.: Aspen, 1996), 667–678.
34. G.L. Lippe, "Operational Underwriting in Managed Care Organizations," in *The Managed Health Care*

Handbook, 3d ed., ed. P.R. Kongstvedt (Gaithersburg, Md.: Aspen, 1996), 679–699.

35. Iglehart, Rapid Changes for Academic Medical Centers: Second of Two Parts.
36. Iglehart, Academic Medical Centers Enter the Market.
37. University Hospital Consortium, Responding to a Dynamic Health Care Marketplace.
38. Employer Groups Rethink Commitment to Big HMOs, *Wall Street Journal* (21 July 1995): B1.
39. University Hospital Consortium, Responding to a Dynamic Health Care Marketplace.
40. Iglehart, Rapid Changes for Academic Medical Centers: Second of Two Parts.
41. Iglehart, Academic Medical Centers Enter the Market.
42. Craig, Practicing Medicine under Capitation.
43. B. Starfield, Is Primary Care Essential?, *Lancet* 344 (1994): 1129–1133.
44. Brown, et al., *Does Managed Care Work for Medicare?*
45. J.E. Billi, et al., Potential Effects of Managed Care on Specialty Practice at a University Medical Center, *New England Journal of Medicine* 333 (1995): 979–983.
46. Iglehart, Academic Medical Centers Enter the Market.
47. University Hospital Consortium, Responding to a Dynamic Health Care Marketplace.
48. J.E. Kralewski, et al., Can Academic Medical Centers Compete in a Managed Care System?, *Academic Medicine* 70 (1995): 867–872.
49. Kralewski, et al., Can Academic Medical Centers Compete in a Managed Care System?
50. Death-Rate Rankings Shake New York Cardiac Surgeons, *The New York Times* (6 September 1995): A1.
51. M. Clare, et al., Reducing Health Care Delivery Costs Using Clinical Paths: A Case Study on Improving Hospital Profitability, *Journal of Health Care Financing* 21 (1995): 48–58.
52. HMOs Are Changing the Face of Medicine.
53. Medicine's Industrial Revolution, *Wall Street Journal* (21 August 1995): A8.
54. E.J. Proenca, Why Outcomes Management Doesn't (Always) Work: An Organizational Perspective, *Quality Management in Health Care* 3 (1995): 1–9.
55. M. Gold, et al., Behind the Curve: A Critical Assessment of How Little Is Known about Arrangements Between Managed Care Plans and Physicians, *Managed Care Research and Review* 52 (1995): 307–341.
56. University Hospital Consortium, Responding to a Dynamic Health Care Marketplace.
57. Fox and Wasserman, Academic Medical Centers and Managed Care.
58. Academic Centers—and GME—Face Growing Market Pressure, *American Medical News* (18 September 1995): 1.
59. Reinhardt, The Bounty Hunters.
60. Market Changes Hasten Oversupply of Physicians, *American Medical News* (8 August 1994): 1.
61. G.T. Moore, et al., The "Teaching HMO": A New Academic Partner, *Academic Medicine* 69 (1994): 595–600.
62. Managed Care and Academia Join To Build "Teaching HMO's," *ACP Observer* (April 1995): 1.
63. Getting Down to Business at Duke's Medical School, *Wall Street Journal* (29 August 1995): B1.
64. Fox and Wasserman, Academic Medical Centers and Managed Care.
65. Kralewski, et al., Can Academic Medical Centers Compete in a Managed Care System?
66. University Hospital Consortium, Responding to a Dynamic Health Care Marketplace.
67. E.A. Kerr, et al., Managed Care and Capitation in California: How Do Physicians at Financial Risk Control Their Own Utilization?, *Annals of Internal Medicine* 123 (1995): 500–504.
68. P.F. Drucker, The Coming of the New Organization, *Harvard Business Review* (January/February 1988): 45–53.
69. B.J. Reilly, et al., Traditional Decision-Making Questioned: It's Time for New Thinking for a New Age, *Business Forum* (Winter/Spring 1993): 25–30.
70. Moore, et al., The "Teaching HMO."
71. HMOs Value Research—If Others Pay for It, *American Medical News* (20 November 1995): 1.
72. Academic Centers—and GME—Face Growing Market Pressure.
73. Managed Care and Academia Join To Build "Teaching HMOs."
74. Sanus Offers Multiple-Option Plan with N.C. Academic Medical Center, *Managed Care Outlook* (17 November 1995): 1–3.

SUGGESTED READING

Nash, D.B. 1994. *The Physician's Guide to Managed Care.* Gaithersburg, Md.: Aspen.

Weitekamp, M.R. and Ziegenfuss, J.T. 1995. Academic Health Centers and HMOs: A Systems Perspective on Collaboration in Training Generalist Physicians and Advancing Mutual Interests. *Academic Medicine* 70(1): S47–S53.

Part III

Medical Management

"You can't always get what you want.
But if you try sometimes
You just might find
You get what you need."

Mick Jagger (1969)

Chapter 13

Managing Basic Medical–Surgical Utilization

Peter R. Kongstvedt

Study Objectives

- Understand what managing utilization means
- Understand the basic categories of utilization management
- Understand the basic differences between managing utilization in the inpatient, outpatient, and specialty services categories
- Understand what basic utilization management techniques are most useful in different situations
- Understand the basic measurements of utilization
- Understand basic roles for different types of professionals in managing utilization

The management of utilization is a critical function of any managed care organization, especially a health maintenance organization (HMO). When one analyzes where the premium dollars go, between 70 percent and 90 percent go into the provision of medical services. While ensuring access and high quality, the fundamental purpose of a managed care plan is to manage utilization, thereby reducing health care costs.

There are many facets to the management of utilization, and these facets are addressed in numerous chapters in this book. As managed care has become more prevalent, the divisions among the management of specialty physician care, inpatient care, outpatient care, and indeed all aspects of health care delivery have become progressively blurred. This chapter will concentrate on basic medical–surgical care. Utilization of primary care services (as well as other professional services) is addressed in the section on demand management. Utilization of specialty services and institutional services is also discussed in later sections of this chapter. The reader is referred to other chapters of the book for discussions of the following:

- large case management (LCM)
- long-term and subacute care
- managing utilization of ancillary and emergency services
- changing provider behavior in managed care plans
- clinical pathways
- managed mental health and substance abuse services
- pharmaceutical services in managed care
- quality management
- reengineering the health care delivery system
- use of data and reports in medical management

ADMINISTRATIVE COST VERSUS MEDICAL LOSS RATIO

Experienced HMO managers know well that investment in utilization management (UM) is well leveraged in the classic sense of the word leverage. In other words, there is a high rate of return for money spent in this activity in the form of lower health care costs. The degree of leverage will vary from plan to plan, but a recent review of 13 quarters of data on 14 large open panel HMOs performed by an investment analyst confirms this finding.[1]

DEMAND MANAGEMENT*

Demand management refers to activities of a health plan designed to reduce the overall requirement for health care services by members. In addition to helping lower health care costs, these services may provide a competitive advantage to a plan by enhancing the plan's reputation for service and by giving members additional value for their premium dollar. Demand management services fall into five broad categories, which are briefly discussed below.

Nurse Advice Lines

Nurse advice lines provide members with access to advice regarding medical conditions, the need for medical care, health promotion and preventive care, and numerous other advice-related activities. Such advice lines have been in use in closed panel HMOs for many years (where they are occasionally referred to as triage nurse lines). Plans may staff these lines with their own nurses or may purchase the service from any one of a number of commercial services. Hours of operation are almost always extended and may be 24 hours (especially if a plan uses a commercial service). A geographically large plan or a commercial service is likely to use a toll-free line to make it easier for members to access the service.

Special market segments, such as Medicare and Medicaid, may benefit from dedicated programs. Attention to the special problems and concerns of seniors will go a long way to improving their health status and can be a major contributor to the overall management of care in this population. Easy access to medical advice in the Medicaid population may allow these members to avoid a trip to the emergency department.

Self-Care and Medical Consumerism Programs

This activity refers to the provision of information to members to allow them to provide care for themselves or to evaluate better when they need to seek care from a professional. Member newsletters with medical advice are used extensively by HMOs. The most common example of a more proactive approach is a self-care guide provided by the plan. These books are generally written in an easy-to-understand manner and provide step-by-step advice for common medical conditions as well as preventive care. Information about the wise use of medical services or how to be an informed consumer would also fall into this category.

Self-care programs have been evaluated since the early 1980s with typical results around $2.50 to $3.50 saved for every dollar invested.[2] A fever health education program at Kaiser decreased pediatric clinic utilization by 35 percent for fever visits and 25 percent for all acute visits.[3] In another study, the combination of a 24-hour nurse advice service with a self-care program (see below) resulted in a savings of $4.75 per dollar invested, and the self-care program alone resulted in a savings of $2.40 per dollar invested.[4]

In another structured study in a staff model HMO, the targeted use of such self-care manuals resulted in decreased outpatient visits and a 2-to-1 return on the cost of the program.[5] Other studies have reported savings of $2.40 to $2.77 per dollar invested.[6] It is unclear if such savings are routinely achievable, though.

Shared Decision-Making Programs

This activity refers to making the member an active participant in choosing a course of care.

---

* The author is indebted to David W. Plocher, M.D., the coauthor of two other chapters in this book, for his invaluable work in summarizing the information paraphrased in the demand management section of the chapter.

Although this general philosophy may be prevalent in routine interactions between patients and physicians, this activity is more focused. Shared decision-making programs provide great depth of information to patients regarding specific procedures. By receiving this information, patients are able to gain a deeper understanding not only of the disease process but also of the treatment alternatives. Some HMOs that use these programs will not finalize authorization for certain elective procedures (e.g., transurethral resection of the prostate) until the member has completed the shared decision-making program.

A number of commercial services have appeared in the past few years to produce these programs. Many use interactive CD-ROM, videotape, and computer programs to provide the information. Supplemental access to a nurse advice line as well as the ability to discuss the alternatives with the physician after the patient has reviewed the material are also routine.

Medical Informatics

Medical informatics is a broad term that applies to the use of information technology in the management of health care delivery. The broader topics of the use of data in medical management are discussed in Chapter 19. For the purposes of this section, medical informatics refers to the use of information technology in helping manage demand for services. There are two broad categories to be mentioned: the use of informatics by the member, and the use of informatics by the plan.

Use of informatics by the member might include access to an on-line service, such as one that provides health-related information to members. Business-related information as well as electronic mail and communications with the plan may also be available. The plan may do this through a dedicated direct dial-in service, or it may do so through a more public arena; several plans have developed sites on the World Wide Web.

Related to this, many plans have placed kiosks in easily accessible locations. These locations might include on the site of a large employer, in the lobby of the health plan, in a large medical facility, or in a public area such as a shopping mall. The kiosk provides information regarding prevention and certain common medical conditions and may also provide access to business information, such as the types of benefits available.

The plan may use information systems to anticipate demand for services or to analyze how demand for services can be better managed. For example, an analysis of the use of urgent care or emergency services may be related to hours of operation, location of primary care, work patterns at a large employer, and so forth. By looking for patterns, the plan may be able to develop strategies for lowering demand for one type of service by substituting another type of service.

Preventive Services and Health Risk Appraisals

Preventive services are a hallmark of the HMO industry. Common preventive services include immunizations, mammograms, routine physical examinations and health assessments, and counseling regarding behavior that the member can undertake to lower the risk of ill health (e.g., smoking cessation, dietary counseling, stress reduction, and so forth). Counseling and education may also be applied to specific clinical conditions; for example, in one study of a managed indemnity plan, an employer held worksite prenatal education programs and found that participants in the educational programs had an average cost per delivery that was $3,200 less than that for nonparticipants.[7]

The health risk appraisal is a tool designed to elicit information from a member regarding certain activities and behaviors that can influence health status. Self-reported information about obvious behaviors, such as smoking and alcohol use, as well as less obvious behaviors, such as the use (or really lack of use) of seat belts, gun ownership, and so forth, is obtained. That information is then used in a computer program to produce a profile of an individual's health risks and what modifications of behavior may improve that individual's life expectancy. This information is usually also provided to the member's primary care physician (PCP), who will then be in a better position to counsel the member.

In plans that have a large Medicare enrollment, the plan may take extra steps in performing an initial assessment. The most common of these extra activities is an in-home assessment of the new Medicare member. A trained nurse or medical social worker may determine, for example, that if the plan gives the new Medicare enrollee a bath mat or shower chair it will significantly reduce the risk of a hip fracture from falling in the bathtub. An inventory of the member's diet may also yield valuable information that will enable the new member's provider to improve health status by lowering sodium intake or lowering saturated fats in the diet. A review of medications may reveal a compliance problem that, if corrected, could prevent complications from a chronic condition.

SPECIALTY PHYSICIAN UTILIZATION MANAGEMENT

The management of utilization of referral physicians and consultants (both physicians and nonphysicians) is an area of great importance. In most managed health care plans, the costs associated with non–primary care professional services will be substantially greater than the cost of primary care services, often between 1.5 and 2.0 times as high. This is due to the increased fees associated with consultant services and to the hospital-intensive and procedure-oriented nature of those services; in other words, more than half the costs of consultant services may be associated with hospital or procedural cases.

Often overlooked are the associated utilization costs generated by consultants. It is not only the fees of the consultants themselves that add to the cost of care but also the cost of services ordered by consultants, such as diagnostic studies, facility charges for procedures, and so forth. One 1987 study in a non–managed care environment found that each referral from a PCP generated nearly $3,000 in combined hospital charges and professional fees within a 6-month period after the referral.[8] It may be safely assumed that the value of a referral has increased considerably since 1987. These costs are not routinely added to the cost of consultant services when data are compiled, but control of consultant services will often lead to control of these outside services as well.

Definitions

The definition of referral or consultant services includes physician fees that are not considered primary care, in other words all physician fees that are not from general internists, family physicians, and general pediatricians. If you have chosen to include obstetrics and gynecology (OB/GYN) as primary care, then you will need to decide which of the services provided by OB/GYN (e.g., surgery, routine Pap smears and pelvic examinations, colposcopy, and so forth) are included as primary care and which are consultant care.

In general, most managed care plans count consultant physicians and nonphysician professionals (e.g., psychologists) in the consultant cost category, and ancillary services (e.g., laboratory, radiology, pharmacy, and the like) are dealt with separately. In keeping with that, control of ancillary services utilization is addressed separately in Chapter 15.

Data

To manage consultant services, you must first be able to capture utilization and cost data in an accurate and timely manner. If you do not have that ability, your efforts to control utilization in this category will be severely hampered. The issue of data capture and reporting is discussed further in Chapter 19.

There is no set standard for reporting data on referral utilization as there is for hospital utilization. Nevertheless, certain measures are used frequently and found useful by managers. In

HMOs that do not have any benefits for services provided without an authorization from a PCP, a useful measure is referrals per 100 encounters per PCP. In this measure, one counts the total number of referrals made by a PCP for every 100 primary care encounters. This correlates to a referral percentage. For example, 11 referrals per 100 encounters per PCP equals a referral rate of 11 percent.

More commonly used is the referral rate per 1,000 members per year. Like the measurement of hospitalization rate, this looks at an annualized referral rate for every 1,000 members. Although this is less directly related to a PCP encounter than referrals per 100 primary care encounters, the nomenclature is standard across many types of plans.

It is important to know whether you are counting initial referrals or total visits to a referral consultant. In other words, if you are only counting the initial referral or authorization, you may be missing a large portion of the actual utilization. It is not uncommon, especially in loosely controlled systems, for a single referral to generate multiple visits to a consultant. For example, if a PCP refers a member with the request to evaluate and treat, this is carte blanche for the consultant to take over the care of the patient, and succeeding visits will be to the consultant and not to the PCP.

It is therefore far more useful to track actual visits. Better yet is to track both initial referrals and actual visits because that will give you a clearer idea of how the consultants are really handling the cases. In a tightly controlled system, such as an HMO with a strict policy granting authorization for one visit only for any referral, the numbers may be close to being the same. In a system with loose controls, the number of actual visits may exceed the initial referral rate by two to three times. Specialty visit rates in commercial HMOs average 1.2 encounters per member per year (PMPY), with a range of 0.8 to 1.3 encounters PMPY; visits to medical specialists were slightly higher than for surgical specialists.[9] Figure 13–1 illustrates specialty visit rates in HMOs.

Selection of Referral and Consulting Providers

As mentioned in Chapter 7 and discussed in Chapter 19, the ability to select providers on the basis of a demonstrated pattern of practice can have a considerable impact on referral expenses. There are large differences in the efficiency of practice among providers within each specialty, and if patients are preferentially sent to those consultants and referral specialists who demonstrate cost-effective practice, the plan can achieve considerable savings.

This is especially important in plans that allow self-referral to consultants by members, such as preferred provider organizations (PPOs) or point-of-service (POS) plans; see Chapter 3 for a description of these types of plans. If you have a loose system that allows open access to any consultant at any time other than through selection of providers, you can exert little control except perhaps by making fee adjustments after enough documentation of overutilization. The problem with using fee adjustments to control utilization (i.e., adjusting a consultant's, or the entire provider panel's, fees downward as utilization goes up) is that it can lead to an "I'd better get mine first" mentality. In that situation, providers may begin churning visits and increasing utilization to increase revenues, worried that next month the fees may be adjusted even lower. This issue is discussed in Chapter 8.

Evaluating referral practice behavior is no easy task and must be done over a long period of time on a significant number of events. See Chapter 19 for further discussion of this topic.

Authorization System

Authorization systems are discussed in detail in Chapter 21. The utility of an authorization system is mentioned here because without one you have a markedly diminished chance of effectively controlling referral utilization. Through educative techniques, you may be able to decrease consultant utilization somewhat, but unless there is a primary care gatekeeper or case

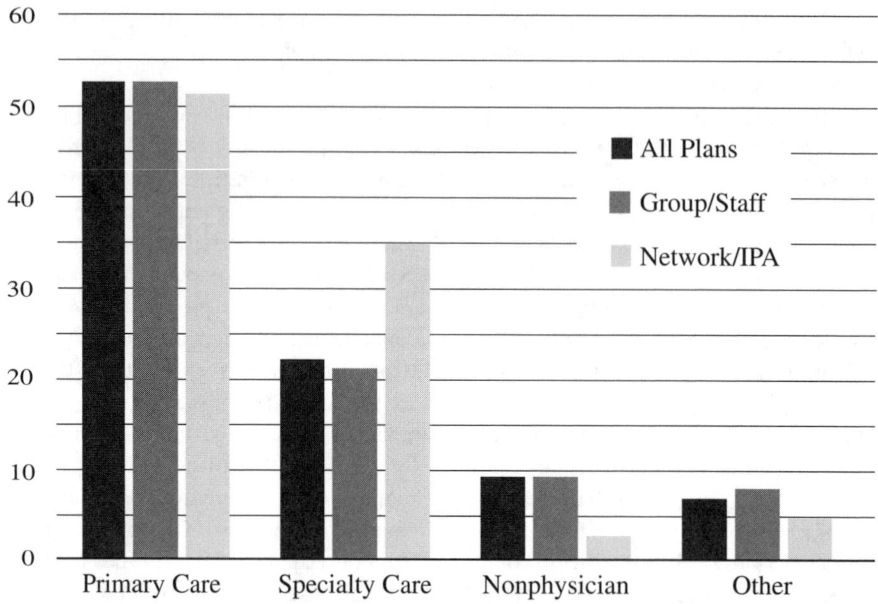

Figure 13–1 Specialty physician visit rates in HMOs as a percentage of total ambulatory encounters. IPA, individual practice association. *Source:* American Association of Health Plans (formerly GHAA/AMCRA) 1992 Utilization Data Supplement to the Eighth Annual HMO Industry Survey (Washington, D.C.).

manager system in place, it is not likely that you will achieve optimal results. If you have been able carefully to select consultants through practice pattern analysis, you may get improvement in referral expenses, but not to the same degree that a PCP authorization system will allow.

The corollary to this is the possibility that a PCP can deliver many of the same services as a consultant, but at considerable savings and in a more appropriate setting. Even in non–managed care systems, PCPs manage a substantial proportion of their patients' care.[10] Therefore, the reason for a PCP authorization system to manage consultant costs is twofold: to reduce consultant utilization through services delivered by the PCP, and to manage those referrals that are made.

The remainder of this chapter will assume that there is some type of authorization system in place. That system can be rigid or loose.

Methods To Achieve Tight Control of Specialty Physician Services

Single Visit Authorizations Only

As discussed in Chapter 21, a system that allows only one visit per authorization is necessary for optimal control. There are common exceptions to that, which are listed below. In essence, every time a member is referred to a consultant, the PCP gatekeepers (or care coordinators, or whatever you choose to call them) must issue a unique authorization. That authorization is good for one visit and will only be used to pay one claim. Claims submitted by the consultant with multiple charges will be compared with what was authorized, and only the authorized services will be reimbursed.

This sounds strong in theory, and it is strong. Unfortunately, it is sometimes difficult to enforce. A mechanism for review of claims that do not exactly match the authorization must be put in place so that you do not penalize members and consultants if the PCP fails to document the authorization correctly. It is also sometimes difficult in practice to pull out overcharges or add-ons to a claim, particularly when the claims adjudicators get overworked. Nonetheless, this system is both workable and necessary for optimal control.

It is vital to inform members through full and fair disclosure of such a system before they enroll in your plan. The usual methods of informing members include enrollment literature, new member kits, the identification card issued by your plan, the evidence of coverage certificate that you issue to a member, the referral form itself, the plan newsletter, and even signs in your consultants' offices. Consultants will usually agree to allow signs in their offices when they understand that improving compliance with authorization procedures will enhance their revenue both by speeding up claims processing and by a decreased bad debt load.

After you have informed members, you must periodically reinform them. Most people will not remember everything they hear, even after hearing it multiple times. There will always be some who deny ever knowing about the need for authorization, but you can only do the best you can.

As noted above, there are common exceptions to the rule of one authorization per visit. These include chemotherapy and radiation therapy for cancer, obstetrics, mental health and chemical dependency therapy, physical therapy, and rehabilitation therapy. You may choose other exceptions in your plan. For example, you may automatically allow one or two home health visits after short-stay obstetrics.

Even for these exceptions, however, you should not have open-ended authorizations. There should be an absolute limit on the number of visits that can be authorized at once. For example, you may wish to limit initial mental health referrals to two or three visits and then require the therapist to discuss the case with the PCP or mental health case manager before any further authorizations are allowed (see Chapter 16). Physical therapy should likewise be limited to an initial number of visits, and then the therapist must discuss the case with the physician before any further authorizations are issued. For chemotherapy cases, the oncologist should discuss the case with the PCP and outline the exact course of treatment, which could then be authorized all at once. The overriding principle is that open-ended authorizations are simply blank checks. If you allow them, you will pay the price.

Prohibition of Secondary Referrals and Authorizations

Another facet of controlling referral utilization is the prohibition of secondary referrals by consultants. This means that a consultant cannot authorize additional referrals for a member. In other words, if a consultant feels that a patient needs to see another consultant, that must be communicated back to the PCP, who is the only one able to issue an authorization for services.

This extends to revisits back to the consultant and to testing and procedures as well. For example, if a consultant has an expensive piece of diagnostic equipment in the office, there may be a subtle pressure to use it to make it pay for itself. One widely noted study looking at physician ownership of radiology equipment documented a fourfold increase in imaging examinations as well as significant increases in charges among physicians who used their own equipment compared with physicians who referred such studies to radiologists.[11] Similar results have been reported for laboratory services and a wide variety of ancillary services.[12,13]

The issue of physician-owned diagnostic and therapeutic equipment or services is a difficult one to address and one that is coming under increasing pressure from government regulation, at least for Medicare.[14] Perhaps the best method for dealing with this issue is simply to prohibit or markedly restrict the use of such services. Most managed care plans contract with a limited number of vendors for such ancillary services and may limit referral to only those vendors. The topic of ancillary services is discussed in Chapter 15.

Even in the absence of those types of pressures, secondary referrals may simply be unnecessary. For example, an endocrinologist may be concerned about a referred patient's chest pain and may refer the patient to a cardiologist when in fact the patient's PCP had worked up the problem and was tracking it carefully. This happens more often than one might think because a patient may not always communicate or even understand the previous care he or she has received, and the PCP may not have considered it necessary to put that information into the referral letter or form.

Last, the prohibition on secondary authorizations extends to procedures, including hospitalizations. A consultant must obtain the authorization from the PCP or the plan (depending on the plan's policy about precertification) before any procedures (e.g., colonoscopy) or admission to the hospital. This is not to be punitive but to ensure that such things are done in the most cost-effective manner possible. For example, a referral surgeon may not be aware of the preadmission testing program, may use a noncontracting hospital, or may be used to admitting the patient the day before surgery simply as a convenience. By requiring authorization, such problems can be detected and dealt with easily.

Review of Reasons for Referral

It is the responsibility of the medical director to review the reasons for referral by the PCPs. In the tightest of all systems, this review takes place before the actual referral is made. In other words, the medical director or associate medical director must approve any authorization prospectively. This system is obviously cumbersome and may be seen as demeaning to the PCPs, but it is definitely tight, even if prohibitively expensive. It is perhaps most suitable for a tightly controlled closed panel plan or a training program where interns and residents are involved.

More acceptable is retrospective review of referrals. In this case, the medical director or associate medical director reviews referral forms after the fact, although preferably not long after. Reviews may be of all referrals, which potentially achieves tight control but is unrealistic, or of randomly selected referrals, which will be less tight but still quite useful. More useful is to evaluate PCP referral rates and patterns as well as utilization patterns of referral physicians to determine where retrospective review will have the greatest potential impact.

The preferred vehicle for review is the referral form (or authorization form), which contains the reasons for referral. If the referral form does not contain clinical information, or if referral authorizations are captured electronically, then periodic chart review, similar to a quality assurance audit, needs to be used.

In this review, the medical director is looking at reasons for referral that are inappropriate or poorly thought out. It is surprising how often one encounters reasons for referral such as "Please evaluate and treat." This is a blank check. Another commonly encountered referral is one in which the patient's complaints are simply echoed (e.g., "Patient complains of pain in foot"). In these cases, one is not sure what the referring physician even bothered to do.

A referral should be made after adequate thought and course of action have been taken. The referring PCP should indicate why the patient is being referred, what the PCP thinks the diagnosis is or what he or she is concerned about, what has already been done, and what exactly the PCP wants the consultant to do. By failing to indicate the results of their own work-up or significant findings on the patient's history and physical examination, PCPs make themselves look lazy and make the job of the consultant that much more inefficient.

When the medical director encounters sloppy reasons for referral, it is not necessary to reprimand or embarrass the PCP. It is more appropriate to discuss the case clinically, suggesting options that the PCP may have tried before referring or ways in which the referral could have been more effective. The ultimate goal of these discussions is to foster that type of internal questioning behavior in the PCP so that the medical director will not have to do it. You want each PCP to consider all the options before making a referral and to make referrals count. This often means breaking old habits, but then that is what medical management is about.

Self-Referrals by Members

It is a chronic problem in managed care plans with authorization systems to have members referring themselves to consultants for care. In POS plans that have benefits for self-referral, plan design allows this. In either an HMO or a POS plan, new members who are not used to the system and signed up because of the benefits offered may not recall or note the requirements for authorization and are more apt to self-refer and later be surprised that there is reduced or no coverage for the service.

In these situations, you need to consider your policy on first offenders. Many HMOs will pay for the first self-referral if it is a new member, if the plan recently changed to an authorization system, or if plan managers want to be nice. In such cases the plan documents a warning so that benefits for self-referral may be denied on subsequent occurrences. Most POS plans do not cover any self-referrals at the higher level of benefits, but some will remind the member via their explanation of benefits statement that the benefits would have been higher if the member had obtained authorization.

LCM by Specialty Physicians

Even in HMO or POS plans, there may be times when the plan may wish to have a referral specialist function as a PCP. This would occur when a member has a chronic and high-cost problem that is clearly outside the scope of a PCP's training and practice. In those events, the plan's LCM function becomes proactive in managing the case (see Chapter 18 in *The Managed Health Care Handbook*). As part of the case management, the patient may no longer be the responsibility of a PCP, but care may be coordinated with a specialist who functions as the PCP for that case only. For example, a member with active and aggressive acquired immune deficiency syndrome may be better cared for by an infectious disease specialist rather than a PCP, although that assumption may not hold in every case. The point is that the plan's LCM function may choose this route on occasion rather than force the PCP to manage catastrophic cases.

Compensation and Financial Incentives for Specialty Physicians

Financial arrangements are discussed in detail in Chapter 10, so only two pertinent issues are reiterated. Capitation is a powerful and effective tool for controlling consultant utilization but can be a trap if not used wisely. You are urged to review the section on capitation in Chapters 8 and 10 before using it. Simple capitation arrangements alone without proper controls on utilization, such as an authorization system and review of reasons for referral, can lead to serious overutilization unless the referral physician is able to exert strong controls on utilization without managerial controls.

Financial incentives or risk/bonus arrangements for PCPs and contracting consultants can be quite useful, especially incentives for PCPs. As discussed elsewhere, this is not an attempt to bribe a physician but to share the savings of cost-effective practice. Incentives should not be so great as to raise the danger of inappropriate underutilization but should be enough to have a genuine effect.

INSTITUTIONAL UM

Utilization of hospital (or, more accurately, institutional) services usually accounts for 40 percent or more of the total expenses in a managed health care plan. That amount can be even greater when utilization is excessive. Control of these expenses is therefore prominent among most managers' priorities.

The expense of any medical service is a product of the price of that service times the volume of services delivered. Pricing for institutional services is discussed in Chapter 11; this chapter focuses on managing the volume of institutional services. Simple reduction of bed days may be of value but can lull the inexperienced manager into a sense of complacency. Control of institutional utilization is therefore to be understood in context with control of other areas of utilization as well.

Measurements

Definition of the Numbers

First, you must choose exactly what you will measure and how you will define that measurement. It is common for most plans to measure bed days per 1,000 plan members per year (a formula to calculate this is given below). Deciding what to count as a bed day is not always straightforward, however.

In some plans, outpatient surgery will be counted as a single day in the hospital. This is done on the assumption that an outpatient procedure will cost the plan nearly the same as or sometimes more than a single inpatient day. Some plans count skilled nursing home days in the total, and some add commercial, Medicare, Medicaid, and fee for service into the total calculation. In some plans the day of discharge is counted; in most it is not (unless it is charged for by the hospital). Whether to count nursery days in the total when the mother is still in the hospital or only if the newborn is boarding over or in intensive care also needs to be decided.

As a general rule of thumb, most plans count commercial days separately from any other days, especially Medicare days. If you have a significant Medicaid population, you may wish to track it both separately and together with commercial. Most plans do not count outpatient surgery as an inpatient day but report out that number separately; likewise, most plans report skilled nursing days separately.

How to count nursery days is a difficult decision. If you use the assumption that skilled nursing days are not counted as hospital days because the cost is so much less, the same assumption may be made for nursery days while the mother is in the hospital. In most hospitals, the nursery charges for a normal newborn are relatively low. If the newborn requires a stay beyond the mother's discharge, the charges usually are higher. If the newborn is in the intensive care unit, charges will obviously be quite high. If you have negotiated an all-inclusive per diem rate or a case rate that takes normal nursery days into account while the mother is in the hospital, you may have no need to count them separately. If you must pay a high rate for nursery, you will probably want nursery days counted in the total. Many plans separate obstetric days from medical–surgical days and report on each. The same issue may apply to mental health days.

Further discussion about utilization reports can be found in Chapter 19.

Formulas To Calculate Institutional Utilization

The standard formula to calculate bed days per 1,000 members per year is relatively straightforward. You may use it to calculate the annualized bed days per 1,000 members for any time period you choose (e.g., for the day, the month to date, the year to date, and so forth).

When calculating bed days per 1,000, use the assumption of a 365-day year as opposed to a 12-month year to prevent variations that are due solely to the length of the month. The formula is as follows:

$$[A \div (B \div 365)] \div (C \div 1{,}000)$$

where A is gross bed days per time unit, B is days per time unit, and C is plan membership.

This may be broken into steps. Exhibit 13–1 illustrates the calculation for bed days per 1,000 on a single day; Exhibit 13–2 illustrates the calculation for bed days per 1,000 for the month to date.

Exhibit 13–1 Example of Bed Days for a Single Day

Assume:	Current hospital census = 10 Plan membership = 12,000	
Step 1:	Gross days	= 10 ÷ (1 ÷ 365) = 10 ÷ 0.00274 = 3,649.635
Step 2:	Days per 1,000	= 3,649.635 ÷ (12,000 ÷ 1,000) = 3,649.635 ÷ 12 = 304 (rounded)

Therefore, the days per 1,000 for that single day equals 304.

Exhibit 13–2 Example of Bed Days for the Month to Date (MTD)

Assume:	Total gross hospital bed days in MTD = 300 Plan membership = 12,000 Days in MTD = 21	
Step 1:	Gross days MTD	= 300 ÷ (21 ÷ 365) = 300 ÷ 0.0575 = 5,217.4
Step 2:	Days per 1,000 in MTD	= 5,217.4 ÷ (12,000 ÷ 1,000) = 5,217.4 ÷ 12 = 435 (rounded)

Therefore, the days per 1,000 for the MTD equals 435.

Expected Utilization and Variations

Inpatient utilization is almost always lower in HMOs than in any other type of health plan. Table 13–1 provides examples of utilization data under a variety of different options. Note that the data in Table 13–1 are for 1993, the most recent year available for analysis at the time of this writing. Utilization figures in some parts of the country are at least 20 percent lower than those illustrated in Table 13–1, even in 1995.

There are two common reasons for variations in hospital utilization rates across the country. One reason is easily understood; the other is not. Easily understood is the relationship between how tight the UM program you have is and its results. The tighter you make the program, and the more actual medical management is going on, the lower your utilization numbers will be. Conversely, if you choose for various reasons not to enforce a UM program stringently (e.g., you may not be marketing a tight system), you will have proportionate increases in the hospitalization rate.

Less easily understood are the profound geographic variations in inpatient utilization. Rates of utilization on the east coast are consistently and significantly higher than those on the west coast.[15] In fact, there are geographic variations in utilization in cities of similar size that are not terribly far apart and even significant geographic variations in a single metropolitan service area[16–20] (Blue Cross/Blue Shield of the National Capital Area, unpublished data). There is no rational explanation for this from the standpoint of the patients. The answer must lie with the practice habits of physicians in different areas. At the very least, this perplexing disparity based on geography points out that significant improvement in utilization may be achieved, especially in the eastern United States.

Despite low utilization in HMOs and other forms of managed care plans, there are researchers who strongly believe that there remains a significant amount of unnecessary utilization even now. The most aggressive of these opinions is found in a report by Milliman & Robertson, in which the authors state that almost 60 percent of inpatient utilization is unnecessary.[21] Table 13–2, adapted from that report, lists "optimally managed" admits per 1,000 and days per 1,000 for commercial and Medicare enrollees.

Reimbursement of Hospitals and Financial Incentives

Financial incentives are important tools for helping manage hospital utilization. This topic is

Table 13–1 Hospital Utilization Rates, 1993

	Commercial			*Medicare*			*Medicaid*		
Type of Plan	*BD/K*	*Discharges/K*	*ALOS*	*BD/K*	*Discharges/K*	*ALOS*	*BD/K*	*Discharges/K*	*ALOS*
Indemnity and HMO	273.1	61.2	4.46	2474	309	8.0	930.1	165.4	5.62
HMO (all plan types)	242.2	66.3	3.8	1526	224.5	7.0	568	132.1	3.8
Staff	251.5	71.1	3.7	1501	209.6	7.0	439	124.9	3.5
Group	242.0	67.0	3.6				N/A	N/A	N/A
Network	197.5	58.9	3.6	1565	228.3	N/A	480	122.0	3.6
Individual practice association	262.9	68.6	4.0				603	142.7	3.7

Note: Indemnity and HMO data cannot be accurately separated. Indemnity and HMO data combined exclude Medicare, Medicaid, workers' compensation, government pay, uninsured, nonpay, and no charge. Indemnity-only utilization is estimated to be approximately 20 percent higher than noted for commercial. For Medicare, staff and group figures are combined, and network and individual practice association numbers are combined.

Abbreviations: BD/K, bed days per 1,000; discharges/K, discharges per 1,000; ALOS, average length of stay.

Source: Courtesy of Ernst & Young LLP, Washington, D.C.

Table 13–2 Optimal Utilization Levels, July 1, 1993

	Commercial Well Managed		*Medicare Well Managed*	
Category of Service	*Admits per 1,000*	*Days per 1,000*	*Admits per 1,000*	*Days per 1,000*
Inpatient Hospital				
Nonmaternity				
Medical	21.24	72.99	132.66	598.27
Surgical	15.23	57.50	66.22	404.48
Psychiatric	2.00	13.78	1.51	14.65
Alcohol/drug	0.70	4.05	0.61	3.97
SNF/ECF	0.50	4.00	32.50	544.10
Maternity				
Mother	15.50	26.14	0.00	0.00
Well newborn		26.14	0.00	0.00
Nondelivery	2.75	5.64	0.00	0.00
Grand Total (excluding SNF/ECF)*	57.42	180.10	201.00	1,021.37
Grand Total (including SNF/ECF)*	57.92	184.10	233.50	1,565.47

Abbreviations: SNF, skilled nursing facility; ECF, extended care facility.

* *Note:* Well newborn included with mother.

Source: Courtesy of Milliman & Robertson, Inc.

addressed in Chapters 6, 8, and 10, and the reader is referred to those chapters.

Common Methods for Decreasing Utilization

Control of institutional utilization may be best presented by discussing the key categories for managing the process: prospective, concurrent, and retrospective review and LCM (i.e., large or catastrophic case management). Prospective review means that the case is reviewed before it happens, concurrent review means that review occurs while the case is active, and retrospective review occurs after the case is finished. LCM refers to managing cases that are expected to result in large costs to provide coordination of care that results in both proper care and cost savings.

Prospective Review

Precertification. Precertification refers to a requirement on the part of the admitting physician (and often the hospital) to notify the plan before a member is admitted for inpatient care or an outpatient procedure. There is a widespread and rather erroneous belief that the primary role of precertification is to prevent unnecessary cases from occurring. Although that may occasionally happen (particularly in workers' compensation cases), it is not the chief reason for precertification.

There are three primary reasons for precertification. The first is to notify the concurrent review system that a case will be occurring. In that way, the UM system will be able to prepare discharge planning (discussed below) ahead of time as well as look for the case during concurrent review rounds. In some instances, the LCM function (see below) may be notified if the admission diagnosis raises the possibility that it will be a highly expensive case (e.g., a bone marrow transplant).

The second major reason for precertification is to ensure that care takes place in the most appropriate setting. Perhaps an inpatient case is diverted to the outpatient department, or a case is diverted from a nonparticipating hospital to a participating one or to a facility that has been designated as a center of excellence for a selected procedure.

The third reason is to capture data for financial accruals. Although it is unlikely that a plan can capture every case before or while it is taking place, a mature plan that is running well can capture the vast majority of cases, perhaps 90 percent to 95 percent. By knowing the number and nature of hospital cases as well as potential catastrophic cases, the plan can more accurately accrue for expenses rather than have to wait for claims to come in. This allows management to take action early and to avoid nasty financial surprises. Accrual methodology is discussed in Chapter 22.

In any case, for inpatient cases the plan usually assigns a length of stay guideline at the time the admission is certified. This topic of length of stay is discussed below. The plan may also use the precertification process to verify eligibility of coverage for the member, although most plans have a disclaimer stating that ultimate eligibility for coverage will be determined at the time the claim is processed.

In the case of an emergency or urgent admission, it is obviously not possible to obtain precertification. In that event, there is usually a contractual requirement to notify the plan by the next business day or within 24 hours if the plan has 24-hour UM staffing. Most plans have contractual language with both the physicians and the hospitals imposing financial penalties (e.g., a percentage of their fee or a flat penalty) for failure to obtain certification. For plans that allow members to seek care from noncontracted providers (e.g., in POS plans), the responsibility to contact the plan rests with the members if they choose not to see a network physician; in such cases, most plans impose benefits penalties (e.g., a higher coinsurance or a flat penalty rate) on a member who fails to obtain proper precertification.

Preadmission testing and same day surgery. One of the easiest, and also one of the most common, methods for cost control is preadmission testing and same day surgery. A member who is going to be hospitalized on an elective basis has routine preoperative tests done as an outpatient and is admitted the same day the surgery is to be performed. Both these policies are confirmed at the time of precertification.

For example, a member has elective gallbladder surgery scheduled for 10:00 A.M. on Thursday. On Tuesday the member goes to the hospital for the preoperative tests. The results are made available to the admitting physician, who performs the admission history and physical as an outpatient and either delivers the results to the hospital or calls them in on an outside line to the hospital's transcription department. The member arrives at the hospital at 6:00 A.M. on Thursday, is admitted, and has surgery as scheduled.

In many health plans, the plan has made arrangements for laboratory work to be done with a contracted laboratory at reduced rates or will have in-house capabilities to perform the laboratory work. Occasionally, a hospital will refuse to accept the results of these laboratories. If the laboratory is accredited and licensed, the hospital has little grounds to require you to use its laboratory, electrocardiography, and radiology services for preoperative admission testing. In these cases it falls to the plan's management team to discuss this with the hospital administrator and negotiate an agreement for the hospital to accept your laboratory work or to agree to perform the work at equivalent costs to you. If the hospital refuses to cooperate, you need to decide whether you want to direct the elective cases to another, more cooperative hospital.

Mandatory outpatient surgery. It has become popular for health plans to produce mandatory outpatient surgery lists. These are essentially lists of procedures that may only be performed on an outpatient basis unless prior approval is obtained from the plan medical director. This is used by so many third party payers that you do not need to make one from scratch if you do not wish to; simply look at what other similar plans (or even Medicare) are using. One byproduct of this popularity is that no two lists are identical, which causes some confusion with physicians and hospitals. Although there is consensus on many common procedures (e.g., a carpal tunnel release), there are always procedures that are migrating from inpatient to outpatient (e.g., at the time of this writing, outpatient cardiac catheterization had become popular only in the last few years). That confusion probably tends to encourage the use of outpatient surgery when physicians are in doubt.

As mentioned earlier in this chapter and elsewhere, be sure that you will actually achieve the desired savings before instituting mandatory outpatient surgery requirements. In some cases, hospitals or free-standing outpatient surgery facilities have charges that are equal to or greater than those for an inpatient day. In other cases, the facility charge may be lower, but the unbundled charges for anesthesia, recovery, supplies, and so on can drive the cost higher than anticipated. These issues are discussed in Chapter 11.

Concurrent Review

Concurrent review means managing utilization during the course of a hospitalization (as opposed to an outpatient procedure). Common techniques for concurrent review involve assignment and tracking of length of stay, review and rounding by UM nurses, and discharge planning. The roles of the medical director, the PCP, and the attending or consulting physicians are discussed later in this chapter, as is the relationship between concurrent review and LCM.

Assignment of length of stay. A common approach to hospital utilization control is the assignment of a maximum allowable length of stay (MaxLOS), which sometimes appears in the guise of an estimated length of stay, but with teeth. With the MaxLOS, the plan assigns a length of stay on the basis of the admission diagnosis, and that is all the plan will authorize for payment. For example, an admission for a routine surgical admission may be assigned 3 days. It is assumed that the patient will be admitted on the day of surgery and will go home 3 days later. Any stay beyond that day is not covered. In those plans that cannot or will not restrict payment, the MaxLOS is used only to trigger greater involvement by the medical director.

The MaxLOS is determined by International Classification of Diseases, Ninth Revision, Clinical Modification code, or diagnostic code, although diagnosis-related groups (DRGs) are similar in concept. Selecting a norm for the MaxLOS is not always easy given regional variations. Looking at the local fee-for-service experience may or may not be helpful, depending on your area's history in achieving good control of utilization. If you have no other source, a number of organizations and companies sell such data.

The advantage of using MaxLOS designations is threefold. First, it allows you to cover a relatively large geographic area with few personnel, which may be necessary in a new start-up open panel plan. Second, such a list has the power of legitimacy and does not require that you negotiate every time. Third, it is relatively mechanical and requires less training of plan personnel. This last may be true for the person issuing the MaxLOS designation, but it is still important to verify, usually through the UM nurse, that the diagnosis is accurate.

The problem with using MaxLOS designations is also threefold. First, it is easy to get complacent. If you choose certain values for MaxLOS designations, you may fail to evaluate continually whether those are in fact the correct values. Second, designated time becomes free time. In other words, there is less incentive to evaluate critically every day in the hospital for appropriateness and alternatives if plan personnel and the physician feel that there is still time on the meter. Third, using such a mechanical system often achieves less than optimal results. Intensive medical management by qualified personnel should produce better control of utilization, but such personnel are not always available. The topic of concurrent review against criteria is discussed below.

You must also know what the consequences of exceeding the MaxLOS will be. In many plans, exceeding the MaxLOS results in either a denial of payment for services rendered after the MaxLOS has been reached or a reduction in payment, usually by a percentage amount. If you have failed to inform your membership of a MaxLOS program and you do not have sole source of payment clauses with your providers and hospitals (see Chapter 29), you may not be able to enforce a MaxLOS designation easily.

Role of the UM nurse. The one individual who is crucial to the success of a managed care program is the UM nurse. It is the UM nurse who will be the eyes and ears of the medical management department, who will generally coordinate the discharge planning, and who will facilitate all the activities of utilization control.

Staffing levels for UM nurses will vary depending on the size of the geographic area, the number of hospitals, the size of the plan, and the intensity with which UM will be performed (e.g., by on-site hospital rounding). It is common for plans to staff one UM nurse for every 6,000 to 8,000 members, assuming that the UM nurses will be making rounds on all hospitalized patients and that utilization is reasonably tightly controlled, but not on a 24-hour basis. Staffing ratios have considerable variation, however, with one study reporting the average number of full-time nurse reviewers at 0.16 per 1,000 enrollees, with a range of 0.01 to 0.8 per 1,000.[22] Plans that perform telephone review only may staff at ratios that are half the average. It is also necessary to provide clerical support to do intake, to follow up on discharge planning needs, to take care of filing, and so forth.

The scope of responsibilities of the UM nurse will vary depending on the plan and the personalities and skills of the other members of the medical management team. In some plans, the role simply involves telephone information gathering. In other plans, there will be a more proactive role, including frequent communication with attending physicians, the medical director, the hospitals, and the hospitalized members and their families; discharge planning and facilitation; and a host of other activities, including active hospital rounding.

The one fundamental function of the UM nurse is information gathering. Information about hospital cases must be obtained in an accurate and timely fashion. It falls to the UM nurse to be the focal point of this information and to ensure that it is obtained and communicated to the necessary individuals in medical management and the claims department.

Necessary information includes admission date and diagnosis, the type of hospital service to which the patient was admitted (e.g., medical, surgical, maternity, and so forth), the admitting physician, consultants, planned procedures (type and timing), expected discharge date, needed discharge planning, and any other pertinent information the plan managers may need.

In some plans, information gathering is done strictly by telephone; in other plans, hospital rounding is done in person by the UM nurse. When the telephone is used, it is used first to check with the admitting office to determine whether any plan members were admitted and then to check with the hospital's own UM department to obtain any further information.

Telephone rounding is usually done in cases where there is too much geographic area to cover and the plan cannot yet justify adding more UM nurses (e.g., in a start-up individual provider association or PPO covering five counties). It may also be done in those instances where a hospital refuses to give the UM nurse rounding privileges on hospitalized plan members. There are certain instances where a plan may in fact delegate rounding and review to the hospital's UM department, but those are rare; examples include arrangements where the hospital is at significant financial risk (e.g., through capitation or DRGs). The other time telephone rounding is used is when there are not tight controls on utilization, and the function is one of looking for clear outliers rather than trying to achieve optimal utilization control.

Rounding in person is far superior to telephone rounding. When rounds are conducted daily by a UM nurse on every hospitalized member, you will obtain the most accurate and timely information, and you will obtain information that you might not get otherwise.

For example, in a good quality management program (see Chapter 17), the rounding UM nurse will be able to watch for quality problems or significant events that would trigger a quality assurance audit. A rounding nurse will also be able to pick up information about a patient's condition that may affect discharge planning, information that the attending physician may have failed to communicate (e.g., the need for home durable equipment that must be ordered).

The UM nurse may also be able to detect practice behavior that increases utilization simply for the convenience of the physician or hospital. For example, a patient may be ready for discharge but the physician missed making rounds that morning and will not be back until the next day, or the hospital rescheduled surgery for its own reasons and the patient will have to spend an extra and unnecessary day. In situations such as these, the UM nurse must not be put into an adversarial position but should refer such cases to the medical director.

Personal rounding by the plan's UM nurse has the added advantage of increasing member satisfaction. Many people feel uncomfortable talking to physicians and welcome the chance to express their fears or feelings to the UM nurse. In other cases, inquiring about how members are feeling can let them know that you care about them as people and that you are not simply trying to get them out as fast as you can.

In the situation where a hospital refuses to grant rounding privileges to the UM nurse (an increasingly uncommon occurrence), a frequent excuse is that there is already a UM department in the hospital. That is usually not adequate for your needs and does not address the specific member satisfaction and quality assurance needs of your plan. Another frequent excuse is protecting the confidentiality of the patients. That does not hold if the plan's UM nurse is only rounding on plan members (who have agreed in their application to allow access to records). If a hospital refuses to cooperate with you on allowing the plan's UM nurse to round, you must seriously question your willingness to do business with that hospital. In most cases, a hospital will cooperate fully and willingly.

The heart of concurrent review is the evaluation of each hospital case against established criteria. Many plans, especially open panel plans and PPOs, use published or commercially available criteria for such reviews to facilitate evaluation by the UM nurses.[23–26] Experienced nurses use such criteria as an aid in managing utilization, but they do not blindly depend on them. It is possible to keep a patient in the hospital for less than adequate reasons but still meet criteria; the seasoned UM nurse is able to evaluate each case on its merits.

Most plans have now automated this function to improve the efficiency of the UM nurses. Software allows the MaxLOS to be generated automatically from the admission diagnosis or procedure. Member and benefit eligibility is checked, diagnostic and procedure codes are generated from entered text, review criteria are automatically displayed for both admission and concurrent review, unlimited text may be entered to allow tracking, census reports are produced, statistics are generated, and so forth. UM software also links to the claims system so that claims are properly processed, including special instructions from the nurses.

Good discharge planning starts as soon as a patient is admitted into the hospital, or even before. The physician and the UM nurse should be considering discharge planning as part of the overall treatment plan from the outset. This planning includes an estimate of how long the patient will be in the hospital, what the expected outcome will be, whether there will be any special requirements on discharge, and what needs to be facilitated early on.

For example, if a patient is admitted with a fractured hip and it is known from the outset that many weeks of rehabilitation will be necessary, it is helpful to contact the facility where the rehabilitation will take place to ensure that a bed will be available at the time of transfer. If it is known that a patient will need durable medical equipment, the equipment should be order-ed early so that the patient does not spend extra days in the hospital waiting for it to arrive.

An often overlooked aspect of discharge planning is informing the patient and family. If the patient and family do not know what to expect, they may be surprised when the physician tells them that the patient is being discharged. This is especially true if the patient has received hospital care in the past and has certain expectations. Informing the patient and family from the start about when they can expect discharge, how the patient will be feeling, what they might need to prepare for at home, and how follow-up will occur will all help smooth things considerably.

In the case of short-stay obstetrics, if the patient and family are not prepared for the homecoming, there may be tremendous pressure on the physician to keep the mother and child in the hospital so that everyone can get a little more rest. Unfortunately, the hospital is far too expensive for that. Active discharge planning for short-stay obstetrics is crucial. If your plan offers a home health visit to mothers who have had a short-stay delivery, that should be confirmed on admission.

Discharge planning is an ongoing effort beginning with admission or preadmission screening. The UM nurse is in the ideal position to coordinate discharge planning. In addition to making sure that all goes smoothly to effect a smooth and proper discharge from the hospital, the UM nurse can follow up with the member by telephone after discharge to ensure that all is well.

PCP model. There are two basic models for managing hospital cases: the PCP model and the attending physician model. In the PCP model, the PCPs are expected to manage the care of their patients in the hospital even when patients are hospitalized for care delivered primarily by consultants or specialists; most commonly this occurs either when the patient is hospitalized for surgery or when the patient has a drawn-out course of treatment (e.g., recovery from a stroke). In the PCP model, the most important functions of the member's PCP are also the most obvious: to make rounds every day and to coordinate the patient's care.

In the first cited instance, care from a consultant, it is all the more important for the PCP to round daily. This serves a number of purposes. First, it helps ensure continuity of care while the patient is in the hospital (e.g., the PCP may be able to add pertinent clinical information as needed). Second, it provides a comforting presence for the patient, a presence that results not only in better bonding between physician and patient but in providing emotional support. Third, it allows for continuity after discharge because the PCP is aware of the clinical course and discharge planning. Fourth, it helps control unnecessary utilization.

Utilization control by the PCP is highly effective in the setting of a member receiving hospital care from a consultant. The PCP is able to discuss the case with the consultant and suggest ways to decrease the length of stay (e.g., home nursing care) that the consultant is not used to considering. The PCP will presumably know the patient well enough to determine the patient's ability to do well in alternative situations.

The PCP will also be able to communicate effectively with a consultant in the event that the consultant failed to see the patient on rounds. For example, if a busy surgeon misses a patient on rounds because the patient was in the bathroom, the surgeon, because of a heavy operating room schedule, may not make it back to see that patient until late at night. If the patient is actually ready for discharge, the PCP can communicate with the surgeon that morning and arrange for discharge.

There will be situations where the PCP is unable to make rounds in person. This happens most frequently when a member is admitted to a tertiary hospital where the PCP does not have privileges. For example, cardiac bypass surgery may be done at a teaching hospital with a closed medical staff. In these situations, it is important for the PCP to be in frequent telephone contact with the attending physician on the case to keep up with developments and to aid in the discharge planning process. For example, the PCP may be comfortable in accepting the patient back in transfer during the recovery period or may be able to suggest home nursing care. In addition to controlling utilization, this helps ensure continuity of care, and the attending physician will almost always remark to the patient about how attentive the PCP has been about the case.

Equally important to good medical management is for the PCP to avoid the trap of "That's the way it's always been done and it's good enough for me!" The PCP has responsibility not only over the physical health of the member but over the financial health of the plan as well. The PCP must be open to evaluating new methods of treatment and to considering high-quality but cost-effective ways of caring for people.

As a corollary, PCPs must be confident and assertive about their own abilities. It is an unfortunate byproduct of the highly specialized nature of medicine that there are times when a PCP is looked down upon by a consultant. Certainly a consultant who depends on the PCP for referrals will not knowingly exhibit behavior that the PCP will find offensive, but there often remains an unspoken agreement that the consultant will call the shots once the patient is admitted.

There are a number of objections that a PCP may raise concerning getting involved with patients admitted to a consultant's service. First, the PCP may feel intimidated by the consultant's knowledge about the medical problem. When this happens, there is no reason why the PCP cannot read up on the subject, at least in a major medical text, and ask questions. Also, it is the PCP's patient, and the consultant is a consultant. It is the role and responsibility of the PCP to follow the care of the patient and to be aware of the medical issues involved. The simple act of asking the consultant questions about that care is appropriate and necessary and will frequently result in improved understanding by all parties as well as improved utilization control.

There is the possibility that the PCP will view such questioning as confrontational and will be unwilling to question the competence of the consultant. It is important to point out that the PCP is not questioning the consultant's competence (assuming that the consultant is indeed competent) but rather is discussing the case and asking the consultant his or her opinion about alternatives. The fear of such confrontations is far greater than the reality. The PCP has nothing to be shy about; PCPs are trained physicians specializing in primary care, and the consultant is helping care for the PCP's patient, not vice versa.

Specialist physician responsibilities. Even in a PCP model, the consultant has responsibilities as well as the PCP. The interaction between consultant and PCP is highly important to good medical management and utilization control. Beyond that, it is reasonable for the plan, through the medical director, to communicate certain expectations of all consultants. It has been clearly shown that even in intensive care units, where little discretion would be expected in treatment decisions, HMOs have 30 percent to 40 percent lower utilization (measured by length of stay, charges, and use of ventilators) compared with fee-for-service plans even when adjusted for case mix, thus pointing out that consultants and specialists in a managed care environment have considerable effect on resource use.[27]

First, you expect all consultants to be aware of and to cooperate with your plan's policy on testing, procedures, and primary care case management. Second, plans that use PCPs as gatekeepers or managing physicians should expect consultants to be in communication with PCPs about their patients and to provide written reports on consultations (some plans go so far as to refuse payment to a consultant until the PCP receives a written report). Third, care should be directed back to the PCP as soon as it is possible to do so, so that the consultant reinforces the plan's philosophy of primary care. Last, the consultant cannot subauthorize further care for the member without first discussing the case with the PCP involved. The PCP may already have worked up a problem that the consultant is seeing for the first time, or the PCP may be able to perform the medical duties that the consultant is requesting; for example, a surgeon may call a cardiologist to evaluate chest pain even though the PCP is an internist who is aware of the patient's condition.

In a loosely controlled plan there will be fewer expectations of the consultant than in a tightly controlled plan. As has been mentioned numerous times, the better the control of utilization you hope to achieve, the more you have to deal with practice patterns and physician behavior. Consultants are able to add significantly to the cost of care not only from their own fees but through additional fees generated by extra days in the hospital and through testing, procedures, and secondary referrals to other consultants.

Rounding physician model. In the rounding physician model, sometimes called the designated admitting physician model, one physician is designated to care for all admissions of a group or health plan to a given hospital or hospital service (e.g., to a medical service). This model is not infrequently found in group and staff model HMOs and is beginning to appear in some open panel HMOs as well. The PCP indeed relinquishes responsibility for the admission, and the rounding physician assumes responsibility.

The rounding or designated physician may be on site on a full-time basis or may simply carry a lighter outpatient load, devoting greater time to rounding on hospitalized patients. In the large closed panels as well as the open panel plans that are adopting this system, it is more common for the designated physician to be on site full time at the hospital.

The reasoning behind this approach is that a dedicated on-site physician will be closer to the care that the patient is receiving and in a better position to coordinate needed services as well as closely monitor care for quality and appropriateness. On a secondary note, large groups find that this increases their overall efficiency because this model avoids many physicians going into the hospital for just one or two visits.

In some plans, it is not practical for the PCP to follow all cases in the hospital even though the plan may not have a formal rounding physician program in place. Reasons may include high use of teaching hospitals with closed medical staffs, communities where PCPs simply do not hospitalize cases (which can occur in both urban and rural areas), and plans that do not use a PCP gatekeeper system. In any case, the attending physician in this situation is usually a specialist or consultant and has responsibility to manage the case and to interact with the plan. The responsibilities of the attending physician in this model are little different from those of the PCP. Interaction with the plan is necessary, and the consultant needs to cooperate with plan policies and procedures. The main difference in this model is the person with whom the UM nurse and medical director interact.

Medical director's responsibilities. In addition to monitoring all the elements discussed in this chapter, there are a few specific functions that the medical director should be performing. The medical director will have to become involved in the most difficult cases from a management standpoint. This does not necessarily refer to those cases where the difficulty is medical but rather to those cases where there is difficulty with the PCP, a consultant, a hospital, or the member or member's family. There are times when the medical director must deal with uncooperative individuals, and this is certainly a difficult responsibility. The medical director must take a compassionate, caring, but firm and fair stance when dealing with difficult people. It is often easiest simply to give in, but that can only be done so many times before it becomes a habit that damages the plan's effectiveness. The ability to empathize and sympathize with someone's point of view and to recognize what the real issues are in a dispute is not the same as acquiescing. Although there are indeed times when the medical director will want to loosen the reins, it is important for the medical director to remain firm when the situation is clear and to back up his or her subordinates and the PCPs when they are right.

If the medical director is only heard from when there is a problem, his or her effectiveness will be diminished. It is important for there to be reasonably frequent contact with PCPs and important consultants even when all is well. This can be especially useful when discussing cases. If the medical director discusses cases, suggesting alternatives if appropriate even when there is no pressing need to make a change, the participating plan physicians will be much more accepting of the medical director's opinions when change is needed (assuming that the medical director has useful opinions in the first place, of course).

The usefulness of frequent contact cannot be overestimated. By asking thoughtful questions in a nonthreatening manner and by constantly stimulating thought regarding cost-effective clinical management, the medical director may slowly reinforce appropriate patterns of care. The most successful outcome of such contacts occurs when physicians begin asking themselves the questions the medical director would ask and begin improving their practice patterns on that basis.

A task that the medical director should perform for optimal utilization control is reviewing the hospital log daily. This may seem an onerous task, and it can be, but it is the only way the medical director will consistently spot problems in time to do something about them. For example, finding that surgery was not done on the same day as admission may prompt a call to the PCP or surgeon to prevent that same thing happening again. If possible, it is even better for the medical director to review the hospital log with the UM nurse early enough in the day for meaningful action to be taken, which is usually before noon, when many hospitals automatically charge for another day. Large plans with highly competent UM nurses and UM departments may get to a point where the medical director need not review every case every day but simply will review any problem cases or outliers. Even in these situations, the medical director should periodically review every case to be certain that the

UM department is performing as well as expected.

Retrospective Review

Retrospective review occurs after the case is finished and the patient is discharged. Retrospective review takes on two primary forms: claims review and pattern review.

Claims review. Claims review refers to examining claims for improprieties or mistakes. For example, it is common for plans to review large claims to verify whether services were actually delivered or whether mistakes were made in collating the claims data. In such large cases, the plan may actually send a representative on site to the hospital to review the medical record against the claims record.

Pattern review. This refers to examining patterns of utilization to determine where action must be taken. For example, if three hospitals in the area perform coronary artery bypass surgery, the plan may look to see which one has the best clinical outcomes, the shortest length of stay, and the lowest charges. The plan may then preferentially send all such cases to that hospital. Pattern review also allows the plan to focus UM efforts primarily on those areas needing greater attention (i.e., Sutton's law: Go where the money is!).

One other use of pattern review is to provide feedback to providers. Although not as powerful as active UM by the plan's own department, feedback can have an effect in and of itself.[28] When combined with other management functions and financial incentives, feedback can be a useful management tool.

Alternatives to Acute Care Hospitalization

There are many instances where patients are ill or disabled but not to the extent that they need to be in an acute care hospital. Despite that, that is where they often stay. The reasons for this are many. In some cases, the patient started out needing the services of an acute care hospital (e.g., a patient had surgery but the recovery phase requires far fewer resources than are available in the hospital). In other cases, there is simply no place for the patient to go (e.g., a patient is recovering from a broken femur but lives alone). In a few cases, a patient is kept in the hospital for the convenience of a physician who does not want to make house calls or rounds at another institution. Last, there are times when a patient is kept in the hospital simply because "That's the way it's always been done!"

Skilled or intermediate nursing facilities and subacute facilities. A useful alternative to consider is the skilled or intermediate nursing facility or subacute facility (subacute care facilities are discussed in detail in Chapter 24 of *The Managed Health Care Handbook*).[29] This is best suited for prolonged convalescence or recovery cases. For example, if a patient with a broken femur requires more traction than can be provided safely at home and requires many months to recover, the cost for a bed day in a nursing facility will be greatly reduced compared with that in the acute care hospital. The same goes for rehabilitation cases, such as stroke or trauma to the brain, when the damage is too extensive for the patient to go home immediately. Although there are few (if any) reasons anymore to admit someone for uncomplicated back pain, if one of your physicians does so, a nursing facility is the most appropriate place for the bed rest to take place.

Recently, the subacute care industry has begun to focus on making its facilities a practical alternative to an acute care hospital for a larger variety of medical cases. For example, some subacute care facilities provide a cost-effective location for the administration of chemotherapy that requires close supervision. The treatment of many medical conditions, such as acute pneumonia or osteomyelitis, when the patient is too sick to be cared for at home, may be done in a subacute facility. In some cases, the patient may be able to be cared for at home, but it is still more cost effective to deliver the therapy in the subacute facility as a result of the more favorable pricing achievable through economies of scale. For a subacute facility to vie effectively for this type of business, it must transform itself into something other than a nursing home.

The main problem with the use of subacute facilities or nursing homes is objections from the patient or the family, particularly in the case of young patients. There is a stigma attached to nursing homes that makes some people associate them with warehouses for the elderly. To overcome this, you need to take a proactive approach.

First, contract only with those nursing and subacute facilities that meet your (and implicitly your members') demands for pleasant surroundings. You may find a better price elsewhere, but try to imagine yourself or your loved ones staying at the facility for a month and see if it would be acceptable. A good nursing facility will be interested in working with you on making the option acceptable by ensuring that your patients will be given a private room (a private room in a nursing facility is still less costly than a semiprivate bed in an acute care hospital) or at least will be placed in a room with another patient with a similar functional status.

Second, discuss the alternative with the patient and the family well in advance of the actual move. Nothing is as distressing as suddenly finding out that you will be shipped out in the morning to a nursing home. If possible, have the family visit the nursing facility to meet the staff and see the environment before the patient is transferred.

Last, do not abandon the patient. In other words, have someone, preferably the physician and the UM nurse, visit the patient on a regular basis. It is easy to rationalize that, because the patient is in the nursing facility for long-term care, you do not need to visit often; after all, the nurse would call if there were a problem. That may be true from a medical standpoint, but it is not true from a human relations standpoint.

How you handle using a nursing facility will have an impact on your marketing. If you coldly shunt people into a nursing facility simply to save money, you will rapidly get a reputation for placing your needs over those of your members. Members will complain to their benefits managers or to other potential members, and you will develop problems in enrollment. If, however, you handle the option with caring and compassion, taking the time to alleviate the emotional distress that may be caused, you will find that most people will be quite understanding and accepting of this alternative.

The other issue to consider in the use of nursing facilities is monitoring the case in regard to your benefit structure. It is easy for a case to go from prolonged recovery to permanent placement or custodial care. It can be emotionally wrenching both for the member's family and for you to face up to the end of benefits. The problem of who will pay for long-term custodial care is a national dilemma, and it becomes personal when a family is faced with high costs because the benefits your plan offers do not continue indefinitely.

If it is possible or likely that benefits will end, it is wise early on to make the benefits structure clear to the family. This does not have to be done in a cold and calculating manner but rather by laying out all the possibilities so that the family members can begin early planning themselves.

Step-down units. As an alternative to freestanding nursing facilities, many hospitals with excess capacity have developed step-down units. Even if they have not, many hospital administrators are willing to consider it in your negotiations.

In essence, a step-down unit is a ward or section of a ward that is used in much the same way as a skilled nursing facility. A patient who requires less care and monitoring, such as someone recovering from a hip replacement (after all the drains have been removed), may need only bed rest, traction, and minimal nursing care. In recognition of the lesser resource needs, the charge per day is less.

The step-down unit has the advantage of being convenient for the physician and UM nurse and is more acceptable to the patient and family. It also does not require transfer outside the facility. Although the cost per day is sometimes slightly higher than that of a nursing facility, the difference may be worth it in terms of member acceptability.

Outpatient procedure units. In many instances, performing a procedure in an outpatient unit is less expensive than admitting a patient for a 1-day stay. This is not always true because, with the increased popularity of outpatient surgery, some hospitals have raised their outpatient unit charges to make up the lost revenue. As discussed in Chapter 11, you must pay attention to outpatient charges when negotiating with hospitals.

Free-standing outpatient facilities are also an alternative. These may be affiliated with a hospital or may be independent. As with hospitals, you can and should negotiate the charge structure so that you indeed save the costs that outpatient surgery should allow.

Hospice care. Hospice care is that care given to terminally ill patients. It tends to be supportive care and is used most often when such care cannot be given in the home. It is not always covered by health plans, but it does sometimes take the place of acute care hospitalization and should be considered when appropriate.

Home health care. Home health agencies are proliferating, and home care is becoming increasingly accepted. Services that are particularly amenable to home health care include nursing care for routine reasons (e.g., checking weights, changing dressings, and the like), home intravenous treatment (e.g., for osteomyelitis, certain forms of chemotherapy, and home intravenous nutrition), home physical therapy, respiratory therapy, and rehabilitation care.

You should have little trouble negotiating and contracting with home health agencies for services. It is becoming popular for hospitals to have home health care services to aid with caring for patients discharged from their facility, and you may be able to negotiate those services with your overall contract. Furthermore, as Medicare continues to tighten down payments for home care, many agencies are looking for alternative sources of revenue. As with hospitals or any other providers of care, home health and high-technology home care agencies need to be evaluated in terms beyond simple pricing breaks. An active quality management program, the presence of a medical director, and evidence of attention to the changes that are constantly occurring in the field are all requisites for contracting.

A warning about home health services is in order. Because the physician and UM nurse seldom visit the patient receiving home health care, it often defaults to the home health nurse to determine how often and how long the patient should receive services, and this can lead to some surprising bills. It is highly advisable to have a firm policy regarding how many home health visits will be covered under a single authorization and stating that continued authorization requires physician review.

LCM

LCM, also referred to as catastrophic case management, refers to specialized techniques for identifying and managing cases that are disproportionately high in cost. For example, active acquired immune deficiency syndrome can be an expensive disease process, as can a high cervical spinal cord injury, a bone marrow transplant, and many other events. Only a brief discussion occurs here in the context of overall management of medical–surgical utilization. (For a more detailed discussion of this highly important subject, see Chapter 18 in *The Managed Health Care Handbook.*)

Identification of large cases may be straightforward because the patients are in the hospital the first time you identify them. This is the case for trauma. Other cases may be identified before they are ever hospitalized. For example, examining the claims system for use of dialysis services may identify an end-stage renal disease patient. Proactively contacting patients with potentially catastrophic illnesses not only can save the plan considerable expense by managing the care cost effectively but can also result in better medical care because the services are coordinated.

Prenatal care is a specialized form of LCM because active coordination occurs before the newborn is delivered. Prenatal LCM involves identification of high-risk pregnancies early enough to intervene to improve the chances of a good outcome. With the staggering costs of neonatal intensive care, it only takes a few improved outcomes to yield dramatic savings. Methods for identifying cases include sending out information about pregnancy to all members, reviewing the claims system for pregnancy-related claims, asking (or requiring) the PCPs and obstetricians to notify the plan when a delivery is expected, and so forth. After the UM department is informed of the case, the member may be proactively contacted, and a questionnaire may be given to assess for risk factors (e.g., very young maternal age, diabetes, medical problems, smoking or alcohol abuse, and so forth). If risk factors are noted, then the plan coordinates prenatal care in a proactive manner. Although it is impossible to force a member to seek care and to follow up on problems, it is possible to increase the amount and quality of prenatal care that is delivered. A special problem exists when the pregnant patient is also abusing drugs; close coordination with the substance abuse program must then occur.

The degree to which the plan can become involved in LCM is in part a function of the benefits structure. In a tightly run managed health care plan, it is common for the UM department to be proactive in LCM; in simple PPOs, LCM is often voluntary on the part of the member (in other words, if the member chooses not to cooperate, there is little impact on benefits). Even in situations requiring strictly voluntary cooperation by the members and physicians, it is surprising how often LCM can be highly effective.

In addition to the standard methods of managing utilization, LCM often involves two other techniques. First is the use of community resources. Some catastrophic cases require support structures to help the member function or even return home. Examples of such support include family members, social service agencies, churches, special foundations, and so forth. The other common technique is to go beyond the contractual benefits to manage the case. For example, if the benefits structure of the group has only limited coverage for durable medical equipment, it may still be in the plan's interest to cover such expenses to get the patient home and out of the hospital. In self-funded groups, the group administrator may actually be willing to fund extracontractual benefits simply as a benefit for an employee or dependent who is experiencing a terrible medical problem.

In any event, the hallmark of LCM is longitudinal management of the case by a single UM nurse or department. Management spans hospital care, rehabilitation, outpatient care, professional services, home care, ancillary services, and so forth. It is in the active coordination of care that both quality and cost-effectiveness are maintained.

CONCLUSION

The provision of basic medical–surgical services involves a broad continuum of care. Managing utilization of these services must focus on managing basic demand, managing referral and specialty services, and managing institutional services.

The control of referral and specialty services affects not only professional expenses but also costs associated with testing and procedures, including hospitalization, that may be generated by the consultant. The ability to select only those consultants and referral specialists who practice cost effectively can yield cost savings, but optimal control depends on an authorization system, and lack of such a system will hamper your abilities to decrease consultant utilization meaningfully over the long term.

The control of hospital or institutional utilization is one of the most important aspects of controlling overall health care costs. The methods used to control hospital utilization vary from relatively weak and mechanical to tightly controlled, longitudinally integrated, and highly labor intensive. The control of hospital utilization is a function that must be attended to every day to achieve optimal results, and special attention must be paid to LCM to produce the greatest savings.

Study Questions

1. Calculate the bed days per thousand in the following situations:

Gross Bed Days per Thousand	Days in Time Period	Plan Membership	Bed Days per Thousand
375	21	25,000	
500	15	35,000	
80	1	100,000	
1,100	10	150,000	
4,500	31	200,000	

2. Develop policies and procedures for an HMO to manage inpatient utilization and outpatient institutional utilization.
3. An open panel HMO with 80,000 members, 400 PCPs, 1,400 specialists, and 11 hospitals currently conducts inpatient utilization primarily through telephonic review. How might that HMO realistically improve its UM?
4. Develop policies and procedures for managing consultant and specialist utilization in a provider-sponsored and owned HMO.
5. Create reports that would be useful to the medical director for managing specialist utilization.
6. Develop a work plan for selecting consultants in a newly formed IPA.
7. Create reports that would be useful for PCPs in managing consultant utilization.

REFERENCES AND NOTES

1. Sherlock Company, *P.U.L.S.E.* Analysis (Gwynedd, Pa.: Sherlock Company, 1995).
2. D.M. Vickery, et al., Effect of a Self-Case Education Program on Medical Visits, *Journal of the American Medical Association* 250 (1983): 2952–2956.
3. J.S. Robinson, et al., The Impact of Fever Education on Clinic Utilization, *American Journal of Diseases of Children* 143 (1989): 698–704.
4. M.A. Goldstein, Emerging Data Show Programs Are Effective, *Modern Healthcare* (21 August 1995): 126–130.
5. V.D. Elsenhans, Use of Self-Care Manual Shifts Utilization Pattern, *HMO Practice* (June 1995).
6. Goldstein, Emerging Data Show Programs Are Effective.
7. W.N. Burton and D.A. Hoy, First Chicago's Integrated Health Data Management Computer System, *Managed Care Quarterly* 1 (1993): 18–23.
8. J.K. Glenn, et al., Physician Referrals in a Competitive Environment: An Estimate of the Economic Impact of a Referral, *Journal of the American Medical Association* 258 (1987): 1920–1923.
9. Group Health Association of America (GHAA), *1995 Sourcebook on HMO Utilization Data* (Washington, D.C.: GHAA, 1995).
10. A.J. Dietrich, et al., Do Primary Physicians Actually Manage Their Patients' Fee-for-Service Care?, *Journal of the American Medical Association* 259 (1988): 3145–3149.
11. B.J. Hillman, et al., Frequency and Costs of Diagnostic Imaging in Office Practice—A Comparison of Self-Referring and Radiologist Referring Physicians, *New England Journal of Medicine* 323 (1990): 1604–1608.
12. Office of the Inspector General, *Financial Arrangements between Physicians and Health Care Businesses: Report to Congress* (Washington, D.C.: Department of Health and Human Services, 1989; Department of Health and Human Services Publication OAI-12-88-01410).
13. State of Florida Health Care Cost Containment Board, *Joint Ventures among Health Care Providers in Florida* (Tallahassee, Fla.: State of Florida, 1991), 2.
14. Omnibus Budget Reconciliation Act of 1989.
15. Health Care Knowledge Resources, *Length of Stay by Diagnosis and Operation* (Ann Arbor, Mich.: Health Knowledge Resources, 1991).
16. M.R. Chassin, et al., Variations in the Use of Medical and Surgical Services by the Medicare Population, *New England Journal of Medicine* 314 (1986): 285–290.
17. H.L. Smits, Medical Practice Variations Revisited, *Health Affairs* (Fall 1986): 91–96.
18. J. Wennberg and A. Gittelsohn, Variations in Medical Care among Small Areas, *Scientific American* (April 1982): 120–135.

19. J. Wennberg, et al., Are Hospital Services Rationed in New Haven or Overutilized in Boston?, *Lancet* 1 (1987): 1185–1189.
20. M.R. Chassin, et al., Does Inappropriate Use Explain Geographic Variations in the Use of Health Care Services? A Study of Three Procedures, *Journal of the American Medical Association* 258 (1987): 2533–2537.
21. D.V. Axene and R.L. Doyle, *Research Report: Analysis of Medically Unnecessary Inpatient Services* (Milliman & Robertson, 1994).
22. S.K. Kelley and J.J. Trutlein, A Survey of Human Resources in Managed Care Organizations, *Physician Executive* 18 (1992): 49–51.
23. R.L. Doyle, *Healthcare Management Guidelines, Vol 1: Inpatient and Surgical Care* (Milliman & Robertson, 1990).
24. InterQual, *The ISD—A Review System with Adult Criteria* (Chicago, Ill.: InterQual, 1991).
25. InterQual, *Surgical Indications Monitoring SIM III* (Chicago, Ill.: InterQual, 1991).
26. Utilization Management Associates, *Managed Care Appropriateness Protocol (MCAP)* (Wellesley, Mass.: Utilization Management Associates, 1991).
27. J. Rapoport, et al., Resource Utilization among Intensive Care Patients: Managed Care vs. Traditional Insurance, *Archives of Internal Medicine* 152 (1992): 2207–2212.
28. J.E. Billi, et al., The Effects of a Cost-Education Program on Hospital Charges, *Journal of General Internal Medicine* 2 (1987): 306–311.
29. K.M. Griffin, "Subacute Care and Managed Care," in *The Managed Health Care Handbook*, 3d ed., ed. P.R. Kongstvedt (Gaithersburg, Md.: Aspen, 1996), 388–399.

SUGGESTED READING

Doyle, R.L. *Healthcare Management Guidelines: Inpatient and Surgical Care*. Milliman & Robertson. Updated periodically.

Doyle, R.L. and Feren, H.P. *Healthcare Management Guidelines: Ambulatory Care*. Milliman & Robertson. Updated periodically.

Gray, B.H. and Field, M.J. (eds.). 1989. *Controlling Costs and Changing Patient Care? The Role of Utilization Management*. Washington, D.C.: National Academy Press.

Hammon, J.L. (ed.). 1993. *Fundamentals of Medical Management: A Guide for New Physician Executives*. Tampa, Fla.: American College of Physician Executives.

Chapter 14

Disease Management

David W. Plocher

Study Objectives

- Understand the meaning of disease management and be able to explain what is new and unique about the term
- Give at least one example of results following a disease management program implementation, expressed in return on investment (ROI)
- Explain how conventional case management differs from disease management
- List three to four key steps in setting up a disease management program
- List two or three important characteristics of a disease that make it appropriate for this model
- Explain why disease management is not enough, with regard to the entire spectrum of care management

---

DEFINITION

The title of this chapter requires careful definition, in view of the common belief that physicians have already been managing patients who have diseases. Disease management redirects the intervention efforts toward the outpatient setting for several chronic disorders, often featuring noncompliance with prescription drugs, and captures information from all sites of care for each patient with that disorder into a single longitudinal episode. It is on this comprehensive knowledge base that patients are tracked continuously, thereby adding new opportunities for patient education at encounter sites other than the hospital or physician's office and opportunities for nonphysician practitioners to give more care. This allows a more prospective approach to managing a disease, improving the likelihood of altering its natural history. That is, exacerbations of the disease can be prevented or reduced in frequency and severity. The resulting performance report is unique for this approach to a disease because it represents resource consumption from all sites of care, values global episode changes over time, and adds to routine economic measures the impact on morbidity, satisfaction, functional status, and, when advanced, population health status.

RATIONALE AND REQUIREMENTS FOR SUCCESSFUL DEMONSTRATIONS

This lengthy definition is necessary to explain the newness of the concept. Figure 14–1 displays schematically where disease management fits on the background of other established interventions in care management.

David W. Plocher, M.D., is a partner in the Minneapolis office of Ernst & Young LLP with the Health Care Consulting practice. His managed care activities include the national direction of development and deployment of care management techniques, including demand management and disease management.

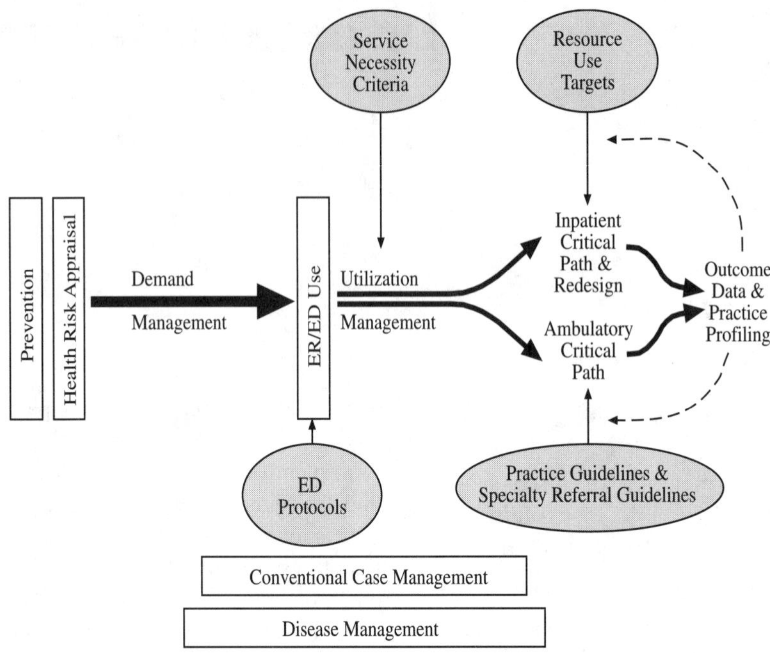

Figure 14–1 Interventions in care management

The connectivity depicted favors a disease manager who is operating within a vertically integrated delivery system with alignment of incentives among all constituents. This permits capture of information from and dissemination of educational material to encounter locations that are physically and geographically discontinuous.

Disease managers are also most motivated if they are at financial risk. Conversely, the fee-for-service physician is not financially rewarded for struggling through the innovations discussed in this chapter. There is one exceptional circumstance: the purchaser mandates. Recently, The Foundation for Accountability, a large purchasing group, has announced intentions to direct market share toward those delivery systems showing measurement and performance capabilities in five conditions: asthma, type I diabetes, cardiovascular disease, acquired immune deficiency syndrome (AIDS), and cancer.

Primary prevention programs have usually been discussed on a continuum that precedes the scope of classic disease management. That is, many primary preventive efforts do not select a single disease to prevent but rather emphasize generic nutrition, exercise, stress reduction, and so on. Conversely, we do not yet have a method for prevention of type I diabetes. Therefore, the prevention theme within disease management is oriented to exacerbation prevention. This includes a more sensitive outpatient detection mechanism, such as the newly designed health risk appraisal instruments, to help discover that emergency-department-visit-to-be.

When this prospective reconnaissance is supplemented by telephone nurse triage services that include directions for self-care, we begin to see an amelioration of the expected course for common disorders. This ranges from a dramatic reduction for office and emergency department visits for pediatric fevers (as in the Harvard

Community Health Plan Pediatric Fever Pilot) to extensive counseling for type I diabetics that reduces annual care costs. These approaches to demand management are discussed further in Chapter 13.

In summary, the disease manager will deploy techniques in secondary prevention, patient empowerment through education, demand management, and enhanced data management. Information systems will be key in determining success, beginning with analysis of practice pattern variants and progressing toward new outcome measures.

The performance requirements of such a data warehouse can be summarized as follows:

- Data are captured from all sites of care.
- Data are edited and cleansed.
- Severity adjustment is conducted with methodology validated independently.
- Reports are generated and benchmarks are provided:
    1. charges and cost
    2. mortality and morbidity
    3. functional status, health status, and satisfaction

There will be a real value in such information for the delivery system medical director who needs to find comparisons, norms, and benchmarks for each disease's annual cost of care and other outcome parameters.

CARVE-OUTS

Although industry analysts often represent carve-outs as a synonym or variation of disease management, this chapter will not incorporate a lengthy discussion of this entity. Chapter 10 addresses specialty-selective contracting in detail. Carve-outs usually produce a separate provider network as a capitated subcontractor. This chapter will instead concentrate on the new approach for managing patients with certain diseases, looking at improving the processes of care inside a delivery system.

For the sake of complete taxonomy, the main disease management carve-outs are divided between common and rare conditions. Common disease carve-outs have been in place for many years for patients with mental illness and substance abuse (see Chapter 16). More recently, oncology carve-outs have replicated this mode.[1–4] Rare diseases are amenable to a carve-out when there is a large enrollment in the delivery system. It then becomes problematic for the medical director to divert care management resources from asthma, congestive heart failure (CHF), and type I diabetes to create new guidelines for conditions such as hemophilia. Recently, vendors have come to the rescue for this purpose, and preliminary performance data are encouraging. For example, the annual cost of care for hemophilia could be reduced by 30 percent.

It must be emphasized that various other forms of specialty contracting (e.g., package pricing for coronary artery bypass) have not risen to the level of disease management. They are concerned about the hospitalization component only. Taxonomists might classify them as single-procedure preferred provider organizations.

CONVENTIONAL CASE MANAGEMENT AND DISEASE MANAGEMENT

The decade of the 1980s featured flourishing case management programs. Table 14–1, a comparison of these two care management techniques, helps answer the case manager's question "What else do we need?" In short, disease managers are better equipped to accomplish what the profession has wanted to do:

- achieve better control of episode cost of care
- reduce morbidity
- improve functional status
- improve patient and physician satisfaction
- acquire more meaningful outcome data (e.g., medication compliance)
- develop an improved ability to bear financial risk for the service

Table 14–1 Comparison of Conventional Case Management and Disease Management

Case Management	*Disease Management*
Goal	*Goal*
Streamlining components	Integrating components
Critical path component cost control	Improving long-term outcome
Emphasis	*Emphasis*
Treatment of sickness, especially in a complex inpatient	Prevention and education • for patients, families, and physicians • for common outpatient conditions • low technology nonsurgical • prescription drug-managed
Scope	Scope
Patient often has multiple diseases	Patient is initially evaluated for a single disease
Timing	*Timing*
Periodic inspection	Prospective and concurrent
Guidelines	*Guidelines*
Generic	Customized to diagnosis
Externally imposed	Internally designed
Caregivers	*Caregivers*
Generalists	Specialists
Nurses (primarily)	Multidisciplinary team
Data sources	*Data sources*
• Primarily inpatient (tracks length of stay, profit margin per confinement, mortality)	• All points of service (tracks annual episode of care cost, medication compliance, functional status)
• Not integrated	• Integrated
Lacks ability to bear financial risk	Increased ability to bear financial risk

SELECTION OF DISEASES

Advanced delivery systems have experimented with this model of care management for a large number of conditions. Pharmaceutical manufacturers have promoted this model for dozens of diseases for which their product represents one of the treatment options. After struggles with cost versus benefit, the feasibility tests have produced the following short list of diagnoses that appear currently to deliver the largest early impact. They are ranked here in approximate order of success.

1. asthma; adolescent, refractory
2. CHF
3. diabetes, type I
4. AIDS
5. cancer, as managed by carve-outs mentioned above

It is important to understand the criteria that these conditions must meet. The following series of observations seem to be most valuable in prioritizing the selection:

- high rate of preventable complications, so that emergency department visits and hospital readmissions can be influenced
- short time frame during which alterations in natural history can show a measurable impact (i.e., 1 to 3 years), coinciding with the most common time interval after which subscribers change health plans

- chronic outpatient-focused conditions that are common, low technology, and nonsurgical
- high rate of variability in patterns of therapeutics from patient to patient and from physician to physician (most variation is easily measured in resource use, but other outcome measures should pertain, such as prescription drug selection)
- high rates of patient noncompliance with the therapeutic regimen (this noncompliance must be amenable to change by education; education is directed at patients, family members, *and* physicians)
- practice guidelines on optimal treatment exist or can be developed
- consensus is achievable on what constitutes good quality, which outcomes to measure, and how to improve them

EXPERIENCE FROM EARLY DEMONSTRATIONS

Adolescent Refractory Asthma

The performance observed in the first pilots of disease management is best described with adolescent refractory asthma. Most pilots begin with refractory adolescents, because of the above tests, and extend to adults later. Less than 5 percent of asthmatics are classified as severe, and nearly half the claims costs for all asthmatics occur in the emergency department and hospital.[5] More important is the observation that only 10 percent to 20 percent of asthmatics receive inhaled steroids, considered the cornerstone of therapy. The reason appears to be that inhaled bronchodilators are overused because of their ability to provide instant relief. Finally, physicians are not the most frequently encountered caregiver. Asthmatics see their pharmacist five times more often. This has raised the position of the pharmacist in disease management programs to that of a true provider and educator, sometimes with financial incentives. Ironically, this opportunity is lost when subscribers are financially motivated to use mail order programs for inhaler refills. Compensatory efforts include visits by home nurses specializing in asthma and various phone and mail prompts.

The entire continuum of asthma care is displayed in Figure 14–2. The contrast between a hospital-based case manager's role and that of the disease manager is dramatic.

Results from individual delivery system implementation of disease management for asthma are consistent over all regions in the United States. The most important observations include the following:

- reduction in hospitalizations by half or more
- reduction in emergency department visits by half or more
- abrupt increase in the use of inhaled steroids
- decrease in reliance on bronchodilators
- improved functional status, as measured by:
    1. ability to work
    2. quality of sleep

Other Conditions

The role of specialized nurse managers and intensive home care is applicable to a variety of conditions, ranging from hemophilia to AIDS. For reasons of space, an abbreviated series for type I diabetes and CHF is described below.

Type I Diabetes

Context. Five percent of Americans are diabetic, and employers pay as much as 20 percent of their medical claims for this disease. The nonmedical claim costs add up a further tally for employers in the form of reduced productivity at work, absenteeism, and short- and long-term disability.

Caregivers. As with asthma, the diabetic will see a pharmacist twice a month but the physician as infrequently as three times a year.

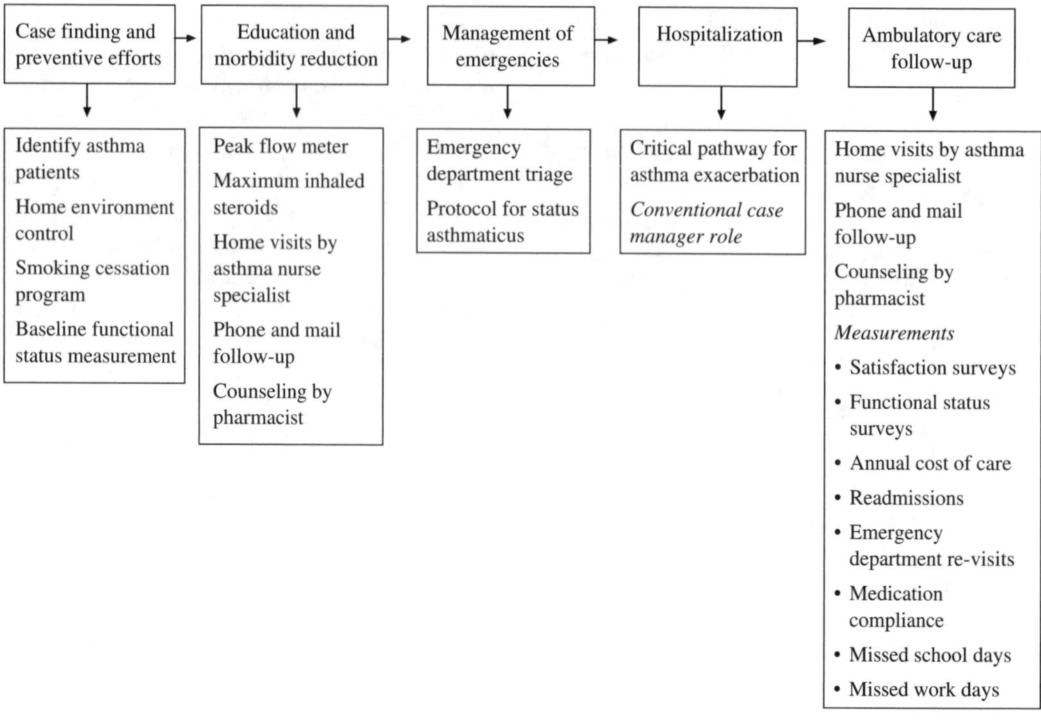

Figure 14–2 Continuum of care for adolescent refractory asthma

Short-term impact. Emergency department visits and hospitalizations for ketoacidosis are reduced. A southwestern health plan has demonstrated half the usual admission rate, attributed largely to intensified educational efforts.

Long-term impact. The literature has recently documented the success of tighter control (beyond intensive education) in reducing retinopathy, neuropathy, and nephropathy;[6] the risk of weight gain; a threefold increase in severe hypoglycemia[7] and at least triple care costs.[8]

CHF

Context. Many primary care physicians have been insufficiently aggressive in using angiotensin-converting enzyme (ACE) inhibitors and other preload and afterload reducers for this population, especially for the CHF subset with systolic dysfunction. There has been further difficulty separating the CHF patient subset with diastolic dysfunction, for which digoxin is not primary therapy and agents that control the heart rate, such as ß blockers or calcium channel blockers, are indicated. Both types of patients have also been subject to excessive diuresis, which makes them refractory to the indicated agents or compromises renal function.

Caregivers. The combination of more direct access to cardiologists as well as clinic nurses and home care nurses specially trained in CHF is changing these episodes.

Short-term impact. CHF readmissions and annual cost of care have been reduced. This success and recent data are displayed at the end of this chapter, serving as examples for measurement when pilots are being constructed.

Long-term impact. Expanded use of ACE inhibitors has reduced mortality from CHF.[9]

CAVEATS FROM THE MARKET

The Skeptical Health Maintenance Organization Medical Director

Several medical directors have adopted a hold-out posture until better data are available. The additional labor embedded in these new processes must be weighed against the suggested annual cost of care reductions. More important for a delivery system trying to be comprehensive in all services is the threat of a carve-out. That is, the conditions best suited for disease management are so common that their services are already completely intertwined with the health maintenance organization's operations. Carving them out to a subcontractor would interrupt the continuity of care and produce disintegration, according to several medical directors.

The Suspect Pharmaceutical Manufacturer

Most delivery systems will not consider allowing a drug supplier to "front" a disease management pilot. This risks using a therapeutic agent that is not the drug of choice. It is also anti-innovation because newer products from competitors, blockbuster drugs or otherwise, must have a chance to prove their worth. The middle ground with some medical directors has been partnering as long as the supplier shares risk and offers some of its competitors' agents.

Poor Prioritization

In an effort to manage high-volume conditions better, several medical directors have selected hypertension and hyperlipoproteinemia as target diagnoses for disease management pilots. Of the criteria that must be met, frequency and variability appear applicable. These are diseases subject to some of the heaviest marketing by pharmaceutical manufacturers, and pilots are underway. These two conditions are not necessarily the best selection for an early success, however.

First, the conditions have no symptoms. Therefore, patients are not going to experience instant gratification through compliance and will be refractory to education efforts, which has been summarized as the primary care physician's quandary: "It's hard to make an asymptomatic patient feel better." Second, there is an early increase in cost of care when randomly screened subscribers acquire these diagnoses and begin drug therapy. Finally, the return on investment for the delivery system cannot be achieved in a 1- to 3-year time frame because the sequelae of those conditions are at least 10 years away. All this is not to suggest that these patients should be abandoned but only to remind the delivery system chief financial officer where the first disease management pilot might be more effectively directed.

GETTING YOUR PILOT PROGRAM STARTED

There are several key steps in the pilot start-up process:

1. Prioritize disease selection:
    - Make it pertinent to the demographics of your covered lives.
    - Begin with two "Top-10" diagnosis lists, one by frequency or volume and one by total charges.
2. For the first condition selected, flowchart care processes across all sites in your delivery system, including self-care.
3. Conduct focus groups with a homogeneous group of patients carrying that diagnosis to validate patient needs and preferences as well as to articulate bottlenecks in the delivery system.
4. Using the flowchart, discover each cost driver.
5. Using the flowchart, discover determinants of important clinical outcome measures.
6. Assign working groups to each cost/outcome driver to engage in formal process

value optimization, including literature search for evidence-based support.

7. Prepare for major information systems investment.
8. Define episode duration and establish performance measures specific to the diagnosis beyond cost and resource use (e.g., morbidity, functional status, and satisfaction).
9. Use data to motivate physicians.
10. Consider restructuring financial incentives for caregivers.

Learning is accelerated by searches and surveys that reveal process and outcome from early efforts around the country. In light of the critical role of information capture and reporting, three examples are offered here. The first example is illustrated in Figure 14–3 and Table 14–2. These episode reports are remarkable in their ability to capture drug and nondrug costs, including drug side effect management. In view of the wide 95 percent confidence intervals, however, the differences among therapeutic agents do not appear significant.

The next example is illustrated in Figures 14–4 through 14–6. These episodes are more completely constructed with narrower confidence intervals, possibly related to large sample sizes. Of further interest, measurement parameters go beyond dollars to variations on patient satisfaction.

Finally, Exhibit 14–1 and Table 14–3 depict advantages for elderly patients, with substantial risk factors beyond age alone, whose CHF is managed using principles of disease management. The main outcomes are a reduction in the rate of readmission due to recurrent heart failure by 56.2 percent, and improved life quality scores.

THE FUTURE

Speculations about the future of disease management include the following:

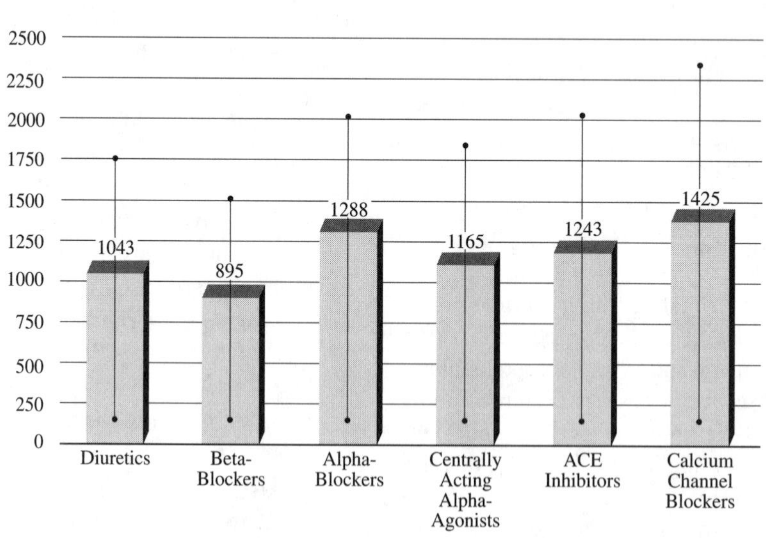

Figure 14–3 Mean annual cost per drug (dollars) for drugs with comparable blood pressure control. ACE, angiotensin-converting enzyme. *Source:* Reprinted with permission from S.H. McBride, Taking a long-term view of hypertension, *Managed Healthcare*, pp. 519–520, © 1995, Advanstar Communications, Inc.

Table 14–2 Mean Annual Cost per Drug per Cost Category for Drugs with Comparable Blood Pressure Control (Values Expressed as Mean ± Standard Deviation)

Drug Category	*Acquisition Cost ($)*	*Supplemental Drug Cost ($)*	*Laboratory Cost ($)*	*Clinic Visit Cost ($)*	*Side Effect Cost ($)*	*Total Cost ($)*
Diuretics	133 ± 107	232 ± 203	117 ± 32	298 ± 102	263 ± 480	1043 ± 667
ß Blockers	334 ± 170	115 ± 192	56 ± 32	187 ± 87	203 ± 418	895 ± 545
α Blockers	410 ± 151	290 ± 290	114 ± 30	227 ± 69	256 ± 485	1288 ± 697
Centrally acting α agonists	285 ± 224	295 ± 338	125 ± 52	267 ± 114	193 ± 390	1165 ± 658
Angiotensin-converting enzyme inhibitors	444 ± 301	291 ± 315	95 ± 33	218 ± 87	195 ± 400	1243 ± 800
Calcium channel blockers	540 ± 219	278 ± 398	87 ± 29	214 ± 84	306 ± 642	1425 ± 962

Source: Reprinted with permission from S.H. McBride, Taking a long-term view of hypertension, *Managed Healthcare*, pp. 519–520, © 1995, Advanstar Communications, Inc.

- Information technology advances hold the greatest promise for improvement, starting with the electronic longitudinal patient medical record and including on-line educational services for patients.
- Continuous updates in optimal treatment guidelines will drive improvements in care.
- Customized programs for Medicare and Medicaid populations will be necessary, relying heavily on outreach programs.
- Interventions must include attention to the patient's psychosocial needs rather than focus only on clinical morbidity because care-seeking behavior is often not directly related to burden of illness. This will raise the value of demand management programs.
- Treatment decision support systems will need to rediscover the role of patient choice in the equation for controversial circumstances.

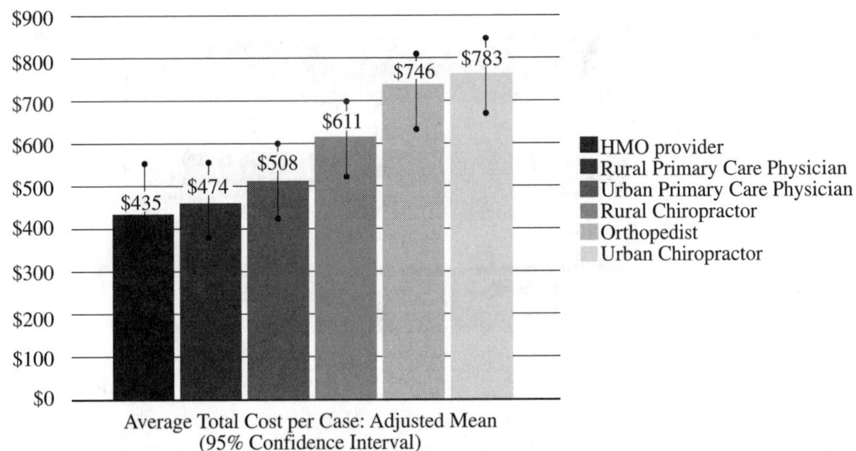

Figure 14–4 Total direct outpatient costs per episode of low back pain, adjusted for baseline functional status, sciatica, income, duration of pain, and workers' compensation. HMO, health maintenance organization. *Source:* Adapted from T.S. Carey et al., *New England Journal of Medicine*, 1995, Vol. 333, p. 916. Copyright 1995. Massachusetts Medical Society. All rights reserved.

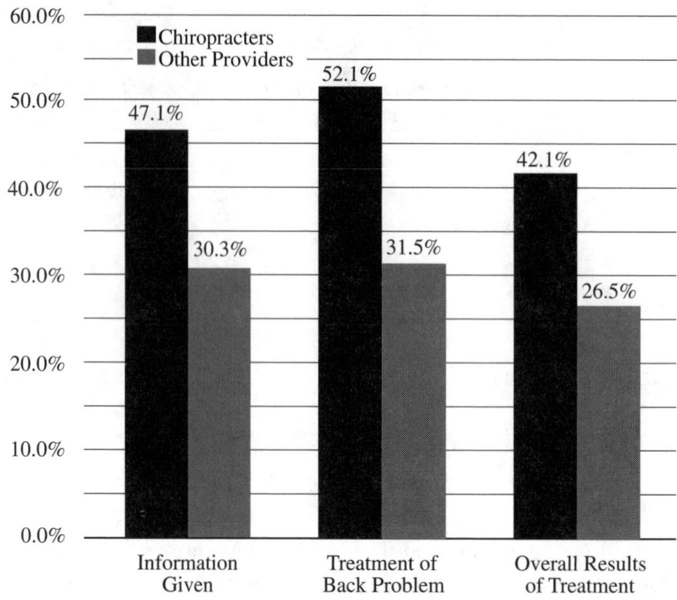

Figure 14–5 Satisfaction with treatment of acute low back pain: Percentage of patients answering "excellent" in response to satisfaction survey. Chiropractors, $n = 606$; other providers, $n = 1{,}027$; $p < .001$. A one-way analysis of variance, or the Kruskal-Wallis test was used for continuous data; the Pearsons chi-square test was used for categorical data; nonparametric Kaplan-Meier methods were used for data on time to functional recovery. *Source:* Adapted from T.S. Carey et al., *New England Journal of Medicine*, 1995, Vol. 333, p. 917.

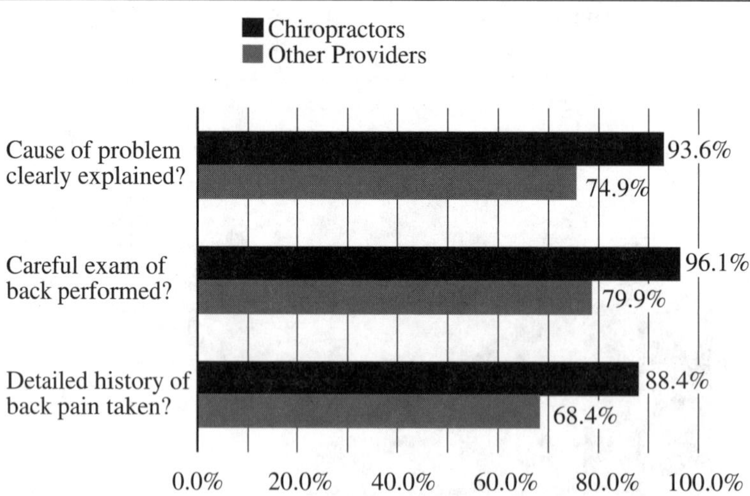

Figure 14–6 Perception of care in treatment of acute low back pain: Percentage of patients answering "yes" to satisfaction survey. Chiropractors, $n = 606$; other providers, $n = 1{,}027$; $p < .001$. A one-way analysis of variance, or the Kruskal-Wallis test was used for continuous data; the Pearsons chi-square test was used for categorical data; nonparametric Kaplan-Meier methods were used for data on time to functional recovery. *Source:* Adapted from T.S. Carey et al., *New England Journal of Medicine*, 1995, Vol. 333, p. 915.

Exhibit 14–1 Disease Management in CHF

Study design
Randomized controlled trial

Population
Seniors older than 70 years ($N = 282$)
Risk factors in addition to age

Duration
90 days

Care patterns
Disease management (treatment group, $n = 142$)
Conventional management (control group, $n = 140$)

Functional status measure
Chronic Heart Failure Questionnaire

- Has shown responsiveness to improvement in health status
- Has demonstrated validity (e.g., in measuring shortness of breath)

Treatment group interventions
Cardiovascular nurse education
Booklet specific for geriatric patients with CHF
Diet instruction
Social services consultation
Medication analysis by geriatric cardiologist
Intensive postdischarge home care

- Visits
- Phone contacts

Survival (for 90 days without readmission from subset of survivors of the initial hospitalization)
Treatment group: 66.9%
Control group: 54.3%
$p = .04$

90-day episode cost

Treatment group:	$4,815	$2,178
Control group:	$5,275	$3,236
Difference:	$460	$1,058*

* $p = 0.03$

Source: Adapted from M.W. Rich et al., *New England Journal of Medicine*, 1995, Vol. 333, p. 1192.

Table 14–3 Disease Management in CHF

Group	*Readmissions*	*More Than One Readmission*	*Hospital Days*	*Drug Compliance*	*Daily Drug Doses*	*Quality of Life Scores*	*Understanding CHF*
Treatment	53	9	556	82.5%	2.7	Greater improvement	Greater
Control	94	23	865	64.9%	3.0	—	—
p	.02	.01	.04	.02	.01	.001	.001

The two study groups were compared by students' t-test for normally distributed continuous variables, by the chi-square test for discrete variables, and by the Wilcox rank-sum test for categorical and abnormally distributed continuous variables.

Source: Adapted from M.W. Rich et al., *New Enland Journal of Medicine*, 1995, Vol. 333, p. 1192,

- Progression is necessary from concentrated efforts on the single disease toward better coordination of care for patients with two or more diseases.
- Health risk appraisals need to become better cost risk predictors.
- Population health management will require using both disease-specific functional status measures and health status measures.

Study Questions

1. What is disease management? What is new and unique about disease management?
2. Please give one example of the results following the implementation of disease management expressed in ROI.
3. How does conventional case management differ from disease management?
4. What are the key steps in setting up a disease management program?
5. What are some characteristics of a disease that make it appropriate for this model?
6. How does disease management fall short, with regard to the entire spectrum of care management?

REFERENCES AND NOTES

1. B. Kurowski, Cancer Carve-Outs: Can They Fulfill the Promise of Managed Care?, *Oncology Issues* (November/December 1994): 10–13.
2. R. Rundle, Salick Agrees To Provide Cancer Care at Fixed Price to Florida HMO Patients, *Wall Street Journal* (14 July 1994): B7.
3. Salick Signs First Capitated Oncology Contract, *Modern Healthcare* 24 (1994): 14.
4. C. Sardinha, Seeking Cancer Know-How, PCA Signs Carve-Out Deal with Salick, *Managed Care Outlook* (1994).
5. National Jewish Center for Immunology and Respiratory Medicine, *Your Guide to National Jewish* (Denver, Colo.: National Jewish Center for Immunology and Respiratory Medicine, 1987).
6. DCCT Research Group, The Effect of Intensive Treatment of Diabetes on the Development and Progression of Long-Term Complications in Insulin-Dependent Diabetes Mellitus, *New England Journal of Medicine* 329 (1993): 977–986.
7. DCCT Research Group, Adverse Events and Their Association with Treatment Regimens in the Diabetes Control and Complications Trial, *Diabetes Care* 18 (1995): 1415–1427.
8. DCCT Research Group, Resource Utilization and Costs of Care in the Diabetes Control and Complications Trial, *Diabetes Care* 18 (1995): 1468–1478.
9. L. Kober, et al., A Clinical Trial of the Angiotensin-Converting Enzyme Inhibitor Trandolapril in Patients with Left Ventricular Dysfunction after Myocardial Infarction, *New England Journal of Medicine* 333 (1995): 1670–1676.

SUGGESTED READING

Disease State Management: Identifying an Rx for Savings. *1995. Business & Health,* 13, pp. 11–15.

Griffin, M. and Griffin, R.B. 1994. Critical Pathways Produce Tangible Results. *Health Care Strategic Management* 12(7): 1, 17–22.

Lumsdon, K. 5 April 1995. Disease Management: The Heat and Headaches over Retooling Patient Care Create Hard Labor. *Hospitals and Health Networks*, pp. 34–42.

Peterson, C. May/June 1995. Disease Management. *HMO Magazine*, pp. 39–47.

Peterson, C. September/October 1994. Pharmaceutical Integration: Going Vertical. *HMO Magazine*, pp. 50–54.

Regardie, J. 30 January–5 February 1995. Providers Turn to "Disease Management" To Cut Costs: Practice Targets Conditions Requiring Pricey Treatment. *Los Angeles Business Journal.*

Rohl, B.J., Meyer, L.C., and Lung, C.L. 1994. Asthma Care Map for Decision Making. *Medical Interface* 7(2): 107–110.

Rohl, B.J., Meyer, L.C., and Lung, C.L. 1994. An Individualized, Comprehensive Asthma Care Treatment Program. *Medical Interface* 7(3): 121–123, 134.

Terry, K. April 1995. Disease Management: Continuous Health-Care Improvement. *Business & Health*, pp. 64–72.

Chapter 15

Managing Utilization of Ancillary and Emergency Services

Peter R. Kongstvedt

Study Objectives

- Understand what is meant by ancillary and emergency services
- Understand basic contracting approaches to different types of ancillary services and which approaches work best under what circumstances
- Understand how emergency services are incurred and approaches to managing them
- Understand how ancillary and emergency services differ from other forms of utilization

This chapter addresses those medical services that are generally considered ancillary services by most managed care plans. These services are a collection of services that are provided as an adjunct to basic primary or specialty services and include almost everything other than institutional services as described in Chapter 11 (although institutions can provide ancillary services). Ancillary services and emergency services are sufficiently different that each must be discussed in its own section. The two categories often cost the health plan roughly the same amount of money, but for different reasons.

ANCILLARY SERVICES

Ancillary services are divided into diagnostic and therapeutic services. Examples of ancillary diagnostic services include laboratory, radiology, nuclear testing, computed tomography, magnetic resonance imaging, electroencephalography, electrocardiography, and cardiac testing (including plain and nuclear stress testing, other cardiac nuclear imaging, invasive imaging, echocardiography, and Holter monitoring). Examples of ancillary therapeutic services include cardiac rehabilitation, noncardiac rehabilitation, physical therapy (PT), occupational therapy, and speech therapy.

Pharmacy services are a special form of ancillary services that account for a significant measure of cost and have been subject to tremendous inflation. This important topic is discussed separately in Chapter 23 of *The Managed Health Care Handbook.*[1] Mental health and substance abuse services may also be considered ancillary from a health plan's standpoint but are really core services, albeit discretely defined. Those services are discussed in Chapter 16.

Ancillary services are unique in that they are rarely sought out by the patient without a referral by a physician. For example, it is certainly possible that an individual could self-refer to a rehabilitation center, but it is likely that the center would require a referral from a physician before accepting the individual into the program. Diagnostic studies almost universally require physician referral. One exception is the free-standing diagnostic center that has medical staff whose sole purpose is to guide a patient through the diagnostic workup that the patient seeks (e.g., a free-standing cardiac testing center whose advertisements appeal to people who want those tests done). Because those types of centers are out of a plan's control, as are free-standing urgent/convenience care centers, the only real way to control them is economically. If those centers do not have a contract with the plan, or if the plan requires authorization from a contracted physician to pay in full, then the plan does not have to pay such free-standing centers. In the case of a health maintenance organization (HMO), the plan does not have to pay at all. For a preferred provider organization (PPO), a point-of-service (POS) plan, or a managed indemnity plan, the plan may or may not have a partial payment liability, depending on the service agreement and schedule of benefits.

Because most ancillary services require an order from a physician, it is logical that control of such services is dependent on changing the utilization patterns of physicians. As discussed below, the other primary method of controlling costs of ancillary services is to contract for such services in such a way as to make costs predictable. Even with favorable contracts, however, controlling utilization of ancillary services by physicians remains an essential ingredient to long-term cost control.

Physician-Owned Ancillary Services

There is compelling evidence that physician ownership of diagnostic or therapeutic equipment or services, whether owned individually or through joint ventures or partnerships, can lead to significant increases in utilization of those services. As mentioned in Chapter 10, there are three studies that documented this phenomenon in diagnostic imaging, laboratory, and a remarkably wide range of other services.[2–4] Physician self-referral is now restricted by the Health Care Financing Administration for Medicare services (see Chapter 26), and many private plans have followed suit, especially if they are enrolling public sector (i.e., Medicare or Medicaid) members.[5]

Actually tracing ownership or fiduciary relationships is not always easy. The ancillary services may have a completely separate provider name and tax identification number, may have a separate billing address (perhaps not even in the same geographic area), and may otherwise appear to be an independent vendor. Tracking unusually high rates of referral to a given provider of ancillary services (see Chapter 19) may be the only clue to such potential utilization abuse. Many plans are also clearly prohibiting physician self-referral in their provider contracts (unless expressly allowed by the plan) and are requiring the physicians to disclose any fiduciary relationship with such providers.

It is neither practical nor desirable to place too heavy a restriction on physicians' ability to use services or equipment that they own to deliver routine care. For example, orthopedists cannot properly care for their patients if they cannot obtain radiographs. In some cases, a physician may be the only available provider of a given service (e.g., in a rural area). In other cases, it may actually be more cost effective to allow physicians to use their own facility. The point here is that physician-owned services must not be allowed to become a lucrative profit center, one that is subject to abuse.

Managed care plans deal with this issue in a number of ways. One method is to have an outright ban on self-referral other than for carefully designated services. For example, a cardiologist may be allowed to perform in-office exercise tolerance testing but be prohibited from referring to a free-standing cardiac diagnostic center with which he or she has a fiduciary relationship. Another method is to reimburse for such physician self-referred services at a low margin (not so low as to cause the physician to lose money but low enough to prevent any profit) or to include it in the capitation payment (see Chapters 8 and 10). The last common method is to contract for all ancillary services through a limited network of providers and require the physicians and members to use only those contracted providers for ancillary services; this is discussed later in this chapter.

The advent of integrated delivery systems (IDSs; see Chapter 4) has complicated this issue somewhat. It is not always clear whether the ancillary services are owned by the physician or the IDS, and those services may be included in an all-encompassing global capitation rate in any event. The regulatory environment is changing in this arena, however, which is particularly important for those managed care organizations (MCOs) that are contracting for public sector business (Medicare and Medicaid; see Chapters 26 and 27). The reader is referred to Chapter 30 for additional discussion of the topic of fraud and abuse in physician-owned ancillary services in the setting of IDSs.

Data Capture

The ability to control utilization of ancillary services will be directly related to your ability to capture accurate and timely data (see Chapters 18 and 19). If you have a tight authorization system (see Chapter 21), you may get prospective data. If your claims management system is capable, you should be able to get retrospective data. If you have no way to capture data regarding ancillary services, you will have great difficulty controlling utilization. Lack of data will also make contracting problematic because no vendor will be willing to contract aggressively without having some idea of projected utilization.

Data elements that you need to capture include who ordered the service [this is sometimes different from the physician of record; for example, a member may have signed up with a primary care physician (PCP), but the referral physician ordered the tests], what was ordered, what is being paid for (in other words, are you paying for more than was ordered?), and how much it is costing.

The ability to look at patterns of usage in ancillary services is quite valuable. For example, it would be useful to know that of 10 family practitioners there is 1 who routinely orders double the number of radiographs compared with the other 9. There may be a perfectly good reason for this, but you will never know unless you can identify that pattern and look for the reasons.

Financial Incentives

Ancillary services utilization is commonly incorporated into primary care reimbursement systems that are performance based (e.g., capitation or performance-based fee for service). In one study, capitation with risk sharing combined with education and feedback (see below) led to a clear reduction in the use of ambulatory testing while having no adverse impact on outcomes.[6] The topic of financial incentives is discussed in Chapters 6, 8, 9, and 10.

Feedback

The issue of monetary gain leading to excessive use of ancillary services has been discussed earlier in this chapter, but there are a number of nonmonetary causes of excessive testing; such causes include the quest for diagnostic certainty, peer pressure, convenience, patient demands, and fear of malpractice claims.[7]

There is evidence that physicians will modify their use of ancillary services when given feedback on their performance. Simple feedback regarding test ordering behavior has led to modest reductions in use.[8] This response has been confirmed for simple feedback, and somewhat greater decreases have been seen when feedback was combined with other written guidelines or peer review.[9,10]

Feedback to physicians regarding their use of ancillary services is therefore a worthwhile endeavor. Feedback should include comparisons with their peers and should be properly adjusted for factors that affect utilization (e.g., age and sex of patients, specialty type, and the like). Feedback should also contain adequate data to allow a physician to know where performance may be improved. See Chapter 19 for further discussion about using reports and practice profiling.

Control Points

Irrespective of physician self-regulation of the use of ancillary services, many plans apply additional controls over ancillary utilization. The most common of these are briefly discussed as follows.

Indications for Use

The first control point to discuss is indications for use of services. This is not an easy means of controlling ancillary services, but it has the potential of producing the best control and fostering high quality. In essence, this means using standards of care. Like protocols and clinical pathways (see Chapter 19 of *The Managed Health Care Handbook*), standards of care outline the events and thought processes that should occur before physicians refer for ancillary or consultant services.

Standards of care are especially useful in certain types of services. Theoretically, one could develop standards of care for virtually any service, but because review of such standards is time consuming, it is not worth it in all cases. For example, unless a plan is experiencing a tremendous cost overrun connected with urinalyses, there will be no marginal benefits to developing a protocol for when a urinalysis is required and when a urine dip test will do.

Cardiac testing is another matter. Cardiac testing, particularly stress testing and imaging, is quite expensive and increasingly common. Indications for cardiac testing have been published in medical journals, and texts and algorithms are available, but the ordering of cardiac testing sometimes defies rationality. As mentioned earlier in this chapter, a scattershot approach may be used by some physicians that results in test ordering simply as an effort to turn something up. Concentration on this service via chart reviews for appropriateness may yield interesting results and give you direction in developing standards for ordering.

There are now multiple sources for clinical protocols. In the example of cardiac testing, a reasonable approach is to enlist several highly respected cardiologists to use published protocols as a beginning and then tailor the algorithms, protocols, or standards rather than simply impose the protocol without input from plan physicians. A well-reasoned, referenced, and well-presented approach to cardiac disease will benefit the patient and result in lower costs.

The problem with using standards of care is that it exposes you to charges of practicing cookbook medicine. If you are imposing arbitrary requirements on physicians, that charge has the ring of truth. If, however, you are using the best and latest in medical intelligence as well as respected journals and experts to develop the standards, then you are simply expecting high-quality medical practice and thoughtful care of the patient. That having been said, some plans have found that adherence to good protocols has such a beneficial effect that those plans require specialists to agree to follow such protocols and guidelines as a condition of their participation with the health plan.[11]

Test of Reasonableness

If you do not have standards developed, or if you choose not to do so, there are still other approaches. The first is a continual test of reasonableness: Will the test or therapy help? In other words, will the test provide a piece of information that will have an effect on the care of the patient, or at least on the diagnosis or prognosis? In too many cases, tests are ordered only because they have always been ordered. A good example of that is the routine admission chest radiograph. Despite multiple articles in the medical literature, admission chest radiographs get ordered for many people who do not need them.[12–14] The same issue may apply to many other routine studies [e.g., preoperative electrocardiograms (ECGs) or laboratory screening for otherwise healthy patients[15,16]].

Another example is long-term PT for patients who no longer show improvement but who continually complain to their physician. For example, a patient complains of lower back pain, but a diagnostic workup has yielded a negative result. The patient may not be losing weight or exercising as instructed but is still demanding that something be done. The physician orders PT because it is easy to do and because the patient likes the attention. This is clearly not cost effective, but it happens.

Limits on Authority To Authorize

Limiting the authority to authorize ancillary services will also help control their use. An HMO can limit the authority to authorize services to the PCP only. In that case, a consultant must discuss the case with the PCP, and the PCP must actually order the test or therapy. This is not always practical, and there are legitimate reasons in some plans to allow certain consultants to order ancillary services; for example, orthopedists need to be able to order radiographs, cardiologists need to be able to do ECGs, and so forth.

On the other hand, as discussed earlier in this chapter, you need to watch out for the physician who has purchased an expensive piece of equipment and is hoping to increase revenue from its use. In those cases, allowing the physician to bill the plan for tests or procedures done with that equipment may cause problems. Again, one must be reasonable in this. Certain specialists use certain pieces of equipment routinely (e.g., gastroenterologists use colonoscopes), and you may not want to hamper that unduly. What you do want to avoid is paying for someone else's amortization needs.

Limits on Services Authorized

Another standard feature of managed care is limiting the number of visits for therapy without prior approval. This refers not only to having a limited number of visits that are covered in your schedule of benefits but also to having a limitation on the number of visits that a member may receive without reauthorization.

For example, you may allow up to three or four visits to PT, but for any more the PCP must receive a case report, or the therapist must discuss the case with the physician or the plan's case manager. At that point a treatment plan is developed, and the correct number of visits is authorized.

There will be exceptions to this last technique. In cases where the absolute treatment need is known, proper authorizations for the entire course of treatment may be made. An example is radiation therapy or home intravenous treatments. In such cases, the treatment plan is worked out in detail before therapy is initiated. The number of treatments required and their duration are known and may be authorized at the beginning.

Failure to control prospectively the use of ancillary therapy may result in the number of treatments or visits required in a particular type of therapy exactly equaling the level of benefits your plan offers. Much preferred is a rational approach to treatment with review of the case by the member's physician or the plan's case management function (as appropriate) and a definite treatment plan with periodic reassessments required.

Contracting and Reimbursement for Ancillary Services

Closed panels have the option of bringing certain ancillary services in house. It is up to management to do the cost/benefit analysis to determine whether that is the best course of action. One thing to keep in mind, though, is that controlling utilization is no less difficult when the service is in house because referral for that service is often seen as free and certainly as convenient.

For open panel plans or closed panels that do not have the services in house, the services must be contracted for. A plan usually has its choice of hospital-based (sometimes that is the only choice), free-standing or independent, or office-based service. The choice will be made on the basis of a combination of quality, cost, access, service (e.g., turnaround time for testing), and convenience for members. Unlike physician services, ancillary services usually may be limited to a small subset of providers. This allows for greater leverage in negotiating as well as greater control of quality and service.

In HMOs or plans that have absolute limitations on benefits for ancillary services, ancillary services often lend themselves to capitation.

When capitating for ancillary services, you need to calculate the expected frequency of need for the service and the expected or desired cost and then spread this over the membership base on a monthly basis. Plans that allow significant benefits for out-of-network use (e.g., a POS plan) may still capitate, but only for the in-network portion; out-of-network costs will have to be paid through the regular fee allowances. If the capitated provider strictly limits access or cannot meet demand, the plan could end up paying twice: once through capitation and a second time through fee for service. It is possible, although uncommon, for a POS plan to have no out-of-network benefits for some ancillary services, thus more easily allowing for capitation; this may be difficult from a regulatory standpoint if the ancillary services are clearly part of the basic medical benefit. Simple PPOs generally are unable to capitate and must therefore depend on fee allowances.

Capitating for ancillary services clearly makes the provider of the service a partner in controlling costs and helps you budget and forecast more accurately. The benefit to the provider of the service is a guaranteed source of referrals and a steady income. In diagnostic services, great economies of scale will often be present (this is especially true for diagnostic laboratory services). In those services where the provider delivering the service may be determining the need for continued services (e.g., PT), capitation will remove the fee-for-service incentives that may lead to inappropriately increased utilization. As with all capitation contracts, you must take care that the service is not seen by the providers as free, which may lead to uncontrolled utilization. Again, as with all capitation arrangements, be sure that you can direct all (or at least a defined portion) of the care to the capitated provider, and do not allow referrals to noncontracted providers.

Certain types of ancillary services require greater skill in capitating than others. If an ancillary service is highly self-contained, then it is easier to capitate; for example, PT usually is limited to therapy given by the physical therapists and does not involve other types of ancillary providers. Home health, on the other hand, is often a combination of home health nurses and aids, durable medical equipment, home infusion and medication delivery (which includes the cost of the drug or intravenous substance as well as the cost to deliver it), home PT, and so forth. Some plans have successfully capitated for home health services, although those have tended to be larger plans with sufficient volume to be able to predict costs accurately in all these different areas. Other plans have been able to capitate only parts of home health (e.g., home respiratory therapy) but have had less success in other forms. In those cases, a combination of capitation and fixed case rates (e.g., for a course of chemotherapy) may yield positive results.

A recent variant on capitation is similar to the single-specialty management organization or specialty network manager discussed in Chapter 10. In this case, a single entity accepts capitation from the plan for all of a particular ancillary service (e.g., PT). That organization then serves as a network manager or even an independent practice association. The participating ancillary providers may be subcontractors to the network manager and be paid either through subcapitation or through a form of fee for service, but in any event, the network manager is at risk for the total costs of the capitated service (the participating ancillary providers are usually at risk as well through capitation, fee adjustments, withholds, and so forth).

Some plans that capitate for ancillary services are employing risk and reward systems to ensure high levels of quality and satisfaction. For example, a plan may withhold 10 percent of the capitation or set up an incentive pool to ensure compliance with service standards, such as accessibility, member satisfaction, responsiveness to referring physicians, documentation, and so forth.

Plans that do not have the option of capitating may still achieve considerable savings from discounts. Because ancillary services are often high-margin businesses, it is usually not difficult to obtain reasonable discounts or to have a negotiated fee schedule accepted for ancillary services. Related to that for therapeutic ancillary providers are case rates or tiered case rates. In this form of reimbursement, the ancillary provider is paid a fixed case rate regardless of the number of visits or resources used in providing services. For home health that is inclusive of high-intensity services such as chemotherapy or other high-technology services, the plan may pay different levels of case rates depending on which category of complexity the case falls into. These types of reimbursement systems are appealing but often quite hard to administer, requiring manual administration by both the plan and the provider.

The exception to being able to obtain substantial discounts and savings is when there is a limited number of providers offering the service. Beyond exotic testing and therapy, this is usually not the case unless the plan is located in a rural area. In general, high savings can be achieved through good contracting.

EMERGENCY DEPARTMENT

Exactly opposite the situation with ancillary services, use of the emergency department (ED) is usually at the discretion of the members themselves rather than due to referral from a physician. Physicians do refer patients to the ED, but that is only a source of inappropriate expense if the physician is using the ED as a way of avoiding seeing the patient. For the most part, when a patient is sent to the ED by a physician, it is because there is a legitimate concern that there may be a significant medical problem. There are, however, concerns about cost-effective use of the ED even in that circumstance, and these are discussed later in this chapter. In those plans where the physicians are at risk for medical services, the cost of ED care must be built into that risk arrangement.

Nurse Advice Lines

As discussed in Chapter 13 in the section on demand management, many plans now use 24-hour nurse advice lines. These advice services may be provided by the plan's own advice nurses, or a plan may contract with a company that expressly provides the service for customers in a wide geographic area. In this form of ED utilization management, members are strongly encouraged to call a toll-free 800 number before going to the ED (unless the member has a truly life-threatening emergency such as a bleeding wound or a heart attack). The member then discusses his or her symptoms and medical history with the advice nurse over the telephone. In virtually all advice services of this kind, the nurse uses a clinical protocol to evaluate the member's complaint and then renders advice about what the member should do, possibly including going to the ED. In the event that a referral to the ED is authorized by the advice nurse, the nurse may then follow up with the ED to determine the member's disposition. This latter feature has the added value to the plan of tracking possible admissions to notify the utilization review system.

This approach is rapidly gaining popularity and appears to be highly beneficial. In one remarkable situation, four competing health plans joined together to form a not-for-profit association to provide the same service to all their combined members not only to manage the cost but also to provide uniform services to all their managed care members.[17]

Prior Approval by the PCP

Managed care plans that use PCPs to coordinate care have the opportunity to bring some measure of control to ED use. There have been some studies documenting decreased usage of ED services in PCP case manager plans, but these studies have been most positive when looking at Medicaid populations.[18,19] There is evidence that good access to primary care in and of itself lowers use of ED services, so that the positive effect in the Medicaid population may be more related to accessibility to care in a population with chronic access problems than to a structural method to lower utilization.[20] In fact, there is one study involving children that was able to document only a modest reduction in ED use despite the presence of a gatekeeper system.[21] Requiring members to seek authorization from PCPs (in an HMO or POS system) may thus yield some savings in utilization, but results may not be what you would hope to see.

Alternatives to the ED

There are alternatives to ED care that you may wish to explore. Late office hours will provide a lot of the care that members go to EDs to receive. If not all physicians or offices offer evening and weekend hours, those that do may wish to cover for those that do not (with appropriate compensation, of course). Free-standing urgent care centers are found in most communities. These are sometimes less expensive than EDs, but not always. Ancillary services or professional fees can erode any savings from the room charge, and again you have no control of the case. Nonetheless, you may consider contracting with an urgent care center if you can negotiate a good fee structure or a flat fee and ensure that the service will not be abused. Urgent care facilities or late office hours have a way of becoming predominantly for convenience care, and that can be expensive.

Know Each ED

Although the ED may be a lesser aggregate cost than some specialties, it is important to bear in mind that a single ED is usually more costly than any single specialist. It is therefore worthwhile for plan management to apply at least as much attention to the relationship between the plan and the ED as it does to the relationship between the plan and individual specialists. It is also important to bear in mind that each ED tends to have its own culture, just as each hospital does. Regular visits by provider relations and utilization management staff may aid in communications between the ED and the plan and help identify problems that can be resolved. It also allows the ED to understand how the plan works beyond simply receiving payment denial notices. This level of communication becomes even more important as a plan takes on a significant Medicaid population because many Medicaid recipients are used to using the ED as a source of primary care.

Contracting

Many plans contract for special rates with both free-standing urgent care centers and EDs of hospitals. A plan may negotiate a flat rate for all cases to remove the incentive to unbundle and upcode charges. That rate may be deeply discounted if the plan agrees preferentially to send urgent care visits to that facility through the plan's after-hours advice line, through the PCPs, or through the provider directory sent to each member. This has the added value of service to the members because, if the discount is deep enough, the plan may be more willing to allow urgent care visits than if it is paying full charges at an ED. In the case of flat rates, occasionally a plan will negotiate several tiers of flat rates to differentiate routine ED visits from severe trauma cases or other forms of high-cost emergencies.

Self-Referral

Except for serious or life-threatening conditions, when a person goes to an ED without seeking advice from the physician or advice nurse first, the cost can be quite high for a problem that did not need to be cared for in that setting unless the plan has negotiated a deeply discounted flat rate, as discussed above. In cases where the plan denies payment for inappropriate self-referral to the ED, the plan must allow the member to appeal that decision (see Chapter 24), especially to avoid charges of arbitrariness. In cases of payment denial, the plan needs a clear policy on whether to allow the ED then to bill the member for the uncovered charges. Although many plans refer to balance billing prohibitions in their contracts and thus require the ED to absorb the cost, it is more fair to allow the ED to bill the member, although collecting that money may sometimes be difficult. This last issue is especially problematic in public sector programs (i.e., Medicare and Medicaid), and the ED may in fact never collect the denied charge.

One effective approach to the problem of members inappropriately self-referring themselves to the ED is a limitation on coverage. It has been shown that adding a deductible or copay for ED visits can reduce ED utilization without having an adverse effect on health.[22] Some plans have a higher copayment or coinsurance for ED visits than for visits to contracting urgent care centers (some of which may actually be hospital EDs) to direct where members seek care. Most plans waive the ED copay if admission is required.

Most plans also review ED claims that come in cold (i.e., when there is no prior authorization). If the ED visit is not found to be medically necessary, then coverage is denied. As of late 1996, there is discussion amongst regulators to attempt to define what a nonmedically trained individual would reasonably assume to be an emergency for purposes of plan payment. The outcome of those discussions had not been finalized. Some plans may elect to pay the claim for the first offense, especially for a new member of the plan. If that happens, the member should always get a letter explaining that payment was made but that hereafter he or she will have to get authorization first (unless it is a life-threatening condition) or future claims will be denied.

Education may have some effect on members' use of ED services. Educating members is done through the usual means of newsletters, pamphlets, the member identification card, and so forth. Some plans also promote self-help through education, self-help medical reference manuals, and the like, as discussed in Chapter 13.

Hidden Costs

There are hidden costs associated with ED visits. The ED charges themselves are made up of the room charge, testing, therapy, a professional component, and take-home items or medication. That in itself routinely runs several hundred dollars. The hidden expenses come from losing control of the patient's care.

When a member is seen in the ED, the care is often rendered by the ED medical staff. If the member needs admission, he or she may be admitted to a physician who is not participating in your plan. When that happens, you have lost control of the care of the patient and will have less impact on future events.

In those cases, the plan may have the option of refusing to pay the charges or paying only part of them. That will help achieve some savings, but at the cost of goodwill from the member, and you have still not controlled the actual use of services. It is far better to work hard to develop and maintain a notification system that functions reliably.

The goal of a notification system is to educate both the plan members and the staff of the local EDs that a plan physician must be notified for all cases involving plan members. When hospital administrators know that the level of reimbursement (or even reimbursement at all) will be dependent on plan notification, that will provide a strong incentive for the staff of the ED to work with you. Notification will allow participating plan physicians to gain immediate control of the case and to direct care in the most appropriate fashion.

You must take care not to make the system so difficult that proper medical care is hampered. The ED staff must understand that in serious cases, or when there is sufficient concern, they must take action as necessary. In those cases, the patient should be evaluated and treatment initiated if necessary, but the plan physician or the plan's utilization management department should be notified as soon as possible without jeopardizing the care of the patient. Certainly the ED receptionist can notify the plan physician in those cases where the ED physician is unable to leave the patient's side.

In cases where the physician has referred the member to the ED, you still want to have a system where the physician is kept aware of the course of events. At an absolute minimum, a plan physician should be required to handle an admission from the ED to avoid losing control of the care of the patient. That requirement also allows for continuity of care, and patients have a positive reaction when their own physician handles the case. Latitude must be given for the realities of covering on call. It will not always be possible for any single physician to handle all admissions, but that physician should have a coverage mechanism worked out that provides for this.

Nonparticipating EDs

Because virtually all HMOs, and even PPOs, do not contract with the entire universe of available hospitals in the community (rural communities being the obvious exception), there will be times when a member is either taken to or self-refers to the ED of a nonparticipating hospital. In the case of self-referral, the plan's most common reaction is to deny payment unless the member had symptoms or signs of a serious, life-threatening emergency or was admitted. In the case of being transported, this most often occurs when an ambulance conveys the member after an accident or a medical call (e.g., the member called 911 to report severe chest pain).

In no case should an HMO or other MCO attempt to move the member until he or she is medically stabilized, an event that may occur in the ED or not until some time after admission to the hospital. In some communities, stable enough to transport will mean very stable indeed, because transport is only available by routine ambulance. In other communities, mobile intensive care units (ICUs) contract with HMOs to assist in transporting patients who are still seriously ill but not so unstable that they cannot be moved at all. In the case of mobile ICUs, it is also common for the physicians of the mobile ICU company to have privileges at all hospitals with a large ED to allow them actually to attend the patient during the period of preparation for transport.

Out-of-Area Emergencies

Out-of-area emergency services are necessary to cover and present special difficulties. Fortunately, the amount of out-of-area expense is usually low in most plans, but the problem can become acute when someone is hospitalized out of area. When that happens and there is little hope that the patient will be discharged quickly, you need to make arrangements to transfer the patient to one of your participating hospitals and physicians as soon as medically feasible.

If the admission is only for a few days, or if the patient is too ill to be transferred, you will not be able to transfer the patient. If you can, however, transferring the patient back to your plan will allow you to control the case, and that can mean cutting the cost of care in half, even when the transportation is taken into account. Many plans, primarily HMOs, have specific language regarding out-of-area coverage that requires the member to cooperate in such transfers to maintain financial coverage.

A few plans will contact the out-of-area hospital and negotiate reimbursement terms over the telephone. Although the hospital may appear to have little incentive to negotiate, the HMO may offer direct and timely payment and not request transfer of the patient, all of which may be seen as valuable to the hospital. Other plans have reciprocity agreements with other HMOs through formal associations or joint corporate ownership that allow the local HMO both to manage the case and to handle the reimbursement to the providers.

CONCLUSION

Control of ancillary services requires controlling physicians' practice behavior. Authorization systems, standards of care, capitation arrangements, limitations of coverage, and risk/bonus arrangements are all useful. Control of the use of emergency services requires controlling member behavior. Copays, limitations on coverage, 24-hour telephone nurse advice lines, member education, and alternative settings for urgent care are all potentially useful.

Study Questions

1. Develop policies and procedures for managing ancillary utilization in an

HMO; be specific regaring the type of ancillary service.

2. Create reports that would be useful to the medical director for managing ancillary utilization.
3. Develop a work plan for selecting ancillary services in an HMO.
4. Create reports that would be useful for PCPs in managing utilization of ancillary services.
5. Which ancillary services lend themselves to capitation? Why?
6. How might an IPA HMO achieve better control over utilization of the emergency department without substantially increasing member complaints?

REFERENCES AND NOTES

1. H.F. Blissenbach and P.M. Penna, "Pharmaceutical Services in Managed Care," in *The Managed Health Care Handbook*, 3d ed., ed. P.R. Konstvedt (Gaithersburg, Md.: Aspen, 1996), 367–387.
2. B.J. Hillman, et al., Frequency and Costs of Diagnostic Imaging in Office Practice—A Comparison of Self-Referring and Radiologist-Referring Physicians, *New England Journal of Medicine* 323 (1990): 1604–1608.
3. Office of the Inspector General, *Financial Arrangements between Physicians and Health Care Businesses: Report to Congress* (Washington, D.C.: Dept. of Health and Human Services, 1989; Dept. of Health and Human Services Publication OAI-12-88-01410).
4. State of Florida Health Care Cost Containment Board, *Joint Ventures among Health Care Providers in Florida* (Tallahassee, Fla.: State of Florida, 1991): 2.
5. Omnibus Budget Reconciliation Act of 1989.
6. M.P. Murray, et al., Ambulatory Testing for Capitation and Fee-for-Service Patients in the Same Practice Setting: Relationship to Outcomes, *Medical Care* 30 (1992): 252–261.
7. J.P. Kassirer, Our Stubborn Quest for Diagnostic Certainty: A Cause of Excessive Testing, *New England Journal of Medicine* 320 (1989): 1489–1491.
8. D.M. Berwick and K.L. Coltin, Feedback Reduces Test Use in a Health Maintenance Organization, *Journal of the American Medical Association* 255 (1986): 1450–1454.
9. K.I. Marton, et al., Modifying Test-Ordering Behavior in the Outpatient Medical Clinic, *Archives of Internal Medicine* 145 (1985): 816–821.
10. A.R. Martin, et al., A Trial of Two Strategies to Modify the Test-Ordering Behavior of Medical Residents, *New England Journal of Medicine* 303 (1980): 1330–1336.
11. Atlantic Information Services, Inc., *Provider Contracting and Capitation* (Washington, D.C.: Atlantic Information Services, 1993).
12. T.G. Tape and A.I. Mushlin, The Utility of Routine Chest Radiographs, *Annals of Internal Medicine* 104 (1986): 663–670.
13. F.A. Hubble, et al., The Impact of Routine Admission Chest X-Ray Films on Patient Care, *New England Journal of Medicine* 312 (1985): 209.
14. Food and Drug Administration, *The Selection of Patients for X-Ray Examinations: Chest X-Ray Screening Examinations* (Rockville, Md.: National Center for Devices and Radiological Health, 1983; Dept. of Health and Human Services Publication 83-8204).
15. B.S. Gold, et al., The Utility of Preoperative Electrocardiograms in the Ambulatory Surgical Patient. *Archives of Internal Medicine* 152 (1992): 301–305.
16. B.J. Narr, et al., Preoperative Laboratory Screening in Healthy Mayo Patients: Cost-Effective Elimination of Tests and Unchanged Outcomes, *Mayo Clinic Proceedings* 66 (1991): 155–159.
17. Health Care Rivals Cooperate To Cut Costs, *Washington Post*, (2 October 1995): F-12.
18. R. Hurley, et al., Emergency Room Use and Primary Care Case Management: Evidence from Four Medicaid Demonstration Programs, *American Journal of Public Health* 79 (1989): 843–846.
19. S. Long and R. Settle, An Evaluation of Utah's Primary Care Case Management Program for Medicaid Recipients, *Medical Care* 26 (1988): 1021–1032.
20. H.R. Kelman and D.S. Lane, Use of Hospital Emergency Room in Relation to Use of Private Physicians, *American Journal of Public Health* 66 (1976): 1189–1191.
21. D. Glotzer, et al., Prior Approval in the Emergency Room, *Pediatrics* 88 (1991): 674–680.
22. K.F. O'Grady, et al., The Impact of Cost Sharing on Emergency Department Use, *New England Journal of Medicine* 313 (1985): 484–490.

SUGGESTED READING

Doyle, R.L. and Feren, A.P. *Healthcare Management Guidelines: Ambulatory Care Guidelines*. Milliman & Robertson. Updated periodically.

Chapter 16

Managed Behavioral Health Care Services

Donald F. Anderson, Jeffrey L. Berlant, Danna Mauch, and William R. Maloney

Study Objectives

- Understand the differences between behavioral health managed care and medical-surgical managed care
- Understand the different forms of managed care treatment in behavioral managed care
- Understand how behavioral managed health care is integrated into the larger health system

Management of behavioral health (BH) treatment and costs presents special challenges. For the purposes of this chapter, BH services include mental health and substance abuse or chemical dependency services. Unique factors contributing to these special challenges include the following:

- destigmatization of mental illness and chemical dependency, which has led to a greater willingness on the part of the general public to seek help for these problems
- erosion of social support systems, including fragmentation of traditional extended and nuclear family structures
- increased complexity and stress in society, which have resulted in increased incidence and manifestation of BH symptoms
- advances in medication and psychological therapeutic techniques, which have promoted more effective treatment of more disorders
- proliferation of private hospitals during the 1970s and early 1980s as a result of high profit margins, cheap capital investment, elimination of certificate-of-need laws in several large states, and exemption from reimbursement by diagnosis-related groups
- tightening during the 1990s of public sector BH funding at the federal level, which resulted in increasing pressure on local government agencies to contain costs

Added to these pressures is the fact that many BH problems tend to be chronic and recurrent,

Donald F. Anderson is national practice leader for behavioral health benefits at William M. Mercer, Incorporated, a human resources consulting organization. He has extensive experience in the evaluation of managed mental health and substance abuse programs.

Jeffrey L. Berlant is William M. Mercer, Incorporated's senior consultant for mental health and substance abuse services. He has broad experience in evaluation of both public and private sector managed mental health and substance abuse programs.

Danna Mauch is a partner in the behavioral health consulting firm of Integrated Health Strategies, Inc. She has extensive experience in strategic planning, operations management, systems evaluation, and the development and implementation of innovative and managed care programs.

William R. Maloney is a principal in William M. Mercer, Incorporated's Behavioral Healthcare Practice in San Francisco. His consulting specialty is the evaluation of information management systems for managed behavioral health applications.

requiring periodic treatment, sometimes intensive in nature, throughout the lifetime of the affected individual. Finally, BH diagnostic categories do not lend themselves to by-the-book utilization management with standardized length of stay and treatment protocols for specified diagnoses. The range of accepted treatment approaches for a given BH diagnosis can be broad, and severity of illness and service requirements cannot be inferred without detailed information about social context and specific symptoms.

Substantial efforts at managing BH treatment and costs first emanated from health maintenance organizations (HMOs). Early HMOs, for the most part, were wary of BH coverage. Some plans offered only diagnosis and consultation; others arranged for discounted fee-for-service care for members. The HMO Act of 1973 required only minimal BH benefits, such as crisis intervention and a maximum of 20 visits for outpatient services. No benefits for inpatient care, chronic or recurrent conditions, and chemical dependency were required. Later in the 1970s and 1980s, increasing numbers of HMOs expanded BH benefits as a result of consumer demand and legislation enacted in a number of states that required richer benefits.[1]

During the late 1970s and 1980s, when insurers and self-insured employers began instituting general utilization management techniques to help control their indemnity plan health benefit costs, it became clear that these approaches were far less effective in controlling BH costs than other medical benefit costs. Thus the scene was set for development of a niche industry of specialized managed BH organizations to contract directly with HMOs, indemnity insurers, and self-insured employers and to apply specialized techniques in managing these costs. Employers traditionally have been the ultimate payers for most BH treatment managed by specialty BH entities (whether in-house HMO, insurance carrier based, or free-standing). Increasingly in recent years, government BH agencies have become purveyors and/or purchasers of managed BH services as budgets have constricted, federal regulations have been administered more flexibly, and accountability has migrated to local government levels. The following describes managed BH care as it undergoes transformation and reinvention during an era of ferment and change.

KEY TREATMENT PRINCIPLES

Special Issues and Common Problems

Any managed care organization (MCO) venturing into management of BH care faces the dilemma of how to address potentially large unmet treatment needs that place demands on scarce resources and may compete for resources from other medical care specialties. Several factors limit BH resources: a historical pattern of poor insurance benefits for BH care, particularly stemming from benefit reductions put into place during the late 1980s; a historical legacy of underinvestment and avoidance of treatment of BH disorders left by pioneering general medical–surgical HMOs; biases underestimating the prevalence, morbidity, and mortality of BH disorders; and apprehension over assuming the moral hazard of coverage for a large and poorly delineated pool of service needs.

On an operational level, it has been difficult to establish the boundaries of BH service obligations. The concept of medical necessity begins to blur when the causes of the disorder encompass social, personality, and biological factors and when necessary services often must address stabilization of social supports; these are factors that are not universally recognized as medical needs. From the perspective of designing a delivery system, this need for social stability as a critical prerequisite for clinical stability requires a broader, more diverse continuum of programs and services than is seen in the general medical–surgical realm.

As a result of recent advances in diagnostics, psychopharmacology, and psychotherapeutic techniques, there is a growing demand for powerful new treatment options during a time of shrinking resources. All these factors enhance the need for incisive management of BH care.

Goals of Treatment

Ideally, the goal of treatment for the health plan should be to improve the BH status of a defined population. A well-managed system should aim to reduce suicide and homicide rates, substance abuse–related impairments, and mortality and morbidity from accidents related to substance abuse or mental disorders. A well-managed system should improve the clinical status of a population in terms of symptomatic distress levels and improve life functioning in several areas.

Another central goal of managed BH care should be conservation and rational allocation of resources to optimize return on expenditures. Finding the correct balance between conservation of resources and provision of the appropriate mix of effective services is the fundamental task for managed care.

Objectives of Treatment

There are a number of important clinical objectives for a managed care system to pursue: rapid symptomatic relief, protection of the physical safety of the patient and others, satisfaction of the patient/client and family, and improved life functioning. To conserve resources, managed care systems need to invest in cost-effective treatments and high-return therapeutic activities and to maximize medical cost offsets (decreased costs for general medical and surgical care).

Strategic Approaches

Historically, MCOs have regarded BH care services cautiously. Coming down strongly on the side of conservation of resources, at least in terms of short-term, direct costs of care, they have pursued two general strategies: controlling demand and controlling supply.

Typical strategies for controlling demand make use of the established fact that demand for mental health services is price sensitive. Techniques employed that are based on this price sensitivity include setting higher copayments and deductibles, delaying access to treatment, and limiting benefits, including imposing lifetime ceilings on BH benefits. Typical strategies for controlling supply have included benefit restrictions, program limitations, gatekeepers, triage systems, and waiting lists.

Benefit and program restrictions have at times been profound, severely limiting or excluding mental health services entirely from the benefit package, excluding certain diagnostic-specific disorders or chronic illnesses, and providing few or no psychiatric inpatient services and little or no long-term outpatient treatment. Some contracts have excluded certain member groups from coverage, such as the mentally retarded and people with organic psychoses, alcoholism, and/or intractable personality disorders. Others have limited or refused to provide court-ordered services, thereby reducing liability for uncooperative clients. Some contracts have excluded geriatric patients, violent or assaultive patients, primary substance abusers, heroin-dependent persons, and people with sexual dysfunction, severe learning disabilities, or attention deficit hyperactivity disorder. Virtually all managed care plans use some form of utilization review (UR). Although many use primary care practitioner (PCP) gatekeeping, large HMOs (those with more than 200,000 enrollees) usually allow self-referral. Large case or catastrophic case management is also used.

Beyond a certain point, however, limitations on services can result in underservice of legitimate needs. To meet the BH care needs of a population better, MCOs are exploring strategies for improving the clinical value received for each BH dollar.

From a clinical perspective, managed care should favor:

- use of multiple clinical pathways, providing simpler treatment plans for uncomplicated cases and more intensive treatment plans for exceptional cases

- development of a network of effective, efficient providers selected and retained on the basis of demonstrated superior clinical performance
- matching of the treatment problem with the optimal provider
- selection of treatment innovations and clinical best practices to optimize effective and efficient patient response
- minimal disruption of everyday social role obligations
- treatment at the least restrictive but most effective level of care, favoring community-based over facility-based services
- measurement and tracking of clinical performance, focusing on clinical outcomes, management of resources, and efficiency of response
- systematic methods for helping treatment-refractory patients gain access to highly skilled, specialized services, including the use of centers of excellence for specific problems
- reducing relapse through identifying and planning for ongoing support for therapeutic and social needs

Finally, there is a need for the collective management of aggregate clinical expenditures in comparison with budgeted resources, concurrently identifying reasons for unexpected excessive expenditures and incisively constructing corrective action plans. It is a powerful strategic concept in managed care to tie useful clinical information to financial information in such a manner that changes in clinical practices can target high-risk areas.

Methods of Treatment

Specialized managed BH care is rooted in four key principles of clinical treatment: alternatives to psychiatric hospitalization, alternatives to restrictive treatment for substance abuse, goal-directed psychotherapy, and crisis intervention.

Alternatives to Psychiatric Hospitalization

Partial hospitalization programs (PHP; i.e., day, evening, and/or weekend nonresidential programs) have been proved to be effective alternatives to hospital inpatient treatment in many outcome studies.[2] In a plan with adequate coverage for alternatives to inpatient services, and with informed decision making as to which patients can benefit from these alternatives, economical and effective treatment can be provided to acutely ill patients in a PHP setting.[3,4]

Alternatives to Restrictive Treatment for Substance Abuse

Research does not provide evidence that inpatient or residential substance abuse treatment is superior to outpatient or PHP approaches.[5,6] The central question of which patients truly need inpatient treatment and which can benefit equally well from outpatient or partial hospitalization has yet to be answered definitively. In the absence of support for the superiority of inpatient programs for the general treatment population, specialized managed BH systems tend to emphasize the more economical alternatives.

Goal-Directed Psychotherapy

The research literature supports the effectiveness of brief, goal-directed psychotherapeutic approaches for a number of problems.[7,8] Specialized managed BH care systems generally emphasize an interpersonal rather than an intrapsychic focus of therapy. These systems also place emphasis on therapy that is designed to be brief and time limited and not just a truncated version of long-term therapy.

Crisis Intervention

Successful managed BH systems are designed to make use of crisis intervention as a key service in the overall constellation of services. Research has demonstrated that short-term, intensive support of individuals during life crises or periodic acute episodes of psychiatric illness is an effective way to diminish the incidence of future crises and can substantially reduce the inappropriate use of psychiatric care.[9]

Additional clinical methods, utilized especially when managed care principles are applied to the care of severely ill persons, include the following:

- accurate behavioral diagnosis and attention to potential medical and neurological diagnostic issues
- detection and management of substance abuse
- prompt access to services for high-risk clients
- effective management of safety issues
- coordination of services from other agencies and multiple providers
- prevention of relapse through specialized clinical and case management services and adoption of a longitudinal treatment perspective for chronic disorders
- integrated use of multidisciplinary providers for exceptional cases, driven by a coherent, comprehensive treatment plan
- intensive community treatment of high-risk patients
- use of social stabilization measures to reduce relapse

Bridging

Integral to effective BH care services is the capacity to bridge from mental health and substance abuse treatment services to closely allied and interactive general health and medical care, social services, and long-term care.

The Ideal Continuum of Care

Despite historical separation of substance abuse and mental health treatment programs, effective systems integrate treatment programs that tailor the appropriate mix of services to each individual's treatment needs.

Basic Core Services

Entry into the system requires an intake function, not necessarily geographically centralized, to triage cases, gather initial data, establish the presence of a BH disorder requiring treatment, determine the clinically appropriate level of care and mix of service types, and refer the patient to appropriate services. Immediate access to emergency evaluation services is also essential.

Mobile emergency services should also be available on a 24-hour basis for on-site evaluations of the need for acute inpatient services and to provide stabilization services as an alternative to hospitalization. Other important emergency services include the capacity to schedule next-day outpatient appointments and to provide psychiatric nursing backup for problems that might arise after hours.

Patients who are not stabilized despite on-site interventions may require 24-hour observation and assessment by a multidisciplinary team in a short-term behavioral crisis unit providing 1 to 5 days of 24-hour voluntary or involuntary observation, containment of assaultive or self-destructive behavior, and treatment of acute psychiatric emergencies. Because of the high prevalence of dual diagnoses, chemical dependency detection and treatment protocols as well as staff with specialized training in both chemical dependency and mental disorders should be standard components for all basic services as well as for inpatient and residential programs.

Specialized Treatment Services

Substance abuse. Few patients with substance abuse problems require inpatient treatment. Patients with mild to moderate withdrawal symptoms or significant drug craving symptoms who need more than social support to maintain abstinence can be referred for ambulatory detoxification with daily medical management and monitoring by a physician–nurse practitioner team, including administration of medications as needed.

Patients with more severe problems need at least three types of alternative treatment levels:

1. social detoxification centers for those who require removal from their usual living environment as a result of an inadequate support system
2. residential rehabilitation for medically supervised detoxification when moderate withdrawal symptoms are present or when there is a problem with compliance with instructions
3. inpatient medical detoxification, usually in a general hospital setting, for patients with severe withdrawal syndromes of an imminently life-threatening nature, such as delirium tremens or withdrawal seizures

A full spectrum of nonintensive outpatient chemical dependency treatment services should be available, including brief alcohol and drug counseling, maintenance counseling for individuals who need long-term support, and medication services for those requiring long-term chemical stabilization.

Most patients who are unable to control substance use despite outpatient efforts can benefit from a PHP or intensive outpatient program, including standardized, systematic group education and therapy, core information about chemical dependency, and development of peer supports. Standard treatment packages may include an initial intensive phase with at least 20 evenings of treatment followed by progressively less intensive treatment for the remainder of at least 1 year. Drug counselors in the intensive outpatient program discourage drop-out by contacting patients who fail to attend meetings to determine whether relapse is occurring and to encourage return to treatment.

For those patients who relapse despite best therapeutic efforts and completion of treatment in the intensive phase of an intensive outpatient program, the continuum of care needs to provide several levels of care and therapeutic programs:

- residential chemical dependency rehabilitation with 24-hour supervision during initial rehabilitation treatment to identify and correct factors interfering with the ability to receive successful treatment at an outpatient level; once these factors have been removed, discharge to an intensive outpatient program can proceed
- relapse prevention programs providing specialized, more individualized techniques to address unmet treatment needs and specialized aftercare for those for whom standard methods are ineffective
- therapeutic halfway houses, linked to participation in a relapse prevention program, for those who repeatedly fail outpatient efforts

Mental health. The vast majority of patients with mental health problems need only outpatient therapy services, including brief (fewer than 12 sessions) individual, group, and family psychotherapy; medication management services; and, for those at risk of relapse and deterioration, long-term maintenance therapy. Complicated cases need a designated primary therapist, who is responsible for formulating and implementing a master treatment plan and for coordinating referrals to other outpatient services. Complicated cases may require individualized services, such as on-site clinical case management assistance, social service interventions, and wraparound services.

Patients who are unable to succeed by using only outpatient therapy services need access to intensive outpatient services. These may consist of crisis services, such as daily intensive individual, group, or family therapy sessions or outpatient medication visits; home-based or school-based therapeutic services, including in-home family therapy; or modular outpatient programs with an array of psychoeducational modules combined with specialized individual outpatient services and interdisciplinary treatment team involvement.

For more severely ill patients who cannot be served adequately by outpatient or intensive outpatient services, multidisciplinary PHPs provide several hours of structured, integrated, modular treatment and psychoeducational services per day throughout the week and weekend. PHP replaces the range and intensity of services, except for 24-hour supervision and security, previously found in inpatient psychiatric programs.

Some patients require brief removal from troubled environments for stabilization of potentially life-threatening situations or situations that may cause family disintegration. As an alternative to acute hospital services or a behavioral crisis unit, the availability of crisis/respite house services may avert the need for a more restrictive and intensive facility placement. Such settings provide brief removal from a destructive or dangerous social situation or from an excessively strained family system for periods up to 2 weeks to allow stabilization of the living environment, placement in a more suitable living placement, or investigation by protective service agencies. Ideal applications of this level of care would be runaway adolescents with oppositional behavior and limited substance abuse problems, battered spouses with highly disruptive adjustment disorders, self-mutilating nonpsychotic patients, and chronically mentally ill patients with families needing respite from excessive care needs or unremitting levels of conflict.

Despite intensive efforts, return home is not feasible in some situations because of excessive long-term danger related to family violence or conflict, risk of violence by the patient, or predatory sexual behavior on the part of the patient. For such patients, community-based residential treatment services, such as a range of residential alternatives for out-of-home placement, need to be available, including therapeutic homes under the care of a family with parenting training and therapeutic group homes for small groups of adolescents and chronically ill adults with frequent disruptive behavior or without the skills to live independently or semi-independently.

Some children or adults may require placement in conventional large residential treatment centers for modification of subacute dangerous behaviors that exceed the skills capacity and security of community-based therapeutic services. Such centers provide 24-hour, tightly coordinated behavioral modification and medication treatment services, preferably with programs designed to prepare patients as rapidly as possible for placement in less restrictive therapeutic settings.

Psychiatric acute care facilities remain essential for patients requiring high-security and highly intensive treatment for imminently life-threatening conditions.

Dual diagnosis. To address the treatment needs of the large population of patients with both mental disorders and substance abuse disorders, the continuum of care should include two general types of program elements: routine surveillance and cross-training in both disciplines at all levels of care, and specialized dual-diagnosis programs to facilitate simultaneous treatment of both types of disorders when simpler treatment methods fail.

For more severely ill dual-diagnosis patients, outpatient programs need to address abuse of a wide range of substances because polysubstance abuse is highly prevalent among dual-diagnosis patients. Intensive day and evening programs are needed for motivated patients with dual diagnoses, including psychotic mental disorders without severe residual symptoms, personality disorders without severe behavioral disturbance, and moderately severe coexisting anxiety, mood, and posttraumatic stress disorders. In these specialized dual-diagnosis treatment programs, abstinence may be a goal rather than a prerequisite for entry. An ideal system will make provision for programs integrating interventions from both psychiatric and substance abuse treatment camps: continuous treatment teams, monitored medication compliance, behavioral skills training to prevent both psychiatric relapse and lapses into substance abuse, close monitoring of drug abuse, modified 12-step groups, behavioral reinforcement programs (such as a token economy) to reward abstinence and healthier behaviors, and assertive case management to reengage poorly compliant participants. Specialized dual-diagnosis treatment programs may exist at the level of the crisis house, social detoxification house, behavioral crisis unit, PHP, community therapeutic residential program, large-scale residential treatment center, or acute inpatient service.

BENEFIT PLAN DESIGN

The starting point for managing benefits in any managed BH program is the underlying benefit plan. BH benefit design, like all health benefit design, needs to address two key issues: coverage limits and incentives.

Coverage Limits

Coverage limits are essentially a fail-safe to limit benefit cost at levels beyond which the plan will not pay, even for medically necessary, cost-effective treatment. Coverage limits can include maximum days, visits, or dollar amounts and can be based on level of care (e.g., inpatient, PHP, or structured outpatient), type of disorder (e.g., acute psychiatric, chronic, custodial, or specific diagnosis), type of treatment (e.g., psychosurgery, psychoanalysis, or nutritionally based therapies), and/or type of provider (e.g., physician, psychologist, social worker, or marriage, family, and child counselor [MFCC]). The optimal benefit design for a managed BH program will provide adequate coverage for inpatient treatment and its alternatives as well as for treatment providers from various professional disciplines.

Levels of Care

Traditional indemnity plans and many HMO plans limit coverage to inpatient hospital care and minimal outpatient care for mental health problems and inpatient detoxification and may cover inpatient rehabilitation for substance abuse. To support a comprehensive managed BH program, the benefit should cover a number of levels of care (Table 16–1).

Day/Dollar Limits

A recent survey of specialized managed BH organizations (D. Anderson and K. Anderson, unpublished data, 1991) revealed current practice regarding coverage limits in plans where some degree of specialized BH management is in effect (Exhibit 16–1). When asked to characterize optimal coverage limits, respondents advocated raising deductibles (to $500 for individuals and $1,200 for families), raising mental health outpatient annual dollar limits (to $6,000 to $8,000), raising substance abuse structured outpatient annual dollar limits (to $6,000 to $12,000), and raising the lifetime BH combined maximum (to $125,000 to $130,000).

Types of Disorders

Another way that some managed BH plans limit plan liability is through limiting covered disorders. Survey respondents indicated considerable variation in the types of disorders covered by plans featuring BH management (Table 16–2). Some plans also exclude coverage for

Table 16–1 Managed Mental Health Benefits: Covered Levels of Care

Mental Health	*Substance Abuse*
Hospital inpatient services	Detoxification (inpatient, noninpatient residential, and outpatient)
Nonhospital residential treatment	Hospital rehabilitation
PHP/day treatment	Nonhospital residential rehabilitation
Individual/group outpatient treatment	Structured outpatient rehabilitation
Crisis intervention	Individual/group outpatient rehabilitation
Outreach services	

Exhibit 16–1 Typical Day/Dollar Limits in Plans with Specialized Mental Health/Substance Abuse Management

Annual deductibles:	$250 individual/$750 family
Annual dollar maximum:	
Mental health	
Inpatient	
Residential	$25,000–$30,000
PHP	
Individual/group outpatient	$1,200–$3,500
Substance abuse	
Inpatient	
Residential	$15,000–$20,000
Structured outpatient	$4,000–$9,000
Individual/group outpatient	$1,300–$1,500
Annual day/session maximum:	
Mental health	
Inpatient	35–40
Residential	45–60
PHP	40–45
Individual/group outpatient	35–40
Substance abuse	
Inpatient	30–40
Residential	35–40
Individual/group outpatient	35–40

Annual family out-of-pocket limit (stop loss): $4,000
Lifetime course of treatment limit (substance abuse): 2
Lifetime maximum (mental health/substance abuse): $45,000–$50,000

Courtesy of William M. Mercer, Inc., San Francisco, California.

specific *Diagnostic and Statistical Manual IV* (DSM-IV) diagnostic categories, such as learning disorders and autism, as well as medical diagnoses with potential psychiatric treatment regimens, such as obesity.

Types of Treatment

Many plans built around specialized BH management limit the specific treatments covered.

Table 16–2 Typical Coverage of Disorders in Plans with Specialized Mental Health/ Substance Abuse Management

Category of Disorder	*Percentage of Plans Offering Coverage*
DSM diagnoses	100
Chronic mental disorders	71
Sexual addiction	21
DSM V codes	7
Codependency	7
Nicotine addiction	7
Custodial care	0

Courtesy of William M. Mercer, Inc., San Francisco, California.

Table 16–3 indicates variation among respondents as to coverage of selected types of treatment. Many plans also exclude from coverage such treatments as biofeedback and electroconvulsive therapy.

Types of Providers

Many traditional indemnity plans have covered only the services of practitioners holding medical and doctoral degrees for outpatient BH psychotherapy. HMOs and managed indemnity BH plans have expanded coverage to a broader range of mental health professionals. Table 16–4 indicates patterns of provider coverage for plans with specialized BH management. Some plans also cover pastoral counselors and family practitioners for BH services.

Incentives

The greater the incentives to access and comply with the managed BH system, the greater the impact of the system. Exclusive of HMO BH coverage, most employers are not comfortable with a plan that offers no BH coverage outside the managed system. For this reason, most managed BH plans tend to offer point-of-service choice with differential coverage. The typical managed indemnity plan offers a zero deductible

Table 16–3 Typical Coverage of Treatment Types in Plans with Specialized Mental Health/Substance Abuse Management

Category of Treatment	*Percentage of Plans Offering Coverage*
Brief problem-focused therapy	93
Long-term psychodynamically oriented therapy	64
Psychosurgery	15
Nutritionally based therapies	7

Courtesy of William M. Mercer, Inc., San Francisco, California.

Table 16–4 Typical Coverage of Provider Types in Plans with Specialized Mental Health/Substance Abuse Management

Category of Provider	*Percentage of Plans Offering Coverage*
MD	100
PhD psychologist	93
MA social worker	87
MA psychiatric nurse	87
MFCC	83
MA psychologist	73
Certified alcoholism counselor	57

Courtesy of William M. Mercer, Inc., San Francisco, California.

in-network benefit with a coinsurance of 20 percent. Out-of-network coverage typically will feature a deductible of $250 with 50 percent coinsurance.

In one survey, respondents indicated that an optimal coinsurance differential would be 40 percent (e.g., 10 percent in network and 50 percent out of network). Managed BH plans typically do not publish a preferred provider list. For practical purposes, then, coverage differentials actually apply to the plan member accessing a gatekeeper and accepting channeling to a network provider rather than accessing a provider directly without going through the gatekeeper.

RISK ASSESSMENT AND CAPITATION

General issues relative to risk contracting and capitation are covered thoroughly in Chapters 8 and 10; our purpose here is to touch on some issues of particular relevance to BH.

Definitions

For our purposes here, we define capitation as the provision of a defined scope of BH services for a defined population for a fixed period of time for a fixed fee per population member. Risk, in this context, is defined as the possibility that BH care expenditures will exceed a specified amount of revenue (i.e., the capitation amount).

Sources of Risk

Whether the payer or provider is at risk, or if there is a sharing of risk, there are a few key factors that determine the magnitude of overall risk:

- *Insufficient information*—Although in some circumstances historical utilization and cost data can form the best basis for predicting future expenditures, these data frequently are neither complete nor easily accessible. To the extent that the data are flawed, risk increases.
- *Excess demand*—Even if historical data are accurate, utilization of services may exceed that which would be predicted based on historical trends. Particularly in instances where real or perceived access to the services covered by the benefit is enhanced, pent-up demand may unexpectedly boost costs, especially in the early stages of implementation of a capitated system.
- *Large claim risk*—The smaller the size of the capitated population, the larger the impact of isolated catastrophic expenses incurred by individual population members. Actuarial principles determining capitation levels are based on having a large enough population over which to spread the risk (see Chapter 23).

Although such factors as population demographics, historical experience, and diagnosis can help predict risk, there are no perfect predictors of risk. It is vitally important that entities accepting risk be equipped with an actuarial analysis of the magnitude of risk and that they establish an adequate dedicated safety net of reserve to deal with likely fluctuations in claims experience.

Special BH Capitation Issues

Given the current state of the BH service delivery system nationally, the following issues must be addressed carefully and seriously as capitation is implemented.

Underservice

In any capitated system, an overarching concern is the possibility of restriction of access and resulting underservice. Although this concern is not restricted to BH systems, it is particularly important that reliable monitoring of access, quality of care, and satisfaction take place. It is also vital that the capitated entity be at risk not only for cost but also for meeting measurable performance standards pertaining to access, quality, and outcomes.

Cost Shifting

As discussed above, it has been difficult to establish the boundaries of BH service obligations. To the extent that treatment of BH problems can involve interventions addressing social, personality, and biological problems, entities capitated for BH services can easily become victims or perpetrators of attempts to shift costs. This issue is particularly sensitive in the emerging public/private partnerships involving public BH agencies, BH integrated delivery systems, and MCOs/HMOs (discussed below). It is of key importance to develop and obtain agreement on clear protocols and processes to determine responsibility among agencies with overlapping constituencies and separate capitation arrangements.

Preparedness

Perhaps the single most important issue for BH is the preparedness of the key players to participate knowledgeably and effectively in capitated service delivery models. The current enthusiasm for implementing capitated arrangements, and thereby for "pushing down" accountability and control to the lowest possible level, must be tempered by taking a hard look at the capacity of the front-line players to accept and sustain risk while managing the care. Whether one focuses on BH provider organizations competing for capitated contracts or on county BH agencies faced with capitation from state and federal funding sources, the issues are the same.

Information

Information is a key determinant of magnitude of risk. Do these entities have access to sufficient and accurate information in the required format? Have they built a sufficient specialized infrastructure, particularly information systems, to analyze and manage the information (see below)? If large claims are a significant driver of risk, do they have a large enough "locked-in" population to make such risk sustainable? Do they have the resources to conduct an actuarial analysis of their level of risk? Do they have sufficient dedicated safety net reserves to cope with possible fluctuations in costs?

UTILIZATION MANAGEMENT

Utilization management in specialized BH programs falls into two general categories: UR and case management. In practice, distinctions between the two disciplines often become blurred, but it will be instructive to discuss them separately.

UR

In the mid-1980s, when an increasing number of employers had installed UR systems to help contain the costs of indemnity plans, it became clear that UR conducted by nonspecialized staff with general medical backgrounds was ineffective when applied to BH cases. As a response, specialized BH UR developed that employed specialized staff applying BH-specific utilization criteria. Specialized UR typically includes preadmission certification of inpatient BH cases and concurrent review of inpatient and residential cases (and sometimes of outpatient cases) to determine the presence or absence of medical necessity of treatment. Operational characteristics of effective specialized UR programs are as follows:

- Telephone-based treatment review is conducted by credentialed BH professional reviewers, usually master's level psychiatric nurses, master's level social workers, and doctoral and master's level psychologists.
- Reviewers as a group are trained and experienced in inpatient and outpatient BH treatment for adults, adolescents, and children.
- Initial and concurrent review episodes involve direct contact with the primary clinician instead of, or in addition to, the facility UR nurse.
- High level backup clinical supervisory staff are readily available for front-line reviewers. Such back-up staff include, at a minimum, board-certified adult and child/adolescent psychiatrists and a certified addictionologist.
- Medical necessity/level of care criteria employed by reviewers are age and diagnosis specific and behaviorally descriptive and encompass all levels of care, including, for example, nonhospital residential programs and PHPs. Criteria are tested and retested continually and modified as needed on an ongoing basis.

UR construed narrowly as determination of medical necessity is typically installed as a means of protecting against abuses in a traditional fee-for-service plan. Although specialized BH UR has proved to be somewhat more effective in containing costs than nonspecialized UR, utilization management has been far more effective in conjunction with a specialized BH network with point-of-service choice.[10] This comprehensive approach to managing BH care generally invokes case management as the utilization management tool of choice.

Case Management

As comprehensive managed BH programs evolved during the late 1980s and early 1990s, the case management function crystallized as a focal point for promoting cost-effective, quality BH care. BH case management encompasses traditional UR but extends beyond it into a broader form of patient advocacy, addressing the longitudinal course of care as well as discrete episodes of intensive treatment. Comprehensive case management includes four overlapping components:

1. promoting correct diagnosis and effective treatment: assisting plan members to access the best level, type, and mix of treatment; keeping alert to opportunities for enhancing the quality and efficacy of care; acting to make the provider and patient aware of these opportunities (UR strives to exclude payment for unnecessarily intensive treatment, whereas case management strives to direct patients into effective forms of treatment at appropriate levels of intensity)
2. promoting efficient use of resources: helping the patient/family access the most effective resources with the minimum depletion of family finances and finite available insurance dollars (directing patients into effective care may be the most potent cost-saving method of all)
3. preventing recidivism: monitoring progress subsequent to intensive treatment

episodes; encouraging and, if necessary, helping arrange for interepisode care to prevent recidivism

4. monitoring for and containing substandard care: identifying potential quality of care defects during treatment; investigating and, when needed, intervening to ensure remediation

Comprehensive case management goes beyond determination of medical necessity and seeks to promote enhancement of the quality, efficacy, and continuity of care. As such, it is a more demanding discipline than simple UR. It is practiced optimally by qualified front-line case management staff with a minimum of 5 to 10 years of relevant clinical experience who are thoroughly trained in case management techniques, backed up by readily available doctoral level advisors with relevant clinical experience (including managed care experience), and supported by well-articulated systems to assist with the case management task. Examples of such systems include the following:

- *Triage systems*—Every managed BH system must devise a mechanism for directing cases to the proper case manager. This includes, for example, ensuring that cases with medical issues are directed to a psychiatric nurse rather than to a social worker and that substance abuse cases are directed to case managers specifically qualified and experienced in this area.
- *Quality screens*—Diagnosis-based criteria for the use of case managers, delineating typical best practice patterns of high-quality care for specific problems as well as screens for common quality of care defects, should be employed routinely as cases are reviewed. Such screens assist in early identification of mismatches between treatment plans and diagnosis as well as pinpoint more subtle opportunities to enhance quality and efficacy of care (e.g., when providers may be unaware of or unwilling to use superior treatment methods).

CHANNELING MECHANISMS

A key aspect of any managed BH system is a channeling mechanism to assess initially and then direct an individual to the appropriate type and intensity of treatment. This gatekeeper function is crucial to the effectiveness of the managed BH program and is fraught with potential implementation problems. Who should conduct the initial assessment to determine whether there is a BH problem for which an evaluation and treatment plan are in order? Who should conduct a thorough clinical evaluation and formulate a treatment plan? Who should carry out the treatment plan? The candidates for some role in the gatekeeper function may include an employee assistance program (EAP), a PCP in a general managed medical system, and/or a specialized BH case manager and designated assessor clinician belonging to a contracted BH provider network.

In practice, the gatekeeper role in a managed BH system is often divided among a number of system participants. EAP counselors may be credentialed to make direct treatment referrals for certain types of cases but may be required to review decisions with a case manager before making other types of referrals. PCPs may have full authority to treat mental health problems, may have authority to refer cases directly for BH treatment with notification to the BH managed care system, or may yield all authority over BH treatment to the BH manager. It is of the utmost importance that protocols detailing roles and responsibilities of all concerned be carefully worked out, understood, and agreed to.

The EAP as Gatekeeper

EAPs play a unique role in corporate America, serving as a wide open point of access for employees and dependents with various problems and concerns. Before the advent of specialized BH systems, EAPs were often the only reliable source of information and guidance for individuals needing BH services. In this role, it has long been one of the functions of the EAP to assess an individual's BH status and, if necessary, to make a referral for treatment.

The positive aspect of involving EAP counselors as gatekeepers for the managed BH benefit is that they are numerous and generally knowledgeable and cast a wide net. They are likely to come in contact with people early, when problems of living have not necessarily grown to become major BH problems. Drawbacks of assigning gatekeeper responsibilities to EAP counselors include the fact that not all are clinically credentialed and qualified, that virtually none has the medical background to enable identification of medical and medication problems that may mimic or underlie BH problems, and that some may not be philosophically in tune with the goals of the managed BH program.

The PCP As Gatekeeper

Many managed medical care programs (including many HMOs) restrict direct access to mental health practitioners and require the approval of the PCP before mental health specialists may be consulted. In some managed care programs, the PCP is expected to diagnose and treat common, uncomplicated mental disorders.

The advantage of investing gatekeeping responsibility in the PCP is that it encourages continuity of care and concentrates authority over preventing unnecessary use of all specialty services in the hands of one person. A major disadvantage of using PCPs as gatekeepers for BH services is that medical clinicians have been shown to be dramatically less likely to detect or treat mental disorders than mental health specialists.[11] Historically, HMOs have gradually acknowledged the value of allowing direct access to mental health services. A recent longitudinal study of a large number of HMOs demonstrated that only 22 percent allowed self-referral for mental health services in their first 2 years of existence, 51 percent allowed self-referral after 2 to 5 years, and 80 percent allowed self-referral after 16 years.[12]

The Mental Health/Substance Abuse Case Manager and Assessor As Gatekeepers

Most specialized managed BH systems are organized to utilize some combination of case managers and designated assessor-clinicians within the contracted provider network as gatekeepers/channelers to appropriate treatment. Some systems rely on case managers to conduct a fairly detailed initial assessment over the telephone and to make referrals for treatment on that basis for all but the most complex cases, which are referred to a field clinician for further evaluation. Other systems routinely channel virtually every case to one of a group of specially designated assessors for detailed face-to-face evaluation and treatment planning.

In either instance, important triaging occurs at the outset. Many systems are able to case-match referrals to assessors or treatment clinicians on the basis of the therapist's specialty interests, gender, language, ethnicity, and so forth. Among systems that encompass a broad spectrum of mental health providers (e.g., those holding degrees in medicine, psychiatry, psychology, social work, or nursing), few have developed a practical theory or usable criteria for matching cases to specific provider disciplines.

PROVIDER NETWORKS

Assembling and administering a specialized BH provider network involves a more labor-intensive selection and monitoring process than is usually required for a general medical provider network. Some of the criteria could apply to any network; examples are geographic accessibility, inclusion of a full continuum of care, willingness to negotiate favorable rates in exchange for channeling of patients, willingness to cooperate with utilization management procedures and standards, and structural evidence of quality, such as appropriate credentials, current licensure, certification, and the like. Some other issues related to continuum of services, practice patterns, and practice philosophy are uniquely relevant to specialized BH networks.

Network Development Staff

All managed BH organizations offering a specialized network-based product employ network development staff dedicated to assembling and administering networks of contracted BH providers. These staff may be located at a central administrative location or at several local offices throughout the region or country, but typically they reside in the local area of a network during its start-up phase. Network development staff typically include experienced BH clinicians, who are responsible for evaluating the clinical skills of prospective network members, and individuals experienced in managed care administration and provider contracting, who are responsible for negotiating contract terms and administering the network after it is established.

Network Development Process

Generally, managed BH organizations adhere to a network development process that includes the following seven steps.

Step 1: Establish the Size and Scope of the Network

To pinpoint the size and scope of the network, the organization must take into account the benefit design to be administered (i.e., the range of provider types covered), the demographic characteristics of the population to be served, area geographic characteristics (e.g., physical or psychological barriers to provider access), and any specific payer requirements related to the size and composition of the network.

The above factors influence the characteristics of a network in any particular area, but certain general rules of thumb apply across most specialized BH networks:

- No plan member has driving time of more than:
  - —1 hour to a full-service hospital
  - —30 minutes to an emergency department
  - —30 minutes to an outpatient substance abuse program
  - —30 minutes to an individual provider
  - —30 minutes to an assessor
- Network coverage ratios should be at least:
  - —1 individual provider per 1,000 covered members
  - —1 assessor per 3,000 covered members
- The distribution of network providers by discipline generally falls within these ranges:
  - —20 percent to 30 percent psychiatrists
  - —20 percent to 30 percent doctoral-prepared psychologists
  - —40 percent to 60 percent master's level providers (psychologists, social workers, nurses, and MFCCs)

Step 2: Assess and Determine Fees/Rates

Providers in the area to be developed are surveyed to determine current prevailing fees by discipline and sometimes by procedure within discipline. From analysis of these data, maximum fees are usually fixed at a standard by discipline across the entire network in the given geographic area. Individual provider fees are usually pegged at a level reflecting approximately a 10 percent discount from the median. Some organizations actually establish the maximum fee at the 75th or 80th percentile, arguing that it is more cost effective to pay close to top dollar to attract the best practitioners but to be vigilant when it comes to evaluating practice philosophy and practice patterns. Hospital and substance abuse treatment program rates typically are not fixed but are negotiated on a program-by-program basis. Typical discounts for these programs are in the range of 25 percent to 40 percent of regular charges and are usually contracted on an all-inclusive per diem basis (see Chapter 11).

Step 3: Identify Targeted Providers

Once the size of the network and the fees are established, the task is to identify providers who will actually be enrolled in the network. Important factors in identifying the targeted group include minimizing disruption of ongoing therapeutic relationships for the plan population to be served, identifying providers who have a good reputation in the community for quality and competence, and identifying providers who are likely to work compatibly in a managed care environment.

Good sources of information about providers include payer (employer or insurer) staff, who can identify providers historically utilized by plan members and who probably have some knowledge of specific BH providers; EAP counselors, who have ongoing relationships with BH providers to whom they have referred patients; and community providers with whom the BH organization itself has had favorable past experience. If these sources are not available or are not sufficient to identify a large enough target group, less selective sources such as professional association listings, state licensing registers, or the phone book are used.

Step 4: Contact Providers

Once a targeted group of providers is identified, contact is made by mail or telephone. Information about network requirements and potential channeling of patients is provided, and providers are invited to indicate interest. Depending on how much advance work has been done to identify likely candidates, response rates range from 10 percent to 50 percent.

Step 5: Obtain In-Depth Information via Application

Providers expressing interest in network membership are asked to complete a detailed application. Although the content and length of application forms vary, forms generally cover such areas as credentials, certification, licensure, specialization/specialized training, years of experience, treatment philosophy, hours available, percentage of practice available to network subscribers, fees, and so forth.

Step 6: Conduct a Site Visit/Interview

Anywhere from 10 percent to 30 percent of providers completing the application typically are eliminated as a result of failure to pass the screening process (most BH organizations have a formalized set of screens that are applied to applications to narrow the field of eligible network participants). Virtually all organizations conduct an in-person site visit to facility-based programs before approving them for network membership. With individual providers, there is considerably more variation. Many organizations rely completely on written applications, some include a telephone interview, some conduct face-to-face site visits/interviews for selected providers, and a few require site visits/interviews for all individual providers admitted to the network. Some common selection criteria are listed in Exhibit 16–2.

Step 7: Select Providers for Network

Results of analysis of applications, interviews, and site visits typically are reviewed formally by a credentialing committee that includes top level clinical and administrative staff. Approved providers receive a contract, the final terms of which are negotiated by network development staff with oversight from top level operations and legal staff. Managed BH contracting issues do not differ significantly from those involved in general managed care contracting, which are dealt with in Chapters 7 and 29.

QUALITY ASSURANCE

Quality management (QM) refers to activities designed to prevent and/or correct quality problems. In managed BH systems, core QM activities are focused on the qualifications and behavior of case managers and providers and (to some extent) on the treatment results achieved by providers. The following is a delineation of common elements of internal QM programs for managed BH organizations.

Exhibit 16–2 Common Selection Criteria for Providers

Facilities
- Must provide a continuum of levels of care (not only acute inpatient)
- Average length of stay for acute inpatient cases < 10 days

Psychiatrists
- Accustomed to filling medication management role in conjunction with other therapists handling individual therapy
- Usual practice pattern involves referring patients to psychologists and social workers for individual therapy
- Work primarily with serious, complicated conditions

Psychologists
- Usual practice pattern involves referring to physician for medication evaluation when appropriate
- Do not routinely test all patients unless specifically indicated

Social workers
- Demonstrated experience in treating sociofamilial issues
- Experienced with assessment, especially in community mental health center settings

Nurses
- Some general medical nursing experience
- Demonstrated current knowledge of psychopharmacology

All practitioners
- Knowledge, experience, and training in goal-focused, brief therapy techniques
- Experienced in multidisciplinary treatment approaches
- Routinely use peer support system to discuss difficult cases
- Demonstrated familiarity with community resources

Courtesy of William M. Mercer, Inc., San Francisco, California.

UR/Case Management

Internal QM programs should include the following elements designed to ensure quality in the UR/case management process:

- *Credentialing/recredentialing*—Typical requirements are that case managers have at least master's level BH clinical credentials, have a minimum of 3 to 5 years of clinical experience, and maintain current licensure and certification to practice. Many organizations consistently exceed these standards in practice; for example, it is not uncommon for incumbent case managers in a given setting to average 10 to 15 years of clinical experience at various levels of care.
- *Clinical rounds*—Staff must participate in educationally oriented interdisciplinary conferences that include senior clinical staff.
- *Formal supervision*—Provision must be made for regular direct supervision and coaching of case managers by clinically qualified supervisors.
- *Clinical audits*—Routine internal audits of case management notes must be performed with attention to administrative and clinical performance, routine feedback to case managers, and individualized remedial activities when standards are not met.
- *Data tracking*—Staff-specific, diagnosis-specific outcome data must be tracked (e.g., average length of stay) with comparison to norms, analysis of implications for case management technique, and feedback to case managers.
- *Inservice training*—Inservice training programs for case managers must be shaped and driven by the findings of the internal QM monitoring system.

Network Providers

Internal QM systems in BH programs should include the following elements to ensure quality in the provider network:

- *Credentialing/recredentialing*—Minimum requirements usually include academic credentialing, licensure, certification, confirmation of criterion level malpractice insurance, and clearing of malpractice history. Some organizations independently check licensure directly with state licensing boards and perform direct checks on legal actions concerning malpractice. Recredentialing should be done on a continual basis (e.g., every 2 years), including systematic reminders to providers when current licensure or insurance is about to expire.

- *Case manager ratings*—Routine global ratings of providers by case managers per contact episode must be based on cost-effectiveness, quality of care, and degree of cooperation with the managed care system.
- *Provider profiling*—Diagnosis-based provider profiling must be based on measures of cost and utilization with feedback to providers on network norms. This topic is also addressed in Chapter 19.
- *Treatment chart audits*—There must be routine audits of provider treatment charts, often focused on profile outliers, with feedback to providers.
- *Provider communications*—These include bulletins, newsletters, memoranda, and so forth to network providers addressing administrative and clinical issues; these are driven by findings of the internal QM system.
- *Provider education*—Provision must be made for formal education programs for providers driven by findings of the internal QM system.
- *Provider satisfaction surveys*—The plan must conduct routine monitoring of network provider satisfaction with clinical and administrative requirements of the managed care system and provide the opportunity for constructive suggestions for system changes.
- *Outcome monitoring*—There must be diagnosis-specific, provider-specific tracking of outcome measures, including patient satisfaction, recidivism/relapse, mental and/or physical health status change, mental and/or physical claims costs, and functional change (through employer-based data such as absenteeism rates and productivity measures).

External Quality Assurance Monitoring

It has been suggested that the incentives and conflicts of interest inherent in a managed BH program are too great to be overcome entirely by internal self-regulation. In recognition of this problem, some state and federal regulatory agencies and employer/payers have instituted routine external quality monitoring of managed BH systems. The results of such external auditing activities reveal considerable variation in performance among managed BH organizations and within organizations over time and at different service delivery locations.

Routine monitoring of the quality of patient care services may be a useful check and balance mechanism. Audits of treatment records and case management records can reveal significant areas for improvement in the service delivery system not otherwise detected by internal quality assurance methods. Determining these areas may help improve the MCO's quality of care and its competitive position. Following are some examples of variation and common weaknesses in systems.

Utilization Criteria

Most organizations have criteria that specify clear, behavioral criteria for various levels of care. Some organizations, however, have adopted criteria that do not provide clear guidance to the case manager. In these cases, general, nonbehavioral criteria are difficult to apply with any precision. In some other instances, criteria are clear but inefficient. For example, some organizations use published 50th percentile norms to assign initial lengths of stay, thus missing the opportunity to influence cases for which earlier discharge would be reasonable and achievable.

As specialized BH MCOs have matured, there has been a growing consensus among organizations concerning the essential criteria for inpatient care. There has also been serious attention paid to indications for outpatient care and elaboration of UR criteria for intermediate levels of care in the continuum of care.

Staff Qualifications

Some organizations lack case managers or even supervisory personnel with relevant BH background and experience. Some lack doctoral level advisors who can engage in matched peer review with doctoral level providers. Some programs have physicians without psychiatric or substance abuse background functioning as psychiatric medical directors.

Inservice Training

Some organizations select inservice training programs on the basis of apparently random or arbitrary topic selection rather than needs identified through an internal QM system. Many have no inservice training, orientation, or QM oversight applied to doctoral level advisors. Some have no discernible inservice training program at all.

Quality of Care Problem Identification

Analysis of random samples of case management notes in more than 100 audits of managed BH systems has consistently identified clinically significant quality of care problems in 25 percent to 50 percent of cases (National Medical Audit, unpublished data, 1994). Identified problems include misdiagnosis, subtherapeutic or toxic medication dosages, unexplored medical complications, mismatch of diagnosis and treatment plan, and mismanagement of dangerous behavior. Over time, the prevalence of such problems has not diminished, and specialized MCOs have yet to devise effective methods for improving care at the point of UR. In general, review programs document detection of and action on these problems in only a small minority of cases, although informal activity is believed to occur in some programs. When problems are identified by case managers in these programs, action by doctoral level advisors can also be too rare an occurrence. The potential for conserving resources through methodical improvement of the quality of care remains unexplored territory.

Provider Credentialing

At the most minimal level of QM for a provider network, the BH system warrants to payers and direct consumers that all network providers meet certain baseline credentialing standards. Some programs fail to document and confirm credentialing thoroughly and independently when providers are admitted to the network, and many programs fail consistently to recredential on a continuing basis to ensure that network members continue to meet basic requirements.

Progress in Outcomes Measurement, Tracking, and Assessment

The ultimate gateway to true continuous quality improvement is keyed to the reliable measurement of treatment outcomes and analysis of the relationship among treatment approach, provider type, case management technique, and treatment outcome. Some BH programs have begun to track treatment outcomes in a number of ways, and joint meetings between MCOs and large provider entities have been held to stimulate consensus on proposed tentative conceptual schemes and data measurement tools. There remains, however, great variation among programs and providers in the degree of conceptual development of these approaches, in the sophistication of information systems available to put data to use, and in the extent of agreement about appropriate measures and methods.

Special Issues and Common Problems in Establishing Effective Utilization Management/QM in an MCO for BH

There has been a progressive homogenization of specialized carve-out BH MCOs. Competitive pressures to provide managed care services at lower prices have made it increasingly difficult to engage in more than narrow UR activity. Yet the larger strategic need is to promote more effective care and to generate more clinical value for every BH care dollar. Increasingly limited MCO dollars also limit investment in clinical information systems (infrastructure) and in processes for data aggregation and analysis necessary for the development of outcomes tracking systems.

PROVIDER STRUCTURES FOR INTEGRATED DELIVERY SYSTEMS TO MEET MANAGED CARE OBJECTIVES

An earlier discussion in this chapter focused on aspects of network formation from the perspective of MCOs. Market changes are rapidly moving the BH delivery system toward mergers of providers themselves into vertically or horizontally integrated systems and toward the integration of providers and MCOs. Therefore, in this section the focus will be aspects of network formation from the point of view of such emerging systems. A detailed discussion of integrated health care delivery systems is also found in Chapter 4.

Importance of Planned Integrated Delivery Systems

The nature of psychiatric and addiction disorders and the secondary disabilities that manifest as a result of the severity and persistence of these disorders underscore the importance of integrated delivery systems. A range of treatment interventions must be simultaneously available to address numerous and discrete demands for crisis intervention, stabilization and relief of acute symptoms, and continuing treatment and psychoeducational support for recovery and relapse prevention.

Historical Structures: Public and Private

Integrated service delivery systems can offer better access and accountability while safeguarding against clinical risk and cost drifting. Historical BH delivery structures in the private sector were one dimensional (a hospital) or two dimensional (a hospital and outpatient clinic). These limited structures were inadequate to address the heterogeneity of the client population and its needs. Interventions more intensive than an outpatient visit were either carried out in expensive hospital settings or not available. Public care systems began to develop a broader range of services in the 1960s under the umbrella of comprehensive community mental health centers (CMHCs).

Until the advent of managed care, CMHCs represented the majority of comprehensive and integrated care systems. Managed BH care organizations adopted community mental health approaches and became leaders in creating integrated service delivery networks, initially for the private sector and for Medicaid and Medicare recipients more recently.

Move to Provider Networks

Integrated service delivery systems have a comprehensive array of services organized to meet the needs of a defined population and geographic base. Fully integrated systems in BH care comprise acute and intensive care services, continuing care and relapse prevention, and community support and long-term care. Integrated care systems provide a single point of clinical and fiscal accountability to patients and payers, promoting access, managing utilization, and ensuring quality.

Integration has been achieved through consolidation and/or affiliation of providers into defined delivery networks. As discussed in Chapter 4, the model of a physician–hospital organization, which is familiar to health practitioners, is less common in BH care. More common are preferred provider organizations, which are designed to link individual and small group practitioners and are established by hospitals, insurers, and MCOs. Horizontal networks, comprising provider organizations in similar lines of business (i.e., a hospital *or* CMHC *or* residential provider) are most often formed to consolidate a broader geographic and client base, to achieve management efficiencies, and to position the combined organizations to compete for managed care business. Vertical networks incorporate hospitals with ambulatory service providers. In the BH arena, this may include acute care services or a combination of acute, continuing, and long-term care services (i.e., hospitals *and* CMHCs *and* residential providers).

Issues in Establishment of Networks

A number of issues must be addressed in the formation of a successful BH services delivery network. Among the steps to be taken are the following:

- Confirm patient and payer demand to ensure an adequate client and financing base for efficient operation of the network.
- Define the terms of membership and governance structure for both core and affiliated members.
- Identify and implement the legal structure(s) that best fit the mission of the network and the culture of the core members.
- Acquire network development staff with capabilities in marketing, system development, and information management.
- Initiate the marketing and development functions in conjunction with core members of the network to attract business that is key to the maintenance and growth of the network.
- Determine the size and scope of the network consistent with the mission and the market.
- Profile, recruit, and select providers based on planning and marketing results.
- Set network provider fees, costs model, and rate structure for capitated reimbursement and risk management.

Key Operational Challenges

Providers contemplating the formation of a network face numerous operational challenges. Although the initial will to coalesce may be driven by external forces in the regulatory, financing, and competitor environment, an internal will must be formulated if the network is to succeed in bringing together previously independent organizations to:

- adopt common practice standards required by multiple payers
- share reporting and information about clients, utilization, and cost of care
- form a firm commitment to quality assurance and improvement
- develop the capacity to demonstrate and evaluate outcomes of treatment and service interventions provided
- set aside individual agency interests and competition to survive in the BH reimbursement environment

Factors in and Constraints on Carve-In and Carve-Out Strategies Varying by Eligibility Population

To succeed in the current reimbursement environment, BH networks require the capacity to integrate internally across programs and facilities and externally with primary health care providers. Carve-out approaches, where both reimbursement and management of BH benefits are administered separately from broader health benefits, persist where payers believe that separate administration strengthens accountability, lowers cost, and/or improves access to care (see Chapter 36 of *The Managed Health Care Handbook*).[13] Carve-outs are most common in the private sector in areas where benefits were historically generous, utilization was high, and the provider community was well developed. In the public sector, the strategy has been focused most often on the disabled population that represents the greatest risk, clinically and financially.

Carve-in approaches are most frequently found in HMOs that provide all health and BH services for a single capitated rate and limit even specialty service utilization to providers within the organization or network. Carve-in strategies are viewed as useful in controlling inappropriate health utilization driven by behavioral disorders and in promoting more integrated care. BH delivery systems must organize to accept payment on a carve-out basis as well as on a carve-in basis if volume is to be maintained and growth achieved. This capacity is particularly important in the short term to preserve continuity with clients whose insurance coverage may shift and to mitigate the financial impact of low HMO expenditures and subcapitated payments for BH. The capacity to play on both terms is considered essential to positioning for the long term, for which the forecast is greater integration between physical health and BH.

Recent Trends in Network and MCO Integration

As the profit margins become thinner and providers gain sophistication in care management, the utility and affordability of carve-out BH care management diminishes. In recognition, MCOs and provider networks have begun to merge. Combined, these new organizations offer service, utilization management, and insurance functions directly to primary purchasers of health care.

INFORMATION SYSTEMS

BH care information systems are a subset of general health care informatics. Consequently, many of the issues facing the automation of BH care processes mirror those facing health care generally. This section focuses on the balance that BH systems must reach between the necessarily unique BH features and those features that both types of systems hold in common. Information systems in managed care are also discussed in Chapter 20.

Unique Features of BH Systems

An information system designed specifically for BH diverges functionally in several ways from similar medical–surgical systems. Good BH systems include, for example, DSM-IV diagnosis codes (including all axes). They allow for residential and partial care settings, nontraditional treatment alternatives, and BH testing. Many of the most important methods for delivering BH services under managed care involve the use of intensive, noninpatient, alternative care settings. These alternatives are incompatible with the basic inpatient/outpatient structure and coding schemes of typical medical–surgical systems.

Developers of the best BH management information systems recognize the more long-term nature of BH problems and have structured system functions to accommodate this reality. These systems smoothly handle issues of multiple and extended authorizations for all levels of care, review and approval of treatment plans, and episodes of care that are routinely longer than those in medical–surgical systems. Contracting and provider modules have well-developed BH credentialing and profiling systems and allow for provider searches on the full range of provider experience, treatment preferences, and education. A wide range of contracting options should be accommodated and utilization against these contracts tracked.

Level of Integration

Although good BH information systems have many features that distinguish them from typical medical–surgical systems, there are many functions that can be shared between the BH and corresponding medical–surgical systems. More important, there are many functions that by definition must be the same. One example is eligibility information. In most cases, the BH benefit is part of a larger medical benefit, and therefore the eligibility information for the two benefits must be the same.

Typically, the BH system relies on the corresponding medical–surgical or employer system for eligibility information. The level of integration between these corresponding systems determines the eligibility file access alternatives. The level of integration can be represented as a continuum with highest level being a single system for both medical–surgical and BH and the lowest level being two independent systems with incompatible eligibility file structures.

At the high integration end of the continuum, BH processing is accomplished on the medical–surgical information system. Historically, this has led to significant functional compromises in the quality and specificity of the BH data, but it does have the positive effect of making access to the eligibility file simple. Because the BH staff are using the same system as the medical–surgical staff, they have access to the same eligibility functions and access the same eligibility file. No transfer of eligibility information between systems is required.

At the other end of the integration continuum, there are many independent BH systems that have varying degrees of compatibility with the employer systems or medical–surgical systems from which they must obtain their eligibility data. In the worst case, the BH staff must either access the medical–surgical system themselves for the eligibility data or rely on paper printouts or phone calls to the medical–surgical staff.

The center point of the integration continuum includes maintaining duplicate eligibility files on each system. This requires transferring the data from one system to the other over a leased line or by tape. Duplicating the files leads to new issues, including scheduling the replication process, reconciling the files, and accessing the original file between replications when eligibility questions arise.

The best integration options utilize client/server approaches. In these cases, there is only one eligibility file that is maintained on its own eligibility server. When either a user of the medical–surgical system or a user of the BH system checks the eligibility of a client, the respective system sends a message or remote procedure call to the eligibility server, which returns with the appropriate eligibility and demographic data. The user is unaware that the system has accessed an external resource to answer the query.

This last approach allows the BH system the independence required to preserve its unique BH functions without requiring the duplication of files that need to be accessible to all systems. It also makes it easy to develop BH-specific data files that contain information not required by medical systems. These files can be accessed by the BH client application at the same time as the shared eligibility file. The result for the user of the BH system is an answer that contains information from both the unique BH file and the systemwide eligibility file.

Key Issues

The key to a successful BH information system is found in the balance between unique system functions and data and those functions and data that must be integrated with the remainder of the benefit plan. Eligibility is an example of a function that must be well integrated. Other examples include accumulators against benefit plan maximums, integrated claims files, member service systems, and contracting.

Many other system functions and data, as indicated above, must be developed independently. The quality of the service provided is compromised when these functions are combined because the medical–surgical information systems do not support the unique needs of BH care. Treatment planning provides a good example. Medical–surgical applications have not been designed to accommodate treatment plans before the delivery of the service. There is much less variability in the possible treatments, and they are typically not delivered over the longer time spans that BH care requires. Consequently, medical–surgical systems do not analyze treatment plans and progress against treatment plans in determining the appropriateness of services delivered. In BH, however, this is the main method of precertification and concurrent review. It is much more efficient and effective to develop this function and the others mentioned above as separate mental health modules or as an entirely independent system.

PUBLIC–PRIVATE SYSTEMS INTEGRATION

BH is unique in the health care world for the dominant role that the public sector has played in the financing and delivery of care. Approximately two public dollars are spent for every private dollar in the financing of psychiatric and addiction treatment services. Moreover, publicly financed and operated systems historically have cared for individuals with the most serious forms of illness, contrary to tertiary care practices in the medical–surgical arena, where the sickest people more often access care in the best staffed teaching hospitals.

The BH field moved from a medical to a psychosocial model of care in the last 30 years to support the decongregation of public psychiatric hospitals and the development of community-based care. Considerable technology was developed in community mental health and addiction services for the management of care in alternative and less costly settings. Adoption of these practices was key to the success of the early managed BH care organizations.

Managed BH care was formally established in response to private sector demand for an alternative to unregulated and growing use of inpatient and outpatient care. Emergence of managed care in the public sector has, in the main, been driven by a desire to manage cost or the benefit combined with aspirations to improve access, quality, and outcomes of the care provided. Despite the fact that first-generation BH managed care developed from public sector approaches, the advent of managed care in the public sector has been accompanied by the notion that the private sector is more consistent and considered in its approach, which can therefore benefit the public sector. This implied notion has created some misunderstanding and disappointment.

Managed care has also been accompanied by a government privatization effort that has (more than managed care techniques) promoted public–private systems integration. Opportunities for a positive fusion of public and private sector technologies and competence are a great benefit accrued to patients at a time when the amount and cost of service benefits are being reduced. Through privatization and managed care initiatives, those with the most serious disorders now have access to the best hospitals at more affordable rates. At the same time, privately insured persons now have access to less restrictive and broader types of care. The interactive effects of public sector community treatment technology and private sector quality improvement and information management hold great promise for consumers of care.

The promise of public–private systems integration can be realized through a deliberate and planned approach to implementation of a reformed system. Steps to be taken include the following:

- Understand the shifting roles of government players in the local environment as public health and medical assistance programs reframe their policy, regulatory, financing, and provider roles
- Analyze the case mix characteristics and utilization patterns among publicly insured persons to identify client risk groups and project utilization and cost associated with their care.
- Assess political and regulatory challenges to implementing new provider arrangements, service models, and reimbursement rates.
- Evaluate the potential for integration of publicly and privately insured persons at the provider level to reduce segregation, maximize resources, and improve access.
- Establish a process and standards for quality assurance and improvement of all care programs.
- Incorporate the voice and interests of consumers in the planning, delivery, and evaluation of accountable services.
- Develop benchmarks to guide monitoring of client utilization and professional prac-

tice patterns as a safeguard against underservice.

- Frame agreements and a plan for allocation of savings as a return on public investments.

EMERGING ISSUES

As with managed health care in general, the field remains highly dynamic, with new issues emerging. Among the more salient emerging issues in BH care are the following.

As noted above, BH providers are challenged to integrate horizontally to achieve comprehensiveness of service continuum, geographic base, and covered lives. They are also challenged to integrate vertically to complete continuums with primary health and tertiary care providers. BH providers/networks require the capacity to operate as, and to accept varying payments on, both carve-in and carve-out bases.

The potential for medical cost offset as a result of timely and targeted psychiatric and addiction treatment is recognized but infrequently measured. As data emerge and full-risk capitation arrangements grow, the demand for behavioral treatment in primary and tertiary care settings grows. A substantial proportion of the highest-cost tertiary care patients have psychiatric and substance abuse disorders that increase morbidity and mortality if left untreated. The implications for redistribution of resources to BH are dependent upon the ability of the BH field to produce data and to educate payers and practitioners.

Legal, ethical, cultural, and values challenges that have been commonplace in public care systems are emerging in managed BH care systems. Legally mandated civil commitment has produced uncontrolled expenses in length of stay and legal representation, driving financial risk to a capitated system. Providers face challenges in rationing care under managed and capitated arrangements, where fiscal incentives promote underservice. As managed care penetration increases, particularly among publicly insured clients, demands increase for providers to be culturally competent, for treatments to be culturally fit, and for programs to be culturally accessible.

CONCLUSION

This chapter has outlined some of the key aspects, issues, and recent developments in specialized managed care programs addressing BH treatment. In overview, BH presents unique management problems that are increasingly being addressed through specialized managed care systems with specific and separate operational guidelines, managed care personnel, provider networks, and QM approaches.

Study Questions

1. Which unique factors present special challenges to behavioral health management as compared to medical-surgical management?
2. Which types of behavioral health treatment methods form the backbone of managed care service?
3. Which additions to the continuum of care for behavioral health problems contribute to the effectiveness of treatment?

REFERENCES AND NOTES

1. M.J. Bennett, The Greening of the HMO: Implications for Prepaid Psychiatry, *American Journal of Psychiatry* 145 (1988): 1544–1549.
2. A.H. Schene and V.P. Gersons, Effectiveness and Application of Partial Hospitalization. *Acta Psychiatrica Scandinavica* 74 (1986): 335–340.
3. J.S. Rosie, Partial Hospitalization: A Review of Recent Literature, *Hospital and Community Psychiatry* 38 (1987): 1291–1299.
4. L.R. Mosher, Alternatives to Psychiatric Hospitalization, *New England Journal of Medicine* 309 (1983): 1579–1580.
5. H.M. Annis, Is Inpatient Rehabilitation of the Alcoholic Cost Effective? A Composition, *Advances in Alcohol and Substance Abuse* 5 (1986): 175–190.
6. L. Saxe and L. Goodman, *The Effectiveness of Outpatient vs. Inpatient Treatment: Updating the OTA Report*

(Hartford, Conn.: Prudential Insurance Company, 1988).

7. R. Husby, et al., Short-Term Dynamic Psychotherapy: Prognostic Value of Characteristics of Patient Studies by a Two-Year Follow-Up of 39 Neurotic Patients, *Psychotherapy and Psychosomatics* 43 (1985): 8–16.
8. M.J. Horowitz, et al., Comprehensive Analysis of Change after Brief Dynamic Psychotherapy, *American Journal of Psychiatry* 143 (1986): 582–589.
9. H.G. Whittington, "Managed Mental Health: Clinical Myths and Imperatives," in *Managed Mental Health Services*, ed. S. Feldman (Springfield, Ill.: Thomas, 1992), 223–243.
10. D. Anderson, How Effective Is Managed Mental Health Care?, *Business and Health* (November 1989): 34–35.
11. K.B. Wells, et al., Detection of Depressive Disorder for Patients Receiving Prepaid or Fee-For-Service Care, *Journal of the American Medical Association* 262 (1989): 3298–3302.
12. M. Shadle and J.B. Christianson, The Organization of Mental Health Care Delivery in HMOs, *Administration in Mental Health* 15 (1988): 201–225.
13. A.M. Kotin and T.J. Kuhlman, "The Employer's View of Managed Health Care: From a Passive to an Aggressive Role," in *The Managed Health Care Handbook*, 3d ed., ed. P.R. Kongstvedt (Gaithersburg, Md.: Aspen, 1996), 580–592.

SUGGESTED READING

Austin, M.J. and Blum, S.R. 1995. Public Sector Planning for Managed Mental Health Care. *Administration and Policy in Mental Health*, 22, pp. 201–356.

Burton, W.N. and Conti, D.J. 1991. Value-Managed Mental Health Benefits. *Journal of Occupational Medicine*, 33, pp. 311, 313.

D'Alesandro, A. (ed.). 1994. *Managed Behavioral Health Care: Provider Training and Development Manual.* Clearwater, Fla.: American Board of Certified Managed Care Providers/Of Course Publications.

Feldman, J.L. and Fitzpatrick, R.J. 1992. *Managed Mental Health Care: Administrative and Clinical Issues*. Washington, D.C.: American Psychiatric Press.

Gartner, L. and Mee-Lee, D. 1995. *The Role and Current Status of Patient Placement Criteria in the Treatment of Substance Use Disorders*. Rockville, Md: U.S. Department of Health and Human Services.

Goodman, M., Brown, J., and Dietz, P. 1992. *Managing Managed Care: A Mental Health Practitioner's Survival Guide*. Washington, D.C.: American Psychiatric Press.

Migdail, K.J. and Youngs, M.T. (eds.). 1995. *1995 Behavioral Outcomes & Guidelines Sourcebook*. New York, N.Y.: Faulkner & Gray.

Milstein, A. 1994. Evaluating Psychiatric and Substance Abuse Case Management Organizations. In S.A. Shueman, W.G. Troy, and S.L. Mayhugh, eds: *Managed Behavioral Health Care: An Industry Perspective,* pp. 222–240. Springfield, Ill.: Charles C Thomas.

Mrazeki, P.J. and Haggerty, R.J. 1994. *Reducing Risks for Mental Disorders*. Washington, D.C.: National Academy Press.

National Advisory Mental Health Council. 1993. Health Care Reform for Americans with Severe Mental Illnesses: Report of the National Advisory Mental Health Council. *American Journal of Psychiatry*, 150, pp. 1447–1465.

Shueman, S.A., Troy, W.G., and Mayhugh, S.L. (eds.). 1994. *Managed Behavioral Health Care: An Industry Perspective*. Springfield, Ill.: Charles C Thomas, Publisher.

Chapter 17

Quality Management in Managed Care

Pamela B. Siren and Glenn L. Laffel

Study Objectives

- Describe the basic structural models of traditional quality assurance programs
- Describe the basic components of quality management program
- Identify the customers of managed care
- Describe the managed care processes and outcomes that meet customer need
- Describe key measures to assess the performance of managed care processes
- Propose a model to report managed care performance measures

There are a variety of approaches to quality management in the managed care setting. These approaches are complementary and employ the principles of measurement, customer focus, and statistically based decision making. This chapter provides an overview of quality management in managed care, from traditional quality assurance to modern performance assessment and continuous improvement. It is hoped that readers will be able to utilize both methods once they have completed this chapter.

TRADITIONAL QUALITY ASSURANCE

Advocacy for performance assessment in health care can be traced to E.A. Codman, a surgeon who practiced at Massachusetts General Hospital in the early 1900s. He was among the first advocates of systematic performance assessment in health care. His efforts included evaluation of the care provided to his own patients.

In the 1960s and 1970s, the introduction of computers and large administrative datasets (used initially to support Medicare claims processing) permitted investigators to use powerful epidemiological methods in their analyses of practice variations and related phenomena. In this period, Avedias Donabedian developed three criteria for the assessment of quality that are still used today: structure, process, and outcome.[1] His approach to quality assessment of care has stood the test of time and remains useful in managed care settings.

Structure Criteria

Structural measures of health care performance focus on the context in which care and serv-

Pamela B. Siren, R.N., is the Director of Clinical Development with Lazo, Gertman & Associates in Waltham, Massachusetts. Her area of expertise is quality management in health care. She has designed strategies to identify and address opportunities for improvement in clinical performance in a variety of health care settings. She is the former Director of Clinical Improvement of Blue Cross and Blue Shield of Massachusetts.

Glenn L. Laffel, M.D., Ph.D., is the Senior Vice President for Medical Affairs at Preferred Health Systems. He is recognized internationally for his work on the health care application of total quality management and is the founding editor of *Quality Management in Health Care*.

ices are provided. These measures provide inferences about the managed care organization's (MCO's) capability to provide the services it proposes to offer. Structural measures include board certification of physicians, licensure of facilities, compliance with safety codes, record-keeping, and physician network appointments. Many such requirements are delineated in federal, state, and local regulations that govern licensing or accreditation and mandate periodic review and reporting mechanisms.

Accreditation and regulatory bodies have traditionally emphasized structural criteria because of their ease of documentation. Purchasers support this tradition by requesting such information in their contract negotiations with MCOs. The role of the MCO's leadership in improving performance is increasing and is evaluated by accrediting agencies through assessment of committee function. The MCO needs a complete understanding of its leadership's role in performance improvement.

As MCOs form into integrated delivery systems, the structural criterion of performance assessment becomes more complex. The regulations and standards that may govern MCOs, such as those of the National Committee for Quality Assurance (NCQA), may be different from the standards to which member hospitals are held accountable, such as those of the Joint Commission on Accreditation of Healthcare Organizations. Reconciliation of at least the minimal and widely accepted standards within the MCO and across an integrated delivery system is the first step to developing structural measures and evaluating structural performance and its impact on the quality and cost of health care delivery.

Structural measures generally do not offer adequate specificity to differentiate the capabilities of providers or organizations beyond meeting minimum standards. In addition, the relationship between structure and other measures of performance, such as outcomes, must be clarified to ensure that enforcing structural standards leads to better results.[2]

Process Criteria

The second traditional criterion for health care quality assessment is process. Process of care measures evaluate the way in which care is provided. Examples of care process measures for MCOs include the number of referrals made out of network, health screening rates (e.g., cholesterol), follow-up rates for abnormal diagnostic results, and clinical algorithms for different conditions. Such measures are frequently evaluated against national criteria or benchmarks. Process of service measures are also frequently used. These include appointment waiting times and membership application processing times.

As with structural measures, it is important to link process measures to outcomes. Although the field of outcomes research is growing, the link between many health care processes and key outcomes has not always been clearly defined.

Outcome Criteria

The third traditional category of quality assessment is the outcome of care or service. Traditional outcomes measurements include infection rates, morbidity, and mortality. Relatively poor outcomes performance generally mandates careful review. Exhibits 17–1 and 17–2 illustrate common outcome criteria used to assess quality of inpatient and outpatient care. Unfortunately, although outcomes measures are purported to reflect the performance of the entire system of care and service processes, they often offer little insight into the causes of poor performance.

Despite the limitations of current outcomes assessment, most MCOs have systems in place to assess for adverse events. These screening criteria are often evaluated during the utilization review process to detect sentinel events. Some of these same measures are being applied to the peer review process within the MCO.

Exhibit 17–1 Examples of Events among Hospitalized Patients That May Indicate Inadequate Quality of Care

Adequacy of discharge planning
- No documented plan for appropriate follow-up care or discharge planning as necessary, with consideration of physical, emotional, and mental status/needs at the time of discharge

Medical stability of the patient at discharge
- Blood pressure on day before or day of discharge: systolic, < 85 mm Hg or > 180 mm Hg; diastolic, < 50 mm Hg or > 110 mm Hg
- Oral temperature on day before or day of discharge > 101°F (rectal, > 102°F)
- Pulse < 50 beat/min (or < 45 beat/min if patient is on a ß blocker) or > 120 beat/min within 24 hours of discharge
- Abnormal results of diagnostic services not addressed or explained in the medical record
- Intravenous fluids or drugs on the day of discharge (excludes the ones that keep veins open, antibiotics, chemotherapy, or total parenteral nutrition)
- Purulent or bloody drainage of postoperative wound within 24 hours before discharge

Deaths
- During or after elective surgery
- After return to intensive care unit, coronary care, or special care unit within 24 hours of being transferred out
- Other unexpected death

Nosocomial infections
- Temperature increase of more than 2°F more than 72 hours from admission
- Indication of infection after an invasive procedure (e.g., suctioning, catheter insertion, tube feedings, surgery)

Unscheduled return to surgery within same admission for same condition as previous surgery or to correct operative problem (excludes staged procedures)

Trauma suffered in the hospital
- Unplanned removal or repair of a normal organ (i.e., removal or repair not addressed in operative consent)
- Fall with injury or untoward effect (including but not limited to fracture, dislocation, concussion, laceration)
- Life-threatening complications of anesthesia
- Life-threatening transfusion error or reaction
- Hospital-acquired decubitus ulcer
- Care resulting in serious or life-threatening complications not related to admitting signs and symptoms, including but not limited to neurological, endocrine, cardiovascular, renal, or respiratory body systems (e.g., resulting in dialysis, unplanned transfer to special care unit, lengthened hospital stay)
- Major adverse drug reaction or medication error with serious potential for harm or resulting in special measures to correct (e.g., intubation, cardiopulmonary resuscitation, gastric lavage), including but not limited to the following:
  1. Incorrect antibiotic ordered by physician (e.g., inconsistent with diagnostic studies or patient's history of drug allergy)
  2. No diagnostic study to confirm which drug is correct to administer (e.g., culture and sensitivity)
  3. Serum drug levels not measured as needed
  4. Diagnostic studies or other measures for side effects not performed as needed (e.g., blood urea nitrogen, creatinine, intake and output)

Source: Health Care Financing Administration, 1986.

Exhibit 17–2 Examples of Inpatient Diagnoses That May Indicate Inadequate or Improper Outpatient Care

- Cellulitis (extremities)
- Dehydration of child with severe diarrhea (younger than 2 years)
- Diabetic coma–ketoacidosis
- Essential hypertension
- Gangrene (angiosclerotic, extremities)
- Hemorrhage secondary to anticoagulant therapy
- Hypokalemia secondary to potassium-depleting diuretic
- Low-birthweight infant (premature, < 2,500 g)
- Malunion or nonunion of fracture (extremities)
- Perforated or hemorrhaging ulcer (duodenal, gastric)
- Pregnancy-induced hypertension (preeclampsia, eclampsia, toxemia)
- Pulmonary embolism (admitting diagnosis)
- Readmission of same condition within 14 days
- Ruptured appendix
- Septicemia (admitting diagnosis)
- Status asthmaticus
- Urinary tract infection (bacturia, pyuria)

Courtesy of Blue Cross and Blue Shield Association, Chicago, Illinois.

Peer Review and Appropriateness Evaluation

In addition to Donabedian's three quality criteria, peer review and appropriateness review have been key components of the traditional quality assurance model. Because of their applicability to managed care, they are discussed here.

Peer Review

Peer review involves a comparison of an individual provider's practice either by the provider's peers or against an acceptable standard of care. These standards may be developed within the MCO (e.g., practice guidelines), be described by national professional associations, or be required by a regulatory or legislative agency. Cases for peer review are identified either as outliers to specific indicators or through audits of medical records. Peer review has traditionally been used as an informal educational tool. It is typified by morbidity and mortality conferences currently in existence.

Peer review has its limitations. First, opportunities for improvement may be missed by a paradigm that rests on conformance with standards. Deming emphasized that meeting specifications does not result in constant improvement but rather ensures the status quo.[3] Second, studies have shown that there is poor interreviewer reliability among panels of physician reviewers and that the level of physician agreement regarding the quality of care is only slightly higher than the level expected by chance alone.[4] Third, peer review is limited by the scope of the indicators or processes under review. Despite these limitations, peer review continues to serve an important role in MCOs' quality management programs.

Appropriateness Evaluation

Appropriateness evaluation reviews the extent to which the MCO provides necessary care and does not provide unnecessary care. Appropriateness review frequently occurs before an elective clinical event (admission or procedure). Procedures or admissions most frequently selected for appropriateness review include those for which there is a wide variation of opinion as to their usefulness or effectiveness and those that have been notably expensive. Examples of procedures frequently selected for appropriateness review include hysterectomy, coronary artery bypass surgery, and laminectomy. The proposed indication for the event is compared with a list of approved indications obtained from a professional society or a specialty vendor or designed by the MCO itself. Appropriateness review is intended to identify and minimize areas of overutilization.

Appropriateness review provides a snapshot of a care decision and does not lend itself to an understanding of the events that may have preceded the admission or procedure in question. In addition, this review does not evaluate the effectiveness of the procedure once it has been authorized.

COMPONENTS OF A QUALITY MANAGEMENT PROGRAM: BUILDING ON TRADITION

The traditional quality assurance model provides a sound foundation for a modern quality management program. The quality assurance model can be improved, however, with an infusion of systems thinking, customer focus, and knowledge for improvement.

First, systems thinking offers a method for assessment and management of performance with a clear aim or purpose. The traditional quality assurance model does not incorporate this important concept. Lacking a shared aim, payers and providers risk forming a disconnected, inefficient network. This disconnected network will eventually engage in contradictory and inefficient behaviors. Organizational goals can be achieved first by identifying customer needs of an organization, unifying the purpose within the organization, and expanding the shared purpose across the integrated delivery system. For further information about systems thinking and organizational goal setting, the reader is referred to the work of Peter Senge.

Second, the cornerstone of a modern quality management program is customer focus. The traditional quality assurance model was driven, in part, by regulations and accreditors without explicit knowledge of what the customer (member, purchaser, provider) needed. The modern quality management program identifies key customers, measures customer needs, and improves processes to meet those needs.

Finally, an enhancement of the traditional quality assurance model is knowledge for improvement. According to Moen and Nolan, three fundamental questions can be used as guides for improvement efforts[5]:

1. What are you trying to accomplish? Information gained from understanding customer needs, the current process and outcome performance, and expected performance will assist the MCO in answering this question.
2. How will you know that a change is an improvement? Establishing performance expectations before implementing an improvement activity assists the MCO in understanding whether a change is an improvement and minimizes any potential confusion between measures of utilization and indicators of quality.
3. What changes can be made that will result in an improvement?

To develop tests and implement changes, the plan-do-study-act cycle is used as a framework for an efficient trial and learning model. The term *study* is used in the third cycle to emphasize this phase's primary purpose: to gain knowledge. Increased knowledge leads to a better prediction of whether a change in a current process will result in an improvement.[6]

A PROCESS MODEL FOR A MODERN QUALITY MANAGEMENT PROGRAM

Figure 17–1 depicts a model for a modern quality management program that enhances the traditional quality assurance model such that it includes the above dimensions. The remainder of this chapter discusses the eight key steps in developing a modern quality management program.

Understand Customer Need

Understanding customer need (Figure 17–2) is the basis of all quality management programs. Juran and Gyrna described a customer as anyone who is affected by a product or process.[7] Three categories of customers are external customers, internal customers, and suppliers. External customers of an MCO include members or benefactors and purchasers. Internal customers include the departments and services within the MCO, such as claims processing and member education, as well as the health care professionals themselves. Customer needs may be clear or disguised, rational, or less than rational. These needs must be discovered and served.[8] Negotiating and balancing the needs of these diverse and sometimes conflicting customer groups represent a challenge for MCOs, as they do for any organization.

Methods to understand customer need are as diverse as the customer groups. Customer complaints are a usual signal of a quality problem. Low levels of complaints, however, do not necessarily mean high satisfaction. Frequently, dissatisfied customers will purchase services elsewhere without ever registering a complaint. Most MCOs have a formal process to survey their membership for satisfaction with care or services (Exhibit 17–3). Yet despite the burgeoning number of satisfaction surveys, a study has shown that only 2 of 10 health care organizations conducting patient satisfaction surveys were using them as a regular feedback device to administrative and clinical departments.[9]

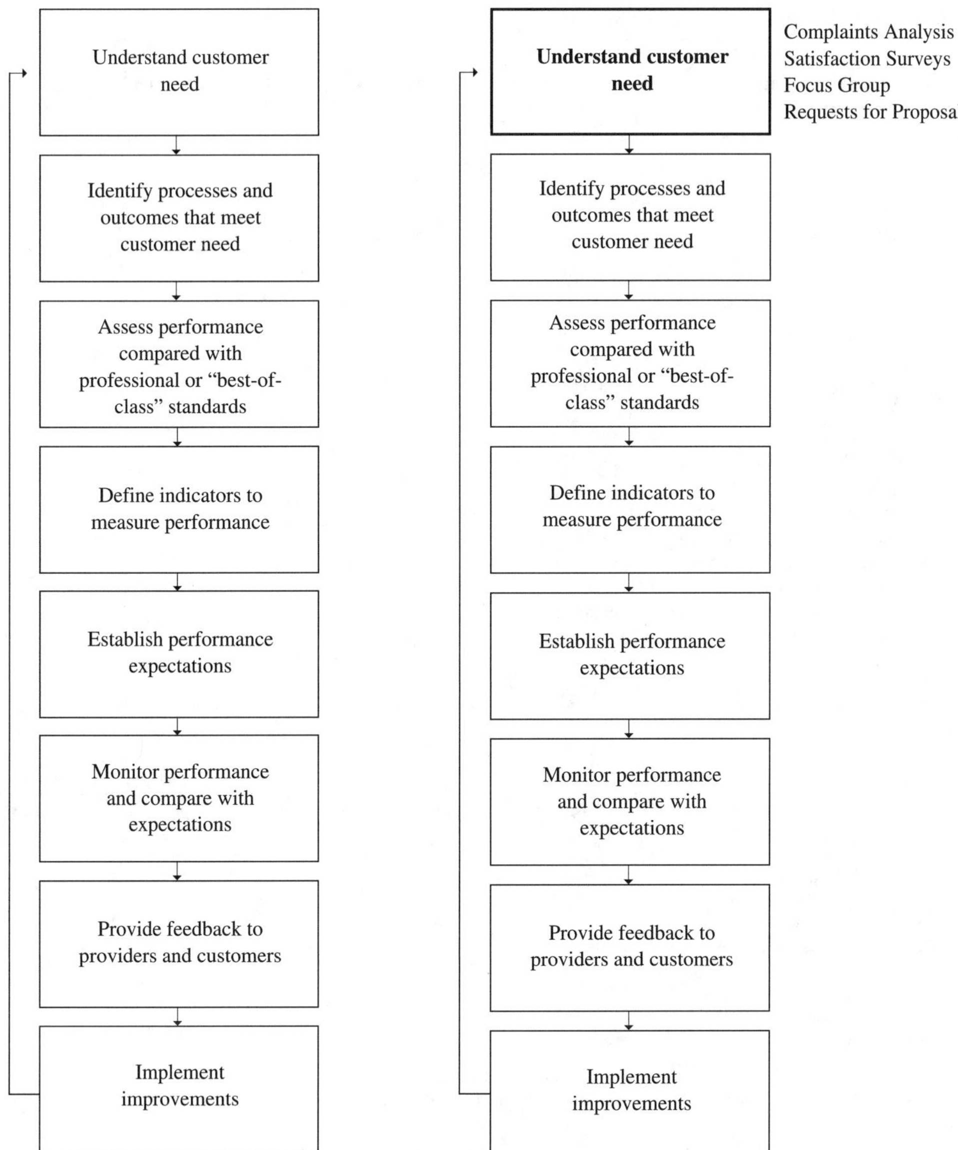

Figure 17–1 Continuous improvement process

Figure 17–2 Continuous improvement process—understand customer need

Through marketing initiatives, MCOs are proactively determining customer needs through focus groups and interviews. These processes are designed to identify customer expectations and real (versus stated) need. The Hospital Corporation of America (now Columbia/HCA) finds it useful to identify several levels of customer expectation. At level I, a customer as-

Exhibit 17–3 Examples of Satisfaction Surveys*

How would you rate:	**Excellent**	**Very Good**	**Good**	**Fair**	**Poor**
The thoroughness and technical skills of the:					
Attending doctor					
Nursing staff					
Consulting doctors					
Other personnel (lab, x-ray, etc.)					
The friendliness and compassion of the:					
Attending doctor					
Nursing staff					
Consulting doctors					
Other personnel (lab, x-ray, etc.)					
The explanations, instructions, and responses to questions by the:					
Attending doctor					
Nursing staff					
Consulting doctors					
Other personnel (lab, x-ray, etc.)					
Admission process (timeliness, friendliness, convenience)					
Explanation of your rights as a patient					
Discharge instructions and arrangements					
Food quality and service					
Appearance and cleanliness of the hospital					
Overall quality of care provided by the attending doctor					
Overall rating of this hospital					
Satisfaction with the outcome of your procedure (if applicable)					

Would you recommend this hospital to a friend or loved one? ❑ Yes ❑ No
Would you recommend your attending doctor to a friend or loved one?

© U.S. Quality Algorithms (USQA), 1991

How would you rate each of the following:	**Excellent 10**	**9**	**8**	**7**	**6**	**5**	**4**	**3**	**2**	**Poor 1**	**No Opinion 0**
Nursing Care											
Emergency Room Services											
Laboratory Department											
Quality Assurance/Improvement Program											
Utilization Review Department											
Social Services/Discharge Planning											
Medical Records											
Bed availibility											
Patient satisfaction with the hospital											

Please rate the following clinical departments:	**Excellent 10**	**9**	**8**	**7**	**6**	**5**	**4**	**3**	**2**	**Poor 1**	**No Opinion 0**
OB/GYN											
General Surgery											
Orthopedics											
Urology											
Cardiology											
ENT											
Other _______________											
Other _______________											

Would you refer a family member to this hospital? ❑ Yes ❑ No © U.S. Quality Algorithms (USDA), 1991

* This example includes selected questions from USQA's survey of members and USQA's survey of physicians.

Source: © *Journal on Quality Improvement*. Oakbrook Terrace, IL: Joint Commission on Accreditation of Healthcare Organizations, 1993, p. 377. Reprinted with permission.

sumes that a basic need will be met; at level II, the customer will be satisfied; at level III, the customer will be delighted.[10] Results from member satisfaction surveys and market analyses are an integral part of strategic quality planning.

A fundamental principle of quality improvement theory is the necessity for economically meaningful partnerships between purchasers and suppliers. Purchasers, MCOs, and hospitals are negotiating contracts based on performance measurement. To illustrate this concept, US Quality Algorithms, Inc., a subsidiary of US Healthcare, has implemented the CapTainer℠ compensation system, which combines base payments with an annual performance-based distribution. The CapTainer℠ system is based on a contracting process that includes the setting of performance targets, the development of a schedule for progress toward them, and the construction of a purchase/compensation schedule that translates improvement into a performance-based distribution.[11] The size of the performance-based distribution is related to progress toward goals and to the financial implications of changes in hospital or MCO operating procedures. Partnerships between MCOs and hospitals, and the positive economic relationships they imply, are only realistic and possible if the values of delivering care in a managed environment are shared.[12]

Negotiating and balancing the diverse groups of customer needs represent a challenge. Juran and Gyrna stated that it is important to recognize that some customers are more important than others. It is typical that 80 percent of the total sales volume comes from about 20 percent of the customers; these are the "vital few" customers who command priority.[13] Within these key customer groups, there is a distribution of individual customers that also may have a hierarchy of importance, such as a government agency, a gold card purchaser account, or an academic teaching center. Explicit understanding of the needs of all the MCO customer groups will minimize situations in which one customer's needs are met to the exclusion of another's.

Identify Processes and Outcomes That Meet Customer Need

Identification of processes and outcomes that meet customer need is the next step of the continuous improvement process model (Figure 17–3). How do customers view the MCO's quality? To begin with, they want to know whether the MCO meets their expectations. MCOs are expected to treat members who are ill and to maintain the health and functional capabilities of those who are not. To treat sick patients, MCOs first have to make it easy for them to access services and second must provide them with appropriate care. Purchasers and members value access and appropriateness.[14] Purchasers also value assessments of disease screening activities, service quality, and encounter outcomes to the extent that they support or embellish information about access and appropriateness.[15] Similarly, purchasers know that to maintain health and functional capacity, MCOs must support prevention of illness and management of health status. Therefore, the two key processes in this step are treating disease and managing health.

Treating Disease

Access. The Institute of Medicine defines access as "the timely use of personal health services to achieve the best possible outcomes."[16(p.4)] In an MCO, access encompasses geographical convenience and availability of providers.

For purchasers and members alike, access is an absolutely critical area. For example, a 1993 study found that 93 percent of Americans considered access to services very important in their choice of a health system, and 76 percent of the same group felt that accessibility might decline given the incentive structure created by capitation.[17] Of related interest, Americans in all demographic categories consistently indicate that they will not accept the waits characteristic of other countries' health systems (up to 6 months for heart surgery in Canada, up to 4 months for a specialist appointment in Britain).[18] Finally, surveys of MCO disenrollees re-

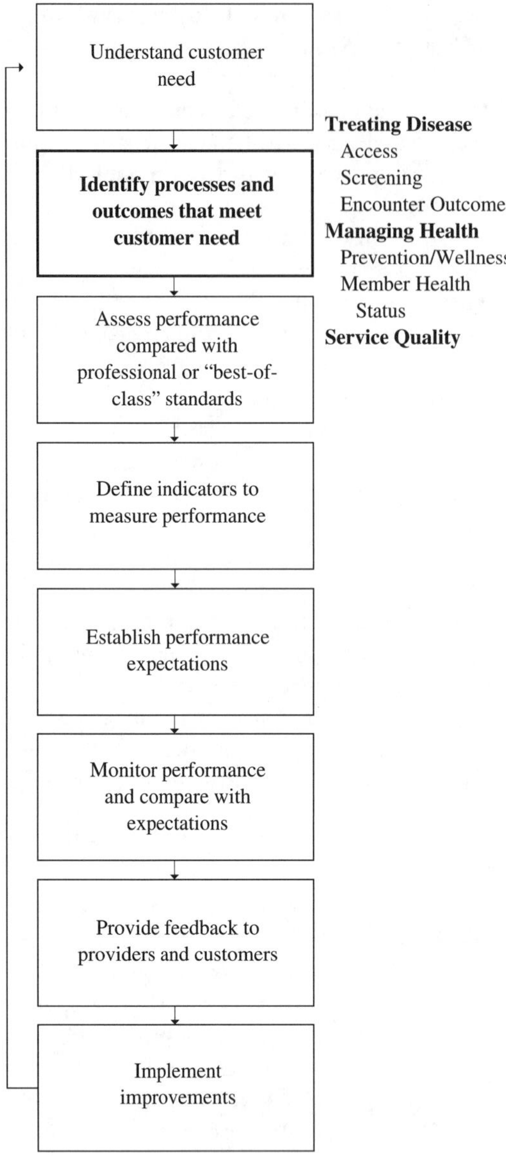

Figure 17–3 Continuous improvement process—meet customer need.

peatedly show that a majority of those who left the MCO of their own volition chose to leave because they were dissatisfied with access to service.

In addition, studies have concluded that communities where people perceive poor access to medical care have higher rates of hospitalization for chronic diseases (asthma, hypertension, chronic obstructive pulmonary disease, congestive heart failure, and diabetes).[19] It has been suggested that improving access to care is more likely to reduce hospitalization rates for chronic disease than changing patients' propensity to seek health care or eliminating variation in physician practice style.[20]

Screening. Disease screening measures assess the MCO's performance in detecting the medical conditions of its membership at an asymptomatic, treatable stage. Familiar examples of disease screening include mammography, Pap smear testing, cholesterol screening, and sigmoidoscopy. Disease screening measures defined as screening rates per eligible population are easy for consumers to understand. The measures, however, are not immune to the controversies of timing of disease screening. In addition, purchasers tend to view screening activities as useful and cost effective even though the evidence to support this is weak. Nevertheless, screening processes are likely to remain important to purchasers.

In the future, outcomes of screening may supersede the quantification of screening in terms of its importance to consumers and purchasers alike. After all, screening does not assess the patient's benefit from early detection. For example, an effectiveness measure in screening breast cancer may someday be two outcome measures—the stage of breast cancer at diagnosis and the 5-year mortality rate for breast cancer—rather than only mammography rates over time.

Encounter outcomes. Encounter outcome measures evaluate the results of specific clinical encounters, such as a hospitalization or an office visit. Included in this category are the traditional assessments of mortality, readmission rates, adverse events, provider empathy, and satisfaction. Traditionally, encounter outcome measures have been confounded by small sample sizes, case mix adjustment issues, and unreliable data collection methods. These problems have made it difficult to compare data across systems or even within an MCO over time. Purchasers are likely to continue asking for encounter outcomes for high-volume clinical conditions. Because of the methodological issues mentioned, however, purchasers are likely to set relatively low performance standards in these areas.

Managing Health

Prevention/wellness. The next set of key processes comprises those associated with prevention of illness. Prevention activities are designed to keep the membership free of disease. Examples of prevention programs include smoking cessation, nutritional counseling, and stress reduction. Measures of prevention include the percentage of eligible patients enrolled in one of the above programs, immunization rates, and first trimester prenatal care visit rates. Such prevention programs assess process performance. As discussed earlier, the effectiveness of such programs is questionable without a link to outcomes. High disenrollment rates make it hard for MCOs to realize long-term benefits from prevention programs. At least in the short term, it appears that consistently poor performance in this area would dampen a purchaser's enthusiasm for a particular MCO.

Member health status. The evaluation of a member's health status may include assessment of functioning in physiological terms (e.g., blood pressure or laboratory tests), physical terms (e.g., activities of daily living), mental or psychological terms (e.g., cognitive skill and affective interaction), social terms (e.g., ability to engage in family work or school), and other health-related quality of life areas (e.g., pain, energy, sleep, and sex).[21] Two purposes are served by health status evaluations. First, members at risk for need of services can be identified before a catastrophic event. Second, a member's health status assessment can serve as an outcome measure for care or treatment received. The recent popularity of health status assessment stems from two ideas. The first is that members' perceptions of their health are both important and easy to obtain.[22] The second is that health systems should be accountable not only for treating disease and managing health, but for enhancing members' well-being as well.

Although it is believed that purchasers will rely heavily on member health status measures in their assessments of MCO quality, the Health Care Advisory Board recently articulated a persuasive countervailing opinion.[23] According to the Advisory Board, health status data are not likely to play a prominent role in MCO selection. The Advisory Board called attention to two facts in presenting its argument. First, member health status is influenced by factors beyond the control of the MCO, including genetic predisposition to illness, sociodemographic factors, dietary and exercise habits, and so forth. Second, most systems exhibit member turnover rates of 10 percent or higher, and this makes it difficult to link health status to activities in any one system. According to the Advisory Board, purchasers are unlikely to hold MCOs accountable for (much less make a decisive negotiating decision in light of) the health status of its members. Only time will tell how much member health status measures will play as a role in MCOs.

Service Quality

Service quality measures evaluate the timeliness, responsiveness, and courtesy with which the MCO serves its members. These attributes are of obvious importance to MCO members. The impact of managed care and the balance of cost and quality will continue to be evaluated. Although there are numerous studies showing high levels of member satisfaction with MCOs, it is worth noting that the results were less than favorable for the MCOs in one recent survey. A total of 2,374 adults were randomly selected and interviewed over an 11-month period. Non-elderly sick persons in managed care plans reported lower out-of-pocket expenses but more problems getting the health service or treatment they or their physicians thought was necessary. The study also found that sick people in managed care plans were more likely to be unhappy with both general and specialist physician care. In addition, managed care enrollees were more likely to report difficulty getting access to specialist care and diagnostic tests and waited longer for medical care. Compared with patients in fee-for-service plans, sick or disabled patients in managed care plans were more likely to complain that their general physician:

- provided medical care that was not correct or appropriate (5 percent fee-for-service patients, 12 percent managed care patients)
- failed to explain what he or she was doing (6 percent fee-for-service patients, 12 percent managed care patients)
- neglected to explain how and when to take prescriptions at home (4 percent fee-for-service patients, 10 percent managed care patients)
- made them wait a long time for an appointment (7 percent fee-for-service patients, 17 percent managed care patients) or a long time in the waiting room (18 percent fee-for-service patients, 26 percent managed care patients)[24]

In addition to these service quality assessments, some MCOs are following their industry counterparts by offering service guarantees for members who are not satisfied with services received during an office visit; for example, qualified member dissatisfiers may result in the repayment of a monthly premium.

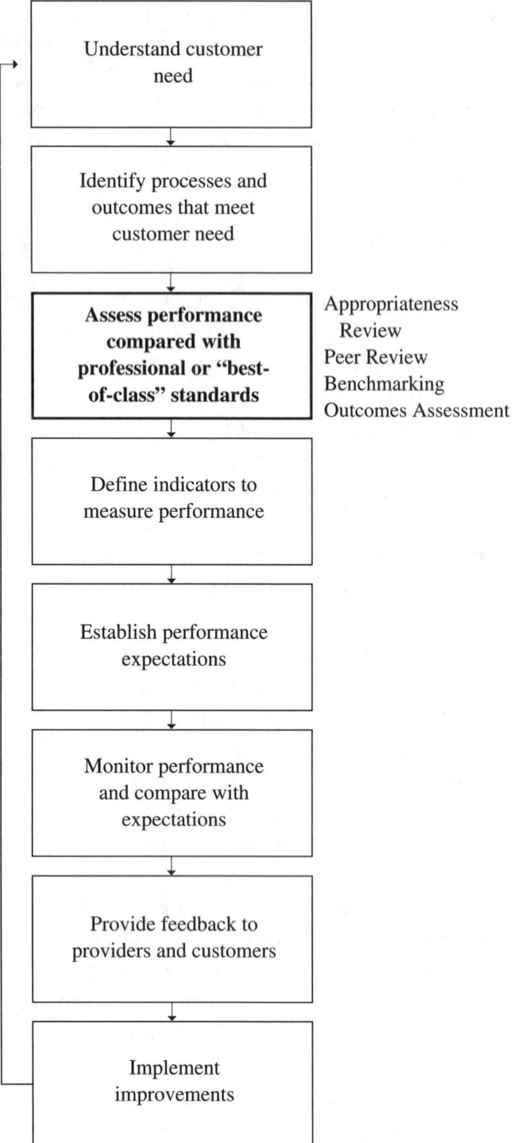

Figure 17–4 Continuous improvement process—compare performance

Assess Performance Compared with Professional or "Best-of-Class" Standards

The third step of the continuous improvement process model (Figure 17–4) is assessing the MCO's performance compared with a professional or "best-of-class" standard. This concept of comparison was discussed earlier. The modern quality management program includes the components of performance assessment as described for appropriateness evaluation and peer review but also includes the processes of benchmarking and outcomes assessment.

Appropriateness Review

As discussed for the traditional quality assurance model, appropriateness indicators evaluate the extent to which the MCO provides necessary care and does not provide unnecessary care in the service location best suited for quality and cost efficiencies. Purchasers understand that they cannot obtain good value from an MCO unless it provides appropriate services, so that these indicators are as important as those for accessibility.

Unfortunately, improving the assessment of appropriateness has been dogged by methodological problems, such as adjusting the data for case mix (discussed later), and the surprising lack of data from controlled trials that would define appropriate care in the first place. This issue affects the evaluation of both overutilization and underutilization of services.

In response to these challenges, the MCO can do two things. First, the MCO can identify minimum performance standards for high-cost diagnoses and use them to select processes having excess utilization. Second, the MCO can demonstrate evidence of consistent success and/or an improvement trend in clinical appropriateness indicators. If these two approaches are employed, purchasers seem inclined to offer MCOs some flexibility in the short run even if some isolated indicators suggest that there may be quality problems.

Peer Review

As discussed previously, peer review involves a comparison of an individual provider's practice against an accepted standard of care. A key difference between peer review in a traditional quality assurance model and that in a modern quality management model is the topic of comparison.

Benchmarking

A third method of assessing and comparing an MCO's performance is benchmarking. Benchmarking was popularized by Robert Camp of Xerox (Rochester, New York) over the last 20 years. Camp and Tweet define benchmarking as "the continuous process of measuring products, services and practices against the company's toughest competitors or those companies renowned as industry leaders."[25(p.229)] Two types of benchmarking may be used by MCOs. First, internal benchmarking identifies internal functions to serve as pilot sites for comparison. This type of benchmarking is particularly useful in newly integrated delivery systems with multiple, diverse component entities.[26] The second type of benchmarking is external or competitive benchmarking. Competitive benchmarking is the comparison of work processes with those of the best competitor and reveals which performance measure levels can be surpassed.[27] The benchmarking process can be applied to service and clinical processes for knowledge of current performance.

Outcomes Assessment

A fourth method for an MCO to assess performance is through outcomes assessment. An outcomes assessment may be performed on the MCO's 10 high-volume or high-cost diagnoses or procedure groups. An outcomes assessment permits the MCO to assess its own performance over time and to identify variation within the MCO. Davies and others have outlined three core activities for an outcomes assessment[28]:

1. Outcomes measurements are "point-in-time" observations.
2. Outcomes monitoring includes the process of repeated measurements over time, which permits causal inferences to be drawn about the observed outcomes.
3. Outcomes management is the application of the information and knowledge gained from outcome assessment to achieve optimal outcomes through improved decision making and delivery.

The purpose of an outcomes assessment is to provide a quantitative comparison among treatment programs, to map the typical course of a chronic disease across a continuum, or to identify variations in the outcome of care as potential markers of process variation.[29]

Define Indicators To Measure Performance

Defining indicators to measure performance is the fourth step of the continuous improvement process model (Figure 17–5). The MCO may apply the quality criteria (structure, process, and outcome) as discussed for the traditional quality assurance model. In addition, it is useful for MCOs to evaluate their process and outcomes by populations of customers served. The MCO quality management matrix (Figure 17–6) is a diagram of how this may occur. A key issue faced by MCOs in indicator definition and analysis is case mix adjustment.

Case mix adjustment is the process to correct data for variations in illness or wellness in patient populations. It is a statistical model that takes into account specific attributes of a patient population (e.g., age, sex, severity of illness, chronic health status, etc.) that are beyond the control of the MCO or health provider.[30] This adjustment is particularly important in comparative analyses between providers or among MCOs.

Case mix adjustment permits fair comparisons among same-population groups because it accounts for preexisting phenomena that may affect the outcome of care. Potentially required variables in a broadly useful risk adjustment system include the following[31]:

- demographic factors
- diagnostic information
- patient-derived health status
- claims-derived health status
- prior use of all services
- prior use of nonelective hospitalization
- prior use of medical procedures

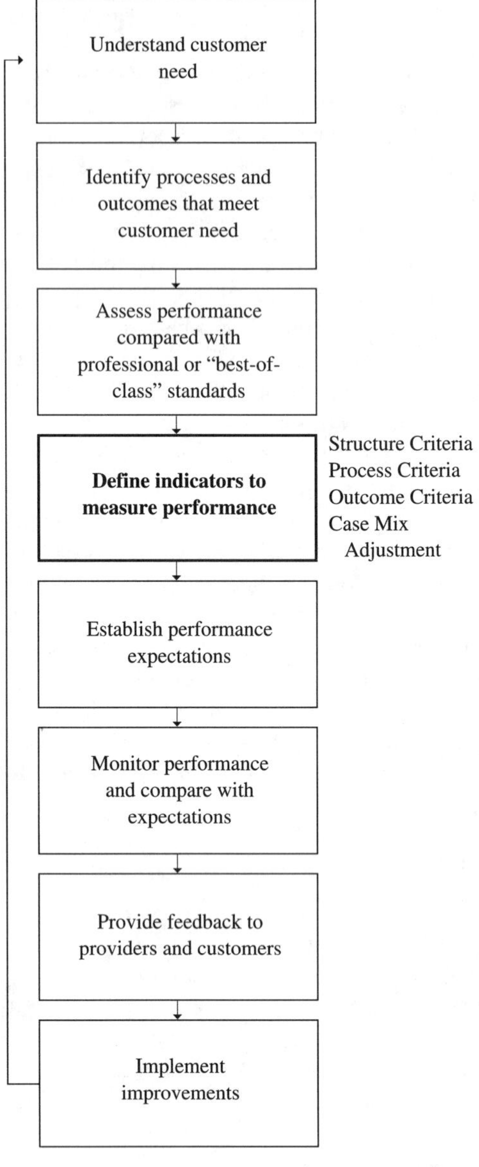

Figure 17–5 Continuous improvement process—measures of performance

Issues of case mix affect the analysis of both inpatient and outpatient care. The problem, however, is more serious for some performance measures than for others. Case mix is important for clinically oriented indicators such as appropriateness and encounter outcomes. It also has a significant impact on assessments of health status, resource use, and member satisfaction. Case mix is not nearly as important for measures of access and prevention and thus these measures should be considered for physician profiles and

Population / Key Function	Access	Appropriateness	Screening	Encounter Outcomes	Prevention	Health Status	Service Quality
	Treatment of Disease				Managing Health		
Primary Care	# of PCPs with open panels # days for routine physical		Mammography Cholesterol		Childhood immunization Adult immunization		Member satisfaction
Senior Care		% seniors with > 7 prescriptions					
Specialty Care							
High Risk OB Care							
Other High-Volume or Special Need Population							

Figure 17–6 Quality management matrix. PCP, primary care physician; OB, obstetrics. *Source:* Adapted from N. Goldfield. Case Mix, Risk Adjustment, Reinsurance, and Health Reform. *Managed Care Quarterly*, Vol. 2, No. 3, p. iv, © 1994, Aspen Publishers, Inc.

report cards. The topic of case mix adjustment exceeds the scope of this chapter; Chapter 19 provides a discussion of this issue.

Establish Performance Expectations

Establishing performance expectations is the fifth step of the continuous improvement process model for an MCO (Figure 17–7). Performance expectations are defined by understanding customer needs (step 1), evaluating the performance of the processes and outcomes designed to meet those needs (step 2), and comparing performance against "best-of-class" standards either internal or external to the MCO (step 3). Purchasers have had an influence on establishing performance expectations. In 1990, Digital Corporation identified priority areas where quality improvement efforts might promote better outcomes. Digital began this effort with the development of health maintenance organization (HMO) standards and by setting expectations in the areas of utilization management, access, quality assurance, mental health services, data capabilities, and financial performance.[32] Digital examined its health care costs and used weightings that drew on multiple data sources to identify priority areas to be considered by the participating plans. Clinical indicators selected for performance measurement and improvement included mental health inpatient readmissions and inpatient days per patient, cesarean section rates, prenatal care in the first trimester, screening mammography rates, asthma inpatient admissions, and blood pressure screenings. The results from these measurements were not meant to be used punitively but rather enabled Digital to gauge the participating managed care plans in terms of their success in managing specific aspects of health care.

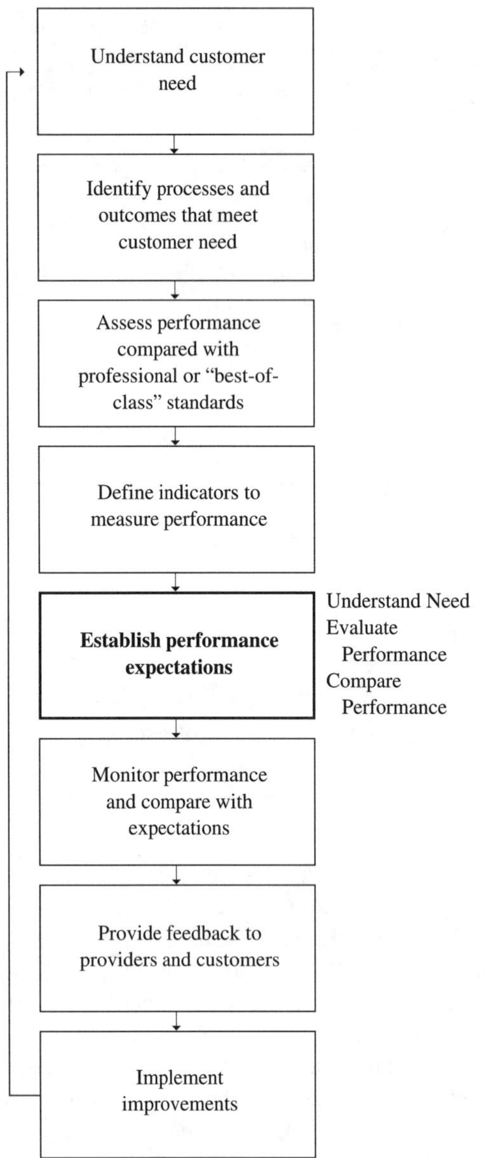

Figure 17–7 Continuous improvement process—establish expectations

Monitor Performance and Compare with Expectations

Following established expectations, the sixth step is the actual monitoring of performance and comparison with expectations. The frequency of monitoring is determined by the indicators the MCO has selected to measure performance. An MCO can compare its performance against its own over time and against other MCOs if the same indicator definitions are used.

Provide Feedback to Providers and Customers

The seventh step of the continuous improvement process model (Figure 17–8) is providing feedback. Two methods of feedback are discussed here: profiling assesses the performance of individual providers, and report cards assess overall MCO performance.

Profiling

Profiling focuses on the patterns of an individual provider's care rather than that provider's specific clinical decisions (see Chapter 19). The practice pattern of an individual provider—hospital or physician—is expressed as a rate or a measure of resource use during a defined period and for a defined population.[33] The resulting profile can then be compared against a peer group or a standard. MCOs are using profiling to measure providers' performance, to guide quality improvement efforts, and to select providers for managed care networks.[34]

The Physician Payment Review Commission (PPRC) has suggested several guidelines for effective physician profiling.[35] According to the PPRC, profiles first must be analyzed for a well-defined population. Second, they must include a sufficient number of observations to ensure that differences are not due to chance. Third, they should include adjustments for case mix. Finally, profiles must be analyzed for a small enough organizational unit that the parties involved can be responsible for the results and take the necessary courses of action for improvement. A successful profiling system defines an episode of care, accounts for severity of illness and comorbidities, and identifies all the resources used per episode of care.[36] Most profiling systems rely heavily on standard billing information, such as diagnosis-related groups,

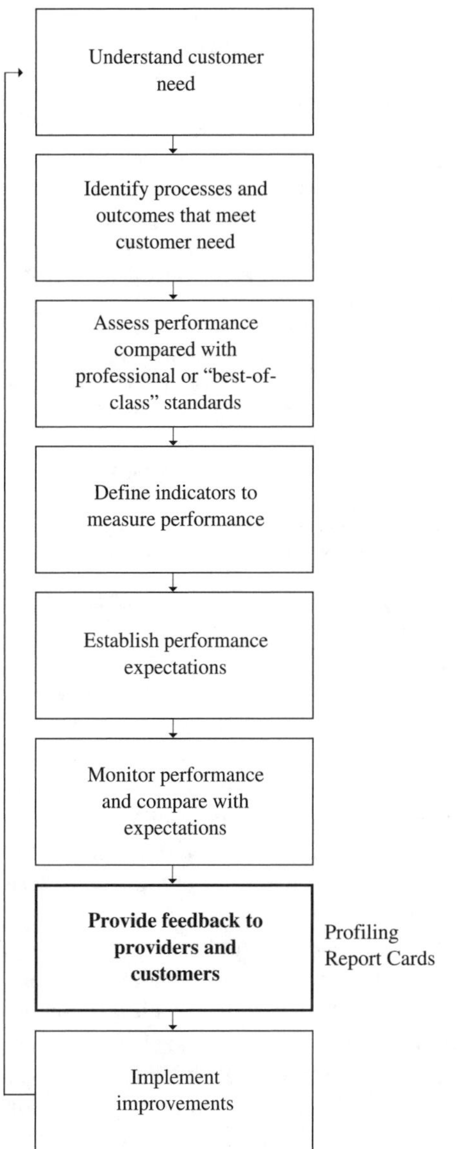

Figure 17–8 Continuous improvement process—feedback

categories in the tenth revision of the *International Classification of Disease*, and current procedural terminology codes.

Examples of measures used in provider profiling include average wait time to schedule a routine physical, number of hospital admissions, number of referrals out of network, number of emergency department visits, member satisfaction, percentage compliance with the MCO's clinical practice guidelines, and, if applicable, the percentage of children receiving appropriate immunizations and the cesarean section rate. Profiling is discussed further in Chapter 19.

Report Cards

Report cards have become a popular method of conveying performance within an individual MCO with multiple geographic sites or across many diverse MCOs. The purpose of a report card is to provide customers (purchasers and consumers) with comparable quality and cost information in a common language for the purpose of selecting a health plan. Purchasers have formed groups across the country to facilitate the development of a standardized approach to health plan performance measurement. For example, in 1993, 27 corporate and government purchasers of health care formed the Massachusetts Health Care Purchaser Group. The group challenged the health plans in Massachusetts to submit data on six clinical indicators: mammography screening, prenatal care, cesarean section rate, hypertension screening, asthma admission rate, and mental health admissions after an inpatient stay[37] (Exhibit 17–4). Each health plan was compared with the clinically significant average range, and a consumer-friendly pie chart graphic was used to summarize performance (Figure 17–9).

The NCQA, a nonprofit group that accredits HMOs, organized a national test pilot report card demonstration for 21 health plans representing 9.6 million enrollees. The NCQA judged the plans on a subset of the Health Plan Employer Data and Information Set (HEDIS; see Chapter 20) measures: standard measures of quality, member satisfaction, membership enrollment, and resource utilization measures.

The report card concept is equally valuable when applied to internal customers of the MCO. Key quality measures can be tracked, trended, and utilized for strategic quality planning and to

Exhibit 17–4 Massachusetts Health Care Purchaser Group Clinical Indicators

Mammography Screening Rate:	Percentage of members aged 52–64 who were continuously enrolled in the plan during 1991 and 1992 who received mammograms.
Hypertension Screening Rate:	Percentage of members aged 52–64 who were continuously enrolled in the plan in 1991 and 1992 who were screened for high blood pressure.
Asthma Admission Rate:	The number of hospital admissions for asthmatics of both sexes between the ages of 1 and 19 and ages 20 and 64 divided by the number of enrollees in the plan of the same age cohorts over a 1-year period.
Prenatal Care Rate:	The percentage of pregnancies among women who delivered babies and who were continuously enrolled for 7 months in 1992 for which prenatal care was received during the first trimester of pregnancy.
Cesarean Section Rate:	The percentage of all deliveries in 1992 that were performed by cesarean section.
Mental Health Readmission Rate:	Males and females aged 18–64 years continuously enrolled in a given health plan for the previous 2 years, and hospitalized with a discharge date in the second year for psychiatric care. There were two measures: the average number of individual hospital admissions per patient, and the average number of mental health hospital days per patient for all hospital admissions.

Source: © *Journal on Quality Improvement*. Oakbrook Terrace, IL: Joint Commission on Accreditation of Healthcare Organizations, 1995, p. 169. Reprinted with permission.

assess the effectiveness of improvement efforts. For example, in 1993, the northern California region of Kaiser Permanente released a self-assessment that it referred to as its report card.[38] This report card is organized into seven categories: childhood health, maternal care, cardiovascular disease, cancer, common surgical procedures, other adult health, and mental health/substance abuse. In designing categories, developers selected areas that affected many enrollees and tried to depict care from the patient's perspective (i.e., what would the patient need during the course of his or her illness?) The report card assessed enrollee satisfaction as a separate entity.

The benefits of the report card movement include the stimulus for MCOs to build the capacity to produce performance information and strengthen data quality. Public disclosure of performance information also lends itself to plan, provider, and hospital accountability. The main limitation of the report card movement continues to be measurement. Although the NCQA and HEDIS have made moves to standardize measurement, there continues to be variation in measurement, coding, and clinical classification. Additionally, there is variation in the administrative source datasets that plans use to obtain their measurements. Risk adjustment and a broader clinical focus are opportunities for improvement. Finally, no conclusion can be drawn about processes or outcomes that are not assessed by the report card measurements.

Implement Improvements

The eighth step of the continuous improvement process model (Figure 17–10) is implementation of improvements. Current strategies employed by MCOs as tools to improve health

	Provider															
	5	8	14	13	2	11	9	6	16	1	10	15	3	4	7	12
Mammography	◑	○	●	◔	○	◕	◑		●	◑		◑	◑	◔	◕	◑
Prenatal Care: NonMedicaid	◑	◑	◑	○	◑	◔	○	◑	●	◑		◑	◑	◔	◑	◑
Medicaid	◑			○	●	◑				◕	◕	◑		◑		
C-Section: NonMedicaid	◑	◑	◑	○	◑	◑	◑	◑	◕	◔		◑	◑	◕	◑	◑
Medicaid	◑			◑	◑					◑	◑	◔	◑	◑		
Hypertension	◕	◑	◔	◑	◑	◑				◑			◑	◑	◑	
Asthma-Adult: NonMedicaid	●	◑	◑		◑	○	◕	◔	○	○		◑	●	●	◑	
Medicaid					◔	◔					●	●	●			
Asthma-Child: NonMedicaid	●	○	◑	◑	●	○	○	○	○	○		●	●	●	◑	
Medicaid	◑		◑	◑	◕	◑					●	●		◑		
Mental Health: Admissions (0 in 1991)	◑	◑	◑	◑	◑	○	◑		◑	◑		◑	◑	◕		◔
(> 0 in 1991)	○		◑		◔	◕			◑				◔	◑		
Mental Health: Days (0 in 1991)	◔	◑	◕	◔	◕	◔	○		●			○	◑	◑		
(> 0 in 1991)	◑		◑	◑	◕	◕	○		●			○	◑	◑		

Legend
○ Better than the average range
◔ Better than the mean, but within the average range
◑ Within the average range
◕ Worse than the mean, but within the average range
● Worse than the average range

Figure 17–9 Massachusetts Health Care Purchaser Group 1992 Summary Table. *Source: Journal on Quality Improvement.* Oakbrook Terrace, IL: Joint Commission on Accreditation of Healthcare Organizations, 1995, p. 171. Reprinted with permission.

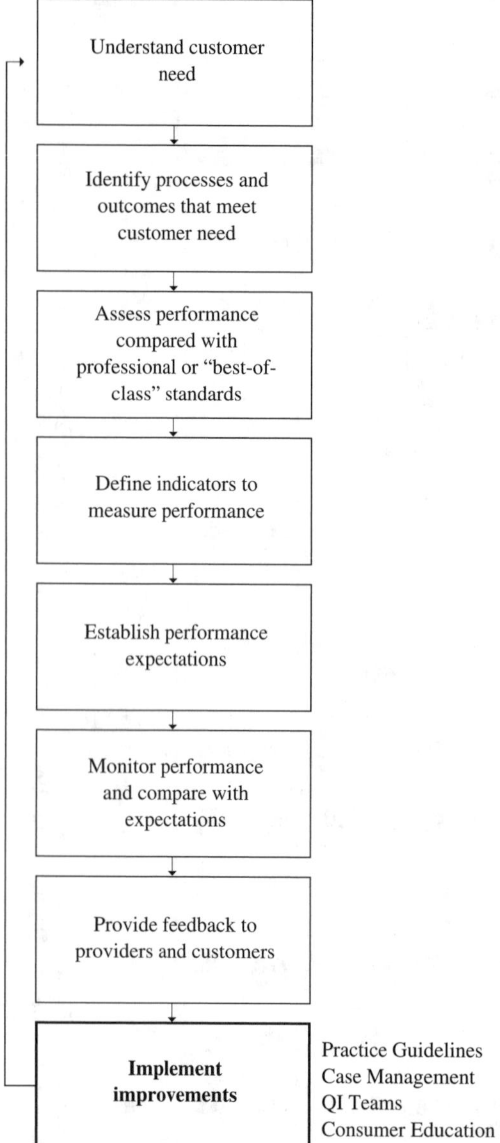

Figure 17–10 Continuous improvement process—implement improvements. QI, quality improvement.

care delivery processes and outcomes are practice guidelines, case management, improvement teams, and consumer education.

Practice Guidelines

Clinical practice guidelines are systematically developed statements to assist practitioners and patients in making decisions about appropriate health care for specific clinical circumstances. Guidelines offer an opportunity to improve health care delivery processes by reducing unwanted variation. An appointed committee of the Institute of Medicine recommended the following attributes of guideline design[39]:

- *Validity:* Practice guidelines are deemed valid if they lead to the health and cost outcomes projected for them.
- *Reliability/reproducibility:* If given the same evidence and development methods, another set of experts would come up with the same recommendations and the guidelines are interpreted and applied consistently across providers.
- *Clinical applicability:* Guidelines should apply to a clearly defined patient population.
- *Clinical flexibility:* Guidelines should recognize the generally anticipated exceptions to the recommendations proposed.
- *Multidisciplinary process:* Representatives of key disciplines involved in the process of care should participate in the guideline development process.
- *Scheduled review:* Guideline evaluation should be planned in advance and occur at a frequency that reflects the evolution of clinical evidence for the guideline topic.
- *Documentation:* Detailed summaries of the guideline development process should be maintained that reflect the procedures followed, the participants involved, the evidence and analytical methods employed, and the assumptions and rationales accepted.

In addition to a development process, guideline programs also have an implementation process. The first step in designing an implementation strategy for clinical guidelines is to identify the forces driving and restraining clinical practice change.[40] Thus, an MCO may want to convene a group of local content experts along with its own medical leadership to initiate guideline planning and adoption. An effective implementation team strengthens the driving forces for the guideline and weakens the restraining forces for a given clinical practice change. Performance assessment is measured on two levels. First, the gap between prior and optimal practice is measured to assess the degree of implementation. Second, feedback may given to providers to reinforce the change in clinical practice. As an example, the following is a summary of United HealthCare's guideline implementation process[41]:

1. Prioritize your objectives.
   - Select guidelines that:
   —are likely to be accepted by physicians
   —have a cost impact for the health plan
   —affect a quality issue for patients
   —affect a large population
   —fulfill a regulatory issue
2. Document the need to change.
3. Look for guideline credibility.
4. Get the word out.
5. Use timely feedback to physicians.
6. Remember, you are dealing with a system.

Practice guidelines are not without limitations. Studies have shown that traditional methods of guideline dissemination have not resulted in significant changes in practice.[42,43] Frequently, guidelines are not designed to be implemented directly into practice. This has a particular impact in preferred provider organizations (PPOs) and individual practice associations (IPAs), where there are multiple and varied processes. An MCO can facilitate the implementation of guidelines through the corresponding development of algorithms, summaries, laminated cards, medical record tools, and reminder systems. Second, as mentioned earlier in this chapter, meeting specifications does not necessarily result in constant improvement but rather may maintain ensuring the status quo.[44] Guidelines should be designed with flexibility to encourage improvement and innovation.

Clinical pathways and protocols are discussed in detail in *The Managed Health Care Handbook, Third Edition.*

Case Management

Case management is a model of patient care delivery that restructures and streamlines the clinical production process so that it is outcome based.[45] Case management, like practice guidelines, can reduce unwanted variation. As a model, case management mobilizes, monitors, and rationalizes the resources a patient uses over the course of an illness. In doing so, case management aims at a controlled balance between quality and cost.[46]

Case management plays an integral part in an MCO's quality management program. First, a case manager is an integral part of the health care team and participates in establishing an individualized treatment plan with the member, physician, and MCO. Second, case management can be applied to the identification of members at risk for high-dollar, catastrophic illness. After identification of these members, case managers monitor their care on an ongoing basis to assess whether quality care is being provided in an appropriate setting. The case manager plays an important role as a resource manager for the MCO. Third, case managers can evaluate the implementation and effectiveness of practice guidelines.

To date, little evidence exists regarding the long-term effectiveness of case management in MCOs or integrated delivery systems. The effectiveness of case management, however, has been studied in preventive services and community mental health. A number of studies have shown that maternity care coordination and preventive services improve child health and are cost effective but are underused.[47–54] Replicated findings suggest that case management during pregnancy increases infant birthweight.[55,56] Other studies have found that community mental health clients who received case management used more community services than those not receiving case management.[57–61] This finding has led researchers to speculate that case management of clients' vocational, educational, housing, social, recreational, and financial needs may improve their quality of life, which consequently reduces their need for rehospitalization.[62,63] These effectiveness evaluations are important to MCOs because the performance of these key functions (prenatal care and mental health care management) is a measure used for evaluation by purchasers in HEDIS.

Large case management is discussed in detail in *The Managed Health Care Handbook, Third Edition*.

Quality Improvement Teams

A third tool employed by MCOs to facilitate improvement of health care delivery is the quality improvement team. MCOs are complex organizations that span job functions and geography. The tasks required to produce the outputs of a quality management program require diverse talents and skill sets. The variety of network configurations (e.g., staff model HMO, PPO, and IPA) requires a method to incorporate provider input from a variety of perspectives. Quality improvement teams offer an alternative in an environment where administrative expense must be controlled and minimized. Teams outperform individuals acting alone or in larger organizational groupings, especially when performance requires multiple skills, judgments, and experiences.[64]

There are several well-known phenomena that explain why teams perform well. First, the broader skill mix and know-how facilitate the team's response to multifaceted challenges, such as innovations, quality, and customer service. Second, in developing clear goals and approaches to problem solving, teams can support real-time resolution and initiative. Finally, teams provide a unique social dimension that enhances the economic and administrative aspects of work. By surmounting barriers to collective performance, team members build trust and confidence in each other's capabilities. This supports the pursuit of team purpose above and beyond individual or functional agendas.[65]

How can teams be applied to quality management in an MCO? Examples include a team consisting of MCO leaders, purchasers, members, and providers setting the evaluation and improvement agendas for the MCO by prioritizing goals. Alternately, a cross functional team may evaluate the disease- or population-specific needs of a member group and test interventions, such as practice guidelines, for care improvement. Finally a team could form to design an MCO's strategy to meet accreditation requirements. Teams can be chartered to address most issues faced by an MCO as long as an explicit purpose and a defined time frame for completion have been identified.

Consumer Education

Many MCOs' quality management programs include evaluation of the effectiveness of consumer education. Consumer education is targeted at beneficiaries so that they can become effective health care consumers and participate in meeting the aforementioned needs of treating disease and managing health. Examples of consumer education utilized by MCOs include telephone resource lines, health risk appraisals, worksite-based consumer education programs, and consumer health education materials. Many MCOs have developed and provide members with self-care guidelines for preventing illness and treating common complaints at the time of enrollment. These topics are also discussed in Chapter 13.

SETTING THE IMPROVEMENT AGENDA

After the implementation of step 8, the MCO must evaluate whether the improvements actually made a change and met customer need. If not, the cycle begins again with step 1. If improvements did occur and customer needs were met, the cycle can begin again for new or unaddressed customer needs.

How can an MCO design such a cycle? MCOs have limited resources with which to assess and improve performance, and strategic decisions must be made to target resources effectively. An MCO's leadership group may begin the cycle of improvement by applying the following criteria:

1. Identify which customer need is being addressed by the proposed project.
2. Evaluate the strength of the evidence for the need to improve.
3. Assess the probability that there will be a measurable impact.
4. Determine the likelihood of success.
5. Identify the immediacy of impact in meeting the customer's need.

CONCLUSION

Consumers and purchasers of health care are demanding quality at a reasonable price. To address this need, a quality management program in a managed care setting must be designed to reflect complex delivery systems and diverse customer groups. Success in managing cost and optimizing health outcomes begins with an understanding of customer needs, assessment of performance to meet those needs, and continuous improvement. Attention focused on the provision of appropriate care in an appropriate setting will continue to shape the quality resource programs in MCOs. The need to assess the impact of these shifts of care from one segment of the delivery system to another will continue to grow as the shifts progress.

As a part of a health delivery system, MCOs have an opportunity to affect the health status of populations through their actions and thus have a responsibility to assess and measure these effects. To achieve these goals, an MCO must have a focused aim and a process for achievement, such as that summarized in Figure 17–11. This eight-step process can be implemented on a diverse scale, such as in an IPA or network model, or at a staff model site. Improvement opportunities have many degrees of success in diverse organizations, as identified in Figure 17–12. A variety of methods—practice guidelines, case management, outcomes management, and others—have been introduced and, no doubt, will continue to evolve.

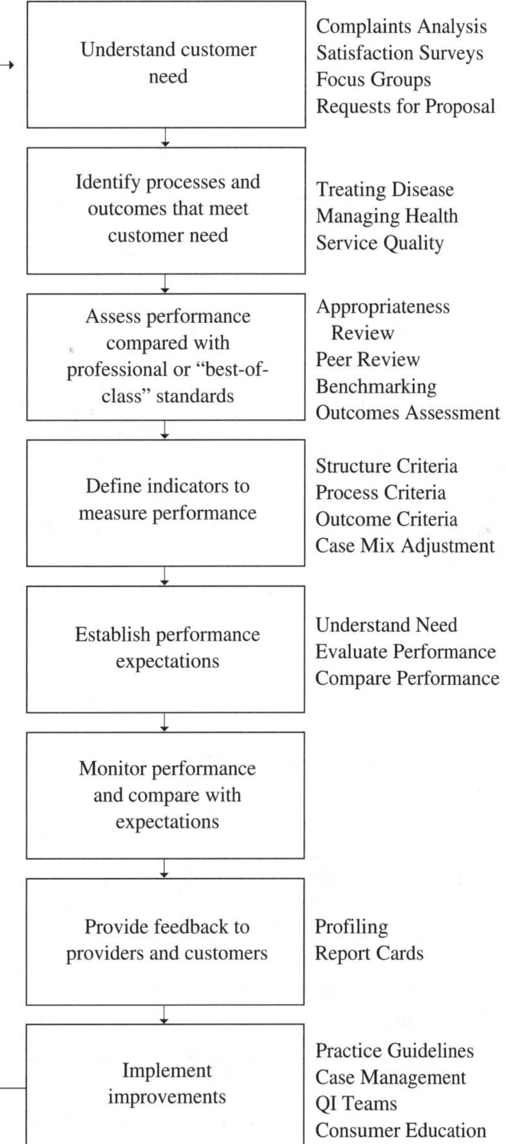

Figure 17–11 Continuous improvement process—summary. QI, quality improvement.

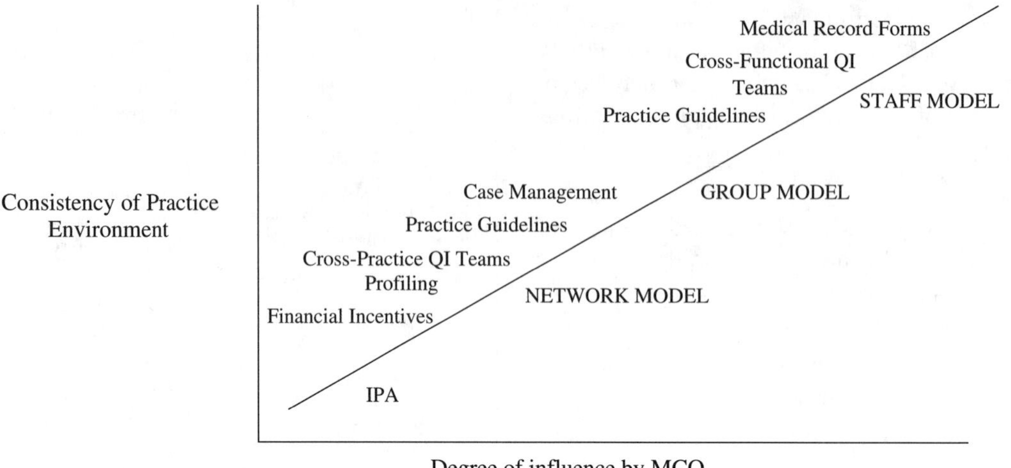

Figure 17–12 Quality management tools for a variety of MCOs. QI, quality improvement.

Study Questions

1. Describe the three criteria Donebedian developed to assess quality and identify circumstances in which they can be applied.
2. What are the key components of a quality management program? What key features distinguish a quality management program from a traditional quality assurance program?
3. Who are the customers of managed care?
4. How can managed care organizations understand cusotmer need?
5. What are the key functions of a managed care organization? How can their performance be evaluated? How can this performance be improved?

REFERENCES AND NOTES

1. A. Donabedian, *Exploration in Quality Assessment and Monitoring: The Definition of Quality and Approaches to Its Assessment*, Vol. 1 (Ann Arbor, Mich.: Health Administration Press, 1980).
2. S.M. Shortell and J.P. LoGerfo, Hospital Medical Staff Organization and Quality of Care: Results from Myocardial Infarction and Appendectomy, *Medical Care* 19 (1981): 1041–1056.
3. M. Walton, "Improve Constantly and Forever the System of Production and Service," in *The Deming Management Method* (New York, N.Y.: Putnam, 1986), 66–67.
4. R.L. Goldman, The Reliability of Peer Assessments of Quality of Care, *Journal of the American Medical Association* 267 (1992): 958–960.
5. R.D. Moen and T.W. Nolan, Process Improvement, *Quality Progress* 9 (1987): 62–68.
6. G.J. Langley, et al., The Foundation of Improvement, *Quality Progress* 6 (1994): 81–86.
7. J. Juran and F. Gyrna, "Understanding Customer Need," in *Quality Planning and Analysis*, 3d ed. (New York, N.Y.: McGraw-Hill, 1993), 240–252.
8. Juran and Gyrna, "Understanding Customer Need," 241.
9. C.W. Nelson and J. Niederberger, Patient Satisfaction Surveys: An Opportunity for Total Quality Improvement, *Hospital Health Service Adminstration* 35 (1990): 409–427.
10. Juran and Gyrna, "Understanding Customer Need," 243.

11. C. Sennet, et al., Performance-Based Hospital Contracting for Quality Improvement, *Joint Commission Journal on Quality Improvement* 9 (1993): 374–383.
12. Sennet, et al., Performance-Based Hospital Contracting, 380.
13. Juran and Gyrna, "Understanding Customer Need," 241.
14. Health Care Advisory Board, *Next Generation of Outcomes Tracking* (Washington, D.C.: Health Care Advisory Board, 1994), 1–57.
15. Health Care Advisory Board, *Next Generation of Outcomes Tracking.*
16. M. Millman, ed., *Access to Health Care in America: Institute of Medicine (U.S.) Committee on Monitoring Access to Personal Health Services* (Washington, D.C.: National Academy Press, 1993), 4.
17. What about Quality of Care?, *PR Newswire* (14 September 1993): 3–6.
18. R.B. Alta, Canadian Way: Universal, But Not Immediate Access, *Modern Healthcare* 6 (1989): 36.
19. A. B. Bindman, et al., Preventable Hospitalization Rates and Access to Health Care, *Journal of the American Medical Association* 274 (1995): 305–311.
20. Bindman, et al., Preventable Hospitalization Rates, 305.
21. P.B. Batalden, et al. Linking Outcomes Measurement to Continual Improvement: The Serial "V" Way of Thinking about Improving Clinical Care, *Joint Commission Journal on Quality Improvement* 20 (1994): 167–180.
22. E.C. Nelson, et al., Patient-Based Quality Measurement Systems, *Quality Management in Health Care* 2 (1993): 18–30.
23. Health Care Advisory Board, *Next Generation of Outcomes Tracking.*
24. Robert Wood Johnson Foundation, *Sick People in Managed Care Have Difficulty Getting Services and Treatment* (Princeton, N.J.: Robert Wood Johnson Foundation, 1995).
25. R.L. Camp and A.G. Tweet, Benchmarking Applied to Health Care, *Joint Commission Journal on Quality Improvement* 20 (1994): 229–238.
26. Camp and Tweet, Benchmarking Applied to Health Care, 230.
27. Camp and Tweet, Benchmarking Applied to Health Care, 230.
28. A.R. Davies, et al., Outcomes Assessment in Clinical Settings: A Consensus Statement on Principles and Best Practices in Project Management, *Joint Commission Journal on Quality Improvement* 20 (1994): 6–16.
29. Davies, et al., Outcomes Assessment in Clinical Settings, 11.
30. M. Pine and D.L. Harper, Designing and Using Case Mix Indices, *Managed Care Quarterly* 2 (1994): 1–11.
31. N. Goldfield, Case Mix, Risk Adjustment, Reinsurance, and Health Reform, *Managed Care Quarterly*, 2 (1994): iv.
32. M.A. Bloomberg, et al., Development of Indicators for Performance Measurement and Improvement: An HMO/Purchaser Collaborative Effort, *Joint Commission Journal on Quality Improvement* 19 (1993): 586–595.
33. P.R. Lee, et al., Managed Care: Provider Profiling, *Journal of Insurance Medicine* 24 (1992): 179–181.
34. L.M. Walker, Can a Computer Tell How Good a Doctor You Are?, *Medical Economics* 71 (1994): 136–147.
35. Physician Payment Review Commission (PPRC), *Conference on Profiling* (Washington, D.C.: PPRC, 1992).
36. Walker, Can a Computer Tell?, 138.
37. H. Jordan, et al., Reporting and Using Health Plan Performance Information in Massachusetts, *Joint Commission Journal on Quality Improvement* 21 (1995): 167–177.
38. Executive Director's Office, Kaiser Permanente Medical Group, *Reporting on Quality KPMG Forum* (Oakland, Calif.: Kaiser Permanente Medical Group, 1993), 1–16.
39. Institute of Medicine, Committee to Advise the Public Health Service on Clinical Practice Guidelines, *Clinical Practice Guidelines: Directions for a New Program* (Washington, D.C.: National Academy Press, 1990).
40. M.R. Handley, et al., An Evidence-Based Approach to Evaluating and Improving Clinical Practice: Implementing Practice Guidelines, *HMO Practice* 8 (1994): 75–83.
41. L.N. Newcomber, Six Pointers for Implementing Guidelines, *Healthcare Forum Journal* (July/August 1994): 31–33.
42. J. Kosecoff, et al., Effects of a National Institutes of Health Consensus Development Program on Physician Practice, *Journal of the American Medical Association* 258 (1987): 2708–2713.
43. J. Lomas, et al., Do Practice Guidelines Guide Practice: The Effect of a Consensus Statement on the Practice of Physicians, *New England Journal of Medicine* 321 (1989): 1306–1311.
44. Walton, "Improve Constantly and Forever," 67.
45. K. Zander, Nursing Case Management: Strategic Management of Cost and Quality Outcomes, *Journal of Nursing Adminstration* 18 (1988): 23–30.
46. K.K. Giullano and C.E. Poirier, Nursing Case Management: Critical Pathways to Desirable Outcomes, *Nursing Management* 22 (1991): 52–55.
47. S.L. Gortmaker, The Effects of Prenatal Care upon the Health of the Newborn, *American Journal of Public Health* 69 (1979): 653–660.

48. J.A. Showstack, et al., Factors Associated with Birth Weight: An Exploration of the Roles of Prenatal Care and Length of Gestation, *American Journal of Public Health* 74 (1984): 1003–1008.
49. D.R. Cohen and J.B. Henderson, *Health, Prevention, and Economics* (New York: Oxford University Press, 1988).
50. R. Currier, Is Early and Periodic Screening, Diagnosis and Treatment (EPSDT) Worthwhile?, *International Journal of Rehabilitation Research* 2 (1979): 508–509.
51. P.H. Irwin and R. Conroy-Hughes, EPSDT Impact on Health Status: Estimates Based on Secondary Analysis of Administratively Generated Data, *Medical Care* 20 (1982): 216–234.
52. W.J. Kelle, Study of Selected Outcomes of the Early and Periodic Screening, Diagnosis, and Treatment Program in Michigan, *Public Health Reports* 98 (1983): 110–119.
53. W.L. Manning, The EPSDT Program: A Progress Report, *Indiana Medicine* 78 (1985): 320–322.
54. J.S. Reis, et al., A Synopsis of Federally Sponsored Preventive Child Health, *Journal of Community Health* 9 (1984): 222–239.
55. C.C. Korenbrot, et al., Birth Weight Outcomes in a Teenage Pregnancy Case Management Project, *Journal of Adolescent Health Care* 10 (1989): 97–104.
56. P.A. Buescher, et al., An Evaluation of the Impact of Maternity Care Coordination on Medicaid Birth Outcomes in North Carolina, *American Journal of Public Health* 81 (1991): 1625–1629.
57. D.A. Bigelow and D.J. Young, Effectiveness of a Case Management Program, *Community Mental Health Journal* 27 (1991): 115–123.
58. A. Borland, et al., Outcomes of Five Years of Continuous Intensive Case Management, *Hospital Community Psychiatry* 40 (1989): 369–376.
59. J.L. Franklin, et al., An Evaluation of Case Management, *American Journal of Public Health* 77 (1987): 674–678.
60. P.N. Goering, et al., What Difference Does Case Management Make?, *Hospital Community Psychiatry* 39 (1988): 272–276.
61. J. McRae, et al., What Happens to Patients after Five Years of Intensive Case Management Stops?, *Hospital Community Psychiatry* 41 (1990): 175–180.
62. Bigelow and Young, Effectiveness of a Case Management Program.
63. Goering, et al., What Difference Does Case Management Make?
64. J.R. Katzenbach and D.K. Smith, *The Wisdom of Teams. Creating the High Performance Organization* (Boston, Mass.: Harvard University Press, 1993), 9.
65. Katzenbach and Smith, *The Wisdom of Teams*, 18.

SUGGESTED READING

Books

Couch, J.B. (ed.). 1991. *Health Care Quality Management for the 21st Century*. Tampa, Fla.: American College of Medical Quality and the American College of Physician Executives.

The Deming Management Method. 1986. New York, N.Y.: Putnam.

Juran, J.M., and Gyrna, F.M. 1993. *Quality Planning and Analysis*. New York, N.Y.: McGraw-Hill.

Goldfield, N., Pine, M., and Pine, J. 1992. *Measuring and Managing Health Care Quality: Procedures, Techniques, and Protocols*. Gaithersburg, Md.: Aspen.

Katzenbach, J.R., and Smith, D.K. 1993. *The Wisdom of Teams: Creating the High Performance Organization*. Boston, Mass.: Harvard University Press.

Senge, Peter, 1993. *The Fifth Discipline: The Art and Practice of the Learning Organization.*

Senge, Peter, and Kleiner, Art. 1994. *The Fifth Discipline Fieldbook.*

Youngs, M.T. and Wingerson, L. 1995. *The 1996 Medical Outcomes and Guidelines Sourcebook*. New York, N.Y.: Faulkner & Gray.

Journals

Joint Commission Journal on Quality Improvement. Joint Commission on Accreditation of Healthcare Organizations, One Renaissance Blvd., Oakbrook Terrace, IL 60181.

Quality Management in Health Care. Aspen Publishers, Inc., 200 Orchard Ridge Dr., Gaithersburg, MD 20878.

Newsletter

Eye on Improvement. Institute for Healthcare Improvement, P.O. Box 38100, Cleveland, OH 44138-0100.

Chapter 18

Changing Provider Behavior in Managed Care Plans

Peter R. Kongstvedt

Study Objectives

- Understand the inherent difficulties in modifying physician behavior
- Understand general approaches to modifying physician behavior
- Understand programmatic and specific approaches to modifying physician behavior, and the strengths and weaknesses of these approaches
- Understand discipline and sanctioning as applied to physicians

The practice behavior of physicians in a managed care organization (MCO) is the most important element in controlling cost and quality. As mentioned in Chapters 6 and 7, this process begins at the front door. Selecting physicians who already practice high-quality, cost-effective medicine is the best way to achieve success, although profiling physicians, as discussed in Chapter 19, is no easy task. Even in the best of worlds, however, one cannot be assured that every physician participating in the plan will be solid gold, and realities of marketing and delivery system needs dictate that adequate geographic coverage be present, even when that means accepting some B players rather than all A players.

The best contractual arrangements in the world will be of little value if there are poor utilization patterns or a lack of cooperation with plan policies and procedures. There will be some physicians in the medical community who will not modify their practice behavior. There will also be some physicians who are frankly hostile and some whom, for various reasons, you will not want participating in your plan regardless of how friendly or cooperative they are. The majority of physicians, however, will want to cooperate and be valued participants.

Given these realities, the purpose of this chapter is to present some of the issues involved in modifying the practice behavior of those participating physicians who can and will work with the plan. Financial incentives are clearly a useful method of aligning financial and behavioral goals and are discussed separately in Chapters 6, 8, and 9; nonfinancial approaches are the topic of this chapter.[1,2]

INHERENT DIFFICULTIES IN MODIFYING PHYSICIAN BEHAVIOR

Physicians are professionals with an inordinately large set of built-in biases. This is due to their training, the current environment of medical practice, and the types of pressures now being brought to bear upon them. There is also great heterogeneity in attitudes and prior training in cost containment.[3] None of these issues is unique to the medical profession, but their combination and depth make for a number of inherent difficulties in changing behavior.

What follows is a brief discussion of some of the more important issues. It is wise for managers to be sensitive to these issues, although that does not mean that they should fail to apply proper management and control techniques.

Strong Autonomy and Control Needs

There is perhaps no more emotionally charged issue than autonomy and control. Physicians are trained to function in an autonomous way, to stand up for themselves, and to be the authority. It is difficult for them to accept a role in which another entity has control over their professional activities, whether it is managed care, peer review, or practice guidelines.[4,5] Because of that, physicians participating in MCOs often feel antagonistic when they perceive that their control has been lost or lessened. By definition, managed care introduces elements of management control into the arena of health care delivery, control that clearly reduces the physician's autonomy. In one large study, physicians who entered into contracts with health maintenance organizations (HMOs) expected lower earnings, lower quality of care, and lessened autonomy; neither earnings nor quality declined, but there remained a general perception that physician autonomy did decline.[6] In a different study, physicians maintained a mildly negative attitude toward practicing medicine in an open panel HMO setting, yet their perceived negative attitudes regarding autonomy and income were not supported by actual facts abut their practice when they were asked specific questions about these issues.[7] At least one other study, however, has shown that practicing under managed care does not produce a uniformly lower level of satisfaction.[8]

There has been an increase in the amount of external control over the years. HMOs, preferred provider organizations (PPOs), indemnity plans with managed care elements (e.g., preadmission authorization requirements), Medicare, and Medicaid are all programs that have been increasing their control over medical practice as health care costs have risen. The degree of control will vary considerably depending on the type of program involved, but managed health care, particularly tightly managed HMOs, currently exerts the greatest degree of external control outside medical residency training. The greater the degree of external control, the greater the danger of overt or covert resistance to achieving the goals of the plan.

Many of the issues discussed in the course of this chapter are pertinent to ameliorating some of the anxieties that arise in dealing with control issues. It is probably not unreasonable to point out that failure of the private sector and the physician community to control medical costs in the nation will lead to even greater interventions by nonphysicians charged with bringing medical costs under control. Enlisting the physician's help in achieving the plan's goals is possible by empowering the physicians within the system. Suggestions for some specific approaches to the issues of control needs follow.

Control of Where Care Is Received

Virtually all managed care plans will have some controls over where members receive their care. In a simple PPO, that control will be confined to a differential in benefits that is based on whether a member uses participating hospitals and physicians. In a tightly managed HMO, the plan will allow only the use of participating providers, and even then only for certain services. For example, the HMO may have an exclusive contract for mammography; even though all the participating hospitals have the ability to perform mammography, only one provider will be allowed to do it and get paid.

If a plan intends to have a highly restricted panel of participating providers, it is sometimes helpful to elicit the opinions of those physicians already in the panel, even though the final decision will still rest with the plan. For example, if the decision has been made to use only two or three orthopedic groups to provide services, the primary care physicians could be canvassed for nominations of groups to approach. The plan should clearly state that it is not having a majority rule vote but is looking for people to approach; the final selection will be based on a combination of the plan's regular credentialing and quality assessment process, the group's willingness to cooperate with plan policies and procedures, and cost.

Control of Patient Care

Much more volatile than the above, control of patient care is a real hot button with most physicians. This control can range from the retrospective review of claims that is found in most plans to the mandatory preauthorization of all nonprimary care services that is found in most HMOs. The greater the degree of plan involvement in clinical decision making, the greater the chances of antagonism between physicians and plan managers, but also the greater the degree of medical cost control.

Because management of medical services is the hallmark of managed care, it is neither possible nor desirable to eliminate it. How that control is exercised will have a great effect on its acceptance and success, however. If the plan intervenes in an arbitrary and heavy-handed manner, there will be problems. If interventions are done with an element of understanding and respect, there should be greater cooperation.

The techniques described in a later section of this chapter are particularly important here. Frequent and regular contact, both positive and negative, will help a great deal. Discussing cases and suggesting and soliciting alternatives for case management will yield better results than arbitrary demands for improvement.

Control of Quality

The most common objection that physicians will actually voice about managed care is that it reduces the quality of care. Regardless of whether that argument is a smoke screen for purely economic concerns, the issue is still a valid one. Any system that requires the use of a restricted network of providers and has an authorization system has the potential of reducing the quality of care delivered. Despite the fact that numerous studies of quality in managed care have shown care to be equal or superior to unmanaged care (see Chapter 8 for references), this feeling persists.

The best approach here is to place responsibility for participating with the plan's quality management (QM) program squarely with the physicians themselves. It is vital to have a properly constructed QM program so that participation is meaningful. A solid QM program will allow the physicians to feel that the plan genuinely does have an interest in quality and should allow for some pride in participation. A more detailed discussion of QM programs is found in Chapter 17.

Role Conflict

It is often stated that physicians are trained to be the patient's advocate. This is partially true, but that notion presupposes a system whereby a patient, like a plaintiff or defendant in a lawsuit, needs an advocate. In fact, physicians are trained to be the patient's caregiver, that is, the coordinator and deliverer of medical care.

The issue of advocacy arises when a physician feels that the needs of the plan and the needs of the patient are in conflict.[9] When that happens, the physician feels genuinely torn between being the patient's advocate and the plan's advocate. This most frequently comes up when the patients request or demand a service that is not really necessary or is medically marginal. Physicians feel on the spot if they must deny the service, putting themselves in a role conflict with their patients: "Just whose side are you on, anyway?" This is a difficult situation that is handled better by some physicians than others.[10]

Plan managers need to acknowledge this conflict, even though there may be less conflict in reality than in perception. Because of poor provider understanding of the insurance function (discussed below), the conflict may come up when the physician feels a service is medically necessary that in fact is not a covered benefit. In some cases, there is poor understanding of the difference between what is actually medically necessary and what is essentially a convenience. The health plan is not in the business of denying truly needed services, assuming that they are covered under the schedule of benefits; denial of such services would be ethically and financially foolish.

What the health plan is in the business of doing is cutting the fat out of the system. The physician is charged with conserving the resources, primarily economic, of the plan to ensure availability of those resources to those who truly need them. It is the physician who will best be able to determine what is really needed and what is really not, and that will help provide more appropriate allocation of those resources. The plan's utilization management efforts are (or should be) aimed at aiding the physician in carrying out that function.

Poor Understanding of the Insurance Function of the Plan

As mentioned above, some of the problems of role conflict stem from a poor understanding of the insurance aspect of the plan. HMOs in particular are marketed as offering comprehensive benefits, even though there are clearly certain exclusions and limitations, just as there are for any form of health coverage. Physicians often do not differentiate between what is medically necessary and what is a covered benefit.

Every plan has certain exclusions and limitations of coverage. For example, a member may require 3 months of inpatient psychiatric care, but the plan only covers 30 days. Another example is an experimental transplant procedure. In each case, an argument can be made that the treatment is necessary, but it is not a covered benefit under the plan's schedule of benefits.

Plan management may make exceptions to the exclusions and limitations policy, but that should only be done rarely and after much thought. In some cases, it will be clearly cost effective to do so (e.g., providing 30 days of home durable medical equipment to avoid a hospitalization). In other cases, it will not be. If frequent exceptions are made, it can lead to an open-ended commitment to provide lifetime noncovered services, a commitment that the plan cannot afford if it is to remain in business.

Helping a physician understand the insurance nature of the plan and that there are limitations to coverage will be a wise investment on the part of the plan managers. It is often of great help for the plan to play the role of the black hat here; in other words, plan management contacts the member in such cases to reinforce that it is a contract (i.e., schedule of benefits) issue and not a matter of the physician being callous and hard hearted.

Bad Habits

All of us have habits and patterns in our lives. Most physicians have habits and patterns in their practices that are not cost effective but are difficult to change. One example is the practice of not seeing patients or making rounds on Wednesdays; the physician's partner may not feel comfortable discharging a partner's patient, so the stay is lengthened by an extra day. Another example is a physician who keeps a routine, uncomplicated surgical patient in the hospital for 4 days, stating "That's the way I've always done it, and it's worked just fine for me!"

This problem is a touchy one. It is usually poor form bluntly to accuse a physician of bad practice habits. The frontal assault is generally met with the indignant question, "Are you questioning my judgment?" You are not, of course; you are questioning a bad habit.

It is preferable to lead physicians to the appropriate conclusion themselves. If you discuss the issue objectively, present supporting information, and ask physicians to examine critically the difference in practice behavior, a number of physicians will arrive at the conclusion that their old habits must change. By allowing physicians gracefully and quietly to make the change, you run less risk of creating the need for a rigid defensive posture on their part.

In some cases, that will not work. If calm and rational discussions fail to effect a change, firmer action is needed; physicians may cooperate but may tell the patient that the health plan is making them do it. In most cases, that type of grumbling will go away after a short while. If it does not, the medical director must counsel these physicians about appropriate behavior, especially in this litigious era. If there is an adverse outcome, even though it had nothing to do with the changed practice pattern, the chances of a lawsuit are probably heightened if those types of comments have been made.

Poor Understanding of Economics

Even though physicians and their business managers are becoming more sophisticated about managed care, there is still a surprising lack of understanding of its economics, especially in capitated or other performance-based reimbursement systems. There may be little understanding of the withholds and incentive pools, or physicians may feel so distant from those pools that there is little or no effect on behavior.

It is worthwhile to have continual reeducation about the economics of the plan as it relates to the physician's income. Related to this is the need for accurate and timely feedback to the physicians about their economic status on the basis of payments and utilization. Inaccurate feedback is far worse than no feedback at all.

The hoary old cliche that money talks is absolutely true. Because of that, plan management should always be aware of the whole dollars involved in compensating physicians. A small number, such as an $11.25 per member per month capitation payment, may seem like "funny money" to a physician, but if that $11.25 per member per month really means $40,000 per year, that has a considerable impact on the financial health of a practice. Helping physicians realize the contribution that the plan is making to their bottom line can be eye opening.

Poor Differentiation among Competing Plans

Considerable difficulty arises when there is little or no differentiation among competing plans; this is essentially a problem in open panels. In many HMOs, particularly when the state or federal government sets standards, the benefits may be the same, and the provider network may be similar or the same; the only difference is the rates (at which point the situation takes on the ominous characteristics of a commodity market).

This becomes a problem when each plan has different internal policies and procedures with which the physicians and their office staff must comply. If a physician is contracting with three or more plans, the frustration involved with trying to remember which one wants what can be quite high. This problem is exacerbated when the same patient changes to a different managed care plan. For example, on Friday Mr. Jones was with the ABC Health Plan, but when he came in for his return appointment on Monday he had switched to the XYZ Health Plan; the office staff did not take notice, which resulted in claims or authorization denials. This can be a real morale problem with the physician's office staff. When frustration rises, compliance fails.

This is best addressed by increased attention and service to the physicians and their office staff. Frequent and timely communications will help, and the more that is done in person the better because newsletters have a way of getting to the bottom of the parakeet cage without being read.

In this area, nonmonetary issues can have as much impact as monetary ones. Examples include difficult-to-use forms that require a lot of unnecessary writing, frequent busy signals on service lines, and inconsistencies in responses to questions. It cannot be overstressed that prompt and courteous responsiveness to questions and concerns is required. You do not have to give the answer that you think physicians will want to hear; you do have to give an answer or response that is consistent, clear, and reasonably fair.

GENERAL APPROACHES TO CHANGING BEHAVIOR

Translating Goals and Objectives

A useful way of looking at communications between plan management and physicians is to consider the concept of translation. It is easy to overlook the fact that managers and physicians may have radically different ways of viewing matters relating to the delivery of health care services to plan members.

For example, the area of cost containment is rife with possibilities for opposing views. Physicians frequently look upon cost containment measures as unnecessary intrusions into their domain, whereas nonphysician managers view the same measures as the only way to control headstrong physicians. Translating the goal of cost containment into terms that are both understandable and acceptable to both parties will take you far toward obtaining cooperation and acceptance. To ensure that the economic resources will be available to compensate providers and to make services available at all to patients, cost containment must take place.

Rewards Are More Effective Than Sanctions

A tenet of behavior modification theory is that positive interactions or rewards are more effective at achieving long-term changes in behavior than negative interactions or sanctions. Furthermore, it is rarely good policy for managers to impose their will on others in an arbitrary manner. In some cases it is necessary, but if it is done as a matter of course, cooperation will not be enthusiastic. In the worst case, it can lead to widespread dissatisfaction and defection from the plan. Even without such attrition, overt cooperation can occur, but covert sabotage undoes any progress made. This can be especially true with physicians. Unlike regular employees, physicians (even in closed panel operations) behave with a great deal of autonomy and power.

In the context of this discussion, rewards refer primarily to forms of positive feedback and communication about good performance. Clearly, good case management should yield economic rewards as well, but positive feedback from plan management will be a reward system all its own. Other rewards could include continuing education seminars about managed care, small gifts or acknowledgments for good work, and so forth.

Although it is unrealistic to expect that every physician will embrace every policy and procedure that plan has, the odds in favor of cooperation will increase when the interactions between the physician and the plan are more positive than negative. This is not to be confused with capitulation on necessary policies and procedures: There were once plenty of physician-friendly health plans that are now little more than smoking rubble. Rather, this is to emphasize that too heavy a hand will eventually cause problems.

Be Involved

It is shocking how often managers of health plans fail to maintain an active involvement with the participating physicians. Frequently the only communications with the physicians are occasional newsletters or memos, claims denials, and calls from the utilization management department harassing the physicians about hospital cases. Those types of interactions will not add to the luster of plan management in the physicians' eyes.

Frequent and regular contact, through scheduled meetings, personal visits, or telephone calls, will help create an environment for positive change. If the only time physicians hear from the plan is when there is a problem, they will try to avoid contact in the future and will tend to have decreased responsiveness to the plan's needs.

Offer advice, suggestions, and alternatives, not just demands to change something. Ask intelligent questions about the clinical issues at hand, and solicit advice about alternative ways to provide the care. Work to get to the point where physicians will be asking themselves the same questions you would ask without your having to ask them.

Involvement is a two-way proposition. It is fair and reasonable to expect the practicing physicians to participate in plan committees to help set medical policy, monitor quality, and so forth.

Soliciting active participation in such functions helps promote a sense of ownership on the part of the involved physicians and will clearly give the plan some valuable input. Whether the plan compensates the physicians for the time spent on such activities is a local decision, but an honorarium is common.

PROGRAMMATIC APPROACHES TO CHANGING PHYSICIAN BEHAVIOR

Formal Continuing Medical Education

Formal continuing medical education (CME) is the provision of additional clinical training through seminars, conferences, home study, and so forth. The hallmark of CME is that it provides CME credits by virtue of the accreditation of the sponsoring body. This method of information dissemination, while traditionally the most prevalent, has mixed effectiveness when it comes to changing behavior. One large review found little evidence that traditional CME changed patient outcomes or behavior.[11] Another study, however, found that changes in behavior did occur when the curriculum was *designed* to change specific types of behavior.[12] A more recent and extensive review of CME (which specifically excluded programs that were tied to financial incentives) supports the conclusion that traditional CME can have a small effect on behavior, with a somewhat greater effect on behavior when the techniques of academic detailing (e.g., one-on-one education focused on specific issues), reminders (e.g., specific reminders at the time of a patient visit), and possibly the additional influence of opinion leaders are brought into play.[13]

Based on this evidence, formal CME will remain a useful tool for disseminating clinical information and will be a useful adjunct in changing physician behavior in general. Formal CME is not currently a useful tool for a managed care plan to use to change specific physician behavior compared with other available methodologies.

Data and Feedback

As mentioned in other chapters, particularly Chapter 19, data regarding utilization and cost are an integral part of a managed care plan. The value of data is not restricted to plan managers; data are equally important to individual physicians. If the only data physicians get are letters at the end of the year informing them that all their withhold is used up, they can credibly argue that they have been blindsided.

Providing regular and accurate data about an individual physician's performance, from both a utilization and (for risk/bonus models) an economic standpoint, is vital to changing behavior. Most physicians will want to perform well, but they can do so only when they can judge their own performance against that of their peers or against plan norms.

The research literature is actually a bit mixed in its support for feedback as a means of changing behavior, although the preponderance of the research data is positive. There are numerous studies showing significant reductions in utilization and costs in response to feedback about individual physician behavior.[14–22] There are, however, some studies that are more ambiguous regarding the role of feedback or report that feedback has little lasting effect unless continuously reinforced.[23–29]

When one is reviewing the possible reasons for feedback being shown to be ineffective (at least in the long run), it is possible to conjecture on some conditions that improve the effectiveness of feedback. First, the physicians must believe that their behavior needs to change, whether for clinical reasons, for economic reasons, or simply to remain part of the participating panel in the plan; if physicians do not believe that they need to change, then feedback provides nothing of value. Feedback must also be consistent and usable; in other words, a physician must clearly understand the data in the report, be able to use that information in a concrete way, and be able to keep using it to measure his or her own performance. Feedback needs to be closely related to what a physician is doing right at that time; in other words, feedback about behavior that is remote in time or infrequent is less likely to be acted upon. Feedback must be regular to sustain the changed behavior; feedback that is sporadic or unsustained is likely to result in behavior returning to the condition before the feedback caused any change to begin with. Last, feedback that is linked to economic performance is more likely to produce substantial change than feedback that is not so linked.

Practice Guidelines and Clinical Protocols

Practice guidelines and clinical protocols refer to codified approaches to medical care. Guidelines may be for both diagnostic and therapeutic modalities, and they may be used to guide physicians in the care of patients with defined diseases or symptoms or as surveillance tools to monitor practice on a retrospective basis. Clinical pathways or protocols are discussed in great detail in *The Managed Health Care Handbook* and the reader is urged to review this chapter.

Many physicians have an initial negative reaction to practice guidelines. They feel that guidelines make for "cookbook medicine" and do not allow for judgment or that guidelines represent a high risk in the case of a malpractice suit (because guidelines provide a template against which all actions will be judged). Nevertheless, practice guidelines have been gaining in popularity, at least among medical managers.

Implementing practice guidelines is not always easy, particularly in an open panel setting. There is frequently a lack of enthusiasm on the part of the physicians, and the plan's ability actually to monitor the guidelines is limited. Generally, the plan's QM process is best able to monitor the use of guidelines (see Chapter 17), although there may be some ability to use the claims system to do so as well.

Attempting to put comprehensive practice guidelines into place in a managed care plan is a daunting task. In an open panel, it will be exponentially more difficult. There is some evidence that simple publication of practice guidelines alone may predispose physicians to consider changing their behavior but that such guidelines by themselves are unlikely to effect rapid change.[30,31] When such protocols are accompanied by direct presentations by opinion leaders (so-called academic detailing), then changes are more sustained.[32] Last, as discussed in *The Managed Health Care Handbook*, clinical pathways that are developed by the physicians who will then use those pathways, especially in the inpatient setting, are most likely to have significant effects, at least for the type of care that the pathway addresses, and there are multiple interventions that can improve compliance with the guidelines.[33]

CHANGING THE BEHAVIOR OF INDIVIDUAL PHYSICIANS

Stepwise Approach to Changing Behavior Patterns

Changing the behavior of an individual provider involves a stepwise approach. The first and most common step is collegial discussion. Discussing cases and utilization patterns in a nonthreatening way, colleague to colleague, is generally an effective method of bringing about change.

Far less common is positive feedback.* This is an even more effective tool for change but one that most managers fail to use to any great degree. Positive feedback does not refer to mindless or misleading praise but to letting a physician know when things are done well. Most managers get so involved in firefighting that they tend to neglect sending positive messages to those providers who are managing well. In the absence of such messages, providers have to figure out for themselves what they are doing right (the plan will usually tell them what they are doing wrong), and that may not be optimal.

* The use of the term *positive feedback* here is different from the use of the term *feedback* regarding data. Although both forms of feedback provide information to the provider regarding performance, data feedback is objective; positive feedback in the context of this section refers to subjective information from plan managers.

Persuasion is also commonly used. Somewhat stronger than collegial discussion, persuasion refers to plan managers persuading providers to act in ways that the providers may not initially choose themselves. For example, if a patient requires intravenous antibiotics for osteomyelitis but is otherwise doing well, that patient is a candidate for home intravenous therapy. Some physicians will resist discharging the patient to home therapy because it is convenient to follow the case; keeping the patient in the hospital is a lot easier in terms of rounding. The physician must then be persuaded to discharge the patient because of the cost-effectiveness of home therapy.

Firm direction of plan policies, procedures, and requirements is the next step after persuasion. If a physician refuses to cooperate with the plan to deliver care cost effectively, and if discussion and persuasion have failed, a medical director may be required to give the physician firm direction, reminding him or her of the contractual agreement to cooperate with plan policies and procedures. Behind firm direction is the implied threat of refusal to pay for services or even more severe sanctions. It is clearly a display of power and should not be done with a heavy hand. When giving firm direction, it is best to not allow oneself to be drawn into long and unresolvable arguments. Presumably the discussions and even the arguments have already occurred, so that it is pointless to keep rehashing them. This is sometimes called a broken record type of response because, rather than respond to old arguments, the medical director always gives the same response: firm direction.

The last steps are sanctions and termination. Sanctioning should rarely be required, and termination is so serious that these topics are discussed separately below.

One last thought in this section: Avoid global responses to individual problems. When managers are uncomfortable confronting individual physicians about problems in behavior, a dysfunctional response is to make a global change in policy or procedure because of the actions of one or two physicians. That type of response frequently has the effect of alienating all the other physicians who have been cooperating while failing to change the behavior of the problem providers. If a policy change is required, make it. If the problem is really just with a few individuals, however, deal with them, and do not harass the rest of the panel.

Discipline and Sanctions

This section discusses the most serious form of behavior modification. Sanctions or threats are only applied when the problem is so serious that action must be taken and when the provider fails to cooperate. In some cases the provider may be willing to cooperate, but the offense is so serious that sanctions must be taken anyway. An example of this is a serious problem of quality care, such as malpractice resulting in death or serious morbidity. In any event, the sanctioning process has legal overtones that must be kept in mind.

Plan management may initiate disciplinary actions short of a formal sanctioning process. In most cases, such discipline is helpful in creating documentation of chronic problems or failure to cooperate. Discipline may involve verbal warnings or letters; in either case, the thrust of the action is to document the offensive behavior and to describe the consequences of failure to cooperate.

One example of discipline is sometimes called ticketing. It is called that because it is similar to getting a ticket from a traffic cop. This is a verbal reprimand about a specific behavior; the behavior and corrective action are described, as are the consequences of failure to carry out the corrective action. The manager refuses to get into an argument at that time and requires the offending provider to make an appointment at a future date to discuss the issue (similar to a court date). This allows tempers to cool off a bit and ensures that the disciplinary message does not get muddied up with other issues. When a manager issues a ticket, there should be a document to file that describes what transpired.

A more formal approach is an actual disciplinary letter. Like a ticket, the letter describes the offending behavior and the required corrective action and invites the provider to make an appointment to discuss the issue. In the case of a verbal ticket or a disciplinary letter, the consequences of failure to change errant ways is initiation of the formal sanctioning process.

Formal sanctioning has potentially serious legal overtones. Due process, or a policy regarding rights and responsibilities of both parties, is a requirement for an effective sanctioning procedure, at least when one is sanctioning for reasons of quality. The Health Care Quality Improvement Act of 1986 has formalized due process in the sanctioning procedure as it relates to quality and must be adhered to in order to maintain protection from antitrust action (see Exhibit 18–1).[34] Although this act was primarily aimed at hospital peer review activities, HMOs are specifically mentioned, and other forms of managed care may be implied in the future.

Following the requirements of the act regarding due process is cumbersome and is obviously the final step before removing a physician from the panel for reasons of poor quality care. Because it is such a drastic step, compliance with the act, including the reporting requirements, is the best protection the plan has against legal action.

It should be emphasized that the act applies to peer review activities that result in actions against physicians for quality problems. If a physician fails to cooperate with contractually agreed-to plan policies and procedures, the plan may have reason to terminate the contract with the physician for cause. Even in that case, it may be wise to have a due process policy that allows for formal steps to be taken in the event that the plan contemplates termination. Presentation of facts to a medical advisory committee made up of physicians who are not in direct economic competition with the involved physician provides a backup to plan management. Such a committee may be able to effect changes by the physician where the medical director may not. Finally, the backing of a committee underscores that severe sanctions are not arbitrary but the result of failure on the part of the physician, not plan management.

There may arise situations where a physician's utilization performance is such that there is a clear mismatch with managed care practice philosophy; in other words, the plan simply cannot afford to keep the physician in the panel. The quality of the physician's medical care may be adequate, and there may have been no gross lack of cooperation with plan policies and procedures, but the physician simply practices medicine in such a style that medical resources are heavily and inappropriately overutilized. In such cases, the medical director must assess whether the physician can change his or her behavior. Assuming that the medical director concludes that the provider in question cannot change (or change sufficiently) or has failed to change despite warnings and feedback, the plan may choose to terminate the relationship solely on the basis of contractual terms that allow either party to terminate without cause when adequate notice is given (see Chapter 29).

When the plan departicipates a physician in this way, it is often not subject to a due process type of review. The reason is that the separation is based on practice style and fit, not accusations of rule breaking or poor quality. Although this may not seem fair at first blush, in point of fact most contracts certainly allow physicians to terminate if they feel the fit is poor; plans have the same right, even if they do not exercise it frequently. Terminating physicians in this manner has the potential for creating adverse relations in the network if there is the perception that the plan is acting arbitrarily and without reason. On the other hand, assuming that the terminated physician does indeed practice profligately, the other physicians in the network are probably aware of it, so that there may not be as much shock and surprise as one might think. Even so, such steps are drastic and should not be taken frequently or lightly.

Exhibit 18–1 Health Care Quality Improvement Act of 1986: Requirements of Due Process

(a)...a professional review action must be taken

(1) in the reasonable belief that the action was in the furtherance of quality health care,

(2) after a reasonable effort to obtain the facts of the matter,

(3) after adequate notice and hearing procedures are afforded to the physician involved and after such other procedures as are fair to the physician under the circumstances, and

(4) in the reasonable belief that the action was warranted by the facts known after such reasonable effort to obtain facts and after meeting requirements of paragraph (3)...

(b)...A health care entity is deemed to have met the adequate notice and hearing requirement of subsection (a)(3) with respect to a physician if the following conditions are met (or are waived voluntarily by the physician):

(1) Notice of Proposed Action—The physician has been given notice stating—

(A) (i) that a professional review action has been proposed to be taken against the physician,

(ii) reasons for the proposed action,

(B) (i) that the physician has the right to request a hearing on the proposed action,

(ii) any time limit (of not less than 30 days) within which to request such a hearing, and

(C) a summary of the rights in the hearing under paragraph (3).

(2) Notice of Hearing—If a hearing is requested on a timely basis under paragraph (1)(B), the physician involved must be given notice stating—

(A) the place, time, and date of the hearing, which date shall not be less than 30 days after the date of the notice, and

(B) a list of the witness (if any) expected to testify at the hearing on behalf of the profession review body.

(3) Conduct of Hearing and Notice—

(A)...the hearing shall be held (as determined by the health care entity)—

(i) before an arbitrator mutually acceptable to the physician and the health care entity,

(ii) before a hearing officer who is appointed by the entity and who is not in direct economic competition with the physician involved, or

(iii) before a panel of individuals who are appointed by the entity and are not in direct economic competition with the physician involved;

(B) the right to the hearing may be forfeited if the physician fails, without good cause, to appear;

(C) in the hearing the physician has the right—

(i) to representation by an attorney or other person of the physician's choice,

(ii) to have a record made of the proceedings, copies of which may be obtained by the physician upon payment of any reasonable charges associated with the preparation thereof,

(iii) to call, examine, and cross-examine witnesses,

(iv) to present evidence determined to be relevant by the hearing officer, regardless of its admissibility in a court of law, and

(v) to submit a written statement at the close of the hearing; and

(D) upon completion of the hearing, the physician has the right—

(i) to receive the written recommendation of the arbitrator, officer, or panel, including a statement of the basis for the recommendations, and

(ii) to receive a written decision of the health care entity, including a statement of the basis for the decision.

Source: Healthcare Quality Improvement Act of 1986, 45 U.S.C. §11101–11152, section 412.

CONCLUSION

Changing physician behavior is crucial to the success of any managed care plan. Physicians are unique in their strong need for autonomy and control, potential for role conflicts, uneven understanding of the economics or insurance functions of managed care, and ingrained practice habits. Plan managers can exacerbate the difficulties in changing physician behavior by failing to be responsive and consistent, failing to differentiate their plan from other plans, failing to provide positive feedback, failing to address specific problems with providers early, and failing to take a stepwise approach to managing change.

Systematic approaches to changing physician behavior can be used successfully for many aspects of practice. Continuing education, creation and dissemination of practice protocols, and data feedback are all useful techniques, especially when combined with financial incentives.

When reasonable efforts to get a physician to change are unsuccessful and the problems are serious, discipline and sanctions must be applied. Due process must be followed before termination for poor quality, and it may be useful in other settings as well. In the final analysis, it is the plan's responsibility to effect changes in provider behavior that will benefit all the parties concerned and to take action when necessary.

Study Questions

1. Describe the routine actions an HMO should take to positively influence provider behavior.
2. What behavior on the part of an HMO would likely engender negative provider behavior?
3. Develop policies and procedures for a physician sanction program to deal with unacceptable physician behavior.
4. Describe common physician perceptions, both negative and positive, of managed care. What steps might an HMO take in regard to those perceptions?

REFERENCES AND NOTES

1. A.L. Hillman, et al., HMO Managers' Views on Financial Incentives and Quality, *Health Affairs* (Winter 1991): 207–219.
2. A.L. Hillman, et al., How Do Financial Incentives Affect Physicians' Clinical Decisions and the Financial Performance of Health Maintenance Organizations?, *New England Journal of Medicine* 321 (1989): 86–92.
3. H.L. Greene, et al., Physicians Attitudes toward Cost Containment: The Missing Piece of the Puzzle, *Archives of Internal Medicine* 149 (1989): 1966–1968.
4. S.J. O'Connor and J.A. Lanning, The End of Autonomy? Reflections on the Postprofessional Physician, *Health Care Management Review* 17 (1992): 63–72.
5. J.W. Salmon, et al., The Futures of Physicians: Agency and Autonomy Reconsidered, *Theoretical Medicine* 11 (1990): 261–274.
6. R. Schultz, et al., Physician Adaptation to Health Maintenance Organizations and Implications for Management, *Health Services Research* 25 (1990): 43–64.
7. G.J. Deckard, Physicians Responses to a Managed Environment: A Perceptual Paradox, *Health Care Management Review* 20 (1995): 40–46.
8. L.C. Baker and J.C. Cantor, Physician Satisfaction under Managed Care, *Health Affairs Supplement* (1993): 258–270.
9. E.J. Emanuel and N.N. Dubler, Preserving the Physician–Patient Relationship in the Era of Managed Care, *Journal of the American Medical Association* 273 (1995): 323–329.
10. R.O Anderson, How Do You Manage the Demanding (Difficult) Patient?, *HMO Practice* 4 (1990): 15–16.
11. D.A. Davis, et al., Evidence for the Effectiveness of CME: A Review of 50 Randomized Controlled Trials, *Journal of the American Medical Association* 268 (1992): 1111–1117.
12. C.W. White, et al., The Effectiveness of Continuing Medical Education in Changing the Behavior of Physicians Caring for Patients with Acute Myocardial Infarction: A Controlled Randomized Trial, *Annals of Internal Medicine* 102 (1985): 686–692.
13. D.A. Davis, et al., Changing Physician Performance: A Systematic Review of the Effect of Continuing Medical Education Strategies, *Journal of the American Medical Association* 274 (1995): 700–706.
14. S.A Myers and N. Gleicher, A Successful Program To Lower Cesarean Section Rates, *New England Journal of Medicine* 319 (1989): 1511–1516.

15. J.E. Wennberg, et al., Changes in Tonsillectomy Rates Associated with Feedback and Review, *Pediatrics* 59 (1977): 821–826.
16. L.M. Frazier, et al., Academia and Clinic: Can Physician Education Lower the Cost of Prescription Drugs? A Prospective, Controlled Trial, *Annals of Internal Medicine* 15 (1991): 116–121.
17. K.I. Marton, et al., Modifying Test-Ordering Behavior in the Outpatient Medical Clinic, *Archives of Internal Medicine* 145 (1985): 816–821.
18. D.M. Berwick and K.L. Coltin, Feedback Reduces Test Use in a Health Maintenance Organization, *Journal of the American Medical Association* 255 (1986): 1450–1454.
19. J.E. Billi, et al., The Effects of a Cost-Education Program on Hospital Charges, *Journal of General Internal Medicine* 2 (1987): 306–311.
20. J.E. Billi, et al., The Effects of a Low-Cost Intervention Program on Hospital Costs, *Journal of General Internal Medicine* 7 (1992): 411–416.
21. L.M. Manheim, et al., Training House Officers To Be Cost Conscious: Effects of an Educational Intervention on Charges and Length of Stay, *Medical Care* 28 (1990): 29–42.
22. E. Zablocki, ed. "Sharing Data with Physicians," in *Changing Physician Practice Patterns: Strategies for Success in a Capitated Health Care System*, (Gaithersburg, Md.: Aspen, 1995), 1–22.
23. F.J. Dyck, et al., Effect of Surveillance on the Number of Hysterectomies in the Province of Saskatchewan, *New England Journal of Medicine* 296 (1977): 1326–1328.
24. J. Lomas, et al., Opinion Leaders vs. Audits and Feedback to Implement Practice Guidelines: Delivery after Previous Cesarean Section, *Journal of the American Medical Association* 265 (1991): 2202–2207.
25. Failure of Information as an Intervention To Modify Clinical Management: A Time-Series Trial in Patients with Acute Chest Pain, *Annals of Internal Medicine* 122 (1995): 434–437.
26. P. Axt-Adam, et al., Influencing Behavior of Physicians Ordering Laboratory Tests: A Literature Study, *Medical Care* 31 (1993): 784–794.
27. T.A. Parrino, The Nonvalue of Retrospective Peer Comparison Feedback in Containing Hospital Antibiotic Costs, *American Journal of Medicine* 86 (1989): 442–448.
28. S.B. Soumerai, et al., Improving Drug Prescribing in Primary Care: A Critical Analysis of the Experimental Literature, *Milbank Memorial Fund Quarterly* 67 (1989): 268–317.
29. A.R. Martin, et al., A Trial of Two Strategies To Modify the Test-Ordering Behavior of Medical Residents, *New England Journal of Medicine* 303 (1980): 1330–1336.
30. J. Kosecoff, et al., Effects of the National Institutes of Health Consensus Development Program of Physician Practice, *Journal of the American Medical Association* 258 (1987): 2708–2713.
31. J. Lomas, et al., Do Practice Guidelines Guide Practice? The Effect of a Consensus Statement on the Practice of Physicians, *New England Journal of Medicine* 321 (1989): 1306–1311.
32. S.B. Soumerai and J. Avorn, Principles of Education Outreach ("Academic Detailing") To Improve Clinical Decision Making, *Journal of the American Medical Association* 263 (1990): 549–556.
33. A.G. Ellrodt, et al., Measuring and Improving Physician Compliance with Clinical Practice Guidelines: A Controlled Intervention Trial, *Annals of Internal Medicine* 122 (1995): 277–282.
34. Healthcare Quality Improvement Act of 1986. 45 U.S.C. §11101–11152, section 412.

SUGGESTED READING

Berenson, R.A. 1991. Commentary: A Physician's View of Managed Care. *Health Affairs* 10:106–119.

Chernov, A.J. 1993 (February). Managed Care and the Doctor–Patient Relationship. *Medical Interface*, 30–32.

Delio, S.A. and Hein, G. 1995. *The Making of an Efficient Physician*. Englewood, Colo.: MGMA.

Eisenberg, J.M. 1986. *Doctors' Decisions and the Cost of Medical Care*. Ann Arbor, Mich.: Health Administration Press.

Greco, P.J. and Eisenberg, J.M. 1993. Changing Physicians' Practices. *New England Journal of Medicine* 329:1271–1274.

Mittman, B.S. and Siu, A.L. 1992. "Changing Provider Behavior: Applying Research on Outcomes and Effectiveness in Health Care." In *Improving Health Policy Management: Nine Critical Research Issues for the 1990s*, eds. S.M. Shortell and U.E. Reinhardt. Ann Arbor, Mich.: Health Administration Press, pp. 195–227.

Moynihan, J.J. 1994. Using EDI for Utilization Management. *Healthcare Financial Management* 48(7): 73.

Nash, D.B., ed. 1994. *The Physician's Guide to Managed Care*. Gaithersburg, Md.: Aspen.

Zablocki, E. 1995. *Changing Physician Practice Patterns: Strategies for Success in a Capitated Health Care System*. Gaithersburg, Md.: Aspen.

Chapter 19

Using Data in Medical Management

Peter R. Kongstvedt

Study Objectives

- Understand general requirements for using data in medical management
- Understand basic report format requirements
- Understand basic types of reports and data for inpatient, outpatient, and ambulatory utilization
- Understand basic concepts and problems of profiling and approaches to dealing with those problems
- Understand the uses of data, and the strengths and weaknesses of different approaches to using data to manage medical care

Of all the activities involved in managing health care, the use of data in medical management continues to take on ever-increasing importance. It is the ability of medical managers to use data intelligently to manage the health care delivery system that will ultimately separate out those plans that truly excel from those plans that are, at best, adequate performers. This is not to say that the other management activities described in this book have less merit; rather, the opposite is the case: The use of data allows those activities to be carried out more effectively (of course, no data in the world can change someone's personality). It is important to bear in mind, however, that information is not magic; one cannot press ALT-F4 and have utilization suddenly drop. Data and information are merely powerful tools for the medical manager to carry out necessary functions.

This chapter should be read in the context of a managed care plan's specific needs and in conjunction with the information presented in other chapters. It is the intention of this chapter not to be highly redundant and review all the possible reports that can be produced by a plan's management information system (MIS) but rather to concentrate on those reports specific to utilization and medical management that will help medical directors carry out their job. Clearly, the need for these types of reports will be influenced by the configuration of your plan and the types of controls and incentives in place. Not all the reports discussed in this chapter will be helpful, and there will certainly be situations where there are necessary utilization reports that are not discussed here. It is up to the medical director to decide what reports are necessary, and it is up to the director of MIS to provide them. The reader is also referred to Chapter 20 for an in-depth discussion of systems issues in managed care.

GENERAL REQUIREMENTS FOR USING DATA TO MANAGE THE HEALTH CARE DELIVERY SYSTEM

Data Characteristics

For data to be used at all for managing health care costs, certain basic requirements must be met. First, the data must have integrity. Errors are common, especially in data that require manual entry (i.e., data entered via keystrokes); such errors must be prevented when possible and identified and corrected when present. In some plans, especially large insurance companies, the database may not even use all the available information; for example, to hold down personnel costs, the plan may only key in the first three digits of the diagnostic code (each keystroke costs money!) and thus may not be able to refine diagnostic data.

It is not unusual for data to come from multiple sources. For example, a health plan may use more than one system to administer different activities (e.g., enrollment and billing on one system, general ledger on another, utilization management on another, and claims on still another). It is also possible that multiple plans, or a combination of a plan and a provider system, such as an integrated delivery system (IDS; see Chapter 4), will desire to combine data to improve the robustness of the database. In such cases, the data must be integrated into a common database, again bringing up the problems of conformance in meaning. This leads to a requirement to standardize a format for use in data analyses.

Data must be consistent and mean the same thing from provider to provider. For example, one provider may code differently from other providers for the same procedure, and a hospital may code an event differently from the attending physician. Diagnostic coding is particularly problematic when one is analyzing data from physician outpatient reports. Because diagnostic coding is not important in determining what a physician is paid (except for those claims systems that match diagnostic code to procedure code), there is a great deal of laxity in diagnostic coding for office visits. Procedure coding tends to be more accurate because there is a direct relationship between what a provider codes as having been performed and what the provider gets paid (except in capitated systems). Accuracy, however, does not rule out creative coding, upcoding, or even fraud in the form of deliberate coding inconsistencies. For example, one surgeon may bill for a hysterectomy, and another surgeon may bill for an exploratory laparotomy, removal of the uterus, removal of the ovaries, and lysis of adhesions, all of which generate a fee. The need for consistency may mean having to change or otherwise modify data to force conformance of meaning.

Data must also be valid: They must actually mean what you think they mean. Even when there is great attention to diagnostic coding, the reason for the visit may not be related to everything that gets done (e.g., a patient is seen with the diagnosis of hypertension but also gets a hearing test), or the diagnostic code may not be the same as the underlying disease (e.g., a patient is seen for an upper respiratory infection, but the relevant diagnosis is emphysema). In addition to coding validity, it is important to validate data against other potential sources of the same data; for example, physician identification data may be kept in two separate databases, which may not match.

The measures must be meaningful. It is of no value (other than academic) to measure things that have no real impact on the plan's ability to manage the system or a physician's ability to practice effectively. Even worse, there is potential harm in producing reports that purport to mean one thing but really mean another.

The sample size must be adequate. Measuring encounters or referral statistics by physician is of little value if a physician has only 20 members in the panel. Even large databases may fall prey to this problem if the claims and clinical data are spread over too large a provider base, so that there are insufficient data for any given provider. Even when there are sufficient outpatient data for participating primary care physicians (PCPs), there frequently are insufficient data regarding inpatient admissions to be meaningful, even in large insurance claims databases.[1,2]

The data must encompass an adequate time period. Simple snapshots in time do not reveal the true picture. This is particularly important when one is looking at total health care resource consumption of patients. It is even more important when one is trying to determine whether a provider's behavior is consistent. Analyses that encompass long periods of time need to be viewed with the knowledge that practice patterns and behavior do indeed change over time, and that must be taken into account when long time periods are compared with short ones for the same types of episodes.

General User Needs

There are certain general needs that must be considered to make data more useful to end users. Raw data have no immediate value to the typical manager. Users must be able to access usable data as directly as possible. If a manager must stand in line to supplicate the priests of MIS to get critical information, opportunities will be lost. Access must also be as timely and easy as possible.

The ability of managers to have considerable flexibility with data is also desirable. If a manager must accept a hard-coded report and cannot cut the data in another fashion without a lot of wasted time and coding expense, then that manager will be trapped into managing only with whatever information the programmers have allowed for.

Ability To Use System Data with Other Tools

It is important that managers be able to obtain data from the system and use those data with other analytic tools. Advanced statistical analysis programs can be useful to the medical department in performing practice profiling (discussed below) or other trend analyses. The ability to export or download data into other plan programs, such as spreadsheets or database programs in personal computers, is also desirable. The ability to transmit analyzed data to physicians' offices is a feature that will become more important over time.

Format

How reports are formatted is a matter of taste and the MIS department's ability to produce the requested format. The easiest type of report for MIS to produce is one that tabulates columns of numbers. That is also usually the type most deadly to a busy manager. An already overburdened medical director has better things to do than sift through 20 pages of printout looking at raw numbers of referrals for each physician to get an idea of the referral rate.

The best types of report formats for senior plan managers usually are ones that can fit onto one or two 8" × 11" sheets of paper. Those reports should summarize the important data, indicate the outliers and deviations from the norm (or from preset standards), and indicate whether the manager will need to seek more detail. If managers need the raw data, they can always ask for them. For example, a two-page report giving the overall referral rate for the plan and the annualized referral rate per 1,000 members per year for each PCP for the month and the year to date may be sufficient by itself. If there are PCPs who are grossly over the norm, the medical director can then ask for the detail behind the report.

Graphic reports (especially color graphics) are highly useful for conveying large amounts of information quickly to busy managers. This is particularly true when one is presenting data to managers and providers who are not used to looking at reports. Unfortunately, most mainframe computer systems are not set up to produce graphic reports, so that data must be entered (or downloaded and then imported) into a personal computer before the graphs can be produced. This is a cumbersome process and not amenable to mass production. As computers and software become more sophisticated and interlinked through client-server systems, production of graphic reports will become more common.

Routine and Ad Hoc Reports

To manage information wisely, you need to decide which reports you will want on a routine basis and which reports you will want to call on an ad hoc or as-needed basis. For example, in a stable open panel plan, it is unnecessary for the medical director to receive a monthly report listing the recruiting activity or membership for each participating physician. That information, if it is needed, could be provided once per quarter. On the other hand, the medical director or associate medical director will usually want a hospital report on a daily basis.

The basic rule of thumb is to ask for routine reports for those functions that require constant management and will provide sufficient data to show trends and aberrations. Routine reports should allow you to decide when to focus on specific areas for further investigation. For example, watching the trend in referral costs could reveal an upswing that would result in your requesting detail about utilization by specialty. That in turn could lead to a need to look at utilization by individual providers in a single specialty. Save the highly detailed reports for infrequent intervals or ad hoc requests. Time spent deciphering cryptic reports is time spent not managing.

Further discussion of what types of summary reports may be useful follows. The message here is that reports for busy managers should be concise, readable, and easily interpreted and allow the manager to request further detail as needed. One common problem is overkill with detail. Judging by the stacks of computer printouts that are seen holding up the ceiling, reports in some plans must be valued by weight. It is easy to believe that the more data and detail the better. When that happens, you get the classic problem of not seeing the forest for the trees, with the manager spending more time grinding through reports than managing. Computers are wonderful tools, but they can smother you with data. Know what to ask for and when to ask for it.

FOCUS

Reports may be focused in a variety of ways to reveal useful information. For example, the overall admission rate for the plan may be normal, but a report focusing on where the patients are admitted may reveal that most of the admissions are to high-cost or even nonparticipating hospitals. What follows is a general guide to the different ways in which data can be focused.

Plan Average

Plan average simply looks at the average performance for the entire plan. It is useful in that it will relate closely to the plan's financial performance. For example, if the plan is over budget in medical expense, a plan average report that reveals hospital admissions to be greatly over budget will allow management to focus on that first. It also allows for comparative data between plans that may have somewhat different types of arrangements for the delivery of care.

Plan average is limited because it is relatively insensitive to specific causes of problems. That can be an advantage in some circumstances, however. In plans that manage by trying to keep performance clustered around a norm, that norm can sometimes be one of mediocrity. If the plan average reports and the provider-specific reports tie closely (i.e., there are no real outliers in performance), and if the plan is not doing as well as it should, then it is clear that there is a general problem of attitude or skills in the managers themselves and not a problem with a few recalcitrant providers or hospitals.

Plan average reports are frequently required by regulatory agencies and are also useful for reporting the overall performance of the plan to participating physicians and corporate parents.

Plan average reports also function as the backdrop against which other reports are viewed. A plan with multiple lines of business, such as commercial, Medicare, and Medicaid, will probably create additional plan average reports that focus on each line of business.

Health Center, Individual Practice Association, Provider Organization, or Geographically Related Center

The purpose of this focus is to provide midlevel managers with data for their own areas of responsibility. In many plans, especially large or geographically diverse ones, it is common to divide up responsibility into manageable units. The problem of span of control in large or diverse plans can be a very real one. In closed panels this often refers to a health center or a small number of geographically related health centers. In open panels, this usually refers to discrete multiple individual practice associations (IPAs), subunits within the overall health plan (e.g., pools of doctors [PODs]), or geographically divided territories. In plans that contract with vertical IDSs, such as physician–hospital organizations or management services organizations (see Chapter 4 for a discussion of such systems), it will be important to develop reports focused on each individual IDS.

Individual Physician

Most managed care plans produce reports that focus on individual physicians. This may refer to PCPs who are functioning as gatekeepers or care coordinators but may apply equally to open access health maintenance organizations (HMOs) or preferred provider organizations (PPOs). Virtually all the types of utilization reports discussed later in this chapter are amenable to focusing on individual physicians.

Physicians become understandably paranoid about the plethora of reports that are produced about them. They feel that they are being judged by machines or by standards that fail to take into account any extenuating circumstances and that their fate will be decided on the basis of sterile reports. In truth, it is the ability to report the behavior of individual physicians that provides managed care plans with their most powerful tool and physicians with their greatest source of both concern and potential help.

Care must be taken when one is using physician-specific reports. The medical director must look behind the data of the report for the reasons for the reported performance. This is not to say that any behavior should be rationalized, and physicians are as adept as anybody in arguing that they are different and should not be held to the same standards as anyone else. Rather, this is to say that individual physician performance reports need to be used intelligently and properly.

Service or Vendor Type

This type of report refers to the entity delivering the service (e.g., a hospital or a type of referral specialist). Focusing reports on those delivering the service (sometimes referred to as vendors) will be of great value when one is negotiating contracts and will allow for improved utilization control. These types of reports also help focus on areas where attention should be directed. Remember Sutton's law: Go where the money is!

Employer Group

This type of report tracks utilization and other data by enrolled group. For those plans that are allowed to experience rate, this will be necessary to develop the actual cost experience; even for those plans that must community rate, these data will tell you whether you have a problem with a particular group that may need to be addressed (see Chapter 23 for a discussion of underwriting). Also, some large employers are demanding such data as a requisite for offering your plan to their employees.

HOSPITAL UTILIZATION REPORTS

Routine hospital utilization management reports may be divided into two categories: the daily log and monthly summaries. Many plans now automate their utilization management systems (see Chapter 13). In addition to producing reports as discussed below, these systems allow for on-line access to far more information than would be practical on a printed report. Nevertheless, printed reports regarding hospital utilization remain useful to medical managers, who may review them in a manner and time not possible if they were required to stare at a computer terminal.

Daily Log

It is almost a requirement for a managed care plan to produce a daily hospital log. This document serves as a working tool for the utilization management nurse and the medical director in controlling institutional utilization. Its design should be directed toward providing the necessary information to manage cases actively that are current or prospective. Data should be sorted and printed by whatever management criteria make sense. For example, you may wish to print each hospital's census separately so that the utilization review nurse can take it when making hospital rounds. In plans where associate medical directors will have primary responsibility, you may want to print the log so that it sorts by geographic region, IPA, IDS, or health center.

Useful information for any daily log includes elements illustrated in Exhibit 19–1. Information on a daily log that is also useful in most types of health plans is illustrated in Exhibit 19–2.

Monthly Summary

A monthly summary report of hospital utilization should also be produced. This differs somewhat from the daily log because it is used to identify patterns for overall management rather than to serve as a mechanism for performing concurrent utilization review. A monthly report might include the data illustrated in Exhibit 19–3 for both the month ended and the year to date.

Exhibit 19–1 Minimum Data Elements for a Daily Hospital Log

Current census
- Name of patient
- Hospital
- Diagnosis and procedures
- PCP
- Admitting physician
- Consultants or specialists
- Admission date
- Length of stay to date
- Free text narrative with clinical information
- In-network compared with out-of-network status

Hospital statistics
- Days per 1,000 today
- Days per 1,000 month to date

Prospective admits and outpatient surgeries

Exhibit 19–2 Additional Useful Data Elements for a Daily Hospital Log

Service type (as part of current census)
- Medicine
- Surgery
- Pediatrics
- Gynecologic surgery
- Obstetrics
- Mental health
- Chemical dependency
- Intensive care unit/cardiac care unit
- Neonatal intensive care unit
- Rehabilitation
- Outpatient surgery

Estimated length of stay or maximum length of stay

Admissions and discharges today and month to date

Authorization or denial status

Catastrophic case report

Line of business code
- Commercial
- Medicare
- Medicaid
- Self-insured versus fully insured
- Special accounts

OUTPATIENT UTILIZATION

Although daily reports are necessary for controlling hospital utilization, in only the most tightly managed health plans will that be neces-

Exhibit 19–3 Sample Data Elements for a Monthly Summary of Hospital Utilization*

Plan statistics
- Days per 1,000
- Admissions per 1,000
- Average length of stay
- Average per diem cost
- Average per case (per admission) cost
- Emergency department visits and average cost

Hospital- and provider-specific statistics
- Days per 1,000
- Admissions per 1,000
- Average length of stay
- Average per diem cost
- Average per case (per admission) cost
- Emergency department visits and average cost

Statistics by service type (see Exhibit 19–2)
- Days per 1,000
- Admissions per 1,000
- Average length of stay
- Average per diem cost
- Average per case (per admission) cost

Retrospective authorizations

Pended cases for review

In-network compared with out-of-network statistics

Number and percentage of denied days

* The plan will want to produce these statistics not only for the entire plan but for major lines of business as well (i.e., commercial, Medicare, Medicaid, self-insured versus fully insured, and so forth). The plan may also want to report year-to-date.

sary for controlling outpatient utilization. In general, outpatient utilization control is usually best done by using monthly reports, both routine and ad hoc. Reports should include data both for the month ended and for the year to date. Data may also be reported by month on a 12-month rolling basis. Data for such reports might include the elements illustrated in Exhibit 19–4, depending on the needs of medical management.

Categories of outpatient or ambulatory care may be divided into several components, each of which has its own unique characteristics. Office visits for primary care, including any testing or procedures, is one such category, as is the related category of office visits for specialty care. Ambulatory procedures are a different matter,

Exhibit 19–4 Sample Data for a Monthly Summary of Outpatient Utilization*

Primary care encounter rates
- Visits per day (closed panels only)
- Visits per member per year (annualized)
- Percentage of new visits
- Revisit interval rates (to look for churning)

Preventive care
- Immunization rates
- Mammography
- Pap smears
- Other

Laboratory/pathology utilization per visit

Radiology utilization per visit
- Total
- Focused (e.g., magnetic resonance imaging)

Prescriptions
- Prescriptions per visit or prescriptions per member per year
- Average cost per prescription
- Percentage generic

Referral utilization
- Referral rate per 100 primary care visits or per 1,000 members per year
- Comparison of PCP referral rate with peer group referral rate
- Initial referrals only compared with total referral visits
- Cost per referral by PCP, plan average, and specialty
- Number of visits and cost by specialty
  1. Top specialty referrals for each PCP
  2. Average cost per visit
  3. Per member per month cost by specialty

Out-of-network specialty care in point-of-service plans
- Percentage of total specialty care
- Cost
- Specialty and utilization categories

Ambulatory procedures
- By ambulatory patient groups
- By ambulatory care groups and ambulatory diagnosis groups
- By diagnostic or procedure code

Ancillary care
- Physical therapy and other rehabilitation therapies
- Podiatry
- Eye care
- Oral surgery
- Other

* The plan will want to produce these statistics not only for the entire plan but for major lines of business as well (i.e., commercial, Medicare, Medicaid, self-insured versus fully insured, and so forth). The plan may also want to report year-to-date.

however, as is the setting for the procedure. The identical procedure may be performed in a physician's office, an ambulatory care center, or the outpatient department of a hospital.

Some plans have addressed the issue of ambulatory care, especially outpatient procedures, by using statistical groupings. One method is ambulatory patient groups (APGs), a method developed under contract by 3M Systems for the Health Care Financing Administration for use in Medicare (Medicare has yet to use them as this chapter is being written, but a number of private health plans have adopted them for reimbursement purposes; see Chapter 11). APGs are to outpatient services what diagnosis-related groups (DRGs) are to inpatient ones, although APGs are based on procedures rather than simply on diagnoses and are considerably more complex. Under APGs, all the services associated with a given outpatient procedure or visit are bundled into the APG reimbursement. More than one APG may be billed if more than one procedure is performed, but there is significant discounting for additional APGs. There are 297 APGs, and if the number of events is quite high, a plan may analyze them all; most plans, however, will probably need to cluster the APGs into sets to achieve statistical validity.

Another statistical approach is to use ambulatory care groups (ACGs), a methodology that focuses on a resource-based measure of burden of illness.[3] Ambulatory patients are monitored for all encounters, and each encounter is classified as one of 34 ambulatory diagnosis groups (ADGs) based on medical resource used over a 1-year period and on the expectation of recurrence of that diagnosis over time. The set of ADGs for each patient is then combined with measures of age and sex to assign the patient to 1 of 51 mutually exclusive ACGs. ADGs and ACGs may also be looked at independently.[4] ACG and ADG methodology requires a high level of statistical sophistication, and the programming is not always found in the plan's MIS.

As has been mentioned earlier, once you decide on the routine reports, you can use those to decide what reports to request on an ad hoc basis. For example, if total expenses for cardiology appear to be high, you could investigate further by requesting reports that show who is ordering the referrals, what ancillary testing is being done, which specialists are seeing the patients and how much are they charging, and so forth.

Open access systems, or systems that do not use a PCP gatekeeper model, present special problems in monitoring utilization. In a PPO or managed indemnity plan, there will be no physician-specific membership base to use as a denominator. In HMOs that allow open access to specialists or allow specialists to self-authorize revisits or secondarily to authorize referrals to other specialists, there will be no way to measure specialist utilization against a fixed membership base (the base is only for the PCPs, not the specialists).

In these situations, you must be willing to accept less precise methods of measuring utilization of referral services and specialist utilization. Reports should focus on those areas under the control of the specialist as well as the PCP. Examples of such data elements are illustrated in Exhibit 19–5.

PROVIDER PROFILING

Closely related to all the issues discussed in this chapter is provider profiling. Profiling means the collection, collation, and analysis of data to develop provider-specific profiles. Such profiles have a variety of uses, but the most important ones are producing provider feedback reports to help the providers modify their own behavior, recruiting providers into the network, and choosing which providers may not be (or are not) the right fit with the plan's managed care philosophy and goals. Other uses include determining specialists to whom the plan will send certain types of cases, detecting fraud and abuse, determining how to focus the utilization management program, supporting performance-based reimbursement systems, and performing economic modeling.

The initial focus of many physician profiling activities has been inpatient care. A hospital case

Exhibit 19–5 Sample Data for an Open Access Model Plan

Outpatient Services

- Average number of visits per member per year
- Average number of visits per member per year to each specialty
- Diagnostic utilization per visit
  1. Laboratory
  2. Radiology and imaging
  3. Other
- Average cost per visit
- Procedures per 1,000 visits per year (annualized)
  1. Aggregate
  2. By procedure for top 10 by specialty type
  3. By individual specialist
- Average cost per episode (as defined for each sentinel diagnosis) over a defined time period, including charges not directly billed by provider

Inpatient Services

- Average total cost per case, including charges not billed by provider, for hospitalized cases
- Average length of stay for defined procedures
- Average rate of performance of a procedure, such as:
  1. Cesarean section rate
  2. Hysterectomy rate
  3. Transurethral prostatectomy rate
  4. Cardiac procedures
- Readmission rate or complication rate
- Use of resources before and after the hospitalization

is usually easily definable (except for cases that are transferred or readmitted), and the physicians delivering care are usually identifiable. The cost of inpatient care has also led to this focus. Basic hospital care profiling (adjusted for case mix and severity; see below) combined with feedback to physicians and active intervention has been shown to reduce length of stay effectively.[5] Recent activity has shifted to considering outpatient care as well because it has been recognized that care occurs across a continuum rather than in isolated episodes.

Some provider profiling systems simply look at the behavior of the provider against certain norms. Comparison against norms is certainly necessary, but it is fraught with difficulties. The chief difficulty is defining the norm, but an attendant difficulty is choosing what to look at. Most profiling activities focus solely on the actions of the provider. It is better to attempt to examine provider behavior from the standpoint of total health care resource consumption and outcome, including resources not directly delivered or billed by the provider, and to look at true episodes of care and outcomes as opposed to constellations of single visits.

Episodes of Care

Episodes of care are defined as time-related intervals that have meaning to the behavior you are trying to measure. Episodes may vary considerably both by clinical condition and by the provider type that is being measured. In the case of obstetrics, obvious measures such as cesarean section rate and average length of stay are important but will not reveal the full picture. Looking at the entire prenatal and postnatal episode may reveal significant differences in the use of ultrasound and other diagnostics or perhaps a great deal of unbundled claims during the prenatal period. In the case of some medical conditions, the episode may extend over the course of years. Furthermore, it is possible in patients with multiple medical conditions to have overlapping episodes of care, making it more difficult to sort out what resources are being used for what episode.

Related to the issue of episode is the problem of identifying which provider is actually responsible for care. As an example, an internist may be responsible for the care of a diabetic but may have little responsibility for managing that patient's broken leg other than to refer the patient to a cost-effective orthopedist. This issue is also difficult regarding hospitalized patients. It is not uncommon for the admitting physician not to be the attending physician, especially when surgery is involved.

The hallmark of episode definition is the ability to link up all the health care resources into a defined event. This may mean diagnostic services (e.g., laboratory or imaging), therapeutic services (e.g., physical therapy), consultations, outpatient visits, and inpatient visits. In other words, it must be a patient-based analysis rather than a provider-based one; the analysis of the behavior of providers is a product of examining what happens to their patients.

Adjusting for Severity and Case Mix

Case mix and severity are always issues of contention when one is profiling providers: Providers with costly profiles will always complain that they have the sickest patients. When you are performing profiling, the issue of severity must be accounted for. One technique for doing so is to use severity of illness indicators. Severity of illness is most often used in hospital cases (using, for example, 3M's all-patient DRGs, which assign patients to DRGs and adjust that based on four levels of severity), but it may be applied to outpatient care as well (with some difficulty by using, for example, APGs, ACGs, and ADGs). Statistical manipulation, such as trimming in outlier cases, is also commonly employed (i.e., if only a few cases are outliers, one brings those cases back to the mean).

Adjusting for severity and case mix is important and cannot be bypassed. It is interesting to note, however, that it probably accounts for only a small amount of the variation noted in practice behavior. At least one study has reported that adjusting for severity and case mix significantly reduced the number of physicians who appeared to be outliers, although there was some discussion as to whether the methodology actually made genuine outliers look normal.[6,7] Other studies have reported that these adjustments accounted for little of the variation in practice that was found.[8–10]

Practices will also have differences in the age and sex make-up of their patient panel that must be accounted for. Geographic differences may also account for utilization variations. These must be factored into any profiling report. Even within a single specialty there will be differences in how "specialized" a specialist is. For example, a specialist may have a larger percentage of primary care or may not care for patients in the intensive care unit. The plan therefore will want to look at the degree to which a physician is truly a specialist in his or her mix of routine and complex cases.

Comparing the Results of Profiling

Practice profiles are of no use unless the results are compared with some type of standard. There are certain problems inherent in comparisons of provider profiles. All these problems are resolvable, but medical managers need to be aware of them before embarking on profiling.

The usual way of comparing profiling results is to provide data for each individual practice in comparison with one or more of the following:

- *Plan average results*—This standard is simply the average for the entire plan. It is the crudest method of comparison.
- *IPA, POD, or IDS*—A variation on plan average, this compares the practice only with other practices within a smaller set of providers than the entire network. This approach may be combined with multiple other approaches when a plan contracts through organized provider systems. Another variation on this is geography even in the absence of organized provider groups.
- *Specialty or peer group*—This compares each practice only with its own specialty. For example, internists are only compared with other internists.
- *Peer group adjusted for age, sex, and case mix/severity of illness*—This is the most complicated approach, as noted earlier, but provides the most meaningful comparative data.
- *Budget*—This compares the profile with budgeted utilization and cost, a necessary activity when providers are accepting full or substantial risk for medical expenses.

It is not always clear what specialty a physician really is practicing. Most plans have provider files that indicate what specialty type a physician has self-indicated, but it is surprising how often that information does not match up with specialty indicators in the claims file. Of course, plans that perform comprehensive verification of board specialty status will have more accurate data than plans that depend on self-reporting by physicians. Even when the specialty designation is accurate, there is no guarantee that the provider actually makes a living at that specialty.

The problem of provider specialty definition is particularly acute when one is looking at primary care. Many board-certified medical specialists actually spend a considerable amount of time performing primary care, whereas others spend the majority of their time practicing true specialty medicine. This has great implications for how a plan will evaluate performance of specialists as well as PCPs when comparisons with peers are used (as they almost always are). A related issue is determining which physicians will be considered specialists at all because the plan may not want to send referrals to a specialist who is not particularly active in his or her designated specialty.

Even when the issue of specialty definition is resolved, there remains the problem that no two practices are exactly alike. As an example, either general internists perform flexible sigmoidoscopies, or they do not. If one looks only at charge patterns, the internist who performs the procedure will look more expensive compared with the internist who does not, but that analysis will fail to pick up the fact that the internist who does not perform flexible sigmoidoscopies instead refers them all to a gastroenterologist who charges more than the first internist (of course, the first internist could be overutilizing the procedure, but that is a separate part of the analysis).

The next issue is the problem of providers who behave as though they are in a group but are not legally connected and do not appear as a group in the plan's provider file. An example would be two physicians who share an office, share on-call duty, and see each other's patients but who have different tax numbers and billing services. The reason that this is important in managed care is that, if the plan contracts with one but not the other, the member may wind up seeing the nonparticipating physician and be subject to balance billing. Even if the physicians agree not to balance bill, the plan still may not actually want the other physician in the network, even on an occasional basis.

Related to the above is the ability to detect linkages between practices and ancillary services. Examples include orthopedists who own physical therapy practices and neurologists who have a proprietary interest in a magnetic resonance imaging center.

Incorporation of Other Data

Many plans incorporate other data into a provider profile analysis. Claims and encounter data are enormously useful, as are data from hospital episodes, but there are additional sources of data as well. Credentialing data (see Chapter 7) may be automated and referenced. Data from member services, such as complaints, transfer rates, or administrative problems, may be incorporated (see Chapter 24). Data from the quality management program (see Chapter 17) and member satisfaction are now included in the profiling reports and even compensation programs of advanced managed care organizations (see Chapter 9).

Feedback

Medical management reports should not be confined to plan managers. As mentioned in several chapters in this book (especially Chapter 18), feedback to providers is a useful adjunct to other medical management activities. Feedback to providers must be clear, easy to understand, and accurate.

Feedback should be meaningful and useful to both parties, not just the plan or the provider. When feedback reports are clearly linked with performance expectations, and when such reports can help a provider alter a behavior in a positive way (which will in turn benefit that provider), then feedback may be successful. This is especially true when feedback is linked to the financial incentive system.

Providers will alter their behavior in response to feedback for a variety of reasons. Natural competitiveness and peer pressure may exert influence. More important, the opportunity to increase market share and to improve their revenue will be a powerful reason to respond to feedback. Fear of possible adverse actions by the plan may also play a role if a provider is a clear outlier and if feedback provides a concrete measure of expectation by the plan.

Hospitals may benefit from feedback reports as well. Hospitals are providers in their own right, even though the physicians on staff give the orders. Nevertheless, hospitals have their own policies and procedures that influence how care is rendered, and hospitals certainly have their own billing practices. Hospitals can also have a strong role in influencing the practice behavior of the physicians on staff and can work effectively with managed care plans to effect changes.

Feedback is not always effective in changing behavior, however. The topic of changing physician behavior, including the use of data and feedback, is discussed in Chapter 18.

Focused Utilization Management

As noted earlier, profiling provides medical managers with the ability to focus utilization management more efficiently. Some providers may perform at such a high level of cost effectiveness that the plan can essentially rely on feedback and case management support rather than on more traditional methods of managing utilization; in other words, those providers would need little oversight or intervention by the plan. In other cases, the plan may determine that heightened levels of utilization review and precertification are required for some providers who are clear outliers.

Profiling and data management may also reveal systemwide issues of utilization that require a broad approach. For example, it may be found that emergency department usage is uniformly high and not due to a small number of outlier physicians. In that case, a focused approach to demand management (see Chapter 13) would have greater utility than focusing on individual physician behavior.

Last, profiling will enable the medical director to determine which specialists should receive more referrals and preferential business in contrast to those specialists who are less cost effective, of lesser quality, or simply too low volume in a competitive market.

CONCLUSION

Medical management reports are powerful and absolutely necessary tools for managers of health plans. Routine reports need to be simple to read and compact and must provide only those data required generally to manage the plan. They need to provide managers with sufficient information to order ad hoc, detailed reports required to solve specific problems that are flagged by the routine reports. Provider profiling is taking on an ever greater role in managed care but remains a complex area. Data overload is a frequent and deadly problem in managed care, but intelligent use of reports should prevent that from occurring. As systems evolve, the ability of managers to access useful information directly and manipulate it as needed will provide a clear competitive edge.

Study Questions

1. Discuss the principles of using data to manage health care delivery systems.
2. List the most important reports a medical director would need by model type and describe the key elements in those reports.
3. Describe the most common problems medical directors face in using data to

manage utilization, and what steps might be taken to deal with those problems.

4. What are the most important principles in provider profiling? What are the most common problems with profiling and how might a plan address those problems?
5. What common sources of data are accessed in producing data for medical management? How can problems with each of these data sources cause problems with the others?

REFERENCES AND NOTES

1. R.D. Lasker, et al., Realizing the Potential of Practice Pattern Profiling, *Inquiry* 29 (1992): 287–297.
2. R. Nathanson, et al., Using Claims Data To Select Primary Care Physicians for a Managed Care Network, *Managed Care Quarterly* 2 (1994): 50–59.
3. B. Starfield, et al., Ambulatory Care Groups: A Categorization of Diagnoses for Research and Management, *Health Services Research* 26 (1991): 53–74.
4. J. Weiner, et al., Development and Application of a Population Oriented Measure of Ambulatory Care Case-Mix, *Medical Care* 29 (1991): 452–472.
5. G. Bennett, et al., Case Study in Physician Profiling, *Managed Care Quarterly* 2 (1994): 60–70.
6. S. Salem-Schatz, et al., The Case for Case-Mix Adjustment in Practice Profiling: When Good Apples Look Bad, *Journal of the American Medical Association* 272 (1994): 871–874.
7. H.G. Welch, et al., Case-Mix Adjustment: Making Bad Apples Look Good, *Journal of the American Medical Association* 273 (1995): 772–773.
8. Bennett, et al., Case Study in Physician Profiling.
9. Nathanson, et al., Using Claims Data To Select Primary Care Physicians.
10. H.G. Welch, et al., Physician Profiling: An Analysis of Inpatient Practice Patterns in Florida and Oregon, *New England Journal of Medicine* 330 (1994): 607–612.

SUGGESTED READING

Betty, W.R., et al. 1990. Physician Practice Profiles: A Valuable Information System for HMOs. *Medical Group Management* 37: 68–75.

Blackwood, M.J. 1994. Utilization Management and Data Acquisition: A Case Study. *Benefits Quarterly* 10(3): 38–42.

Boll, A. and McCafferty, C. 1994. Why Managed Care Needs Encounter-based Systems. *Healthcare Infomatics* 11(2): 78, 80.

Braham, R.L., and Ruchlin, H.S. 1987. Physician Practice Profiles: A Case Study of the Use of Audit and Feedback in an Ambulatory Care Group Practice. *Health Care Management Review* 12: 11–16.

Doubilet, P., et al. 1986. Use and Misuse of the Term "Cost Effective" in Medicine. *New England Journal of Medicine* 314: 253–256.

Eisenberg, J.M. 1989. Clinical Economics: A Guide to the Economic Analysis of Clinical Practices. *Journal of the American Medical Association* 262: 2879–2886.

Goldfield, N., and Boland, P. 1996. *Physician Profiling and Risk Adjustment*. Gaithersburg, Md.: Aspen.

Gotowka, T.D., et al. 1993. Health Data Analysis and Reporting: Organization and System Strategies. *Managed Care Quarterly* 1: 26–34.

Harris, J.S. 1991. Watching the Numbers: Basic Data for Health Care Management. *Journal of Occupational Medicine* 33: 275–278.

Hughes, R.G., and Lee, D.E. 1991. Using Data Describing Physician Inpatient Practice Patterns: Issues and Opportunities. *Health Care Management Review* 16: 33–40.

Kenkel, P.J. 1995. *Report Cards: What Every Health Provider Needs to Know about HEDIS and Other Performance Measures*. Gaithersburg, Md.: Aspen.

Nathanson, P., Noether, M., et al. 1994. Using Claims Data To Select Primary Care Physicians for a Managed Care Network. *Managed Care Quarterly* 2(4): 50–59.

Physician Payment Review Commission. 1992. *Physician Payment Review Commission Conference on Profiling*. Washington, D.C.: Physician Payment Review Commission.

Wang, H., Sharp, V., and Coulter, C. 1994. Creating an Information System for Evaluating HMO Performance. *Managed Care Medicine* 1(5): 43–44, 46–49.

Part IV

Selected Topics in Health Plan Operational Management

"We could manage this matter to a T."

Sterne
Tristram Shandy, bk. II, ch. 5, 1760

Chapter 20

Information Systems Operations and Organization Structures

Robert Reese

Study Objectives

- Understand the role of information services in a managed care organization
- Understand the basic activities of the information systems area
- Understand different approaches to delivering services, and the advantages and disadvantages of those approaches
- Understand some of the future initiatives in information systems

Numerous contributing items have caused many health care organizations to view their information systems (IS) operations differently from other operations. The lack of enterprise-wide technology-enabled systems and the focus of available applications on internal operating procedures led many health care organizations in the past to view their IS operations as an operating expense. As efforts have been made to control or reduce costs, many organizations have focused on reducing their operating costs by targeting IS operations in the budget wars.

Today, health care organizations, specifically managed care organizations (MCOs), better understand the ability of technology-enabled systems to lower their operating costs and manage the entire enterprise. Technology-enabled systems are now viewed as an investment in the future of the enterprise rather than an expense. As a result, many health care organizations are exploring the most efficient means of building and supporting technology-enabled systems throughout their enterprises.

The health care industry, however, lags behind other industries, such as manufacturing and banking, in its investment in information technology. In fact, health care organizations spend, on average, about 2 percent of their operating expenses on information technology, whereas heavy manufacturing companies spend 6 to 8 percent and banking firms spend from 8 to 12 percent.[1] As a result of minimal investment, information technologies in many hospitals can be characterized as disjointed service-specific applications with little internal or external connectivity.

The managed care industry is no exception to this low level of investment. In a review of Ernst & Young managed care clients conducted in the fall of 1994, IS expenditures were expected to be in the range of 1.4 percent to 2.2 percent of revenues. The bulk of the expenditures in this study was expected to be in the areas of application software. The focus was to be enhancing clinical competency, particularly outcomes analysis and demand management. Additionally, money was to be used to expand the use of technology to enhance the primary and specialty physicians' knowledge and use of established regional and national practice guidelines to improve overall patient care.

This low level of investment is quickly changing, as evidenced by the 1995 Health Informa-

Robert Reese is a partner with Ernst & Young LLP in Detroit, Michigan. He specializes in information technology issues relative to managed care.

tion Management Systems Society survey.[2] In that survey, 80 percent of the chief information officers (CIOs) who responded indicated that their IS budgets were growing. In addition, the vendor marketplace for health care information technology is growing. In October 1995, the *New York Times* noted that "health care could be the biggest growth market [for vendors of information technology] in the 1990s, exceeding $20 billion in sales annually by the turn of the century."[3(p.41)]

As managed care contracting and capitation expand to dominate the U.S. market, low-cost health care providers who can quickly and efficiently share information will have a distinct advantage. MCOs and integrated delivery systems (see Chapter 4) have already begun to transition themselves toward reduced cost by leveraging new technologies and providing value through information management among physicians and patients and between payers and providers.

GENERAL ORGANIZATION STRUCTURE AND REPORTING RELATIONSHIPS

Organizational structure and reporting relationships are vital to the successful management of the IS operations within the MCO. A CIO is necessary to oversee the entire MCO as well as to represent IS operations on the enterprise's strategic planning committee. The CIO's main responsibility is to align the IS operations with the strategic direction of the MCO as well as to ensure that targeted efficiencies are achieved.

An IS strategic planning committee should be established to oversee the continuum of IS operations. This committee should identify a vision statement that is consistent with the MCO's operations to direct all business decisions and initiatives within the IS department. The MCO's chief operating officer and a representative from finance should participate on this committee to help ensure alignment with the MCO's strategic and financial direction.

Directors of IS operations, depending on the size of the organization, should have responsibility for each of the separate operating entities (e.g., claims and benefits administration, ambulatory care services, etc.) within the MCO. Their primary responsibility is to ensure alignment with the strategic direction within their entity and to oversee the day-to-day IS operations. The directors should be members of the IS strategic planning committee. Within each entity, IS teams should be established to support and meet the needs of a specific customer base.

Purchasing, hardware support and maintenance, employee training, and application support should function independent of the MCO's operating entities and should operate under the leadership of individual directors. As members of the IS strategic planning committee, these directors should be under the direction of the committee. A sample organizational structure is illustrated in Figure 20–1.

ANNUAL OPERATING GOALS WITH QUARTERLY UPDATES FOR REFINEMENTS

Because of the strong alignment between effective technology-enabled systems and the success of the MCO, it is important that IS operations, the means of building and supporting the technology-enabled systems, be included in the MCO's strategic plan and be given specific operating goals that help move the MCO in the direction of its strategic plan. The IS operating goals should be developed annually in conjunction with the MCO's strategic plan. Goals should include at least the following: the MCO's strategic goals, the IS divisions' supporting strategic goals, a list of approved IS projects that have been included in the annual capital budget, IS staffing and educational requirements, the annual IS budget, and long-term (3- to 5-year) IS plans. Built-in quarterly reviews and updates prevent getting off track or falling behind.

COST MANAGEMENT

When structuring contractual agreements with their customers (or internal departments) in

Figure 20–1 Sample IS organizational structure

the past, many organizations closely examined the operating procedures of the primary business and included IS operations as free or set-fee support for the primary business process. This type of IS cost structuring increases the difficulty of IS providing quality service and provides no means to link the size of the customer base supported to the level of information technology provided.

As an effective component of cost accounting, a mechanism to help manage IS costs is to charge each customer or department for the relative amount of IS services utilized on a per member per month (PMPM) basis. The PMPM effectively increases or decreases IS revenues as the customer base, and the resulting amount of IS support, grows or shrinks.

CLIENT RELATIONSHIPS

The IS department generally has more customers than any other department within the MCO. Its customers or clients include every staff member who uses the IS and every staff member who utilizes the data (reports and so forth) produced by the IS. All the constituencies may make requests to the IS department about the format and content of reports, the format and content of user workstation screens, and application errors. This flexibility places a significant responsibility on the department to manage its staff and prioritize user requests.

One of the goals of a progressive IS organization is to help users become more proactive, responsible, and accountable for identifying systems needs and assisting with implementations. To meet the daily and long-term needs of the users and the members of the MCO, an effective IS department must develop an enterprisewide user support philosophy.

Client Support Philosophy

In the past, most IS departments have operated in a reactive mode to client end-user requests for application enhancements and/or support. Often, the end-user would have to track down an individual within the IS division to issue a request. The schedule of the IS department would often determine the priority level of the request. IS would then react to the request by developing and implementing a solution. Most commonly, the solution would address only the immediate request and not the long-term impact as time became a limiting factor and more requests were being made. In this scenario, the end-user had little input into how the IS department prioritized or completed user requests, and users often became disillusioned and frustrated.

In an effort to provide quality community service today, MCOs are implementing quality initiatives throughout their organizations. Effective IS services, whether owned or outsourced, are beginning to develop service level agreements, customer teams, and user satisfaction surveys to provide the level of service expected by their customers.

Service Level Agreements

Under the direction of the CIO, the IS strategic planning committee should develop service level agreements that clearly define the expected level of service that IS operations are to provide to their customers and a recourse for scenarios where the level of service falls short. Service level agreements, also known as guiding principles, serve as boundaries regarding expectations, roles, and responsibilities for senior management, the user community, and the IS department. The agreement should address such areas as expectations of support provided by each party, the working relationships among the three parties, how IS-related projects are coordinated from project initiation through postimplementation, and benefits realization. The agreement should also drive the philosophy of the customer teams and satisfaction surveys.

Customer Teams

Today, MCOs are assigning teams to work with each constituency. These teams develop an understanding of the business issues facing the customer and work with the customer to develop systems (people, processes, and technology) to improve the business process. In this manner, MCOs are taking a proactive approach to improving operations and reducing costs.

User Satisfaction Surveys

User satisfaction surveys are tools that review the effectiveness of the IS operations and provide insight into possible operational improvements within the MCO. User satisfaction surveys should be used annually or semiannually and should include questions relating to the following: IS operations improvement opportunities, upcoming legislative or client issues that could affect the business, and training requirements. When used effectively, user satisfaction surveys can provide a tremendous amount of information.

INTELLECTUAL PROPERTY

In many organizations, it is common practice to develop applications in house and then interface those applications with a packaged application or make modifications to the packaged application directly. For legal reasons, the organization adding to the package application needs to understand fully the issues of ownership and support.

When an organization develops an application and then integrates it with a packaged solution, the vendor that developed the original package may gain ownership rights to the application. The same holds true for modifications made to the source code of the package solution in that the organization that developed the original package gains the ownership rights of the modifications. Before signing the software licensing agreement, the organization should negotiate with the vendor to retain the right to any software developed by the organization.

Support agreements can also be affected by in-house source code and/or package modifications. In almost all cases, when modifications are made to any source code or package by anyone other than the company that originally produced the package, the vendor will no longer support the product. Support issues are important to understand because in-house modifications to an application may adversely affect the IS operations and thus the MCO.

OUTSOURCING VERSUS OWNERSHIP

Although many readers may assume that information technology is an internally managed function, this is not always strictly the case. As a result of the expertise required to purchase, install, and manage IS operations within an organization, many health care companies choose to contract with outside vendors to provide the information technology to meet their needs. For some MCOs, outsourcing all or part of their IS operations has significant potential to provide quality customer service while reducing operating costs. The central issue is to examine closely each function that the IS division performs, compare those functions with vendors' products and services, and identify areas that may benefit from outsourcing.

The level of outsourcing, as in other industries, can vary significantly from providing limited application support to providing complete IS staff and technology. Similarly, the types of organizations that provide outsourcing services range from consulting firms, to health care IS hardware and software vendors, to neighboring (noncompeting) or organizationally related health care organizations with excess resources.

Outsourcing has (or can have) many benefits. The most notable benefit is when another company, whose service is its core competency, can provide the service in a more cost-effective and cost-efficient manner than can be achieved by providing the service in house. Outsourcing can allow an organization to focus on its core business while providing access to state-of-the-art technology and scarce resources. From a cost standpoint, it can preserve capital resources while reducing and providing for predictable operating costs. Some additional benefits include guaranteed levels of service, shared risk, and improved user satisfaction.

Areas that commonly reap benefits from outsourcing are management, purchasing, hardware support and maintenance, employee training, specific application support, and application development. Outsourcing the purchasing function often leads to volume discounts, consistencies among purchased equipment, and better inventory tracking and control. Outsourcing other areas often improves quality while reducing necessary staffing levels. Again, each area being considered for outsourcing should be examined closely and weighed against the value of ownership of that area.

Many of the outsourcing contracts over the past 5 years have involved some form of upfront payment by the vendor. Some of the payments provided cash for capital equipment acquired as part of the contract. In return, the vendor received a long-term annuity agreement. The term, usually 10 to 15 years, enabled the vendor to begin to expect a certain level of cash flow. It was this guaranteed cash flow that enabled many of the vendors to experience substantial increases in the value of their companies. Because the cost of technology (most notably hardware) has dropped dramatically, however, clients now realize that they are paying far more than the vendor's true cost plus margin. It is for this reason, along with other lesser issues, that many of the outsourcing agreements of the past are being renegotiated. MCOs should regard outsourcing as an option when deciding to focus on core services.

HARDWARE CONSIDERATIONS

Mainframes, Minis, and Personal Computers

A variety of hardware environments, including mainframes, midrange systems, minis, and personal computers (PCs), exist for today's MCO. As would be expected, support issues vary among these environments. In general, mainframe and midrange systems require greater support resources than minis and PCs. Mainframe and midrange systems are often proprietary systems, making little or no use of industry standards and requiring a great deal of time and effort to interface with other systems. Most mainframe and midrange applications are written in a first- or second-generation programming language and do not maximize the potential of the powerful development tools and commercial applications that are available for the mini and PC environment.

Conversion/Migration

Although most organizations simply cannot afford to replace all their legacy systems at one time, migration of these legacy systems to more open, distributed network models is common. It should be noted that, during the migration period, both environments must be supported.

A support consideration when the organization is moving from a mainframe or midrange system to a more distributed system is the migration (conversion) itself. This process is complex and requires numerous resources, both user and IS operations involvement, and a strong organizational commitment to be successful. Conversion strategies and work plans should be developed in advance for all the following: infrastructure migration, application migration, process improvement (developing new procedures to capitalize on the efficiencies of the new applications), training schedules, and job definitions.

"Throw-Away" Solutions

Once the decision has been made to migrate from one environment to another, IS resources should focus on performing the migration. As is often the case, organizations will attempt to migrate to a new platform while continuing normal operation on the existing platform. Attention should be paid to reducing the number of throw-away solutions, that is, those solutions made specifically for a system that will soon be obsolete. Efforts should also be made continuously to eliminate the development of short-lived (single-use) system solutions. This is more likely to occur in the mini and PC environments because thousands of commercial applications can be purchased and installed quickly to fulfill immediate needs.

INTERCONNECTIVITY

The term *interconnectivity* refers to an enterprise's ability to allow multiple, disparate systems to share information from department to department, from the hospital to other entities in the enterprise, and from the enterprise to the insurance company or employer. The opportunities are significant. The following sections discuss some of the current and emerging trends in interconnectivity.

Types of Interconnectivity

Some in the health care IS industry have noted that the lack of spending in health care information technology has resulted in the technical and financial impossibility of acquiring a single system solution to meet all an MCO's needs. One study noted "Given the multitude of competing interests, a single, monolithic IS is a virtual impossibility in the near future."[4(p.189)] Therefore, methods for integrating disparate systems are essential to develop effective enterprisewide solutions.

System interconnectivity is occurring within institutions through system integration and between provider institutions and MCOs through electronic eligibility verification, authorizations, claim submission, and remittance advice receipts. In addition, interconnectivity exists between MCOs and banks through electronic reimbursement (electronic funds transmission [EFT]) and between hospitals and suppliers through electronic inventory management. In health care today, interconnectivities that occur among health care applications are primarily financial in nature (e.g., submitting a claim for payment, transferring funds electronically, and sending automated remittance advice to providers).

Managed care has already seen significant advances in interconnectivity with the development of patient eligibility and provider referrals. As the health care industry emerges into the information age, interconnectivity will include the exchange of financial and clinical information within and external to the enterprise and the full support of a computer-based patient record.

System Integration

The goal of integrating the various system platforms is seamless access to any network application and/or data through a single workstation. Although it is possible to maintain disjointed hardware and software systems, successful integration of all systems in the managed care network is vital to cost-effective support of interconnectivity. With disjointed hardware and software systems, building and managing the network interfaces necessary for seamless access are labor intensive.

Successful systems integration includes all the following components: universal cabling plans, integrated network electronics and components, telecommunication systems, an application integration gateway (interface system), application services (E-mail and file transfer), and enterprise network management tools.

Integration requires connectivity or the ability to plug any device into the system (network). Connectivity is not possible without common, enterprisewide (universal) cabling because various systems must be able to communicate at the lowest possible level. Integrated network electronics and components are necessary to achieve seamless access (i.e., the ability for users to traverse the network without needing to know where the information resides).

Managed care systems, at a minimum, must support the integration of multivendor applications and key strategic applications. The application integration gateway, necessary for traversal across the network, refers to the point where independent application services are reduced to their lowest common denominator. Enterprise network management tools give system administrators the ability to manage network security and transactions at each access point across the network.

Electronic Data Interchange Initiatives

Electronic data interchange (EDI) is a means for IS operations to exchange information in a common, standard methodology. Although many organizations, such as the American National Standards Institute (ANSI) and the Workgroup on Electronic Data Interchange, are working toward EDI standards, EDI is not yet fully developed for the health care industry. Numerous providers and MCOs are aiding in the definition and development process. Reportedly, 13 percent of all hospital IS budget increases in 1995 were attributable to advances in EDI.[5]

When EDI permeates the health care industry, the need for individual interface applications will be eliminated, thus allowing virtually all systems to share information more easily. More important, with the successful implementation of EDI, critical work flow procedures within health care facilities and the industry could be reengineered to eliminate and streamline many of the existing paper- and labor-intensive functions. As a result of EDI, the entire manner in which health care providers deliver services could change, leaving only the basic mission statement—to improve the health of our communities—unchanged.[6]

Implementing EDI across the enterprise continuum can be a difficult task. Once implemented, however, further EDI requirements can be expanded with little effort. One common example of an EDI initiative outside the health care industry is bar coding. Walk into a grocery store and look at the bottom or side of any product on the shelves, and you will see a one-inch square bar code with a number of lines varying in width and a series of numbers. The bar code is a standard in the industry, and a product can be taken to any grocery store and recognized by the bar code scanner. In the food services industry, the bar code allows both suppliers and grocers to inventory their products easily, and the grocer's need to maintain a large inventory is virtually eliminated. The status of the grocer's supply is electronically routed to the distributor. In addition, both the grocer and the supplier can easily track the purchasing patterns of their customers.[7] The distributor can deliver goods "just in time" to the grocer, eliminating labor- and paper-intensive inventorying.

The same EDI scenario can apply in a health care provider organization (e.g., in a hospital system or a closed panel health maintenance organization) in the daily provision of medical treatment. For example, while treatment is being administered to the patient, the caregivers can record the information into wireless, hand-held computers as opposed to making notes on paper. This information is critical to the ongoing treatment of the patient, and its usefulness can be maximized through the interconnected computerized medical record. The medical information can be sent instantaneously to appropriate caregivers throughout the facility, significantly reducing charting time, missing charts, and unnecessary or duplicated tests and facilitating the next steps in the treatment process. In addition, supplies could be ordered, treatment charts and work orders outlined and distributed, progress reports updated, surgeries and radiologic tests scheduled, and billing information accumulated and submitted. If necessary, providers from other facilities could also be notified. All this is happening at the same time as treatment is being administered.[8]

Electronic transfer of information is already occurring between and within institutions through nonstandard, proprietary formats. Individual interface programs are being written to exchange information between applications and organizations. Although EDI is not fully developed within the health care industry, standards are emerging for appointment scheduling, electronic eligibility verification, automated authorization and referrals, electronic claims submission, EFT, electronic remittance advice (ERA), and computerized medical records.

Eligibility Verification

In a managed care setting, various means of electronic verification are important to give health care service providers immediate and accurate service parameters for the patient, such as enrollment, eligibility, and benefits information. The utilization of electronic eligibility verification at the service entry point significantly reduces efforts to verify these service parameters, thus reducing manual intervention to obtain the information and reducing the number of noncovered treatments performed.

Although some argue that the patient can present an identification card indicating coverage, it is often the case that coverage has terminated without adequate notification to the provider. The provider must contact the MCO at each patient registration or risk providing services to ineligible patients, thus raising administrative costs and hassles for both organizations. Frequently, providers must write off services performed because the patient did not have coverage at the time of service or needed prior authorization or because the wrong amount of copayment was collected. With electronic eligibility verification, when the clerk enters the patient's name, up-to-date eligibility status is received, and the provider can be assured of payment. This reduces unnecessary ineligible claims for both the provider and the payer, along with the attendant costs and frustrations.

Within the industry, the electronic eligibility and benefits inquiry standard being developed is the ANSI ASC X12 (270 and 271).

Authorizations and Referrals

A key component in managed care is the presence of a system to monitor care for medical necessity. Interconnected information systems can greatly increase the effectiveness and efficiency of managed care authorization systems. As with electronic eligibility verification for members (patients), the MCO can provide an immediate automated authorization, or permission, to the provider of care.

The MCO determines which types of services and providers require preauthorization. To receive reimbursement, the provider (primary care physician [PCP] or specialist) must obtain authorization from the MCO to perform a service or refer a patient to another physician. The request to the managed care company can be made electronically at the provider site. The electronic request may be as simple as an electronic form that the provider completes on line and transmits to the plan. Most electronic authorization systems are more complex, however, containing editing fields to ensure that the referral or admission is to a participating provider and requiring that key data elements be provided. An electronic authorization system may also provide automatic information transfer (e.g., member status and demographics). More sophisticated systems could ensure that the referral provider is participating and can gather clinical information (from the patient's electronic medical record) and compare it with standard protocols before processing the authorization.[9]

The MCO may review the request and electronically provide authorization or denial for the service, or in some cases it may automatically issue an authorization number (e.g., in many MCOs, the PCP has the ability to refer to any participating specialist without prior review by the MCO). The authorization number can become part of the patient's master file and can be attached to the electronic claim when it is submitted. As a result, the need for hospital and physician office personnel to enter data, mail information, and speak directly with the MCO is significantly reduced. In addition, automated authorization systems can easily provide reports to the MCO for provider profiling (usage patterns) and to estimate incurred but not reported (IBNR) costs. The standard for electronic referrals is in development.

Electronic Claims Submission

Electronic claims submission is a mechanism that the Health Care Financing Administration (HCFA) and payers are utilizing to reduce paper flow and increase the accuracy and timeliness of claim submission. As patients receive treatment throughout the integrated delivery network, health care service providers electronically produce and submit the appropriate claim forms to the appropriate payer. As noted above, much of the patient and treatment information necessary for proper submission of the claim is generated from the provider's information system, thus reducing the labor necessary to complete paper forms as well as inadvertent data inaccuracies. Delays from using a mail service are also eliminated. The electronic claim forms flow directly into the payer's system while other MCOs' databases are queried and checked for duplicate benefit requests. Specific claim and cost information of MCOs can also be made available to enable a health care facility to manage its claims appropriately.[10] For the MCO, this reduces the need for claim processors, as discussed in Chapter 31 of *The Managed Health Care Handbook*.[11]

Over the past 5 years, the HCFA has been phasing in mandatory electronic claims submission for both Medicare A and Medicare B. As MCOs began to see the benefits and became more technology enabled, many also began accepting electronic claim submissions. The HCFA and payers are using many different standards for claims submission, however. This variability requires providers (hospitals and physicians) to spend many hours of programming time and funds to meet the data format requirements of the payers to which they send claims. Fortunately, an EDI standard, ANSI ASC X12 (837), is being developed for electronic claims and is a major step in the attempt to reduce health care administrative costs nationwide.

EFT/ERA

After proper claim submission and adjudication, reimbursement to providers can be sent electronically. Funds can be transferred from the payer's financial institution to the provider's financial institution, and an electronic notice of reimbursement or ERA can be sent directly to the provider. In addition, concurrent updates of payer and provider database information can reduce operating costs.

HCFA implemented EFT and ERA in 1993 for Medicare A and Medicare B. Again, as a result many payers also began to reimburse and notify providers in this manner. The electronic processing saves printing and mailing costs for the payer, and providers can save data entry costs when they automatically post the remittance voucher within their own systems. An EDI standard, ANSI ASC X12 (835), has been developed and is in use for EFT and ERA.

Computerized Medical Records

A common, enterprisewide medical record supports the concept of data integration. Immediate, accurate information is vital to controlling operating costs. By developing one common computerized medical record, the ability to reduce unnecessary, duplicative procedures is significantly enhanced, paper flow is reduced, the number of lost documents is reduced, and more accurate and reliable treatment is administered. Because a patient's history and medical information can be accessed at any time in an organized, legible format, the computerized medical record can also help clinical staff provide better care to the patient. Unnecessary tests resulting from unavailable patient records are eliminated.

According to an Institute of Medicine report, a computerized medical record should do the following[12]:

- record and organize clinically all transactions, encounters, and events
- streamline and guide the business of the caregiver or caregiving team
- add substantively to the body of medical knowledge
- support population and epidemiological studies

The report defined the computer-based patient record as an "electronic record that resides in a system specifically designed to support users through availability of complete and accurate data, practitioner reminders and alerts, clinical decision support systems, links to bodies of medical knowledge, and other aids."[13(p.110)] The report also noted that a patient's medical record is unavailable 30 percent of the time during clinical evaluation and that 11 percent of laboratory tests are reordered because the first test results are lost.

According to Kenneth McCarty, director of the Pittsburgh Cancer Institute's (PCI's) Endocrine Laboratories, "Participating physicians could access necessary patient records instantly, regardless of where and when the clinical and laboratory information was generated."[14(p.131)] By connecting with the networking infrastructure at PCI, community physicians can analyze the various diagnostic and treatment alternatives available to their patients and can readily access experts. An alarms-and-alerts subsystem of the network will notify health care professionals when they have not entered all the information necessary for each patient or when they need to order additional procedures.

The EDI standard for electronic medical records is HL7.

Claim Liability of IBNR Services

IBNR refers to the amount of money that the plan needs to accrue for services that have been performed by providers but not yet reported to the MCO (see Chapter 22). This lapse results from a lag in the provider's process between providing a service and submitting a claim to the MCO. IBNR is determined actuarially from past experience and the MCO's IS operations, including authorization information, and represents a liability to the MCO.

The MCO's management IS should provide regular reporting of actual claims paid statistics. The most common method of reporting claims paid statistics is through system-generated lag reports. A lag report summarizes claims paid by the month of service and the month of payment. The lag report is so named because of the lag, or lapse of time, between when services are rendered (date of service) and when the MCO actually receives the billing for such services.[15]

In an MCO with EDI links to all its providers, IBNR will be significantly reduced. Each time a service is provided, the information will be directly submitted to the MCO, and the lag will be minutes instead of days or months. This is particularly true for participating providers, but it holds the potential to be true even for emergency or urgent services provided by nonparticipating providers as well.

DATA REPOSITORIES

Enterprisewide data repositories are relational databases that bring together snapshots of transactional data from multiple systems to provide a single source of data for executive decision making, customer management, patient care, and end-user applications. According to Inmon, a data repository or warehouse is a collection of data in support of management's decisions. The data are subject oriented rather than application oriented; integrated or transformed into a consistent format; nonvolatile, meaning that the snapshot never changes; and time variant, with snapshots over a period of 5 years or more.[16]

MCOs have historically led the way in developing large repositories of encounter data. In the early 1980s, MCOs, specifically those linked with health care–focused teaching institutions, began to analyze the data contained in these repositories to improve their negotiating position with payer organizations and employers. At that time, computer hardware was not capable of sufficiently managing the huge volumes of data contained in a repository. As technology advanced, MCOs began to review more broadly the large-scale data repositories of clinically related services.

Although still in its infancy stages, data warehousing is becoming more popular. The Gartner Group has predicted that more than 90 percent of all information processing organizations will implement this technology within 5 years, and some industry analysts feel that its implementation is a key success factor for competing in the managed care environment.[17] The implementation of central data repositories is considered a key success factor primarily because data warehousing supports business process redesign and has been, in many cases, the first step in the reengineering process.

Data within a repository are stored according to the structure of the database model, either central or relational. Central databases are characterized by centralized control through a single hardware platform with a database management system serving both operations and enterprise decision support. With central databases, end-user functional needs are more difficult to meet. This is especially apparent when the community physician user group and other user groups are not utilizing the same central hardware platform. Relational databases, although efficient in enabling storage and extraction functions, do not meet enterprise decision support needs for analysis and comparisons because decision support functions frequently involve complex queries and comparisons of cross-tabulated data.

Development of the data warehouse often occurs in opposite sequence to the standard systems development life cycle: implementation followed by data integration, testing, programming, design of the decision support system, analysis, and requirements definition. For this reason, cost justification is difficult because benefits are not understood at the outset. Historically, benefits of established data warehouse implementations have been measured in terms of differentiation of product/services with increases in market share, improved production efficiency as evidenced by increased revenue per unit cost, and improved management through a better understanding of the profitability of products and services.

Data warehousing supports on-line transaction processing, on-line analytical processing, enterprise decision support, executive IS, business process redesign, legacy refurbishment, clinical workstation development, clinical decision support, distributed processing, and client-server implementation. Although distributed client-server standards-based environments are supported fully by many data warehouse vendors, specific characteristics such as management preferences, technology infrastructures, products and services, and market volatility make each data warehouse organizationally specific. Individual organizational characteristics and long-term strategic plans will drive the structure of the storage of information within the database because each type of database is suited to meet different needs.

THE NATIONAL COMMITTEE FOR QUALITY ASSURANCE AND THE HEALTH PLAN EMPLOYER DATA AND INFORMATION SET REPORTING

The National Committee for Quality Assurance (NCQA) in 1993 revised the data reporting standard for MCOs. This topic is discussed in detail in Chapter 37 of *The Managed Health Care Handbook*.[18] The standard known as the Health Plan Employer Data and Information Set (HEDIS 3.0) established performance criteria in more than 75 measures, with an additional 30 measures included as a testing set for further evaluation. These performance measures establish a baseline for commercial and government purchasers in their effort to evaluate MCOs in terms of provision of health care services to their employees and family members. Significantly, as part of Medicare reform, Medicare risk plans will be required to report HEDIS 3.0 measures in future years.

Any discussion here of the individual data elements in HEDIS is bound to become outdated within a relatively brief period of time because NCQA has revised HEDIS frequently. Nonetheless, it is important for the reader to understand HEDIS and to be aware of the increasing importance of HEDIS in the purchaser and regulatory communities. As one reviews the data elements in HEDIS, it becomes clear that most MCOs should be, and usually are, collecting these data and producing similar reports for internal uses. By way of example, Exhibit 20–1 lists the basic data elements in HEDIS 3.0; the reader is urged to obtain the most recent release of HEDIS from the NCQA (2000 L Street, N.W., Suite 500, Washington, D.C. 20036) and to become familiar with the required data reports and their interpretation.

HEDIS requires a significant level of IS technology and staff support to represent effectively the performance of the MCO. The clinically focused user of IS requires an enhanced ability not only to display data in the aggregate but also to perform a "drill-down" through the information.

Related to this issue is the difficulty in interpretation of what the data are actually supposed to report. It is obviously of great value to any external body in reviewing data to have consistency of meaning and report integrity on a plan-to-plan comparative basis. As HEDIS continues to mature, the ability of plans to capture and report data in a consistent manner will continue to improve.

The data analysis necessary to support HEDIS reporting requires a thorough understanding of the business requirements of the MCO. This is critical given that the interpretation of the data is influenced by the behavior of the MCO in relating to the purchasers of health care in the community. From this understanding of the business, a high-level data model can be constructed. The data model should depict each data value and the interrelationships that exist. An iterative process of reviewing the data, interpreting their use, and refining the model is critical to the development of the HEDIS report set.

Development of a robust data model will permit the use of relational database tools to support the creation of the clinical and financial analysis reports necessary to support HEDIS reporting. These relational database tools will enable the managed care leadership to perform detailed longitudinal studies of its experience with a defined population and to identify possible interventions. An example is determining the impact of implementing an early intervention program for children younger than 5 years living in a cer-

Exhibit 20–1 Categories of Performance Measures in Draft of HEDIS 3.0

Effectiveness of Care

- Advising smokers to quit
- Beta blocker treatment after a heart attack
- Use of appropriate medications for people with asthma
- The health of seniors
- Eye exams for people with diabetes
- Flu shots for older adults
- Flu shots for high-risk adults
- Cervical cancer screening
- Breast cancer screening
- Childhood immunization status
- Adolescent immunization status
- Treating children's ear infections
- Prenatal care in the first trimester
- Low birth-weight babies
- Checkups after delivery
- Follow-up after hospitalization for mental illness

Testing Set:

- Number of people in the plan who smoke
- Smokers who quit
- Cholesterol management of patients hospitalized for coronary artery disease
- Aspirin treatment after a heart attack
- Outpatient care of patients hospitalized for congestive heart failure
- Controlling high blood pressure
- Prevention of stroke in people with atrial fibrillation
- Colorectal cancer screening
- Follow-up after abnormal pap smear
- Follow-up after abnormal mammogram
- Stage at which breast cancer was detected
- Functional assessment of brest cancer therapy
- Continuity of care—substance abuse
- Substance abuse counseling for adolescents
- Availability of medication management—schizophrenia
- Patient reported behavioral health measure
- Family visit for children 12 years of age or younger undergoing mental health treatment
- Treatment failure—substance abuse
- Chemical dependency screening
- Diagnosis supporting the use of psychotherapeutic drugs
- Rate of continuation treatment of depression
- Monitoring diabetes patients
- Chlamydia screening
- HIV patient management

Access to/Availability of Care

- Appointment access
- Telephone access
- Availability of primary care providers
- Children's access to primary care providers
- Availability of mental health/chemical dependency providers
- Annual dentist visit
- Availability of dentists
- Adults' access to preventive/ambulatory health services
- Initiation of prenatal care
- Availability of obstetrical/prenatal care providers
- Low birth weight deliveries at facilities for high-risk deliveries and neonates
- Availability of language interpretation services

Testing Set:

- Problems with obtaining care

Satisfaction with the Experience of Care

- The annual member health survey
- Survey description information

Testing Set:

- Member disenrollment survey
- Satisfaction with breast cancer treatment

Health Plan Stability

- Member disenrollment
- Physician turnover
- Narrative information on rate trends, financial stability, and insolvency protection
- Performance indicators
- Years in business/total membership

Exhibit 20–1 continued

Use of Services
- Well-child visits in the first 15 months of life
- Well-child visits in the third, fourth, fifth, and sixth year of life
- Adolescent well-care visit
- Frequency of selected procedures
- Inpatient utilization—non-acute care
- Inpatient utilization general hospital/acute care
- Ambulatory care
- C-section and vaginal birth after C-section rate
- Discharge and average length of stay for females in maternity care
- Births and average lengths of stay
- Frequency of ongoing prenatal care
- Mental health utilization—percentage of members receiving inpatient day/night and ambulatory services
- Readmission for specified mental health disorders
- Chemical dependency utilization—inpatient, discharges and average length of stay
- Chemical dependency utilization—percentage of members receiving inpatient, day/night care and ambulatory services
- Mental health utilization—inpatient discharges and average length of stay
- Readmission for chemical dependency
- Outpatient drug utilization

Testing Set:
- Use of behavioral health services

Cost of Care
- High-occurrence/high cost DRGs
- Rate trends

Testing Set:
- Health plan costs per member per month

Informed Health Care Choices
- Language translation services
- New member orientation/education

Testing Set:
- Counseling women about hormone replacement

Health Plan Descriptive Information
- Board certification/residency completion
- Provider compensation
- Physicians under capitation
- Recredentialing of physicians
- Pediatric mental health network
- Chemical dependency services
- Arrangements with public health, educational, and social service entities
- Weeks of pregnancy at time of enrollment
- Family planning
- Preventive care and health promotion
- Quality assessment and improvement
- Case management
- Utilization management
- Risk management
- Cultural diversity of Medicaid membership
- Unduplicated count of Medicaid members
- Enrollment by payer (member year/months)
- Total enrollment

Courtesy of the National Committee for Quality Assurance, Washington, D.C., 1996. HEDIS is a registered trademark of NCQA.

tain geographical region. The reporting tools can perform the detailed analysis necessary to determine the value of the program in assessing the overall level of health care in the area.

CONCLUSION

> "Health care delivery systems need flexibility with empowered users to meet and surpass the competition in managed care entrainments. Ideally, enterprise data could be transformed into strategic information and implemented via package parameters. Clerical workers would be converted to knowledge workers, empowered with preconceived information that would be used during the operations of health care delivery."[19(p.98)]

Health care in the 1990s has been characterized by tremendous change, the need to reduce costs overall within the industry, and the development of new processes and methods to provide better patient care. In 1994, Wendy Herr, vice president of the Healthcare Financial Management Association, testified before the House Ways and Means Health Care Subcommittee. In urging Congress to adopt standard electronic patient and processing practices for health care, Herr advocated "the development of legislation to simplify health care administrative processes rather than waiting for a complete reform package."[20] Even without such legislation, MCOs and providers throughout the United States have been diligently working to streamline their processes and invent new ways to reduce operating costs while providing high-quality care to the patient. IS and information technology are key to an MCO's ability to thrive and compete successfully in the health care marketplace.

Study Questions

1. Describe key attributes for the information systems area in an MCO.
2. Discuss the main issues concerning intellectual property as they involve information services.
3. Discuss the merits of in-house or owned versus outsourcing.
4. What is a data warehouse, and what are the key attributes?
5. What is HEDIS? Why is HEDIS important?

REFERENCES AND NOTES

1. T. Reynolds, Informatting the IDS, *HIMSS News* 6 (1995).
2. Health Information Management Information Systems Society (HIMSS), *Conference Survey* (HIMSS, 1995).
3. L.M. Fisher, Health Care Is Being Pulled into the Computer Age, *New York Times* (21 October 1995).
4. J.D. Ladd and R.D. Reese, Traveling the Information Superhighway, *Michigan Hospitals* (1994).
5. HIMSS, *Conference Survey.*
6. Ladd and Reese, Traveling the Information Superhighway.
7. Ladd and Reese, Traveling the Information Superhighway.
8. Ladd and Reese, Traveling the Information Superhighway.
9. P. Kongstvedt, ed., *The Managed Care Handbook*, 2d ed. (Gaithersburg, Md.: Aspen, 1993).
10. Ladd and Reese, Traveling the Information Superhighway.
11. R.S. Eichler and R.L. McElfatrick, "Claims and Benefits Administration," in *The Managed Health Care Handbook*, 3d ed., ed. P.R. Kongstvedt (Gaithersburg, Md.: Aspen, 1996), 491–531.
12. Institute of Medicine, *The Computer-Based Patient Record: An Essential Technology for Health Care* (Institute of Medicine, 1991).
13. Institute of Medicine, *The Computer-Based Patient Record.*
14. Ladd and Reese, Traveling the Information Superhighway.
15. Kongstvedt, *The Managed Health Care Handbook.*
16. W.H. Inmon, *Building the Data Warehouse* (New York, N.Y.: Wiley, 1993).
17. R.E. Gilbreath, Health Care Data Repositories: Components and a Model, *Healthcare Information Management* 9 (1995).
18. Eichler and McElfatrick, "Claims and Benefits Administration."
19. Reynolds, Informatting the IDS.
20. Ladd and Reese, Traveling the Information Superhighway.

SUGGESTED READING

Austin, C.J. and Sobczak, P.M. 1993. Information Technology and Managed Care. *Hospital Topics* 71(3): 33–37.

Coady, S.F. 1993. Where Are the Data? *Managed Care Quarterly* 1(3): 40–44.

Gotowka, T.D., Jackson, M., and Aquilina D. 1993. Health Data Analysis and Reporting: Organization and System Strategies. *Managed Care Quarterly* 1(3): 26–34.

Kenkel, P.J. 1995. *Report Cards: What Every Health Provider Needs To Know About HEDIS and Other Performance Measures.* Gaithersburg, Md.: Aspen.

Rontal, R. 1993. Information and Secision Support in Managed Care. *Managed Care Quarterly* 1(3): 3–14.

Strategies for Transitioning from Legacy Systems to New Systems. *The Singer Report.* Boston, Mass.: Charles Singer, Inc.

Wang, H., Sharp, V., and Coulter, C. 1994. Creating an Information System for Evaluating HMO Performance. *Managed Care Medicine* 1(5): 43–44, 46–49.

Chapter 21

Authorization Systems

Peter R. Kongstvedt

Study Objectives

- Understand what an authorization system is, and what the basic types of authorizations are
- Understand the uses of authorization systems
- Understand what types of benefits designs and health plans have an effect on authorization systems and how those issues are addressed
- Understand basic data elements captured in authorization systems
- Understand basic operational issues in authorization systems

One of the definitive elements in managed health care is the presence of an authorization system. This may be as simple as precertification of elective hospitalizations in an indemnity plan or preferred provider organization (PPO) or as complex as mandatory authorization for all non–primary care services in a health maintenance organization (HMO). It is the authorization system that provides a key element of management in the delivery of medical services.

There are multiple reasons for an authorization system. One is to allow the medical management function of the plan to review a case for medical necessity. A second reason is to channel care to the most appropriate location (e.g., the outpatient setting or to a participating specialist rather than a nonparticipating one). Third, the authorization system may be used to provide timely information to the concurrent utilization review system and to large case management. Fourth, the system may help finance estimate the accruals for medical expenditures each month (see Chapter 22).

DEFINITION OF SERVICES REQUIRING AUTHORIZATION

The first requirement in an authorization system is to define what will require authorization and what will not. This is obviously tied to the benefits design and is part of full and fair disclosure marketing requirements in that, if services require authorization, the plan must make that clear in its marketing literature.

There are no managed care systems that require authorization for primary care services. PPOs and HMOs require members to use providers on their panels, and most HMOs require members to choose a single primary care physician (PCP) to coordinate care, but this does not require an authorization. Defining what constitutes primary care services is another issue and is addressed in Chapters 6 and 7.

The real issue is determining what non–primary care services will require authorization. In a tightly controlled system, such as most HMOs (with a few rare exceptions), all services not rendered by the PCP require authorization. In other words, any service from a referral specialist, any hospitalization, any procedure, and so forth require specific authorization, although there may be certain exceptions, such as an optometry visit or a routine Pap smear from a gynecologist. In less tightly controlled systems, such as many PPOs and most indemnity plans, the requirements are less stringent. In those cases, it is common for authorization only to be required for elective hospitalizations and procedures, both inpatient and outpatient.

The tighter the authorization system, the greater the plan's ability to manage utilization. An authorization system per se will not automatically control utilization, although one could expect some sentinel effect. It is the management behind the system that will determine its ultimate effectiveness. If the medical director is unable or unwilling to deal with poor utilization behavior, an authorization system will have only a marginal effect. If the claims department is unable to back up the authorization system, it will quickly be subverted as members and providers learn that it is little more than a burdensome sham.

In any plan, there will be times when a member is unable to obtain prior authorization. This is usually due to an emergency or an urgent problem that occurs out of area. In those cases, the plan must make provision for retrospective review of the case to determine whether authorization may be granted after the fact. Certain rules may also be defined regarding the member's obligation in those circumstances (e.g., notification within 24 hours of the emergency). Be careful that such requirements do not allow for automatic authorization if the plan is notified within 24 hours but only for automatic review of the case to determine medical necessity.

DEFINITION OF WHO CAN AUTHORIZE SERVICES

The next requirement of an authorization system is to define who has the ability to authorize services and to what extent. This will vary considerably depending on the type of plan and the degree to which it will be medically managed.

In PPOs that are tightly controlled, there may be a requirement for PCP authorization (the so-called "gatekeeper" PPO). In loosely controlled PPOs and in managed indemnity plans, there is usually only a requirement for authorization for elective hospitalizations and procedures, but that authorization comes from plan personnel and not from the PCP or any other physician.

For example, if a participating surgeon wishes to admit a patient for surgery, the surgeon first calls a central telephone number and speaks with a plan representative, usually a nurse. That representative then asks a number of questions about the patient's condition, and if predetermined criteria are met, and after the member's eligibility is confirmed (if the plan has that capability), an authorization is issued. In most cases, the surgery must take place on the day of admission, and certain procedures may only be done on an outpatient basis.

It is common practice in HMOs to require that most or all medical services be authorized by the member's PCP. Even then, however, there can be some dispute. For example, if a PCP authorizes a member to see a referral specialist, does that specialist have the ability to authorize tests, surgery, or another referral to himself or herself or to another specialist? Does a PCP require authorization to hospitalize one of his or her own patients?

A relatively common exception to this practice is in the area of mental health and substance abuse (MH/SA). As discussed in detail in Chapter 16, MH/SA services are unique and often lend themselves better to other methods of authorization. Plans or even the accounts themselves may carve out MH/SA from the basic health plan and treat it as a stand-alone function.

Another exception to the PCP-only concept occurs in HMOs that allow specialists to contact the plan directly about hospitalizations. In these cases, the referral to the specialist must have been made by the PCP in the first place, but the specialist may determine that hospitalization is required and obtain authorization directly from the plan's medical management department. Plans that operate this way generally do so because the PCPs have no real involvement in hospital cases anyway and because there is no utility in involving them in that decision.

In any type of managed care plan, there may be services that will require specific authorization from the plan's medical director. This is usually the case for expensive procedures such as transplants and for controversial procedures that may be considered experimental or of limited value except in particular circumstances. This is even more necessary when the plan has negotiated a special arrangement for high-cost services. The authorization system not only serves to review the medical necessity of the service but ensures that the care will be delivered at an institution that has contracted with the plan.

As mentioned above, the tighter the authorization system, the better the plan's ability to manage the care. For optimal control, only the PCP should be able to authorize services, and that pertains to all services except those that specifically require the approval of the plan's medical director or to MH/SA services in those plans that have carved out that piece. In other words, even if a member is referred to a specialist, only the PCP can actually authorize any further services, such as diagnostic tests, rereferral, or a procedure. This is the tightest form of a gatekeeper or case management model. As discussed below, it requires the use of unique authorization numbers that tie to specific bills, and the claims department must be able to back that up. As one backs away from that degree of tight control, utilization will tend to increase.

CLAIMS PAYMENT

A managed care health plan does not exist as an absolute dictator; you cannot issue blindfolds and cigarettes to members who fail to obtain authorization for services. The only recourse a plan has is to deny full payment for services that have not been authorized. This pertains equally to services obtained from nonparticipating providers (professionals or institutions) and to services obtained without required prior authorization.

In an HMO, payment can be completely denied for services that were not authorized. Point of service (POS) is unique and is discussed below. In most PPOs and in indemnity plans, if an inpatient admission is not authorized but is considered a covered benefit, payment may not be denied, but the amount paid may be significantly reduced. For example, a plan pays 80 percent of charges for an authorized admission but only 50 percent of charges for a nonauthorized admission or perhaps imposes a flat dollar amount penalty for failure to obtain authorization.

In certain cases, a plan may deny any payment for a portion of the bill but will pay the rest. For example, if a patient is admitted the day before surgery even though same-day admission was required, the plan may not pay the charges (both hospital and physician) related to that first day but will pay charges for the remaining days.

In a PPO where a contractual relationship exists between the provider and the plan, the penalty may fall solely on the provider, who cannot balance bill the member for the amount of the penalty. In the case of an indemnity plan (or a PPO in which the member received services from a nonparticipating provider), the penalty falls on the member, who must then pay more out of pocket.

POS is a special challenge for authorization systems and claims management. (A discussion of claims management may be found in Chapter 31 of *The Managed Health Care Handbook.*)[1] It is necessary to define what is covered as an authorized service and what is not because services that are not authorized will still be paid, albeit at the lower out-of-network level of benefits. Because POS is sold with the expressed intent that members will use out-of-network services, it is not always clear how a service was or was not authorized.

Common examples of this issue are illustrated as follows. If a PCP makes a referral to a specialist for one visit and the member returns to that specialist for a follow-up, was that authorized? If a PCP authorizes three visits but the member goes four times, does the fourth visit cascade out to an out-of-network level of benefits? If a PCP refers to a specialist and the specialist determines that admission is necessary but the member is admitted to a nonparticipating hospital, is that authorized? What if the member is admitted to a participating hospital but is cared for by a mix of participating and nonparticipating physicians? What if a member is referred to a participating specialist who performs laboratory and radiology testing (even though the plan has capitated for such services); is the visit authorized but not the testing? What if the member claims that he or she had no choice in the matter?

The list of "what ifs" is a long one. Most plans strive to identify an episode of care (e.g., a hospitalization or a referral) and to remain consistent within that episode. For example, the testing by the specialist referenced above would be denied and the specialist prohibited from balance billing, or an entire hospitalization would be considered either in network or out of network. In any case, the plan must develop policies and procedures for defining when a service is to be considered authorized (and when it is considered in network in the case of hospital services that require precertification in any event) and when it is not.

CATEGORIES OF AUTHORIZATION

Authorizations may be classified into six types:

1. prospective
2. concurrent
3. retrospective
4. pended (for review)
5. denial (no authorization)
6. subauthorization

There is value in categorizing authorization types. By examining how authorizations are actually generated in your plan, you will be able to identify areas of weakness in your system. For example, if you feel that all elective admissions are receiving prospective authorization and discover that in fact most are being authorized either concurrently or, worse yet, retrospectively, you will know that you are not able to intervene effectively in managing hospital cases because you do not know about them in a timely manner. A brief description of the authorization categories follows.

Prospective

Sometimes referred to as precertification, this type of authorization is issued before any service is rendered. This is commonly used in plans that require prior authorization for elective services. The more prospective the authorization, the more time the medical director has to intervene if necessary, the greater the ability to direct care to the most appropriate setting or provider, and the more current your knowledge regarding utilization trends.

Inexperienced plan managers tend to believe that all authorizations are prospective. That naive belief can lead to a real shock when the manager of a troubled plan learns that most claims are actually being paid on the basis of other types of authorizations that were not correctly categorized. This is discussed further below.

Concurrent

A concurrent authorization is generated at the time the service is rendered. For example, the utilization review nurse discovers that a patient is being admitted to the hospital that day. An authorization is generated, but by the nurse and not by the PCP. Another example is an urgent service that cannot wait for review, such as setting a broken leg. In that case, the PCP may contact the plan, but the referral is made at the same time.

Concurrent authorizations allow for timely data gathering and the potential for affecting the outcome, but they do not allow the plan medical managers to intervene in the initial decision to render services. This may result in care being inappropriately delivered or delivered in a setting that is not cost effective, but it also may result in the plan's being able to alter the course of care in a more cost-effective direction even though care has already commenced.

Retrospective

As the term indicates, retrospective authorizations take place after the fact. For example, a patient is admitted, has surgery, and is discharged, and then the plan finds out. On the surface, it appears that any service rendered without authorization would have payment denied or reduced, but there will be circumstances when the plan will genuinely agree to authorize services after the fact. For example, if a member is involved in a serious automobile accident or has a heart attack while traveling in another state, there is a clear need for care, and the plan could not deny that need.

Inexperienced managers often believe not only that most authorizations are prospective but that, except for emergency cases, there are few retrospective authorizations. Unfortunately, there are circumstances when there may be a high volume of retrospective authorizations. This commonly occurs when the PCPs or participating providers fail to cooperate with the authorization system. A claim comes in cold (i.e., without an authorization), and the plan must create one after the fact if it finds out that the service was really meant to be authorized. The plan cannot punish the member because it was really the fault of the PCP, so that claim gets paid.

Most plans have a no balance billing clause in their provider contracts (see Chapter 29) and may elect not to pay claims that have not been prospectively authorized, forcing the noncompliant providers to write off the expense. That will certainly get their attention, but it comes at some cost in provider relations. Even so, sometimes it becomes necessary if discussions and education attempts fail.

If the plan's systems allow an authorization to be classified as prospective or concurrent regardless of when it is created relative to the delivery of the service, it is a sure thing that retrospective authorizations will occur but not be labeled retrospective; for example, the PCP or specialist will say "I really meant to authorize that" or "It's in the mail" and will call the authorization concurrent. Another possibility is that claims clerks may be creating retrospective authorizations on the basis of the belief that the claim was linked to another authorized claim (see below).

In a tightly managed plan, the ability to create a retrospective authorization is strictly limited to the medical director or utilization management department, the ability to create prospective authorizations does not exist once the service has actually been rendered, and concurrent authorizations cannot be created after 24 hours have passed since the service was rendered.

Pended (for Review)

Pended is a claims term that refers to a state of authorization purgatory. In this situation, it is not known whether an authorization has been or will be issued, and the case has been pended for review. This refers to medical review (for medical necessity, such as an emergency department claim, or for medical policy review to determine whether the service is covered under the schedule of benefits) or to administrative review. As noted above, if a plan is having problems getting the PCPs or participating providers to cooperate with the authorization system, there will be a significant number of pended claims that ultimately lead to retrospective authorizations.

Denial

Denial refers to the certainty that there will be no authorization forthcoming. As has been discussed, you cannot assume that every claim coming into the plan without an associated authorization will be denied because there are reasons that an unauthorized claim may be paid.

Subauthorization

This is a special category that allows one authorization to hitchhike on another. This is most common for hospital-based professional services. For example, a single authorization may be issued for a hospitalization, and that authorization is used to cover anesthesia, pathology, radiology, or even a surgeon's or consultant's fees.

In some plans, an authorization to a referral specialist may be used to authorize diagnostic and therapeutic services ordered by that specialist. Great care must be taken to control this. If not, the phenomenon of linking will occur. Linking refers to claims clerks linking unauthorized services to authorized ones and creating subauthorizations to do so. For example, a referral to a specialist is authorized, and a claim is received not only for the specialist's fees but for some expensive procedure or test as well, or a bill is received for ten visits even though the PCP intended to authorize only one. The claims clerk (who is probably being judged on how many claims he or she can process per hour) may then inappropriately link all the bills to the originally authorized service through the creation of subauthorizations, thereby increasing the costs to the plan.

STAFFING

Plan personnel required to implement an authorization system properly are the medical director, an authorization system coordinator (whatever that person's actual title), and the utilization review nurses. Various clerks and telephone operators will also be required; the number of these depends on the size of the plan and the scope of the system.

The medical director has three primary roles. The first is to interact with the plan's PCPs and specialty physicians to ensure cooperation with the authorization system. Second, the medical director is responsible for medical review of pended claims. That does not mean that the medical director will have to review every claim personally but rather that it is ultimately the medical director's responsibility. In some instances the case will be reviewed by the member's PCP; in others it will be more appropriate for a nurse reviewer or even the medical director (or designee) to perform the primary review. Third, the medical director will sometimes have interactions with members when payment of a claim is denied. Although the claims department usually sends the denial letters and responds to inquiries, it is common for members to demand a review of the denied claim on the basis of medical necessity or a belief that the PCP really authorized the service. In those cases, the medical director will often be involved.

The authorization system needs a coordinator to make sure that all the pieces fit together. Whether that responsibility falls to the claims department, the utilization department, the medical director's office, or general management is a local choice. In a small plan, the role of coordinator usually falls to a manager with other duties as well, but as the plan grows it is best to dedicate that function.

The coordinator's primary purpose is to track the authorization system at all its points. All systems can break down, and the coordinator must keep track of where the system is performing suboptimally and take steps to correct it. In some cases that will require the intervention of others because an authorization system has ramifications in the PCP's office, the hospitals, the utilization review department, the claims department, member services, and finance. If no one is in charge of maintaining the authorization system, people will tend to deny their responsibilities in making it work.

Some thought must be given to the relationship of the authorization system to the utilization review coordinators. Specifically, how much can the utilization review coordinator authorize? It makes sense to allow some ability to create authorizations, especially subauthorizations for hospital services, but you must decide whether you will allow the utilization review coordinators to create primary authorizations, particularly for hospital cases. It is common in large HMOs for nurse case managers involved in large case management to have the ability to authorize services without the need to go through a

PCP (see *The Managed Health Care Handbook* for a discussion of this activity).

COMMON DATA ELEMENTS

The needs of your plan will dictate what data elements you actually capture. In some plans, the management information system will be able automatically to provide some of this information, so you would not have to capture it at the time the authorization is created. The data elements that are commonly captured in authorization systems are illustrated in Exhibit 21–1.

In systems where there are clinical requirements for authorization, the system then must determine what the requirements are on the basis of the diagnosis. For example, if a plan has preset criteria for authorization for cataract surgery, those requirements may be reviewed with the physician when he or she calls in for authorization. The same issue applies to mandatory outpatient surgery: If admission is being requested, the procedure may be compared with an outpatient surgery list to determine whether the physician needs to justify an exception. Such reviews should only be done by medically trained personnel, usually nurses. In the case of disagreements with the requesting physician, the medical director must be able to contact the physician at that time or as soon as possible. It becomes less common for a plan to deny authorization based on medical necessity as the plan matures and the participating physicians become more conversant in definitions of medical necessity; the other values of the authorization system remain important, however.

When an authorization is made, the system also must be able to generate and link an authorization number or identifier to the data, so that every authorization will be unique. In tightly controlled plans, any claim must be accompanied by that unique authorization number to be processed.

Exhibit 21–1 Data Elements Commonly Captured in an Authorization System

Member's name

Member's birth date

Member's plan identification number

Eligibility status

- Commercial group number or public sector (i.e., Medicare and Medicaid) group identifier
- Line of business (e.g., HMO, POS, Medicare, Medicaid, conversion, private, or self-pay)
- Benefits code for particular service (e.g., noncovered, partial coverage, limited benefit, full coverage)

PCP

Referral provider

- Name
- Specialty

Outpatient data elements

- Referral or service date
- Diagnosis (ICD-9-CM, free text)
- Number of visits authorized
- Specific procedures authorized (CPT-4, free text)

Inpatient data elements

- Name of institution
- Admitting physician
- Admission or service date
- Diagnosis (ICD-9-CM, diagnosis-related group, free text)
- Discharge date

Subauthorizations (if allowed or required)

- Hospital-based professionals
- Other specialists
- Other procedures or studies

Free text to be transmitted to the claims processing department

METHODS OF DATA CAPTURE AND AUTHORIZATION ISSUANCE

There are three main methods of interacting with an authorization system: paper based, telephone based, and electronic.

Paper-Based Authorization Systems

Paper-based systems generally work in plans that allow the PCP to authorize the service without prospective review by the plan. If plan preapproval is necessary before an authorization is issued (except for infrequent services, such as transplants), a paper-based system will not be responsive enough. If, however, the PCP has the authority to authorize services, a paper-based system will be adequate, although not state of the art.

This type of system depends on the PCP (or other authorizing provider) filling out an authorization form, which may be used as a referral or admission form as well. A copy of the form is sent to the plan, which enters the authorization data into its system. Claims submitted to the plan may or may not require a copy of the authorization form, depending on plan policy.

The advantages of paper-based systems are as follows. They are less labor intensive than telephone-based systems and therefore require less overhead for the plan. Although electronic systems are even more labor efficient, they require a higher level of sophistication and support than paper-based systems. Data entry can be done in batch mode because there is little need for real-time interaction. They also tend to be more acceptable to physicians because they are less intrusive regarding clinical decision making, run less risk of violating patient confidentiality, and do not have the problem of busy signals or a physician being placed on hold during a busy day in the office.

The main disadvantage of paper-based systems is that there is less opportunity to intervene at the time the authorization is made. Once an authorization is issued, it is nearly impossible to reverse it. You may be able to alter future behavior, but neither the physician nor the member will easily accept an after-the-fact reversal of an authorization. Another disadvantage is that it increases the administrative burden on the physician, particularly if he or she is participating in multiple plans, each with its own complicated set of forms. Paper authorizations can also get lost in the mail (or mail room) and lend themselves to data entry errors (e.g., digit transpositions). Lastly, as noted earlier, paper authorizations may arrive at the plan after an electronic claim has been received and adjudicated.

Telephone-Based Authorization Systems

Telephone-based systems rely on the PCP or office staff to call a central number and give the information over the phone. If clinical review is required, it is done at that time. Telephone-based systems have the built in potential of clogging up and leading to poor service. If the system is unresponsive, or if PCPs get frequent busy signals or are put on hold, they will stop calling. The investment in a responsive telephone-based system will be paid back in a reduction of pended claims and retrospective authorizations.

Collecting the data and issuing an authorization number may be done either manually or by an automated system. It is extremely rare for a health plan not to use computers for claims payment, although a new start-up plan could certainly perform this function manually for a brief period. Because authorization is linked to claims payment, there must be an interface between the two systems.

One approach is to collect all the data on manual logs and then enter them into the claims system through batch processing. Another approach is to automate the entire process. If you have systems capabilities to do so, you may wish to have your authorization clerks or nurses enter the data directly into the computer. Be aware, though, that computer systems can delay you with slow screens, complicated menus and entry screens, downtime, training problems, and a host of other problems. Some computer systems are made for batch entry, making real-time entry too inefficient. In those situations, you may wish to use a manual log for data capture and authorization issuance until your automated system is well tested. You should also be able to use a manual system as a backup on a moment's notice.

The advantages of telephone-based systems are that they can be more responsive and timely, have greater potential for directing care to the appropriate location and provider, and have the potential of reducing the administrative burden on the PCP's office staff. The disadvantages are that they increase the administrative burden on the plan and, if not run efficiently, can generate great ill will with the PCPs.

Electronic Authorization Systems

Electronic authorization systems are still not as common as paper- or telephone-based systems, but their popularity is growing. Electronic systems require participating physicians and hospitals to interface electronically with the plan, usually through a personal computer or a dumb terminal in the office. Generally, electronic communications with providers focus on claims submission and payment, but authorizations are equally possible.

Electronic authorizations may be nothing more than an electronic form that the provider completes on line and transmits to the plan. The authorization system may be more complex, using editing fields to ensure that the referral or admission is to a participating provider and requiring key data elements to be provided. An electronic authorization system may also provide automatic information transfer (e.g., member status and demographics). It is also possible for an electronic system to gather clinical information and to compare it with protocols before processing the authorization, but currently that is more conjecture than fact.

Electronic systems generally enter the authorization data directly (or via electronic batch entry) into the management information system, so that the need for personnel to enter data is reduced. Such systems require a high level of expertise by the plan and a certain level of sophistication by the providers themselves. Electronic systems and data interchange are discussed in Chapter 20.

AUTHORIZATION SYSTEM REPORTS

The reports needed from an authorization system will depend on the complexity of the system and your management needs. Obviously, the one absolutely necessary report function is linking incoming claims to authorized services.

Hospital logs and reports are discussed in greater detail in Chapter 13. The authorization system should be able to print out a report indicating prospective admissions and procedures, current admissions and procedures, and retrospectively authorized cases. Cases pended for review should also be reported, with data indicating when the claim was received, when it was reviewed, and its current status.

Outpatient reports are also discussed in greater detail in Chapter 19. Reports from the authorization system could include summaries of authorizations by type for each PCP expressed as ratios, for example total authorizations per 100 encounters per PCP or per 1,000 members per year (annualized), with a breakdown of prospective compared with concurrent compared with retrospective, and so forth. Authorization types may also be expressed as a percentage of the total number of authorizations for that PCP. For example, the total authorization rate may be 8 per 100 encounters per PCP with 50 percent prospective, 40 percent concurrent, 6 percent retrospective, and 4 percent pended (if it is denied, it is not an authorization, although it is still quite useful to report denial statistics by provider as well).

A valuable report is a comparison of authorization types with paid claims. This is basically looking at the percentage of claims that have been authorized prospectively, concurrently, and so forth. This is valuable in determining your ability to capture the data in a timely fashion. It will be inversely proportional to your plan's rate of incurred but not reported claims.

These reports will allow you to identify noncompliant providers or providers who comply but not in a timely fashion. The medical director will be able to focus on those providers who either do not obtain authorizations or do so in a way that does not allow for active medical management by the medical director (if that is needed). These reports, along with a report on the number and nature of open authorizations (i.e., authorizations for services for which a claim has not yet been received), will also allow the finance department to calculate more accurately the accruals and incurred but not reported factor for the plan, reducing the chances of nasty surprises later.

CONCLUSION

An effective authorization system is a requirement of any managed care plan. Whether that system is all encompassing or pertains only to certain types of services is dependent on the type of plan. Key elements to address are what services require authorization, who has the ability to authorize, whether secondary plan approval is required, what data will be captured, how they will be captured, and how they will be used.

Study Questions

1. Describe the similarities and differences in authorization systems between inpatient and specialist referral authorization.
2. Describe similarities and differences in authorization system requirements between various model types.
3. Describe the key advantages and disadvantages of different types of open panel HMO authorization systems. What conditions would influence an HMO to adopt one type over another?
4. If a managed care organization contracts with a foundation type of integrated delivery system, how might the authorization system needs change? How might they not change?

Reference

1. R.S. Eichler and R.L. McElfatrick, "Claims and Benefits Administration," in *The Managed Health Care Handbook*, 3d ed., ed. P.R. Kongstvedt (Gaithersburg, Md.: Aspen, 1996), 491–531.

Chapter 22

Operational Finance and Budgeting

Dale F. Harding

Study Objectives

- Understand the basic flow of funds in a typical managed care organization
- Understand the basic types of revenues and expenses
- Understand some of the key issues involved in statutory accounting
- Understand basic regulatory requirements as they pertain to financial activities
- Understand the budgeting process

The challenge to manage successfully a managed care organization (MCO) lies in the financial manager's ability to produce timely, accurate financial reports. The interaction between operational managers and financial managers is key to achieving this goal. Overall financial management of an MCO begins with the MCO's product pricing strategies. Strategic pricing is based on an assessment of the competition, targeted profitability, the MCO's estimate of costs incurred for the provision of health care, and its ability to control costs, in particular, medical costs. Detailed operating budgets are then developed under the same assumptions used in the pricing strategy. Financial managers rely significantly upon information captured and monitored by operational departments to develop the detailed budgets.

Information provided by operational departments is also used as the basis for certain accounting estimates recorded in financial statements. The financial manager's ability to report on actual results, analyze budget variances, and assess the reasonableness of pricing strategies in a timely manner is dependent upon the support of operating functions.

In this chapter, through a review of the components of the financial statements of a health maintenance organization (HMO), key information and operational procedures that the financial manager will need and rely upon are discussed. The discussion addresses typical problems that occur in gathering information and provides insight into challenging the integrity of information.

BACKGROUND

Accounting policy for MCOs is set by many regulatory entities. MCOs are primarily regulated at the state level, although certain federal regulations may be imposed if an MCO offers federally regulated products such as Medicare risk contracts. State regulation may be imposed by both the Department of Insurance and the Department of Health. Additionally, there are many publicly held MCOs that are subject to the rules and regulations of the Securities and Exchange Commission (SEC).

Dale F. Harding is a senior manager in the East/Great Lakes Healthcare Practice of Ernst & Young LLP. Dale has been with the firm for over 11 years, focusing on the insurance and health care fields. She spends most of her time working on financial audits and financial management projects for managed care organizations.

The state's Department of Insurance is generally concerned with the fiscal solvency of the MCO to ensure that the health benefits of enrollees will be provided. The state's Department of Health is generally concerned with quality of care issues as well as access to care issues, including the location of providers within specific geographic boundaries and the mix of primary care physicians and specialists to serve the population within these boundaries.

Financial management of MCOs must consider the interests of each of the users of financial information, whether they be senior management, insurance regulators, the SEC, tax authorities, or investors. Balancing the concerns of each interested party represents a challenge for the financial manager. Senior management is concerned with the profitability of products and market segment performance. Management will require internal reporting that focuses on line of business management and also meets regulatory reporting requirements. Regulators are concerned with protecting the insured members and focus on liquidity of the MCO. The SEC is concerned with the protection of investor interests. Balancing conservatism and positive performance with the best return on investment is a difficult task.

The requirements imposed by the state's Department of Insurance and Department of Health can be found in the state laws and regulations. The National Association of Insurance Commissioners (NAIC) is an organization comprising the state commissioners of insurance, who set guidelines at a national level. The NAIC has no governing authority over the individual states, however. Generally, states will introduce legislation modeling NAIC guidelines. The NAIC has adopted an annual statement report format that has been adopted by most states. The financial information is prepared in accordance with statutory accounting practices (SAP). Other financial statement users (lenders, the SEC, and investors) require that financial statements be prepared in accordance with generally accepted accounting principles (GAAP). The American Institute of Certified Public Accountants (AICPA) issued an audit and accounting guide for health care providers that provides additional guidance on audit, accounting, and reporting matters for prepaid health plans.

The financial manager should also be aware of the continuous changes taking place in the regulatory arena. For many states, managed care market penetration has historically been minimal, and legislation has not kept pace with recent growth in managed care. Many varieties of MCOs or managed care strategies are emerging, such as physician–hospital organizations (PHOs), integrated delivery systems, management services organizations, direct contracting arrangements among employers and providers, and so forth (see Chapters 3 and 4), and regulators acknowledge that there is little or no legislation governing these emerging areas (see Chapters 28 and 30). For example, many regulators have imposed policy (absent legislative authority) to exercise financial restrictions on PHOs or other provider organizations that contract directly with self-insured plans. Other developments include the NAIC's committee to develop risk-based capital requirements for health insurers, including HMOs, which will impose stricter minimum capital requirements. An exposure draft was issued by the AICPA updating the audit and accounting guide for health care providers and is slated for an effective date in late 1996. In 1994, expanded financial disclosure requirements regarding changes in claims reserves were imposed on health insurers. Although these new requirements are not yet required for MCOs, they may be required in the future.

FINANCIAL STATEMENT COMPONENTS

Operating Statement

A typical profit and loss statement for an HMO is depicted in Exhibit 22–1. For internal management reporting purposes, the ability to develop profit and loss reports by product line/market segment is critical to the financial management process. Assumptions and financial

Exhibit 22–1 Sample Profit and Loss Statement for an MCO—Percentage of Total Revenue

Revenue
Premiums earned: 95
Other income: 5
Total revenue: 100

Expenses
Health care expenses: 84
General and administrative expenses: 11
Total expenses: 95

Income or loss before income taxes: 5

benchmarks may vary widely by product or market segment. For example, medical cost estimates are based on utilization patterns and provider reimbursement strategies that will differ by product and market segment. Likewise, administration of lines of business may be different. For example, the costs associated with supporting a Medicare or Medicaid product will differ from those associated with the commercial population because the customers have unique service needs and because dedicated staff with specific skill sets will be needed to service Medicare and Medicaid enrollees. Pricing is based on the medical cost and administrative cost components; therefore, premium pricing by product will vary consistent with the variations in these cost components. In the following discussion of the components of the financial statement, keep in mind the importance of segregating the reporting by product line or market segment. Analyzing financial results by line of business not only will enhance management's ability to understand the fluctuations from budgeted results but will provide information needed to redirect strategies to preserve the overall success of the operation.

Premium Revenue

Premium revenue is the primary revenue source for HMOs. Premiums are generally received in advance of the coverage period, which is usually monthly. Premium rates are generally effective for a 12-month period. Rates or rating methodologies are usually filed with and must be approved by the state's Department of Insurance. MCOs may file revisions to the rates or methodology, which will also be subject to approval by the Department of Insurance. New rates will not be effective for existing groups until the renewal of the annual contract.

Premiums are actuarially determined, as discussed in Chapter 23. Premiums are intended to cover all medical and administrative expenses as well as to provide a profit margin (Exhibit 22–2). Premium rates are therefore directly related to medical expense and administrative expense projections. If the premium rates are not adequate to cover the actual medical expenses and administrative costs, expected profit margins will diminish. If losses for a line of business are anticipated, a premium deficiency exists. Under GAAP accounting, because premium rates are fixed until the end of the coverage period, the aggregate anticipated net loss for the line of business may need to be recorded immediately, not ratably over the remaining coverage period.

Certain premium rates may not be controlled by the MCO, such as those for Medicare risk contracts or Medicaid. These rates are set by the government. For example, Medicare premium rates are based upon the adjusted average per capita cost (AAPCC) rates set by the federal

Exhibit 22–2 Allocation of Operating Revenue Dollar (Median Results as of December 1993)

Health care expenditures:	79% (HMOs with fewer than 50,000 enrollees); 84% (HMOs with 50,000 enrollees or more)
Administrative expenses:	11%
Profit margin:	3–5%

Source: Courtesy of Hoescht Marion Roussel, 1994, Cincinnati, Ohio.

government. The sufficiency of these rates therefore is dependent, in part, on the federal government's ability to capture and analyze data when determining the AAPCC rates and also on the ultimate product benefit design and the ability of the MCO to manage benefits and expenses to the rates. It is then the responsibility of the MCO to be able to perform medical management and administrative expense management so that the premium is sufficient to cover costs and yield a profit (see Chapter 26).

Rating methodologies derive rates based on an evaluation of demographic data (e.g., the age and sex mix or geographic location) of the population to insure. Rates may be determined using a community rating methodology or an experience rating methodology. Community rating is often used for small groups (less than 50 subscribers) or individuals, and experience rating is used for large groups. In many states community rating is mandatory for small groups and individuals. States may also mandate community rating for all groups regardless of size.

Basic community rating entails the application of a standard rate to all groups within the community being underwritten. The standard rate is applied to groups on the basis of the number of rate tiers quoted, the average family size, and the contract mix assumed for the group. Rate tiers are developed based on the age and sex of members as well as the classification of single versus family. Community rating by class considers an adjustment to the basic rate for specific demographics and/or industry classification of the group. Adjusted community rating allows for adjustments to the base rate for group-specific information other than demographics and industry classification.

The experience rating methodology develops a group rate based on a group's actual experience. After determining actual past experience, expenses are trended forward. Experience-rated contracts can be retrospectively rated or prospectively rated. Retrospective rate adjustments allow for an adjustment to the current period premium based on actual experience. The premium adjustment should be accrued in the current financial statement period and may need to be estimated if the settlement date is subsequent to the end of the accounting period. Prospectively rated premiums provide for increases in rates in the next contract period based on the actual experience of the previous period. When premium adjustments are prospectively rated, there are no accounting entries required in the current reporting period. Rating and underwriting are discussed in greater detail in Chapter 23.

Revenues are recorded in the financial statements as a function of the underlying billing process. The effectiveness of the billing process is further dependent upon the membership or enrollment process. Membership data must be gathered in sufficient detail from the enrollment forms to allow for the proper classification of the enrollee to ensure that the appropriate rates are charged. Timely updating of enrollment records for changes in membership status not only ensures the accuracy of rates charged but also ensures that medical services are only provided to active enrollees. Furthermore, compliance with billing and enrollment procedures may affect whether the MCO will incur costs for health care services provided to inactive enrollees. Subscribers, providers, and the MCO each have contractual obligations related to updating and verification of the enrollee's status. Failure to meet contractual obligations to maintain enrollment records properly and accurately could result in additional costs to the MCO. Therefore, the financial manager should have the information needed to ensure that revenue is being billed for all active enrollees and that business processes are functioning in a manner to prevent loss due to noncompliance with contract terms.

Premium billing may occur under two methods: self-billing or retroactive billing. The self-billing method permits the subscriber (or the group) to adjust the invoice for changes in enrollment. In this situation, the amount billed and recorded as premium revenue receivable will differ from the actual amounts paid by the group. Differences in the amount billed and received require adjustment to revenue and accounts receivable records. A secondary process should include communication of changes to ensure timely updating of enrollment records and notification of enrollment changes to providers. If processes are not in place to ensure that such differences are reconciled and resolved on a timely basis, revenue and accounts receivable may not be recorded properly in the financial statements, and health care benefits may be provided to individuals who are no longer insured.

The retroactive billing method results in adjustments to be recorded in the next month's billing cycle. Under this method, payments made by the group should equal amounts billed. Any changes in enrollment will be adjusted on the next billing. Any changes in enrollment noted should also be forwarded to the appropriate department to ensure updating of enrollment records.

For either billing method, the financial manager must develop a methodology of estimating adjustments affecting the current accounting period. Because the actual adjustments are not known until payment is received or reported in the next billing cycle, an estimate of expected adjustments should be accrued in the current reporting cycle.

Certain large commercial or government clients remit payment without detailed hard copy explanation of the adjustment. These customers often request electronic data transfer for billing purposes. Financial managers should be aware that significant resources may be needed to service these customers. Information systems personnel will be needed to deal with technical aspects of the electronic data transfer process. Support personnel with specific training will be needed to handle the unique challenges associated with large accounts. The process of reconciling the MCO's records with the customer's records can be time consuming but is absolutely necessary. The financial manager should monitor the status (timeliness and completeness) of the reconciliations of these accounts to ensure that any potential problems with the reconciliations do not also affect other financial statement components, such as medical expense accruals.

Other Revenue Sources

Because many HMOs offer preferred provider organization (PPO) products, a growing revenue source is fee revenue derived from PPO members. Subscribers selecting a PPO product generally pay an access fee for use of the provider network established by the MCO. For example, PPO product fees are generally based on a specified per member per month charge. Fees for PPO products vary depending upon the level of service. There is a base fee for accessing the provider network, but enhanced services such as utilization management or providing a gatekeeper mechanism to manage utilization would increase the PPO access fee charged. Pricing of access fees should consider costs of performing administrative functions related to maintaining the provider network, such as credentialing, contract negotiations, and monitoring physician practice patterns.

Coordination of benefits (COB) recoverable is another source of revenue for the HMO. MCOs must have sufficient procedures in place to identify recoveries of costs under COB. COB usually exists when there is a two-wage earner family and individuals will have insurance coverage under two policies with a different insurer or health plan. Policies and procedures are established by insurance organizations to determine which insurer or health plan will serve as the primary or secondary payer. Procedures need to be in place to ensure that costs that are the responsibility of the other carrier are recovered. The data necessary to perform this procedure are usually gathered during the enrollment and billing process. Again, accuracy and completeness during the enrollment process are key to securing the data necessary to determine the amounts recoverable.

There are two primary methods of recovering COB: pay and pursue, and pursue and pay. Under the pay and pursue method, claims are paid, and COB recovery is sought later from the other carrier. Under pursue and pay, the claim net of any COB is paid. To ensure that medical expenses are not recorded net, it is important that gross claim costs and COB recoverable are identifiable by the financial manager. This topic is discussed in detail in Chapter 32 of *The Managed Health Care Handbook*.[1]

Reinsurance recoverable is another source of income to the MCO. Reinsurance against catastrophic claims or claims in excess of specified dollar limits is often obtained to reduce the risk of individual large losses for the MCO. MCOs may forego obtaining reinsurance based on the cost versus benefit of the coverage. The financial manager needs to perform a risk assessment to determine whether stop-loss insurance is appropriate. Procedures need to exist to ensure that costs recoverable under reinsurance are identifiable, so that the MCO receives the full benefit to which it is entitled under the reinsurance arrangement. Reinsurance premiums should be recorded as health care costs, and reinsurance recoverable should be shown net of health care costs.

Another source of income for HMOs is interest income. Excess cash is generally invested in short-term instruments to ensure cash availability for the payment of claims.

Medical Expenses

Table 22–1 summarizes the breakdown of medical costs among hospital, physician, and ancillary services. Medical expenses may be incurred on a capitated basis, fee schedule, or per diem arrangement. Another form of reimbursement that is similar to capitation is percentage of premium. Capitation and percentage of premium represent risk transfer arrangements. Risk transfer arrangements place the providers at risk if utilization exceeds expected results. Reimbursement strategies are discussed in more detail in Chapters 8, 10, and 11.

Medical expenses reported in the financial statements should represent paid claims plus accruals for claims reported but unpaid and claims incurred but not reported (IBNR). The development of the accruals for both reported and unreported claims is an accounting estimate whereby the accuracy of the estimate is dependent upon the data captured by operations personnel and communicated to the financial managers. For reported claims, the incidence of claims is known (e.g., estimated length of stay for inpatient service, number of referred visits for outpatient services, etc.), and the type of claim is known (e.g., inpatient procedure codes, type of outpatient service, etc.). The costs related to the claim incident must be estimated. For reported claims there is less unknown, and there can be more accuracy when ultimate costs are projected, although the ultimate disposition of the claims must still be estimated.

For IBNR claims, both the incidence of claims and the type of claims are unknown and must be estimated. IBNR estimates are often developed with the assistance of actuaries. A preferred methodology for estimating IBNR is the development of loss triangles (Table 22–2). These triangles graphically depict the lag between either the date of service and the payment date or the date of service and the date the claim is reported. From the lag analysis, completion factors are developed to estimate the remaining claims to be reported or paid at each duration. Claim severity, or the estimated average claim

Table 22–1 Typical Health Plan Medical Costs

Category	*Percentage of Expenses*
Hospital	
Inpatient:	28
Outpatient:	11
Total hospital:	39
Physician services	
Primary care:	12
Specialty care:	20
Total physician services:	32
Other medical services:	5
Ancillary services:	15
Prescription drugs:	9
Total health care expenditures:	100

Source: Data from Milliman & Robertson *Health Cost Guidelines* 1993.

Table 22–2 Loss Triangles

Inpatient Services
Claims Paid by Month of Receipt

Service Month	*Jan*	*Feb*	*Mar*	*Apr*	*May*	*Jun*	*Jul*	*Aug*	*Sep*	*Oct*	*Nov*	*Dec*
Jan	10	100	150	50	35	2	1		1		4	1
Feb		7	126	164	44	22	1	1		6		
Mar			24	89	201	33	46	53			5	1
Apr				12	109	177	3	25	2	2	1	
May					1	188	156	45	59	3	4	2
Jun						3	255	189	67	55	4	1
July							9	163	198	84	54	8
Aug								33	127	199	87	62
Sep									27	244	149	88
Oct										17	155	205
Nov											5	104
Dec												12
Total	10	107	300	315	390	425	471	509	481	610	468	484

Inpatient Services
Completion Factors by Month of Receipt

Service Month	*Cur*	*+1*	*+2*	*+3*	*+4*	*+5*	*+6*	*+7*	*+8*	*+9*	*+10*	*+11*	*Total*
Jan	0.03	0.31	0.73	0.88	0.97	0.98	0.98	0.98	0.99	0.99	1.00	1.00	
Feb	0.02	0.36	0.80	0.92	0.98	0.98	0.98	0.98	1.00	1.00	1.00		
Mar	0.05	0.25	0.69	0.77	0.87	0.99	0.99	0.99	1.00	1.00			
Apr	0.04	0.37	0.90	0.91	0.98	0.99	1.00	1.00	1.00				
May	0.00	0.41	0.75	0.85	0.98	0.99	1.00	1.00					
Jun	0.01	0.45	0.78	0.90	0.99	1.00	1.00						
Jul	0.02	0.33	0.72	0.88	0.98	1.00							
Aug	0.06	0.31	0.71	0.88	1.00								
Sep	0.05	0.53	0.83	1.00									
Oct	0.05	0.46	1.00										
Nov	0.05	1.00											
Dec	1.00												
Jan–Jun	0.02	0.36	0.78	0.87	0.96	0.99	0.99	0.99	1.00	1.00	1.00	1.00	

costs, is then used to calculate the total projected costs yet to be incurred. The total projected costs are the basis for accruals to be recorded in the financial statements for the IBNR claims.

Loss triangles are often developed separately for hospital and physician claims. Physician claims can also be further analyzed by type of specialty claim where appropriate. Also the IBNR claims analysis should be segregated by line of business. Although greater level of details can assist in a more refined estimate, caution should be used when one is developing estimates from small population sizes. The smaller the base population, the less precise the estimates. It is prudent to limit the level of detail used in the analysis.

As discussed above, the adequacy of the estimates for reported claims developed by financial managers is dependent upon the availability of data from the operating areas within the MCO. These data are usually developed from the utilization management program. Inpatient care, excluding nonemergency care, typically requires preauthorization; therefore, if the utilization managers are keeping accurate records of admissions and length of stay statistics, the data needed by the financial managers to estimate admissions and cost of services should be readily available. For outpatient services and specialist services, referrals are usually required for more services. Again, if the utilization management program is properly monitoring outpatient and specialist utilization and is maintaining accurate records of referrals, the data needed to estimate outpatient and specialist visits should be readily available to the financial manager. To be usable, the authorization information must be carefully controlled so that authorizations unlikely to be used are eliminated before ultimate utilization is estimated. It is extremely important that the utilization managers understand the significance of their responsibilities in that utilization managers not only are vital to controlling overall utilization but also provide necessary information to predict medical costs accurately, prepare reports on financial results, and develop budgets and financial forecasts. See Chapter 21 for a detailed discussion of authorization systems and types of authorizations.

Because the tools used by the financial managers to estimate medical costs also rely heavily on the accuracy of paid claims data, the claims processing department also plays an important role in financial management. The accuracy of claims data and the timely processing of claims will affect the reliability of the data used to develop the loss triangles. The extent of any backlogs in claim processing must be communicated in timely fashion to the financial manager. Claims management is discussed in detail in Chapter 31 of *The Managed Health Care Handbook.*[2]

Loss triangles represent the most frequently used method to estimate claim costs. Other analyses can also be performed to substantiate further the reasonableness of the estimates for IBNR claims. Analyzing the monthly trends in claims costs or loss ratios by service type (inpatient, outpatient, physician services by specialty, etc.) within product lines and on a per member per month basis provides a basis for determining whether the overall trends in claim costs are consistent with expected results and, where appropriate, industry benchmarks. Factors that may affect the trends include:

- significant changes in enrollment
- unusual or large claims (isolated occurrences versus changes in utilization/cost patterns)
- changes in pricing or product design
- seasonal utilization or reporting patterns
- claim processing backlogs
- major changes to the provider network or reimbursement methods

Each of these factors provides a basis for explaining fluctuations when one is preparing trend analyses. It is important to note, however, that significant changes in enrollment also affect the financial manager's ability to determine reasonable estimates used in financial statements. For example, during periods of enrollment growth, it is difficult to estimate medical cost trends because there is little history associated with the current enrollment base and revenue begins on the first day of enrollment but medical costs generally do not; this may lull an inexperienced financial manager into believing that the medical costs ratio is low. In times of significant disenrollment, there is a risk of adverse selection. Adverse selection exists when the characteristics of the remaining population of insureds are weighted toward a high-risk group. Significant disenrollment often occurs when it is generally not an optimal condition for the enrollee to maintain the current coverage. Usually, those insureds with less choice (e.g., those who are unable to opt for other coverage because of current health status) remain enrolled. Medical cost estimates must be adjusted under these circumstances.

Administrative Expenses

Administrative expenses include salaries as well as sales, marketing, and other operating expenses. Administrative expenses also vary by product and market segment. Administrative expenses can be measured using percentage of premium and per member per month benchmarks. Administrative expenses may also be tracked by functional area (e.g., finance, sales, underwriting, member services, etc.). Administrative expenses will vary with volume as a result of economies of scale. In growth periods, administrative expenses tend to be high as a percentage of premium.

Tracking of administrative expenses by product and market segment allows management to identify whether the appropriate resources are being allocated to product lines. Additionally, if the HMO experience rates certain groups, management needs to track adequately costs associated with a particular group's business to ensure that costs are appropriately allocated to the group and are recovered. The financial manager should also be aware that certain products or market segments, such as government groups and Medicare or Medicaid, place limits on administrative expense allocations to these product lines.

Balance Sheet

Cash and Investments

Cash and investments represent a significant balance sheet account for an HMO. The major source of cash is premium revenue. An HMO's investment portfolio usually consists of short-term investments because cash outlays for claims are frequent. As a result, the financial manager is not significantly affected by investment strategies, and typically there is limited investment risk associated with an HMO's investment portfolio. Because cash does churn quickly through the HMO, management may benefit from implementing strong cash management practices, such as using lock-box arrangements for premiums.

Premium Receivable

Another significant balance sheet account is premium receivable. Premiums are generally collected monthly; therefore, problems with the aging of accounts will probably arise from many old items that are not reconciled often. Unreconciled differences may occur when billing problems exist or as a result of discrepancies in the enrollment records of the MCO in comparison with customer records.

Timely update of membership records ensures the accuracy of premium billings and further ensures that claims are paid appropriately. Policies and procedures to ensure timely updating of membership records protect the MCO from paying claims for terminated members or ensures the recoverability of amounts paid incorrectly. In general, if membership records are not up to date and the MCO bills incorrectly for terminated or inactive members, upon remittance a group will adjust the payment accordingly. If the MCO does not have procedures in place to reconcile remittances to billed amounts, premium receivable records will show amounts outstanding and past due. Because of the large number of individual members within a group and the potentially large number of billings, management must monitor closely the status of premium reconciliation procedures.

The reconciliation process related to premium receivable for government accounts is usually a more complex problem. For example, federal and state employers often remit premium on a cycle that differs from the normal billing cycle of the MCO. The remittances by these institutions are consistent with the institution's payroll cycles. Premium is remitted only for those employees noted as active on the payroll. There are many events that affect the active status of federal and state employees (e.g., leave of absence, summer recess for educators, etc.), but these employees may still be eligible for health benefits. For this reason, the MCO will bill and accrue for premium that will not be paid until the employee's status on the institution's records is reinstated to active status. Often, MCOs that provide coverage to federal and state groups will have dedicated resources to support the reconciliation process.

The reconciliation process for certain large groups may also be complex. The high enrollment volume or the need to accept enrollment data in compatible electronic format may present a challenge for the MCO.

Other Assets

The significance of other assets of an MCO will vary. Another typical large asset may be fixed assets, particularly if the HMO is organized as a staff model HMO and owns and operates physician offices.

Unearned Premiums

Unearned premiums are premiums received by the MCO that at the close of the financial reporting period have not been earned, principally because the premiums are for the ensuing month and are in actuality premiums received in advance. Because most MCOs bill on a monthly basis, unearned premium is generally not a major accounting issue. If premiums are billed and collected other than monthly (e.g., quarterly), an unearned premium reserve would be required.

Claims Payable and IBNR

As discussed earlier, the basis for the recording of claim reserves, including IBNR, is dependent upon information provided by other operating areas of the MCO. Claim liabilities are separated between hospital claims and physician claims. In addition to the matters discussed for medical expenses, the financial manager should prepare further analyses of claim reserves and IBNR estimates.

The financial manager should compare the actual claim payments since the close of the accounting period with the original estimates. Significant differences in the actual results compared with estimated results should be investigated. Information obtained from the investigation should be considered when the sufficiency of current estimates is evaluated.

Risk Pool Liabilities

As discussed in Chapter 8, reimbursement strategies may provide for risk pools, which will require the MCO to maintain accurate records of payment withholds from hospitals and physicians. Amounts payable to the providers from the withhold should be maintained in separate accounts. In addition, shortfalls in the risk pool that must be recovered from the providers need to be evaluated to ensure that the amounts are recoverable, and where necessary the financial manager should consider the need for a provision for unrecoverable amounts. Additionally, any contributions to be made by the MCO for its participation in a risk pool should be appropriately accrued in the financial statements.

Equity

The MCO will need to track its SAP and GAAP basis equity. The statutory balance sheet may permit certain surplus notes to be classified as equity for purposes of determining statutory net worth (issues regarding statutory net worth are discussed below). Surplus notes are obligations to investors that meet certain requirements of the state insurance laws, which are generally subordinated to all obligations of the MCOs. Repayment of surplus notes is subject to the approval of the state's commissioners of insurance. Other transactions affecting equity that are subject to the approval of the state's commissioners of insurance include restrictions on the payout of dividends.

REGULATORY REPORTING CONSIDERATIONS

Generally, HMOs are required to file quarterly financial statements with the state Department of Insurance, which are due 45 days after the close of the quarter. An annual statement filing is also required. The annual filing is due March 1. Many states also require the filing of a certification on claims reserves prepared by a licensed actuary. Audited financial statements are also required; the filing deadline may vary by state but is generally June 1. Any differences in the amounts reported in the audited financial statements and the annual filing due on March 1 must be disclosed in the footnotes to the audited financial statements. Depending on the applicable state's requirements, the audited financial statements may be prepared on either an SAP basis or a GAAP basis.

GAAP focuses more on the matching of revenue and expenses in a given reporting period to measure the earnings of an entity. The state insurance departments that have jurisdiction over the MCO are concerned with the MCO's ability to pay claims in the future. For example, certain expenditures (e.g., capital assets) may benefit future earnings ability and therefore are likely to be capitalized and expensed ratably over future periods for GAAP. However, such costs are expensed immediately in accordance with SAP because monies expended are no longer available to pay future liabilities.

There are many differences between SAP and GAAP accounting that are generally based on the premise of the state insurance department's ability to determine liquidity of the MCO. Some of the major differences include the following:

- treatment of certain assets and investments as nonadmitted under SAP (e.g., fixed assets other than electronic data processing equipment, past due premium receivables, certain loans and other receivables, and investments not authorized by statute or in excess of statutory limitations)
- deferred tax accounts
- carrying value of investments in subsidiaries (which is primarily affected by limitations in the carrying amount and the amortization period of goodwill)

The state Department of Insurance imposes minimum statutory capital requirements for HMOs. The NAIC adopted a model act for HMOs that specified that minimum capital for HMOs should be determined as follows:

- the greater of $1,000,000, or
- 2 percent of annual premium as reported on the most recent annual financial statement filed with the commissioners of insurance on the first $150 million of premium and 1 percent of annual premium on premium greater than $150 million, or
- an amount equal to the sum of 3 months' uncovered health care expenditures as reported on the most recent financial statement filed with the commissioners, or
- an amount equal to the sum of:
  1. 8 percent of annual health care expenditures except those paid on a capitated basis or a managed hospital payment basis as reported on the most recent financial statement filed with the commissioner, and
  2. 4 percent of annual health care expenditures paid on a managed hospital payment basis as reported on the most recent financial statement filed with the commissioner

Managed hospital basis means agreements wherein the financial risk is primarily related to the degree of utilization rather than to the cost of services. *Uncovered expenditures* means the costs to the HMO for health care services that are the obligation of the HMO, for which an enrollee may also be liable in the event of HMO insolvency and for which no alternative arrangements have been made that are acceptable to the commissioner.

Many states are in the process of adopting the NAIC model act. Other states maintain separate minimum surplus requirements. The requirements of each of the states generally call for plans of action when an entity's capital falls within a close range of the minimum requirement.

Although the states' minimum requirements have provided a means to measure the financial viability of an insurance entity, the states' requirements were often a flat minimum and disregarded the size of an entity or the differing degrees of risk to which different entities are exposed. Insurance entities' exposure to risk has become more diverse, and although some are conservative in investment and underwriting practices, others have been more aggressive. The NAIC began examining existing capital requirements and concluded that consumers should be further protected by having companies that assume a more aggressive, risk-taking approach be subject to higher capital requirements. Risk-based capital requirements have been developed for life and health insurers and property/casualty insurers. A working group was formed in 1993 to develop a separate risk-based capital formula for health organizations, including traditional health insurers, HMOs, Blue Cross/Blue Shield plans, and health service plans.

Integrated delivery systems have some risk characteristics that may differ from those of other insurers. Traditional indemnity insurance companies in general invest extensively in marketable securities, and the risk-based capital formulas currently in place address the risks associated with this investment strategy. Although MCOs may invest excess cash in low-risk, short-term securities, they also will often invest directly in the provider operation (e.g., they will own and operate hospitals, medical groups, or outpatient facilities), which contributes directly to the MCO's ability to control quantity and cost of services. MCOs may also control costs through risk transfer arrangements with providers, such as negotiated fee schedules, budgets, and capitation rate agreements. These reimbursement arrangements are not generally available to the traditional indemnity carrier.

The goals of the working group are to develop a seamless system of risk-based capital requirements that will be appropriate for the existing environment and will accommodate future evolution as well. The goals are aimed at facilitating an even playing field for health insurers, Blue Cross/Blue Shield plans, HMOs, and others while not compromising the development of innovations in the health care finance field. A health organization risk-based capital formula proposed by the American Academy of Actuaries is under review by the working group. The working group has been asked to work with the academy to develop a simplified formula to be presented to the NAIC at its March 1996 meeting. Any changes to the formula will probably not be approved before mid-1996. If this timetable is met, changes that would affect HMOs will probably be effective for calendar year end 1997, but HMOs would be able to measure where they stand using the formula that is expected to be proposed in mid-1996.

The regulatory environment under which MCOs operate is continuously changing to meet market changes, and entities need to prepare themselves in particular to meet the challenges imposed by new or expected legislation.

BUDGETING AND FINANCIAL FORECASTING

The importance of maintaining detailed budgets has been discussed throughout this chapter. Financial forecasts, which project activity and results beyond the current period, are also important management tools. Financial forecasts often are prepared when new product lines are introduced, particularly for the purposes of determining capital needs to invest in new lines of business.

When one is preparing current year budgets or projecting results for future periods, it is important to build the projections at a detailed level. This would include developing projections by product line. A baseline projection representing the best estimate of results should be developed first and variations from the baseline projection that are more conservative or optimistic can be developed later and evaluated. Building the projections begins with detailed enrollment projections developed from an analysis of the market and total targeted population for each market segment. Management should then estimate the market share anticipated to be captured. The enrollment projections should be reviewed with the sales and marketing departments and compared with the detailed sales plan. Where possible, membership projections for targeted accounts should be reconciled to the overall enrollment projections.

Based on historical experience or, for new products, industry benchmarks, medical costs should be extended from the enrollment projections. Medical cost estimates should be developed at a detailed level with separate calculations for inpatient costs, outpatient costs, and ancillary benefits costs, such as mental health and substance abuse, vision, dental, and pharmacy. Inpatient cost projections should be benchmarked against an overall per member per month cost and should identify the assumed days per thousand, overall length of stay targets, or, where appropriate, per case or per diem costs. Outpatient and ancillary benefit costs will probably be compared with per member per month cost benchmarks and, where applicable, per case costs. These projected costs should be evaluated for consistency with historical experience and negotiated or proposed (but realistic) changes in reimbursement arrangements. For future years, medical costs should be trended for inflation and also should consider the impact of utilization management and reimbursement strategies that may change over time.

Administrative costs should be developed from detailed staffing plans and detailed budgets for supplies and system development costs. The operating departments should prepare staffing requirements that consider the need for additional staff as enrollment grows. Once the detailed budgets are developed, the overall costs on a per member per month basis and as a percentage of premium should be determined and compared with historical experience and industry benchmarks.

The MCO also needs to consider pricing of products. As previously discussed, certain pricing, such as the pricing of Medicare risk products, is not controlled by the MCO. Pricing will therefore be a function of enrollment projections and mandated rates. For products under the control of the MCO, the financial manager should consider the desired profit margin and determine the premium to charge to achieve a profit margin based on the medical costs and administrative costs developed as discussed above. The premium rates then must be evaluated against competition, and the process of reevaluating the initial set of enrollment assumptions begins. For example, based on desired rates and competitor rates, will the market retention used in enrollment projections be achievable?

The process of financial forecasting is an iterative process. Management will begin to reevaluate all initial assumptions. Targeted profit margins may need to be adjusted to revise the premium rates for competitive purposes. Management will probably challenge the aggressiveness or conservativeness of administrative budgets.

The financial forecasting process must also include the development of a projected balance sheet. This is particularly important to evaluate the impact of the projected growth in operations on minimum capital requirements. Additionally, the forecasting process should require variations from the baseline projections to determine the risks and exposures if the actual results fall short of the baseline and also to project the impact if actual results are better than expected. Cash flow analyses are also important to ensure that cash will be generated from operations or to determine the extent to which cash reserves will be needed, particularly as new lines of business are pursued.

CONCLUSION

Whether the financial manager is developing budgets or financial forecasts or preparing financial statements, he or she must depend on the information prepared and maintained by the operating departments. This information is an integral part of the financial manager's decision-making process. Communication among the various functional areas in the MCO will be key to the successful operation of the entity. Timely financial reporting enhances management's ability to determine performance against anticipated results and redirect its strategies to minimize exposure to loss and preserve a favorable financial performance.

Study Questions

1. What regulatory agencies/organizations govern HMO? Describe the different aspects of their governance.
2. How should the profit and loss and forecast information be segregated and why? Why is it important to analyze the results using PMPM data?
3. Describe the key elements an HMO finance officer needs to properly set the claims accruals.
4. What is a lag report and what are completion factors? What are the strengths and problems associated with completion factors?
5. How are premiums billed and received?
6. What is a premium deficiency; why is its identification important and how should this be reflected in the accounting records?
7. How does enrollment affect the financial statement components?
8. What are some of the more significant issues related to Risk Pool Liabilities?
9. What is the minimum capital requirement under the NAIC Model Act?
10. What is Statutory Accounting? What are a few of the key differences between Statutory Accounting Principles and Generally Accepted Accounting Principles? Why is this important to an HMO?

REFERENCES AND NOTES

1. B.S. Scheur, R.L. McElfatrick, and R.S. Eichler, "Other Party Liability and Coordination of Benefits," in *The Managed Health Care Handbook*, 3d ed., ed. P.R. Kongstvedt (Gaithersburg, Md.: Aspen, 1996), 532–544.
2. R.S. Eichler and R.L. McElfatrick, "Claims and Benefits Administration," in *The Managed Health Care Handbook*, 3d ed., ed. P.R. Kongstvedt (Gaithersburg, Md.: Aspen, 1996), 491–531.

SUGGESTED READING

Coyne, J.S. 1993. Assessing the Financial Performance of Health Maintenance Organizations: Tools and Techniques. *Managed Care Quarterly* 1(3): 63–74.

Mensah, Y.M., Considine, J.M., and Oakes, L. 1994. Statutory Insolvency Regulations and Earning Management in the Prepaid Healthcare Industry. *Accounting Review* 69 (1): 70–95.

Peterson, C.E. 1994. Standards for Capitilization and Solvency. *HMO Magazine* 35 (4): 13–14, 16.

Chapter 23

Rating and Underwriting

Stephen M. Cigich

Study Objectives

- Understand the basic forms of premium rate development in managed care plans
- Understand the basic issues involved in underwriting
- Understand the basic elements that go into rate development
- Understand how per member per month medical costs are calculated

INTRODUCTION

Successful rating and underwriting create a balance among adequacy, competitiveness, and equity of rates in every case-specific rating situation. It can be a difficult and delicate balance to achieve. Moving too far in any direction could spell disaster for a health plan.

Rates are adequate when they are high enough to generate sufficient revenue to cover all plan expenses and yield an acceptable return on equity or contribution to reserves. Competitive rates are low enough to sell enough cases or enroll enough members to meet health plan growth goals. Rates are equitable when all factors that affect case-specific costs are appropriately reflected in the rating and underwriting process.

It is important for a health plan to assess continually its success in each of these areas. This is particularly true for a newly established plan or product offering. Until such a review, the plan cannot be certain whether a high volume of sales or successful renewals is good news or bad. After all, competitive, and perhaps equitable, rates are not necessarily adequate.

Each market segment contains different case-specific risk aspects that require different approaches to rating and underwriting. Major market segments include individual, commercial group, Medicare, and Medicaid. Each major segment has several components with unique risk characteristics that require rating and underwriting modifications. Without these modifications, the balance in rating and underwriting is not likely to be achieved.

This chapter addresses the commercial group market segment. Although the other market segments are important, most health plans offer products in the commercial market. Applying the ideas discussed here to tailor rating and underwriting tools to achieve rate adequacy, competitiveness, and equity in the other market segments will result in successful health plan operation.

Employer size, measured by number of employees, further segments the commercial group market. Small employers possess different risk characteristics than large employers. The rating and underwriting process must recognize that

Stephen M. Cigich, F.S.A., is an actuary with the Milwaukee office of Milliman & Robertson, Inc. His area of expertise is in managed health care programs. He has assisted clients in the areas of medical delivery system design and evaluation, product and rate manual development, experience analysis, and actuarial projections.

small employers can choose not to provide coverage for their employees. This voluntary nature of coverage presents an opportunity for the small employer to select adversely against a health plan that does not rate and underwrite this risk prudently.

Adverse selection is not unique to the small employer market segment. Employees of large employers will typically get to choose among competing health plans through an open enrollment process. Adverse selection may also occur, for example, within a plan with a poorly designed preferred provider organization plan design. Again, the design, rating, and underwriting process employed by the health plan must recognize the adverse selection risk and treat it in a way that will result in rates that are adequate, competitive, and equitable.

RATING VERSUS UNDERWRITING

Rating is the formula that solves for the expected case-specific price for a medical service product. The case-specific price will depend on the unique values that an employer group has for each cost generating variable recognized by the rating formula. This formula is sometimes called the book rate formula or manual rating structure. Underwriting will use the result of this formula alone or with case experience to produce the final rates. The underwriting process may modify the book rates and/or provide certain conditions to be satisfied by the employer or members before risk is accepted.

The rating structure must recognize all costs associated with the health plan, calculate premium rates, and be flexible to allow easy application in most situations. Health plan costs include medical services, sales/marketing, administrative, and return on equity. The rating formula will represent each cost by a specific, measurable cost generating variable. The results of the rating structure, which is typically expressed as a per member per month (PMPM) cost, must be transformed into premium rates for each employer using the employer's preferred billing basis (i.e., employee only, employee with one dependent, and employee plus two or more dependents).

The rating structure itself, or reports used to support the rating structure, will have other important applications in managing a health plan. These include establishing budgets by medical service category or department, establishing funding for provider-based risk pools, and identifying, quantifying, and ranking medical management opportunities within the health plan. Timely analysis of these data will allow the health plan to establish the proper provider-based education and incentives necessary to realize opportunities within the health plan.

Underwriting is the process used to arrive at the final rate and conditions or contingencies for accepting the employer group or individual members of the group. It modifies the results from the rating structure based on other quantitative or qualitative considerations. For small employer groups, it may consider the result of medical underwriting, the application of preexisting conditions limitations, or minimum participation requirements. For large employer groups, it may include evaluating prior claims experience or minimum penetration requirements in dual-choice offerings to employees.

RATE STRUCTURE DEVELOPMENT

The use of a rate structure will decide its construction. PMPM medical cost and revenue targets are established on a basis that allows recognition of several cost generating variables. Case-specific premium rates, the final output of the rate structure, are the translation of the PMPM targets into an employee billing basis. The most common approaches in use to establish case-specific PMPM revenue targets and premium rates are community rating, community rating by class (CRC), and adjusted community rating (ACR).

Community-rated PMPM revenue targets are the same for every group. The PMPM revenue requirements are set using community-wide data only. CRC rating uses case-specific data and the rate structure cost relativity factors to create unique revenue targets for each case situation. ACR is an extension of CRC but will also consider the employer's projected claims experience to modify the CRC rate structure result. ACR is normally reserved for large groups.

The process to translate PMPM revenue targets into premium rates is separate from the process to calculate PMPM targets, and much variation is possible. Premium rates for groups typically reflect only differences in employee billing bases using community-wide demographics. The small employer market may use a further modification by establishing billed premium rates that vary by the age and/or gender of the enrolled employees. Large cases may modify this result to reflect case-specific demographics yet still may vary final premium rates by employee billing basis only.

Medical Cost and Revenue Targets PMPM

The construction of a rating structure to develop PMPM revenue targets begins by choosing the rate structure variables and their interaction. The variables must consider all important determinants of costs yet be easy to measure and use. Given the design of the rate structure, the task turns to obtaining the necessary data to support the selected variables. Historical data will require adjustment to reflect future conditions.

Table 23–1 illustrates typical output for an actuarial cost model that details medical costs and revenue targets on a PMPM basis. A unique set of procedure codes defines each benefit service category (e.g., hospital inpatient services contain diagnosis-related group [DRG] groupings while current procedural terminology [CPT] code groupings define physician services). Further groupings may be done of the benefit service categories by existing or planned risk allocation pools. For example, Table 23–1 presents the cost for a core of narrowly defined primary care physician services in a separate section to support the capitation of those services.

The bottom of Table 23–1 presents administrative costs, coordination of benefits, and the net cost of reinsurance. Administrative revenue requirements must be sufficient to cover all functions, which may be all inclusive for a full service health maintenance organization (HMO) or just a subset of functions if the targets are for a physician–hospital organization or other provider-based group. Coordination of benefits (see Chapter 32 of *The Managed Health Care Handbook*[1]) results in revenues back to the health plan for providing services to members who have their primary insurance elsewhere. The net cost of reinsurance is the actual cost to the health plan for providing protection against catastrophic loss and equals reinsurance premium net of reinsurance claims. Reinsurance cost may appear elsewhere in Table 23–1 if its cost is the responsibility of a specific risk pool.

Columns 1, 2, and 4 in Table 23–1 are the cost driving variables that measure the cost to deliver medical services. Annual utilization per 1,000 members is the measure of service usage. Average cost per service is based on the fee level expectation required by the health plan and is the result of analyzing billed charges, maximum discount from billed (i.e., a fee floor acceptable by the health plan), and/or provider fee schedules. The impact of copays depends on the benefit plan design and the health plan policy for their collection.

The cost driving variables are dependent upon the values of other explanatory variables measured using formulas that are not shown in Table 23–1. Explanatory variables are either explicit (i.e., they are readily measured and reflected in the rating structure) or implicit (i.e., either their measurement or their impact is less well defined). Table 23–2 provides examples of the types of rate structure variables.

Explicit explanatory variables quantitatively measure different attributes of the rated risk and provide a measure of their impact on the cost of medical services. The member's distribution by age and gender is perhaps the best example of an explanatory variable. The rate structure will reflect the impact on various benefit groupings of the member's demographics. For example, a young, female population will have high mater-

Table 23–1 Actuarial Cost Model: Required Revenue for Calendar Year 19xx

Benefit	(1) *Utilization per 1,000*	(2) *Allowed Average Charge*	(3) *Per Capita Monthly Claim Cost*	(4) *Frequency of Copay*	(5) *Copay*	(6) *Per Capita Monthly Cost Sharing Value*	(7) *Per Capita Monthly Net Claim Costs*
Hospital inpatient							
Medical–surgical	247 Days	$1,276.76	$26.28				$26.28
Psychiatric/substance abuse	67 Days	657.31	3.67				3.67
Extended care	5 Days	250.00	0.10				0.10
Total hospital inpatient	319 Days	$1,130.56	$30.05				$30.05
Hospital outpatient							
Emergency department	261 Visits	$159.99	$3.48	196	$25.00	$0.41	$3.07
Surgery	85 Visits	1,172.46	8.30				8.30
Other outpatient services	512 Services	149.53	6.38				6.38
Total hospital outpatient			$18.16			$0.41	$17.75
Physician							
Primary care capitated							
Office and inpatient visits	2,152 Visits	$42.77	$7.67	2,035	$10.00	$1.70	5.97
Immunizations and injections	154 Procedures	17.14	0.22				0.22
Total primary care capitated			$7.89			$1.70	$6.19
Fee for service							
Surgery	374 Procedures	$266.63	$8.31				$8.31
Anesthesia	78 Procedures	575.38	3.74				3.74
Office and inpatient visits	1,025 Visits	45.78	3.91	944	$10.00	$0.78	3.13
Total fee for service			$36.44			$0.78	$35.66
Total physician			$44.33			$2.48	$41.85
Other							
Prescription drugs	5,209 Scripts	$36.00	$15.63	5,209	$5.00	$2.17	$13.46
Home health care	29 Visits	228.21	0.55				0.55
Ambulance	15 Runs	322.43	0.40				0.40
Durable medical equipment/ prosthetics	32 Units	269.54	0.72				0.72
Total other			$17.30			$2.17	$15.13
Total medical costs			$109.84			$5.06	$104.78
Administration							18.00
Coordination of benefits							(4.19)
Net cost of reinsurance							1.41
PMPM revenue required							$120.00

Table 23–2 Explanatory Rate Structure Variables

Explicit	*Implicit*
Member age	Medical management impact on
Member gender	• Utilization of services
Industry	• Average charge of services
Time period trend	Population overall health level
Benefit level	
Geographic service area	

nity costs yet low prescription drug costs, and each benefit grouping will be adjusted using different factors.

Implicit explanatory variables are equally important in the rate structure, although by their nature they are more qualitative. The level of medical management in a health plan is a good example of an implicit explanatory variable. It is important to understand and measure the level of medical management in the data used to develop the rate structure and to make adjustments to reflect the impact of specific health plan initiatives. The overall level of health of the population modeled by the rate structure is also an important consideration. For example, the use of health care costs in a loosely managed care environment will be different for a Medicare population than for a commercial group population. Such measurements require careful consideration, and special expertise is required to make prudent adjustments.

A premium rating structure will typically support many different benefit plan design options. It should also include adjustments necessary to reflect risk selection in dual-choice situations. Different plan designs, such as benefit rider selections, will probably be handled through adjustments to the base table costs. Selection adjustments are normally handled as multiplicative adjustments to the overall PMPM cost.

Many data sources are available to establish rate structure tables. Typically, no one data source can be used exclusively. Combining results from different data sources must be done with care. Health plan data are the best long-term source as a result of their relevance to the health plan, but newly established plans lack a credible amount of data. As a result, many health plans look to published sources or actuarial consulting firms to provide initial targets based on outside data in a structured form to allow substitution, over time, of their own health plan data.

When health plan data are used, they are summarized in 12-month segments to provide a more stable base and to avoid any seasonal conditions from influencing the results. Encounter and claim payment data (including any capitation payments to providers) are matched with health plan exposure measured in member months. Characteristics of the exposure must also be analyzed, such as member age, gender, benefit design, service area, and time period exposed. Calculations are performed to ensure that the claim data are on an incurred basis and are well matched with the exposure data.

Summarizing the results depends on both data quality and form as well as the health plan's financial organization. The definition of provider payment pools, capitated services, and any case rate arrangements must all be considered. As an example, Table 23–1 could be for a health plan where four risk pools are operating: hospital, primary care capitated services, physician fee for service, and ancillary. The hospital pool has a budget of \$47.80 PMPM for both inpatient and outpatient services. Primary care physicians are paid a capitation of \$6.19 PMPM for a limited grouping of CPT codes and fee for service from the physician fee-for-service pool for their remaining services. Noncapitated physician services are budgeted \$35.66 PMPM. The ancillary pool has a budget of \$15.13 PMPM. PMPM funding and operational fee-for-service and capitation payments can be made from these pools, and at the end of the year an accounting can be performed to decide individual pool gains or losses. These gains or losses are typically shared between the provider risk pools and the health plan in a predetermined fashion. Bonus payments to individual providers are then made from any pool gains, again on a predetermined basis.

As another alternative, the health plan might capitate mental health and substance abuse benefits. In this scenario, inpatient and outpatient mental health and substance abuse services would be removed from the various payment pools and placed in the ancillary pool as a special capitation.

Further data summaries will quantify adjustments for the explanatory variables. Details of the utilization and cost data can be allocated into the procedure code groupings. For example, physician inpatient surgery costs can be allocated by member status and age to develop relative cost relationships. Table 23–3 illustrates physician inpatient surgery costs by employee age and gender, all spouses, and all children categories compared with costs for an average member. Note that the composite adjustment across all categories is equal to 1.0 when the standard rate structure demographics are used. Thus physician inpatient surgery costs assumed in the rate structure are replicated when standard demographics are used.

After historical data have been analyzed and placed into the structure required to model health plan operations, they must then be adjusted from their historical period to the pricing period for which they will be used. This adjustment is called trending. Exhibit 23–1 presents elements to consider that may change between these time periods. The elements of trend may be offsetting; for example, the underlying demand to use more health care services may be offset by anticipated improvements in the efficiencies achieved by specific medical management programs. Care must be exercised in reflecting lower projected cost in the future because this may lead to revenue shortfalls to the plan or in the unintended use of provider withhold funds (see Chapter 8) to eliminate any shortfall.

The rate structure may be used in its Table 23–1 summary form for community rating, or the details behind Table 23–1 may be used for CRC. CRC will set group-specific rates using the total HMO's revenue targets adjusted using rate structure relationships for the group's unique risk characteristics. Examples of these unique risk characteristics include the following:

- employer industry classification
- age of member or subscriber
- gender of member or subscriber
- average number of members per contract type
- health status (e.g., smoker or nonsmoker, lifestyle habits, etc.)

Table 23–3 Physician Inpatient Surgery Cost Relativities by Age and Gender*

	Member Status			
	Employee			
Member Age (Years)	*Male*	*Female*	*Spouse: All*	*Child: All*
< 30	0.42	0.75		
30–39	0.53	1.30		
40–49	0.97	1.75		
50–59	2.30	2.15		
≥ 60	4.35	3.00		
Composite	1.19	1.49	1.50	0.32

* Overall composite of factors = 1.00.

Exhibit 23–1 Components of Trend

> ***Utilization***—Actual or anticipated changes in:
> - underlying demand for medical services
> - contractual benefit levels or member cost sharing
> - underwriting guidelines
> - utilization management program
> - delivery system or provider risk-sharing arrangements
>
> ***Charges***—Actual or anticipated changes in:
> - fee schedules or billing practices
> - intensity of services
> - structure of provider contracts (e.g., per diem contracts may be expected to have different trend components than those with discount arrangements)

The purpose of CRC is to set rates closer to the rates expected given the risk characteristics of the group without using prior experience. Illustrative age and gender factors by employee contract type are shown in Table 23–4. These factors reflect the expected revenue requirements for an employee of a particular age, gender, and contract status compared with the HMO's total PMPM revenue target. For example, the expected revenue for a single male employee younger than 30 years is 50 percent (i.e., 0.5 from Table 23–4) of the HMO's average PMPM revenue target. Note that the composite of all factors from Table 23–4 is equal to 2.32, the average number of members per employee contract. This ensures that the overall PMPM revenue is obtained when these factors are applied to the number of employee contracts.

Premium Rate Development

Several options are available for transforming the PMPM revenue targets into premium rates. The option selected will depend on the billing basis required by the employer and the level in which employer data are used to develop the premium rates. This section assumes that the case-specific PMPM revenue targets are already established.

The billing basis for employers is some form of employee contract. The contract holder (i.e., subscriber) is the employee, and the premium rates reflect all the members associated with that particular employee. Rates are sometimes expressed on a per employee basis only but are usually expressed with finer breakouts of employees by their dependent status. Table 23–5 presents common billing bases.

Community-rated premium rates are developed using community or plan assumptions regarding average number of members per employee contract type. Modified community rating will use employer membership characteristics by contract or perhaps competitive contract relativity information. Either method can develop premium rates to be charged to the group on a contract basis (e.g., all employees with spouses have the same rate) or on an age and/or gender basis by contract type (e.g., male employees age 30 have a different rate than female employees age 45). The contract basis is more common, but many small group plans will bill on an age/gender basis where allowed by law.

Despite the method employed, premium rates depend on the PMPM revenue requirements, demographic assumptions underlying their development, and targeted premium relationships. The demographic assumptions include the distribution of contracts (e.g., single employee, employee plus spouse, etc.) and the average number of members per contract. As noted above, the demographic assumptions may be expected HMO demographics (community rating) or employer demographics (modified community rating or CRC). Targeted premium relationships relate to the cost relativity among the various contract types and usually reflect competitive requirements.

Table 23–6 shows the development of a four-tier [i.e., single, employee and spouse, employee and child(ren), and family] community rating billing basis. In this example, the plan demographics assume 2.32 members per employee contract. Additionally, the average number of members within each contract type is also

Table 23–4 Illustrative Age/Gender Factors*

Employee Age (Years)	*Employee*		*Employee with Family*	
	Male	*Female*	*Male*	*Female*
< 30	0.5	1.2	2.9	2.8
30–39	0.7	1.3	2.8	2.6
40–49	1.0	1.4	2.7	2.5
50–59	1.4	1.5	2.9	3.1
> 60	1.9	1.8	3.4	3.5

* Overall composite of factors = 2.32.

Table 23–5 Common Employer Billing Bases

*Type**	*Separate Premium Rates Calculated for*
One tier	Employee
Two tiers	Employee Employee with family
Three tiers	Employee Employee with one dependent Employee with two or more dependents
Four tiers	Employee Employee with spouse Employee with child(ren) Employee with spouse and child(ren)

* These structures may also be list billed in the small case market, with premium rates being calculated by employee age and/or gender.

shown. Column 1 presents the distribution of employees by contract type. Column 2 presents the members for each contract type and illustrates that the weighted average of members per contract equals the total average members per contract of 2.32. Column 3 presents the premium load necessary to rate each contract type adequately and illustrates that the weighted average equals total average members per contract. Column 4 presents the HMO PMPM revenue required, and column 5, the target premium rate by contract, is the multiplication of the premium load and the PMPM revenue.

The premium load in column 3 relates to a member cost relativity of 1.00 and is based on an analysis of claims costs among the various contract types. Alternatively, the premium load may reflect competitive considerations. The single premium load in Table 23–6, the ratio of the single premium to the PMPM revenue, is estimated to be 1.19. The single premium is an adult (actually an employee) only rate, whereas the PMPM revenue reflects HMO average member costs when adults and children are combined. Because child costs are expected to be much lower than adult costs, the employee contract premium is set higher than the PMPM revenue.

In competitive situations, an HMO wishing to enter a large employer account may modify the premium load to reflect the rating relativity used by the employer's current insurance plan. For example, the employer may insist that family rates equal 3.0 times the single rate (i.e., $142.80 × 3 = $428.40). Table 23–7 illustrates how the HMO can accomplish this and still collect the community PMPM revenue requirement of $120.00. Note the change in the relativity of all premium loading factors from Table 23–6. This is necessary to ensure that the required PMPM revenue ($278.40 divided by 2.32) is obtained.

An example of modified (or CRC) premium rating is provided in Table 23–8 using the age/gender factors from Table 23–4. The example is for an employee only contract, and the process is similar to that for other contract types. The resulting premium rate in this example is 15 per-

Table 23–6 Four-Tier Premium Rate Development

Contract Type	(1) *Contract Distribution (%)*	(2) *Members Per Contract*	(3) *Premium Loading Factor*	(4) *PMPM Target Revenue Requirement*	(5) *Target Premium Rate ($)*
Employee	41	1.0	1.19	120.00	142.80
Employee with spouse	15	2.0	3.08	120.00	369.60
Employee with child(ren)	10	2.5	2.04	120.00	244.80
Employee with spouse and child(ren)	34	4.0	3.42	120.00	410.40
Composite	100	2.32	2.32	120.00	278.40

Table 23–7 Competitively Adjusted Premium Loading Factors

Contract Type	*Contract Distribution (%)*	*Standard Premium Loading Factor*	*Competitive Premium Loading Factor**	*Resulting Competitive Premium Rate ($)*
Employee	41	1.19	1.19	142.80
Employee with spouse	15	3.08	2.86	343.20
Employee with child(ren)	10	2.04	1.89	226.80
Employee with spouse and child(ren)	34	3.42	3.57	428.40
Composite	100	2.32	2.32	278.40

* Employee with spouse and child(ren) is set equal to 3.0 times the employee rate. Other contract factors are adjusted to maintain their standard relationship to each other.

cent above the PMPM revenue target (premium loading factor equals 1.15) and 3 percent below the community-rated employee premium (1.15 divided by 1.19). CRC will, of course, result in more rate variability than community rating. Table 23–8 could be modified to illustrate the type of calculation used to determine the premium required of individuals of a small employer group. For example, the premium rate to charge all male employees younger than 30 years would be $60.00 (i.e., $120 × 0.5 = $60).

UNDERWRITING

Underwriting is the pragmatic side of rating. Underwriting can occur at various points in an employer group's life cycle:

- at quotation, through rating adjustments
- at issue, through participation (based on work or time employed requirements)
- at time of claim, through applying preexisting contract coverage or coordination of benefits interpretations
- at renewal, through new participation requirements

This section will only discuss underwriting adjustments made at the time of quotation.

Rating adjustments made through the quotation process are made using data and judgments regarding the risk associated with enrolling a specific employer group or, in dual-choice situations, a subset of employees. The rating structure is the basis for these adjustments.

Table 23–8 Community Rating by Class Example (Health Plan PMPM Revenue Target, $120.00)

Employee Age (Years)	*Employee*	
	Male	*Female*
< 30	5	6
30–39	4	5
40–49	3	4
50–59	2	3
> 60	1	2
	15	20

Employee
only premium = $120.00 × [(5)(0.5)+(4)(0.7)+(3)(1.0)+(2)(1.4)+(1)(1.9)+(6)(1.2)+(5)(1.3)+(4)(1.4)+(3)(1.5)+(2)(1.8)]÷(15+20)
= $120.00 × (40.4 ÷ 35)
= $138.51

The underwriting process begins with data collected to allow premium rate calculation using the rating structure. The development of rate structure premium rates assumes that all aspects of a particular employer group have the same characteristics as the rate structure. The underwriting process will correct this assumption, as necessary and allowed by regulation, and make adjustments using qualitative and quantitative analyses. Perhaps the most notable of the adjustments made is through the experience-rating process, which uses past employer data.

Experience rating develops claims costs, revenue targets, and premium rates based entirely or partially on a group's experience. Experience rating methods may rely on actual claim costs, utilization statistics, loss ratios, or some combination of these approaches. If less than full credibility is given to the group based on too few members or other considerations, then the results of using the group's experience will be weighted with results from the rate structure to yield final results.

Experience rating is generally done on larger groups, where the experience is judged to be credible enough to justify the effort involved. The purpose is to achieve the goals introduced at the beginning of this chapter: to produce rates that are adequate, competitive, and equitable in every case-specific rating situation.

Careful judgment must be used when case-specific information is used. The data reviewed must be scrutinized carefully for inconsistencies. Similar questions must be asked of the data as when the health plan's total revenue targets were established because the process of experience rating is similar.

Many methods are available to rate an employer group based on prior claims experience. The method chosen should be based on the quality and type of information available. A simplified example of claims-based experience rating is shown in Exhibit 23–2. Two years of claims information is used in this example to illustrate the weighing of more than 1 year of data. Multiple years are often used to reduce the impact of fluctuation that may occur in a group's year-to-year claims experience. Large claims are pooled to reduce the impact of fluctuation in the group's experience due to an unexpected number of such claims. The pooling adjustment replaces actual claims above the pooling point with the health plan's expected amount.

No explicit adjustments are made between the time periods for trend, benefit design, or demographics. Any differences are accounted for in steps 6 and 7, with the actual-to-expected ratio being calculated using the plan's expected claims based on the group's characteristics in each of the experience periods. The group's data are ratioed to the expected claims calculated using a manual rate structure for each experience year (step 7). Generally, different credibility adjustments will be applied to each year of experience, with more weight being given to the most current year. The plan's expected PMPM revenue target (step B) is calculated from the manual rate structure given the plan's current benefit design, demographics, and other rating factors reflected by the manual rate structure. Step C is the calculation that combines the employer's experience ratio for each year with

Exhibit 23–2 Claim Cost Experience Rating Example

Step A: Group-Specific Experience

Category	Year* *t*	*t–1*
1. Paid claims	$68.00	50.00
2. Incurred claims	82.00	65.00
3. Pooling charge	8.00	7.00
4. Pooled claims	(10.00)	(2.00)
5. Claims charged (2+3+4)	$80.00	$70.00
6. Employer expected claims	$75.00	$60.00
7. Experience ratio (5 ÷ 6)	1.07	1.17
8. Credibility	60%	20%

* *t*, most recent year; *t–1*, next most recent year.

Step B: Plan Expected PMPM Revenue Target = $120

Step C: Group Experience Rating Development

PMPM Revenue Target = $120 × [(1.07)(60%)+ (1.17)(20%)+ (1.00)(20%)]

= $129.12

the expected cost calculated from the manual rate structure. In this example, 60 percent, 20 percent, and 20 percent weight is given to the employer's most recent, the employer's second most recent, and the manual rate structure result, respectively.

Exhibit 23–3 is a simplified example of another experience rating method based on case-specific utilization statistics. Experience rating in this situation uses utilization statistics to develop an actual-to-expected utilization (as opposed to cost) ratio for the group that is multiplied by the expected revenue target. Again, the expected revenue target is adjusted to reflect the group's benefit plan and demographics for the pricing period.

Exhibit 23–3 Utilization Experience Rating Example

Step A: Group Specific Utilization

Category	Year* *t*	*t*–1
Inpatient days per 1,000		
Group (*G*)	300	350
Health plan (*H*)	280	300
Ratio (*G* ÷ *H*)	1.07	1.17
Weight	40%	40%
Office visits per 1,000		
Group	3,100	3,300
Health plan	2,900	3,000
Ratio	1.07	1.10
Weight	50%	50%
Scripts per 1,000		
Group	4,900	5,000
Health plan	4,600	4,800
Ratio	1.07	1.04
Weight	10%	10%
Average ratio	1.07	1.12†
Credibility	60%	20%

* *t*, most recent year; *t*–1, next most recent year.

† 1.12 = (1.17)(40%)+(1.10)(50%)+(1.04)(10%)

Step B: Plan Expected PMPM Revenue Target = $120

Step C: Group Experience Rating Development

PMPM Revenue Target = $120.00 × [(1.07)(60%)+(1.12)(20%)+(1.00)(20%)]

= $127.92

These are but two examples of experience rating methods. Others can be used, but care should always be exercised to ensure that the results are consistent with expectations and reflect the nature of the rated risk. The reader is referred to Chapter 42 of *The Managed*

Health Care Handbook for a discussion of actuarial services in managed care organizations and integrated delivery systems.[2] The reader is also referred to Chapter 44 of *The Managed Health Care Handbook* for an in-depth discussion of operational underwriting issues.[3]

CONCLUSION

The success of rating and underwriting methods is measured in the ability of the health plan to meet growth and profitability goals. As shown in this chapter, there are many methods to employ for establishing revenue and premium targets. The right combinations must be selected and the resulting experience closely monitored to guarantee better the chances of success. Successful plans will employ systems that achieve the appropriate balance in rates that are adequate, competitive, and equitable on a group-specific basis.

Study Questions

1. Describe the differences between rating and underwriting.
2. Describe the basic forms of rates for MCOs.
3. Describe the basic elements that go into typical rate development formulas.
4. Describe at what points that underwriting may occur.

REFERENCES AND NOTES

1. B.S. Scheur, R.L. McElfatrick, and R.S. Eichler, "Other Party Liability and Coordination of Benefits," in *The Managed Health Care Handbook*, 3d ed., ed. P.R. Kongstvedt (Gaithersburg, Md.: Aspen, 1996), 532–544.
2. S.M. Cigich, "Actuarial Services in an Integrated Delivery System," in *The Managed Health Care Handbook*, 3d ed., ed. P.R. Kongstvedt (Gaithersburg, Md.: Aspen, 1996), 659–666.
3. G.J. Lippe, "Operational Underwriting in Managed Care Organizations," in *The Managed Health Care Handbook*, 3d ed., ed. P.R. Kongstvedt (Gaithersburg, Md.: Aspen, 1996), 679–699.

SUGGESTED READING

Chollet, D.J. and Paul, R.R. 1994. *Community Rating: Issues and Experience*. Washington, D.C.: Alpha Center.

Dowd, B. and Feldman, R. 1995. Premium Elasticities of Health Plan Choice. *Inquiry* 31 (4): 438–444.

Chapter 24

Member Services and Consumer Affairs

Peter R. Kongstvedt

Study Objectives

- Understand the goals of member services in a managed care organization
- Understand basic staffing and management issues in member services
- Understand the basics of how a plan addresses member concerns and grievances
- Understand proactive approaches a plan may take to measuring and maintaining member satisfaction

All managed health care plans need a member services, customer services, or consumer affairs function. For purposes of discussion, in this chapter the term *member services* is used synonymously with the terms *customer services* and *consumer affairs*. Member services are not to be confused with membership services; the latter term is sometimes used to describe the operational area responsible for processing enrollment applications and sending out membership cards and evidence of coverage documents. Member services, in the context of this chapter, refers to the department responsible for helping members with any problems, handling member grievances and complaints, tracking and reporting patterns of problems encountered, and enhancing the relationship between the members of the plan and the plan itself.

Managed care plans are far more complicated than simple indemnity insurance plans (as if those were simple!). Members are required to choose a primary care physician (PCP), to follow rules for accessing health care (e.g., obtaining an authorization from their PCP for referral services), to understand complex benefits structures, and so forth. Health maintenance organizations (HMOs) are complicated enough; point-of-service (POS) plans are even more complicated and have different levels of coverage depending on how the member accesses services (intentionally or not). See Chapter 3 for a description of these types of plans.

The central point is that plans that manage access to care through the use of a restricted provider panel and an authorization system need to have a system to help members use the plan, a system to monitor and track the nature of member contacts, and a mechanism for members to express dissatisfaction with their care because members have less ability simply to change providers. Likewise, plans that have the ability to deny or reduce coverage for nonauthorized services need a mechanism for members to seek review of claims that have been denied or covered at a lower than expected level of benefits. Managed care or not, any plan that provides for the financing of health care must have a system to manage member problems with those payments. This topic is discussed in detail in Chapter 58 of *The Managed Health Care Handbook*.[1] Last, the plan must have a mechanism for members to get help addressing routine business issues, such as change of address, issuance of identification cards, and so forth.

When a plan has delegated a large measure of responsibility to an integrated delivery system (IDS; see Chapter 4), then some care needs to be taken as to how member services will function. The IDS will have a higher than normal level of control over all aspects of the medical encounter, including access to care, the authorization system, availability of providers, and so forth. In some cases, the IDS will actually perform many traditional member services functions. It is important that there be consistency between the plan and the IDS and that there be clear distinctions between the responsibilities of the plan and those of the IDS. It is preferable for the plan to perform all member services functions, but if the IDS is to perform some of them, then it is necessary that the plan receive accurate and timely data from the IDS member services department. It is equally important for the plan to share its member services data with the IDS.

TRAINING AND STAFFING

The amount of training required for member services representatives before they are allowed to interact with members varies from plan to plan. It is common for large and complicated plans to require new representatives to spend 2 to 3 months in training before they begin actually interfacing with members, and even then the first few weeks are monitored by the supervisor. Smaller or less complicated plans generally require less training. It is a clear mistake to skimp on training because how the member services representative performs will have a direct impact on member satisfaction and perhaps on the legal risk profile of the plan. Remember: Each and every interaction that members have with the plan will either reaffirm their decision to join or cause them to wonder whether they made a mistake; that goes for member services encounters as well as for medical encounters.

Staffing of this department is a function of both the scope of responsibilities of the representatives and the complexity of the plan. For highly complex plans with significant growth, complicated products such as POS, and active outreach (discussed below), staffing ratios may be as generous as 1 representative for every 3,500 members. Plans with benefits designs that are simpler and more consistent, those that have stable membership levels, and those that generally have good service levels may staff at a ratio of 1 representative for every 7,500 members.

The degree to which a plan can automate certain routine customer calls may have a substantial effect on staffing ratios as well and can clearly improve responsiveness in the eyes of the member. If the member services representative is required to look up information manually, such as benefits (base plan and riders), claims history, the provider directory, and so forth, that will reduce efficiency and the member's satisfaction with the interaction. In addition, if the member services representative is required to access multiple, awkward screens, many of which may actually add no value to the transaction, then work required will be disproportionately high. Automation will also help the member services representative resolve the problem or issue on that first call, thereby lowering the amount of follow-up work required and thus administrative cost.

It is common in large plans to organize the department into dedicated service units. Such units are responsible for a limited number of accounts, particularly if those accounts are large. In that way, the representatives working in the unit are better able to be familiar with a limited set of benefits issues, to gain knowledge about particular problems unique to an account, and to be more responsive to the accounts. Dedicated service units are sometimes required by large employers before you can obtain their business.

ACCESSING MEMBER SERVICES

How a member accesses the plan is also important to understand and manage. Traditional telephone lines must be adequate in number and must be properly automated in function (e.g., automatic call distribution, sequencing, etc.), depending on plan size. Large plans usually also have a toll-free line for use by members outside the local area code of the plan's service center. The use of direct inward dialing can relieve a member from having to grind through several automated menus. This means that the member's identification card or member handbook lists different numbers for different needs. For example, a plan may have a dedicated, direct inward dial-in line for members to select a new PCP, to obtain a new identification card, or to resolve a problem.

Some plans allow members access by personal computer through bulletin boards or dedicated on-line services. A few large plans and insurers have also developed Web sites on the World Wide Web of the Internet, allowing E-mail through that vehicle as well as access to nonconfidential information. Plans that provide for such electronic communications from members must be careful about security, and members are usually limited to sending E-mail and other routine transactions.

Related to communication by personal computer is the electronic kiosk, which the plan may place in its lobby, on site at a large employer, or in a public area such as a shopping mall. This kiosk allows access to generally available plan information and, in the case of a kiosk at an employer site, may allow the member to perform certain functions such as choosing a PCP or sending an electronic message.

Mail and paper communication remains highly important and must be managed properly. All correspondence must be logged and tracked, policies and procedures must be in place regarding the routing of correspondence, and master files need to be kept of both incoming and outgoing correspondence. In a small plan, this is usually done with the actual paper documents; large plans frequently use imaging technology to store the massive amounts of paper documents, the originals of which may then be stored off site for a number of years. It is important to ensure that paper correspondence receives the same attention that telephone calls do and have time standards for response.

PERFORMANCE STANDARDS

Member services departments generally have responsiveness requirements as part of their performance standards. Such standards generally revolve around a few simple measures. Performance standards must be tailored to meet the standards that the members would expect, not simply what the plan chooses to measure. For example, a plan may measure telephone responsiveness by measuring how long it takes an operator to answer once that operator receives the call; such a measurement might fail to capture the fact that the member had to wade through seven menus of a voice-response unit to get there, resulting in 3 minutes of frustration by the member.

Telephone responsiveness is usually measured by how many times the telephone rings on average, the elapsed time (in seconds) before it is answered by a representative, and what percentage of calls are abandoned before they are ever answered. For example, a plan may have a goal of less than 2 percent of callers hanging up because their call did not get through and 80 percent of all calls being answered in 20 seconds or less.

Timeliness of response is also measured against standards. This is done by tracking the percentage of calls that are resolved on the spot (i.e., no follow-up is required); for example, the standard may be that 90 percent of calls require no follow-up. For problems or questions that require follow-up, there are usually standards for how long that takes (e.g., 90 percent of outstanding inquiries or problems are resolved within 14 days and 98 percent within 28 days). Similar standards apply to written correspondence.

Individual service representatives are usually monitored for both productivity and quality. Productivity may be measured by tracking the number of contacts per day or per hour, the length of time each contact takes to complete, and the percentage of contacts that are resolved on the first call. Quality is usually monitored through silent monitoring of the calls themselves. This refers to the supervisor or manager listening to random calls for each service representative and then making a qualitative judgment about how well the service representative handled the call. It is not enough to take and give information when a member has a problem or complaint; the representative must apply communication techniques developed for customer service to be optimally effective.[2] Some plans routinely send follow-up questionnaires to members after the member services inquiry or complaint is resolved to solicit feedback about the process as well as to reinforce the notion that the member is important.[3]

SERVICE AND HELP

Member services is responsible for helping members use the plan. New members commonly have less than complete (or even no) understanding of how the plan operates, how to access care, how to obtain authorization for specialty services (in a PCP case manager type of plan), and so forth. These are services to members as opposed to complaint and concern resolution, which is discussed later. Although the broad issues are generally the same across product lines, plans often find differing levels of need for each of these types of services in the commercial, Medicare, and Medicaid markets.

PCP Selection

In plans that use PCPs to access care, member services will frequently be called on to help members select a PCP. This may occur because the member failed to select a PCP in the first place, particularly in a POS plan in which the member has no intention of using the HMO part of the plan. Even in POS, it is best to require the member to select a PCP because it is not known whether the member will change his or her mind later and because the plan really does want to encourage the member to use the managed care system.

Another reason that a member may need to select a new PCP is if a participating PCP leaves the network for any reason or if the PCP's practice closes because it is full but that information did not get into the most recent provider directory (or the member did not realize that a tiny, asterisk superscript meant that the practice was closed). One other common reason for change is that the member and the PCP simply were not the right match for each other, and the member is requesting a change to another PCP. This often occurs when a member is new to the system, and it occurs particularly often when managed care is installed as a replacement for all other insurance (as with most POS plans), thus requiring new members who never wanted to go into a managed care plan to select a PCP.

In any event, member services is generally responsible for helping the members with this problem. Many plans have more information about PCPs available on line to the member services representative than is available in the directory, and representatives may be able to help the member select a PCP on the basis of special information, such as languages spoken, training, hours available, and so forth. Some plans, especially closed panel plans, have highly informative physician directories available for this purpose that they mail to the member.

Identification Cards

Although this chapter does not address the basic issues of entering enrollment information and issuing identification cards, it is inevitable that some members will have problems with their cards, and then member services will need to resolve those problems. Common problems include lost cards, cards that were sent to the wrong address, incorrect information on the card, and changes required because of change of status (e.g., the subscriber got married).

Outreach

An outreach program can be of great benefit in preventing member complaints and problems. An outreach program is one that proactively contacts new members and discusses the way the plan works. By reaching out and letting members know how the authorization system works, how to obtain services, what the benefits are, and so forth, the plan can reduce confusion.

Virtually all HMOs, as well as other types of plans, mail an information pack to new members. This pack typically includes not only the new identification card but also descriptive language about how to use the plan, how to access care, and how the authorization system works; information about coordination of benefits (see Chapter 32 of *The Managed Health Care Handbook* for a detailed discussion[4]); an updated provider directory (possibly with maps in the case of a closed panel); and a description of how the pharmacy benefit works (see Chapter 23 of *The Managed Health Care Handbook* for a detailed discussion[5]) if the member has such a benefit. Some plans may also include a copy of the benefits description and even possibly the group master contract or legal schedule of benefits. Some plans also include a "Member Bill of Rights" outlining the member's rights and responsibilities. Closed panels also include hours of operation and telephone numbers for the health centers as well as how to access urgent care. Medical groups in network model plans, medical groups in open panel plans, and IDSs may also provide such information on a direct basis and not as part of materials sent by the HMO.

Many plans accomplish a more aggressive and effective outreach program by conducting a telephone-based outreach program. Telephone outreach requires a carefully scripted approach during the contact. Development of scripts allows the plan to use less thoroughly trained personnel to carry out the program; when questions arise that are not easily answered from the script or when problems are identified, the member may be transferred to an experienced member services representative. This also gives the member a chance to ask questions about the plan, especially when those questions do not come up until the member has heard about the plan from the outreach personnel. It is worthwhile to bear in mind that, for many members who are low utilizers, this contact may be the most important one; clearly, it is in the plan's interest to retain such members. Outreach is most effective when carried out during both daytime and early evening hours to ensure that contact is made.

Telephone outreach is especially useful when the plan undergoes a large enrollment surge. The level of problems that members experience with a managed care plan is generally highest during the initial period of enrollment (because new members are still unfamiliar with the way the plan operates), and outreach can help ameliorate that issue. The sooner the members understand how to access the system, the sooner the burden on the plan to deal with complaints and grievances will diminish.

MEMBER COMPLAINTS AND GRIEVANCES

Complaints Compared with Grievances

Complaints by members may be generally defined as problems that members bring to the attention of the plan; they differ from grievances in that grievances are formal complaints demanding formal resolution by the plan. Complaints that are not resolved to the satisfaction of the member may evolve into formal grievances. It is clearly in the best interest of the plan to try and resolve complaints before they become formal grievances because there are greater legal implications and member satisfaction issues involved with grievances.

Resolution of complaints is usually informal, although the plan should have a clear policy for investigating complaints and responding to members. Despite the informal nature of complaint resolution, it is extremely important for the member services department, or in fact any staff member, to document carefully every contact with a member when the member expresses any dissatisfaction. For complaints, the member services representative should keep a log of even casual telephone calls from members as well as notes of any conversations with members while he or she is trying to resolve complaints. Concise and thorough records may prove quite valuable if the complaint turns into a formal grievance. Such documentation also helps in data analysis, as discussed later in this chapter.

Grievance resolution is distinctly formal. State and federal regulations require HMOs to have clearly delineated member grievance procedures, to inform members of those procedures, and to abide by them. Clearly defined grievance and appeals procedures are usually required in insurance and self-funded plans as well. (This topic is discussed in detail in Chapter 59 of *The Managed Health Care Handbook.*[6]) As a general rule, members may be contractually prohibited from filing a lawsuit over benefits denial until they have gone through the plan's grievance procedure. Conversely, if a plan fails to inform a member of grievance rights or fails to abide by the grievance procedure, the plan has a real potential for liability. Suggested steps in formal grievance resolution follow later in this chapter.

Claims Problems Compared with Service Problems

Member complaints and grievances fall into two basic categories: claims problems and service problems. Service problems fall into two basic categories as well: medical service and administrative service.

Claims Problems

Claims problems generally occur when the member seeks coverage for a service that is not covered under the schedule of benefits or is not considered medically necessary or when the member had services rendered without authorization and the plan denied or reduced coverage. In the first two situations, the plan must rely on both the schedule of benefits and determinations of medical necessity by the medical department. In the case of denial or reduction in payment of claims already incurred, the issue of plan policy and procedure is also present because this situation arises from cold claims received without prior PCP authorization.

For prospective denial or reduction of coverage, the plan should respond to the member with the exact contractual language upon which it bases its denial of coverage. There also needs to be a mechanism in place for second opinions by the medical director or designee in those cases where there is a dispute over medical necessity. The medical director must be careful not to confuse these two issues: There may be times when a service can be considered medically necessary but the plan does not cover it under the schedule of benefits.

Cases involving denial or reduction in coverage for services already incurred are a bit more complex. The claims department of the plan will receive a claim without an authorization for services. As discussed in detail in Chapter 31 of *The Managed Health Care Handbook*, the plan must have clear policies and procedures for processing such claims.[7] In the case of an HMO without any benefits for out-of-network services, the plan may pend or hold the claims to investigate whether an authorization actually does exist (or should have been given). If an authorization for services ultimately is given, the claim is paid; if no authorization is forthcoming, the claim is denied. The plan may occasionally wish to pay the claim even without an authorization in certain circumstances, such as a genuine emergency, an urgent problem out of the area, or a first offense of a new member.

In POS plans an unauthorized claim is not denied (assuming that it is covered under the schedule of benefits), but the coverage is substantially reduced. As discussed in Chapter 21, it is not always clear when a service was actually authorized and when the member chose to self-refer. The plan must have clear policies to deal with these claims because it is impractical to pend every unauthorized claim, POS being predicated on a certain level of out-of-network use.

In those instances where the claim is ultimately denied or coverage is reduced, members need an appeal mechanism. It is conceivable that the plan's claims payment policies will not envision every contingency, that the claims investigation mechanism will not always be accurate, or that there may be mitigating circumstances involved. There may be a genuine conflict of opinion over whether the member followed plan policies or over issues such as medical necessity. In the case of denial of a claim, the member needs to be informed of appeal rights; whether such information is required when one is processing POS claims is not clear, but most plans do not do so under the assumption that nonauthorized claims are a result of voluntary self-referral by the member and that coverage has not been denied but only paid at the out-of-network level.

Service Problems

Service problems include medical service and administrative service problems. Medical service problems could include a member's inability to get an appointment, rude treatment, lack of physicians located near where the member lives, difficulty getting a needed referral (difficult at least in the opinion of the member), and, most serious, problems with quality of care. Administrative problems could include incorrect identification cards, not issuing an identification card at all, poor responsiveness to previous inquiries, not answering the telephone, lack of documentation or education materials, and so forth.

Member services personnel need to investigate service complaints and get a response to the member. When the complaint alleges quality of care problems, the medical director needs to be notified. If investigation reveals a genuine quality of care problem, the matter requires referral to the quality assurance committee or peer review committee (see Chapters 5 and 17). In most cases, the real problem may be one of communication or of a member demanding a service that the physician feels is unnecessary. In those cases, the member services personnel need to communicate back to the member the results of the investigation or to clarify plan policy regarding coverage.

In all cases of service problems, the key to success is communication. If member services communicates clearly and promptly to all parties, many problems can be cleared up. Such communication must not be confrontational or accusatory. It is important for member services always to keep in mind that there are at least two ways of looking at any one situation and that there is rarely a clear-cut right or wrong.

FORMAL GRIEVANCE PROCEDURE

As indicated earlier, plans (HMOs at least) are required to have a formal grievance procedure, and the responsibility for implementing it falls to the member services department. State regulations (and federal regulations for federally qualified HMOs and competitive medical plans) often spell out the minimum requirements for the procedure. Such requirements may include timeliness of response, who will review the grievance, what recourse the member has, and so forth. Plans are also usually allowed to have a limitation on how long a member has to file a grievance; for example, if a member fails to file a grievance within 90 days after the problem arises, he or she may lose the right under the plan's grievance procedure to file. Such restrictions may not ultimately prevent lawsuits, but they probably serve to strengthen the plan's position.

Each plan must review applicable state and federal regulations to develop its grievance procedure; the procedure should also be reviewed by the plan's legal counsel to evaluate its utility as a risk management function. A general outline of a suggested grievance procedure follows.

Filing of Formal Grievance

Assuming that the plan has been unable satisfactorily to resolve a member complaint, the member must be informed of and afforded the opportunity to file a formal grievance. This is usually done with a form specific to that purpose. The form usually asks for essential information (e.g., name, membership number, parties involved, and so forth) and a narrative of the problem. The form may also contain space for tracking the grievance and responses by other parties.

Investigation of Grievance

During the time period that begins when the form is received and ends when the plan responds, the grievance needs to be investigated. This may include further interviews with the member, interviews with or written responses from other parties, and any other pertinent information. The time period may be set by law or may be set by the plan, but it should not exceed some reasonable period (e.g., 60 days). At the end of that time period, the plan responds to the member with its findings and resolution. The response includes the requirements for the member to respond back to the plan if the resolution is not satisfactory.

Appeal

If the member's grievance is not resolved to his or her satisfaction, the member has the right to appeal. This appeal may involve having the case reviewed by a senior officer of the company or by an outside reviewer. This first appeal is usually done without any formal hearings or testimony but rather is based on the material submitted for review by both the plan and the member. Again, the plan usually sets a reasonable time period for requesting the appeal (e.g., 30 days) and a reasonable time period for the review to occur (e.g., 30 days).

Formal Hearing

If the plan's response is still not satisfactory to the member, some plans afford the member a right to request a formal hearing. There is usually a time limitation (e.g., 15 working days), during which the member must request the hearing or forfeit the right to a hearing. If the plan has a formal hearing right, then once the plan receives a request for a formal hearing the plan has an obligation to respond in a timely manner (e.g., 15 working days). The response is notification of when and where the hearing will take place. The hearing should be scheduled within a reasonable time period (e.g., 15 working days).

The purpose of a formal hearing is to afford the member a chance to present his or her case in person to an unbiased individual or a panel of unbiased individuals. To that end, the hearing officer or the voting members of the hearing panel should not have participated in the earlier decisions, if possible; plan managers who have been involved before will surely participate, but not necessarily as the hearing officer or as voting members.

It is common to use a panel for formal hearings. Panels may be made up of board members, providers (who are not involved with the member on a professional basis), lay members of the plan, or managers from the plan who do not participate in member services issues except for grievances. It is best to use a panel size of odd numbers, preferably five or seven, to prevent ties. There should be a panel chairperson to function as the hearing officer. If a single hearing officer is used, that individual should be the board chairperson, the president of the corporation, or an independent person capable of understanding the issues (e.g., an attorney specializing in health care).

The hearing provides the member the opportunity to present the grievance and any pertinent information. The plan does likewise, usually by having the member services representative present the plan's case. The executive director and medical director may likewise present testimony.

It is a bad idea to ask the member's provider to appear at the hearing in those cases where the provider has been involved in the grievance. This carries the potential of disrupting the physician–patient relationship and of placing the provider in a no-win situation, and it can have implications for future legal action against the provider or plan. Any information from the provider should be presented by the medical director.

A resolution of the grievance is rarely given to the member at the close of the hearing. When the hearing is over, the member is told that he or she will be informed of the results within a set time period (e.g., 15 working days). After the member and staff have left, the voting members of the panel discuss the case and reach a resolution. That resolution is communicated in writing to the member and any other pertinent parties, along with the statement that the member has the right of further appeal to arbitration or the government agency, as appropriate.

Arbitration

In some states, arbitration is allowed. This may occur before or after appeal to the state agency (see below). In those states where arbitration is allowed, and if the plan wishes to pursue it (or if it is required), the plan would comply with the regulations regarding arbitration in terms of selection of the arbitrator(s) and the form of the hearing.

Appeal to Government Agencies

In all cases, if the member is not satisfied with the results of the formal hearing, he or she has the right to appeal to the appropriate government agency. Usually, most members are commercial members; that is, they are members who are neither federal employees nor beneficiaries of entitlement programs but who enroll through a private company or are employees of the state or municipal government. For commercial members, the state insurance department has jurisdiction. In cases where the grievance involves quality of care, the health department may have jurisdiction.

Federal employees, or those who are covered under the Office of Personnel Management (OPM), have the right of appeal to the OPM. The OPM specifically reserves the right in its contract with health plans to resolve and rule on grievances by members who are federal employees. Members who are covered under entitlement programs (Medicare and Medicaid) have the right to appeal to the respective government agency; for Medicare that means the Health Care Financing Administration, and for Medicaid it refers to the state's human services (or welfare) department.

Lawsuits

Although not a part of a plan's grievance procedure, the last legal remedy for a disgruntled member is legal action. If the plan carefully follows its grievance procedure, the chances of a successful lawsuit against it are small. If the plan fails to follow proper policy and procedure, the chances become pretty high. See Chapter 38 of *The Managed Health Care Handbook* for a full discussion of risk management.[8]

DATA COLLECTION AND ANALYSIS

The member services department should be responsible for collecting, collating, and analyzing data. Data may be considered in two broad categories: data regarding general levels of satisfaction and dissatisfaction, and data regarding medical and administrative problems (trends analysis).

Satisfaction Data

Satisfaction data may include surveys of current members, disenrollment surveys, telephone response time and waiting time studies (these may be done in conjunction with the quality management department, but they are essentially patient satisfaction studies), and surveys of clients and accounts (although marketing rather than member services may perform many of these studies).

Member surveys are particularly useful when done properly. Even when a managed care plan is the sole carrier in an account (e.g., a replacement POS plan), surveys help the plan evaluate service levels and ascertain what issues are important to the members. Surveys may be focused on a few issues that the plan wants to study, or they may be broad and comprehensive.[9]

In an environment where members have multiple choices for their health care coverage, member surveys will be geared toward issues that influence enrollment choices. It is easier and less expensive to retain a member than it is to sell a new one. Of special importance are those members who do not heavily utilize medical services because their premiums pay for the expenses of high utilizers and because such members tend to disenroll more often than members who utilize services heavily.[10] Surveys designed to analyze what makes those low-utilizing members leave or stay (or join in the first place) can lead to the development of targeted member retention programs. Some plans develop direct mail campaigns that include giveaways or promote services available to low utilizers (e.g., health promotion) to have those members place a sense of value on their membership in the plan.

Trends Analysis

Problems that are brought to the plan's attention not only require resolution but need to be analyzed to look for trends. If a problem is sporadic or random, there may be little required other than helping the individual member as needed. If problems are widespread or stem from something that is likely to cause continual problems, then the plan must act to resolve the problems at the source. Such resolution may mean changing a policy or procedure, improving education materials to the members, dealing with a difficult provider, or any number of events. The point is that plan management will not know of chronic problems if the data are not analyzed.

Many plans now automate their member services tracking systems. Such automation not only serves to help member services track and manage individual problems but also serves as a method to collect and collate data. Each member contact with the plan is entered into the computerized tracking system and assigned a category (or multiple categories if necessary); issues involving providers are generally tracked not only by category but by provider as well. Repeat or follow-up calls are also tracked but usually still count as only one problem or inquiry.

Producing regular reports summarizing the frequency of each category as well as the frequency of problems or complaints by provider (along with monitoring of the rate at which members transfer out of a provider's practice) allows management to focus attention appropriately. An example of the types of categories that a plan may track is given in Exhibit 24–1. This example applies primarily to HMOs or POS plans and is by no means exhaustive; conversely, it is unlikely that a plan would use all these categories.

PROACTIVE APPROACHES TO MEMBER SERVICES

Most member services departments become complaint departments. When that happens, the plan not only loses a valuable source of member satisfaction but runs the risk of burning out the personnel in the department. It is emotionally draining to listen to complaints all day. Even the satisfaction of successfully resolving the majority of complaints can be inadequate if there is nothing else the plan is doing to address satisfaction. In addition to analyzing the sources of dissatisfaction and complaints to resolve the problems at the source, the plan might consider the following suggestions.

Member Suggestions and Recommendations

Soliciting member suggestions and recommendations can be valuable. This may be done along with member surveys, or the plan may solicit suggestions through response cards in physicians' offices or in the member newsletter. There are times when the members will have ways of viewing the plan that provide valuable insight to managers. Although not all the suggestions may be practical, they may at least illuminate trouble spots that need attention of some sort.

Exhibit 24–1 Examples of Categories for a Member Contact Tracking System

Enrollment issues

- Selecting a PCP
  - —Practice closed
  - —Never selected
  - —Special needs
- Changing PCP
  - —Dissatisfied with PCP
  - —PCP no longer participating with plan
  - —Geographic reasons
- Identification card(s)
  - —Never received
  - —Errors on card
  - —Change in information
  - —Lost card
- Change in enrollment status
  - —New dependent
  - —Delete dependent
  - —Student or disabled dependent verification
- Change in address
  - —Subscriber
  - —Dependent(s)
- Need evidence of coverage or other documentation
- Need new directory of providers

Benefits issues

- Questions
  - —Physician services (primary care, specialty care)
  - —Hospital or institutional services
  - —Emergency services
  - —Ancillary services (pharmacy, other)
  - —POS benefits questions
- Complaints
  - —Copayment or coinsurance levels
  - —Limitations on coverage
  - —Did not know benefits levels

Claims issues

- In-network
  - —Claims denied (HMO)
  - —Claim cascaded to lower level of benefits (POS)
  - —Unpaid claim (provider submitted, member submitted)
  - —Received bill from provider
  - —Coordination of benefits
  - —Subrogation/other party liability
- Out of network
  - —Claim denied (HMO)
  - —Claim cascaded to lower level of benefits (POS)
  - —Unpaid claim (provider submitted, member submitted)
  - —Received bill from provider
  - —Coordination of benefits
  - —Subrogation/other party liability

Plan policies and procedures

- Authorization system for specialty care
- Precertification system for institutional care
- Second opinion procedures
- Copayments and coinsurance
- Unable to understand printed materials or instructions
- Complaint and grievance procedures

Plan administration

- Personnel rude or unhelpful
- Incorrect or inappropriate information given
- Telephone responsiveness problems
  - —On hold
  - —Unanswered calls
  - —Call not returned
- Complaints or grievances not addressed satisfactorily

Access to care

- Unable to get an appointment
- Too long before appointment scheduled
- Office hours not convenient
- Waiting time too long in office
- Problems accessing care after hours
- Too far to travel to get care
- No public transportation
- Calls not returned

Physician issues

- Unpleasant or rude behavior
- Unprofessional or inappropriate behavior
- Does not spend adequate time with member
- Does not provide adequate information
  - —Medical
  - —Financial
  - —Administrative (e.g., referral process)
- Lack of compliance with use of plan network
- Lack of compliance with authorization policies
- Does not speak member's language
- Speaks negatively about the plan

Perceived appropriateness and quality of care

- Delayed treatment
- Inappropriate denial of treatment
- Inappropriate denial of referral
- Unnecessary treatment
- Incorrect diagnosis or treatment
- Lack of follow-up
  - —Physician visit
  - —Diagnostic tests

continues

Exhibit 24–1 continued

Medical office facility issues
- Lack of privacy
- Unclean or unpleasant
- Unsafe or ill equipped
- Lack of adequate parking

Institutional care issues
- Perceived poor care in hospital
- Discharged too soon
- Hospital or facility staff behavior
  —Rude or unpleasant behavior
  —Unprofessional or inappropriate behavior
  —Speak negatively about the plan
- Facility unclean or unpleasant
- Facility unsafe or ill equipped
- Problems with admission or discharge process
- Other administrative errors

Affiliations with Health Clubs and Health Promotion Activities

Managed care plans frequently develop affiliations with health clubs and other types of health-related organizations. This serves to underscore the emphasis on prevention and health maintenance, allows for differentiation with competitors, and provides value-added service to the member. Access to or sponsorship of various health promotion activities falls into the same category.

A special type of health promotion is the provision of health advice from nurses available on the telephone. This is meant not as a replacement for physician advice but rather as a supplement. Advice may range from helping a member deal with a minor illness to explaining and educating about surgical procedures. This may be done in tandem with distribution of self-help medical books and other health promotion literature. Some closed panel plans are providing this type of service to a remarkable degree. These plans have well-designed education materials, such as interactive videos, literature, and personal education. For certain types of procedures, such as transurethral prostatectomy, the member must participate in an interactive video before making a choice regarding an elective procedure. Some open panel plans are also providing such services either through their own personnel or through contracts with outside firms. Many advanced managed care plans are using this type of service to help reduce the demand for physician-related services; see Chapter 13 for more discussion of this topic.

CONCLUSION

Member services are a requirement of any managed care plan. The primary responsibility of member services is to help members resolve any problems or questions they may have. Member services must also track and analyze member problems and complaints so that management can act to correct problems at the source. Mechanisms to resolve complaints and grievances not only are required by law but make good business sense. Plan management should not be satisfied with a reactive member services function but should take a proactive approach as well.

Study Questions

1. Explain the basic goals of a member services department.
2. Describe the typical types of steps that member services would take to address a member injury, problem, a complaint, and a formal grievance.
3. Describe actions a plan may take to enhance member satisfaction.

4. Construct an outreach program for an HMO that has just undertaken a new Medicare contract.

REFERENCES AND NOTES

1. J.L. Touse, "Medical Management and Legal Obligations to Members," in *The Managed Health Care Handbook*, 3d ed., ed. P.R. Kongstvedt (Gaithersburg, Md.: Aspen, 1996), 930–943.
2. C.R. Bell and R. Zemke, Service Breakdown: The Road to Recovery, *Management Review* 76 (1987): 32–35.
3. S.W. Hall, Targeting Member Needs with Technology, *HMO Magazine* (July/August 1993): 55–56.
4. B.S. Scheur, R.L. McElfatrick, and R.S. Eichler, "Other Party Liability and Coordination of Benefits," in *The Managed Health Care Handbook*, 3d ed., ed. P.R. Kongstvedt (Gaithersburg, Md.: Aspen, 1996), 532–544.
5. H.F. Blissenbach and P.M. Penna, "Pharmaceutical Services in Managed Care," in *The Managed Health Care Handbook*, 3d ed., ed. P.R. Kongstvedt (Gaithersburg, Md.: Aspen, 1996), 367–387.
6. J.M. Saue and G.H. Dooge, "ERISA and Managed Care," in *The Managed Health Care Handbook*, 3d ed., ed. P.R. Kongstvedt (Gaithersburg, Md.: Aspen, 1996), 944–966.
7. R.S. Eichler and R.L. McElfatrick, "Claims and Benefits Administration," in *The Managed Health Care Handbook*, 3d ed., ed. P.R. Kongstvedt (Gaithersburg, Md.: Aspen, 1996), 491–531.
8. B.J. Youngberg, "Risk Management in Managed Care," in *The Managed Health Care Handbook*, 3d ed., ed. P.R. Kongstvedt (Gaithersburg, Md.: Aspen, 1996), 608–621.
9. Group Health Association of America (GHAA), *GHAA's Consumer Satisfaction Survey*, 2d ed. Washington, D.C.: GHAA, 1991.
10. W. Wrightson, et al., Demographic and Utilization Characteristics of HMO Disenrollees. *GHAA Journal* (Summer 1987): 23–42.

SUGGESTED READING

Furse, D.H., Bucham, M.R., et al. 1994. Leveraging the Value of Customer Satisfaction Information. *Journal of Health Care Marketing* 14(3): 16–20.

Gold, M. and Woolridge, J. 1995. Surveying Consumer Satisfaction To Assess Managed-Care Quality: Current Practices. *Health Care Financing Review* 16: 155–173.

Hall, S.W. 1993. Targeting Member Needs with Technology. *HMO Magazine* 34(4): 55–56.

Kenkel, P., ed. 1995. Centered Information. *Managed Care Quarterly* 3(4).

Noe, T.J. 1994. Bypassing the Busy Signal. *HMO Magazine* 35(3): 81–82, 83.

Polonski, G.J. 1995. Customer Complaints: A Managed Care Firm's Best Weapon in CQI. *Medical Interface* 8(1): 111–117.

Youngs, M.T. and Wingerson, L. 1995. *The 1996 Medical Outcomes & Guidelines Sourcebook*. New York, N.Y.: Faulkner & Gray.

Chapter 25

Common Operational Problems in Managed Health Care Plans

Peter R. Kongstvedt

Study Objectives

- Understand common operational problems that managed care organizations can develop
- Understand how managed care organizations can avoid those problems
- Understand basic approaches that managed care organizations can take to deal with these common problems should they occur

As in most enterprises, managed health care plans are prone to problems that are common to their own industry. The most common problem for start-up plans is inability to gain market share. That problem, languishing in the market, is not addressed in this chapter. The reader is referred to Chapter 35 of *The Managed Health Care Handbook* for an in-depth discussion of marketing issues, including common pitfalls and problems.[1] The focus of this chapter is operational problems rather than the problems of gaining membership.

Whether a problem occurs and how serious that problem is will depend on a variety of factors. None of the problems and common mistakes that are discussed in this chapter occurs in a vacuum. Certain problems will be exacerbated by the presence of other, concurrent problems. In some types of plans the relative dangers will be far less than in others. The purpose of this chapter is to discuss these common problems and mistakes to help make a manager aware of them. Early detection could prevent severe damage to the plan.

Not all these problems would be found in the same plan at the same time, and rarely will only one problem exist at a time. In general, troubled health plans will have problems in logical combinations. For example, if significant problems are occurring with expenses that are incurred but not reported (IBNRs), it is likely that the plan will be having problems with claims processing and inaccurate utilization reports as well.

In some cases, the problems discussed in this chapter will be serious only in plans that assume full financial risk (i.e., health maintenance organizations [HMOs], full risk-bearing preferred provider organizations [PPOs], and individual practice associations [IPAs] that take full responsibility for enrolling members, collecting premiums, paying providers, and so forth). Other problems, especially those that relate to medical management, may be found in organizations that accept limited risk as well as organizations accepting full risk (e.g., medical groups, contracting IPAs within an HMO, or any other organization responsible for delivering medical services).

Regardless of how a particular organization is configured, it is worthwhile understanding the potential common problems that any health plan can encounter. This may allow you to see whether a plan is running into trouble, even if you yourself do not have responsibility for that particular area of management. It will also allow you to analyze the competition better and develop strategies for success.

UNDERCAPITALIZATION OF NEW PLANS

A classic problem in business, undercapitalization is just as troublesome for health plans as for any other business. Losses can mount more quickly than anticipated, and if the pricing strategy was too low, losses can continue for quite some time. It is not uncommon for new plans to spend between $2 million and $7 million before getting to breakeven status. The best way to handle this is to prevent it by using an experienced actuary and financial consultant to estimate losses before breakeven and to do so under a number of different scenarios.

Once a plan is operational, if it is undercapitalized and not amenable to fast repairs (e.g., sharp reductions in administrative cost or medical cost or rapid increases in premium revenue), there are a limited number of responses available to management. One response is to try to get the providers to assume the expenses, perhaps through mandatory fee reductions or promissory notes, or to use a reimbursement methodology that places provider systems at full risk for medical expenses (which is a complicated strategy that is discussed in detail in Chapter 5 of *The Managed Health Care Handbook*).[2] The other routes involve obtaining money from outside sources, either as debt or by selling equity. In any of these cases, you are obviously dealing from a position of weakness and will usually pay the price of failing to obtain adequate capital before commencement of operations. Failing even that, the plan may wind up in a forced merger with a healthy plan, in receivership to creditors, seized by the state insurance department, or having to declare bankruptcy or even fold. All these last options may be considered a career limiting move on the part of management.

PREDATORY PRICING OR LOW-BALLING

This refers to premium rates that are intentionally well below the actual cost of delivering care. This is usually found in start-up plans, although a mature plan may low-ball to preserve or rapidly gain market share in response to a competitor's rates. Price undercutting is a venerable tradition in a capitalistic system and has great utility in enhancing one's competitive stance. Buying market share is not necessarily a mistake under all circumstances, but it is a risky strategy that must be undertaken with great care.

There is a crusty old cliché in business that goes "You can't buy widgets for a dollar, sell them for eighty cents, and make it up on volume." This is even more true in managed health care than in manufacturing. The manufacturer may hope to sell a service contract with the widget and recoup the loss or raise the price of widgets after a few months. In a health plan, all you sell is service; there are no benefits riders that will make up for a grossly underbid base premium. Furthermore, once you sign up a group for a set premium rate, you usually have to live with that rate for at least a year. Even in accounts in which the plan is not bearing financial risk for medical expenses (such as an administrative services only account), the plan may suffer a financial penalty if it has guaranteed medical expense trends, and it will doubtless suffer a tarnished reputation for effective management, veracity, or both.

The purpose of low-balling is to drive enrollment up and buy market share. If you low-ball a rate so that you lose $5 per member per month (PMPM), and if you succeed in increasing enrollment by 5,000 members, you have succeeded in increasing your losses to 5,000 × $5 PMPM, or $25,000 per month, or $300,000 per year. You cannot make it up on volume.

Occasionally, managers may low-ball primarily to cover high overhead costs (in other words, to get some cash flowing in) rather than as an attempt to get market dominance. In those cases, the losses from the fixed overhead are in fact attenuated by the premium revenue brought in, at least initially, even though the medical loss ratio is unacceptably high. Low-balling may provide a short-term fix for highly leveraged plans such as closed panels, but the long-term result is the same: As enrollment increases, the overhead required to provide service increases as well, leading to a continuing loss situation that may become more severe than anticipated.

In addition to sustained losses, low-balling is a market strategy that appeals to the most price-sensitive consumers. That can be a set-up for a raid by a competitor who low-balls the rates even further. Unless another strategy is available, the plan could then end up in a price war and never recoup its losses.

None of this is to say that a plan may not have to hold rates down or even lower them for competitive reasons. It is to say that low-balling should never be the only competitive strategy. It should really be used only as an adjunct to a long-range strategy, and even then only with caution. Far too many plans have found that their pockets were not as deep as they thought or that they underestimated how deep those pockets would need to be.

A common and critical mistake by plan managers facing price competition is to lower the rates to unrealistic levels and simply budget expenses lower, usually medical expenses. Unless there is a clear and believable strategy for lowering those expenses, the savings will not materialize. It is not enough to order the medical director to harass the physicians and get costs down; there needs to be a more cogent plan for reducing expenses. Sadly, a manager under pressure frequently indulges in a combination of magical thinking and rule by decree. In other words, by decreeing that expenses must be reduced, the other managers will magically figure out how to do that despite not having succeeded the previous year. The lesson here is that, if the rates are intentionally lowered, managers had better figure out specifically how they are going to reduce expenses in each category. If they cannot come up with a clear plan for each category, they should budget the loss.

Assuming that the decision has been made to try to recover some of the losses, the main question is whether to raise the rates in one breathtaking rate hike or to phase in the rate increase over a number of years. That decision must be made by analyzing the plan's financial resources, the market conditions, the customers' willingness to put up with a rate hike, the danger of losing significant enrollment in that group (which may or may not be a bad thing, depending on the degree of losses you are sustaining in the group; in turn, this may lead to adverse selection, which is discussed below), and the plan's ability to control expenses. Of course, if the situation is bad enough, the state insurance commissioner may wind up making the decision unilaterally.

OVERPRICING

The antipode of low-balling, overpricing simply refers to rates that are unacceptably high in the marketplace. This is usually found in mature plans, but occasionally it occurs in new plans that anticipate high costs or that have incurred unusually high preoperational expenses. Overpricing is becoming more rare in the current, highly competitive marketplace because purchasers simply will not overpay when good, less expensive alternatives exist. Nevertheless, overpricing is not extinct, and it remains an identifiable and even predictable problem for health plans.

There are five primary reasons for overpricing:

1. a panic response to previous low-balling
2. excessive overhead
3. failure to control utilization properly
4. adverse selection
5. avarice

The fifth reason, avarice, is obvious and will not be addressed in this chapter except to note that the competitive marketplace may help hold down excessive prices that are based on greed.

A panic response to previous low-balling is not unusual. As losses mount, plan management feels unable to weather the losses and tries to make up the revenue quickly. This is particularly true when a plan is being pressured by investors or regulators or when the plan's financial reserves are projected to be dangerously low. If the low-balling strategy has driven out competition (not a likely event), exorbitant rate hikes may occur simply as a natural course.

Excessive overhead may also lead to overpricing. If plan management is unable to improve efficiency, the price must be paid. Excessive overhead may occur in any plan. It occurs in new starts when required administrative support has been estimated on the basis of enrollment projections that fail to materialize. In mature plans, excessive overhead usually is traced to a combination of internal politics, or turf battles, and management's unwillingness or inability to explore new methods of managing the plan. An additional cause of excessive overhead in a mature plan is the plan developing multiple and creative products and/or reimbursement systems that require significant manual intervention.

Excessive medical expense is the most common reason for overpricing. It is far easier to raise prices than to deal with the causes of overutilization. The usual rationalization goes something like this: "The reason we have the highest rates is that we have the best physicians, and so we have the sickest patients. It's all adverse selection!" In these cases, the plan has often marketed benefits comparable to or better than those of competing HMOs and has assumed utilization rates similar to those of tightly run HMOs (after all, if you call yourself an HMO, you should perform like one, right?) but has imposed fewer controls on physicians and hospitals. Rather than impose restrictions and tighten management, administrators indulge in the common fantasy that they are doing the best they can and it is all the fault of external events.

Bear in mind, however, that excessively high rates do indeed lead to adverse selection. This is especially true in two situations. The first situation is when an account allows more than one health plan to market to employees, in contrast to a total replacement account, where no competing health plans are allowed to market. In a multiple-choice environment, if the plan becomes too expensive for most people, only those facing high medical costs will choose to enroll because the plan's premiums are still less than the coinsurance and deductibles they would face with the competition. A related phenomenon has been a classic problem with indemnity insurance when multiple HMOs are offered: Despite high premium rates in the indemnity plan, individuals with high medical costs and an affinity with a provider not in the managed care plan will enroll at almost any premium cost.

The second common situation is in a free-choice environment, such as is found in a purchasing cooperative or in the public sector market (i.e., Medicare). In this situation, analogous to what was just described above, each individual can choose among several alternatives. A high-priced plan with a large provider panel will remain attractive to sick individuals, and healthy individuals may choose a less expensive plan despite a smaller network because they feel healthy and have bills to pay (and can thus use the savings for other needs). This situation is especially dangerous for provider-sponsored health plans that may easily enroll existing patients but not attract members with few health problems.

UNREALISTIC PROJECTIONS

Any and all categories of revenue and expense are subject to unrealistic projections and expectations, but two stand out: overprojecting enrollment and underprojecting medical expenses.

In new plans, it is common to overestimate enrollment. The reasons are probably a combination of high optimism, inexperience of the marketing director, failure to forecast and reforecast enrollment correctly on an account-specific basis, and an unrealistic start date. Unless the marketing director is a seasoned veteran, the forecast may include accounts considered sold that were only being polite, a factor may be added for new business even when the source and probability of that business are in doubt, or a standard penetration factor may be used that fails to address competitiveness in the account. If the plan does not go operational when anticipated, or if the delivery system is weaker than the anticipated delivery system used to forecast enrollment, significant negative variations in projected growth can occur.

Certainly unanticipated events can blindside even the most experienced marketing director. Competing or invading plans may spark a price war, or a regulator may delay certification for unexpected reasons. For all these reasons, the best marketing projections are conservative ones. Some executive directors feel that enrollment projections should always be high to motivate the director of marketing through his or her bonus. Unfortunately, enrollment projections drive financial projections, so that care must be taken, especially in new plans.

Underprojecting medical expenses, or overestimating the ability to manage utilization, is equally common in new plans. As has been mentioned earlier, naive managers sometimes assume that if they call themselves an HMO or a PPO and put some rudimentary controls in place, they will have the same results as an experienced and successful plan. If the medical director is inexperienced, or if the physicians in the panel are not used to tight medical management, it is unlikely that good utilization results will occur, unless by good luck.

Luck can also be bad. During the early stages of a plan's life, enrollment will be small enough that a few bad cases can have an excessive impact on expenses. A common and critical mistake for new plan managers to make is to project utilization as though there will be few serious cases. When the cases occur, management keeps factoring out the cost of caring for those sick patients and measures utilization on the basis of the remaining members. Clearly, if one factors out sick patients, utilization will always look reasonable. This mistake can be partially offset by purchasing adequate reinsurance, but that comes at a cost.

UNCONTROLLED GROWTH

Rapid growth is usually greeted with applause. In fact, many readers of this book may be saying to themselves "I wish we had such problems," but rapid growth is not always a good thing (dandelions come to mind). Certainly growth is a necessary ingredient to long-term success, but if growth is too rapid it can lead to problems that are long in resolving.

Closely related to the problem of overextended management (see below), the problem of uncontrolled growth is a bit more generalized: Rapid growth not only may quickly outstrip the ability of the plan's managers to keep up but may outstrip the system's capabilities as well. Dysfunctional patterns can set in, such as referral patterns or utilization behaviors that are more difficult to change after the fact than if they were addressed early on. Because the systems and management capabilities in the plan may now be inadequate, the developing problems will not be picked up until they are serious.

Rapid growth also means rapid expansions in the delivery system. The same attention paid to recruiting and credentialing in the development stages may not be present, and there may be little or no time spent properly orienting new providers to the plan's policies and procedures. That ultimately leads not only to inefficient practice patterns but to frustration on the part of those new providers.

Conversely, rapid growth can lead to saturation of the delivery system before there is adequate recruiting to take up the volume. This becomes especially problematic when practices begin to close more quickly than directory printing can accommodate, and new groups are enrolled with inaccurate directories of providers (or directories are distributed with addendums falling out onto the floor). In many cases, the physician practices will decide to close before they even notify the plan, and new members are signed up for those practices only to be turned away when calling for an appointment.

Service erosion is common when growth has been too rapid. Identification cards are not produced on time (or are produced inaccurately), claims are not paid properly, telephone calls to the plan are not answered in a timely or quality manner, evidence of coverage statements are not sent out on time, inadequate information is given to new members, and so forth. Poor service leads to a vicious cycle of ever-escalating problems resulting in a poor reputation from which it takes a long time to recover.

Rapid growth may also result in insufficient claims reserves. In periods of rapid growth, the usual methods of calculating claims reserves and IBNR become less reliable. This issue is discussed below. Last, rapid growth may lead to inadequate reserves. If reserves were adequate for a small plan, utilization in a plan suddenly grown large may take those reserves down to a dangerously low level. A plan's ability to withstand the cyclic nature of the insurance business, or just a run of bad luck, is tied directly to the amount of reserves available.

One approach to the problem of rapid growth is to limit increases in enrollment through decreased offerings and marketing. This has been done by a few plans in the past and is a viable approach. The risk in this is that your competition may pick up the members, and you will never catch up. For that reason, most plan managers are reluctant to turn off the tap unless it is a critical situation.

It is preferable to have plans for dealing with rapid growth before your back is against the wall. Plan for expansion of the plan's information and computer systems. Groom potential candidates for managerial promotion; you may even consider delegating certain responsibilities before such delegation is required. Some amount of physician recruiting activity should always be occurring, especially in areas without a great deal of capacity, although the rate of actual contracting needs to be coordinated with projected enrollment increases. Careful attention to staffing levels and training lead times in service areas such as claims and member services will help a great deal, although if projected enrollment does not occur, the overhead to the plan can become crushing.

IMPROPER IBNR CALCULATIONS AND ACCRUAL METHODS

As discussed in Chapter 22, the calculation and booking of liabilities in managed care plans are different from those found in most other industries. There have been quite a few health plans where accruals were based on the bills that came in the mail that month or on historical data only. A health plan that is standing risk for medical services must estimate accurately the cost of those services and accrue for them. If the costs are simply booked as they come in, disaster is certain.

The usual culprit here is failure to accrue properly for expenses that are IBNR. With data from lag studies and the plan's information system (i.e., the authorization and encounter data systems) as well as prior experience, sufficient accruals must be made each month for all expenses regardless of whether the bills came in. Calculation of proper accruals and IBNRs becomes especially difficult in plans that are experiencing rapid growth. A new member contributes to revenue on day 1 but generally does not incur medical services until some later date. Also, new members are not familiar with the plan and may not comply with policies and procedures, incurring medical costs that the plan will ultimately have to pay but are not well controlled. If the plan fails to perform good lag studies, the problem can be compounded. For all the reasons discussed earlier, a rapidly growing plan will have a diminished capacity to capture data accurately and will have lessened efficacy of utilization controls. Rapid growth should always lead management to consider boosting IBNRs.

In plans that have failed to accrue properly for expenses, actual expenses may exceed accruals as early as the first 6 months. The malignant feature of this problem is that it can go inexorably on for another 6 months or even more, especially if the plan is experiencing a claims processing problem, as most plans undergoing rapid growth do. Each month's accruals have to be adjusted for expenses related to past months, and financial performance suffers not only for performance to date but for past periods as well. The plan cannot stop the financial hemorrhage quickly because the expenses were already incurred and will keep rolling in. Monthly performance gets muddied up with adjustments for prior performance, and managers find themselves chasing their tails. This problem becomes intensified if the plan is generating inadequate premium revenue either through intentional low-balling or through faulty rate calculations.

This problem has accounted for a disproportionate number of health plan failures. It does not occur as an isolated problem and is usually accompanied by serious claims processing problems and inadequate controls on utilization. Failure to accrue properly is preventable with vigilance and early detection.

FAILURE TO RECONCILE ACCOUNTS RECEIVABLE AND MEMBERSHIP

Typical managed care plans have considerable changes occurring in membership each month. When the plan is standing risk for medical expenses, capitates providers, capitates administration fees, books some accruals based on PMPM historical cost, and so forth, it is vital to have as accurate a reconciliation of membership as possible. Most important, accounts receivable are tied directly to membership and billing.

It is common for plans to have difficulty with this activity. In some accounts (e.g., the federal employee health benefit program), the account is chronically late in providing accurate enrollment information. In other cases, the plan receives information from an account but never properly reconciles it every month because it is such a labor-intensive process. In any case, if the plan pays medical expenses for members who are no longer eligible or fails to collect premiums for members who are newly enrolled, losses are sure to follow. Even more devastating is the need to make a huge downward adjustment on the balance sheet to write off an uncollectible receivable.

OVEREXTENDED MANAGEMENT

What may have been appropriate or even generous staffing at the start-up stage can become understaffing after significant growth, especially if that growth has been rapid. The problem is more complex than the number of management bodies available; it is really one of span of control and experience of managers.

It is not uncommon in any industry for management requirements to change over time. Frequently, the methods used by the pioneers become dysfunctional as plans reach significant size. Tight control concentrated in a few managers, overreliance on central decision making, heavy hands-on involvement by senior managers, and so forth all can lead to paralysis and calcification as a plan becomes large and complex. The few managers with the control are unable to keep up with all the necessary details and demands of running operations, and failure to delegate properly prevents the plan from recruiting and retaining talented second level managers.

As a plan grows, its ability to change and adapt to the competitive environment becomes diminished. All the details necessary for proper operations become overwhelming. If senior managers are personally responsible for all these details, they may be unable to keep up, and things will get missed. Change becomes even less likely when overloaded managers cannot handle the prospect of having to learn yet another set of management skills while still having to use the old ones. This becomes demoralizing to subordinates and providers when plan management is seen as unresponsive, inattentive, or both.

A full discussion of appropriate delegation of authority and responsibility is beyond the scope of this chapter. Here it is sufficient to point out the dangers inherent in failing to create proper tiers of management as a plan grows. This is not to imply that senior managers should insulate themselves from the operations of the plan, overdelegate, or drive up administrative costs for no good reason. Rather, it is to emphasize that health plans are complex organizations, and nobody can do it all.

FAILURE TO USE UNDERWRITING

As this book is being written, the topic of small group market reform is being actively debated both at the federal level and in many states. Such reforms would sharply limit the degree to which a plan may medically underwrite accounts (i.e., choose whether to offer coverage and under what terms). That is, plans would not be able to turn down any valid group for coverage because of medical conditions, although the plan may be able to use such information in premium rate development. Such market reform is currently sporadic but is likely to become more widespread.

Even in the face of market reform, underwriting has a place, and in the desire to grow proper underwriting guidelines may be neglected. This is most likely to occur in a new plan that is trying to grow, but it can occur in any plan where marketing representatives and managers are inadequately supervised at the same time that they are being pressured to produce growth. Proper information must be obtained and acted upon both to determine what product to offer (or even whether the group qualifies for coverage under any circumstances) and to determine proper premium rates.

The plan's approach to rate setting must also occur in the context of the market, or problems in adverse selection are bound to occur. If a plan uses standard book rates or basic community rating (see Chapter 23) but the competition uses more advanced rating methodologies, then it is likely that the risk selection will be skewed. Conversely, if advanced approaches to rating are used simply to lower the price, then the plan will not obtain the required premium revenue in the budget.

FAILURE TO UNDERSTAND SALES AND MARKETING

When the plan is offered in an account with multiple other carriers or plans competing to enroll employees, then marketing managed care is essentially retail selling. It is much harder to assess the actuarial risk accurately in a multiple choice environment because it is possible to enroll only those members who have high medical needs, or vice versa. In other words, the possibility of adverse selection occurring within a group is very real. This is a particular problem in a highly competitive market, where the pressure on the marketing department is high. If the sales representative is on a pure commission basis, the pressure may be overwhelming. If emphasis is placed on the ease of access to high-cost specialists and hospitals, and if any restrictions to that access are downplayed, it can lead to adverse selection within an otherwise normal risk group.

This issue is especially important to provider-sponsored health plans. Provider-sponsored plans often look at members as patients and fail to understand that a health plan needs more members than patients. There will always be a pool of relatively young and healthy people who will choose price over provider selection because they have pressures on their lives greater than health-related issues (e.g., they feel healthy and need to pay their mortgage). A provider-sponsored health plan that markets primarily to the patients of the providers will never enroll enough new members who are not patients of anybody and thus will have adverse selection.

FAILURE OF MANAGEMENT TO UNDERSTAND REPORTS

Difficult as it may be to believe, managers may not always understand how reports are developed and written. A report may be labeled as one thing, but the data that are put into the report are really something else. For example, there may be a report that gives the rate of disenrollment from the plan. Depending on how the management information services (MIS) department inputs the data or how the computer was programmed, the disenrollment rate may include any member who changes status (e.g., goes from single to family) or coverage (e.g., changes jobs but continues with the plan under the new group). If that is the case, the disenrollment rate will be spuriously high. Failure to understand the meaning behind the disenrollment rate can lead to inaccurate forecasting and budgeting. Failure to understand the data elements in medical management and utilization reports is obviously far more serious.

To prevent this, senior management should be involved in developing the formats of reports and deciding what data will be used. The decisions about how to collect data and how to input them should not be made solely by the MIS department. In the event that the plan has experienced changeover in managers, it is important for the new manager not to assume anything and to ask explicitly what data go into each report. This last may seem embarrassing to a manager, but that type of compulsive behavior could prevent a serious mistake in the future.

FAILURE TO TRACK MEDICAL COSTS AND UTILIZATION CORRECTLY

This is a special subset of the problem just discussed, that of failure of management to understand reports. The problem of tracking medical expenses and utilization is so important that it merits discussion by itself.

As growing plans develop problems with operations (the authorization system, claims, or data gathering in general), medical expense and utilization reports frequently suffer. If the plan is accruing for IBNRs based on historical data because current data are inaccurate, expenses may be allocated to categories primarily because that is where the expenses have been found before. For example, if a plan historically has had high costs in orthopedics, and if the data system is unable reliably to provide current utilization data, finance may accrue expenses to orthopedics even if the medical director has been able to reduce costs in that area. It may take 6 months for the data to come through the system that show a reduction in orthopedics expenses, but by that time the medical director has resigned in frustration.

Another example would be a plan that has an authorization system for referrals but that system allows for subauthorizations, automatic authorization of return visits, and self-referral. Because of the loose nature of the system, the finance department cannot rely on it when calculating accruals. If there is a concomitant problem with claims processing, then there will be no timely and accurate data about utilization. In that case, finance will calculate accruals by using lag studies and best guess numbers and will assign the expenses where they fell as the claims were processed. In this way, high expenses may really be reflective of a combination of two things: what was happening in utilization some time back, and what types of claims were processed that month.

If the calculation of these numbers is sufficiently removed from senior management, and if the medical director does not know how the numbers are derived, tremendous efforts may be expended in dealing with problems that are neither timely nor high priority. As mentioned in Chapter 17, a plan's ability to implement continuous quality improvement in its business operations will be hampered if efforts are wasted trying to solve problems that are not indicative of the true problems facing management.

Closely related is the problem of not properly tracking utilization. For example, if a plan has an authorization system for referrals that tracks initial referrals from the primary care physician but fails to track subauthorizations, self-referrals, and repeat visits adequately, the referral rate may be grossly inaccurate. Another example would be a plan that is able to report high rates of utilization but is unable to provide the details about who is responsible.

In a perverse twist, in those cases where data are presented in an inaccurate or inadequate form but the medical director understands why that is so, a false sense of complacency can develop. For example, if a hospital utilization report consistently and inaccurately reports high utilization for a certain physician (perhaps because that physician represents a three-physician group), the medical director may continually make adjustments when reviewing the report and fail to recognize a genuine increase in utilization.

SYSTEMS INABILITY TO MANAGE THE BUSINESS

As a health plan grows in the marketplace, it must continue to evolve to meet ever-changing needs. When the plan does so, it is not uncommon that the MIS is unable to change at the same pace without a prohibitively high cost in programming and time. Manual workarounds are put into place, custom programming is undertaken, and soon MIS is a cat's cradle of code and administrative costs have escalated. Multiple systems are used to manage different parts of the business, and they do not tie or even match up. This problem is quickly compounded when innovative managers invent new ways of doing business (e.g., invent a new reimbursement system) that appears to make sense but cannot be supported by MIS. Eventually the plan ends up migrating to an entirely new system, with the attendant headaches that accompany any conversion.

Unfortunately, the most obvious way to prevent this problem is also the least useful: Never change anything. A health plan that fails to change and innovate soon becomes stale in the market and begins losing to the competition. Therefore, what is most important is for information systems managers to be involved in management policies and procedures so that alternative approaches are explored and the entire team understands the systems implications of policy changes. Even more important, the information systems managers need to be able to engage in strategic planning to stay in front of the demands of the industry. As discussed in Chapter 20, MIS must be flexible and designed such that change is accommodated at an acceptable cost.

FAILURE TO EDUCATE AND REEDUCATE PROVIDERS

An all-too-common sin of omission is the failure to educate providers properly. As discussed in Chapters 6 and 7, proper orientation of new providers and office staff is an important success factor. All too often, the providers are simply given a procedure manual and a metaphorical kiss on the cheek. Even in those situations where proper orientation has taken place, it is unlikely that the information will stick unless there are already a large number of patients coming in through the plan. This is even more of a problem when there are a number of competing health plans, each with its own unique way of doing things.

Just as important as the initial orientation is a program of continuing education in the procedures and policies of the plan. Regular maintenance of the knowledge base of the providers and their office staff will help prevent problems caused solely by lack of communication.

Examples of this problem abound in most open panels. Physicians may fail to use the authorization system properly, may provide or promise benefits that the plan does not cover, may allow open-ended authorizations to specialists, and so forth. Although none of these occurrences is dangerous in itself, all can be additive. In a large plan, failure to communicate properly with providers can lead rapidly to a loss of control. Far more energy is spent trying to repair damage than would have been spent in maintenance.

FAILURE TO DEAL WITH DIFFICULT OR NONCOMPLIANT PROVIDERS

Perhaps the most difficult of all the tasks of a medical director is dealing with difficult and noncompliant physicians. The same task applies to nonphysician providers, but that is generally easier for most medical directors. Because dealing with difficult physicians is so onerous to physician managers, they tend to avoid it or at least procrastinate. Assuming that the plan is reasonably well run and not subject to a justified physician mutiny, difficult physicians, like difficult patients, make up only a tiny minority of the total panel but consume an inordinate amount of managerial energy. Failure to deal with such physicians has both direct and indirect ramifications.

The direct result of failing to deal with an uncooperative physician is the expense associated with that physician's utilization of resources. This problem is obvious, although easy to rationalize away ("Well, maybe they have sicker patients"). If the physician's utilization behavior really is a problem, it may be worthwhile to calculate in whole dollars the cost of that overutilization.

The indirect results are less obvious. The most important is the effect on members. If the physician has a truly bad attitude, that will be transmitted to members. For example, the physician may tell members that they need services but the plan will not allow it. A little bit of this "blame the bogeyman" behavior can be tolerated and understood, but if it becomes chronic, the plan can find itself fighting off unwarranted attacks by members and employee benefits managers. Other indirect effects include promoting a poor attitude among the other physicians and lowering the morale of the plan staff who have to deal with that particular physician.

The most frequent objection to dealing with difficult physicians is that the plan needs them because they are so prestigious or popular. In many cases, that physician also has a large number of members, and there are fears that if the physician leaves or is kicked out, the plan will lose membership. It is up to plan management to determine whether the plan is worse off with or without the physician. Do not let numbers of members alone make that determination (remember, if you are losing on each member, you cannot make it up on volume). Regarding the issue of prestige, it is far worse to have that physician bad mouthing your plan directly to the members than it is to have him or her deriding you in the hospital lounge (where he or she is probably doing it anyway). You may also find that the members stick with the plan and agree to change physicians.

If education and personal appeals fail to effect the needed change, you must take action. Failure to take action is the mark of weak and ineffectual management.

CONCLUSION

This chapter presents some of the common problems that can occur in managed care plans. There are few plans in existence today that have not experienced at least a few of these difficulties at some point. The list is not exhaustive, and there are certainly many other difficulties that a plan can experience. The important point is to recognize that managed care plans do indeed develop predictable problems and must be ever-vigilant for their emergence.

Study Questions

1. A hospital sponsored integrated delivery system (IDS) that currently employs 50 primary care physicians and contracts with 150 specialists, accepts a full risk capitation contract with an HMO. What are the most likely problems the IDS will encounter, assuming the capitation rate was reasonable; why?
2. An open panel HMO has grown rapidly through underpricing its product. It has

controlled utilization poorly and is now losing money. What steps must the HMO managers take to rectify the problems? What consequences and new problems will occur as a result of these actions? How might the HMO attenuate those consequences?

3. What are the problems most likely encountered in an HMO that has experienced rapid growth even though premium rates were not underpriced?
4. What steps should a medical director take proactively to prevent anticipated problems with the delivery system? What are the risks of those steps? How can the medical director attenuate those risks?
5. What monitoring activities might an HMO CEO take to prevent her or his plan from falling prey to a serious but common problem?

REFERENCES AND NOTES

1. J.P. Anton, "Marketing Managed Health Care Plans," in *The Managed Health Care Handbook*, 3d ed., ed. P.R. Kongstvedt (Gaithersburg, Md.: Aspen, 1996), 567–579.
2. P.R. Kongstvedt and D.W. Plocher, "Acquisitions, Joint Ventures, and Partnerships between Providers and Managed Care Organizations," in *The Managed Health Care Handbook*, 3d ed., ed. P.R. Kongstvedt (Gaithersburg, Md.: Aspen, 1996), 66–77.

SUGGESTED READING

Christianson, J.B., et al. 1991. State Responses to HMO Failures. *Health Affairs* 10: 78–92.

Coyne, J.S. 1993. Assessing the Financial Performance of Health Maintenance Organizations: Tools and Techniques. *Managed Care Quarterly* 1: 63–74.

Health Care Financing Administration. 1995. *Best Practices of Managed Care Organizations*. Baltimore, Md.: HCFA.

Meigham, S.S. 1994. Managing Conflict in an Integrated System. *Topics in Health Care Financing* 20 (4): 39–47.

Part V

Public Sector Managed Care

"We're one, but we're not the same."

Bono
(1991)

Chapter 26

Medicare and Managed Care

Carlos Zarabozo and Jean D. LeMasurier

Study Objectives

- Understand how Medicare HMOs are paid
- Understand the requirements for an entity to contract as a Medicare HMO
- Understand how Medicare processes HMO applications
- Understand some of the issues related to how an HMO administers a Medicare contract
- Understand possible legislative and other changes in store for the Medicare managed care program

Carlos Zarabozo is a social science research analyst in the Special Analysis Staff, Office of the Associate Administrator for Policy. He previously held a number of positions in the managed care office of the Health Care Financing Administration (HCFA), including Director of the Operational Analysis Staff and Special Assistant to the Director.

Jean D. LeMasurier is Director of the Division of Policy and Program Improvement of the HCFA's Office of Managed Care. She has developed policy, legislation, and regulations for Medicare contracts with health maintenance organization (HMOs) and federally qualified HMOs and other coordinated care initiatives in the HCFA's Office of Research and Demonstrations, Office of Legislation and Policy, and Office of Prepaid Health Care. In addition, she developed legislation for Medicare HMOs while serving on the U.S. Senate Finance Committee.

The views expressed in this chapter are the authors' and not those of the HCFA. All addresses and telephone numbers listed were accurate at the time of publication, but such numbers and addresses occasionally change, so that the authors make no warranty as to their currency.

TGIF (THE GOVERNMENT IS FRIGHTENING) UNLESS YOU KNOW YOUR ACRONYMS

Although you do not need to know too many acronyms for some dealings with the government, such as buying a postage stamp or paying taxes, it helps to know an acronym or two in dealing with Medicare. On the subject of health maintenance organizations (HMOs) and Medicare, some of the acronyms that you can use at cocktail parties to sound knowledgeable (and no doubt boring) are HCFA, TEFRA, CMP, ACR, APR, and, especially, AAPCC. These acronyms are all addressed in this chapter.

All acronyms aside, what the government is attempting to do through its emphasis on managed care options, one of which is HMO* contracting, is bring down health care costs while improving the quality of care. Traditional Medicare was at one time a strictly fee-for-service system with reimbursement based on cost or charges. In the past few years the government

* Throughout this chapter, the term *HMO* is generally meant to refer to both federally qualified HMOs and organizations that are determined to be competitive medical plans (CMPs) as defined in the Tax Equity and Fiscal Responsibility Act legislation introducing the concept of CMPs. The initial discussion deals exclusively with risk-sharing HMOs and CMPs. It is also possible for an HMO or CMP to contract with the Health Care Financing Administration under a cost-reimbursement arrangement that limits the risk exposure of the HMO or CMP, as discussed in the latter part of the chapter.

has radically changed its reimbursement for Medicare services through such means as the well-publicized prospective payment system of inpatient reimbursement based on diagnosis-related groups (DRGs) rather than reasonable cost reimbursement. In the case of HMOs, the government looked at what was happening in the private sector and found that HMOs (which in their early history had been promoted, in a sense, by the federal government) had the potential for decreasing health care costs while bringing about possible improvements in the quality of care through managed care.

UNDERSTANDING THE ADJUSTED AVERAGE PER CAPITA COST

If acronyms are not your favorite subject of discussion, we can get down to business and talk instead about money. As one would expect, money usually determines whether an HMO or CMP will want to contract with the government. Under the risk payment methodology established in the law, a contract is expected to be financially advantageous to both the HMO/CMP and the government. HMOs with a Medicare risk contract are paid 95 percent of what the government's actuaries estimate to be the cost of medical services if the services had been obtained in traditional fee-for-service Medicare. The government should save, actuarially speaking, at least 5 percent compared with what would have been the fee-for-service costs for those Medicare beneficiaries who choose to enroll in an HMO, and the health plan is paid at 95 percent of the fee-for-service rate with the expectation that because HMOs, as organized health care delivery systems, are able to provide services more efficiently than fee for service, their cost of providing care will be at or below the 95 percent level.

The government pays risk-based HMOs a prospective monthly capitation payment for each Medicare member that is akin to the premium paid to an HMO by an employer for coverage of its employees. In exchange for this capitation payment, the HMO is required to provide the full range of health care services covered under the federal Medicare program. The adjusted average per capita cost (AAPCC) is the basis of payment to HMOs and CMPs under contract to the HCFA. For each county of the United States, for each Medicare member, an HMO or CMP is paid 1 of 142 possible monthly capitation amounts (which can vary significantly by county).

You can think of these 142 rate cells as 142 amoebalike creatures floating around aimlessly in space, or you can think in the less daunting terms of the 6 (yes, a mere 6) variables used to create 140 rate cells: the demographic factors of age, sex, Medicaid eligibility, institutional status; and the entitlement factors of working aged status (i.e., aged Medicare beneficiaries with other insurance coverage that is primary in relation to Medicare), and whether a person has both parts of Medicare (part A being inpatient hospital, inpatient skilled nursing services, and home health services and part B being all other services, such as physician and outpatient services). A separate computation is made for individuals entitled to Medicare on the basis of disability, but this category is redundant with the age category, because all such individuals are under age 65. This is illustrated in Exhibit 26–1.

To restate the illustration in Exhibit 26–1, once the age and sex are established, the part A and part B rates are different for institutionalized and noninstitutionalized individuals. The noninstitutionalized are reimbursed at different rates depending on whether they have other insurance coverage and whether they are eligible for Medicaid, factors that do not affect the level of payment for the institutionalized. There are also two rate cells for each state for individuals with end-stage renal disease, making a total of 142 possible rate cells.

The AAPCC represents an actuarial projection of what Medicare expenses would have been for a given category of Medicare beneficiary had the person remained in traditional fee-

Exhibit 26–1 The 140 Rate Cells That Make Up Medicare Capitation

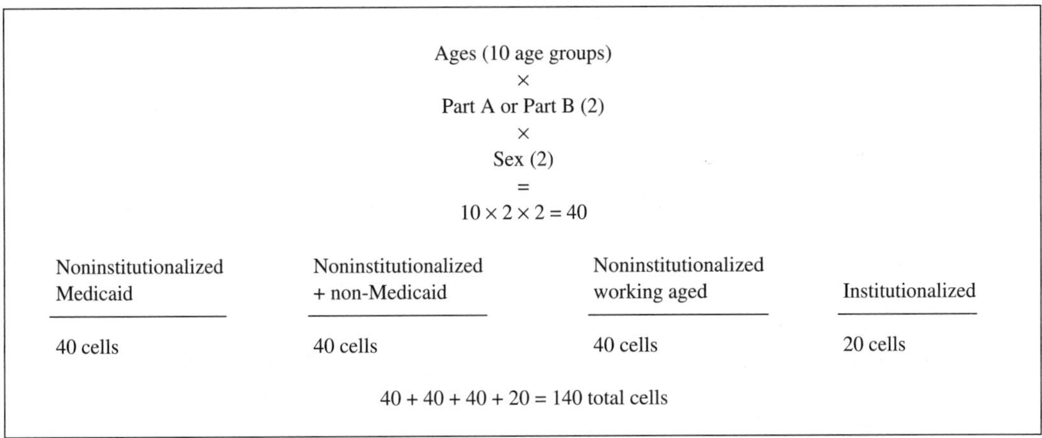

for-service Medicare. The AAPCC rates change every calendar year.

Under the law, the HCFA's actuary is required to publish each calendar year's AAPCC rates by 7 September of the preceding year. Each July, the HCFA's Office of the Actuary is also required to publish information about the methodology and assumptions related to the AAPCC announcement for the following year. The announcement of rates is required to contain sufficient information for any HMO to reconstruct the manner in which AAPCC rates for the counties served by the HMO were derived. The HCFA's actuary also determines the actuarial equivalent of Medicare beneficiary liability amounts, expressed as a monthly average amount that Medicare beneficiaries have to pay for out-of-pocket expenses in fee-for-service Medicare (such as the coinsurance for physician services or the deductible a person pays on entering a hospital). When a Medicare beneficiary joins an HMO, the beneficiary deductible and coinsurance requirements are satisfied by having the beneficiary pay a monthly premium to the HMO and/or copayments for services. This actuarial equivalent is the maximum total of premiums and copayments that an HMO may charge its Medicare members to cover Medicare beneficiary liability amounts for covered services (other than under a point-of-service [POS] option).

The format of the published AAPCC rates consists of a listing, for all U.S. counties, of Medicare part A and part B base rates for the aged and the disabled (beneficiaries younger than 65 years entitled to Medicare because of their disability) together with a table of nationally used demographic factors, by which the county rates are multiplied to determine payment for a given rate cell. The published AAPCC rates are not the total projected fee-for-service rates. As published, they are 95 percent of the projected rates. As noted above, the upper limit of payment to a risk-based HMO/CMP contracting with the HCFA is the 95 percent rate.

To determine how much an HMO will be paid for its Medicare members, an HMO that is considering entering into a contract with the HCFA needs to be able to project the make-up of its Medicare population. The HMO will project how many members it will have in each rate cell of each county of its service area to determine the total payment rate and the average payment rate (APR) from the HCFA. The HCFA is able to provide a report of the demographic make-up of each U.S. county by rate cell. The same report states how many Medicare beneficiaries are currently HMO members. This type of report can be obtained through the HCFA's Office of the Actuary.

THE ADJUSTED COMMUNITY RATE/APR COMPARISON

Let us assume that you are the chief financial officer of an HMO and that, having nothing better to do one morning while reading the latest *Federal Register*, you decide to figure out how much money the government will pay you under a Medicare contract. After a little bit of effort, you have figured out that the HCFA is willing to pay you an average of, let us say, $200 per member per month (PMPM), more than any employer group ever considered paying you. You cannot wait to phone the HCFA and ask that a signed contract be sent to you immediately. The HCFA is more than happy to oblige, provided that you understand that you may not really be getting $200 PMPM. After you have determined your APR (per person) from the HCFA, the law requires that you compare this APR with your adjusted community rate (ACR) to determine whether $200 PMPM is an appropriate payment from the government. Your community rate is your premium for a commercial group. Your ACR computation is a statement to the HCFA's accountants of what premium you would charge for providing exactly the same Medicare-covered benefits to a community-rated group account, adjusted to allow for the greater intensity and frequency of utilization by Medicare recipients (because most Medicare beneficiaries are elderly). The ACR includes the normal profit of a for-profit HMO or CMP.

If your projected premium (your ACR) equals or exceeds your projected payment (your APR)—that is, if you expect your Medicare revenue to be less than or equal to your cost of providing care—then you will receive the $200 PMPM, or whatever the exact 95 percent AAPCC payment happens to be, and no more. If, however, your ACR is lower than your projected APR—if you project, for example, that you can deliver the Medicare-covered services to the population you expect to enroll at $175 PMPM—then you are required to return the surplus to the government or to your Medicare beneficiaries by accepting a reduced payment rate averaging $175 PMPM, or by returning the difference between the ACR and the APR to Medicare beneficiaries in the form of a reduced premium that would otherwise be collectible from the Medicare members, or by enriching the benefit package offered by the dollar equivalent of the surplus. That is, in the last case, if your ACR is $175 PMPM and your APR is $200, you would return $25 PMPM to the Medicare members of your HMO by providing $25 worth of additional benefits not covered by Medicare (such as drugs and routine eye care and glasses), by reducing the premium by $25 per month, or by offering any combination of premium reduction and benefit enrichment.

A health plan may also use what is referred to as a benefit stabilization fund, through which the government withholds a portion of the difference between the ACR and the APR if the APR exceeds the ACR. The withholds can be withdrawn by the health plan in a future year so that the plan is able to offer its Medicare beneficiaries the same benefit package as in the previous year in the event that there is a reduction in the AAPCC or an increase in the ACR that would otherwise result in a reduction in the benefits available. Only a few plans have used this method of disposing of savings.

WHAT IF YOU MAKE A MISTAKE IN COMPUTING THE ACR/APR?

An HMO must sign a contract lasting at least 1 year. All HMOs with Medicare contracts currently operate on a calendar year cycle to match the AAPCC cycle because the AAPCC payment rates change each year beginning on 1 January. Contracts are automatically renewable at the end of each contract period. During the contract term, there can be no increase in the premium an HMO charges its Medicare members, nor can there be any reduction in the enriched benefits offered to Medicare members.

As a newly contracting HMO, you can either overestimate or underestimate the ACR and APR. As noted above, the HCFA will not pay you more than the 95 percent AAPCC rate, but if you have overestimated an element of the ACR computation—let us say, for example, that you have overestimated the degree to which Medicare members will require more frequent visits to their primary care physicians—you pocket the difference. If you underestimate, you lose money.

Of course, the HCFA requires that you submit a new ACR computation for each year. During the first year of contracting, you are permitted to use utilization data from other HMOs to come up with a Medicare ACR. After the first year you must use internal data, however, and in the case of pocketing the difference your internal data should show that the ACR of the first year had overestimated figures, leading to a windfall that will not be repeated in the coming year. If your ACR calculation had underestimated your cost, your recalculation would yield a higher ACR.

A LITTLE BIT OF HISTORY

Because you have now mastered the accounting aspects of Medicare contracting, we will take up the subject of history. The current body of law treating Medicare HMOs was passed in September 1982 as part of the Tax Equity and Fiscal Responsibility Act of 1982 (TEFRA). There were to be no TEFRA Medicare contractors until publication of final HCFA regulations on TEFRA contracting, however, which appeared in the 10 January 1985 *Federal Register*. The regulations became effective 1 February 1985.

There did exist pre-TEFRA risk contractors (as well as cost-reimbursed contractors) under rules in existence before TEFRA. From the beginning of the Medicare program in 1965, Medicare has recognized the unique nature of HMOs and HMO-like entities and has provided for alternative payment methodologies appropriate for such organizations. The original Medicare amendments to the Social Security Act included the authority for prepaid plans to receive payment for physician services on a basis other than individual charges (through the cost reimbursement mechanism used by what are now referred to as health care prepayment plans, HCPPs). Even before the enactment of the federal HMO Act in 1973, the 1972 amendments to the Social Security Act provided authority to contract with HMOs (as defined in the amendments) on a risk-sharing basis and on a cost basis.

The largest of the pre-TEFRA risk contractors was the Group Health Cooperative of Puget Sound. There were never more than a few health plans that chose to contract with the HCFA under the pre-TEFRA rules, although as of mid-1995 there were nearly 200 HMOs or CMPs with TEFRA risk contracts. Why the difference? TEFRA simplified the contracting requirements and brought them more in line with the way in which HMOs normally operate. Under pre-TEFRA rules, an HMO was reimbursed at 100 percent of the AAPCC, but it was required to file cost reports with the government to establish whether there was a loss or whether there were excess government payments at the 100 percent rate. If the cost of providing services was below the 100 percent rate, the HMO could keep only a portion of the profit or savings. If the cost of providing services (as determined through submission of a cost report by the HMO) was below the 100 percent level, the HMO and the government split the savings unless savings exceeded 20 percent. If savings exceeded 20 percent, the HMO retained 10 percent of the savings, and the government kept the remainder. Losses, however, could be carried over into future years to offset the amount of savings that had to be shared with the government.

In 1982, the HCFA awarded demonstration contracts to try out the concepts of TEFRA type risk HMOs through what were referred to as Medicare competition demonstration projects. These demonstration projects, some of which were operating under a variety of waivers of parts of Section 1876 of the Social Security Act (the section entirely reworked by TEFRA), were all required to convert to TEFRA status. By the time TEFRA implementing regulations were published in January 1985, there were about 300,000 members (out of a total of about 30 million Medicare beneficiaries then) of these types of organizations. In mid-1995, Medicare membership in TEFRA risk HMOs was nearly 3 million.

What TEFRA Did

On the payment side, TEFRA introduced the concept of sharing the wealth, to use Huey Long's phrase, whereby savings are returned to Medicare beneficiaries rather than to the government, as explained in the section above on the AAPCC. The computation of savings would be done on a prospective basis, and there would be no retrospective adjustment and thus no cost reports filed by an HMO. As far as changes in contracting provisions, before TEFRA only plans that were federally qualified HMOs could have Medicare contracts. TEFRA modified HMO contracting rules to permit the HCFA to contract with a new type of entity, the CMP. A CMP is defined as an entity that:

- is state licensed (organized under the laws of any state, to use the terminology of the regulations)
- provides health care on a prepaid, capitated basis
- provides care primarily through physicians who are employees or partners of the entity (or the services are provided through groups of physicians or individuals under contract to the CMP), primarily being defined under HCFA policy to be at least 51 percent of the services provided through the CMP (thus allowing preferred provider organizations [PPOs] to be CMPs)
- assumes full financial risk on a prospective basis, with provisions for stop loss, reinsurance, and risk sharing with providers
- meets the Public Health Service Act requirements of protection against insolvency

As of mid-1995 there were 50 CMPs with Medicare contracts. As a result of the 1988 amendments to the HMO Act (the 1973 law authorizing federally qualified HMOs, Title XIII of the Public Health Service Act), the major differences that existed between federally qualified HMOs and CMPs at the time TEFRA was passed no longer exist: Federally qualified HMOs are no longer required to be separate legal entities, and they may set premium levels based on the utilization experience of groups (as opposed to the pre-1988 community-rating requirement). The major remaining differences that continue to make the CMP option more feasible for certain organizations are the level at which services may be provided through noncontracting providers; the limitations that a CMP, but not an HMO, may impose on the scope of services; and the fact that employers may prefer to deal with non–federally qualified HMOs because of the requirement that employer contributions toward HMO coverage be nondiscriminatory (i.e., at levels similar to those for other health plan options). The 1988 HMO Act amendments introduced a provision allowing a federally qualified HMO to provide up to 10 percent of physician services outside the HMO (i.e., a self-referral option for members not wishing to use an HMO physician), whereas the requirement for the provision of medical services in a CMP is that the services be provided primarily through the CMP.

Although under a Medicare contract a CMP and an HMO would both be required to provide all Medicare-covered services, the commercial members of a CMP need not be offered certain benefits that the law requires an HMO to offer, such as home health care, mental health services, and substance abuse treatment. A CMP may also limit the scope of some of the services it is required to offer (the required services being physician services; inpatient hospital services; laboratory, radiology, emergency, and preventive services; and out-of-area coverage) and is permitted to require deductibles and copayments. A federally qualified HMO may only charge nominal copayments, a deductible for the 10 percent of physician services that the HMO is permitted to cover as out-of-plan services. A federally qualified HMO may not limit the scope of coverage except as specifically allowed in regulations (20 outpatient mental health visits per year being an example of a reduced scope of service permitted in HMO regulations).

What Congress Did after TEFRA

Over the brief history of Medicare risk contracting, a number of new provisions of the law and regulations have been added. For example, the 25 May 1984 publication of the proposed TEFRA risk contracting regulations contained a provision that required all marketing material to be reviewed and approved by the HCFA before an HMO could use the material. This requirement was dropped in the 10 January 1985, publication of the final rules, only to be added later by Congress through the Consolidated Omnibus Budget Reconciliation Act (COBRA) of 1986. COBRA also required that HMOs immediately disenroll Medicare beneficiaries who requested disenrollment as of the first day of the month after the beneficiary's request; previously an HMO could retain a Medicare member for up to 60 days before disenrollment was effective.

The Omnibus Budget Reconciliation Act of 1985 (OBRA-85) introduced more requirements and restrictions on HMOs. The importance of the 50/50 requirement was reemphasized because Congress limited the availability of waivers to government entities or to HMOs serving areas in which the Medicare/Medicaid population exceeds 50 percent of the total area population. Sanctions are to be imposed if an HMO fails to meet the 50/50 requirement: New enrollment can be prohibited, or the HCFA can permit new enrollment but the HMO will not be paid for the new enrollees.

OBRA-85 requires HMOs to inform Medicare members of their rights when the beneficiaries join the HMO and annually thereafter. It was also OBRA-85 that brought about the option of disenrollment at Social Security offices for Medicare HMO members.

OBRA-85 expanded the role of peer review organizations (PROs) in monitoring the quality of care at HMOs by requiring PRO review of HMO inpatient care and ambulatory care. PROs are charged with the responsibility of investigating any complaint submitted to a PRO by a beneficiary regarding the quality of care rendered by an HMO. OBRA provides for fines against an HMO if it is found that the HMO substantially failed to provide adequate care.

OBRA-85 also mandates that there be a study of the physician incentive arrangements in hospitals reimbursed through the Medicare prospective payment system (DRGs) as well as incentive arrangements in HMOs with a view toward imposing restrictions on the types of incentive arrangements that have an adverse effect on patient care. After several years of pondering the issue, Congress, in OBRA-90, imposed added restrictions on Medicare-contracting HMOs that prevent them from having incentive arrangements that put physicians at substantial financial risk for services that the physicians did not directly provide. If an HMO has incentive arrangements that the HCFA finds to involve such substantial financial risk, the HMO is required to have stop-loss provisions for its physicians, and the HMO must conduct beneficiary surveys to determine whether the risk arrangements affect the services members receive.

OBRA-87 required that HMOs that were terminating or not renewing a contract or were reducing their Medicare service area arrange for supplemental (Medigap) coverage to replace HMO coverage for Medicare beneficiaries affected by the HMO's decision. If an insurer imposes a waiting period for coverage of preexisting conditions, the HMO must arrange to have the waiting period waived or must otherwise provide for coverage, for up to 6 months, of services related to the preexisting condition.

OBRA-90 required Medicare-contracting HMOs to comply with Medicare requirements imposed on hospitals and other providers to make Medicare beneficiaries aware of the right to have their medical care subject to advance directives (living wills) and to have the beneficiary's instructions made part of the HMO medical record. OBRA-90 also permitted retroactive enrollment of Medicare beneficiaries who enroll in a Medicare-contracting risk HMO as retirees through an employer-sponsored health plan; individual Medicare beneficiaries may only be enrolled prospectively. The same law afforded risk HMOs hold-harmless protection limiting their liability for the coverage of services that Medicare might add during a calendar year but were not considered in determining AAPCC rates for the year. Another added provision requires risk HMOs to make prompt payment (under the same time frames as Medicare carriers and intermediaries) on claims for services provided by nonnetwork providers.

THE REQUIREMENTS TO OBTAIN A TEFRA CONTRACT

To obtain a TEFRA Medicare contract, a plan must be either a federally qualified HMO or designated by the HCFA as a CMP. For an entity that wishes to become eligible as a CMP, the only type of application that may be submitted is a combined application to be found eligible as a CMP and to be granted a Medicare contract. An HMO or CMP must meet the following TEFRA requirements to obtain a risk contract.

Membership

A nonrural plan must have at least 5,000 prepaid capitated members for which the organization is at risk for the provision of comprehensive services (although risk may be shared by providers); enrollment must be 1,500 members for a rural plan. The 5,000 rule may be satisfied by a parent organization that assumes responsibility for the financial risk and adequate management and supervision of health care services furnished by its subdivision or subsidiary, to cite the regulations. Even though the 5,000 rule may be met by a parent organization, there is a further requirement that there be a minimum membership of 1,000 at the subsidiary location before the plan may enter into a Medicare contract to establish that the subsidiary is viable and to have a valid basis for determining a Medicare ACR for the subsidiary.

An organization must have a membership that at all times during the contract does not exceed 50 percent combined Medicare and Medicaid enrollees. This provision (referred to as the 50/50 rule) can be waived only for government entities or if the HMO serves an area in which the population exceeds 50 percent Medicare/Medicaid.

Medical Services

The organization must be able to render, directly or through arrangements, all the Medicare services available in its service area. It must use Medicare-certified providers, that is, hospitals, skilled nursing facilities, and home health agencies. Physicians and suppliers used by the HMO may not include persons who have been barred from participation in either Medicare or Medicaid because of program abuse or fraud.

The HMO must be able to provide 24-hour emergency services and must have provisions for the payment of claims for emergency services within the service area and for out-of-area emergency or urgently needed services. All services that the HMO is required to render must be accessible with reasonable promptness, and there must be a recordkeeping system that ensures continuity of care.

Range of Services

The HMO must provide all the Medicare part A and B services available in the service area through staff providers or providers under contract with the HMO. Additional, non–Medicare-covered services may also be provided in several ways: as additional benefits, which are the enriched benefits provided when a risk HMO's ACR is less than its APR; as optional supplemental benefits, which any Medicare beneficiary may choose to purchase from the HMO; as mandatory supplemental benefits, which are benefits a Medicare beneficiary must purchase as a condition of enrollment (e.g., because Medicare does not cover preventive care, a standard HMO benefit, the benefit for Medicare beneficiaries is financed by mandatory premiums); as premium waivers by HMOs that choose not to charge for non–Medicare-covered benefits even though their ACR/APR computation would permit charging such a premium; and as benefits offered only to employer group retirees.

Open Enrollment

The law requires that a Medicare HMO have a 30-day open enrollment every year. An HMO must also open its enrollment to Medicare enrollees who were disenrolled from another Medicare HMO in the area as a result of a contract nonrenewal or termination. Aside from these required open enrollment periods, the HMO may have any other open enrollment period, including continuous open enrollment. During an open enrollment period, the organization must enroll any Medicare beneficiary with Part B coverage who is eligible to enroll and lives in the organization's service area. Medicare beneficiaries who are also Medicaid recipients may also enroll. Medicare beneficiaries who have end-stage renal disease (whether aged, disabled, or entitled to Medicare solely because of their disease), however, must be denied enrollment unless they are already an enrollee of the HMO. Medicare beneficiaries who have elected to be cared for in a Medicare-certified hospice are also prohibited from enrolling. If a person acquires end-stage renal disease after enrollment or elects hospice after enrollment, the HMO may not disenroll the individual.

The open enrollment requirement may be waived in one of three circumstances: The organization will exceed 50 percent Medicare/ Medicaid enrollment; the organization will enroll a disproportionate share of enrollees in a particular AAPCC category, in which case the HCFA will permit the organization to discontinue enrollments in that AAPCC category; or the organization does not have the capacity to render services to any more enrollees, either commercial or Medicare. If an organization is going to limit enrollment under the third option, the HCFA must be informed 90 days before the open enrollment period so that HCFA approval can be given. In determining capacity for Medicare enrollees, the organization may set aside vacancies for expected commercial enrollees during each Medicare contract period.

Marketing Rules

An HMO must market its Medicare plan throughout the entire service area specified in the Medicare contract. All marketing materials, including membership and enrollment materials, must be approved by the HCFA before use. Prospective enrollees must be given descriptive material sufficient for them to make an informed choice in enrolling in an HMO. Prohibited marketing activities include door-to-door solicitation, discriminatory marketing (avoiding low-income areas, for example), and misleading marketing or misrepresentation. These activities are subject to sanctions, including suspension of enrollment, suspension of payment for new enrollees, or civil monetary penalties (the government's euphemism for fines). The HCFA has 45 days to review marketing materials. If 45 days pass without HCFA comments on the material, it is deemed approved.

Ability To Bear Risk

An HMO or CMP must be able to bear the potential financial risk under a Medicare contract. The statute authorizes the HCFA to determine that an otherwise qualified HMO or CMP may not have the ability to bear the risk inherent in a Medicare risk contract; such an organization would only be permitted to contract on a cost reimbursement basis.

Administrative Ability

An organization must have sufficient administrative ability to carry out the terms of a Medicare contract. The same section of the regulations dealing with this provision mentions that an organization may not have any management, agent, or owner who has been convicted of criminal offenses involving Medicare, Medicaid, or Title XX (the regulations are silent about what the HCFA thinks of other types of felons).

Quality Assurance

HMOs are required under the Public Health Service Act to have quality assurance programs that are evaluated as part of the HMO qualification process. CMPs are required to have quality assurance programs to be granted a Medicare contract. The quality assurance program of a CMP must stress health outcomes to the extent consistent with the state of the art, must provide for peer review, must collect and interpret data systematically to make necessary changes in the provision of health services, and must include written procedures for remedial action to correct problems. Another new development is that Medicare HMOs will be required to comply with HEDIS 3.0 reporting requirements (see Chapter 20) as of the 1997 contract year and will also be required to have Medicare member satisfaction surveys.

The Right To Inspect and Evaluate Records

The government has the right to inspect financial records as well as records pertaining to services performed under the contract and pertaining to enrollment and disenrollment of individuals. The right to inspect extends to entities related to the HMO, a right that was expanded in scope in OBRA-86.

Confidentiality of Records

The organization must adhere to relevant provisions of the Privacy Act and is required to maintain the confidentiality of the medical and nonmedical records of its Medicare members.

Limitations on Physician Risk

In 1996, the Office of the Inspector General of the Department of Health and Human Services issued final regulations placing limitations on the amount of risk a health plan may put a physician at in a Medicare or Medicaid program. These new regulations effectively limit the amount of risk to 25 percent, and place additional requirements on the health plan regarding stop-loss insurance and member surveys. The reader is referred to Chapter 8 for a discussion of these new regulations.

FLEXIBILITY IN CONTRACTING

The HCFA's view of the requirements for Medicare contracting has evolved since the early days of the risk-contracting program. Certain changes in policy have permitted expansion of Medicare risk contracting or have ensured the continuing participation of contractors. At the beginning of the TEFRA program, the HCFA maintained that there should be no difference between Medicare contracting and contracting with commercial groups with regard to the providers available to each type of member and the service area in which the HMO was being offered. In 1987, however, two changes were made that gave HMOs more flexibility in their Medicare-contracting options. One change was to allow HMOs to contract initially for less than their commercial service area as well as to drop counties from their service area at the end of any contract year. Because the HCFA's AAPCC payment rates vary from county to county, one consequence of this change was that, in Minnesota, for example, HMOs that included rural counties in their service area were able to discontinue their Medicare contracts in the rural counties in which AAPCC payment rates were relatively low.

Another change has permitted HMOs to have differential premiums for different groups of Medicare enrollees. Under one Medicare HMO contract, premiums may vary by county. In any case in which there are differential premiums among Medicare enrollees in an HMO, however, every Medicare beneficiary must receive the level of benefits and be charged no more than the maximum premium computed through the

HMO-wide Medicare ACR process. That is, an HMO must treat all its Medicare members equally in computing its ACR to be submitted for HCFA approval. If the ACR requires that the HMO charge no more than $20 as a monthly Medicare premium, then all Medicare enrollees must be charged $20 or less. As long as all members are charged no more than $20, members who reside in certain counties may be charged less than $20. The HMO would waive all or a portion of the otherwise collectible premium if the competitive situation in a particular county dictated such a practice.

Employer group retirees represent a special case for which differential premiums are permitted. Often, employers or unions include, in their retiree benefit packages, additional services not covered by Medicare, and the union or employer contributes toward the individual's premium. Medicare beneficiaries who wish to enroll in a Medicare-contracting HMO offered through their employer or union may pay a higher or lower premium than individual Medicare enrollees. As of 1995, group retirees could also have different copayment structures, as long as the copayment structure offered to a group was also available to any individual Medicare beneficiary. For example, if a group asked a Medicare HMO that was charging all Medicare enrollees a $5 copay for physician office visits to increase the charge to $10 for the group's retirees, the HMO could do so (and necessarily would have to reduce the Medicare premium amount in recognition of the increased revenue) as long as a $10 copay option was offered to any Medicare enrollee of the plan.

The most recent change, dating from October 1995, is the clarification of the HCFA's policy regarding a POS option for Medicare risk HMO enrollees. This option, increasingly popular in the commercial marketplace, is permitted under the TEFRA statute. HMOs may offer a POS benefit (coverage of care obtained out of network) to their Medicare enrollees as an additional benefit, a mandatory supplemental benefit, an optional supplement, or a benefit solely for employer group retirees. HMOs offering a POS option are subject to additional monitoring by the HCFA to ensure continued compliance with standards pertaining to financial solvency, availability and accessibility of care, quality assurance, member appeals, and marketing.

WHICH OFFICE DOES WHAT, WHERE TO WRITE, AND WHOM TO CALL

To obtain a contract, you must submit an application to the HCFA. You can obtain an application by writing to:

HCFA Office of Managed Care
(OMC)
Operations and Oversight
Room 3-02-01, South Building
7500 Security Boulevard
Baltimore, MD 21244-1850
(410) 786-1147

Write to the same office to obtain information about and an application for federally qualified HMO status or to obtain Medicare contract eligibility as a CMP.

For information about the ACR process, you should contact:

Medicare Payment and Audit Team
OMC
Room 3-02-01, South Building
7500 Security Boulevard
Baltimore, MD 21244-1850
(410) 786-7634

The Medicare Payment and Audit Team reviews and approves ACR submissions and is also responsible for payment activities and systems activities, such as enrollment and disenrollment from HMOs.

There are 10 regional offices of the HCFA. An applicant would initially send an application for a Medicare contract (HMO or CMP) to the HCFA's regional offices, which have primary responsibility for processing Medicare contract applications and are the principal point of contact for HMOs after they have a Medicare contract. The regional offices and the HCFA central office together monitor the performance of contracting HMOs through on-site visits that occur at least biannually (and more frequently if fortune shines on your HMO). Any marketing material that an HMO prepares that is not submitted with the original application has to be reviewed by the servicing HCFA regional office. The regional offices answer most beneficiary inquiries and investigate complaints about an HMO. They perform valuable technical assistance functions in the day-to-day Medicare operations of an HMO, including resolving problems that an HMO may be having with membership data being submitted to the HCFA, Medicare coverage issues, and liaison with Social Security offices and Medicare fiscal intermediaries. In other words, the regional office contact person is a good person to get to know, although you will also have HCFA central office contact people for systems and financial functions, and each HMO will have a central office overall plan manager.

THE STEPS OF THE CONTRACTING PROCESS

Before submitting a request for a Medicare contract as a part of a federal qualification or CMP eligibility determination, the applicant usually contacts the HCFA, if for no other reason than to obtain the most current application forms and accompanying explanatory material. The purpose of an application for a Medicare contract is to allow the HCFA to determine whether you meet all the requirements for the granting of a contract, as listed above, and whether you have a sufficient understanding of how the requirements are to be implemented. The following are some of the questions included in the application:

- types and numbers of providers the plan will use
- listing of benefits
- description of the Medicare marketing strategy
- copies of marketing material to be used
- evidence of coverage or subscriber agreement listing membership rules, enrollee rights, and plan benefits:
    1. how to use the plan to obtain services
    2. information about obtaining services after hours or in an emergency in or out of the service area
    3. how to file claims from nonplan providers
    4. the lock-in requirement
- quality assurance plan
    1. enrollment and disenrollment procedures, including a description of how the plan will meet the open enrollment requirement
    2. the plan's grievance and Medicare appeals procedures
    3. other information as necessary

If the organization wishes to apply as a CMP, you submit a combined application to the OMC. The Medicare sections of the application are reviewed by the HCFA regional office staff, and the financial and legal aspects (i.e., the structural and contractual requirements imposed by the law) are reviewed by the OMC central office staff. There will also be a site visit to decide whether you meet the criteria for designation as a CMP. If you wish to become a federally qualified HMO, you may also submit a combined application for HMO qualification and the granting of a Medicare contract; there will be a site visit to qualify you as an HMO (the qualification process is discussed in detail in Chapter 54 of *The Managed Health Care Handbook*).[1] If you are already a federally qualified HMO, you submit a freestanding application for a Medicare contract. The evaluation of the Medicare contract application will also involve a site visit in many cases. For any of these situations, an ACR proposal must be submitted to the Medicare Payment and Audit Team. Then you wait.

The Medicare application, or the Medicare portion of your combined application, is reviewed by the regional office, and comments are sent back to you. Then they wait.

You submit a reply to the comments, fix up your marketing material, promise to obey every law in the books and whatever new laws Congress passes, and so forth. Then you wait.

In the meantime, your able accountants have submitted a beautifully done ACR proposal to Baltimore. You insisted that it be beautifully done because you know that, until the ACR proposal is accepted, the HCFA will not sign a contract. Also in the meantime, you have had your management information systems staff talking with the OMC systems staff to make sure that, when you have members to accrete to your Medicare plan, your data submission will be compatible with the HCFA's requirements. Alternatively, you may choose to submit your accretions and deletions through Litton or CompuServe, each of which has a contract with the HCFA for the processing of health plan accretions and deletions. One advantage to using CompuServe or Litton is that you can have immediate verification of Medicare eligibility and identifying data, so that your submission of an accretion will be accepted by the HCFA on the first try, and you will be paid immediately for the new member. As far as how the government pays the plan, once you have a contract you will be paid through electronic funds transfer from the Treasury Department on the first day of each month.

Assuming that you have qualified your HMO or have been deemed eligible as a CMP, the HCFA finally tells you that, yes, you can have a contract. It mails you three copies of a contract to sign and return. You are done waiting. You now mobilize your Medicare marketing forces, deluge the HCFA regional office with brand new innovative marketing material on a daily basis, and (alas) wait again for the hordes of new Medicare enrollees.

BENEFICIARY RIGHTS AND RESPONSIBILITIES

If you are a commercial member of an HMO, you know that you cannot go to any physician anywhere and expect your HMO to cover the cost of the care (other than in a POS case). If you are a Medicare beneficiary, you may not know this, even if you enrolled in a Medicare-contracting HMO. Explaining to Medicare beneficiaries how lock-in HMOs work has been a major problem. This is true partly because Medicare beneficiaries are accustomed to fee-for-service Medicare, in which a beneficiary may use almost any provider and can be assured that Medicare will pay some, if not all, of the costs of the services. It is also the case that some HMOs have enrolled Medicare beneficiaries in ways that do not adequately explain lock-in provisions (e.g., mail-in applications). The HCFA strongly recommends that there be a face-to-face discussion of the requirements of HMO membership with prospective Medicare members. To ensure that the lock-in provision is understood, and to confirm enrollment, the HCFA sends every Medicare beneficiary a notice of HMO enrollment when the HCFA computer records are changed to annotate the individual's new HMO status.

Among the beneficiary rights is the right to remain enrolled in the health plan for the duration of the contract with the government. Involuntary disenrollment is permitted only if the person loses entitlement to part B of Medicare, commits fraud in connection with the enrollment process or permits abuse of his or her membership card, permanently leaves the HMO's service area, fails to pay premiums or copayments, or (people who write regulations like to mention the obvious) dies. There is a provision allowing disenrollment for cause or for disruptive behavior that prevents the health plan from rendering services to the member or other members; such disenrollments have to have the prior approval of the HCFA.

Beneficiaries are guaranteed certain appeal rights for decisions made by an HMO regarding liability for Medicare services or coverage of Medicare services. The appeal rights include a provision that requires HCFA review of any decision that is adverse or partly adverse to a Medicare member. The HCFA review (which is actually done by a private entity under contract to the HCFA) can be followed by appeal to an administrative law judge (if the amount is $100 or more) and, for cases involving amounts of $1,000 or more, appeal for review at the federal court level.

Beneficiaries may voluntarily disenroll from an HMO whenever they wish. COBRA-85 requires the disenrollment to be effective the first day of the month after the month of the request. As of July 1987, beneficiaries may also disenroll from an HMO through any Social Security office.

WHAT IS DIFFERENT ABOUT HAVING A MEDICARE MEMBER?

Evaluating whether the payment an HMO will receive from the government is adequate is a necessary step in determining whether an organization will contract with the HCFA to enroll Medicare members. Another factor to be considered, which may be looked at as a cost, is that enrolling Medicare members and providing services to them are not identical to enrolling and serving a commercial population. In the commercial market, an HMO signs up a group and enrolls members through the group; in Medicare, the HMO must sign up individuals one by one (i.e., retail selling). Thus the marketing strategy is different, the product is different, the means of making potential enrollees aware of the product is different, and the target of marketing is no longer a group and its representative but instead is an individual potential enrollee. These differences require an HMO to expand its marketing staff, and most HMOs with risk contracts have established a completely separate marketing department for Medicare.

There will also have to be a significant increase in the member relations staff of an HMO, again perhaps by establishing a totally separate department to deal with the Medicare membership. For a variety of reasons, Medicare beneficiaries require more hand-holding than commercial members. For example, either the member relations staff or the marketing staff will be responsible for ensuring that Medicare members understand the concept of lock-in or exclusive use of HMO providers, which is an especially difficult concept to convey to Medicare beneficiaries. The member relations staff will also be responsible for dealing with Medicare member grievances, and, along with the claims staff and medical or legal staff in the HMO, the member relations staff will probably be involved in the processing of Medicare appeals cases, which under the law must be reviewed by the HCFA when the HMO wishes to deny payment for claims or when the HMO denies a requested service.

Medicare enrollment records are not solely internal to the HMO. To be paid by the HCFA, an HMO must send its enrollment and disenrollment information to the HCFA on a monthly basis via magnetic tape or by using a commercial firm (CompuServe or Litton, currently) under contract with the HCFA to process membership data. Medicare members may disenroll at any time and may do so not only at the HMO or by writing to the HMO but also at any Social Security office. For both enrollment and disenrollment processes, there are specific regulatory requirements regarding written notice to the member and provisions regarding the timeliness of an HMO's actions.

The claims department of an HMO will be affected by a Medicare contract in that claims volume will increase for nonplan claims. For one thing, given that Medicare beneficiaries are higher utilizers of medical services, there will be a greater number of out-of-plan claims for emergency and urgently needed services. When a Medicare member uses an out-of-plan provider, a claim may be submitted to a Medicare carrier or intermediary as though the person were a fee-for-service Medicare beneficiary, but the claim will be transferred to the HMO from the Medicare carrier or intermediary (the Medicare fiscal agent for processing claims). Regulations require that an HMO process each claim received for its Medicare members and determine whether payment is appropriate. In its coordination of benefits activities, the claims department will have to become aware of Medicare coordination rules because, under a risk contract, the HMO is in a sense acting as a Medicare fiscal agent in making payment decisions.

The services that are covered under the federal Medicare program are broader than the services that a federally qualified HMO is required to provide to serve a commercial population. For example, durable medical equipment and skilled nursing facility services are not benefits usually available in a commercial group package. In addition to having to arrange such services, the HMO has to ensure that its utilization review staff are aware of what is and is not covered under Medicare.

All the above differences require the HMO either to expand its staff or to increase the responsibilities of its existing staff, which in either case usually means increased costs.

Another significant difference that will have to be considered when one is thinking about the consequences of obtaining a Medicare contract is the difference in the method of payment for Medicare members. The government does not pay an HMO in the same way that an employer group does, as explained above in the section on AAPCC payment. Consequently, an HMO may need to revise reimbursement arrangements with its existing providers and develop reimbursement arrangements with new providers (additional providers to expand capacity as well as new provider types, such as skilled nursing facilities and suppliers of durable medical equipment).

In establishing its guidelines for the ACR/APR computation explained above, the HCFA recognized that utilization by Medicare members is more frequent and more intensive than that of commercial enrollees. For example, if a physician is paid a capitation by the HMO to treat HMO commercial members, the same capitation would not be a reasonable payment to the physician for a Medicare member. If hospitals are paid a per diem rate for commercial HMO members, that same per diem may not be appropriate for Medicare members. The new reimbursement arrangements to take into account Medicare member utilization patterns need not result in a decrease in revenue on a per member basis, but it is important to know that there is more to Medicare contracting than just signing a contract and watching the AAPCC rates go up every year.

WHATEVER HAPPENED TO BIG BROTHER?

As of now, payments to HMOs are a minuscule part of the HCFA's budget. Of course, one person's minuscule is another person's majuscule: Payments to HMOs are minuscule in the context of a budget for Medicare health care expenditures that totals more than $175 billion. In a program that involves government payments of more than $1 billion each month, there is bound to be at least a slight amount of interest in having some government oversight.

Once any HMO, whether Medicare contracting or not, is qualified, or once a CMP is granted eligibility for a Medicare contract, the HCFA maintains ongoing monitoring of the plan. The monitoring is accomplished through self-reporting of financial and other information by the HMOs and CMPs on a quarterly basis, although if certain criteria are met, this information may be reported on a yearly basis. The information is reported to the OMC on a special reporting form known as the National Data Reporting Requirements form.

Specific to Medicare is a monitoring process that is performed by the OMC and, principally, by the ten regional offices of the HCFA. By the end of the first year of contracting, each plan will have a monitoring visit conducted jointly by the OMC and the regional offices, during which the reviewers will determine whether the health plan is complying with regulatory requirements in such areas as insolvency arrangements, legal and financial requirements for the entity as a whole, quality of care issues, marketing practices, enrollment/disenrollment, claims payment, and grievance and appeals procedures. The reviewers follow a specific written protocol in conducting the review.

After such a monitoring visit, a report is prepared, and if necessary the HMO is required to submit a corrective action plan. Close monitoring of the plan continues until the HCFA is satisfied that the problems have been resolved. If the initial review goes well, there may not necessarily be a review of the same HMO for another 2 years.

As previously noted, Medicare risk-contracting HMOs are subject to external review of the quality of care they render. PROs, which also review the quality of care of hospitals in fee-for-service Medicare, review a risk HMO's inpatient and ambulatory care. This review requirement has been the subject of a great deal of controversy among HMOs. The HMOs maintain that the review procedures are overly burdensome for the results they produce and that the methodology should be more tailored to the care rendered in a managed care system. As a result, the HCFA has revised the methodology, in part on the basis of comments from the HMO industry and other outside groups such as hospital groups and the American Association of Retired Persons. The revised methodology moves away from review of individual cases and toward a collaborative approach focusing on patterns of care. This approach should be more successful in improving the care provided to Medicare beneficiaries in HMOs. [An entire issue of the *Health Care Financing Review* (volume 16, number 4, Summer 1995) is devoted to advances in quality measurement.]

ALTERNATIVES TO RISK CONTRACTING FOR THE RISK AVERSE

HMOs that are risk averse may decide to contract with the HCFA on a cost basis. Cost contracts provide that the HMO is reimbursed by the HCFA for the reasonable cost of all services actually provided to Medicare enrollees, with the only significant cost that is not reimbursed being the profit of a for-profit contractor. Medicare enrollees of a cost reimbursed organization are not locked into the plan. If a beneficiary chooses to use a nonplan provider, Medicare fee-for-service carriers and intermediaries will pay any claims without regard to the person's Medicare cost HMO status.

An HMO may obtain a cost contract under two different statutory provisions: the Social Security Act provision that also authorizes risk contracting (Section 1876), and a provision that constitutes a fragment of a sentence in Section 1833 of the Medicare law. The latter arrangement, an HCPP agreement, has minimal regulatory requirements and, beginning in 1996, also is subject to state Medigap (Medicare supplemental insurance) regulation requirements. A Section 1876 contractor must be a federally qualified HMO or a CMP and must adhere to all the requirements that risk contractors follow other than PRO review of services (because there is no lock-in and no risk on the part of the cost HMO) and the requirement of holding an open enrollment to enroll beneficiaries leaving a risk HMO that is terminating its contract. An HCPP, on the other hand, may health screen, need not have an open enrollment, need not provide the full range of Medicare-covered services (only certain physician and supplier services are required), and is not financially responsible for emergency care. Any organization that provides services to enrolled members through staff or contracted physicians may become an HCPP. Many of the HCPPs contracting with the HCFA are in fact labor or employer organizations that arrange for the provision of services exclusively to their members. As of August 1995, there were 30 HMO/CMP cost contractors with 181,000 enrollees and 56 HCPP contractors with 541,000 Medicare enrollees.

MEDICARE'S DUAL OPTION STRATEGY SHIFTS TO MEDICARE CHOICES

Overview

In 1985, Medicare policymakers positioned Medicare as a dual-option program: fee for service and the risk HMO option (where the plan is at full financial risk and beneficiaries are locked into the plan's network for all services except emergency or urgently needed care). The expectation was that large numbers of Medicare beneficiaries would be enrolled in HMOs by the end of the decade. By 1991, however, only 3 percent of Medicare beneficiaries were enrolled in a risk contract HMO, and only 6 percent were enrolled in any type of managed care plan.

In contrast, by 1991, according the Health Insurance Association of America, 49 percent of employees younger than 65 years who received their health benefits from an employer-sponsored health plan were enrolled in a managed care plan. Managed care plans offered by employers included a broader array of options than were available to Medicare beneficiaries, such as PPOs and POS options in addition to HMOs.

Medicare policymakers noted the divergent trends between private sector managed care enrollment and Medicare enrollment in managed care. Three perspectives were considered: the beneficiary, the HMO, and the Medicare program (discussed below). The result of this analysis was a revised managed care strategy for Medicare. The strategy incorporates three prongs based on lessons learned from the private sector: improving the Medicare risk HMO program, making the choice of managed care more widely known to Medicare beneficiaries, and adopting an incremental approach to managed care that includes offering a wider choice of hybrid managed care products.

By 1995, this strategy (together with the effects of health care reform at the federal and state levels and evolution of the market) had a substantial impact on increasing the number of HMO contracts and applicants. In addition, the percentage of Medicare beneficiaries enrolled in any type of managed care plan rose to 10 percent. Between 1993 and 1994, Medicare enrollment in risk contracts alone increased by 25 percent.

Several initiatives in 1995 also resulted in the availability of more flexible managed care models to Medicare beneficiaries: Congress extended the Medicare Select program to all 50 states (P.L. 104-18), the HCFA issued guidelines on how Medicare risk contracts could offer a POS option (a limited out-of-plan option); and the HCFA announced a new Medicare Choices demonstration program to test new managed care models (such as PPOs and provider-sponsored integrated delivery systems) and to test partial risk reimbursement methods. In addition, the HCFA supported legislation for Medicare PPOs and initiated several new research and demonstration projects to improve the payment method.

Projecting current trends forward, the HCFA estimates that the number of HMO contracts will increase from 221 to 357 by fiscal year 1998 and that the number of enrollees will increase from 3.1 to 7.4 million. In late 1995, however, Congress was considering legislation to reform Medicare. If this legislation is adopted, there may be additional incentives for beneficiaries to choose managed care plans. Congressional proposals also include provisions to expand the number and type of choices available.

MEDICARE MANAGED CARE (THE HMO MODEL)—1985–1995

The Beneficiary Experience

Although 74 percent of beneficiaries live in areas served by at least one Medicare managed

Table 26–1 Medicare Managed Care Contracts, 1985 to 1995 (Cost Includes HCPPs)

Month	*Number of Risk Contracts*	*Number of Cost Contracts*
April 1985	32	109
December 1985	87	87
December 1986	149	78
December 1990	96	66
December 1994	148	86
October 1995	179	87

Source: Health Care Financing Administration.

care plan, by 1995 less than 3 million beneficiaries (almost 8 percent of the total Medicare population) were enrolled in a risk HMO, and an additional 2 percent were enrolled in cost plans. These statistics suggest that the demand from Medicare beneficiaries for enrollment in HMOs is low. More careful analysis, however, reveals that demand was high in some markets. Fifty percent of all Medicare beneficiaries are enrolled in an HMO in Portland, Oregon. Fifty-seven counties had Medicare enrollment of at least 40 percent. More than one third of Medicare beneficiaries were enrolled in HMOs in southern California, and 27 percent were enrolled in HMOs in south Florida. These penetration rates were similar to the rates for the nonelderly in these market areas and in some cases were higher. Tables 26–1 and 26–2 illustrate Medicare enrollment trends for both risk contract and cost contract HMOs.

Why do beneficiaries choose a lock-in HMO? Most beneficiaries are attracted by the lower out-of-pocket costs. For example, half of all risk plans waive the plan premium (which covers Medicare coinsurance and deductible payments), and most plans offer additional benefits not available in Medicare fee for service, such as prescription drugs, prevention services, eyeglasses, and hearing aids. As of 1993, 55 percent of all Medicare risk HMO enrollees were enrolled in a zero-premium plan, and 65 percent of beneficiaries were enrolled in plans offering prescription drugs (of which 69 percent charged no premium for the drugs).

Why is beneficiary enrollment low in most areas? First of all, the HMO option is not available in many areas. By 1995, only 35 percent of HMOs had Medicare risk or cost contracts. In addition, Medicare did not offer beneficiaries a choice when they became entitled to Medicare. Marketing was left to the HMO. Information from focus groups suggests that beneficiaries do not necessarily understand that the HMO may offer higher coverage at lower costs. In addition, older and sicker persons are committed to their current physician. Unless this physician retires or they move, Medicare beneficiaries are reluctant to change their known source of health care. The concept of managed care, where one is locked into a health care delivery system, is not familiar to the senior population.

A recent trend that is already influencing the growth of Medicare HMO enrollment is the increasing number of beneficiaries who age in to a Medicare risk contract from an employer group contract. More employers are offering risk products to their retirees when a contract is available. In some cases, employers are leveraging their commercial HMO contracts to require Medicare risk contracts. For example, in 1994 CalPERS (the California Public Employees Retirement System, which purchases health care for state and local employees in California) required that all its contracting HMOs offer a risk contract. In some cases, employers are offering a zero-premium risk contract as the only retiree option as a method of reducing health care liability.

The HMO Experience

HMO interest in Medicare managed care can be described as a roller coaster. In 1987, 152 of more than 500 HMOs in the country had Medicare risk contracts. By 1992, the number of risk contracts declined to 87. By 1995, the number had increased to 171 with an additional 40 new applications pending. Although four HMOs

Table 26–2 Medicare Managed Care Enrollment, 1985 to 1995 (Cost Includes HCPPs)

Month	*Number of Risk Enrollees*	*Number of Cost Enrollees*	*Total Enrollment*
April 1985	300,000	916,215	1,216,215
December 1985	440,923	731,191	1,172,114
December 1986	813,712	767,982	1,581,694
December 1990	1,263,547	731,918	1,995,465
December 1994	2,268,364	756,936	3,025,300
October 1995	2,968,791	716,036	3,684,827

Source: Health Care Financing Administration.

continue to enroll the majority of Medicare HMO members, new plans in new areas of the country are entering the business in record numbers.

HMOs are interested in Medicare contracts for several reasons. A primary reason is that HMOs want a way to keep enrollees in their plan after they become eligible for Medicare. During the last decade, many HMOs have been successful in managing the risky Medicare population, especially through enrolling large numbers of beneficiaries (more than 25,000 to spread the risk), reducing hospital and other unnecessary service utilization, and making a corporate commitment to the Medicare line of business. These successful HMOs also learned how to manage the care of an older and sicker population (e.g., by developing special services and programs to manage or coordinate the care of the elderly). A number of these organizations are now expanding their Medicare risk contracts to new markets. As market competition increases, new plans are applying to be risk contractors.

Experience with the significant drop in risk contracts during the 1980s identified a number of issues. In many plans, the number of enrollees was insufficient to spread the risk. Others found marketing the Medicare product on an individual rather than a group basis to be expensive. A number of the contracts were victims of the merger and acquisition trend in the late 1980s. Many plans could not manage the special needs of the elderly population.

The key reason cited by plans for dropping a risk contract is that Medicare payment levels are too low. Analysis of 1994 payment rates revealed, however, that the level of Medicare HMO penetration does not necessarily vary by the level of HMO payment. Among the top 15 AAPCC counties, only southern California and south Florida counties have high HMO enrollment (Los Angeles and Orange counties in California ranked 10th and 13th in AAPCC levels, and Dade County in Florida ranked 7th). Detroit, New York (with the three highest AAPCC rates), and Philadelphia (ranking 6th) had negligible Medicare risk enrollment. In addition, two areas with low AAPCC rates—Portland, Oregon and Minneapolis, Minnesota—have high Medicare enrollment.

Medicare's Experience

Medicare's interest in managed care started with two objectives. The first was to allow Medicare beneficiaries the opportunity to choose an HMO option (the predominant managed care model in 1982 when the legislation was passed), and the second was to ensure that the Medicare payment formula realized the efficiencies of managed care. The issue of savings must be viewed from several perspectives, including the savings to the Medicare Trust Fund and the savings to the enrollee.

By law, the Medicare risk program is designed to return most of the savings to the beneficiary through additional benefits or reduced costs. In 1995, beneficiaries enrolled in risk HMOs received up to $245 per month in additional benefits or reduced premiums, with a weighted plan average of $66 per month per beneficiary.

By law, the only savings that the Medicare Trust Fund can realize is a 5 percent discount from fee-for-service expenditures (i.e., the HMOs are paid 95 percent of the fee-for-service rate). Studies based on the early years of the risk program showed a net cost increase (almost 6 percent) to the Medicare program because the payment rates did not properly adjust for the health status of the beneficiaries. HMOs tend to enroll younger and healthier beneficiaries, especially plans that focus on beneficiaries who age in from employer groups or who retire to Sun Belt areas. A number of studies are currently underway to update the analysis of the savings to Medicare to reflect an older and sicker enrolled population and the maturity of many markets (i.e., a number of competing HMOs and a relative large beneficiary enrollment).

Improvements to the Medicare Risk Contract Option and Risk Payment Method

Medicare has worked aggressively to be a better business partner with HMOs that choose to enter risk contracts. These changes address both the supply side (i.e., the number of HMOs that choose to enter risk contracts) and the demand side (i.e., the number of Medicare beneficiaries who are interested in choosing a risk plan). Medicare has forged partnerships with the industry to resolve a variety of problems in the business relationship between the purchaser and supplier, from reforming payment to improving administrative systems.

Payment Reform

Since the beginning of the TEFRA risk program, the AAPCC payment method has been considered flawed. Over time the problems have increased to the point that a number of serious options for reform are under review. If Congress does not act, the HCFA currently has statutory authority to make changes in the AAPCC to include risk adjusters and to use alternative geographic areas.

The HCFA's research and demonstration program has been the focus for testing refinements to the current AAPCC formula as a short-term strategy and for testing new payment methods as a long-term strategy. As managed care penetration increases, the preferred strategy is to separate Medicare's managed care payment from the fee-for-service base.

Health Status Adjusters

Mathematica Policy Research, in its evaluation of the Medicare risk program, found that, because of the absence of a health status adjuster, Medicare pays on average 5.7 percent more for enrollees of risk HMOs compared with what those enrollees would have cost had they remained in fee-for-service Medicare. The General Accounting Office attributed the relatively better health status of Medicare HMO enrollees to self-selection by healthier Medicare beneficiaries into HMOs. To address this issue, and to provide fairer payment to HMOs (properly compensating HMOs with adverse selection and ensuring that HMOs in competitive areas have payments adjusted to reflect the relative health status of enrollees), the HCFA has sponsored research and demonstrations over the past several years aimed at developing usable health status adjusters for Medicare HMO enrollees.

Ambulatory care groups and diagnostic cost groups are two diagnosis-based risk adjustment methodologies for which the HCFA has funded research and that may be tested in demonstrations in 1996; these methods are discussed briefly in Chapter 19. Another approach is to base health status payment adjustments on an individual's history of illness. Mathematica has recommended the use of the history of stroke, cancer, and heart disease as a simple and reliable risk adjuster. The HCFA has funded research to study this approach using those illnesses, their severity, the length of time since the last hospital stay, and comorbidities. Other research will examine the feasibility of self-reported health status as a risk adjustment mechanism.

A demonstration of an individual high-cost outlier pool is underway in Seattle, Washington and is expected to be completed in 1997. Risk HMOs in Seattle will be paid 97 percent of the AAPCC, with the additional 2 percent being used to fund a reinsurance pool for the payment of high-cost cases. Although reinsurance is common, the demonstration is expected to provide the HCFA with utilization and cost data and information about mechanisms that may be applicable to partial capitation models (favored by Joseph Newhouse and others), in which HMOs are paid partly on a prepaid capitated basis and partly on a retrospectively determined cost basis.

Alternative Geographic Areas

Although HCFA-sponsored research has shown that using a geographic unit other than the county is not necessarily a clearly superior basis for payment to HMOs, there have been proposals to change from a county-based payment to payments based on metropolitan statistical areas. Such larger areas, or market areas, are especially appropriate if payment rates are to be set through a competitive pricing mechanism in which all health plans are expected to operate throughout a wide geographic area.

Competitive Pricing

The AAPCC is often criticized as an administered pricing mechanism that does not take advantage of competition in the marketplace to set the optimum premium for HMO coverage. In September 1995, the HCFA awarded a contract to begin development of a competitive pricing demonstration for Medicare HMO contracting. This would be a managed competition model in which the government payment to HMOs would be based on a bidding process involving all HMOs in a given geographic area. The government payment would be set at the lowest bid or some average amount. All HMOs in an area willing to submit bids would be allowed to accept Medicare enrollees (i.e., it is not a winner-take-all situation). Beneficiaries could choose any participating health plan, but the government contribution toward the premium would be limited to the competitively determined rate. The government contribution toward the HMO premium would be divorced from the AAPCC (although the AAPCC might be an upper limit on payment). A competitive pricing demonstration might include standardization of benefit packages, coordinated enrollment periods, and third party (e.g., broker) enrollment and information dissemination.

Earmarked Medicare Payments

The AAPCC payment includes all Medicare program expenditures. Among those expenditures are payments to hospitals for graduate medical education (GME), indirect medical education, and disproportionate share payments. The argument has been made that, to the extent that such earmarked payments do not represent actual costs incurred by HMOs (e.g., disproportionate share payments) or are payments intended for a particular purpose but not employed for that purpose (e.g., GME payments to HMOs that do not use teaching hospitals), the AAPCC should not include those amounts or, if they are included, they should be paid only to HMOs with GME programs, for example.

Reducing Geographic Variation

There is nearly a fourfold difference between the highest and lowest AAPCCs in the United States. The AAPCCs reflect the differences among counties in Medicare's historical fee-for-service costs. The county-to-county variation reflects variation in input prices as well as other factors, such as the supply of physicians (primary care versus specialists), hospital beds, and practice styles. Some payment reform proposals call for the narrowing of this regional variation to bring counties closer to a national average.

Beneficiary Demand

On the demand side, Medicare is implementing a number of activities to ensure that Medicare beneficiaries understand that their choices for Medicare include not only fee for service but also managed care. For example, all Medicare publications have been revised to emphasize the theme of choice, and materials were provided to Social Security offices and beneficiary groups to ensure that information about beneficiary options is available. Medicare is conducting a number of focus groups and is supporting a demonstration project to understand better how to present information about Medicare choices.

Medicare is contacting employers to ensure that they understand the advantages of offering managed care options for retirees. In addition, Medicare is working with other payers, such as state Medicaid agencies, the Office of Personnel Management of the federal government, and the Department of Defense, to streamline policies for dual eligibles.

An Incremental Strategy

In 1995, 34 million Medicare beneficiaries remained in fee for service. Fee for service will continue to be an option under Medicare. Ultimately, Medicare would like all Medicare beneficiaries to have a choice between fee for service and several managed care plans (PPOs, POS, and full-risk HMOs).

The realities in 1995, however, were that many organizations were not ready to provide services on a full-risk basis to Medicare beneficiaries throughout the nation. In addition, many beneficiaries were not ready to enroll with a comprehensive care organization that provides services through a specified network and will not pay anything when routine services are received out of plan. Thus the Medicare program, following the lead of successful efforts initiated in the private sector, has adopted an incremental managed care strategy that offers a range of managed care products. Figure 26–1 displays the continuum currently envisioned by Medicare. This continuum of complementary managed care choices will allow beneficiaries to choose the arrangement that best suits them, from fee for service to PPO models to opt-out models to risk HMO models.

Medicare Select

Medicare Select permits Medicare supplemental insurance companies to offer a PPO network-type product in conjunction with their Medicare supplemental insurance (Medigap). Medigap is private insurance that covers medical costs that Medicare does not pay, such as deductibles and coinsurance. In exchange for a reduced premium, Medicare Select policies provide a financial incentive for Medicare beneficiaries to use their network of providers. For example, if a network physician is used, the Medicare Select policy will pay 20 percent coinsurance; if a nonnetwork physician is used for nonemergency services, however, the Medicare Select policy may pay no coinsurance or a reduced amount.

Medicare Select policies are considered an incremental managed care product because the financial penalty to the Medicare enrollee for

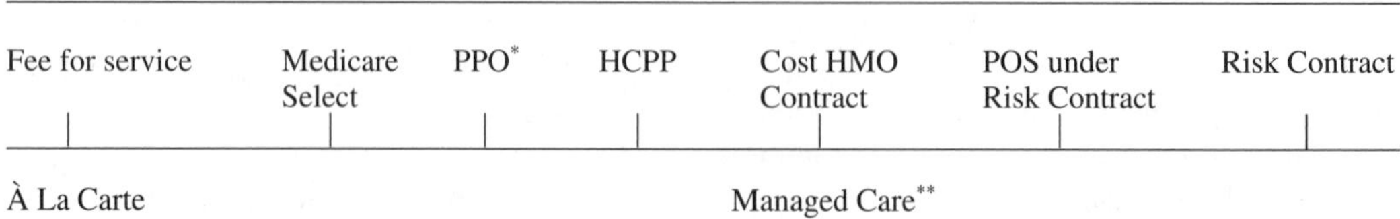

Figure 26–1 Range of Medicare options. *Proposed law; **continuum reflects the range of services under managed care. *Source:* Health Care Financing Administration.

using out-of-network services is minimal. Medicare will continue to pay its share (e.g., the 80 percent of the physician bill in the example cited above).

Originally approved as a pilot project in 15 states, Medicare Select was extended to June 1998 and expanded to all 50 states. The pilot program demonstrated that beneficiary premiums averaged 15 percent to 25 percent less than the premium for a comparable non-Select Medigap policy; Select insurers rarely establish aggressive case management or utilization management programs and tend to rely on discounts (waiver of the hospital deductible) to reduce costs. The final evaluation is not yet complete, but early results suggest that in some plans hospital utilization was higher for Select enrollees than for beneficiaries with non-Select policies. Many companies indicated that they did not offer a Select product because it only offered the insurer the opportunity to manage a small amount of the premium.

PPO

Medicare supports legislation that will authorize a PPO option for Medicare beneficiaries. Under a PPO, a Medicare beneficiary will pay a small amount (not more than 20 percent coinsurance) to use a provider outside the network on a self-referral basis. The PPO could choose to be paid under a partial risk basis (i.e., Medicare and the PPO will share risk over and under a specific target). The plan would be paid on a fee-for-service basis. The PPO model that Medicare prefers is a third-generation model, where the plan uses sophisticated managed care techniques such as case management, quality assessment, and utilization management to increase efficiency and lower costs. PPOs have been successful in the private sector in providing lower premium costs and larger provider choice for persons younger than 65 years.

Improved Cost Contracting Models

Cost contracts are Medicare's outmoded hybrid managed care models. As currently designed, these options often result in higher costs than those for fee-for-service Medicare (i.e., through duplicate payment), lack of beneficiary protections, and lack of incentives for cost contractors to manage the full continuum of the patient's care. Under the incremental strategy, Medicare is proposing to replace cost contracts with an improved PPO model and to redesign the HCPP to serve union and employer retirees.

POS Option

POS models are frequently offered by employers because they provide the savings of full-risk managed care while offering the employee the flexibility to use a nonnetwork provider on a service-by-service basis. Employers use two types of POS models. The first model is a POS option offered in conjunction with an HMO product. The other model is a replacement for fee-for-service care. Experience shows that under both models most employees continue to use the plan's network, where care is coordinated and unnecessary or inappropriate care is minimized. POS provides peace of mind for the employee and allows the employer to offer a mandatory managed care product.

In 1995, Medicare issued guidelines for a POS model in conjunction with a Medicare risk contract. The Medicare POS option will be available to beneficiaries under a variety of options, depending upon the plan choice and local market conditions. For example, the Medicare POS could be offered to all enrollees or just employer groups. The POS can also be marketed as an additional benefit, a mandatory supplemental benefit, or an optional supplemental benefit. The HMOs will have flexibility to structure their POS product in a variety of ways, for example by limiting the types of benefits that may be available through POS or by placing a financial cap on the amount of services that may be received out of plan.

Medicare Choices Program

In 1995, Medicare announced a Medicare Choices program to offer Medicare beneficiaries a broad range of health plan options similar to those available in the private sector. The demonstration program will test a variety of innovative delivery systems and risk-sharing arrangements, primarily in target markets where commercial enrollment is high and Medicare managed care enrollment is low, and in rural areas. Some of the models include integrated delivery systems, provider-sponsored networks, managed care models targeted to rural areas, PPOs, and triple-option models. The health care system is changing rapidly, and Medicare wants to be able to contract with all types of high-quality organizations that can serve beneficiaries.

CONCLUSION

As a purchaser as well as a regulator, Medicare is committed to ensuring that managed care plans offered to Medicare beneficiaries provide only the highest quality and value. Beneficiaries will have an increased choice of options to receive their health care services, ranging from fee for service to hybrid plans to full-risk lock-in HMOs. Beneficiaries will be given information that will allow them to compare their choices and make a selection based on individual preference and market conditions. Managed care plans will also have a wider array of contract options to serve the senior population. These contract options will offer partial as well as full risk payment. Medicare fee for service and the wider array of managed care plans are expected to compete on price, benefits, and, most important of all, quality. Medicare will hold all plans accountable to high standards: Each plan must be fiscally solvent, ensure appropriate access and availability of services, select quality providers and have programs in place to improve quality over time, ensure that beneficiaries have appropriate grievance and appeals processes, and ensure that beneficiaries have sufficient information to make an informed plan choice.

Study Questions

1. How are Medicare risk HMOs paid? How is this payment method different from the way in which HMOs are paid for commercial enrollees? What are the major weaknesses of the current Medicare risk payment system?
2. What kinds of health plans can receive cost reimbursement under Medicare and what is their current statutory status? Why would an HMO eligible for a risk contract choose to be paid on a cost reimbursement basis for Medicare enrollees?
3. What were the principal innovations in Medicare prepaid health plan contracting introduced by TEFRA? Did TEFRA have the effect of increasing the number of Medicare risk contractors, or do other factors seem to have benn more important in increasing Medicare risk HMO enrollment?
4. From a health plan perspective, what are the differences between Medicare HMO enrollees and commercial HMO enrollees?

REFERENCE

1. C.C. Boesz, "Federal Qualification: A Foundation for the Future," in *The Managed Health Care Handbook*, 3d ed., ed. P.R. Kongstvedt (Gaithersburg, Md.: Aspen, 1996), 835–848.

SUGGESTED READING

Law and Regulations

The law governing Medicare risk and cost contracts with HMOs and CMPs is found at Section 1876 of the Social Security Act or Section 1395(mm) of the U.S. Code. The fragment of a sentence that authorizes health care prepayment plans is found at Section 1833(a)(1)(A) of the Social Security Act. Title XIII of the Public Health Service Act (42 U.S.C. 300e) is the law that deals with federally qualified HMOs.

Regulations for all these entities are found in Title 42 of the Code of Federal Regulations, Sections 417.100 through

417.180 (federally qualified HMOs), Sections 417.400 through 417.694 (cost and risk HMOs and CMPs), and Sections 417.800 through 417.810 (HCPPs). Current editions of the Code of Federal Regulations also contain Sections 417.200 through 417.292, which are obsolete in that they contain only pre-TEFRA contract provisions.

For the voracious reader, the *Federal Register* of 25 May 1984, and of 10 January 1985, contains, respectively, the proposed and final versions of the TEFRA contracting regulations, which are relevant to those interested in seeing the changes between the proposed and final versions of the regulations and in knowing the types of public comments received on the regulations. Also published in the *Federal Register* was a 6 January 1986, notice (pp. 506–510) outlining the HCFA's AAPCC payment methodology. Explaining the AAPCC (and studying it) is a cottage industry of its own, as is evident from the list of additional reading materials below.

The law and regulations are available at any federal depository library, at law libraries, and through compendiums such as the Commerce Clearing House *Medicare and Medicaid Guide*. CD-ROM versions of the HCFA's regulations and manuals are also now becoming available.

Manuals

The *Medicare HMO/CMP Manual* (HCFA Publication 75) generally explains (in layperson's language), or expands on, the requirements contained in the law and regulations. All Medicare-contracting HMOs/CMPs/HCPPs receive the Manual and any updates. The Manual may be purchased through:

National Technical Information Service
Department of Commerce
5825 Port Royal Road
Springfield, VA 22161
(703) 487-4630
Publication PB 85-953899

Some information, including AAPCC rates, is available on the Internet at HCFA's address: http://wwwhcfa.gov.

Reports of the General Accounting Office Related to Medicare HMOs

The first two digits indicate the year in which the report was issued.

- **96-63** *Medicare HMOs: Rapid Enrollment Growth Concentrated in Selected States*
- **95-155** *Increased HMO Oversight Could Improve Quality and Access to Care*
- **95-81** *Medicare: Opportunities Are Available To Apply Managed Care Strategies*
- **94-119** *Medicare: Changes to HMO Rate Setting Method Are Needed To Reduce Program Costs*
- **92-11** *HCFA Needs To Take Stronger Actions against HMOs Violating Federal Standards*
- **91-48** *PRO Review Does Not Assure Quality of Care Provided by Risk HMOs*
- **89-46** *Medicare: Health Maintenance Organization Rate Setting Issues*
- **89-03** *Reasonableness of HMO Payments Not Assured*
- **88-12** *Physician Incentive Payments by Prepaid Health Plans Could Lower Quality of Care*
- **88-08** *Experience Shows Ways To Improve Oversight of HMOs*
- **88-07** *Issues Concerning the HealthChoice Demonstration Project*
- **88-05** *Improving Quality of Care Assessment and Assurance*
- **87-11** *Uncertainties Surround Proposal To Expand Prepaid Health Plan Contracting*
- **87-07** *Preliminary Strategies for Assessing Quality of Care*

General Accounting Office reports can be obtained from:

General Accounting Office
PO Box 6015
Gaithersburg, MD 20877
(202) 512-6000

The Office of the Inspector General of the Department of Health and Human Services has also issued reports on Medicare HMOs, including the following, which can be obtained by calling the Office of Public Affairs at (202) 619-1343:

- **OEI-06-91-00730** *Beneficiary Perspectives of Medicare Risk HMOs* (March 1995)
- **OEI-06-91-00731** *Medicare Risk HMOs: Beneficiary Enrollment and Service Access Problems* (April 1995)

Books and Journal Articles

The following monographs, all by Susan Jelley Palsbo, formerly of Group Health Association of America (now with Coopers and Lybrand), are the most lucid and thorough explanation of the AAPCC:

- *The USPCC Explained* (June 1988)
- *The AAPCC Explained* (February 1989)
- *The Demographic Factors Explained* (February 1990)

- *Medicare Capitation Explained* (March 1990)

The monographs, which are all AAHP (formerly GHAA/AMCRA) publications, are available from:

American Association of Health Plans
1129 20th Street, N.W.
Suite 600
Washington, D.C. 20036
(202) 778-3200, fax (202) 331-7487

As noted in the chapter, the Summer 1995 issue of the *Health Care Financing Review* deals entirely with the issue of new initiatives and approaches in health care quality, including several articles on Medicare and Medicaid managed care.

Adamache, K., and Rossiter, L. 1987. The Entry of HMOs into the Medicare Market: Implications for TEFRA's Mandate. *Inquiry* 23:1314–1418.

Anderson, G.F., et al. 1990. Setting Payment Rates for Capitated Systems: A Comparison of Various Alternatives. *Inquiry* 27:225–233.

Ash, A., et al. 1989. Adjusting Medicare Capitation Payments Using Prior Hospitalization Data. *Health Care Financing Review* 10:17–29.

Ash, A., et al. 1990. *Clinical Refinements to the Diagnostic Cost Group Model.* Boston, Mass.: Health Policy Research Consortium, Cooperative Research Center.

Barnett, B. 1989. How To Take the Risk out of Medicare HMO Management: Opportunities and Challenges in the 1990s. *Group Pract Journal* 38:29–30, 32–33, 36.

Bergeron, J., and Brown, R. 1992. *Why Do the Medicare Risk Plans of HMOs Lose Money?* Princeton, N.J.: Mathematica Policy Research, Inc.

Brown, B. 1989. The Structure of Quality Assurance Programs in Risk-Based HMOs/CMPs Enrolling Medicare Beneficiaries. *GHAA Journal* 10:68–82.

Brown, R., et al. 1993. Do Health Maintenance Organizations Work for Medicare? *Health Care Financing Review* 15:7–24.

Dowd, B., et al. Issues Regarding Health Plan Payments under Medicare and Recommendations for Reform. *Milbank Memorial Fund Quarterly* 70:423–449.

Health Care Financing Administration (HCFA). 1991. *Expanding Medicare Coordinated Care Choices for Employer Group Retirees.* Baltimore, Md.: HCFA Office of Coordinated Care Policy and Planning.

Hill, J.W., and Brown, R.S. 1992. *Health Status, Financial Barriers and the Decision to Enroll in Medicare Risk Plans.* Princeton, N.J.: Mathematica Policy Research, Inc.

Hill, J.W., and Brown, R.S. 1990. *Biased Selection in the TEFRA HMO/CMP Program: Final Report.* Baltimore, Md.: Health Care Financing Administration.

Hill, J.W., et al. 1992. *The Impact of the Medicare Risk Program on the Use of Services and Costs to Medicare.* Princeton, N.J.: Mathematica Policy Research, Inc.

Langwell, K. 1990. Structure and Performance of Health Maintenance Organizations: A Review. *Health Care Financing Review* 12:71–79.

Langwell, K.M., and Hadley, J.P. 1990. Insights from the Medicare HMO Demonstrations. *Health Affairs* 9:74–89.

Langwell, K.P., and Hadley, J.P. 1989. *National Evaluation of the Medicare Competition Demonstrations: Summary Report.* Baltimore, Md.: Health Care Financing Administration.

Langwell, K., et al. 1987. Early Experience of Health Maintenance Organizations under Medicare Competition Demonstrations. *Health Care Financing Review* 8:37–56.

Lichtenstein, R., et al. 1992. HMO Marketing and Selection Bias: Are TEFRA HMOs Skimming? *Medical Care* 30:329–346.

Lichtenstein, R., et al. 1991. Selection Bias in TEFRA At-Risk HMOs. *Medical Care* 29:318–331.

Lubitz, J. 1987. Health Status Adjustments for Medicare Capitation. *Inquiry* 24:362–375.

Luft, H., ed. 1994. *HMOs and the Elderly.* Ann Arbor, Mich.: AHSR Health Administration Press.

Manton, K.G., and Stallard, E. 1992. Analysis of Underwriting Factors for AAPCC. *Health Care Financing Review* 14:117–132.

McCombs, J.S., et al. 1990. Do HMOs Reduce Health Care Costs? A Multivariate Analysis of Two Medicare HMO Demonstration Projects. *Health Services Research* 25:593–613.

McGee, J., and Brown, R. 1992. *What Makes HMOs Drop Their Medicare Risk Contracts?* Princeton, N.J.: Mathematica Policy Research, Inc.

McMillan, A. 1993. Trends in Medicare Health Maintenance Organization Enrollment: 1986–1993. *Health Care Financing Review* 15:135–146.

McMillan, A., and Lubitz, J. 1987. Medicare Enrollment in Health Maintenance Organizations. *Health Care Financing Review* 8:87–94.

Morrison, E.M., and Luft, H.S. 1990. Health Maintenance Organization Environments in the 1980s and Beyond. *Health Care Financing Review* 12:81–90.

Nelson, L., and Brown, R. 1989. *The Impact of the Medicare Competition Demonstrations on the Use and Cost of Services: Final Report.* Baltimore, Md.: Health Care Financing Administration.

Newhouse, J.P. 1994. Patients At Risk: Health Reform and Risk Adjustment. *Health Affairs* 13:132–146.

Palmer, R.H. 1995. Securing Health Care Quality for Medicine. *Health Affairs* 14:89–100.

Porell, F.W., and Turner, W.M. 1990. Biased Selection under an Experimental Enrollment and Marketing Medicare HMO Broker. *Medical Care* 28:604–615.

Porell, F.W., and Wallack, S.S. 1990. Medicare Risk Contracting: Determinants of Market Entry. *Health Care Financing Review* 12:75–85.

Porell, F.W., et al. 1990. Alternative Geographic Configurations for Medicare Payments to Health Maintenance Organizations. *Health Care Financing Review* 11:17–30.

Riley, G., et al. 1991. Enrollee Health Status under Medicare Risk Contracts: An Analysis of Mortality Rates. *Health Services Research* 26:137–164.

Rossiter, L.F., and Adamache, K.W. 1990. Payment to Health Maintenance Organizations and the Geographic Factor. *Health Care Financing Review* 12:19–30.

Rossiter, L.F., et al. 1989. Patient Satisfaction Among Elderly Enrollees and Disenrollees in Medicare Health Maintenance Organizations. *Journal of the American Medical Association* 262:57–63.

Siddharthan, K. 1990. HMO Enrollment by Medicare Beneficiaries in Heterogeneous Communities. *Medical Care* 29:918–927.

Welch, W.P. 1992. Alternative Geographic Adjustments in Medicare Payment to Health Maintenance Organizations. *Health Care Financing Review* 13:97–110.

Welch, W.P. 1991. Defining Geographic Areas To Adjust Payments to Physicians, Hospitals and HMOs. *Inquiry* 28:151–160.

Welch, W.P. 1989. Improving Medicare Payments to HMOs: Urban Core versus Suburban Ring. *Inquiry* 26:62–71.

Welch, W.P., and Welch, H.G. 1995. Fee-for Data: A Strategy to Open the HMO Black Box. *Health Affairs* 14:104–116.

Wilensky, G.R., and Rossiter, L.F. 1991. Coordinated Care and Public Programs. *Health Affairs* 10:62–77.

Chapter 27

Medicaid Managed Care

Robert E. Hurley, Leonard Kirschner, and Thomas W. Bone

Study Objectives

- Review the past evolution of Medicaid managed care and its rapid recent growth
- Identify the models of Medicaid managed care in use and the reasons why these have been adopted by states
- Recognize some of the advantages and limitations of managed care for Medicaid beneficiaries
- Understand a number of the operational management challenges of providing Medicaid managed care
- Become aware of current and emergent future trends in Medicaid managed care

The number of Medicaid beneficiaries enrolled in managed care arrangements increased more than fivefold from 1990 to 1995, from 2.1 million to nearly 12 million.[1] In 6 years the joint federal–state program for low-income and disabled individuals grew from less than 10 percent managed care penetration to more than 35 percent. Virtually every state in the country has implemented some type of managed care arrangement for at least some of its eligible populations. Every indicator suggests that this growth will accelerate as states move into an era in which they are granted more program flexibility in return for a substantially reduced growth rate in federal financial support.

The rapid expansion reflects the convergence of several trends. Medicaid eligibility growth and overall cost inflation have contributed to state financial distress. Widening acceptance and availability of managed care options in the commercial sector have made public policymakers eager to avail themselves of the cost savings opportunities being reported by private buyers. There has been a dramatic upsurge in interest among commercial managed care plans to build their membership by entering the Medicaid market, a market viewed with considerable hesitancy and trepidation in the past.

In this chapter, relevant background and history that have led up to these important recent developments are examined. Some distinctive characteristics of the Medicaid program and its beneficiaries are discussed to identify how challenging crafting models to serve them has been. The principal models in use are introduced, and some experience from them is reviewed. Operational issues associated with designing and managing the Medicaid product line are examined in some depth, and the chapter concludes with an assessment of the major trends that are likely to be evident in a block grant environment.

Robert E. Hurley, Ph.D., is an Associate Professor in the Department of Health Administration at the Medical College of Virginia.

Leonard Kirschner, M.P.H., M.D., is with Electronic Data Systems and is the former Director of the Arizona Health Care Cost Containment System.

Thomas W. Bone, M.C.H.A., is with Electronic Data Systems and is the former Director of Managed Care for the Virginia Medicaid program.

BACKGROUND AND HISTORY

Enrollment in managed care arrangements has been permitted in Medicaid almost from the beginning of the program in 1966.[2] As a result of lack of enthusiasm among health maintenance organizations (HMOs), disinterest and/or caution among state officials, and hesitancy among beneficiaries, the numbers grew slowly. By 1981, there were only about a quarter of a million enrollees out of the roughly 20 million persons with Medicaid coverage.[3]

There had also been a notable failure of a major managed care initiative in the California Medicaid (MediCal) program in the early 1970s that had had a chilling effect on efforts to extend managed care to low-income persons.[4] Hasty, ill-considered arrangements by state officials led to shabby and fraudulent behavior by prepaid health plans, many of which were formed solely to exploit this opportunity. Marketing and network abuses resulted in beneficiaries going unserved and providers unpaid. Although this was a unique situation in many respects, the experience raised many concerns about the feasibility and desirability of promoting enrollment, especially rapid and unregulated enrollment, of low-income persons in managed care arrangements.[5]

The Waiver and Demonstration Era

A major change occurred in 1981 when, in the face of rising Medicaid expenditures and growing interest in giving states more flexibility, Congress expanded the waiver-granting authority of the Health Care Financing Administration (HCFA) to allow states to experiment with many new approaches to using alternative financing and delivery arrangements.[6] Many new approaches were introduced, including the most notable: the Arizona Health Care Cost Containment System (AHCCCS), built statewide entirely on prepaid health plans. The AHCCCS program is described below.

Many other states pursued waivers for substate pilot and demonstration programs using varying levels of risk and contracting with different provider configurations.[7] This activity continued through the 1980s, and enrollment grew to about 2 million by the end of the decade, with nearly half the states introducing some form of managed care. The growth provided for much of the knowledge base and experience on which the most recent dramatic surge in managed care has drawn.

Arizona: The First of the Next Generation

The state of Arizona initiated its version of the Medicaid program in July 1982, 17 years after passage of federal Medicaid legislation. State policymakers were intent on developing a new model for health care for the poor using an innovative, alternative health care system that facilitated cost containment, improved patient access, and delivered quality health care in a managed care setting. This approach rejected traditional fee-for-service arrangements in favor of private sector capitation-based contracts and was called the AHCCCS rather than the state Medicaid program. It was implemented using the Section 1115 waiver authority that the federal government issues for the purpose of conducting research and demonstration projects. For the past 14 years the program has continued as a waivered demonstration program, and the current approval allows it to continue to 1997.

Program Structure

As the first Medicaid program to implement a mandatory statewide program based solely on prepaid health plan enrollment, the AHCCCS had four key objectives:

1. competitive bidding for prepaid capitated contracts
2. development of a primary care physician gatekeeper network
3. copayments to control inappropriate utilization of medical services
4. restriction on freedom of choice after selection of a health plan

The state initially engaged a private contractor to run the day-to-day operations. After serious difficulties with this arrangement, however, the AHCCCS was established as a separate state agency with regulatory authority and operational oversight given to the agency director. During its first 13 years, the AHCCCS evolved into a national model providing capitated care to all categories of Medicaid beneficiaries as well as state-funded medically indigent and medically needy individuals.

The current program waiver permits the AHCCCS to require mandatory enrollment of all individuals in prepaid health plans with a 1-year lock-in and a 1-month open enrollment period each year. First-time enrollees get a 6-month guarantee of eligibility. Flexibility in financing allows the state to establish actuarial ranges for competitive bidding rather than having to set a rate as a percentage of fee-for-service experience. The state does not have to require plans to meet federal mandates of the "75/25 rule," meaning that a plan's AHCCCS enrollment could exceed 75 percent of total membership.

Competitive Bidding and Plan Participation

Arizona has used competitive bidding strategies to award acute care medical services contracts since the inception of the AHCCCS. Using encounter data reported by the health plans, actuarially valid rate ranges are established for various demographic groups. These include Aid to Families with Dependent Children (AFDC), Supplemental Security Income (SSI) with and without Medicare, children covered by federally mandated expansion, and state-funded medically needy and medically indigent residents. Health plans develop responses to the request for proposal and compete to serve the Medicaid population. During the 1994 competitive bidding cycle, 95 proposals were submitted to serve the state's 15 counties, and 42 contracts were awarded. The bidding resulted in a decline of 11 percent in capitation payment rates across the state. A recent federal General Accounting Office (GAO) report noted that health plans contracting with the AHCCCS accumulated substantial profits and that the state and federal governments were experiencing substantial costs savings compared with an aggregate of several other states with predominantly fee-for-service Medicaid programs.[8]

As of 1995, 14 health plans were contracting with the AHCCCS program, with the most common model being an individual practice association (IPA); staff and mixed model HMOs also were present. Plans owners included eight for-profit companies, three not-for-profit companies, two county governments, and one state agency. Plan enrollment ranged from 2,000 members in a small rural plan to more than 100,000 in a large IPA that covers multiple counties. A strong commitment to primary care gatekeeping can be found in most of the plans, and this is viewed as effective in promoting high-quality, cost-effective care to this population. The state medical and hospital associations have been and continue to be strong supporters of Arizona's unique model.

Impacts and Implications

The AHCCCS was established as and has continued to be a research and demonstration model and as such has had thorough, continuous assessments performed by outside evaluators commissioned by the HCFA. These evaluations have chronicled nearly every aspect of the successes, problems, and lessons learned from the experience and have systematically studied cost, utilization, quality, access, and client and provider satisfaction. The overall impact on cost has been well documented and is quite positive. Total cost savings averaged 7 percent per year over the first 11 years of the program, with annual savings growing to approximately $72 million in fiscal year 1993.[9] Of particular note is the finding that aged, blind, and disabled SSI beneficiaries showed the greatest cost savings compared with the benchmark states used to derive the cost savings estimates. The GAO reported that, although "the amounts that Arizona spends to administer its program are higher than what other states spend, these additional expenditures more than pay for themselves in net program savings."[10(p.5)]

The GAO also notes "though each state's Medicaid program is different, other states that are considering implementing or are currently operating a managed care program can benefit from Arizona's experience."[11(p.3)] It appears that the innovative model implemented in Arizona in 1982 can be a road map for many other states to follow as they gain greater flexibility to redesign their Medicaid programs in the future. There are many important lessons that can be gleaned from what Arizona has accomplished. Perhaps most important, a successful program requires substantial initial investment in developing data collection and information systems and sufficient start-up time to ensure a smooth transition from a retrospective vendor payment system to a new model of health care delivery and financing.

Rapid Recent Enrollment Growth

The past 5 years have seen enrollment grow exponentially (Figure 27–1). As Medicaid expenditures reached nearly 20 percent of the typical state budget, pursuit of cost control through managed care expansion has become nearly a frenzy for states.[12] States with established programs have rapidly expanded enrollment by making it mandatory and by attempting to cover more and more categories of eligibility. They are also moving beneficiaries toward tighter models of managed care, such as fully capitated HMOs, and away from looser models. Other states with little managed care penetration have initiated low-intensity primary care case management (PCCM) programs to begin the evolution toward more extensive models as the commercial managed care market begins to mature. Even predominantly rural areas have seen a surge of interest in managed care. An example of such an approach is described below.

Most recently, states have exploited the opportunity to obtain Section 1115 waivers from the HCFA to introduce major and multiple changes in their Medicaid programs, including expanding coverage to previously uninsured individuals.[13] Some of the states with 1115 waivers, such as Oregon and Tennessee, have achieved both notability and notoriety for their ambitious designs and implementation schedules. By the end of 1995, more than 15 states had received permission to make massive overhauls in their Medicaid programs, and every one of them proposed to use managed care models as the basic delivery system reform.

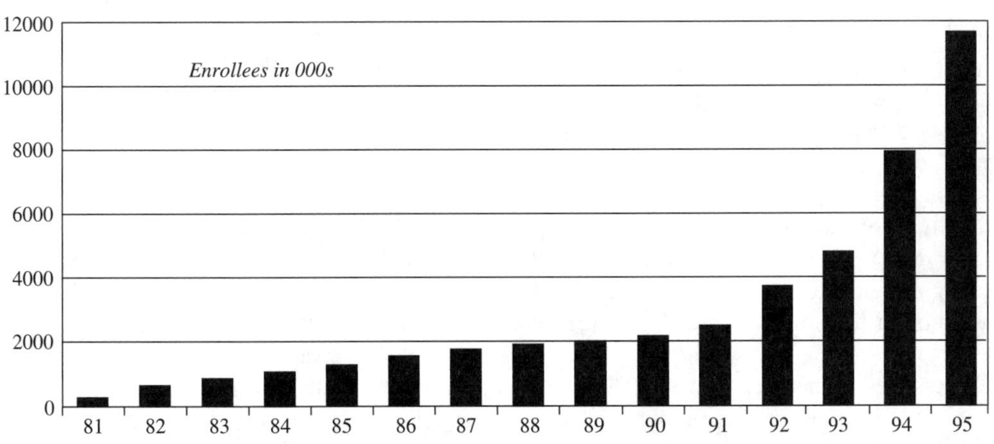

Figure 27–1 Medicaid/managed care enrollment, 1981–1995. *Source:* Health Care Financing Administration.

Virginia: An Incremental Approach

States without substantial commercial managed care plan penetration have usually had to adapt their program design and implementation plans to a pace where Medicaid advances along with the broader market rather than trying to lead it. The experience of Virginia illustrates this approach and contrasts sharply with the Arizona approach of nearly a decade earlier and the more recent Tennessee initiative. State legislation passed in 1990 required the establishment of a managed care program for AFDC beneficiaries. Because the legislation did not specify a model, the state Medicaid agency conducted a feasibility study and concluded that an incremental strategy was needed because commercial managed care penetration was low (less than 10 percent) and only present in urban areas, the state has a large nonurban population, and influential interested parties, including the state professional associations, were averse to managed care in general and HMOs in particular. The Medicaid agency established a small managed care unit to direct the program efforts and introduced the following implementation strategy.

Phase 1

In 1991, the state obtained a federal waiver to restrict freedom of choice and implemented a mandatory fee-for-service PCCM program called Medallion for AFDC beneficiaries in four diverse pilot sites with approximately 40,000 targeted enrollees. The program provided a platform for developing various operating systems and conducting extensive educational efforts for beneficiaries and providers who had limited familiarity with managed care. Once the pilot programs demonstrated program feasibility, the agency was directed to begin statewide implementation of the program on a staged, regional basis.

Program enrollment reached 350,000 by mid-1995. At that same time, the program was extended, on a mandatory basis, to nearly all noninstitutionalized Medicaid beneficiaries.

Phase 2

As HMO penetration in the commercial sector grew larger within the state, the Medicaid agency implemented in 1994 a program called Options, a voluntary HMO choice for persons wishing to opt out of Medallion. The intention of this program was to introduce mainstream managed care models to the Medicaid population and to provide the state with experience in contracting and rate setting. A master contract for HMOs was developed, and a regionalized rate structure based on the fee-for-service equivalent was set. Plans were invited to apply to qualify and were required to accept, rather than negotiate, the rates set by the state. Substantial interest was shown in the three major metropolitan areas in the state, and by late 1995 Medicaid HMO enrollment reached nearly 80,000 members in six plans.

Phase 3

The voluntary program laid the foundation for the next phase of incremental implementation, called Medallion II, which is to be a mandatory HMO enrollment program for virtually all beneficiaries.

The state plans to sequence the implementation of this program in the urban markets with multiple competing HMOs in early 1996 and within a year to have mandatory enrollment in the major metropolitan areas. Future extension of the program will depend on how fast nonurban areas progress in terms of HMO penetration or in the emergence of provider-sponsored integrated delivery systems that can accept full risk.

Impacts and Implications

The Virginia experience demonstrates how the evolution from solely fee-for-service care toward fully capitated managed care could be accomplished on an essentially statewide basis in 4 years in a state with limited commercial managed care penetration when the process was started. The Medicaid agency worked hard to preserve beneficiary–primary care physician relationships, first through aggressive recruitment of physicians into the PCCM program and then through phasing to voluntary and finally mandatory HMO enrollment as the physicians themselves began to migrate into managed care plans. The HMO industry itself has grown over this period, with eight plans participating by late 1995 and another dozen plans in some stage of discussion with state Medicaid officials.

MEDICAID AND ITS BENEFICIARIES

Understanding the opportunities and challenges for managed care in Medicaid requires an appreciation for Medicaid itself and, in particular, for the populations covered and the distribution of expenditures. The program covered 33 million persons in 1994 with costs exceeding $150 billion and more than half the support coming from the federal government. Approximately 70 percent of the persons eligible are women and children receiving assistance from the AFDC and related assistance programs. The remainder are aged, blind, and disabled individuals whose eligibility is a function of a combination of their income, their disabilities, and their medical expenses.

Variation in Expenditures

The 70/30 percent relationship in numbers of eligibles is almost completely reversed when one looks at program expenditures by eligibility category (Figure 27–2). The reason for this discrepancy can be found in the costs of eligible groups. AFDC beneficiaries in 1993 averaged approximately $950 per year for children and $1,700 for adults, and non-AFDC beneficiary costs reached nearly $8,000. Even this high average masks enormous differences within subgroups of this high-need population. Some of these individuals are nursing home residents for whom annual costs may exceed $30,000; others are in institutions for the profoundly retarded and disabled.

Cost variability for aged, blind, and disabled beneficiaries residing in the community can also be extraordinary. Kronick et al. demonstrated in 1995 that in one state the average cost of approximately $5,000 for noninstitutionalized, non-AFDC beneficiaries included large numbers of persons with no expenses and others, such as quadriplegics or people with advanced acquired immune deficiency syndrome (AIDS) with costs in excess of $20,000.[14] Most experi-

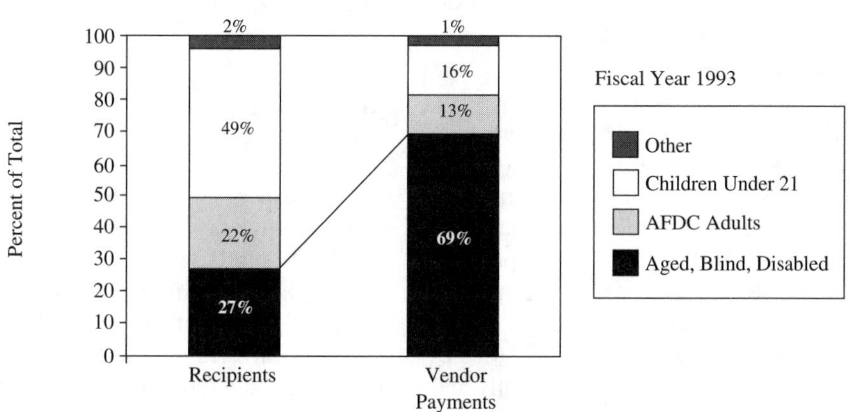

Figure 29–2 Percentage distribution of Medicaid and vendor payments by basis of eligibility. *Source:* Health Care Financing Administration.

ence, and nearly all research, on the impacts of Medicaid managed care have focused on the AFDC population. For AFDC beneficiaries, rate development and medical management have been more similar to those for commercial HMO members and more generally acceptable to health plans. Extending managed care to Medicaid populations with special needs remains the next frontier to be addressed by states, plans, and beneficiaries.

Problems in Traditional Medicaid

Meeting the needs of AFDC beneficiaries in traditional Medicaid has itself been a major challenge. This population, comprising mainly adult women and children under the age of 18, has, by definition, limited resources and a relatively narrow spectrum of medical needs, including obstetrical and perinatal services and well-child care. These individuals also have other social and sociomedical challenges that influence their ability to access care (such as transportation), and they are particularly vulnerable to impoverished, urban-based life style hazards such as violence, substance abuse, inferior housing, and related concerns. Also, intermittent eligibility for cash assistance and medical benefits leads to discontinuity in coverage and service use.

The traditionally low payment rates of the Medicaid program have long discouraged many providers from participating. This compromises access and, in effect, channels beneficiaries to a limited set of providers that would not or could not refuse to serve them. Among these providers are inner city hospitals, especially emergency departments, community health centers, public health programs, and a declining number of indigenous private practitioners who have remained in areas with major Medicaid population concentrations. Reliance on the emergency department as a major source of primary care has typified the interlocking nature of this "Medicaid syndrome" because it is both clinically and economically unsuitable for the provision of routine, continuing, first-contact medical care.[15] Because the emergency department has always been available and accessible, however, its use has led to higher than necessary program expenditures for both ambulatory and inpatient services.

The Appeal of Managed Care

Managed care models have been seen as a natural antidote to this syndrome of reliance on inappropriate and excessively costly sites for uncoordinated, episodic care. Most initiatives have targeted reductions in such care and promotion of the availability of an appropriate "medical home" to improve access to primary care through either primary care gatekeeper models or fully capitated HMO enrollment.

Two persistent challenges for applying managed care principles and experience to Medicaid, however, have been lack of cost participation by beneficiaries who qualify for eligibility because of their limited income and assets, and episodic, income-based eligibility, which makes it difficult to effect sustained changes in use and outcomes of services. Altering undesirable patterns of use and promoting more desirable ones are problematic because of the minimal economic leverage providers and plans have with members. They must rely more on education and exhortation than on financial incentives and penalties. Intermittent eligibility dilutes or may undermine altogether the benefits of preventive care and early intervention, which are key parts of managed care.

MODELS AND APPROACHES TO MANAGED CARE

Early experience with managed care for Medicaid beneficiaries was exclusively with voluntary HMO enrollment in a number of well-established plans that limited enrollment to small fractions of their total membership.[16] Beginning with the waivered programs of the early 1980s, the models and types of programs showed considerable innovation and variation, offering arrangements that were not easily compared to HMOs and the emerging form of managed care called preferred provider organizations. This variation grew until the 1990s, when Medicaid arrangements began to blend more with commercial, mainstream managed care arrangements once again.

PCCM Models

Probably the most notable form of managed care, largely pioneered in Medicaid, was the PCCM model, which enrolled beneficiaries on a mandatory basis with a provider who became the exclusive portal of entry for all nonemergency services. Patterned after a private insurance company primary care gatekeeper initiative, this model was initially adopted in Medicaid programs in Michigan and Utah, which obtained waivers to allow them to restrict beneficiary choice of provider.[17,18] Primary care physicians were paid fee for service plus a case management fee (commonly $2 to $3 per member per month) to compensate them to be available 24 hours per day, 7 days per week and to deliver or authorize all nonemergency care. These programs demonstrated the ability to guarantee access and to control excessive emergency department use and "doctor-shopping" without forcing providers or beneficiaries to join organized delivery systems such as HMOs, and there were modest cost savings associated with them. The PCCM model spread rapidly to many other states.[19] Some states, such as Maryland and Massachusetts, have augmented primary care fees in lieu of paying an explicit case management fee. Other states, such as Texas, have delegated much of the program design and implementation to their fiscal intermediary.

In some states, the lack of risk sharing in PCCM models led developers to promote enhanced models that placed physicians at risk for primary care services by paying a partial capitation rate for primary care and/or allowing the physicians to share in savings in reduced referral care. Other models created pooling mechanisms to group physicians or physicians and hospitals to permit them to bear risk and for the state to pay more inclusive capitation rates.[20] Like the more modest fee-for-service PCCM model, the basic instrument of care management was the physician gatekeeper, who offered access assurance and improved care coordination. Nevertheless, these models still did not represent bona fide integrated delivery systems, nor did they permit states to shift full financial risk through a capitation payment for the full scope of Medicaid services.

Fully Capitated Managed Care Plan Model

Arizona's AHCCCS program represented the first large-scale effort to enroll beneficiaries on a mandatory basis in prepaid health plans. Other substate programs were also attempted in California, Missouri, Minnesota, and New York and later in Wisconsin and Ohio. Beneficiaries were permitted choice among plans, but traditional Medicaid was not an option for the covered eligibility groups. Despite much concern about restricting choice only to prepaid plans, the experience of most beneficiaries did not repeat the California scandals. This was due in part to federal requirements that Medicaid members could not exceed more than 75 percent of total plan membership, although waivers were granted to permit some plans to transition to this level.[21,22] Expanded oversight and better selection of contracting plans, however, also played a role in improved experience.

States reported savings and utilization experience consistent with expectations in most mandatory HMO programs, and the feasibility of executing the marketing and enrollment functions of a multiple choice program was demonstrated. In addition to these mandatory programs, a number of states began to offer HMO enrollment on a voluntary basis as an opportunity to opt out of either traditional Medicaid or a baseline PCCM program. Despite concerns about marketing abuses in some states, these programs have also proven that the choice-making process for low-income persons can be successful and that plans can adequately meet the service needs of their enrollees, nearly all of whom are AFDC adults and children. Voluntary programs are susceptible to biased selection dynamics, however, which indicate that the plans may be enrolling low-cost beneficiaries as high-cost persons remain in traditional Medicaid or PCCM programs.[23]

There are some new carve-out programs that are being developed for selected non-AFDC subpopulations or for selected services for all populations. These models are likely to be prototypes for the next generation of Medicaid managed care as we see interest in enrolling those beneficiaries who are major consumers of Medicaid expenditures.[24,25] A discussion of these programs is beyond the scope of this general presentation, but they suggest that generic managed care models may be increasingly adapted to extend coverage to persons with special needs, including chronic mental illness, physical and developmental disabilities, and other chronic, debilitating conditions such as AIDS.

IMPACTS OF MANAGED CARE

Like findings from most managed care research, the available evidence from Medicaid is relatively uneven and somewhat out of date. As public sector initiatives, however, the evaluation results are readily available, and some efforts have been made to collate the accumulated findings from the Medicaid experience.[26,27]

Cost Savings

The evidence of cost savings comes mostly from federal and state financed evaluations, which are required on waiver renewal. One problem with the reliability of these studies is that states often have had a strong interest in demonstrating savings to ensure that their waiver renewal is granted. The findings suggest savings ranging from 5 percent to 15 percent per enrolled beneficiary, which means in nearly every case AFDC beneficiaries. It is notable that savings can be guaranteed in mandatory HMO enrollment models by virtue of setting rates below expected fee-for-service expenditures, but they must be earned in PCCM programs by reducing service volumes because fee-for-service payments remain in play. Voluntary HMO enrollment programs have rarely been studied in depth because states do not need to obtain a waiver or to commission an external assessment for waiver renewal. Because selection bias is likely to occur in voluntary programs, unless this is adequately adjusted for it is difficult to ascertain whether a state achieved savings, even if plans are paid less than the expected fee-for-service–equivalent rate.

It should be emphasized again that the AFDC population incurs only about 30 percent of Medicaid costs. The only large-scale evaluation of non-AFDC beneficiaries comes from Arizona, where savings well in excess of those for AFDC enrollees have been reported, although making comparative analyses is complicated there by virtue of the fact that there was no prior Medicaid program and no in-state comparison group.[28] A recent study of Massachusetts' carved-out, single-vendor mental health program is another illustration of promising savings for such models, but more study is needed to assess the durability of reported savings.[29]

Utilization, Satisfaction, and Quality

Utilization effects indicate that both HMO and PCCM programs are reducing emergency department use and inpatient services by substantial amounts, as would be expected, although most findings indicate that further reductions in emergency department use are attainable. The effects on physician service use are more mixed, depending on the incentives in place, with some evidence showing that primary care is being substituted for specialty care and that beneficiaries see primary physicians as their medical home more frequently and receive a higher proportion of their care from them.[30] A persistent problem in measuring effects on utilization changes associated with managed care is that data availability is very uneven because

PCCM programs and health plans that make capitation payments may not get reliable encounter or claims data.

Implications for satisfaction and quality effects are limited and inconclusive. Although satisfaction remains relatively high for Medicaid beneficiaries in managed care, just as in commercial managed care, there is evidence to suggest that dislocation and disruption of established provider relations in mandatory enrollment programs engender some dissatisfaction.[31,32] It should be noted, however, that there are relatively few studies of satisfaction in fee-for-service Medicaid to provide a reliable benchmark. Studies of quality of care in Medicaid managed care programs suffer from the same problem: little baseline evidence from traditional Medicaid. The limited amount of work in this area suggests neither quality gains nor losses.[33] This may be because the models of managed care in Medicaid are disparate and some have little quality improvement built into them. In addition, episodic eligibility for beneficiaries may undermine even the most diligent efforts to improve outcomes.

Administrative Costs and Efforts

The final areas of importance in assessing the Medicaid managed care experience from a state perspective are the level of administrative effort and the ability to get budget predictability in future cost expenditures.[34] In both instances, the PCCM programs have serious limitations. In the PCCM model, many of the administrative functions associated with provider recruitment and selection, enrollment, provider payment, performance monitoring, and customer service remain within the purview of the Medicaid agency because it is contracting with individual physicians rather than with a managed care entity. A few states, such as Massachusetts, contract out for management of the PCCM network, but most attempt to perform this with limited staff and other resources. Others, such as Texas, use their fiscal intermediary to handle PCCM selection and ongoing provider relations activities.

HMO enrollment programs afford the opportunity to shift many of the administrative functions and their accompanying costs from the state agency to the contracting plan. Likewise, contracting with a plan for a fixed, prepaid capitation payment for the full scope of Medicaid benefits facilitates risk shifting and greatly improved budget predictability in future costs for state agencies. Future increases become subject to negotiation rather than driven by inflation and volume trends. It is for these reasons that interest in contracting with prepaid health plans has grown enormously in recent years. Coupled with the eagerness of many established plans to grow their membership from all payer sources, there has been a dramatic shift toward HMO enrollment as the major form of Medicaid managed care in recent years.

OPERATIONAL ISSUES FOR THE MEDICAID PRODUCT LINE

The key operational matters in Medicaid managed care programs vary greatly depending on the model or models that states adopt and implement. The PCCM models typically are launched off the same administrative systems and infrastructure as conventional Medicaid. Fee for service is normally maintained, with reliance on the existing set of participating providers and limited efforts to foster a true network-based delivery system. Some additional quality monitoring or beneficiary education programs may be overlaid on the PCCM program, but this is limited. Contracting with prepaid health plans represents a different approach to most operational issues, with perhaps the most crucial challenge being determination of rate structure and contracting strategies.

Rate Setting and Contracting

State Medicaid programs have operated under a federal requirement that their payments to capitated health plans may not exceed the expected fee-for-service–equivalent costs. To comply with this requirement, rates are commonly developed with actuarial assistance based on the fee-for-service equivalency, and then a factor of 95 percent or less is applied to determine what plans will receive on a per member per month basis. Various adjustments for selected service carve-outs or stop-loss contributions may be made, and then, depending on the complexity of the rate book developed by the state, eligibility category, demographic, and regional adjusters are applied to arrive at a final payment rate. This may be the rate paid, or it may represent an upper bound against which bids might be evaluated.

Who qualifies to receive capitation payments is determined by the contracting strategy of the states.[35] Some states develop a master contract and allow all plans that meet qualifications to participate; others set a limit on the number of plans with which they wish to contract and make a selection based on a variety of criteria. Voluntary enrollment programs typically have taken this latter approach because the plans are given the opportunity to entice as many of the eligible population to leave either the traditional Medicaid program or a PCCM program. Mandatory programs are more likely to limit the number of plans that can be offered and to select them based on a competitive process. A good illustration of this approach is the use of competitive bidding by plans to qualify as noted in the discussion of the AHCCCS. Other states are likely to use this approach in the future to enable them to exercise leverage with a limited number of plans, to follow downward trends in the managed care market, and to manage better the choice-making environment for beneficiaries. Medicaid buying will parallel the strategies of private employers that winnow down choices for their employees for the same reasons. As noted in the description of the AHCCCS, however, many years may pass before a program is mature and stable enough to experience bona fide competitive bidding.

Eligibility, Marketing, and Enrollment

Managed care enrollment with plans or primary care physicians is significantly affected by the intermittent nature of eligibility for Medicaid beneficiaries. Income fluctuations may disrupt eligibility and thereby sever members' connection with a prepaid plan or make it necessary for them to seek care from other providers if Medicaid coverage is lost. On the front end, the enrollment process is affected by how well an individual understands the options offered at the time of gaining eligibility and how a Medicaid agency has organized the choice-making process. A growing number of states have selected independent enrollment broker or benefits counselor contractors to manage this process on behalf of the state. Brokers may disseminate information and respond to inquiries from new eligibles as well as screen the marketing and other promotional material made available to beneficiaries to promote an informed choice.

Efforts to regulate the marketing behavior of managed care plans have been controversial in the Medicaid program ever since the MediCal scandals of the early 1970s, and they continue up to the present time. As an individual choice situation, plans invest substantial resources in member acquisition activities. Some plans estimate that it may cost the equivalent of 1 month's capitation to acquire a new member.

In light of intermittent eligibility, the turnover among members is high, and aggressive marketing is used to replenish membership by many plans. Many concerns and complaints have arisen in states where enrollment grows rapidly. Critics suggest that new members are poorly informed or purposely misinformed to get them to sign up or that frivolous gimmickry is employed to cause beneficiaries to switch from one plan to another. State oversight roles vary dramatically, and it appears that some states have done a better job than others in devising prudent marketing policies and vigorous regulation and enforcement of them. Again, it is useful to look upon the role of Medicaid as the equivalent of the employee benefit manager in a private company, who negotiates with plans, makes available a limited set of choices, and then orchestrates the actual choice-making process.

A distinct challenge in enrollment in mandatory programs (and an increasing proportion of programs are becoming mandatory for many eligibles) is that a large percentage of Medicaid beneficiaries may fail to exercise a choice of plan or PCCM when offered an opportunity. Assignment techniques are used to complete this connection of a beneficiary with a source of care. Some approaches may be purely random assignment rotated across participating providers, or the process may be more systematically guided by using information about prior contact with providers by claims review, geographic proximity, specialty suitability, and other approaches. Distribution of assignees is significant, especially in prepaid arrangements, because these persons appear to be low-cost users and thus are attractive members for plans to gain.[36] Some states use this distribution process to reward plans for being low bidders or agreeing to additional service concessions, such as covering a broader territory. Other target assignees for certain types of plans may include, for example, "safety net" providers that the state may be interested in supporting or protecting.

Provider Network Issues

Most efforts to extend managed care to Medicaid beneficiaries have involved a concerted attempt to incorporate traditional providers of services to these populations into provider networks. The reasons for this are obvious because the preponderance of beneficiaries reside in areas with limited numbers of provider options. Major sources of care, such as community health centers, urban hospital outpatient programs, and indigenous community-based physicians, have provided the bulk of care both for Medicaid beneficiaries and for persons without insurance coverage, who are often the same individuals who move from periods of eligibility to ineligibility. PCCM programs typically recruit these providers to play major roles, and many prepaid health plans have incorporated them into their networks because of their location and established relationships. Inclusion of providers with strong ties to beneficiaries is an effective way to grow enrollment rapidly.

Some of these traditional providers have in fact sponsored their own health plans, although they often struggle to gain sufficient non-Medicaid members to meet the 75/25 federal mandate on maximum Medicaid membership. As more well-established commercial plans enter into the Medicaid market, new controversies have arisen about the inclusion of traditional, "safety net," or essential community providers in networks and the terms and payment rates they will receive. Past public policies have given special consideration to selected providers, such as health centers and hospitals with disproportionately high levels of uncompensated care. New contracting with private health plans may no longer perpetuate such considerations, however, and this clearly places these providers in jeopardy. Policymakers will be drawn into these issues because the demise of many of these providers could create serious access problems for persons without any coverage.

A final issue that is sure to grow in importance as managed care is extended to non-AFDC populations, such as persons with chronic mental illness and developmental or physical disabilities, is how well conventional prepaid health plans or PCCM models can serve these beneficiaries. Some states permit specialists to qualify as PCCM providers for people with disabilities. Others make enrollment by special need beneficiaries voluntary rather than mandatory. In others, PCCM appears to avoid confrontations by liberally authorizing contacts with specialty providers. Special carve-out programs have been commonly used for the mentally ill in many instances; sometimes these are carved out by the state or, in other instances, by the health plans that subcontract for managed behavioral and mental health care. Plans have had limited experience with people with chronic illness or substantial disabilities, so that their existing networks and other systems may be inadequate to serve them.[37] Whether plans can and will augment their operations to expand their capacity or whether special subplans built around traditional specialty providers will arise remains to be seen.

Limitations on Physician Risk

In 1996, the Office of the Inspector General of the Department of Health and Human Services issued final regulations placing limitations on the amount of risk a health plan may put a physician at in a Medicare or Medicaid program. These new regulations effectively limit the amount of risk to 25 percent, and place additional requirements on the health plan regarding stop-loss insurance and member surveys. The reader is referred to Chapter 8 for a discussion of these new regulations.

Delivery and Utilization Management Systems

Designing delivery and utilization management systems for the Medicaid product line is challenging for plans whose membership has come from employed individuals and their dependents. Medicaid beneficiaries typically require supportive services to enable them to overcome access barriers to care, including transportation and community-based outreach and other social service efforts. Financial, safety/security, and other impediments to obtaining services on a timely basis require plans to adopt active interventions to deliver care in nontraditional locations, sometimes with diversely skilled personnel. High rates of teen pregnancy and other preventable conditions among eligible members place additional demands on HMOs that believe early intervention, health promotion, and preventive services are crucial elements of successful managed care plans.

Promoting more discreet and appropriate use of high-cost services such as emergency departments is a major goal of most plans and PCCM programs. Because hospitals are reluctant to deny care and because beneficiaries do not have cost-sharing responsibilities, hospitals frequently feel that plans and PCCM models do not do enough to reduce unneeded use despite the widespread evidence of reduced emergency department use in these programs.[38] Some plans have developed nurse call systems for off-hour coverage; others may penalize physician compensation for inappropriately authorized care. Many observers believe, however, that the availability of a bona fide primary care provider, in time, should wean most beneficiaries off the emergency department toward a legitimate medical home.

Member Education and Satisfaction

The emergency department issue also illustrates another area in which Medicaid-serving plans report added challenges: member education. For persons without prior managed care experience, the structure and operations of organized delivery systems can be confusing and distressing. Obtaining care on a planned, regimented basis may be new for those low-income persons who have sought care on an episodic basis from as-available providers. Also, they may have lingual or educational disadvantages to overcome to access care. Orientation programs for new members are seen as crucial, as is ready access to culturally sensitive customer relations and provider personnel. Well-established commercial plans frequently find the need to hire additional multicultural and multilingual staff and to develop targeted programs to adapt their operations to serve this new customer base.

Relatively little is known about the enrollment and disenrollment patterns of Medicaid beneficiaries in managed care arrangements, especially in mandatory enrollment programs. Few states have systematically collected data on this, and many plans do not separate information about Medicaid from other enrollment/disenrollment data. The high level of involuntary disenrollment due to loss of eligibility makes it important to isolate and explore the reasons for voluntary disenrollment among Medicaid health plan members. Studies of satisfaction have typically found that Medicaid members are generally satisfied, but an important question for plans to examine in the future will be how Medicaid and commercial plan members may be similar and/or different in their levels of satisfaction. As plans are asked to enroll beneficiaries with higher or multiple needs, tracking satisfaction among such subgroups will be a focus for state purchaser and advocacy groups.

Quality Assurance/Improvement

As with other buyers of managed care, Medicaid has struggled with how to promote accountability and continuous improvement among its managed care contractors. Ironically, quality in the PCCM models has received little attention, in part because of the minimal changes these models make in the traditional fee-for-service delivery systems despite the potential barrier to care that the gatekeeper represents. Most quality concerns have focused on contracting with prepaid health plans because of the concern that the incentives may produce underserving and that the lack of financial resources of Medicaid beneficiaries impedes their ability to go out of network to get care, as is assumed to be possible among HMO members in the employed sector.

The HCFA has promoted the Quality Assurance Reform Initiative as a set of standards and policies for states to adopt and follow in their contracting with health plans. These standards require plans to have established quality improvement programs that systematically address problems that are particularly endemic to Medicaid eligibles and state Medicaid agencies to conduct oversight of these programs. In addition, states are required to have an external quality review organization conduct periodic audits of quality improvement efforts at the plan level. Some states are now exploring regional quality review organizations using the model established by Tennessee, where the organization is a contractor of the state that oversees the quality of care in HMOs. A regional quality review organization concept would establish an entity capable of conducting clinical assessments with proven methodologies to make sound comparisons of care between fee-for-service providers and HMOs and among HMOs. The regional feature would allow states to share costs and to make state-to-state managed care program comparisons using identical assessment methodologies.

A related development has been the addition of several new performance indicators in the Health Plan Employer Data Information Set (see Chapter 20) that are intended to produce uniform measures that are particularly pertinent to Medicaid beneficiaries, including stage of pregnancy at time of enrollment, cultural diversity of membership, and children's access to primary care providers. The previously discussed concerns with intermittent eligibility are particularly problematic in computing meaningful performance rates for plans serving Medicaid enrollees. In addition, discontinuity in enrollment makes it difficult to attribute accountability to a plan for effects on the health outcomes of Medicaid members.

Clearly, however, a number of states acting as aggressive purchasers are pushing plans both to report more detailed data and to demonstrate more convincingly the effects that they have on the well-being of Medicaid members. Some states are now demanding that plans submit detailed encounter level data to permit the state to compare HMO enrollee experience with non-HMO beneficiary fee-for-service experience.[39] Once again, this parallels the same types of pressures that health plans are facing from private purchasers seeking demonstrated value for their money.

Information System Sophistication and Infrastructure

Undergirding the performance of virtually all these operational functions is the presumption that states will have the data and data management capacity to make informed programmatic decisions. Rate setting and refinement, contract monitoring, eligibility and enrollment tracking, service cost and use information, member experience assessment, and evaluation of evidence of quality performance and improvement all require a systematic and sustained investment in flexible information systems. The dramatic shift from passive payer to active purchaser and sponsor has compelled state agencies and their contractors to make a major investment in these systems, without which states will fail to exploit the opportunities available to them in a buyer's market.

Some states have already made major investments in this area and are ably transitioning to this new-found status as megabuyer. Others are likely to struggle through the process of assembling the components of a bona fide managed care initiative but will fail to invest adequately in the crucial "control panel" that a sophisticated information system represents. Still other states will probably conclude that subcontracting many of these functions will be a sensible approach, one that can permit them to maintain control but not have to devote limited staff and other resources to carrying out these functions directly. The experience from Arizona suggests that an aggressive purchasing strategy may contribute to higher administrative costs, but these costs can be more than offset by greater reductions in service expenditures.[40]

FUTURE TRENDS

Major changes in Medicaid will come with the shifting of far greater administrative flexibility in return for a slowing in the rate of growth in federal support for the program. These changes will profoundly affect the extent to which states will rely on managed care models for their beneficiary groups.

Greater Variability among and within States

Approaches to adopting managed care in Medicaid programs have varied significantly among states subject to the general requirements imposed by the HCFA through the waiver granting process. The demise of much of the federal oversight role will permit states to exercise greater flexibility, resulting in less uniformity from state to state and even within states. Contracting strategies may become more focused, possibly using only a sole source in some locales, and beneficiaries may no longer have a choice of plans. The selection of risk-bearing contractors may not be limited only to established managed care organizations. Plans may also serve only Medicaid beneficiaries because the 75/25 rule will no longer exist. Relaxing these and other traditional requirements may make it possible for states to promote innovation and experimentation, but it will also make it challenging for existing plans to anticipate and respond to state strategies. For beneficiaries, it is not clear how strong state commitment to consumer protection will be.

Prepaid Managed Care Everywhere

An unprecedented cap on growth of federal financial support for Medicaid would send states a powerful and unequivocal message: Reduce the growth rate of Medicaid spending to the capped rate, or contribute more state dollars to finance the program. For many states this will mean a fierce commitment to fixing the growth rate for as much of the program as possible. One way to achieve this, in principle, is to enroll beneficiaries in prepaid managed care arrangements where future rates of growth in capitation payments are negotiated and thus fully predictable. Traditional fee-for-service PCCM models cannot provide this guarantee. As a result, it is likely that prepaid arrangements will be pursued nearly across the board for all beneficiary groups and in all locations within a state. This pressure will push managed care initiatives faster and further than they have previously gone in most states, with the exception of Arizona.

Mainstreaming versus Special Plans and Models

The frenzied pursuit of risk-bearing contractors with which to enroll beneficiaries will raise several challenges. Chief among them will be the extent to which state agencies attempt to achieve enrollment of beneficiaries in established, commercial HMOs that have a broad base of membership. Such arrangements offer the opportunity to mainstream beneficiaries in plans that serve a broad spectrum of members and have recruited into their networks those providers that have traditionally served persons covered by Medicaid. Other states may choose to contract with plans with limited or no commercial membership either because the managed care market is underdeveloped, such as in Tennessee, or because they may wish to give special opportunities to traditional "safety net" providers to develop targeted managed care programs for low-income persons, such as in California. This same issue will be played out for persons with special needs, with whom conventional HMOs have had little experience, and for the specialty providers serving these groups, which have had limited exposure to managed care. Moving into uncharted territory will be trying for all parties concerned.

Vulnerable Populations and Endangered Providers

As managed care moves from an alternative to a mainstream delivery system status in Medicaid, its fitness for Medicaid's distinct beneficiary and provider constituencies will be tested. As noted above, some of these concerns relate to whether states aspire to and can achieve mainstreaming of beneficiaries in conventional plans. It also relates to whether the distinct character of a public "safety net" program such as Medicaid that serves populations with complex, chronic needs for multiple social and sociomedical services is compatible with the traditional medical model of plans serving mostly healthy persons.

It is also instructive to recognize that Medicaid's methods of payments to its core providers of care have become a means to cross-subsidize care for persons without coverage who rely on these same providers. Managed care contracting for Medicaid beneficiaries profoundly threatens this arrangement because it privatizes the decisions about network inclusion and methods of provider payments. Providers that serve large numbers of uninsured may not be incorporated into networks, or, if they are, payment arrangements negotiated with plans may not provide sufficient resources to support the delivery of uncompensated care. Consequently, many "safety net" providers will become genuinely endangered species as states rush into managed care arrangements.

Public–Private Purchaser Convergence

Aligning Medicaid's purchasing posture toward managed care with what is occurring in the private sector and elsewhere in the public sector has considerable appeal, despite the caveats raised above. Some states, such as Massachusetts and Minnesota, participate actively in cross-sector purchaser alliances and initiatives, thereby adding their lives as additional leverage in health plan–buyer negotiations. Areas such as quality improvement and consumer information are especially well served when reporting requirements can be conformed across several major purchasers. Plans can develop uniform reporting mechanisms, and buyers can obtain comparable data across plans and across buyers to assess performance and promote improvement. Greater flexibility in a block grant environment should further contribute to these developments because some states will align purchasing efforts across all public programs for which they are responsible, and the step to conform their actions with those of private buyers becomes a natural one. Nevertheless, it will be important to track how private purchasers respond to what is likely to be growing pressure on plans to cross-subsidize their Medicaid product from the private customers or even from state employee contracts.

Sustainable Profitability of the Medicaid Product Line

The new era of state flexibility and reduced federal roles does present an area of considerable uncertainty and concern for managed care plans that contrasts with the otherwise bright prospects. It is not clear whether rates paid by states to enroll Medicaid beneficiaries will be sufficient, especially in future years, when the rate of program expenditure increases will flatten dramatically. Plans are legitimately anxious about this, in part because of the history of low payments in the fee-for-service Medicaid program and declining political support for public programs.

Plans are currently prepared to accept Medicaid rates apparently because they believe they can reduce utilization to outperform capitation payments; or because the additional lives that Medicaid enrollment brings them produce additional leverage that they can use in provider negotiations, or because states have made enrolling Medicaid beneficiaries a precondition to serving other publicly sponsored groups, such as state employees. Plans also have realized, however, that states may refuse to grant increases or even may demand rollbacks in rates, and plans will have to live within budget constraints in future years. This strategy is even more likely to arise if states attempt to expand or maintain the number of persons eligible for Medicaid while they face declining federal support. There will be a level below which credible plans cannot agree to go if they are to serve enrolled populations. What this actual threshold level is cannot be predicted but will have to be discovered mutually by plans and states.

CONCLUSION

Medicaid has witnessed the same kind of transformation in its financing and delivery systems as the private sector has witnessed, despite a somewhat slower pace of transition. The pace has been modulated in part because of distinct features of a public program, its core providers, and its beneficiary populations. In addition, because Medicaid is a national program, the rate of change has varied dramatically as a result of local market conditions and developments. Current activity has taken on an accelerated pace as both purchasers and health plans are successfully overcoming many obstacles to and compunctions about contracting with one another to meet beneficiary needs.

Far greater change looms on the horizon, however, given the fundamental restructuring of the federal–state partnership on which Medicaid has been based. This restructuring will impel states to move to managed care more quickly and more inclusively, bringing managed care arrangements to many subpopulations that have not previously been exposed to managed care. The uncertainty is likely to intensify in future years as financial support for the program becomes more stressed and states face hard choices about populations and services to cover. Expanded managed care has considerable promise for state Medicaid agencies and for the beneficiaries for whom they provide coverage. For managed care plans, these developments represent both great opportunities and large risks.

Study Questions

1. In what ways have the Arizona and Virginia Medicaid managed care programs differed in design and development and why have these differences occurred?

2. What problems is managed care expected to solve for state Medicaid programs and for beneficiaries?
3. Why has the primary care case management model been so popular in Medicaid and why is it likely to begin decline in its use in the states?
4. What are some of the key ways in which Medicaid managed care differs from commercial managed care?
5. What factors are contributing to current and future rapid growth of managed care in Medicaid?

REFERENCES AND NOTES

1. Health Care Financing Administration (HCFA), *Medicaid Managed Care Enrollment Report* (Baltimore, Md.: HCFA, 1995).
2. R. Stevens and R. Stevens, *Welfare Medicine in America* (New York, N.Y.: Free Press, 1974).
3. D. Freund and R. Hurley, Medicaid Managed Care: Lessons for Health Reform, *Annual Review of Public Health* 16 (1995): 473–496.
4. D. Chavin and A. Treseder, California's Prepaid Health Plans, *Hastings Law Journal* 28 (1977): 685–760.
5. H. Luft, *Health Maintenance Organizations: Dimensions of Performance* (New York, N.Y.: Basic Books, 1981).
6. D. Freund and R. Hurley, Medicaid Managed Care: Selected Issues in Program Origins, Design, and Research, *Annual Review of Public Health* 8 (1987): 137–164.
7. Freund and Hurley, Medicaid Managed Care: Lessons for Health Reform.
8. General Accounting Office (GAO), *Arizona Medicaid: Competition among Managed Care Plans Lowers Program Costs* (Washington, D.C.: GAO, 1995).
9. N. McCall, et al., Medicaid Managed Care Cost Savings: The Arizona Experience, *Health Affairs* 2 (1994): 234–245.
10. General Accounting Office, *Arizona Medicaid.*
11. General Accounting Office, *Arizona Medicaid.*
12. Kaiser Commission on the Future of Medicaid, *The Medicaid Cost Explosion* (Washington, D.C.: Kaiser Commission, 1993).
13. S. Rosenbaum and J. Darnell, *Medicaid Statewide Demonstrations: Overview of Approved and Proposed Section 1115 Proposals, Policy Brief* (Washington, D.C.: Kaiser Commission on the Future of Medicaid, 1994).
14. R. Kronick, et al., Making Risk Adjustment Work for Everyone, *Inquiry* 32 (1995): 41–55.
15. R. Hurley, et al., *Medicaid Managed Care: Lessons for Policy and Program Design* (Ann Arbor, Mich.: Health Administration Press, 1993).
16. Freund and Hurley, Medicaid Managed Care: Selected Issues.
17. S. Moore, Cost Containment through Risk-Sharing by Primary Care Physicians, *New England Journal of Medicine* 300 (1979): 1359–1362.
18. D. Freund, *Medicaid Reform: Four Studies of Case Management* (Washington, D.C.: American Enterprise Institute, 1984).
19. Hurley, et al., *Medicaid Managed Care.*
20. Hurley, et al., *Medicaid Managed Care.*
21. Kaiser Commission on the Future of Medicaid, *Medicaid Managed Care: Lessons from the Literature* (Washington, D.C.: Kaiser Commission, 1995).
22. National Academy for State Health Policy, *Medicaid Managed Care: Guide for the State*, 2d ed. (Portland, Me.: National Academy for State Health Policy, 1995).
23. Freund and Hurley, Medicaid Managed Care: Lessons for Health Reform.
24. J. Christianson, et al., Utah's Prepaid Mental Health Plan: The First Year, *Health Affairs* 14 (1995): 160–172.
25. J. Callahan, et al., Mental Health/Substance Abuse Treatment in Managed Care: The Massachusetts Medicaid Experience, *Health Affairs* 14 (1995): 173–184.
26. Hurley, et al., *Medicaid Managed Care.*
27. Kaiser Commission, *Medicaid Managed Care.*
28. McCall, et al., Medicaid Managed Care Cost Savings.
29. Callahan, et al., Mental Health/Substance Abuse Treatment.
30. Hurley, et al., *Medicaid Managed Care.*
31. R. Hurley, et al., Rollover Effects in Gatekeeper Programs: Cushioning the Impact of Restricted Choice, *Inquiry* 28 (1991): 375–384.
32. M. Gold, et al., *Managed Care and Low-Income Populations: A Case Study in Tennessee* (Washington, D.C.: Mathematica Policy Research, 1995).
33. Kaiser Commission, *Medicaid Managed Care.*
34. National Academy for State Health Policy, *Medicaid Managed Care.*

35. National Academy for State Health Policy, *Medicaid Managed Care.*

36. R. Hurley and D. Freund, Determinants of Provider Selection or Assignment in a Mandatory Case Management Program and Their Implications for Utilization, *Inquiry* 25 (1988): 402–410.

37. S. Tanenbaum and R. Hurley, The Disabled and the Managed Care Frenzy: A Cautionary Note, *Health Affairs* 14 (1996): 213–219.

38. Hurley, et al., *Medicaid Managed Care.*

39. K. Piper and P. Bartels, Medicaid Primary Care: HMOs or Fee-for-Service?, *Public Welfare* (Spring 1995): 18–21.

40. General Accounting Office, *Arizona Medicaid.*

SUGGESTED READING

Crandal, P. and Troutman, J. 1994. Member Education: Communicating to Diverse Membership Populations–Reaching into the Medicaid Population. Public Relations in Managed Care: Communicating in an Era of Health Care Consumerism, Section 13, 9 pp. San Francisco, Calif., 17–18 March. Washington, D.C.: American Association of Health Plans (formerly GHAA).

Freund, D. 1984. *Medicaid Reform: Four Studies of Case Management.* Washington, D.C. American Enterprise Institute.

Hurley, R., D. Freund, and J. Paul, 1993. *Medicaid Managed Care: Lessons for Policy and Program Design.* Ann Arbor, Mich.: Health Administration Press.

Health Care Financing Administration, Medicaid Bureau. 1992. *A Health Care Quality Improvement System for Medicaid Coordinated Care: A Product of the National Quality Assurance Reform Initiative.* McLean, Va.: U.S. Department of Health and Human Services National Clearinghouse of Primary Care Information.

Health Care Financing Administration. 1995. *Medicaid Managed Care Enrollment Report.* Baltimore: HCFA.

Kaiser Commission on the Future of Medicaid. 1995. *Medicaid Managed Care: Lessons from the Literature.* Washington, D.C.

McCall, Nelda, et al. 1994. Medicaid Managed Care Cost Savings: The Arizona Experience, *Health Affairs*, 2: 234–245.

Monfiletto, E. 1994. Assimiliating the Medicaid Population. *Medical Interface* 7(7): 59–62.

National Academy for State Health Policy. 1995. *Medicaid Managed Care: Guide for the States*, 2nd ed. Portland, Me.: National Academy.

Part VI

Regulatory and Legal Issues

"A wise government knows how to enforce
with temper or to conciliate
with dignity."

George Grenville
(1712–1770)
Speech against expulsion of John Wilkes, in Parliament (1769)

Chapter 28

State Regulation of Managed Care

Garry Carneal

Study Objectives

- Describe how various managed care organizations are regulated by state agencies
- Identify what steps state regulators take to safeguard the interest of consumers
- Provide a detailed overview of how HMOs are licensed and recertified
- Discuss the problems associated with anti-managed care legislation
- Highlight the inter-relationship between state and federal regulation
- Understand how regulation is driven by market segmentation and the challenges of maintaining a level regulatory playing field among various forms of managed care

Integration and innovation by managed care organizations (MCOs) are rapidly changing the health care marketplace. These changes pose significant challenges for state and federal regulators charged with protecting consumer interests and maintaining a level regulatory playing field. A central goal of licensure requirements is to ensure that consumers receive the medical coverage that they have been promised.

Regulators, through appropriate statutory authority, must issue and update regulations continually and revitalize efforts to oversee health plan operations to provide strong consumer protections for all health plan enrollees. These efforts are necessary to ensure a fair and level competitive environment. The organizational structure of managed care plans, however, usually determines how they are regulated by government officials, especially in the states. In addition to enabling statutes and regulations, other sources of authority govern MCO operations. Regulators supplement their regulations with written policy statements, and internal office policies help them address specific issues. Federal oversight also may play an important role, depending on the managed care product offering.

In most cases, the key to state regulation is the fact that the MCO has assumed insurance risk for the provision of medical services [e.g., health maintenance organizations (HMOs) and physician–hospital organizations (PHOs)], or the MCO provides one or more services pursuant to a fully insured arrangement [e.g., preferred provider organizations (PPOs) and utilization review organizations (UROs)].

This chapter highlights the role of state regulation and MCO operations. In particular, it de-

Garry Carneal is President of Utilization Review Accreditation Commission in Washington, D.C. Formerly, he was Vice President of the American Association of Health Plans (recently formed through the merger of the Group Health Association of America, Inc. and the American Managed Care Review Association, Inc.).

scribes governance of HMO operations. HMOs serve as the best case study of state-based managed care regulation because they have been regulated the most extensively by the states. Many of the regulatory concerns detailed below are based on the HMO Model Act and the *HMO Examination Handbook*, both of which were adopted by the National Association of Insurance Commissioners (NAIC).[1] The NAIC represents insurance departments in the 50 states and U.S. territories. In 1972, the NAIC adopted the HMO Model Act. The NAIC wanted to create a model bill that clearly authorized the establishment of HMOs and provided for an ongoing regulatory monitoring system. The HMO Model Act, or substantial portions thereof, has now been enacted by 28 states. The NAIC, along with the National Association of Managed Care Regulators, continues to develop new regulatory guidelines for the MCO and insurance industries.

STATE OVERSIGHT: THE REGULATORY PROCESS

HMOs

On the state level, HMOs usually are regulated by more than one agency. Typically, regulatory supervision is shared by the departments of insurance and health. Insurance regulators assume principal responsibility for the financial aspects of HMO operations. Health regulators focus on quality of care issues, utilization patterns, and the ability of participating providers to provide adequate care. In a few instances, other state subdivisions may be charged with some supervisory duties. For example, whereas California's Department of Insurance is charged with overseeing PPOs, the state's Department of Corporations regulates HMOs, which are organized under the California Knox Keene Act. In a few states, only one agency oversees all MCO questions. For example, the North Carolina Department of Insurance regulates HMOs, PPOs, and indemnity plans.

Licensure

HMOs obtain licensure by applying for a certificate of authority (COA). An organization may be incorporated for the sole purpose of becoming licensed as an HMO, or an existing company may sponsor an HMO product line through a subsidiary or affiliated organization. Applications usually are processed by the insurance department and, among other items, include the following documents: corporate bylaws, sample provider and group contract forms, evidence of coverage forms, financial statements, financial feasibility plan, description of service area, internal grievance procedures, and the proposed quality assurance program. Payment of licensing fees is usually required, and about one third of the states assess premium taxes against HMOs.[2]

The licensure and recertification process provides state officials with a mechanism to ensure that the HMO is operating properly and is in compliance with all the applicable laws and regulations. If an HMO or other health plan fails to submit to this oversight, it probably will be considered by regulators as engaging in the unauthorized practice of insurance and may be subject to criminal and civil penalties.

Certificate of Need

In addition to obtaining a COA, HMOs may be subject to a state's certificate of need (CON) law. Thirty-four states and the District of Columbia have CON statutory provisions that regulate the construction, alteration, or licensing of a health care facility. About 25 state CON laws can apply to HMOs.[3] CON approval also may be required for the acquisition of equipment and changes in the level of services or beds. Insofar as HMOs operate and run health care facilities, regulatory permission may be required to carry out these types of activities.

Enrollee Information

The HMO Model Act sets forth requirements for communicating health plan information to HMO enrollees. Enrollees are entitled to receive a copy of individual and group contracts. Misleading, confusing, and unjust provisions are prohibited. Each contract must contain basic information describing eligibility requirements, covered benefits, out-of-pocket expenses, limitations and exclusions, termination or cancellation of policies, claims processing, grievance procedures, continuation of benefits, conversion rights, subrogation rights, terms of coverage, and grace period after nonpayment of premiums. Regulators require these documents to be filed with and approved by the regulatory body in charge of reviewing contracts.

In addition to individual and group contacts, the HMO Model Act requires HMOs to make other disclosures. Every enrollee is entitled to receive a document referred to as the evidence of coverage, which describes essential features and services of the HMO. Plans also must provide details about how services can be obtained through the HMO network and a telephone number at the plan for answers to additional questions. Upon enrollment or reenrollment, members must receive a list of all health plan providers. Within 30 days after a material change in the plan, HMOs must notify enrollees of the change if it has a direct impact on them.

Access to Medical Services

HMOs must ensure the availability and accessibility of medical services. HMO patients should have access to medical care during reasonable hours; emergency care should be provided 24 hours a day, 7 days a week. Regulators limit an HMO's COA to designated service areas (usually established by ZIP code regions or counties) where a determination has been made that the HMO has a sufficient provider network. Regulators also establish protocols governing HMO specialty referrals to ensure appropriate accessibility. In addition, most states require HMOs to offer an annual open enrollment period to prospective enrollees or in the event of another health plan's insolvency.[4]

Provider Issues

HMOs are required to execute written contracts with providers that join the HMO's network, commonly referred to as participating providers. Upon initial application for a COA, and periodically thereafter, regulators review sample contracts for primary care, specialty care, and ancillary services. Contracts must contain a number of provisions, including a list of covered services, details about how physicians will be paid, hold-harmless language, the contract term, termination procedures, and an obligation to adhere to HMO quality assurance and utilization management programs.

Regulators also are concerned about provider risk-sharing arrangements. Most HMOs share the risk for the cost of health care with their providers (principally primary care physicians) through performance-based reimbursement, including capitated payment mechanisms, and periodically through withholds and pooling arrangements. Under capitation, a provider usually is compensated on a fixed, prepaid basis (e.g., per member per month). In addition, providers may participate in a withhold arrangement under which the HMO withholds a portion of the provider's payment (e.g., 5 percent) during a 12-month period to cover excess medical expenses; providers receive any funds that remain in the pool at the end of the contract period. Regulators carefully scrutinize these types of reimbursement formulas to ensure that quality of care is not compromised and that provider solvency is not jeopardized.

Reports and Rate Filings

State regulators employ a number of methods to ensure that licensed HMOs remain in compliance with the law. Typically, HMOs must file an annual report with the insurance department. This report must include audited financial statements, a list of participating providers, an update and summary of enrollee grievances handled during the year, and any additional information that regulators deem necessary to make a proper review of the organization.

The HMO Model Act also requires HMOs to file a schedule of premium rates or a methodology for determining premium rates with the insurance department. Regulators normally will approve the schedule or methodology if premiums are not excessive, inadequate, or unfairly discriminatory.

In addition, states require HMOs to update regulators automatically if there are changes in documents that were part of the initial COA application filing (or part of the annual filings). Regulators keep permanent records, including primary care physician agreements, specialist provider contracts, group and individual contracts, certificate of coverage, and other pertinent information.

Quality Assurance and Utilization Review

The NAIC's model requires HMOs to file a description of their proposed quality assurance program before obtaining state licensure. HMOs must also establish procedures to ensure that the health care services provided to their enrollees are "rendered under reasonable standards of quality of care consistent with prevailing professionally recognized standards of medical practice."[5] In most states, statutory and regulatory quality assurance requirements are supplemented with internal departmental guidelines, as exemplified in the NAIC's *HMO Examination Handbook*.

Examination of an HMO's quality assurance program begins with a review of relevant documents, including a comprehensive description of the program. Regulators then assess how well the HMO is carrying out its quality assurance responsibilities. Preventive care activities, program administration, provider credentialing, utilization review (UR) procedures, risk management, provider payment mechanisms, access to HMO services, medical records, claims payment procedures, and management information services are reviewed carefully in the quality assurance evaluation. Some states, notably Kansas and Pennsylvania, require an HMO to obtain an independent external review of its quality assurance program from approved review agencies, such as the National Committee for Quality Assurance (NCQA).

HMOs often are subject to a higher level of regulatory oversight for quality assurance activities than other MCOs and indemnity health plans, in part because HMOs were the first plans to link prepaid health care delivery systems and financial insurance. Furthermore, HMOs are subject to multiple quality assurance regulations. Sources of quality assurance oversight include a state's HMO enabling law, the federal HMO Act, the Medicare risk-contracting program, Medicaid managed care laws, and private accrediting organizations such as the NCQA.

Grievance Procedures

The HMO Model Act requires establishment of a grievance procedure to help resolve enrollee complaints (see Chapter 24 for an example). States often specify how these grievances should be handled. Typically, regulators require each HMO to form a grievance committee to hear complaints. Enrollees must be informed of their right to a hearing, usually in writing, when they join the HMO. Decisions by the committee may be appealed within the HMO, and if necessary the state may step in to hear the complaint. The number of grievances filed and processed by an HMO also must be reported on a regular basis to the appropriate regulatory body.

Solvency Protection

The HMO Model Act establishes specific capital, reserve, and deposit requirements for HMOs to protect consumers and other interested parties against insolvency. Before a COA is issued, an initial net worth requirement of $1.5 million is required. After issuance, a minimum net worth must be maintained by the HMO equal to the greater of $1 million, the sum of 2 percent of annual premiums on the first $150 million of premiums and 1 percent on the excess, the sum of 3 months' uncovered health care costs, or the sum of 8 percent of annual health expenditures (except those paid on a capitated basis or a managed hospital payment basis) and 4 percent of annual hospital expenses paid on a managed payment basis.

The HMO Model Act also requires a minimum deposit of $300,000 with the insurance department. The deposit is considered an admitted asset of the HMO in the determination of its net worth, but it is used to protect the interests of HMO enrollees or to cover administrative costs if the HMO goes into receivership or liquidation. As mentioned above, most states also require HMOs to include hold-harmless clauses in their provider contracts. In situations where the HMO fails to pay for covered medical care, such clauses prohibit providers from seeking collection from the enrollees. California and New York have statutory hold-harmless requirements protecting enrollees even in the absence of a contractual provision. Many states also require that HMOs enter into reinsurance arrangements to cover liabilities in the event of an insolvency.

A few states (Alabama, Florida, Illinois, Vermont, Virginia, and Wisconsin) also require HMOs to participate in guaranty fund programs.[6] These state programs provide funding to cover an HMO's potential liabilities for health care services if it becomes insolvent. Regulators may use this money to reimburse nonparticipating providers, to pay for the continuation of benefits, and to cover conversion costs. Guaranty funds have been implemented almost universally for life, health, and accident insurance policies. Only one or two states, however, require HMO participation in their life and health guaranty associations. In four states, HMOs reinsure each other through a standalone HMO guaranty association or insolvency assessment fund. The NAIC HMO Model Act also includes a provision to establish an insolvency assessment fund based on a law in the Commonwealth of Virginia. The NAIC drafting notes accompanying this section in the HMO Model Act, however, specifically state that this mechanism is not recommended for all states because there may be inadequate premium volume or too few HMOs to make an assessment feasible.

States often require HMOs to establish contingency plans for insolvency that allow for the continuation of benefits to enrollees during the contract period for which premiums have been paid. If necessary, insurance departments require HMOs to take further precautions to safeguard enrollee benefits. These additional measures might include purchasing additional insurance, entering into contracts obligating providers to continue delivering care if the HMO ceases operation, setting aside additional solvency reserves, or securing letters of credit.

If a regulator determines that an HMO's financial condition threatens enrollees, creditors, or the general public, the regulator usually has broad discretion to order the HMO to take specific corrective actions. Such actions may include reducing potential liabilities through reinsurance, suspending the volume of new business for a period of time, or increasing the HMO's capital and surplus contributions.

Financial Examinations and Site Visits

Regulators also can conduct specialized inquiries, which often examine HMO finances, marketing activities, and quality assurance programs. In part, the objective of these regulatory reviews is to determine the HMO's financial solvency and statutory compliance and whether any trends can be identified that may cause problems in the future. For example, the HMO Model Act requires the insurance department to complete a detailed examination of the HMO's financial affairs at least once every 3 years. The NAIC's *HMO Examination Handbook* sets forth specific procedures for examining HMO balance sheet assets and liabilities. The goals are to verify ownership and stated asset amounts and to ensure the adequacy of the HMO's net worth to meet current and future liabilities. Examiners may review an HMO's existing cash resources; investments; premium receivables; interest receivables; prepaid expenses; restricted assets; leasehold arrangements; accounts payable; unpaid claims; unearned premiums; outstanding loans; statutory liability; building, land, equipment, and inventory lists; and other company assets and costs.

If the HMO is undercapitalized or otherwise short of funds, regulators usually provide an opportunity for the HMO to take corrective action. Regulators take financial shortfalls seriously, however, and will suspend or revoke an HMO's license if necessary to protect consumer interests.

As part of the examination process, regulators may conduct a site visit to see the HMO's operations first hand, to review health plan documents, and to assess the efficiency and soundness of plan operations. The site visit may be relatively brief, or it can take place over a period of days or weeks. Occasionally, regulators contact participating providers and enrollees directly to determine how the HMO is operating.

Point-of-Service Offerings

Interest in coverage that includes a point-of-service option has grown in recent years; more than 10 million HMO enrollees now participate in such a plan.[7] This interest has been fueled by employers, which are seeking better control over their health care expenditures while trying to provide their employees the freedom to choose whether to seek health care within or outside the HMO provider network. HMOs prefer to market point-of-service products on their own by underwriting out-of-plan benefits, referred to as a standalone product. Most state laws, however, prohibit HMOs from offering a point-of-service product without entering into an agreement with an insurance company to cover the out-of-plan usage, referred to as a wraparound product.

In 1993, Group Health Association of America (GHAA; now known as The American Association of Health Plans (AAHP)) examined the ability of HMOs to offer point-of-service products at the state level.[8] Eleven states (Alabama, Iowa, Maine, Michigan, Minnesota, North Carolina, Oklahoma, Pennsylvania, Utah, Virginia, and Wisconsin) have adopted laws, regulations, or published other guidelines allowing HMOs to market standalone point-of-service products, where the HMO underwrites out-of-plan usage. Five states (Indiana, Kentucky, Louisiana, Maryland, and New Jersey) permit a standalone HMO point-of-service offering if approved by the appropriate state agency. The remaining 34 states and the District of Columbia either do not expressly regulate or prohibit HMOs from offering point-of-service products on a standalone basis.

Thirty-seven states, however, may allow HMO-sponsored point-of-service products on a wraparound basis through statute, regulation, or rule or after an agency review. Thirteen states and the District of Columbia either do not expressly regulate or prohibit HMOs from offering a point-of-service product on a wraparound basis. GHAA's 1993 survey identified the following corporate relationships underpinning wraparound offerings:

- *HMO-controlled offerings*, where the HMO contracts with an indemnity carrier directly (the employer signs one contract with the HMO and pays one premium)
- *shared venture offerings*, where the HMO and the indemnity carrier contract separately with the employer (the employer signs two contracts and pays two premiums)
- *multiple licensed parent company offerings*, where the HMO and the indemnity carrier are affiliates or subsidiaries of the same parent company, which offers both plans to the employer
- *insurance company offerings*, where the HMO must be a licensed insurance company
- *indemnity trust agreements*, where the indemnity carrier issues the indemnity portion to a trust, which then contracts with employer groups

In the states that regulate HMO-sponsored point-of-service products, the following provisions are typical: a limit on the percentage (5 percent to 20 percent) of total health care expenditures for enrollees who obtain services outside the plan; an increased net worth requirement; a tracking system to measure in-network and out-of-network utilization separately; authority and encouragement to use increased copayments, deductibles, and limits on covered out-of-plan benefits as disincentives to the use of out-of-plan services; and a mechanism for processing and paying for all out-of-plan service claims.

In 1995, three states adopted laws mandating that HMOs offer point-of-service products in certain situations. Oregon's SB 979 and Maryland's SB 449 require HMOs to offer point-of-service options to employer groups if the HMO offers a traditional closed panel option, and New York passed SB 5469A requiring all HMOs to offer individuals (i.e., nongroup coverage) a point-of-service option. Previously, New York also adopted a law mandating that HMOs offer a closed panel product to individuals under the state's 1992 community rating/open enrollment law. Ironically, these new laws fail to provide the same consumer protections as those in states that have adopted voluntary point-of-service provisions, as described in the preceding paragraph. This situation is a byproduct of recent Provider Protection Act (PPA) initiatives, which are discussed later.

Multistate Operations

With many HMOs now operating in more than one state, HMOs must comply with the regulations of each jurisdiction. Other multistate MCOs can face the same regulatory challenge when complying with the rules in more than one state as well. Most states mandate that foreign HMOs meet the same requirements applicable to domestic HMOs. States also may require that out-of-state HMOs register to do business under the appropriate foreign corporation law and appoint an agent in the state for receipt of legal notifications.

Multistate operations can become expensive if plans are subject to numerous financial examinations and other regulatory requirements. To alleviate this concern, some states permit regulators who are considering the application of a foreign HMO to accept financial reports and other information from the HMO's state of origin. The NAIC also has established guidelines for coordinating examinations of HMOs licensed in more than one state. The coordinated examination is called for by the lead state, where the HMO is domiciled; other states where the HMO operates are encouraged to participate. Occasionally, regulations in one state may adversely affect or hinder the operations of an HMO licensed in another state.

Historically, group insurance policies generally have been subject to the law of the state of issuance. A policy issued in state A would be subject to that state's insurance laws and regulations, including mandated benefits. This general rule has been eroded by extraterritorial application of state insurance law. The laws of state B may require that any state B resident covered under a group health policy, even if issued in state A, receive the same coverage that would be required had the group policy been issued in state B.

PPOs

PPOs are created when a health insurer contracts with a group of providers to provide medical care. PPOs are open panel or point-of-service arrangements where consumers can choose between participating providers and nonparticipating providers outside the network. By staying in the PPO network, the consumer's out-of-pocket costs are lower and benefit levels higher.

PPOs are regulated on the state level, usually by the state insurance department. In 29 states, PPO enabling legislation has been adopted.[9] In the remaining states and the District of Columbia, PPO activities are regulated by insurance laws governing indemnity plans and managed care functions. PPO regulatory supervision is not as intense as HMO oversight. For example, the NAIC's HMO Model Act has 34 sections covered in 31 pages, whereas the NAIC's PPO Model Act has nine sections covered in four pages. Many regulators believe that fewer regulations are needed to govern PPO operations because PPOs already are regulated through other insurance laws and regulations. Furthermore, PPOs often are less structured than HMOs. For example, a PPO could be just a contractual arrangement without being formally incorporated.

Of the states that have enacted specific PPO laws, the most common areas of regulatory oversight include provider participation requirements (21 states), UR (19 states), restrictions on provider incentives (18 states), access to providers (16 states), and benefit level differentials (15 states). Other areas include manner of provider payments (12 states), emergency care (12 states), quality assurance and improvement (12 states), grievance procedures (10 states), enrollee contracts (8 states), solvency requirements (6 states), and unlicensed insurers (5 states).[10]

Some experts have expressed concerns about the inequities between PPO and HMO regulation. For example, noticeably absent from the NAIC's PPO Model Act is oversight of quality assurance, including credentialing requirements for PPOs. This may explain why most states do not regulate the quality assurance activities of PPOs and why, in the 12 states that do, such regulations are less stringent than those applied to HMOs.

Inequities between PPO and HMO regulations may begin to diminish in the near future, however. For example, the NAIC is currently drafting eight new regulatory standards dealing with quality assurance, credentialing, UR, grievance procedures, provider contracting, data reporting, confidentiality, and accessibility. If adopted, these standards would serve as a baseline for HMOs, PPOs, and other MCOs.

PHOs

PHOs are joint ventures between physicians and hospitals that contract with employers and health plans to provide medical services and other functions. The PHO may be organized for a single purpose, such as acting as a single agent for managed care contracting, or it may be organized for multiple purposes. A PHO may perform the same functions as an HMO, including the promise to provide comprehensive coverage on a prepaid capitated basis. A PHO also could function in a fashion similar to a PPO or other MCO arrangements. There are also other forms of integrated delivery systems as described in Chapter 4, but the issues that pertain to all of them will be discussed here in the context of PHOs.

The NAIC has called attention to the rising number of unregulated, risk-bearing PHOs and recently issued a model bulletin for use by state insurance commissioners calling for the licensure of such plans. In circumstances where PHOs assume full or limited insurance risk directly from the employer, most state regulators believe that they have the statutory authority to require the licensure of a PHO as a health plan to safeguard consumer interests. Simply put, regulators use the "duck test": If a PHO looks, waddles, and quacks like an HMO, it should be licensed as an HMO.

A 1995 survey, however, revealed that some gaps in state oversight exist, particularly when PHOs assume full or partial insurance risk directly from employers.[11] Regulators in 25 states in 1995 responded that they have no affirmative policy to require licensure of a PHO when the transfer of risk to a PHO from an employer is limited (e.g., up to 110 percent of an annual predetermined budget). Regulators in nine states reported that they have no affirmative policy to require PHOs to become licensed as an HMO or to meet similar requirements if the PHO assumes full financial risk (i.e., the PHO contracts directly with the employer on a prepaid capitated basis for all medical services). In addition, most regulators replied that no state licensure is necessary for PHOs if they accept downstream transfers of insurance risk or if they assume no risk because the employer self-funds in accordance with the Employee Retirement Income Security Act (ERISA) of 1974.

Even in states where regulators said that PHO licensure would be required under one or more of the proposed scenarios, regulators often did not know how many risk-bearing PHOs were in operation within their respective states. In many states, actual enforcement of regulatory standards for PHOs is often passive or nonexistent.

Enforcement patterns have begun to improve in some states, however, as regulators become more aware of the existence of risk-bearing entities (PHOs and similar unregulated entities) and strive to maintain a level regulatory playing field. As a result, active regulatory oversight should increase the level of consumer protections, including solvency and quality of care safeguards.

Prepaid Limited Health Service Organizations

A prepaid limited health service organization is a corporate venture that contracts on a prepaid basis to provide or arrange for provision of one or more limited health services to enrollees. Health services are usually limited to mental health, substance abuse, dental services, pharmaceutical services, podiatric care, and vision care. According to the NAIC, only seven states have enacted legislation authorizing these limited managed care businesses.[12] General regulatory requirements for prepaid limited health service organizations are similar to, but not as comprehensive as, those in the HMO Model Act. Requirements include licensure and issuance of a COA, filing requirements, review of payment methodologies, development of a complaint system, periodic examinations, financial and investment guidelines, insolvency protections, oversight of agents, confidentiality rules, issuance of a fidelity bond for officers and employees, and provider contracting standards.

UROs

With the growing demand by employers to manage utilization of health care services and to control costs, independent UROs have proliferated quickly. At least 28 states have enacted comprehensive UR laws that require specific protocols and mandate licensure of individuals or corporate entities that conduct UR.[13,14] At least 16 of the states include full or partial exemptions for HMOs that conduct their own UR activity because HMOs' UR activity is regulated through state HMO laws.

One example of a comprehensive UR law is Connecticut's statute that requires UROs to be licensed and meet strict minimum standards. Licensed UROs in Connecticut must do the following:

- maintain and make available procedures for providing notification of admissions or coverage determinations to the provider or plan enrollee
- maintain and make available a written description of the appeal procedure by which either the enrollee or the provider may seek review of determinations not to certify an admission, service, procedure, or extension of stay
- provide for an expedited appeals process for emergency or life-threatening situations
- use established, written clinical criteria and review procedures that are to be periodically evaluated and updated with provider input
- ensure that nurses, practitioners, and other licensed health professionals making UR decisions have current licenses
- ensure that, in cases where an appeal to reverse a determination not to certify is unsuccessful, a practitioner in a specialty related to the condition is reasonably available to review the case
- make review staff available by a toll-free telephone number at least 40 hours per week during normal business hours
- comply with all federal and state laws to protect the confidentiality of individual medical records
- allow a minimum of 24 hours after an emergency admission, service, or procedure for an enrollee or his or her representative to notify the URO and request certification or continuing treatment for that condition

If a URO contracts on an exclusive basis with self-funded employers, its operations are regulated by ERISA, and state law does not apply. Currently, however, ERISA does not regulate UR activities. Many state regulators argue that, if a URO has even one commercial contract where a health plan is assuming the insurance risk (not the employer), all the URO's operations are subject to state laws.

Unfortunately, the combination of standalone UR laws and UR requirements in HMO laws (i.e., in states where HMOs are not exempted from the comprehensive UR law) can create confusion and be unnecessarily duplicative. For example, single-state HMOs can become subject to interstate UR regulations, thereby creating numerous problems. Several states require that all UR agents who inquire about a patient's treatment be licensed in that particular state to gain access to medical records and other pertinent information.[15] Occasionally, an HMO primary care physician cannot obtain his or her enrollee's medical information because the enrollee is injured in another state, and the physician is not a licensed UR agent where the patient is hospitalized. Such interpretations would require single-state HMOs to apply for UR licensure in dozens of states simply to gain access to HMO members' files should individuals need out-of-area emergency treatment.

Third Party Administrators

A third party administrator (TPA) is an organization that administers group benefits and claims for a self-funded company or group. A TPA normally does not assume any insurance risk. Thirty-six states require licensure of TPAs if they do business in a state.[16] Almost half these states require licensure even if there only is one plan participant residing in the state. Approximately five states require licensing if a certain percentage or number of plan participants reside in the state. About one third of all states provide for an exemption for state licensure if the TPA administers only single-employer self-funded plans. State TPA laws typically govern the following[17]:

- the TPA's written agreement with insurers, including a statement of duties
- payment methodology
- maintenance and disclosure of records
- insurer responsibilities, such as determination of benefit levels
- fiduciary obligations when the TPA collects charges and premiums
- issuance of TPA licenses and grounds for suspension or revocation
- filing of annual reports and payment of fees

Self-Funded Plans

Under self-funded arrangements, where the employer assumes the financial risk of its employees' health care costs, state regulators can do little to supervise employer efforts to manage its health plan. Self-funded arrangements usually are defined as employee benefit plans under ERISA and thus are exempt from state regulation. In essence, these plans are not considered in the business of insurance for the purpose of any state law governing insurance activities. With the growing trend by employers to self-fund, state regulators have expressed concern over the lack of authority to protect consumers under these arrangements. It is now common for large employers to use managed care in a self-funded arrangement, thereby avoiding state regulations such as mandated benefits and premium taxes.

MCOs that otherwise have state-licensed products usually can offer limited services under self-funded arrangements in at least two ways:

1. *Administrative services only*—Regulated entities such as insurance companies and HMOs can offer a nonregulated managed care product under an administrative services only arrangement with an employer that assumes the financial risk of

the benefits plan. The MCO handles administrative functions for the employer group.

2. *Exclusive provider organizations*—By definition, exclusive provider organizations are not regulated because they coordinate health services in self-funded plans and administrative services-only arrangements. Under these circumstances, an HMO or PPO could rent out its provider panel to a self-funded employer. The employer would pay the MCO on a fee-for-service basis for medical services rendered to avoid any transfer of insurance risk from the employer to the MCO or providers.

ANTI–MANAGED CARE LEGISLATION

According to operators of HMOs and other MCO delivery systems, these organizations cannot operate successfully—that is, provide high-quality, cost-effective care—in the absence of certain features, including quality assurance procedures, prepayment for services, and selective contracting. Recently, however, many states have moved toward redefining the ground rules and interfering with the basic underpinnings of MCO operations.

PPA Proposals

In 1995, the American Medical Association and state medical societies aggressively promoted provider protection initiatives, the so-called PPA, in most states and in Congress. Under the guise of consumer protection, these bills call for regulatory controls over HMOs and other MCOs. Much of this regulation, however, already exists at both state and federal levels. When these duplicate requirements are stripped away from most PPA proposals, the remaining provisions are primarily special preferences that physicians are seeking for themselves, not consumers. Specific PPA components include the following[18]:

- mandatory point-of-service offerings
- burdensome due process protocols for aggrieved physicians as well as restrictions on a health plan's ability to remove physicians from their network
- any willing credentialing requirements (mandating health plans to credential all providers who apply to become a "participating provider" even if the health plan is not expanding its network) and disclosure of credentialing standards
- prohibition of certain generally accepted financial incentives as well as disclosure of all financial incentives
- establishment of duplicate health plan standards and state certification requirements

Generally, PPA regulations would damage the ability of HMOs and other MCOs to select the physicians who are best suited to the needs of their members by providing physicians with unprecedented rights to affiliate with managed care plans. PPA bills were introduced in more than 25 states during 1995. At the time of this writing, PPA bills were defeated in 20 states, and two scaled-back versions were adopted in Oregon and Maryland.

Any Willing Provider Initiatives

The creation of selective provider panels is a cornerstone of MCO operations. Many states, however, have enacted laws, commonly referred to as any willing provider (AWP) laws, that prevent MCOs from selectively contracting with a limited group of providers. The classic AWP law requires an MCO to accept into its network any nonparticipating provider willing to meet the terms and conditions of the MCO. The Federal Trade Commission concurs with MCO professionals' opinion that such legislation threatens the viability of MCOs. Thus in nine states (California, Illinois, Massachusetts, Montana, Nevada, New Hampshire, Pennsylvania, South Carolina, and Texas) that have considered AWP legislation, the Federal Trade Commission has written opinion letters indicating that AWP bills pose a serious anticompetitive threat. The NAIC and the National Governors Association also have issued statements opposing AWP laws.[19]

Furthermore, several studies have documented the potential costs of implementing AWP laws. In June 1994, Atkinson & Company, an actuarial firm retained by GHAA, published a study of AWP laws. Among other findings, the study reported that the combined increases in administrative and health care costs resulting from AWP provisions would force HMOs to increase premiums by 9.1 percent to 28.7 percent. This would translate into premium increases of up to $458 per individual and $1,284 per family, thus totaling more than $45 billion per year.[20]

Another 1994 study published by Arthur Anderson & Company, an actuarial firm commissioned by the state of Florida House of Representatives Committee on Appropriations, assessed the potential cost effects of several health reform proposals, including an AWP mandate in Florida. Among its findings, the study indicated that HMO premiums in Florida were 25 to 30 percent less than premiums of indemnity plans. If the AWP law were implemented, most savings attributable to provider discounts and reduced utilization would probably be lost. As a result, the study predicted that per member per month costs for private sector managed care plans would increase by approximately 15 percent.[21]

Approximately 33 AWP laws affecting MCOs have been adopted in 27 states.[22,23] Fifteen states have full or partial exemptions for HMOs. AWP laws often apply to certain designated providers, such as chiropractors, optometrists, pharmacists, nurse practitioners, nurse-midwives, podiatrists, psychologists, and other allied health professionals. The most popular type, adopted in 14 states, requires health plans to accept into the plan's network nonparticipating pharmacists willing to meet the terms and conditions of the MCO. In seven states, HMOs receive full or partial exemptions from such open pharmacy requirements.

It is important to note that ten states (Arkansas, Georgia, Idaho, Illinois, Indiana, Kentucky, Texas, Utah, Virginia, and Wyoming) have adopted AWP laws that include physicians as possible beneficiaries. Most states traditionally have exempted HMOs from such requirements. This can be explained in part because such a law would violate the federal HMO Act, which prohibits state laws designating the number or percentage of physicians who must participate in an HMO network.[24] Four states (Arkansas, Idaho, Kentucky, and Wyoming), however, recently failed to exempt federally qualified HMOs. This lack of exemption represents a disturbing new trend by state legislatures.

State AWP laws may be subject to challenge on the basis of federal preemption under at least two theories. First, as noted, an attempt to implement an AWP provision with respect to physicians is in violation of federal law (as applied to physician services).[25] Second, federal courts have found that HMOs are not in the business of insurance for the purpose of ERISA's savings clause.[26] In either case, a state's AWP law as applied to HMOs may be ruled unenforceable because federal law supersedes state law.

Two AWP legal challenges currently underway are testing these and other legal theories. The state of Louisiana is appealing a federal district court decision holding that the state's AWP law is preempted under ERISA.[27] The district court found that the law affects employers' and sponsors' discretion as to the structuring of health benefits under employee benefit plans because it explicitly directs plan administrators not to structure their plans so as to exclude any provider willing and qualified to participate in the network. In July 1995, the Prudential Insurance Company filed a federal lawsuit seeking to prevent the state of Arkansas from enforcing its AWP law.[28] The lawsuit contends that the state AWP law is preempted by several federal statues, including ERISA, the federal HMO Act, and the Federal Employee Health Benefits Act. The suit further alleges that the AWP law would interfere with the private relationship between health plans and employers, thereby impeding health plans' ability to offer high-quality, affordable health care to Arkansas consumers.

Direct Access Legislation

With growing frequency during the 1990s, states have considered direct access legislation (sometimes referred to as freedom of choice initiatives), which would give MCO enrollees unbridled authority to seek care outside MCO participating provider networks. Like AWP laws, these laws can be inconsistent with managed care principles and thus may threaten the viability of HMOs. Direct access initiatives can take several forms: "requiring insurers to offer an indemnity plan if they offer a network plan; preventing the designation of a single source provider (e.g., a pharmacy or medical equipment supply chain); or requiring MCOs to cover services rendered by non-participating providers."[29] Fourteen states have enacted direct access laws that apply to many types of health plans, including traditional indemnity insurance, Blue Cross/Blue Shield plans, PPOs, and HMOs.[30] Three states have implemented provisions that apply only to HMO operations; Louisiana, Mississippi, and New Jersey limit the ability of HMOs to designate pharmacies or pharmacy mail order houses.[31]

Mandated Benefits Requirements

State laws governing HMOs require that their enrollees be offered comprehensive health care services. In fact, the industry's ability to provide broad coverage has been one of its distinctive trademarks. Nevertheless, many states now require coverage of specialty and nonessential services, too. States now require more than 1,000 specific benefits to be offered by health plans; at least 200 of these apply to HMOs.[32–34] Recently, bills setting minimum requirements for coverage of postpartum hospital length of stay and bills requiring payment for emergency department services even in nonurgent circumstances have gained popularity during the 1995 legislative session. As of 1 October 1995, mandatory length-of-stay laws were enacted in Maryland, New Jersey, and North Carolina. During 1995, three states (Arkansas, Louisiana, and Virginia) enacted legislation governing how plans cover emergency services. These laws typically seek either to redefine emergency services or to limit HMOs and other managed care plans authorizing procedures to approve payment for emergency services.

Where state legislatures mandate coverage of expensive services or mandate medical protocols that may not always be necessary, a point of diminishing returns is quickly reached. Many fear that less money will be spent on basic health care as funds are rerouted to cover the nonessential mandates. Mandated benefits also reduce HMOs' flexibility in structuring benefit packages to suit the needs of a particular group.

INSURANCE REFORM INITIATIVES

While the congressional health reform debate ebbs and flows, states are actively considering a variety of health care measures. During the last 4 years alone, more than 2,000 health care proposals were introduced in state legislatures that would have expanded coverage to the uninsured and underinsured.[35] This section examines small group and individual market reforms and their impact on HMO operations.

Since 1990, 46 states have adopted small group reform measures, many based on the model laws adopted by the NAIC (the NAIC first adopted the Premium Rate and Renewability Model Act in 1991; the Small Employer Health Insurance Model Act in 1991, which was revised in 1994; and the Model Regulations To Implement the Small Employer Health Insurance Availability Model Act in 1993). Typical changes in the NAIC's latest small group model (specifically, the Small Employer Health Insurance Availability Model Act, for prospective reinsurance with or without an opt out) to increase the availability of health insurance coverage to small employers include the following: an open enrollment period and a guarantee issue requirement for all products that a small group carrier offers to the small group market (i.e., businesses with up to 50 employees); a community-rating requirement that adjusts for geographic location, age, and family composition; limits on waiting periods for preexisting conditions; and choice of at least two standardized benefit packages.

HMO participation in the small group market has increased dramatically in recent years. For example, from 1992 to 1993 alone, the percentage of HMOs offering small group coverage rose from 52.7 percent to 71.4 percent. The aggregate percentage of HMO business comprising of small groups also increased from 10.0 percent to 13.1 percent during the same period.[36]

Although the HMO industry supports small group reforms, several problems can arise after a state adopts such a measure. For example, federally qualified HMOs "shall provide, without limitations as to time or cost . . . basic and supplemental health services to its members."[37] Many HMO experts interpret this provision as a prohibition on the use of waiting periods for preexisting medical conditions for HMO coverage. Moreover, the way HMOs do business does not lend itself to excluding an HMO enrollee from coverage because of a preexisting medical condition. As a result, 12- or 6-month waiting periods commonly are used by indemnity carriers but not by federally qualified HMOs. This can place HMOs at a competitive disadvantage because federally qualified HMOs must offer full coverage to new enrollees of a small group immediately. The NAIC recently recognized this dilemma by adding to its model the option of imposing a postenrollment or affiliation waiting period for health plans that do not use waiting periods for preexisting conditions. Few states explicitly recognize this option, however.

Another concern relates to rating methodologies used by small group carriers. In compliance with both federal and state requirements, HMOs use community rating more than 80 percent of the time.[38] Most states that have adopted small group reforms, however, still permit health plans to use a modified form of experience rating that limits variation in premiums charged to different small groups.[39] As a result, HMOs sometimes are placed at a competitive disadvantage because they often must make community-rated policies available to small groups, whereas other health plans can sell experience-rated policies.

It also can be difficult for HMOs to satisfy a state's requirement for standardized benefit packages for small businesses. Typically, a state adopts a requirement that two standardized policies must be available. Usually, one is a "bare bones" option. Many HMOs cannot offer such a benefit package, however, because HMOs must offer comprehensive policies pursuant to state and federal HMO laws. For example, federally qualified HMOs must offer comprehensive health services as defined by the federal HMO Act and regulations.

Similar issues may arise as the states, and possibly the federal government, attempt to provide better access and more affordable coverage to individuals who are not employed or who choose not to purchase coverage through a group policy. Since 1992, about a dozen states have adopted individual reforms, and the NAIC may propose a model act to address this issue in 1995.[40] Interestingly, the percentage of HMOs selling individual coverage increased from 24.6 percent in 1992 to 41.9 percent in 1993, although individual policies still represent only a small portion of HMO business.[41]

REGULATION BY MARKET SEGMENTS

It is important to note that, because regulation is driven by market segments, a typical MCO is regulated by several entities, depending on the combination of product lines it offers. The primary regulatory bodies responsible for protecting consumers are the following:

- *state insurance and health departments* for health care coverage purchased by individuals, offered to state employees, and provided to employees of a business where the health plan retains the insurance risk

- *U.S. Department of Labor* for coverage offered to employees when employers retain the insurance risk, either on a standalone basis or through a multiple employer welfare arrangement (i.e., self-funding pursuant to ERISA)
- *the Health Care Financing Administration* for Medicare and Medicaid coverage and all policies sold by federally qualified HMOs
- *state welfare departments*, which share responsibility with the Health Care Financing Administration for Medicaid coverage
- *U.S. Office of Personnel Management* for coverage sold to federal employees (i.e., the Federal Employees Health Benefits Program)
- *U.S. Department of Defense* for coverage offered to active and retired military personnel

Because so many regulatory agencies have statutory authority to oversee managed care and other health plan operations, the percentage of the entire marketplace that states regulate exclusively is estimated at between 15 percent and 20 percent of the U.S. population. In contrast, most health care policies now issued are regulated by the federal government. For example, about 45 percent of the U.S. population is regulated through ERISA. When one adds other federal programs, such as the Federal Employees Health Benefit Program and the Civilian Health and Medical Program of the Uniformed Services, the total exceeds 50 percent. In some cases, the state and federal governments share responsibility. For instance, under the Medicare and Medicaid programs, state and federal regulators share jurisdiction. In any circumstance where there is a conflict between federal and state oversight under these joint oversight programs, however, federal law preempts state law.

THE STATE EXPERIENCE

Throughout the years, states have retained the lion's share of regulatory authority over commercially insured products. The McCarran-Ferguson Act of 1945 reaffirmed the states' primary role. As a result of the recent expansion of managed care and the increasing complexity of state and federal oversight of all health plan operations, however, traditional notions and boundaries of how managed care and other insurance products should be regulated by government officials are being challenged.

Although different regulatory standards may be applied to different managed care offerings depending on the various market segments, many of the core health care services and functions are the same (e.g., the emphasis on primary care services). Therefore, why have so many different regulatory agencies overseeing similar, if not identical, product lines? This is a question that is not easily answered and may be more a result of the U.S. political system than anything else. In any event, regulatory inconsistency is a problem that needs further evaluation to safeguard consumers and to ensure fair competition among managed care plans.

A central goal of future health reform initiatives should be to achieve a seamless regulatory system, wherever possible, that focuses on the activities of each managed care plan rather than on how a health care entity is licensed through the state or federal government. Additional objectives should include establishing the proper equilibrium between federal and state oversight and between regulatory centralization and regional oversight.

Study Questions

1. What are some of the most critical components of state oversight of HMO operations?
2. When does state regulation apply to health coverage sold by managed care arrangements?

3. Is state regulation driven by what is best for consumers or what is best for special interest groups?
4. What is the best way to create a seamless regulatory system for all managed care organizations?

REFERENCES AND NOTES

1. National Association of Insurance Commissioners (NAIC), *HMO Examination Handbook* (NAIC, 1990). In addition to the HMO Model Act and *HMO Examination Handbook*, the NAIC has adopted other model regulations for HMOs, including the Model Regulation To Implement Rules Regarding Contract and Services of HMOs, the HMO Producer Model Regulation, and the *HMO Investment Guidelines*.
2. National Association of Insurance Commissioners (NAIC), *Compilation of State Laws: Premium Taxation of HMOs* (Kansas City, Mo.: NAIC, 1993).
3. Aspen Systems Corporation, *A Report to the Governor on State Regulation of Health Maintenance Organizations* (Rockville, Md.: Aspen Systems Corp., 1993).
4. National Association of Insurance Commissioners (NAIC), *Open Enrollment Periods for HMOs* (Kansas City, Mo.: NAIC, 1993).
5. National Association of Insurance Commissioners HMO Act, Section 7(A).
6. National Association of Insurance Commissioners (NAIC), *Health Maintenance Organization: Coverage by Guaranty Fund* (Kansas City, Mo.: NAIC, 1994). Florida's HMO Consumer Assistance Plan, Virginia's Insolvency Assessment Fund, and Wisconsin's Insurance Security Fund for all insurers are specific examples of guaranty fund programs in which HMOs are required to participate.
7. Group Health Association of America (GHAA), *Patterns in HMO Enrollment* (Washington, D.C.: GHAA, 1995), 36, American Association of Health Plans (AAHP), 1996 database.
8. Group Health Association of America (GHAA), *Stateside Report* (Washington, D.C.: GHAA, 28 January 1993), 2, 16–42.
9. D. Marsan and R. Quigley, *Guide to State PPO Laws and Regulations* (Washington, D.C.: Group Health Association of America/AMCRA, 1995).
10. Marsan and Quigley, *Guide to State PPO Laws and Regulations*.
11. Group Health Association of America (GHAA), *PHOs and the Assumption of Insurance Risk: A 50-State Survey of Regulators' Attitudes toward PHO Licensure* (Washington, D.C.: GHAA, 1995).
12. National Association of Insurance Commissioners Prepaid Limited Health Service Organization Model Act, Appendix.
13. Group Health Association of America (GHAA), *Stateside Report* (Washington, D.C.: 8 September 1993), 6, 46–68.
14. National Association of Insurance Commissioners (NAIC), *State Laws Regarding Utilization Review Agents/Standards* (Kansas City, Mo.: NAIC, 1994).
15. G. Carneal and D. Marsan, The Need for UR Standardization, *HMO Magazine* (November/December 1993): 13–17.
16. National Association of Insurance Commissioners (NAIC), *Society of Professional Benefit Administrators Survey and Third Party Administrator Licensure and Bond Requirements* (Kansas City, Mo.: NAIC, 1994).
17. National Association of Insurance Commissioners Model Third Party Administrator Statute (1977, revised 1991). This model (or similar legislation) has been adopted in 22 states.
18. Group Health Association of America (GHAA), *In the States* (Washington, D.C.: GHAA, 28 February 1995).
19. National Association of Insurance Commissioners, letter to congressional leadership, 10 August 1994; NGA Policy Statement, 21 July, 1994.
20. Atkinson & Company, *The Cost Impact of Any Willing Provider Legislation* (Silver Spring, Md.: Atkinson & Company, 1995).
21. Arthur Anderson & Co., *Florida Health Security Program: Actuarial Report* (Tampa, Fla.: Arthur Anderson & Co., 1994).
22. Group Health Association of America (GHAA), (Washington, D.C.: GHAA, 1994).
23. Blue Cross/Blue Shield Association, *State Legislative Health Care and Insurance Issues: 1994 Surveys of Plans* (Washington, D.C.: Blue Cross/Blue Shield Association, 1994).
24. 42 U.S.C. 300e-10 (1994).
25. 42 U.S.C. 300e-10 (1994).
26. *Pomeroy v. Johns Hopkins Medical Services*, Lexis 16418 (U.S. Dist. Ct. Md., 1994); *O'Reilly v. Ceuleers*, 912 F.2d 1383 (11th Cir. 1990); *McGee v. Equitable HCA Corp.*, 953 F.2d 1192 (10th Cir. 1992); *Dearmas v. Av-Med, Inc.*, 814 F. Supp. 1103 (S.D. Fla. 1993); and *In re International Medical Centers, Inc.*, 604 So. 2d 505 (Fla. App., 1st Dist. 1992). See also *Hollis v. Cigna Health Care of Connecticut, Inc.*, no. 705357 (Sup. Ct., Hartford–New Britain Judicial District, Ct. 5 December 1994).
27. *Cigna Healthplan of Louisiana, Inc. v. State of Louisiana*, No. 94-885 (M.D. La., 17 April 1995).
28. *Prudential Insurance Company v. State of Arkansas*, No. LR-C-95-514 (W.D. Ark., 21 July 1995).

29. Blue Cross/Blue Shield Association, *State Barriers to Managed Care: Results of a National Survey of Blue Cross and Blue Shield Association Plans* (Washington, D.C.: Blue Cross/Blue Shield Association, 1991), 13.
30. Blue Cross/Blue Shield Association, *State Barriers to Managed Care*, 13.
31. Blue Cross/Blue Shield Association, *State Barriers to Managed Care*, 13.
32. *Mandated Benefits Manual* (Alexandria, Va.: Scandlen, 1992).
33. Health Care Financing Administration, *Annual Report to the Governor on State Regulation of Health Maintenance Organizations* (Rockville, Md.: Aspen Systems Corp., 1993).
34. Group Health Association of America (GHAA), *Stateside Report* (Washington, D.C.: GHAA, 17 November 1993), 3–5.
35. Data based on Commerce Clearing House's and StateNet's state legislative tracking computer system, 1991–1994.
36. Group Health Association of America (GHAA), *Annual HMO Industry Survey* (Washington, D.C.: GHAA, 1994).
37. 42 U.S.C. 300e(b) (1994).
38. Group Health Association of America (GHAA), *HMO Industry Profile* (Washington, D.C.: GHAA, 1994), 101. Of all HMOs, 28.5 percent use standard community rating, 26.9 percent use community rating by class, 26.1 percent use adjusted community rating, 12.6 percent use prospective experience rating, and 5.9 percent use retrospective experience rating.
39. Blue Cross/Blue Shield Association, *State Small Group Insurance Reform Legislation* (Washington, D.C.: Blue Cross/Blue Shield Association, 1994).
40. Blue Cross/Blue Shield Association, *State Individual Insurance Reform Legislation* (Washington, D.C.: Blue Cross/Blue Shield Association, 1994).
41. Group Health Association of America, *Annual HMO Industry Survey*.

SUGGESTED READING

Carneal, G., and Marsan, D. 1993. State Oversight of HMO-Sponsored Point-of-Service Products. *Medical Interface* (August): 105–106, 108.

In the States, a periodical published by the American Association of Health Plans, Washington, D.C.

Chapter 29

Legal Issues in Provider Contracting

Mark S. Joffe

Study Objectives

- Understand the necessary steps and considerations in negotiating a managed care contract
- Understand the typical format of a managed care contract
- Understand common clauses and provisions in managed care contracts
- Understand the key issues to consider with regard to the common terms of a managed care contract

The business of a managed health care plan is to provide or arrange for the provision of health care services. Most managed health care plans, such as health maintenance organizations (HMOs) and preferred provider organizations, provide their services through arrangements with individual physicians, individual practice associations (IPAs), medical groups, hospitals, and other types of health care professionals and facilities. The provider contract formalizes the managed health care plan–provider relationship. A carefully drafted contract accomplishes more than mere memorializing of the arrangement between the parties. A well-written contract can foster a positive relationship between the provider and the managed health care plan. Moreover, a good contract can provide important and needed protections to both parties if the relationship sours.

This chapter is intended to offer to the managed health care plan and the provider a practical guide to reviewing and drafting a provider contract. Appendixes 29–A and 29–B are a sample HMO–primary care physician agreement and a sample HMO–hospital agreement, respectively. These contracts, which have been provided solely for illustrative purposes, have been annotated by the author. Although these agreements are used by an HMO, most provisions have equal applicability to other managed care plans.

Contracts need not be complex or lengthy to be legally binding and enforceable. A single-sentence letter agreement between a hospital and a managed health care plan that says that the hospital agrees to provide access to its facility to enrollees of the managed health care plan in exchange for payment of billed charges is a valid

---

Mark S. Joffe is an attorney in private practice in Washington, D.C., and specializes in legal and business issues affecting managed health care delivery systems, including HMOs and PPOs.

Mr. Joffe was previously the Associate Counsel, Group Health Association of America (now known as The American Association of Health Plans); the HMO trade association. Prior to that position, he was a Senior Attorney with the Office of the General Counsel, Department of Health and Human Services.

Mr. Joffe has a Masters of Arts degree in Health Services Administration at The George Washington University. He is Assistant Professorial Lecturer in Health Services Administration at The George Washington University and a guest lecturer at the Center for Managed Health Care, University of Missouri-Kansas City. Mr. Joffe also publishes *Federal Health Bulletin*, a weekly newsletter summarizing current federal legislative and regulatory developments affecting health care.

contract. If a single-paragraph agreement is legally binding, why is it necessary for managed health care plan–provider contracts to be so lengthy? The answer is twofold. First, many terms of the contract, although not required, perform useful functions by articulating the rights and responsibilities of the parties. As managed care becomes an increasingly important revenue source to providers, a clear understanding of these rights and responsibilities becomes increasingly important. Second, a growing number of contractual provisions are required by state licensure regulations (e.g., a hold-harmless clause) or by government payer programs (e.g., Medicare and Medicaid).

An ideal contract or contract form does not exist. Appropriate contract terms vary depending on the issues of concern and the objectives of the parties, each party's relative negotiating strength, and the desired degree of formality. Although the focus of this chapter is explaining key substantive provisions in a contract, the importance of clarity cannot be overstated. A poorly written contract confuses and misleads the parties. Lack of clarity increases substantially the likelihood of disagreements over the meaning of contract language. A contract not only should be written in simple, commonly understood language but also should be well organized so that either party is able to find and review provisions as quickly and easily as possible.

The need for clarity has become more important as contracts have become increasingly complex. Many managed health care plans may act as an HMO, a preferred provider organization, and a third party administrator. Those health care plans will frequently enter into a single contract with a provider to provide services in all three capacities. In addition, this single contract may obligate the provider to furnish services not only to the managed health care plans enrollees but to enrollees of a number of affiliates of the managed health care plan.

The following discussion is designed to provide a workable guide for managed health care plans and providers to draft, amend, or review contracts. Much of the discussion is cast from the perspective of the managed health care plan, but the points are equally valid from the provider's perspective. Most of the discussion relates to contracts directly between the managed health care plan and the provider of services. When the contract is between the managed health care plan and an IPA or medical group, the managed health care plan needs to ensure that the areas discussed below are appropriately addressed in both the managed health care plan's contract and the contract between the IPA or medical group and the provider.

GENERAL ISSUES IN CONTRACTING

Key Objectives

The managed health care plan should divide key objectives into two categories: those that are essential and those that, although not essential, are highly desirable. Throughout the negotiation process, a managed health care plan needs to keep in mind both the musts and the highly desirables. Not infrequently, a managed health care plan or a provider will suddenly realize at the end of the negotiation process that it has not achieved all its basic goals. The managed health care plan's key objectives will vary. If the managed health care plan is in a community with a single provider of a particular specialty service, merely entering into a contract on any terms with the provider may be its objective. On the other hand, the managed health care plan's objectives might be quite complex, and it may demand carefully planned negotiations to achieve them.

"Must" objectives may derive from state and federal regulations, which may require or prohibit particular clauses in contracts. Managed health care plans need to be aware of these requirements and make sure that their contracting providers understand that these provisions are required by law.

Beyond the essential objectives are the highly desirable ones. Before commencing the drafting or the negotiation of the contract, the managed health care plan should list these objectives and have a good understanding of their relative importance. This preliminary thought process assists the managed health care plan in developing its negotiating strategy.

Annual Calendar

Key provider contracts may take months to negotiate. If the contemplated arrangement with the provider is important to the managed health care plan's delivery system, the managed health care plan will want to avoid the diminution of its bargaining strength as the desired effective date approaches.

The managed health care plan should have a master schedule identifying the contracts that need to be entered into and renewed. This schedule should include time lines that identify dates by which progress on key contract negotiations should take place. Although such an orderly system may be difficult to maintain, it may protect the managed health care plan from potential problems that may arise if it is forced to operate without a contract or negotiate from a weakened position.

Letter of Intent Compared with a Contract

The purpose of a letter of intent is to define the basic elements of a contemplated arrangement or transaction between two parties. A letter of intent is used most often when the negotiation process between two parties is expected to be lengthy and expensive (e.g., a major acquisition). A letter of intent is a preliminary, nonbinding agreement that allows the parties to ascertain whether they are able to agree on key terms. If the parties agree on a letter of intent, the terms of that letter serve as the blueprint for the contract. Some people confuse a letter of intent with a letter of agreement. Because a letter of intent is not a legally binding agreement, regulators will not consider them in evaluating whether a managed care organization meets availability and accessibility requirements. Therefore, the use of a letter of intent should be limited to identifying the general parameters of a future contract.

Negotiating Strategy

Negotiating strategy is determined by objectives and relative negotiating strength. Depending on the locale or market dynamics, either the managed health care plan or the provider may have greater negotiating strength. Except in circumstances in which the relative negotiating strength is so one-sided that one party can dictate the terms to the other party, each party should identify for itself before beginning negotiations the negotiable issues, the party's initial position on each issue, and the extent to which it will compromise. Because a managed health care plan may use the same contract form as the contract for many providers, the managed health care plan needs to keep in mind the implications of amending one contract for the other contracts that use the same form.

A recurring theme presented at conference sessions discussing provider contracting and provider relations is the need to foster a win–win relationship, where both parties perceive that they gain from the relationship. The managed health care plan's objective should be fostering long-term, mutually satisfactory relationships with providers. When managed health care plans have enough negotiating strength to dictate the contract terms, they should exercise that strength cautiously to ensure that their short-term actions do not jeopardize their long-term goals.

CONTRACT STRUCTURE

As mentioned above, clarity is an important objective in drafting a provider contract. A key factor affecting the degree of clarity of a contract is the manner in which the agreement is organized. In fact, many managed health care plan contracts follow fairly similar formats. The contract begins with a title describing the instrument (e.g., "Primary Care Physician Agreement"). After this is the caption, which identifies the names of the parties and the legal action taken, along with the transition, which contains words signifying that the parties have entered into an agreement. Then, the contract includes the recitals, which are best explained as the "whereas" clauses. These clauses are not intended to have legal significance but may become relevant to resolve inconsistencies in the body of the contract or if the drafter inappropriately includes substantive provisions in them. The use of the word *whereas* is merely tradition and has no legal significance.

The next section of the contract is the definitions section, which includes definitions of all key contract terms. The definitions section precedes the operative language, including the substantive health-related provisions that define the responsibilities and obligations of each of the parties, representations and warranties, and declarations. The last section of the contract, the closing or testimonium, reflects the assent of the parties through their signatures. Sometimes, the drafters of a provider contract decide to have the signature page on the first page for administrative simplicity.

Contracts frequently incorporate by reference other documents, some of which will be appended to the agreement as attachments or exhibits. As discussed further below, managed health care plans frequently reserve the right to amend some of these referenced documents unilaterally.

The contract's form or structure is intended to accomplish three purposes: to simplify a reader's use and understanding of the agreement, to facilitate amendment or revision of the contract where the contract form has been used for many providers, and to streamline the administrative process necessary to submit and obtain regulatory approvals. Clarity and efficiency can be attained by using commonly understood terms, avoiding legal or technical jargon, using definitions to explain key and frequently used terms, and using well-organized headings and a numbering system. The ultimate objective is that any representative of the managed health care plan or the provider who has an interest in an issue will be able to find the pertinent contract provision easily and understand its meaning.

Exhibits and appendixes are frequently used by managed health care plans to promote efficiency in administering many provider contracts. The managed health care plan, to the extent possible, could design many of its provider contracts or groups of provider contracts around a core set of common requirements. Exhibits may be used to identify the terms that may vary, such as payment rates and provider responsibilities. This approach has several advantages. First, it eases the administrative burden in drafting and revising contracts. Second, if an appendix or exhibit is the only part of the contract that is being amended and has a separate state insurance department provider number, the managed health care plan need only submit the amendment for state review. Third, when a contract is under consideration for renewal and the key issue is the payment rate, having the payment rate listed separately in the appendix lessens the likelihood that the provider will review and suggest amending other provisions of the contract.

COMMON CLAUSES, PROVISIONS, AND KEY FACTORS

Names

The initial paragraph of the contract will identify the names of the parties entering into the agreement. It is always a good idea to ensure that the parties named in the opening paragraph are the parties that are signing the agreement. If a managed health care organization is signing the agreement on behalf of affiliates, the provider may want to have the signing party represent and warrant that it is authorized to sign on behalf of the nonsigning party. If the nonsigning party is much stronger financially than the signing party, it would be worthwhile to have a representation directly from the nonsigning party that the signing party may enter into the agreement on its behalf. In reviewing a contract, providers should be particularly sensitive to the responsibilities of nonparties to the agreement and the ability of the provider to enforce these responsibilities. For example, if a managed care organization is offering services to self-insured employers, is the self-insured employer a party to the agreement? If not, what assurances does the provider have that the self-insured employer will fulfill its responsibilities?

Recitals

A contract will typically contain, in rather legalistic prose, a series of statements describing who the parties are and what they are trying to accomplish. These recitals should be general statements. Periodically, however, contract drafters insert substantive requirements in the recitals section. Contract reviewers should be sensitive to this possibility.

Table of Contents

Although a table of contents has no legal significance, the reader will be greatly assisted in finding pertinent sections in a long contract by referring to the table of contents. One common failing in contract renegotiations is neglecting to update the table of contents after the contract has been amended.

Definitions

The definitions section of a contract plays an essential role in simplifying the structure, and the reader's understanding, of a contract. The body of the contract often contains complicated terms that merit amplification and explanation. The use of a definition, although requiring the reader to refer back to an earlier section for a meaning, simplifies greatly the discussion in the body of the agreement. A poorly drafted contract will define unnecessary terms or define terms in a manner that is inconsistent with their use in the body of the agreement.

Defined terms are frequently capitalized in a contract to alert the reader that the word is defined. Definitions are almost essential in many contracts, but their use may complicate the understanding of the agreement. Someone who reads a contract will first read a definition without knowing its significance. Later, when he or she reads the body of the contract, he or she may no longer recall a term's meaning. For this reason, someone reviewing a contract for the first time should read the definitions twice: initially and then in the context of each term's use. Definitions sections tend to err on the side of containing too many definitions. A term that is used only once in a contract need not be defined. On the other hand, a critical reader of a contract will identify instances in which the contract could be improved by the use of additional definitions.

In reviewing a contract, managed health care organizations and providers should not underestimate the importance of definitions of the parties' responsibilities.

An occasional defect in some contracts is that the drafter includes substantive contract provisions in the definitions. A definition is merely an explanation of a meaning of a term and should not contain substantive provisions. This does not mean that a definition that imposes a substantive obligation on a party is invalid. In reviewing a contract, if a party identifies a substantive provision in a definition, the party should ensure that its usage is consistent with the corresponding provision in the body of the contract.

Terms that are commonly defined in a managed care context are *member*, *subscriber*, *medical director*, *provider*, *payer*, *physician*, *primary care physician*, *emergency*, *medically necessary*, and *utilization review program*. Some of these terms, such as *medically necessary*, are crucial to a party's understanding of its responsibilities and should be considered carefully in the review of a contract. In many managed care agreements, payers and not the managed health care organization are responsible for payment under the contract. In this case, who is a payer and how a payer is selected and removed become important to the provider. The definition of *member* or *enrollee* is also important. The contract should convey clearly who is covered under the agreement, but it should be clear as to whom the managed health care organization can add in the future. The managed health care plan and provider should ensure that these terms are consistent, if appropriate, with those in other contracts (e.g., the group enrollment agreement).

Provider Obligations

Provider Services

Because the purpose of the agreement is to contract for the provision of health services, the description of those services in the contract is important. As mentioned above, the recitation of services to be furnished by the provider could be set out either in the contract or in an exhibit or attachment. An exhibit format frequently allows the party more flexibility and administrative simplicity when it amends the exhibited portion of the agreement, particularly when the change requires regulatory approval.

Contracts may use the term *provider services* to denote the range of services that is to be provided under the contract. Managed health care organizations frequently adapt physician contracts to apply to ancillary providers. In so doing, the managed health care organization may not revise language that is applicable only to physicians and apply it to an ancillary provider. Nonphysician providers should consider this issue in reviewing a contract.

The contract needs to specify to whom the provider is obligated to furnish services. Although the answer is that the provider furnishes services to covered enrollees, the contract needs to define what is meant by *covered enrollee*, explain how the provider will learn who is covered, and assign the responsibility for payment if services are furnished to a noncovered person. Managed health care organizations and providers frequently disagree on this issue. The providers' view is frequently that if the managed care organization represented that the individual was covered, the managed care organization should be responsible for payment. In contrast, the managed care organization frequently asserts that it should not be responsible for the costs of services provided to noncovered enrollees and that the provider should seek payment directly from the individual. This issue is oftentimes resolved based on relative negotiating strength.

Provider contracts should also cover adequately a number of other provider responsibilities, including the provider's responsibilities to refer or to accept referrals of enrollees, the days and times of days the provider agrees to be available to provide services, and substitute on-call arrangements, if appropriate. Provider contracts may also specify the qualifications necessary for the provider of backup services when the provider is not available. Some of these functions may be prescribed as conditions of participation in public programs, such as the Medicare risk-contracting program.

If the provider is a hospital, the contract will include language identifying the circumstances in which the managed health care plan agrees to be responsible or not responsible for services provided to nonemergency patients. A fairly common provision in hospital contracts states that the hospital, except in emergencies, must as a prerequisite to admit have the order of the participating physician or other preadmission authorization. The hospital contract also should have an explicit provision requiring that the managed health care plan be notified within a specified period after an emergency admission. A related policy and contracting issue is whether the hospital should be entitled to reimbursement for performing the initial screen that is required when a patient goes to the emergency department.

A good provider contract must be supplemented by a competent provider relations program to ensure that problems that arise are resolved and that the providers have a means to answer questions about their contract responsibilities. Providers will frequently be given the opportunity to appeal internally claim denials and decisions of non–medical necessity by the managed care organization.

Nondiscriminatory Requirements

Provider agreements frequently contain clauses obligating the provider to furnish services to the health care plan's patients in the same manner as the provider furnishes services to non–managed health care patients (i.e., not to discriminate on the basis of payment source). In addition, a clause is used to prohibit other types of discrimination on the basis of race, color, sex, age, disability, religion, and national origin. Government contracts may require the use of specific contract language, including a reference to compliance with the Americans with Disabilities Act. As an alternative, the managed care organization and provider may want to add a second contract clause that requires compliance with all nondiscrimination requirements under federal, state, and local law. These obligations may also apply to subcontractors of the provider.

Compliance with Utilization Review Standards and Protocols and the Quality Assurance Program

The success of the managed care organization is dependent on its providers being able and willing to control unnecessary utilization. To do so, the providers need to follow the utilization review guidelines of the managed health care plan. The contract needs to set out the provider's responsibilities in carrying out the managed health care plan's utilization review program. The managed health care plan's dilemma is how to articulate this obligation in the contract when the utilization review program may be quite detailed and frequently is updated over time. One option used by some managed care organizations is to append the utilization review program to the contract as an exhibit. A second option is merely to incorporate the program by reference. In either case, it is important for the managed health care plan to ensure that the contract allows it to amend the utilization review standards in the future without the consent of the provider. If the managed health care plan does not append a cross-referenced standard, the managed health care plan should give each provider a copy of the guidelines and any amendments. Without this documentation, the provider might argue that it did not agree to the guidelines or subsequent amendments.

The contract needs to inform providers of their responsibilities to cooperate in efforts by the managed health care plan to ensure compliance and the implications of the provider not meeting the guidelines. Contracts differ on whether the managed health care plan is seeking the provider's cooperation or compliance. The current Health Care Financing Administration (HCFA) guidelines for provider contracts require that the provider cooperate with and participate in the managed health care plan's quality assurance program, member grievance system, and utilization review program. Providers generally favor an obligation to cooperate with these programs rather than one to comply because a requirement to comply with the programs decisions seems to preclude the right to disagree.

The same basic concepts and principles apply to the provider's acceptance of the managed health care plan's quality assurance program. Some managed health care plans tend to equate their utilization review and their quality assurance programs. This attitude not only reflects a misunderstanding of the objectives of the two programs but is likely to engender the concern or criticism of government regulators, which view the two programs as being separate. In the last several years, as managed health care plans have placed greater emphasis on their quality assurance/quality improvement programs, provider compliance responsibilities have increased correspondingly. To provide some guidance on the nature of these responsibilities, some managed health care organizations have appended summaries of these quality programs to the contracts to give providers a better idea of their responsibilities.

The contract should include a provision requiring the provider to cooperate both in furnishing information to the managed health care plan and in taking corrective actions, if appropriate.

Acceptance of Enrollee Patients

A provider contract, particularly with a physician or physician group, will need a clause to ensure that the provider will accept enrollees regardless of their health status. This provision is more important when the risk-sharing responsibilities with the providers are such that the physician has an incentive to dissuade high utilizers from becoming part of his or her panel. Most provider contracts with primary care physicians also include a minimum number of members that the physician will accept into his or her panel (e.g., 250 members). The contract should also include fair and reasonable procedures for allowing the provider to limit or stop new members from being added to his or her panel (at a point after the provider has accepted at least the minimum number of members) and a mechanism to notify the managed health care plan when these changes take place. The managed health care plan needs to have data regarding which providers are limiting their panel size to comply with regulatory requirements.

The contract should also specify the circumstances in which the provider, principally a primary care physician, can cease being an enrollee's physician. Examples may be an enrollee's abusive behavior or refusal to follow a recommended course of treatment. This contract language would need to be consistent with language in the member subscriber agreement and in compliance with licensure requirements, which frequently identify the grounds on which a physician may end the physician–enrollee relationship.

Enrollee Complaints

The contract should require the provider to cooperate in resolving enrollee complaints and to notify the managed health care plan within a specified period of time when any complaints are conveyed to the provider. The provider should also be obligated to advise the managed health care plan of any coverage denials so that the managed health care plan can anticipate future enrollee complaints. To the extent that governmental payer programs require special enrollee grievance procedures, the language in the contract should be written sufficiently broadly to ensure provider cooperation with those procedures.

Maintenance and Retention of Records and Confidentiality

Provider contracts should require the provider to maintain both medical and business records for specified periods of time. For example, these agreements could provide that the records must be maintained in accordance with federal and state laws and consistent with generally accepted business and professional standards as well as whatever other standards are established by the managed health care plan. If the managed health care plan participates in any public or private payer program that establishes certain specific records retention requirements, those requirements should be conveyed to the providers. The contract should state that these obligations survive the termination of the contract.

The managed health care plan also needs a legal right to have access to books and records. The contract will want to state that the managed health care plan, its representatives, and government agencies have the right to inspect, review, and make or obtain copies of medical, financial, and administrative records. The provider would want the availability of this information to be limited to services rendered to enrollees, after reasonable notice, and during normal business hours. The cost of performing these services is often an issue of controversy. If there are no fees for copying these records, the contract should so state. When the managed health care organization is acting on behalf of other payers, it is desirable to have language acknowledging that the other payers have agreed to comply with applicable confidentiality laws.

In addition to the availability of books or records, the managed health care plan might also want the right to require the provider to prepare reports identifying statistical and descriptive medical and patient data and other identifying information as specified by the managed health care plan. If such a provision is included in the contract, the managed health care plan should inform the provider of the types of reports it might request to minimize any future problems. Finally, the provider should be obligated to provide information that is necessary for compliance with state or federal law.

An often neglected legal issue is how the managed health care plan obtains the authority to have access to medical records. Provider agreements periodically contain an acknowledgment by the provider that the managed health care plan is authorized to receive medical records. The problem with this approach is that the managed health care plan might not have the right to have access to this information, and, if it does not, an acknowledgment of that right in the contract has no legal effect. Some state laws give insurers and HMOs, as payers, a limited right of access to medical records. This right may arise if the managed health care organization is performing utilization review on behalf of an enrollee. Managed health care plans should review their state law provisions on this issue and their procedures for obtaining the appropriate consents of their members to have access to this information. Many managed health care plans obtain this information through signatures that are part of the initial enrollment materials. These consents could also be obtained at the time health services are rendered.

Managed health care organizations frequently include provisions in contracts in which the provider acknowledges that the managed health care organization has the right of access to enrollee records. The provider should be reluctant to agree to this provision without consulting state law. Although the clause acknowledging the right of access may make it easier to persuade a reluctant provider to release an enrollee's medical records, the managed health care plan needs to remember that that statement, or for that matter similar statements in the group enrollment agreement, do not confer that right. Finally, the contract should state explicitly that the provisions concerning access to records survive the termination of the agreement.

A related provision almost always included in provider contracts is a requirement that the provider maintain the confidentiality of medical records. A common clause is a provision that the provider will only release the records in accordance with the terms of the contract, in accordance with applicable law, or upon appropriate consent. State law will frequently allow disclosure of information without patient identifiers for purposes of research or education. Managed health care plans and providers need to be sensitive to confidentiality concerns with regard to minors, incompetents, and persons with communicable diseases for which there are specific state confidentiality statutes governing disclosure of information.

A medical record issue may arise when a managed health care plan wants the right to perform certain medical tests outside the hospital before an enrollee's admission. The contract between the managed health care plan and the hospital may allow for such tests and the inclusion of the test results into the hospital's medical record. The hospital may insist that the results of the tests be in a format acceptable to the hospital's medical record committee, that the laboratory results be properly certified, and that the duties performed shall be consistent with the proper practice of medicine.

Payment

The payment terms of the agreement often represent the most important provision for both the provider and the managed health care plan. As mentioned earlier, the payment terms are frequently set forth in an exhibit appended to the contract and are cross-referenced in the body of the agreement. A number of payment issues should be covered in the contract. For example, who will collect the copayments? If the managed health care plan pays the provider on a fee-for-service basis, a provision needs to state that unauthorized or uncovered services are not the responsibility of the managed health care plan. To avoid members' receiving unexpected bills from providers for noncovered services, contracts may say that the provider must inform the member that a service will not be covered by the health plan before providing the service. In addition, the contract may preclude the provider from ever billing an enrollee when the managed health care organization has determined that the service is not medically necessary.

From the provider's perspective, he or she needs a clear understanding of what is necessary for a service to be authorized. If the provider submits claims to the managed health care plan, the contract should set out the manner in which the claim is to be made and either identify the information to be provided in the claim or give the managed health care plan the right to designate or revise that information in the future. If the contract specifies the information to be included in a claim, the managed health care plan should also have the unilateral right to make changes in the future.

The agreement should also obligate the provider to submit claims within a specified period and obligate the managed health care plan to pay claims within a certain number of days. The latter requirement should not apply to contested claims. Also, special provisions will apply to claims for which another carrier may be the primary payer. A common way to address this issue in a balanced manner is to allow a 2-month period for collection from the purported primary carrier. If unsuccessful, the managed health care plan would pay while awaiting resolution of the dispute.

At issue is the time in which the managed health care organization is required to pay on claims. Contracts frequently identify a specific time period (e.g., 30 to 60 days) during which payment on clean claims is to be made. Provider contracts rarely impose an interest penalty for late payment, reflecting the greater bargaining strength of the managed health care organization. Some contracts require the managed health care organization to make a good faith effort to pay within a specified period. From the provider's perspective, the weakness of this provision is that a good faith standard is probably too ambiguous to be enforceable. Some states have laws requiring insurers and HMOs to pay interest on late claims.

The contract needs also to address reconciliations to account for overpayments or underpayments. To avoid these issues from lingering for an inordinately long period of time, some managed health care plans limit the adjustment period to a specified period (e.g., 6 months). Also, some managed health care plans use contract provisions that do not allow for a reconciliation if the amount in controversy falls below a specified amount.

The most complex aspects of provider contracts are often the risk-sharing arrangements (see Chapters 8, 10, and 11). Risk can be shared with providers in significantly varying degrees depending on the initial amount of risk transferred, the services for which the provider is at risk, and whether the managed health care organization offers stop-loss protection. Risk pools with complicated formulas determining distributions are frequently used both when services are capitated and when payments are based on a fee schedule. Although the primary objective of these arrangements is to create incentives to discourage unnecessary utilization, the complexity of many of these arrangements has confused providers and engendered their distrust when their distribution falls below expectations. Some managed health care plans that had complex risk-sharing arrangements are now realizing that simpler, more understandable arrangements are preferable. If the arrangement designed by the managed health care plan is somewhat complex, the provider's understanding will be greatly enhanced by the use of examples that illustrate for providers the total payments they will receive in different factual scenarios.

The most significant trend in provider payment arrangements has been the growth of arrangements where physician–hospital organizations (PHOs) or other integrated delivery systems are willing to accept a percentage of the managed health care plan premium as compensation for the services they provide (see Chapter 4). An important, related issue is the extent to which state regulators will want to oversee these arrangements directly or indirectly through licensure requirements applicable to the licensed entities to which the PHOs contract (see Chapter 28). The PHO assumes the role of a super-IPA as it becomes responsible for providing, or arranging for the provision of, all or almost all the managed health care plan's services for enrollees assigned to it. In fact, the PHO does not typically provide services itself; the PHO arranges for the health services through affiliated hospitals, physician groups, and other health care providers. In developing its relationships with a managed health care plan, the PHO must be mindful of how it is transferring the obligations to provide services to its subcontractors.

The compensation arrangements typically provide that the PHO will receive a specified percentage of the amount that the managed health care plan or other payer receives. To reduce the risk of inappropriate adverse or favorable selection, the payment amounts may be adjusted to account for expected utilization based on demographic factors, such as age, sex, and other predictors of health care utilization. Also, the amount of risk assumed by the PHO might be limited until the number of enrollees assigned to the PHO reaches a critical size. The amount of compensation received by the PHO would be reduced to reflect the cost of services that the PHO does not assume responsibility for or stop-loss coverage that is provided by the managed health care plan.

Another issue to consider is whether the managed health care plan will have the right to have the services performed by other providers if it is not satisfied with the contracted provider's performance. Because the PHO is assuming virtually all the risk for the defined population, the PHO needs to consider carefully the assumptions that have been made regarding the demographics and health needs of the covered population.

In recent years, as providers gain more experience with managed health care plans, they are becoming more sophisticated in analyzing and evaluating payment arrangements and are more aware of the ability or inability of managed health care plans to produce the volume promised. A growing number of contracts are being renegotiated in light of the actual volume of patients that a managed health care plan is able to deliver to the provider. Contracts are also now beginning to allow volume as a factor affecting payment amount.

Some of the payment-related issues that should be addressed in a contract are as follows: What if services are provided to a person who is no longer eligible for enrollment? What if services are provided to a nonenrollee who obtained services by using an enrollee's membership card? Who has the responsibility to pursue third party recoveries? What are the notice requirements when the nonresponsible party finds out about a potential third party recovery? Some managed health care plans allow their providers to collect and keep third party recoveries, whereas others will require that the information be reported and the recovered amount deducted. One sensitive issue is the potential liability of a managed health care plan if a provider collects from Medicare inappropriately when another carrier under the Medicare secondary payer rules had primary responsibility. Under the regulations of the HCFA, the managed health care plan is legally responsible and may be forced to pay back the HCFA even if the payment was received by the provider without the knowledge of the managed health care plan. Managed health care plans should include a contract provision transferring the liability to the provider in this circumstance.

Another issue that should be addressed in the contract is the responsibility of the managed health care plan as a secondary carrier if the provider bills the primary carrier an amount greater than the amount the provider would have received from the managed health care plan. From the managed health care plan's perspective, it will want a contract provision relieving the managed health care plan of any payment responsibility if the provider has received at least the amount that he or she would have been entitled to under the managed health care plan–provider contract.

Hold-Harmless and No Balance Billing Clauses

Virtually all provider contracts contain a hold-harmless clause, under which the provider agrees not to sue or assert any claims against the enrollee for services covered under the contract, even if the managed health care plan becomes insolvent or fails to meet its obligations. A no balance billing clause is similar (and may be used synonymously) and states that a provider may not balance bill a member for any payment owed by the plan, regardless of the reason for nonpayment; the provider may bill the member for any amount that the member is required to pay, such as copayment or coinsurance, or for services not covered under the schedule of benefits (e.g., cosmetic surgery). Many state insurance departments (or other agencies having regulatory oversight in this area) will not approve the provider forms without inclusion of a hold-harmless clause containing specific language. HCFA also has adopted recommended model hold-harmless language applicable to federally qualified HMOs that was approved by the National Association of Insurance Commissioners.

Relationship of the Parties

Provider contracts usually contain a provision stating that the managed health care plan and the provider have an independent contractual arrangement. The purpose of this provision is to refute an assertion that the provider serves as an employee of the managed health care plan. The reason is that, under the legal theory of respondeat superior, the managed health care plan would automatically be liable for the negligent acts of its employees. Although managed health care plans frequently include a provision such as this in their provider contracts, it has limited value. In a lawsuit against the managed health care plan by an enrollee alleging malpractice, the court is likely to disregard such language and to focus on the relationship between the managed health care plan and the provider and the manner in which the managed health care plan represented the provider in evaluating whether the managed health care plan should be vicariously liable.

A related clause frequently used in provider contracts states that nothing contained in the agreement shall be construed to require physicians to recommend any procedure or course of treatment that physicians deem professionally inappropriate. This clause is intended, in part, to affirm that the managed health care plan is not engaged in the practice of medicine, an activity that the managed health care plan may not be permitted to perform. Another reason for this clause is to protect the managed health care plan from liability arising from a provider's negligence.

Use of Name

Many provider contracts limit the ability of either party to use the name of the other. This is done by identifying the circumstances in which the party's name may or may not be used. Contract clauses may allow the managed health care plan the right to use the name of the provider for the health benefits accounts, the enrollees, and the patients of the participating providers. Otherwise, the party needs the written approval of the other party. The use applies not only to the name but also to any symbol, trademark, and service mark of the entity. The managed health care plan and the provider will want to ensure that proprietary information is protected. The contract should require that the provider keep all information about the managed health care plan confidential and prohibit the use of the information for any competitive purpose after the contract is terminated. With medical groups frequently switching managed care affiliations, this protection is important to the managed health care plan.

Notification

The managed health care plan needs to ensure that it is advised of a number of important changes that affect the ability of the provider to meet his or her contractual obligations. The contract should identify the information that needs to be conveyed to the managed health care plan and the time frames for providing that information. For example, a physician might be required to notify a managed health care plan within 5 days upon loss or suspension of his or her license or certification, loss or restriction of full active admitting privileges at any hospital, or issuance of any formal charges brought by a government agency. Although specific events should be identified in the contract, a broad catch-all category should also be included, such as an event that, if sustained, would materially impair the provider's ability to perform the duties under the contract. The contract should require immediate notification if the provider is sanctioned under the Medicare or Medicaid programs. If the managed care organization is contracting with a provider who has been sanctioned, the organization may no longer be eligible to receive Medicare and Medicaid funds.

In a hospital contract, the corresponding provisions would be when the hospital suffers from a change that materially impairs its ability to provide services or if action is taken against it regarding certifications, licenses, or federal agencies or private accrediting bodies.

Insurance and Indemnification

Insurance provisions in contracts are fairly straightforward. The obligations in the contract may be for both professional liability coverage and general liability coverage. The managed health care plan wants to ensure that the provider has resources to pay for any eventuality. The contract will state particular insurance limits, provide that the limits will be set forth in a separate attachment, or leave it up to the managed health care plan to specify. A hospital agreement may require only that the limits be commensurate with limits contained in policies of similar hospitals in the state. From the managed health care organization's perspective, it will probably want a specific requirement to ensure adequate levels of insurance. There also should be a provision requiring the provider to notify the managed health care plan of any notification of cancellations of the policy. Another needed notification in a physician context is notification of any malpractice claims.

Cross-indemnification provisions, in which each party indemnifies the other for damages caused by the other party, are common in contracts. One weakness of the clause is that some professional liability carriers will not pay for claims arising from these clauses because of general exclusions in their policies for contractual claims. Although these clauses are frequently used, this limitation and the fact that a provider should still be liable for his or her negligent acts suggest that these indemnification clauses are not essential.

Term, Suspension, and Termination

One section of most contracts identifies the term of the contract and the term of any subsequent contract renewals. Many contracts have automatic renewal provisions if no party exercises its right to terminate. Both managed health care plans and providers should give careful thought to the length of the contract and the renewal periods.

Some contracts give a right of suspension to the managed health care plan. In suspension, the contract continues, but the provider loses specific rights. For example, if a provider fails to follow utilization review protocols a specified number of times, the provider will not be assigned new HMO members or perhaps will receive a reduction in the amount of payment. The advantage of a suspension provision is that total termination of a contract might be counterproductive for the managed health care plan, but a suspension might be sufficiently punitive to persuade the provider to improve.

Termination provisions fall into two categories: termination without cause, and termination with cause. The value of having a provision that allows the managed health care plan to terminate without cause is that the managed health care plan need not defend a challenge by the provider on the substantive issue of whether the grounds were met. A 90-day period is fairly common. If the managed health care plan has the right to terminate without cause, frequently the provider will also be given that right. A regulatory issue to be aware of is that some state laws require providers to continue to provide services for a specified period of time after their contract has terminated. These requirements relate to the state's requirements for the managed health care plan to have protections against insolvency and have to be reflected in the contract.

Terminations with cause allow the health plan to terminate faster and should be used in situations where the managed health care plan needs to act quickly. The contract might establish two different categories: one for immediate termination and another for termination within a 30-day period. Many contracts give either party a period of time to cure any contract violations. This time period, although useful to the managed health care plan if it has allegedly violated the agreement, extends the period of time in which it can terminate the contract. Grounds for termination for cause may be suspension or revocation of a license, loss of hospital privileges, failure to meet accreditation and credentialing requirements, failure to provide services to enrollees in a professionally acceptable manner, and refusal to accept an amendment to the contract agreement. A general clause also allows for termination if the provider takes any actions or makes any communications that undermine or could undermine the confidence of enrollees in the quality of care provided by the managed health care plan. This last clause has been variably interpreted by health plans and has been the subject of some state regulation. The clause should make clear that a physician is free to make medical recommendations, but is not free to disparage the plan.

The contract should be clear that a provider, upon termination, is required to cooperate in the orderly transfer of enrollee care, including records, to other providers. The provider also should cooperate in resolving any disputes. Finally, the provider should continue to furnish services until the services being rendered to enrollees are complete or the managed health care plan has made appropriate provisions for another provider to assume the responsibility. The contract should also be clear that the provider is entitled to compensation for performing these services.

In general, too little consideration has been given to preparing for contract terminations. When the provider and the managed health care plan enter into a contract, little thought is given to what will occur when the contract ends. Often, relationships end acrimoniously, and it is in both parties' best interest to consider how their interests will be protected in the event that the contract is terminated.

Declarations

In declarations, the parties provide answers to a number of "what if" questions. These clauses are common to all contracts.

A *force majeure* clause relieves a party of responsibility if an event occurs beyond its control. In a provider contract, this instance is more likely to arise if the provider is no longer able to provide services. In considering *force majeure* clauses, the parties need to distinguish between events that are beyond a party's control and those that disadvantage a party but for which the party should still be obligated to perform the contract's responsibilities.

A choice of law provision identifies the law that will apply in the event of a dispute. Absent a violation of public policy in the state in question, a court will apply the agreed-upon law. Frequently, lawyers draft contracts using the state in which their client is located without consideration of the advantages and disadvantages of the underlying law. In provider contracts where the managed health care plan and the provider are located in the same state, this clause has little relevance.

A merger clause specifies that only the language in the agreement shall constitute the contract. Such a clause prevents a party from arguing that oral conversations or other documents not included in the contract modify the contract's terms.

A provision allowing or not allowing parties to assign their rights is frequently included in contracts. Provider contracts usually prohibit a provider from assigning its rights under a contract. Some contracts are silent on the right of the managed health care plan to assign the contract. Silence would allow the managed health care plan to assign the contract. An option is to allow the managed health care plan to assign the contract only to an affiliate or a successor without the written consent of the provider.

A clause identifying how the contract will be amended is almost always included in a provider contract. A contract will frequently give the managed health care plan the unilateral right to amend the contract absent an objection by the provider. This procedure is necessary when the managed health care plan has a large provider panel and it is administratively difficult to obtain the signatures of all the providers.

A severability clause allows the contract to continue if a court invalidates a portion of the contract. This is a common provision in a contract, but it is unlikely that the problem will arise.

Contracts also set forth a notice requirement identifying how notices are provided to parties and to whom. The manner in which notice is provided is important. If a notice requires that the communication be conveyed by certified mail with return receipt requested, an alternative form of delivery is not valid. Parties should consider what is administratively feasible before agreeing on how notice will be given.

Closing

Both parties need to confirm that the parties identified at the beginning of the contract are the parties that sign the contract. Also, if a corporation is one of the parties, the signatory needs to be authorized on behalf of the corporation to sign the agreement.

CONCLUSION

The provider contract establishes the foundation for the working relationship between the managed health care plan and the provider. A good contract is well organized and clearly written and accurately reflects the full intentions of the parties. In drafting and reviewing provider contracts, the managed health care plan and the provider need to keep in mind their objectives in entering the relationship, the relationship of this contract to other provider contracts and agreements, and applicable regulatory requirements.

Study Questions

---

1. Describe important payment issues that should be addressed in a managed care agreement. What is a significant trend in provider payment agreements?
2. Describe "Hold Harmless" and "No Balance Billing" clauses in managed care contracts.
3. Describe insurance and cross indemnification clauses in managed care contracts.
4. What are common provider obligations included in managed care contracts? Describe these obligations.
5. What terms would be considered essential from the standpoint of a physician? A hospital? Under what circumstances would any of these terms be considered unacceptable by the HMO?

Appendix 29–A

Sample Physician Agreement

AGREEMENT BETWEEN

____

AND

PRIMARY CARE PHYSICIAN

THIS AGREEMENT, made and entered into the date set forth on the signature page hereto, by and between _____________________, Inc., a _________ corporation (hereinafter referred to as "HMO"), which is organized and operated as a health maintenance organization under the laws of the State of _________ and the individual physician or group practice identified on the signature page hereto (hereinafter referred to as "Primary Care Physician").

WHEREAS, HMO desires to operate a health maintenance organization pursuant to the laws of the State of _________; and

WHEREAS, Primary Care Physician is a duly licensed physician (or if Primary Care Physician is a legal entity, the members of such entity are duly licensed physicians) in the State of _________, whose license(s) is (are) without limitation or restriction[1]; and

WHEREAS, HMO has as an objective the development and expansion of cost-effective means of delivering quality health services to Members, as defined herein, particularly through prepaid health care plans, and Primary Care Physician concurs in, actively supports, and will contribute to the achievement of this objective; and

WHEREAS, HMO and Primary Care Physician mutually desire to enter into an Agreement whereby the Primary Care Physician shall provide and coordinate the health care services to Members of HMO.

NOW, THEREFORE, in consideration of the premises and mutual covenants herein contained and other good and valuable consideration, it is mutually covenanted and agreed by and between the parties hereto as follows:

[1] Although there is nothing wrong with having a statement here that the primary care physician's license is not restricted, the body of the contract, as is the case in this contract in Part IV (H), needs to contain this requirement and provide that the failure to maintain the license is grounds for termination.

PART I. DEFINITIONS

A. *Covered Services* means those health services and benefits to which Members are entitled under the terms of an applicable Health Maintenance Certificate which may be amended by HMO from time to time.[2]

B. *Emergency Services* means those Medically Necessary services provided in connection with an "Emergency," defined as a sudden or unexpected onset of a condition requiring medical or surgical care which the Member secures after the onset of such condition (or as soon thereafter as care can be made available but which in any case is not later than twenty-four (24) hours after onset) and in the absence of such care the Member could reasonably be expected to suffer serious physical impairment or death. Heart attacks, severe chest pain, cardiovascular accidents, hemorrhaging, poisonings, major burns, loss of consciousness, serious breathing difficulties, spinal injuries, shock, and other acute conditions as HMO shall determine are Emergencies.[3]

C. *Encounter Form* means a record of services provided by Physician to Members in a format acceptable to the HMO.[4]

D. *Health Maintenance Certificate* means a contract issued by HMO to a Member or an employer of Members specifying the services and benefits available under the HMO's prepaid health benefits program.

E. *Health Professionals* means doctors of medicine, doctors of osteopathy, dentists, nurses, chiropractors, podiatrists, optometrists, physician assistants, clinical psychologists, social workers, pharmacists, occupational therapists, physical therapists, and other professionals engaged in the delivery of health services who are licensed, practice under an institutional license, and are certified or practice under other authority consistent with the laws of the State of ____________.

F. *Medical Director* means a Physician designated by HMO to monitor and review the provision of Covered Services to Members.

G. *Medically Necessary* services and/or supplies means the use of services or supplies as provided by a hospital, skilled nursing facility, Physician, or other provider required to identify or treat a Member's illness or injury and which, as determined by HMO's Medical Director or its utilization review committee, are: (1) consistent with the symptoms or diagnosis and treatment of the Member's condition, disease, ailment, or injury; (2) appropriate with regard to standards of good medical practice; (3) not solely for the convenience of the Member, his or her physician, hospital, or other health care provider; and (4) the most appropriate supply or level of service which can be safely provided to the Member.[5] When specifically applied to an inpatient Mem-

---

[2] This definition notes the HMO's right to revise the covered services that the primary care physician is required to provide. If the physicians were capitated for those services, a mechanism would need to be available to revise the capitation rate accordingly. If the services were not limited to HMO enrollees (e.g., covered persons under an administrative services only arrangement with a self-insured employer), this definition would have to be written more broadly.

[3] The definition for emergency services would be coordinated with the definition used in the HMO's group enrollment agreement. The examples are a useful method of illustrating the types of conditions that are considered emergencies. Some contracts will exclude deliveries during the last month of pregnancy while the mother is traveling outside the service area.

[4] By stating that the encounter form must be acceptable to the HMO, the contract allows the HMO to change its requirements in the future.

[5] This clause gives the HMO the authority to deny coverage for a medically appropriate procedure where another procedure is also appropriate. Although this clause does not explicitly address the subject, it is intended to give the HMO the right to cover the most cost-effective, medically appropriate procedure. An alternative way of addressing the issue is to state explicitly as one of the criteria that the procedure performed is the "least costly setting or manner appropriate to treat the Enrollee's medical condition."

ber, it further means that the Member's medical symptoms or condition requires that the diagnosis or treatment cannot be safely provided to the Member as an outpatient.[6]

H. *Member* means both a Subscriber and his or her eligible family members for whom premium payment has been made.[7]

I. *Participating Physician* means a Physician who, at the time of providing or authorizing services to a Member, has contracted with or on whose behalf a contract has been entered into with HMO to provide professional services to Members.

J. *Participating Provider* means a Physician, hospital, skilled nursing facility, home health agency, or any other duly licensed institution or Health Professional under contract with HMO to provide professional and hospital services to Members.

K. *Physician* means a duly licensed doctor of medicine or osteopathy.

L. *Primary Care Physician* means a Participating Physician who provides primary care services to Members (e.g., general or family practitioner, internist, pediatrician, or such other physician specialty as may be designated by HMO) and is responsible for referrals of Members to Referral Physicians, other Participating Providers, and, if necessary, non-Participating Providers. Each Member shall select or have selected on his or her behalf a Primary Care Physician.

M. *Referral Physician* means a Participating Physician who is responsible for providing certain medical referral physician services upon referral by a Primary Care Physician.

N. *Service Area* means those counties in _________ set forth in Attachment A and such other areas as may be designated by HMO from time to time.

O. *Subscriber* means an individual who has contracted, or on whose behalf a contract has been entered into, with HMO for health care services.

PART II. OBLIGATIONS OF HMO

A. *Administrative Procedures.* HMO shall make available to Primary Care Physician a manual of administrative procedures (including any changes thereto) in the areas of recordkeeping, reporting, and other administrative duties of the Primary Care Physician under this Agreement. Primary Care Physician agrees to abide by such administrative procedures including, but not limited to, the submission HMO Encounter Forms documenting all Covered Services provided to Members by Primary Care Physician.[8]

B. *Compensation.* For all Medically Necessary Covered Services provided to Members by Primary Care Physician, HMO shall pay to Primary Care Physician the compensation set forth in Attachment B.[9] Itemized statements on HMO Encounter Forms, or approved equivalent, for all Covered Services rendered by Primary Care Physician must be submitted to HMO within ninety (90) days of the date the service was rendered in order to be compensated by HMO. The purpose of the risk sharing/incentive compensation arrangement set forth in Attachment B is to monitor utilization, to control costs of health services, including hospitalization, and to achieve utilization goals while maintaining quality of care.

---

[6] This last sentence is a good addition to the definition. It makes clear the preference of outpatient care over inpatient care.

[7] *Member* is usually regarded as synonymous with *enrollee*. The definition of *member* would be consistent with the definition used in the group enrollment agreement.

[8] This paragraph allows the HMO to designate and amend the information, including the claims form, that the primary care physician provides the HMO without obtaining the prior approval of the primary care physician.

[9] This contract reimburses primary care physicians on a fee-for-service basis. Attachment B also sets forth alternative language if an HMO pays its primary care physicians on a capitated basis.

C. *Processing of Claims.* HMO agrees to process Primary Care Physician claims for Covered Services rendered to Members. HMO will make payment within thirty (30) days from the date the claim is received with sufficient documentation. Where a claim requires additional documentation, HMO will make payment within thirty (30) days from date of receipt of sufficient documentation to approve the claim.[10]

D. *Eligibility Report.* HMO shall provide Primary Care Physician with a monthly listing of eligible Members who have selected or have been assigned to Primary Care Physician.

E. *Reports.* HMO will provide Primary Care Physician with periodic statements with respect to the compensation set forth in Attachment B and with utilization reports in accordance with HMO's administrative procedures. Primary Care Physician agrees to maintain the confidentiality of the information presented in such reports.

PART III. OBLIGATIONS OF PRIMARY CARE PHYSICIAN

A. *Health Services.* Primary Care Physician shall have the primary responsibility for arranging and coordinating the overall health care of Members, including appropriate referral to Participating Physicians and Participating Providers, and for managing and coordinating the performance of administrative functions relating to the delivery of health services to Members in accordance with this Agreement. In the event that Primary Care Physician shall provide Member non-Covered Services, Primary Care Physician shall, prior to the provision of such non-Covered Services, inform the Member:

1. of the service(s) to be provided,
2. that HMO will not pay for or be liable for said services, and
3. that Member will be financially liable for such services.[11]

For any health care services rendered to or authorized for Members by Primary Care Physician for which HMO's prior approval is required and such prior approval was not obtained, Primary Care Physician agrees that in no event will HMO assume financial responsibility for charges arising from such services, and payments made by HMO for such services may be deducted by HMO from payments otherwise due Primary Care Physician.[12]

B. *Referrals.* Except in Emergencies or when authorized by HMO, Primary Care Physician agrees to make referrals of Members only to Participating Providers, and only in accordance with HMO policies. Primary Care Physician will furnish such Physicians and providers complete information about treatment procedures and diagnostic tests performed prior to such referral. Upon referral, Primary Care Physician agrees to notify HMO of referral. In the event that services required by a Member are not available from Participating Providers, non-Participating Physicians or Providers may be utilized with the prior approval of HMO. HMO will periodically furnish Primary Care Physician with a current listing of HMO's Participating Referral Physicians and Participating Providers.

C. *Hospital Admissions.* In cases where a Member requires a non-Emergency hospital admission, Primary Care Physician agrees to secure authorization for such admission in accordance with

---

[10] This paragraph allows the HMO to delay payment to the physician while waiting for sufficient documentation.

[11] This prior notification requirement is an important requirement and often is required by state law.

[12] It is important for the HMO to make sure that the physicians know the circumstances or conditions in which prior HMO approval is required.

HMO's procedures prior to the admission. In addition, the Primary Care Physician agrees to abide by HMO hospital discharge policies and procedures for Members.[13]

D. *Primary Care Physician's Members*. The Primary Care Physician shall not refuse to accept a Member as a patient on the basis of health status or medical condition of such Member, except with the approval of the Medical Director. Primary Care Physician may request that he/she does not wish to accept additional Members (excluding persons already in Primary Care Physician's practice who enroll in HMO as Members) by giving HMO written notice of such intent thirty (30) days in advance of the effective date of such closure. Primary Care Physician agrees to accept any HMO Members seeking his/her services during the thirty (30) day notice period. Primary Care Physician agrees to initiate closure of his/her practice to additional Members only if his/her practice, as a whole, is to be closed to additional patients or if authorized by HMO. A request for such authorization shall not be unreasonably denied. HMO may suspend, upon thirty (30) days prior written notice to Primary Care Physician, any further selection of Primary Care Physician by Members who have not already sought Primary Care Physician's services at the time of such suspension.

   In addition, a physician who is a Participating Provider may request, in writing to HMO, that coverage for a Member be transferred to another Participating Physician. Participating Physician shall not seek without authorization by HMO to have a Member transferred because of the amount of services required by the Member or because of the health status of the Member.

E. *Charges to Members*. Primary Care Physician shall accept as payment in full, for services which he/she provides, the compensation specified in Attachment B. Primary Care Physician agrees that in no event, including, but not limited to, nonpayment, HMO insolvency, or breach of this Agreement, shall Physician bill, charge, collect a deposit from, seek compensation, remuneration, or reimbursement from, or have any recourse against Subscriber, Member, or persons other than the HMO acting on a Member's behalf for services provided pursuant to this Agreement. This provision shall not prohibit collection of copayments on HMO's behalf made in accordance with the terms of the Health Maintenance Certificate between HMO and Subscriber/Member. Primary Care Physician further agrees that:

   1. this provision shall survive the termination of this Agreement regardless of the cause giving rise to termination and shall be construed to be for the benefit of the HMO Member, and that
   2. this provision supersedes any oral or written contrary agreement now existing or hereafter entered into between Primary Care Physician and Member, or persons acting on their behalf.[14]

F. *Records and Reports*.

   1. Primary Care Physician shall submit to HMO for each Member encounter an HMO Encounter Form which shall contain such statistical and descriptive medical and patient data as specified by HMO. Primary Care Physician shall maintain such records and provide such medical, financial, and administrative information to HMO as the HMO determines may be necessary for compliance by HMO with state and federal law, as well as for pro-

---

[13] Here, again, it is important for the HMO to ensure that the primary care physicians have full notice of all the requirements for prior authorization and discharges.

[14] State regulatory agencies often dictate the precise language of this clause.

gram management purposes. Primary Care Physician will further provide to HMO and, if required, to authorized state and federal agencies, such access to medical records of HMO Members as is needed to ensure the quality of care rendered to such Members. HMO shall have access at reasonable times, upon request, to the billing and medical records of the Primary Care Physician relating to the health care services provided Members, and to information about the cost of such services, and about copayments received by the Primary Care Physician from Members for Covered Services. Utilization and cost data relating to a Participating Physician may be distributed by HMO to other Participating Physicians for HMO program management purposes.

2. HMO shall also have the right to inspect, at reasonable times, Primary Care Physician's facilities pursuant to HMO's credentialing, peer review, and quality assurance program.
3. Primary Care Physician shall maintain a complete medical record for each Member in accordance with the requirements established by HMO. Medical records of Members will include the recording of services provided by the Primary Care Physician, specialists, and hospitals and other reports from referral providers, discharge summaries, records of Emergency care received by the Member, and such other information as HMO requires.[15] Medical records of Members shall be treated as confidential so as to comply with all federal and state laws and regulations regarding the confidentiality of patient records.[16]

G. *Provision of Services and Professional Requirements.*

1. Primary Care Physician shall make necessary and appropriate arrangements to ensure the availability of physician services to his/her Member patients on a twenty-four (24) hours per day, seven (7) days per week basis, including arrangements to ensure coverage of his/her Member patients after hours or when Primary Care Physician is otherwise absent, consistent with HMO's administrative requirements. Primary Care Physician agrees that scheduling of appointments for Members shall be done in a timely manner. The Primary Care Physician will maintain weekly appointment hours which are sufficient and convenient to serve Members and will maintain at all times Emergency and on-call services. Covering arrangements shall be with another Physician who is also a Participating Provider or who has otherwise been approved in advance by HMO. For services rendered by any covering Physician on behalf of Primary Care Physician, including Emergency Services, it shall be Primary Care Physician's sole responsibility to make suitable arrangements with the covering Physician regarding the manner in which said Physician will be reimbursed or otherwise compensated, provided, however, that Primary Care Physician shall ensure that the covering Physician will not, under any circumstances, bill HMO or bill Member for Covered Services (except copayments), and Primary Care Physician hereby agrees to indemnify and hold harmless Members and HMO against charges for Covered Services rendered by physicians who are covering on behalf of Primary Care Physician.

---

[15] This paragraph contains an important requirement. The primary care physician serves as a gatekeeper and the coordinator of care for this HMO. To serve this function, the primary care physician needs information from referral providers. Of course, there needs to be a requirement in the contracts with referral physicians that this information shall be provided to the applicable primary care physician.

[16] For this sentence to be effective, the HMO needs to ensure that its staff and the primary care physician understand state and federal confidentiality laws. Special requirements often arise in some areas, such as acquired immune deficiency syndrome and mental health and substance abuse services.

2. Primary Care Physician agrees:

   (a) not to discriminate in the treatment of his/her patients or in the quality of services delivered to HMO's Members on the basis of race, sex, age, religion, place of residence, health status, disability, or source of payment, and
   (b) to observe, protect, and promote the rights of Members as patients. Primary Care Physician shall not seek to transfer a Member from his/her practice based on the Member's health status, without authorization by HMO.

3. Primary Care Physician agrees that all duties performed hereunder shall be consistent with the proper practice of medicine, and that such duties shall be performed in accordance with the customary rules of ethics and conduct of the applicable state and professional licensure boards and agencies.
4. Primary Care Physician agrees that, to the extent he/she utilizes allied Health Professionals and other personnel for delivery of health care, he/she will inform HMO of the functions performed by such personnel.
5. Primary Care Physician shall be duly licensed to practice medicine in _________ and shall maintain good professional standing at all times. Evidence of such licensing shall be submitted to HMO upon request. In addition, Primary Care Physician must meet all qualifications and standards for membership on the medical staff of at least one of the hospitals, if any, which have contracted with HMO and shall be required to maintain staff membership and full admission privileges in accordance with the rules and regulations of such hospital and be otherwise acceptable to such hospital. Finally, Primary Care Physician shall be a duly qualified provider under the Medicare program. Physician agrees to give immediate notice to HMO in the case of suspension or revocation, or initiation of any proceeding that could result in suspension or revocation, of his/her licensure, hospital privileges, or Medicare qualification status or the filing of a malpractice action against the Primary Care Physician.

H. *Insurance*. Primary Care Physician, including individual Physicians providing services to Members under this Agreement if Primary Care Physician is a legal entity, shall provide and maintain such policies of general and professional liability (malpractice) insurance as shall be necessary to insure the Primary Care Physician and his/her employees against any claim or claims for damages arising by reason of personal injuries or death occasioned, directly or indirectly, in connection with the performance of any service by Primary Care Physician. The amounts and extent of such insurance coverage shall be subject to the approval of HMO. Primary Care Physician shall provide memorandum copies of such insurance coverage to HMO upon request.[17]

I. *Administration*.

1. Primary Care Physician agrees to cooperate and participate in such review and service programs as may be established by HMO, including utilization and quality assurance pro-

[17] The HMO should have this insurance information on file. Thus the HMO, as a matter of course, should request this information and require notification of changes in the insurance coverage.

grams, credentialing, sanctioning, external audit systems, administrative procedures, and Member and Physician grievance procedures. Primary Care Physician shall comply with all determinations rendered through the above programs.

2. Primary Care Physician agrees that HMO may use his/her name, address, phone number, picture, type of practice, applicable practice restrictions, and an indication of Primary Care Physician's willingness to accept additional Members, in HMO's roster of physician participants and other HMO materials. Primary Care Physician shall not reference HMO in any publicity, advertisements, notices, or promotional material or in any announcement to the Members without prior review and written approval of HMO.
3. Primary Care Physician agrees to provide to HMO information for the collection and coordination of benefits when a Member holds other coverage that is deemed primary for the provision of services to said Member and to abide by HMO coordination of benefits and duplicate coverage policies. This shall include, but not be limited to, permitting HMO to bill and process forms for any third party payer on the Primary Care Physician's behalf for Covered Services and to retain any sums received. In addition, Primary Care Physician shall cooperate in and abide by HMO subrogation policies and procedures.
4. Primary Care Physician agrees to maintain the confidentiality of all information related to fees, charges, expenses, and utilization derived from, through, or provided by HMO.
5. In the event of:

   (a) termination of this Agreement,
   (b) the selection by a Member of another Primary Care Physician in accordance with HMO procedures, or
   (c) the approval by HMO of Primary Care Physician's request to transfer a Member from his/her practice,

   Primary Care Physician agrees to transfer copies of the Member's medical records, radiographs, or other data to HMO when requested to do so in writing by HMO, at the reasonable, customary, and usual fee for such copies.

6. In the event that this Agreement is terminated by either HMO or Primary Care Physician, Primary Care Physician shall return to HMO any and all materials used by Primary Care Physician in the provision of services to HMO Members. Upon termination of the Agreement, the Primary Care Physician shall not use any information obtained during the course of the Agreement in furtherance of any competitors of the HMO.
7. Primary Care Physician warrants and represents that all information and statements given to HMO in applying for or maintaining his/her HMO Primary Care Physician Agreement are true, accurate, and complete. The HMO Physician application shall be incorporated by reference into this Agreement. Any inaccurate or incomplete information or misrepresentation of information provided by Primary Care Physician may result in the immediate termination of this Agreement by HMO.
8. Primary Care Physician shall cooperate with HMO in complying with applicable laws relating to HMO.

PART IV. MISCELLANEOUS

A. *Modification of this Agreement.* This Agreement may be amended or modified in writing as mutually agreed upon by the parties. In addition, HMO may modify any provision of this Agreement upon thirty (30) days' prior written notice to Primary Care Physician. Primary Care Physician shall be deemed to have accepted HMO's modification if Primary Care Physician fails to object to such modification, in writing, within the thirty (30) day notice period.[18]

B. *Interpretation.* This Agreement shall be governed in all respects by the laws of the State of _________. The invalidity or unenforceability of any terms or conditions hereof shall in no way affect the validity or enforceability of any other terms or provisions. The waiver by either party of a breach or violation of any provision of this Agreement shall not operate as or be construed to be a waiver of any subsequent breach thereof.

C. *Assignment.* This Agreement, being intended to secure the services of and be personal to the Primary Care Physician, shall not be assigned, sublet, delegated, or transferred by Primary Care Physician without the prior written consent of HMO.

D. *Notice.* Any notice required to be given pursuant to the terms and provisions hereof shall be sent by certified mail, return receipt requested, postage prepaid, to HMO or to the Primary Care Physician at the respective addresses indicated herein. Notice shall be deemed to be effective when mailed, but notice of change of address shall be effective upon receipt.[19]

E. *Relationship of Parties.* None of the provisions of this Agreement is intended to create nor shall be deemed or construed to create any relationship between the parties hereto other than that of independent entities contracting with each other hereunder solely for the purpose of effecting the provisions of this Agreement. Neither of the parties hereto, nor any of their respective employees, shall be construed to be the agent, employer, employee, or representative of the other, nor will either party have an express or implied right of authority to assume or create any obligation or responsibility on behalf of or in the name of the other party. Neither Primary Care Physician nor HMO shall be liable to any other party for any act, or any failure to act, of the other party to this Agreement.

F. *Gender.* The use of any gender herein shall be deemed to include the other gender where applicable.

G. *Legal Entity.* If Primary Care Physician is a legal entity, an application for each Physician who is a member of such entity must be submitted to and accepted by HMO before such Physician may serve as a Primary Care Physician under this Agreement.

H. *Term and Termination.* The term of this Agreement shall be for three (3) years from the "effective date" set forth on the signature page. This Agreement may be terminated by either party at any time without cause by prior written notice given at least sixty (60) days in advance of the effective date of such termination. This Agreement may also be terminated by HMO effective immediately upon written notice if Primary Care Physician's (or, if a legal entity, any of the entity's physicians') medical license, Medicare qualification, or hospital privileges are suspended, limited, restricted, or revoked, or if Primary Care Physician violates Part III(E), (G)(3), (G)(5), (H), (I)(1), or (I)(4) herein. Upon termination, the rights of each party hereunder shall terminate, provided, however, that such action shall not release the Primary Care Physician or HMO from their obligations with respect to:

(1) payments accrued to the Primary Care Physician prior to termination;

---

[18] This is a common provision and useful in simplifying the administrative work associated with amending the agreement. Needless to say, it is important for the HMO to explain clearly the nature of the amendment to the primary care physician.

[19] Before adopting this paragraph, an HMO should consider whether it is necessary to require that all notifications be sent by certified mail, return receipt requested. If the HMO has a large provider panel, it might prefer the right to send information by regular mail.

(2) the Primary Care Physician's agreement not to seek compensation from Members for Covered Services provided prior to termination; and
(3) completion of treatment of Members then receiving care until continuation of the Member's care can be arranged by HMO.

In the event of termination, no distribution of any money accruing to Primary Care Physician under the provisions of Attachment B shall be made until the regularly scheduled date for such distributions. Upon termination, HMO is empowered and authorized to notify Members and prospective Members, other Primary Care Physicians, and other persons or entities whom it deems to have an interest herein of such termination, through such means as it may choose.

In the event of notice of termination, HMO may notify Members of such fact and assign Members or require Members to select another Primary Care Physician prior to the effective date of termination. In any event, HMO shall continue to compensate Primary Care Physician until the effective date of termination as provided herein for those Members who, because of health reasons, cannot be assigned or make such selection during the notice of termination period and as provided by HMO's Medical Director.

IN WITNESS WHEREOF, the foregoing Agreement between ______________________ and Primary Care Physician, is entered into by and between the undersigned parties, to be effective this ____ day of _______________, 19___.

PRIMARY CARE PHYSICIAN

_____________________________ By:_________________________

(Name of Individual Physician or of Group Practice—Please Print)

_____________________________ _________________________

(Mailing Address) (Date)

____

(City, State, ZIP)

____

(Telephone Number)

____

(Taxpayer Identification Number)

____

(DEA #)

____

(Signature)

____

(Name and Title if signing as authorized representative of Group Practice)

____

(Date)

ATTACHMENT B
COMPENSATION SCHEDULE

PRIMARY CARE PHYSICIAN AGREEMENT

I. *Services Rendered by Physicians*

For Covered Services provided by Primary Care Physician in accordance with the terms of this Agreement, HMO shall pay Primary Care Physician his/her Reimbursement Allowance, less any applicable copayment for which the Member is responsible under the applicable Health Maintenance Certificate, and less the Withhold Amount, as described below. "Reimbursement Allowance" shall mean the lower of (i) the usual and customary fee charged by Primary Care Physician for the Covered Service, or (ii) the maximum amount allowed under the fee limits established by HMO.

II. *Withholds from Reimbursement Allowance*

HMO shall withhold from each payment to Primary Care Physician a percentage of the Reimbursement Allowance ("Withhold Amount") and shall allocate an amount equal to such withhold to an HMO Risk Fund. HMO shall have the right, at its sole discretion, to modify the percentage withheld from Primary Care Physician if, in its judgment, the financial condition, operations, or commitments of the HMO or its expenses for particular health services or for services by any particular Participating Providers warrant such modification.

III. *Withhold Amount Distributions*

HMO may, at its sole discretion, from time to time distribute to Primary Care Physician Withhold Amounts retained by HMO from payments to Primary Care Physician, plus such additional amounts, if any, that HMO may deem appropriate as a financial incentive to the provision of cost-effective health care services. HMO may, from time to time, commit or expend Withhold Amounts, in whole or in part, to ensure the financial stability of or commitments of the HMO or health care plans or payers with or for which the HMO has an agreement to arrange for the provision of health care services, or to satisfy budgetary or financial objectives established by HMO.

Subject to HMO's peer review procedures and policies, a Primary Care Physician may be excluded from any distribution if he/she does not qualify for such distribution, for example, if he/she has exceeded HMO utilization standards or criteria. No Primary Care Physician shall have any entitlement to any funds in the HMO Risk Fund.

IV. *Accounting*

Primary Care Physician shall be entitled to an accounting of Withhold Amounts from payments to him/her upon written request to HMO.

ATTACHMENT B (ALTERNATIVE)
CAPITATION PAYMENT

PRIMARY CARE PHYSICIAN AGREEMENT

Compensation

I. *Capitation Allocation*

The total monthly amounts paid to Primary Care Physician will be determined as follows:
For each Member selecting Primary Care Physician ("selecting" also includes Members assigned to a Primary Care Physician), 90 percent of the monthly Primary Care Service capitation set forth below for Primary Care Services shall be paid by HMO to Primary Care Physician by the 5th day of the following month. The capitation shall be set according to the particular benefit plan in which each Member is enrolled. Where the capitation is not currently adjusted for age and/or sex, HMO reserves the right to make such age and/or sex adjustment to the capitation rates upon thirty (30) days' notice. In consideration of such payments, Primary Care Physician agrees to provide to Members the Primary Care Services set forth in Attachment C hereto.
Health Plan shall allocate the remaining 10 percent of the monthly capitation payments to a Risk Reserve Fund, which fund is subject to the further provisions of this Attachment. The capitation payments to Primary Care Physician for Primary Care Services, subject to the above withhold, are as follows:

Coverage Plans

Age/Sex	Commercial Plan __ Capitation Payment	Commercial Plan __ Capitation Payment	Commercial Plan __ Capitation Payment
0–24 Months/M/F	$ _____	$ _____	$ _____
2–4 Years/M/F	$ _____	$ _____	$ _____
5–19 Years/M/F	$ _____	$ _____	$ _____
20–39 Years/F	$ _____	$ _____	$ _____
20–39 Years/M	$ _____	$ _____	$ _____
40–49 Years/F	$ _____	$ _____	$ _____
40–49 Years/M	$ _____	$ _____	$ _____
50–59 Years/F	$ _____	$ _____	$ _____
50–59 Years/M	$ _____	$ _____	$ _____
>60 Years/F	$ _____	$ _____	$ _____
>60 Years/M	$ _____	$ _____	$ _____

Primary Care Physician is financially liable for all Primary Care Services rendered to Members under the above capitation. If Primary Care Physician fails to do so, HMO may pay for such services on behalf of Primary Care Physician and deduct such payments from any sums otherwise due Primary Care Physician by HMO.

Appendix 29–B

Sample Hospital Agreement

HEALTH MAINTENANCE ORGANIZATION

PARTICIPATING HOSPITAL AGREEMENT[1]

THIS AGREEMENT, made and entered into on the date set forth on the signature page hereto, by and between (the "Hospital"), a facility duly licensed under the laws of the State of ____________ and located at ____________________, and ____________________________ ("HMO"), a corporation organized under the ________ law, and located at ____.

WHEREAS, HMO provides a plan of health care benefits (the "Plan") to individuals and their eligible family members and dependents who contract with HMO or who are the beneficiaries of a contract with HMO for such benefits ("Members"), and in connection with such Plan, arranges for the provision of health care services, including Hospital Services, to such Members; and

WHEREAS, the Hospital desires to provide Hospital Services to Members in accordance with the terms and conditions of this Agreement as hereinafter set forth; and

WHEREAS, HMO desires to arrange for the services of the Hospital for the benefit of the Members of the Plan.

NOW, THEREFORE, in consideration of the foregoing recitals and the mutual covenants and promises herein contained and other good and valuable consideration, receipt and sufficiency of which are hereby acknowledged, the parties hereto agree and covenant as follows:

PART I. DEFINITIONS

A. *Covered Services* means those health services and benefits to which Members are entitled under the terms of the applicable Health Maintenance Certificate, which may be amended by HMO from time to time.
B. *Emergency Services* means those Medically Necessary services provided in connection with an "Emergency," defined as a sudden or unexpected onset of a condition requiring medical or surgical care which the Member receives after the onset of such condition (or as soon thereafter

---

[1] For consistency, the HMO has used the same definitions for this agreement and the primary care physician agreement shown in Appendix 29–A. This agreement also uses some of the same provisions as in the primary care physician agreement. Comments made to those provisions in the primary care physician agreement are not repeated here.

as care can be made available but not more than twenty-four (24) hours after onset) and in the absence of such care the Member could reasonably be expected to suffer serious physical impairment or death. Heart attacks, severe chest pain, cardiovascular accidents, hemorrhaging, poisonings, major burns, loss of consciousness, serious breathing difficulties, spinal injuries, shock, and other acute conditions as HMO shall determine are Emergencies.

C. *Health Maintenance Certificate* means a contract issued by HMO to a Member or an employer of Members specifying the services and benefits available under the HMO's prepaid health benefits program.

D. *Hospital Services* means all inpatient services, emergency department, and outpatient hospital services that are Covered Services.

E. *Medical Director* means a Physician designated by HMO to monitor and review the provision of Covered Services to Members.

F. *Medically Necessary* services and/or supplies means the use of services or supplies as provided by a hospital, skilled nursing facility, Physician, or other provider required to identify or treat a Member's illness or injury and which, as determined by HMO's Medical Director or its utilization management committee, are: (1) consistent with the symptoms or diagnosis and treatment of the Member's condition, disease, ailment, or injury; (2) appropriate with regard to standards of good medical practice; (3) not solely for the convenience of the Member, his or her Physician, hospital, or other health care provider; and (4) the most appropriate supply or level of service which can be safely provided to the Member. When specifically applied to an inpatient Member, it further means that the Member's medical symptoms or condition requires that the diagnosis or treatment cannot be safely provided to the Member as an outpatient.

G. *Member* means both an HMO subscriber and his/her enrolled family members for whom premium payment has been made.

H. *Participating Physician* means a Physician who, at the time of providing or authorizing services to a Member, has contracted with or on whose behalf a contract has been entered into with HMO to provide professional services to Members.

I. *Participating Provider* means a Physician, hospital, skilled nursing facility, home health agency, or any other duly licensed institution or health professional under contract with HMO to provide health care services to Members. A list of Participating Providers and their locations is available to each Member upon enrollment. Such list shall be revised from time to time as HMO deems necessary.

J. *Physician* means a duly licensed doctor of medicine or osteopathy.

K. *Primary Care Physician* means a Participating Physician who provides primary care services to Members (e.g., general or family practitioner, internist, pediatrician, or such other physician specialty as may be designated by HMO) and is responsible for referrals of Members to referral Physicians, other Participating Providers, and if necessary, non-Participating Providers.

PART II. HOSPITAL OBLIGATIONS

A. Hospital shall provide to Members those Hospital Services which Hospital has the capacity to provide. Such services shall be provided by Hospital in accordance with the provisions of its Articles of Incorporation and bylaws and medical staff bylaws and the appropriate terms of this Agreement.

B. Hospital shall render Hospital Services to Members in an economical and efficient manner consistent with professional standards of medical care generally accepted in the medical community. Hospital shall not discriminate in the treatment of members and, except as otherwise required by this Agreement, shall make its services available to Members in the same manner as to its other patients.[2] In the event that an admission of a Member cannot be accommodated by Hospital, Hospital shall make the same efforts to arrange for the provision of services at another facility approved by HMO that it would make for other patients in similar circumstances. In the event that Hospital shall provide Member non-Covered Services, Hospital shall, prior to the provision of such non-Covered Services, inform the Member:

(i) of the service(s) to be provided,
(ii) that HMO will not pay for or be liable for said services, and
(iii) that Member will be financially liable for such services.

C. Except in an Emergency, Hospital shall provide Hospital Inpatient Services to a Member only when Hospital has received certification from HMO in advance of admission of such Member. Services which have not been so approved or authorized shall be the sole financial responsibility of Hospital.[3]

D. If, and to the extent that, the Hospital is not authorized to perform preadmission testing, the Hospital agrees to accept the results of qualified and timely laboratory, radiological, and other tests and procedures which may be performed on a Member prior to admission. The Hospital will not require that duplicate tests or procedures be performed after the Enrollee is admitted, unless such tests and procedures are Medically Necessary.

E. In an Emergency, Hospital shall immediately proceed to render Medically Necessary services to the Member. Hospital shall also contact HMO within twenty-four (24) hours of the Emergency treatment visit or emergency admission. HMO has 24-hour on-call nurse coverage for notification of emergency services or admits.
If Hospital fails to notify HMO within the required time period, neither HMO nor the Member shall be liable for charges for Hospital Services rendered subsequent to the required notification period that are deemed by HMO not to be Medically Necessary.[4]

F. Hospital shall cooperate with and abide by HMO's programs that monitor and evaluate whether Hospital Services provided to Members in accordance with this Agreement are Medically Necessary and consistent with professional standards of medical care generally accepted in the medical community. Such programs include, but are not limited to, utilization management, quality assurance review, and grievance procedures. In connection with HMO's programs, Hospital shall permit HMO's utilization management personnel to visit Members in the Hospital and, to the extent permitted by applicable laws, to inspect and copy health records (including medical records) of Members maintained by Hospital for the purposes of concurrent and retrospective utilization management, discharge planning, and other program management purposes.

G. Hospital shall cooperate with HMO in complying with applicable laws relating to HMO.

PART III. LICENSURE AND ACCREDITATION

Hospital represents that it is duly licensed by the Department of Health of the State of _________ to operate a hospital, is a qualified provider under the Medicare program, and is

---

[2] This requirement serves the same purpose as its counterpart in the primary care physician agreement of requiring the hospital to treat HMO members in the same manner as fee-for-service patients.

[3] A growing issue, not addressed in this provision, is the HMO's responsibility for hospital charges incurred to provide a medical screening examination, as required by Section 1867 of the Social Security Act, to enrollees seeking care from the hospital's emergency department. The hospital may want to seek an explicit statement requiring the HMO to cover the cost of that examination.

[4] To avoid disputes, the hospital and HMO need a common understanding of the meaning of the term *medically necessary*. The definition of that term used in this contract favors the HMO by allowing for its interpretation.

accredited by the Joint Commission on the Accreditation of Healthcare Organizations ("Joint Commission"). Hospital shall maintain in good standing such license and accreditation and shall notify HMO immediately should any action of any kind be initiated against Hospital which could result in:

(i) the suspension or loss of such license;
(ii) the suspension or loss of such accreditation; or
(iii) the imposition of any sanctions against Hospital under the Medicare or Medicaid programs.

Hospital shall furnish to HMO such evidence of licensure, Medicare qualification, and accreditation as HMO may request.

PART IV. RECORDS

A. Hospital shall maintain with respect to each Member receiving Hospital Services pursuant to this Agreement a standard hospital medical record in such form, containing such information, and preserved for such time period(s) as are required by the rules and regulations of the _________ Department of Health, the Medicare program, and the Joint Commission. The original hospital medical records shall be and remain the property of Hospital and shall not be removed or transferred from Hospital except in accordance with applicable laws and general Hospital policies, rules, and regulations relating thereto; provided, however, that HMO shall have the right, in accordance with paragraph (B) below, to inspect, review, and make copies of such records upon request.

B. Upon consent of the Member and a request for such records or information, Hospital shall provide copies of information contained in the medical records of Members to other authorized providers of health care services and to HMO for the purpose of facilitating the delivery of appropriate health care services to Members and carrying out the purposes and provisions of this Agreement, and shall facilitate the sharing of such records among health care providers involved in a Member's care. HMO, and if required, authorized state and federal agencies, shall have the right upon request to inspect at reasonable times and to obtain copies of all records that are maintained by Hospital relating to the care of Members pursuant to this Agreement.

PART V. INSURANCE AND INDEMNIFICATION

A. Hospital shall secure and maintain at its expense throughout the term of this Agreement such policy or policies of general liability and professional liability insurance as shall be necessary to insure Hospital, its agents, and its employees against any claim or claims for damages arising by reason of injury or death, occasioned directly or indirectly by the performance or nonperformance of any service by Hospital, its agents, or its employees. Upon request, Hospital shall provide HMO with a copy of the policy (or policies) or certificate(s) of insurance which evidence compliance with the foregoing insurance requirements. It is specifically agreed that coverage amounts in general conformity with other similar type and size hospitals within the State of _________ shall be acceptable to HMO and be considered satisfactory and in compliance with this requirement.[5]

[5] This paragraph reflects the difference in relative bargaining strength that the HMO has with hospitals and physicians. Although the HMO–primary care physician agreement gives the HMO the right to approve malpractice coverage, no such right is contained in the HMO–participating hospital agreement. Another factor may be that the concern for inadequate coverage may be greater for a physician than a hospital.

B. Hospital and HMO each shall indemnify and hold the other harmless from any and all liability, loss, damage, claim, or expense of any kind, including costs and attorney's fees, arising out of the performance of this Agreement and for which the other is solely responsible.

PART VI. MEDICAL STAFF MEMBERSHIP

Notwithstanding any other provision of this Agreement, a Participating Physician may not admit or treat a Member in the Hospital unless he/she is a member in good standing of Hospital's organized medical staff with appropriate clinical privileges to admit and treat such Member.[6]

PART VII. HMO OBLIGATIONS

A. HMO shall provide to or for the benefit of each Member an identification card which shall be presented for purposes of assisting Hospital in verifying Member eligibility. In addition, HMO shall maintain other verification procedures by which Hospital may confirm the eligibility of any Member.
B. HMO shall provide thirty (30) days' advance notice to Hospital of any changes in Covered Services or in the copayments or conditions of coverage applicable thereto.
C. HMO will, whenever an individual, admitted or referred, is not a Member, advise Hospital within thirty (30) days from the date of receipt of an invoice from Hospital for services to such an individual. In such cases, Hospital shall directly bill the individual or another third party payer for services rendered to such individual.
D. In the event that continued stay or services are denied after a patient has been admitted, HMO or its representative shall inform the patient that services have been denied.

PART VIII. USE OF NAME

Except as provided in this paragraph, neither HMO nor Hospital shall use the other's name, symbols, trademarks, or service marks in advertising or promotional material or otherwise. HMO shall have the right to use the name of Hospital for purposes of marketing, informing Members of the identity of Hospital, and otherwise to carry out the terms of this Agreement. Hospital shall have the right to use HMO's name in its informational or promotional materials with HMO's prior approval, which approval shall not be unreasonably withheld.

PART IX. COMPENSATION

Hospital will be compensated by HMO for all Medically Necessary Covered Services provided to Members in accordance with the provisions of Attachment A annexed hereto and incorporated herein.[7]

PART X. PAYMENT TO HOSPITAL BY HMO

For Hospital Services rendered to Members, Hospital shall invoice HMO at Hospital's current charges. [Alternative: For Hospital Services rendered to Members, Hospital shall invoice HMO.[8]] Except for Hospital Services which HMO determines require further review under

---

[6] Requiring the HMO's physicians to comply with the hospital's medical staff requirements is important and reasonable.

[7] Attachment A provides for payment as a percentage of charges. By structuring the agreement in this manner, the HMO is able to negotiate different payment arrangements with hospitals without revising the body of the agreement.

[8] This broader alternative language, along with the cross-reference to Attachment A in the preceding paragraph, allows the body of the contract to be used for any type of payment arrangement. An alternative Attachment A is offered that establishes per diem rates for inpatient stays and a percentage of charges for outpatient services.

HMO's utilization management procedures, or when there are circumstances which are beyond the control of HMO, including submission of incomplete claims, HMO shall make payment of invoices for Hospital Services within thirty (30) calendar days after the HMO's receipt thereof. HMO authorized copayments shall be collected by the Hospital from the Member and the Member shall be solely responsible for the payment of such copayments. All billings by Hospital shall be considered final unless adjustments are requested in writing by Hospital within sixty (60) days after receipt of original billing by HMO, except for circumstances which are beyond the control of Hospital.[9] No payment shall be made unless the invoice for services is received within sixty (60) days after the date of discharge of the Member or date of service, whichever occurs later. Hospital shall interim bill HMO every thirty (30) days for patients whose length of stay is greater than thirty (30) days.

PART XI. PROHIBITIONS ON MEMBER BILLING

Hospital hereby agrees that in no event, including, but not limited to, nonpayment by HMO, HMO's insolvency, or breach of this Agreement, shall Hospital bill, charge, collect a deposit from, seek compensation, remuneration, or reimbursement from, or have any recourse against a Member or persons other than HMO acting on a Member's behalf for services provided pursuant to this Agreement. This provision shall not prohibit collection of copayment on HMO's behalf in accordance with the terms of the Health Maintenance Certificate between HMO and Member. Hospital further agrees that:

(i) this provision shall survive the termination of this Agreement regardless of the cause giving rise to termination and shall be construed to be for the benefit of the Member; and

(ii) this provision supersedes any oral or written contrary agreement now existing or hereafter entered into between Hospital and Member, or persons acting on their behalf.

PART XII. INSPECTION OF RECORDS

Upon request, and at reasonable times, HMO and Hospital shall make available to the other for review such books, records, utilization information, and other documents or information relating directly to any determination required by this Agreement. All such information shall be held by the receiving party in confidence and shall only be used in connection with the administration of this Agreement.

PART XIII. COORDINATION OF BENEFITS

Hospital agrees to cooperate with HMO toward effective implementation of any provisions of HMO's Health Maintenance Certificates relating to coordination of benefits and claims by third parties. Hospital shall forward to HMO any payments received from a third party payer for authorized Hospital Services where HMO has made payment to Hospital covering such Hospital Services and such third party payer is determined to be primarily obligated for such Hospital Services under applicable Coordination of Benefits rules. Such payment shall not exceed the amount paid to Hospital by HMO. Except as otherwise required by law, Hospital agrees to permit HMO to bill and process forms for any third party payer on Hospital's behalf, or to bill such third party directly, as determined by HMO. Hospital further agrees to waive, when requested, any claims against third party payers for its provision of Hospital Services to Members and to execute any further documents that reasonably may be required or appropriate for this

[9] To avoid potential disputes, the hospital and the HMO should have some general understanding of the meaning of the term *beyond the control of Hospital*.

purpose. Any such waiver shall be contingent upon HMO's payment to Hospital of its (HMO's) obligations for charges incurred by Member.

PART XIV. TERM AND TERMINATION

A. This Agreement shall take effect on the "effective date" set forth on the signature page and shall continue for a period of one (1) year or until terminated as provided herein.

   1. Either party may terminate this Agreement without cause upon at least ninety (90) days' written notice prior to the term of this Agreement.
   2. Either party may terminate this Agreement with cause upon at least thirty (30) days' prior written notice.

B. HMO shall have the right to terminate this Agreement immediately by notice to Hospital upon the occurrence of any of the following events:

   (i) the suspension or revocation of Hospital's license;
   (ii) the suspension, revocation, or loss of the Hospital's Joint Commission accreditation or Medicare qualification; or
   (iii) breach of Part II(E) or Part XI of this Agreement.

C. HMO shall continue to pay Hospital in accordance with the provisions of Attachment A for Hospital Services provided by Hospital to Members hospitalized at the time of termination of this Agreement, pending clinically appropriate discharge or transfer to an HMO-designated hospital when medically appropriate as determined by HMO. In continuing to provide such Hospital Services, Hospital shall abide by the applicable terms and conditions of this Agreement.

PART XV. ADMINISTRATION

Hospital agrees to abide by and cooperate with HMO administrative policies including, but not limited to, claims procedures, copayment collections, and duplicate coverage/subrogation recoveries. Nothing in this Agreement shall be construed to require Hospital to violate, breach, or modify its written policies and procedures unless specifically agreed to herein.

PART XVI. MEMBER GRIEVANCES

Hospital agrees to cooperate in and abide by HMO grievance procedures in resolving Member's grievances related to the provision of Hospital Services. In this regard, HMO shall bring to the attention of appropriate Hospital officials all Member complaints involving Hospital, and Hospital shall, in accordance with its regular procedure, investigate such complaints and use its best efforts to resolve them in a fair and equitable manner. Hospital agrees to notify HMO promptly of any action taken or proposed with respect to the resolution of such complaints and the avoidance of similar complaints in the future. The Hospital shall notify the HMO after it has received a complaint from an HMO Member.

PART XVII. MISCELLANEOUS

A. If any term, provision, covenant, or condition of this Agreement is invalid, void, or unenforceable, the rest of the Agreement shall remain in full force and effect. The invalidity or unenforceability of any term or provision hereof shall in no way affect the validity or enforceability of any other term or provision.

B. This Agreement contains the complete understanding and agreement between Hospital and HMO and supersedes all representations, understandings, or agreements prior to the execution hereof.

C. HMO and Hospital agree that, to the extent compatible with the separate and independent management of each, they shall at all times maintain an effective liaison and close cooperation with each other to provide maximum benefits to Members at the most reasonable cost consistent with quality standards of hospital care.
D. No waiver, alteration, amendment, or modification of this Agreement shall be valid unless in each instance a written memorandum specifically expressing such waiver, alteration, amendment, or modification is made and subscribed by a duly authorized officer of Hospital and a duly authorized officer of HMO.
E. Hospital shall not assign its rights, duties, or obligations under this Agreement without the express, written permission of HMO.
F. None of the provisions of this Agreement is intended to create nor shall be deemed to create any relationship between HMO and Hospital other than that of independent entities contracting with each other hereunder solely for the purpose of effecting the provisions of this Agreement. Neither of the parties hereto, nor any of their respective employees, shall be construed to be the agent, employer, employee, or representative of the other.
G. This Agreement shall be construed in accordance with the laws of the State of _________.
H. The headings and numbers of sections and paragraphs contained in this Agreement are for reference purposes only and shall not affect in any way the meaning or interpretation of this Agreement.
I. Any notice required or permitted to be given pursuant to the terms and provisions of this Agreement shall be sent by registered mail or certified mail, return receipt requested, postage prepaid, to:

____
____
____

and to Hospital at:

____
____
____

IN WITNESS WHEREOF, the foregoing Agreement between ______________________________ and Hospital is entered into by and between the undersigned parties, to be effective the _____ day of ___________, 19_____.

By:______________________________

Title:____________________________

Date:____________________________
HOSPITAL

By:______________________________

Title: Administrator

Date:____________________________

ATTACHMENT A
PARTICIPATING HOSPITAL COMPENSATION

Subject to the terms and conditions set forth in this Agreement, HMO shall pay Hospital (____ %) of Hospital's schedule of charges effective __________ as submitted and approved by HMO, for Medically Necessary Covered Services provided to Members.

ATTACHMENT A [ALTERNATIVE]
PARTICIPATING HOSPITAL COMPENSATION

Subject to the terms and conditions set forth in this Agreement, HMO shall pay Hospital as follows:

Service	Type of Reimbursement	Total Reimbursement
Inpatient care		
Nonmaternity–Secondary	Per Diem	$_____
Nonmaternity–Tertiary	Per Diem	$_____
Maternity	Per Diem	$_____
Psychiatric	Per Diem	$_____
Well newborn children	Per Diem	$_____
Outpatient care		
Other than outpatient surgery	Percentage Discount	_____%
Outpatient Surgery	Hospital will be reimbursed (1) the percentage discount stated above, (2) any guaranteed maximum "global" rate program adopted by the Hospital for ambulatory surgical procedures,[10] or (3) 125 percent[11] of the per diem payment amount had the Enrollee been admitted to the Hospital, whichever is least.	

[10] If Medicare adopts a global fee for reimbursement of outpatient hospital costs, an increasing number of HMO–hospital contracts are likely to adopt a similar approach.

[11] This percentage commonly varies from 100 percent to 125 percent.

Chapter 30

Legal Issues in Integrated Delivery Systems

Jerry R. Peters

Study Objectives

- Propose alternative organizational structures, and explain the goals of each structure
- Identify and analyze the legal risks of establishing an IDS
- Identify the major business issues relevant to developing an IDS
- Identify tax and reimbursement issues affecting the development of an IDS

DEFINITIONS

An integrated delivery system (IDS; see also Chapter 4) is an organization or group of legally affiliated organizations in which hospitals and physicians combine their assets, activities, risks, and rewards to deliver comprehensive health care services. This classic definition of an IDS is often confused in two ways.

First, there are numerous terms that are used in place of *IDS*, including *integrated health care organization*, *integrated health care system*, *integrated health care network*, *integrated service network*, and *organized delivery system*. The particular label one gives to the IDS is unimportant, the fundamental question is whether there is a legally affiliated system that controls the delivery of hospital and physician services.

The second, and more recent, area of confusion arises from the use of the term *IDS* to describe arrangements that are actually physician–hospital organizations (PHOs) or management services organizations (MSOs). From a legal perspective, the PHO and MSO are both arrangements in which a hospital is not legally affiliated with the physician practice but enters into a joint venture (the PHO) or contractual arrangement (the MSO) with the legally separate physician organization.

To get a better understanding of the differences among an IDS, PHO, and MSO, one must first identify the two types of integration: structural integration and operational integration. Structural integration occurs when previously separate businesses combine into either a single organization or a group of affiliated organizations that are under common ownership and control. This may occur when a hospital and physician practice merge into a single organization or when a hospital or physician practice places itself under the common control of a single parent holding company.

Operational integration is the merger and consolidation of previously separate business operations into a single business operation. Typically,

Jerry R. Peters, Esq., is a partner practicing in the San Francisco office of Latham & Watkins' health care practice group. He has spoken extensively and published several books and numerous articles on physician–hospital business arrangements, including integrated delivery systems. He was an adjunct professor in health care law, and graduated Phi Beta Kappa in economics from the University of California, Berkeley. He received his law degree from Hastings College of the Law.

it is evidenced by factors such as the common development of operational systems, the consolidation of management into a single management team, the joint planning and implementation of services by the hospital and physician practice, and the general consolidation of staff and other functions. There is no clear standard to determine when an operational integration has occurred. Instead, there are degrees or levels of operational integration. A hospital and physician practice achieve more operational integration when they operate under a consolidated budget, consolidated management and governance, a consolidated strategic plan, a unified marketing program, a single payer contracting process, and a coordinated operating system.

Structural integration is often the first focus of developing an IDS. As difficult as the merger of a hospital business into a physician practice may be, such structural integration is often more simple than operational integration. In fact, many current IDS efforts are foundering in the waters of operational integration, and there is a growing backlash developing against IDSs because of the costs, time, and lost opportunities associated with operational integration.

Given this distinction between operational integration and structural integration, the difference among an IDS, PHO, and MSO is that the IDS includes both structural and operational integration between a hospital and a physician practice. Both the PHO and the MSO do not undergo structural integration; instead, the hospital and the physician practice maintain separate businesses from each other. This lack of structural integration in a PHO and MSO means that such arrangements have additional legal risks (compared with an IDS), and there is less economic incentive to implement operational integration between the parties (a hospital may not be willing to invest significant capital in a medical practice that is free to leave the hospital's sphere of influence or otherwise use the capital to the detriment of the hospital).

It should be noted that, in the current environment, the terms *IDS*, *PHO*, and *MSO* are often used interchangeably. To differentiate among these terms, it is important to determine whether the parties intend to integrate structurally (i.e., merge their businesses into a single economic enterprise—IDS) or whether each party will remain a separate business (i.e., each retains the right to its own revenue stream and controls its own means of production—PHO and MSO). In addition, one should determine what level of operational integration the parties intend to implement, recognizing that it is possible (even if not always economically preferable) to implement a significant degree of operational integration regardless of the level of structural integration between the parties.

IDS MODELS

There are several variables that combine to create numerous IDS models (e.g., nonprofit model, for-profit model, foundation model, integrated health care organization model, etc.). Important variables include the number of organizations in the IDS, whether the organizations are nonprofit or for profit, whether the organizations are taxable or tax exempt, the degree to which the organizations are operationally integrated, the relationship between the IDS and the physicians (i.e., employees or independent contractors), who controls the IDS (physicians, shareholder-investors, or nonprofit community directors), and how physicians are compensated. In developing an IDS, an advisor should examine each of these issues with his or her clients to determine what structure best meets the clients' goals. A few examples are illustrative of how one might structure an IDS.

The California foundation model typically involves a parent holding company, which is a nonprofit corporation that obtains tax exempt status. This parent holding company has two subsidiaries: one that operates the hospital and another that operates a medical practice (the medical practice corporation is typically called the foundation). The California foundation model is inherently a nonprofit, tax exempt model because California's corporate practice of medicine doctrine/licensure laws require that the physician practice organization (i.e., the foundation) be tax exempt. In the Friendly Hills determination letter, the Internal Revenue Service (IRS) imposed certain requirements (see below) upon the foundation, including restrictions on the number of physicians who may serve on the board of directors of the foundation. California's corporate practice of medicine doctrine also requires that the physicians be independent contractors to the foundation (thus the physicians are not employees of the foundation but instead organize their own professional corporation, which enters into a professional services agreement with the foundation under an independent contractor arrangement). Under this model, the IDS is ultimately controlled by nonprofit community directors (who typically control the parent holding company and the subsidiaries). Although this model has been copied in other states, there is no legal requirement that the structure be adopted in states that either do not have a corporate practice of medicine doctrine or have a more lenient doctrine than California.

In some states (other than California), the parties might establish a single for-profit IDS organization that is exclusively or predominantly owned by physicians (often called an integrated health care organization). This organization may acquire a hospital and then enter into contracts with payers to provide comprehensive hospital and physician services. This model is a for-profit organization whereby physicians own and are employed by the organization.

Another alternative is for physicians to own their medical practice and to establish a separate organization that owns the means of production (i.e., space, equipment, staff, etc.) for the physicians to operate their practice. This separate organization is often referred to as an MSO. The MSO may acquire a hospital and its assets. In addition, the MSO may have investors (in addition to the physician owners, who typically control a majority of the MSO). The MSO leases its assets to the physician practice, and the physician practice pays a fee to the MSO that must, at a minimum, equal the cost of operating the MSO.

This alternative illustrates the blurry distinction between an IDS and an MSO. In this example, the physician practice effectively functions as an IDS (it controls the revenues of both the physician and hospital practice and controls the operations of the hospital through the MSO lease arrangement), even though the hospital is technically owned by a separate organization. The common control by the physicians over both organizations, however, combined with the unification of economic incentives between the hospital and physicians, arguably makes this arrangement an IDS.

Given the various options for structuring an IDS, there are numerous models that can be developed. It is important for the parties to begin their integration process by identifying their goals and structuring the IDS to meet those goals. If the parties encounter significant differences in their goals or are unable to agree on the fundamental structural issues (nonprofit or for-profit, physician controlled or community director controlled, etc.), the parties should not be afraid to postpone or discontinue their integration discussions. It is most often better to use these warnings signs to avoid a bad marriage than to embark upon integration efforts with an incompatible partner.

GOVERNANCE

If the IDS is organized as a professional corporation (or some other type of professional organization under state law), the state's corporate practice of medicine doctrine or other licensing laws may restrict who may serve on the board of directors of the organization (typically, only physicians or other licensed persons may serve on the board). If the IDS is formed as a nonprofit corporation under state law, state corporate law may again restrict the number or types of persons who may serve on the board (e.g., some laws require that no more than 49 percent of the board members be interested directors, as that term is defined in the state corporate law). Finally, if the IDS applies for federal tax exempt status under Internal Revenue Code Section

501(c)(3), it will most likely need to address the safe harbor requirements regarding governance that are imposed by the IRS. The IRS has set forth its safe harbors in its 1994, 1995, and 1996 Continuing Professional Education Exempt Organizations Technical Instruction Program (CPE guidelines), copies of which may be obtained from the IRS.

To meet the safe harbor requirements, no more than 20 percent of an IDS board should consist of physicians who are financially related, directly or indirectly, to the IDS. (The IRS has allowed physician representation to exceed 20 percent where the physicians at issue have no past or present financial interest in the IDS organization.) The 20 percent rule includes physicians who have retired from a medical group and, until recently, also included anyone else who is financially related to the IDS. Although in certain cases the IRS applied the safe harbor to include salaried managers or administrators of the hospital participants, it now applies the safe harbor only to physicians selling assets to or providing professional services in conjunction with the IDS organization. In the IRS's view, any physician who sells assets to, is employed by, or receives significant referrals from an IDS is "tainted" and can never serve as a disinterested physician on the board of directors.

Historically, the 20 percent limitation applied to the chief executive officer and other key employees of the IDS. Recently, however, the IRS has begun to exclude IDS employees and is only focusing its 20 percent limitation on physicians who contract with the IDS. In the 1996 CPE guidelines, the IRS clarified its current position:

> The Service has, under certain circumstances, allowed physician representation on the board of directors of an IDS organization to exceed 20 percent where the physicians at issue have no past or present financial interest in the IDS. Also, while in one or two IDS cases the Service may have applied the 20 percent safe harbor to include salaried managers or administrators of hospital participants, the Service now applies the 20 percent safe harbor only to physicians selling assets to or providing professional services in conjunction with the IDS organization.
>
> For example, in a particular case involving a 10 person board of directors, the Service approved the inclusion of three physicians as members. Two physicians were allowed to have a direct or indirect financial interest in the IDS organization. The third physician did not and could not have any direct or indirect financial interest in the IDS organization. In this situation, the third physician member was an employee of the hospital, the sole corporate member of the IDS organization. Another situation where the safe harbor was allowed to be exceeded was when the third physician on a 10 person board was retired and had no past or present direct or indirect financial interest in the IDS organization or any acquired physician practice.
>
> In general, any physician selling assets to, employed by, or providing professional services to or on behalf of an IDS organization is "tainted" and can never serve as a "disinterested" physician on an IDS organization's board of directors. Also, any physician receiving significant referrals from an IDS organization may be considered financially interested and precluded from being considered a disinterested physician member.[1]

The 20 percent limitation applies to an IDS regardless of whether it seeks tax exempt financing. Until recently, only an organization that sought tax exempt financing was restricted by bond counsel to the 20 percent physician director rule set forth in the safe harbor of Revenue Procedure 82-15 (as replaced by Revenue Procedure 93-19). Now, this 20 percent rule applies to all IDSs and possibly to all exempt organizations. IRS officials have informally indicated their willingness to examine the application of the safe harbor on a case-by-case basis. Although the 1996 CPE guidelines admit to a limited exception allowed by the IRS, counselors should prepare their clients to possible strict imposition of this 20 percent safe harbor by the IRS in granting a determination letter. The ultimate resolution of this issue is yet to occur.

IDS participants should also note that the 20 percent limitation applies to quorum and voting requirements on the board. Thus an IDS may not require a supermajority vote that effectively gives the physicians the power to block an activity. The overall principle is that the community members of the board must have control over the activities of the IDS.

If physician participation on the board is an important issue in consummating a transaction, legal counsel should carefully consider exceeding the 20 percent limitation pursuant to the following legal analysis:

- *Legal authority*—Neither the CPE guidelines nor Revenue Ruling 69-545 cited any legal authority that limits physician participation to 20 percent.
- *Influence*—IRS analysis appears to confuse the concept of influence with that of control. The IRS has conceded that physicians may have influence on the board (by allowing 20 percent physician board members). Physician control of the board would not begin until physicians had 50 percent or more of the board positions. Arguably, physicians should be allowed up to 49 percent of the board seats with increasing legal risk to the IDS (because the physicians would still only have influence, not control, over the IDS). Once physicians have 50 percent or more of the board seats, the physicians arguably control the organization, and the legal arguments favoring revocation of tax exempt status are more significant. The IRS has given no rationale explaining the difference between influence and control or any explanation as to why 20 percent physician participation is safer for the IDS than 49 percent or less participation.
- *Private benefit*—The IRS's best argument supporting the 20 percent safe harbor is that physicians benefit more than incidentally if they sell their practices, enter into a professional services agreement with the IDS, and receive influence over the organization in an amount exceeding 20 percent. There are two problems with this argument:
  1. The IRS has opined numerous times that the benefit of forming an IDS outweighs the incidental private benefit to physicians when their practices are sold, a professional services agreement is entered into, and 20 percent of the board comprises physicians. The issue is whether giving the physicians an additional 29 percent of the board seats is the "straw that breaks the camel's back." The IRS may have a difficult time convincing a court that the additional 29 percent of board seats suddenly creates incidental private benefit, especially because the physicians still would not have control over the organization.
  2. The IRS has already granted tax exempt status to many physician organizations that have more than 50 percent physician board composition. The IRS has shown no inclination to revoke those exemptions or require modifications. One must question whether the IRS would now litigate a case in which less than 50 percent of the board comprised physicians.
- *Proposed legislation*—It should be noted that congressional committees have pro-

posed that legislation be enacted limiting the board of directors of tax exempt organizations to 20 percent or less of financially interested persons (which would include physicians in an IDS setting). It also should be noted that such legislation has not become law as of the time this chapter was written. Nonetheless, strict adherence to the IRS's safe harbor would have the effect of making this 20 percent guideline into a law (even though Congress has thus far not found it appropriate to enact such a law). One must question the significance of Congress' failure to enact a 20 percent limitation into the actual law of the land.

- *Unenforceability*—After an IDS obtains tax exempt status by acquiescing to the 20 percent safe harbor rule, it could reconstitute its board so that physicians have 49 percent or less of the board seats. (The IDS should report this change in its subsequent Form 990 report or in a separate notice to the IRS.) If the organization has a conflict of interest policy that excludes physician board members from all votes in which they have a conflicting financial interest and no actual act of inurement occurs, one must wonder whether a court would uphold the IRS's attempt to revoke exemption.
- *Physician expertise*—The purpose of establishing an IDS is to merge the interests of hospitals and physicians into a single organization that motivates providers to deliver high-quality, cost-efficient health care services. Physicians control the delivery (i.e., the quality and efficiency) of most services. By restricting physician participation in the IDS governance structure, the IRS is mandating that physicians be alienated from decisions that affect the delivery process. This limits the IDS's use of physician expertise in certain areas and imparts a message to physicians that they are no longer responsible for organizational performance. This alienation of physicians from the IDS can result in reduced efficiency and quality of care. Physicians are not a single person; the diversity of their opinions often requires more than 20 percent representation on the board.
- *Acquisition costs*—Finally, removing physicians from governance raises the costs of developing an IDS. Physicians typically require a greater purchase price in exchange for their assets if they have little control in the resulting IDS.

One alternative to the IRS's 20 percent limitation is to structure the IDS as follows:

- A majority of the IDS board must comprise persons who do not have a material financial interest in the IDS. Thus a chief executive officer director and any physicians who provide services for the IDS must make up a minority of the board. A quorum for voting must consist of a majority of noninterested directors.
- A financially interested director may not participate in discussions, or vote, regarding any matter in which the director has a financial interest. The director may answer questions from the board before leaving the room.
- Physician directors should be allowed to vote on the IDS's budget, but physician compensation should be separately voted upon by nonphysician directors only.

These safeguards ensure that the IDS will not make decisions that excessively benefit private individuals. At the same time, these safeguards allow physicians to participate in the overall governance of the IDS and allow the IDS to benefit from the physicians' expertise in areas where no conflict of interest exists. See also Chapter 5 for additional governance-related discussion.

COMMITTEES

Any committee or subcommittee created to consider the business or charitable operations of the IDS must be independent and broadly representative of the community. Although the meaning of the phrase *independent and broadly representative of the community* was previously unclear, the IRS now requests that IDS committees, with a few exceptions, comply with the 20 percent safe harbor.[2]

Again, the IRS and/or legal counsel should carefully consider the strength of the IRS's position before enforcing it against an IDS (for the same reasons as those set forth above with respect to the 20 percent safe harbor limit for directors). This is particularly true when the committees are advisory to the board (but see below). Nonetheless, the IRS's rationale for limiting committee participation should be reviewed and understood by the client before the client decides to assume the risk of noncompliance (IRS rationale is addressed in the 1996 CPE guidelines).

There are two committees that the IRS has made particular statements regarding: the compensation committee and the fee committee. The IRS insists that physicians who have (or have had) a financial relationship with the IDS (or the predecessor physician group) may not serve on any committee that recommends or determines physician compensation. The problem with this limitation is that it prevents the IDS from utilizing physician expertise regarding compensation and physician incentives. As long as the compensation committee is advisory to the board and the board has the full power to accept, reject, and/or modify the committee's recommendations, some physician representation on this committee might be beneficial. In general, the physicians are likely to know more about physician compensation than the average person. This expertise should not be lost to the IDS.

At the same time, the IDS board cannot simply accept the committee's recommendation without scrutiny. The board should have outside expertise to verify the committee's report. The board should also examine regional or national compensation surveys. If the committee's report is unreasonable, the board must appoint nonphysicians to negotiate physician compensation with the physicians and reject the committee's recommendation.

This issue may be a red herring in that physicians might not serve on the committee directly but will participate via their negotiations with the committee. Practically speaking, physicians will participate in compensation deliberations however the organization is structured. Nonetheless, if the parties intend to go outside the safe harbors with respect to other issues (e.g., 49 percent of the directors will be physicians), they might carefully consider complying with this particular safe harbor to reduce the probability of an IRS challenge (and to increase the probability of a court victory if a challenge does occur). Legal counsel should weigh the risks of going outside too many safe harbors and should advise clients to be moderate and establish safeguards that protect the organization's charitable assets against excessive private benefit.

The IRS safe harbor also requires that physician participation in the committee that determines IDS fees be limited to a minority of the total committee members. Physician participation on the committee may not be equal to nonphysician participation. Because the IRS is allowing significant physician participation on the fee committee, its position is more palatable to physicians and most likely would be defensible in court. Therefore, IDS participants should consider compliance with this particular safe harbor requirement.

Finally, the 1996 CPE guidelines specifically differentiate between the board-delegated authority committees and advisory committees:

> Most IDS organizations have provisions in their bylaws for the creation and operation of various committees. Normally, an IDS organization will have an executive committee, finance

and planning committee, and provisions for various other committees or subcommittees. Often these committees have substantial authority to study, create, implement, and review charitable and business activities as well as the clinical aspects of the organization's operations. Generally, a committee has either advisory authority or specific powers delegated to it by the board of directors.[3]

DELEGATED BOARD AUTHORITY

In situations where an organization's bylaws grant board of directors powers to a committee or subcommittee, the IRS requests that the organization's bylaws state that no more than 20 percent of its committee members may be physicians who are financially interested or related, directly or indirectly, to any owner, partner, shareholder, or employee of the medical group or other physicians providing services in conjunction with the IDS organization. It should be noted that the IRS's position allows unlimited physician representation on any committees or subcommittees that have authority over the clinical aspects of the organization's activities.[4]

ADVISORY COMMITTEES

Committees that do not have board of directors powers but are merely advisory in nature may also create concerns for the IRS. To elucidate these issues, some background information may be useful. The tax exempt status of the IDS presents several difficult issues. Generally speaking, IDS organizations are created through the purchase of one or more existing private medical practices, and the individual physicians become employees or contractors of the IDS organization. These are factually intensive cases with important issues that the IRS must address. The benefit to the community from the formation of the IDS must be carefully weighed against the benefit to the physicians from the sale of their practices and subsequent professional services agreements. Unless there is a significant community benefit, these transactions may benefit the physicians more than unsubstantially.

Integration also raises serious concerns for physicians. After integration, physicians face a totally different employment or service environment; they may be hesitant to relinquish control of their former medical practice. The IRS, on the other hand, is concerned that the community receive a substantial benefit because of the large amount of charitable assets involved in the purchase of physicians' medical practice assets. In contrast, the physicians may believe that, as the former owners of a valuable business, they should continue to exert considerable control. The IRS acknowledges this expertise but seeks to ensure that there is a significant community benefit, which in certain situations may conflict directly with the interests of the physicians.

Because of the perceived loss of control, physicians often seek to become designated members of committees having substantial day-to-day operational powers as well as considerable influence over business and charitable programs. In many cases, these committees are the important bodies that weigh all the facts and circumstances in a complicated proposed action. These committees often make recommendations based upon complex fact patterns to the board of directors. Typically, the full board of directors meets infrequently. Because of workload demands, the limited expertise of board members, and the complexity of issues, the board often is unable to give detailed attention to every item that comes before it for a vote. Under certain circumstances, the IRS is concerned that the board will routinely accept the recommendations of committees that have significant control by financially interested parties. Because the IRS has no accurate tool to measure the actual control exercised by physicians or other financially interested individuals who are members of committees, it will, under appropriate circumstances, apply the 20 percent safe harbor to committees.

CONFLICT OF INTEREST POLICY

The IDS should be careful to comply with state law regarding the development of a conflict of interest policy and its operations. This is particularly important if the IDS is a nonprofit organization because most states regulate conflicts of interest with respect to nonprofit directors and officers. In addition, if the IDS seeks tax exempt status, the IRS has set forth guidelines as to how it prefers to see the conflict of interest policy developed for the IDS. In the 1996 CPE Guidelines, the IRS states:

> The Service has expressed concerns about interested party control of IDS organizations through its 80 percent community board safe harbor. The Service is also concerned about private benefit and inurement issues that may arise because of the relationship between an exempt organization providing IDS services and its physician employees/contractors, officers, directors and key employees. In most situations, the best protection for a charitable trust is well-defined, written policy governing conflicts of interest. This serves to educate effected individuals and limit their activities under appropriate circumstances. Because most IDS organizations include some financially interested individuals on their governing boards, they may wish to adopt a clear conflicts of interest policy.[5]

Although not required, the IRS favorably views organizations having policy statements in their bylaws that clearly identify situations where a conflict might arise. The IRS believes that directors of tax exempt IDS organizations must exercise their powers in good faith and in a manner that they believe to be in the organization's best interests. Furthermore, organizations that educate their new directors, employees, and officers regarding conflicts of interest and concerns about private benefit and inurement help eliminate problems arising from lack of knowledge.

An example of a conflict of interest policy that is viewed favorably by the IRS is one that requires that, in the event that the board of directors considers entering into any transaction or arrangement with a corporation, entity, or individual in which a director has an interest:

- the interested director must disclose the potential conflict of interest to the board
- the board may ask the interested director to leave the meeting during the discussion of the matter that gives rise to the potential conflict
- the interested director will not vote on the matter that gives rise to the potential conflict
- the board must approve the transaction or arrangement by a majority vote of the directors present at a meeting that has a quorum, not including the vote of the interested director
- the board meeting minutes must state which directors were present for the discussion and vote, the content of the discussion, and any roll call of the vote

In addition, if a director has any interest in a transaction or arrangement that might involve personal financial gain or loss for the director, the policy should contain the following provisions:

- If appropriate, the board may appoint a noninterested person or committee to investigate alternatives to the proposed transaction or arrangement.
- To approve the transaction, the board must first find, by a majority vote of the directors then in office without counting the vote of the interested director, that the proposed transaction or arrangement is in the IDS organization's best interest and for its own benefit, that the proposed transaction is fair and reasonable to the IDS organization,

and, after reasonable investigation, that the board had determined that the IDS organization cannot obtain a more advantageous transaction or arrangement with reasonable efforts under the circumstances.

- The interested director will not be present for the discussion or vote regarding the transaction or arrangement.
- The transaction or arrangement must be approved by a majority vote of the directors, not including interested directors.

TAX EXEMPTION AND CHARITABLE BENEFIT

In addition to the restrictions mentioned above, the IRS will impose additional requirements on an IDS that seeks federal tax exempt status under Internal Revenue Code Section 501 (c)(3). For this reason, many parties should consider carefully whether tax exemption is in their best interest. Some of the advantages of tax exemption are that net income is not subject to federal income taxes (except unrelated business income tax); that the organization may qualify for exemption from state, sales, and/or property tax; that the organization may qualify for tax exempt bond financing; and that contributions to the organization are tax deductible (thereby increasing the probability of the organization receiving grants). The disadvantages include the restrictions placed by the IRS on the organization, the requirement to disclose the tax exemption application and Form 990 to the public (thereby disclosing the salaries of key employees and officers), limitations on the organization's ability to dissolve, and limitations on the use of facilities that were financed by tax exempt bond proceeds.

If the IDS decides to seek exemption from federal taxation under Internal Revenue Code Section 501(c)(3), it must demonstrate that it serves a charitable purpose more than incidentally. This is a facts and circumstances test in which the IRS (or the court) considers all the activities of the IDS to determine whether its primary function is charitable.

The IRS has set forth several requirements, based on Revenue Ruling 69-545 [which sets forth guidelines for a hospital to qualify for Section 501(c)(3)], for an IDS to qualify for tax exempt status under Section 501(c)(3). Although no single factor is determinative, certain factors are more important (and the probability of obtaining tax exempt status is low if such factors are not present):

- *Open medical staff*—Any hospital operated by an IDS must have an open medical staff. Although clinic facilities (in which physicians practice medicine) are not required to have an open medical staff, this policy has created some controversy because of the need for an IDS to control hospital utilization (which is best done by the IDS physicians, not independent physicians who have no economic incentive to control hospital utilization).
- *Medicare/Medicaid patients*—The IDS must be receptive to providing services to all Medicare and Medicaid patients in a nondiscriminatory manner at IDS sites. This has been generally interpreted to mean that the IDS may not open specific Medicaid clinical facilities and refer all Medicaid patients to those facilities. If the IDS is in a state that has a Medicaid contracting program, the IDS must negotiate in good faith to enter into such a contract with the government. Although this is a financially difficult requirement for an IDS to meet, it is a significant factor that the IRS is likely to treat as mandatory.
- *Emergency services*—All IDS facilities must treat emergency or urgent care patients regardless of their ability to pay. This applies to both the hospital facilities and the physician clinical facilities. Exceptions might be available where emergency services are not offered, but this requirement is relatively important to the IRS.

- *Charity care*—Although the IRS does not always require that an IDS provide a specific amount of charity care, in those situations where the IRS determines that the organization is unlikely to provide charity care, the IRS may require the IDS to budget a specific amount of charity care to be provided each year. If the IDS can show that it benefits the community in significant other ways (see the other requirements), there is a chance that the IRS will not require charity care by the IDS.
- *Miscellaneous*—The 1995 CPE guidelines listed the following factors as indicators of community benefit:
    1. All medical functions and records are integrated for each individual patient.
    2. Anyone in need of care is treated at any clinic location without regard to ability to pay.
    3. The IDS treats patients seeking urgent care at its urgent care centers without regard to ability to pay.
    4. The clinic participates in, or has made good faith efforts to participate in, the Medicaid program in a nondiscriminatory manner.
    5. Contract physicians do not discriminate against patients based on ability to pay and will see Medicaid patients on a nondiscriminatory basis.
    6. A specified minimum amount is spent each year for charity care.
    7. The IDS conducts health education programs.
    8. A substantial number of the physicians provide coverage in the hospital emergency department and render care in those emergency departments without regard to the patients' ability to pay.

PHYSICIAN COMPENSATION

An IDS must be careful that it distributes its income to physicians in a manner that complies with the Ethics and Patient Referrals Act of 1989 (the Stark law) as amended (Stark II); (Currently, proposed legislation will significantly reduce the scope of Stark II and make it much easier for an IDS to operate outside the scope of this law). In addition, any state anti-referral laws should be examined before a physician compensation arrangement is finalized.

Generally, the IRS is concerned that a tax exempt IDS does not share its net profits with physicians or otherwise use the IDS organization as a joint venture with physicians. This leaves significant leeway for a tax exempt organization to develop a physician compensation plan based on production, quality of care delivered to patients, and other quantifiable measures (other than the net profits of the organization).

The IRS has made clear that it will closely scrutinize situations where an IDS pays significant amounts for the intangible value of the acquired practice and, at the same time, pays significant annual compensation to the physicians. In the 1996 CPE guidelines, the IRS discusses its concerns regarding compensation and sets forth a list of the data that it will examine to determine whether compensation paid to the physicians is reasonable under all of the circumstances. The 1996 CPE guidelines state "Compensation issues often arise in IDS organizations, faculty group practice plans, clinics, hospitals converting from for-profit to nonprofit status, and joint ventures and partnerships involving exempt organizations, as well as ruling requests regarding these entities. Compensation arrangements often provide for base salaries, fringe benefits, deferred payments, income guarantees, contingencies to compensation, and incentive bonuses."[6]

In most situations, the IRS wants to review certain basic information involving compensation arrangements. Although the compensation arrangements and the accompanying professional services agreement may be included in the file, they are complex, and often it is difficult ultimately to determine actual compensation. Thus the IRS often requests more specific information, adding additional time to the rulings process. The following is a reproduction of the typical compensation questions that the IRS asks (it expedites matters if this information is included in the original submission to the IRS):

- How many physicians do you employ, and how many do you contract with for professional services?
- Please submit a compensation contract for each physician employee. You may black out the physician's name and assign a letter or number to each contract if you are concerned about privacy issues.
- For each compensation arrangement, please provide the following:
  1. A realistic estimate of *total* projected physician's compensation (including base, bonus, benefits, and managed care risk pool withholds or other risk pool participation) for a *3-year period* (the estimate could be for 1 year of actual operation and 2 years of projections, depending upon how long you have been operational). The estimate must be based on the terms contained in the compensation agreement.
  2. A realistic estimate of 3 years' projected gross receipts (the estimate could be for 1 year of actual operation and 2 years of projections, depending upon how long you have been operational). The estimate must be supported by data used in preparing actual or future financial reports or projections.
  3. A statement establishing that the physician's total compensation is reasonable based on the geographic locale and the physician's specialty. You can establish reasonableness by the use of compensation data for the physician specialty based upon compensation studies produced by local, regional, or national medical associations; the American Hospital Association, the Medical Group Management Association, the Hay Group, or other knowledgeable consultants.
  4. Are there any caps (ceilings) on total compensation?
  5. Before total compensation of all physicians (base and benefits minus bonus and risk pool withholds) is determined, how much surplus remains for the exempt organization? After *total* compensation is determined, how much surplus remains? What percentage of surplus do the physicians receive? What percentage does your organization receive?

PRACTICE ACQUISITIONS/ VALUATION

If the IDS will acquire assets from an existing physician practice, the parties must structure the transaction (i.e., sales, lease, etc.). A tax specialist should be consulted as to the tax consequences of the transaction to any for-profit organization (either the IDS or the physicians). Tax issues for managed care organizations and IDSs are discussed in Chapter 41 of *The Managed Health Care Handbook*.[7]

If the IDS is a tax exempt organization, the parties should consult the guidelines set forth in the 1996 CPE guidelines with respect to physician practice acquisitions. These guidelines include a discussion of how the IRS would prefer to see valuations performed. Nonetheless, they indicate a variety of methods recognized by the IRS as to how valuations may be performed. Instead of insisting on the discounted cash flow valuation method, the IRS is recognizing (and is evidencing its own sophistication in this area) that various valuation methods are appropriate in different situations.

One particularly difficult situation occurs when an IDS acquires a small practice or solo practice (especially in a rural area, where the intangible value of the practice is low). In these situations, the IDS does not wish to pay for a valuation fee (often, the valuation fee is higher than the intangible value to be paid to the physician). In these situations, the IDS should obtain an independent valuation for this first practice acquisition. Thereafter, someone employed by the IDS should use the same procedures used by the independent valuation association (and should pay careful attention to the 1996 CPE guidelines) and document the value of the practice. As long as the IDS has carefully demonstrated the reason why it has paid fair market value to the physician, the IRS is unlikely to challenge the arrangement in court.

MEDICARE/MEDICAID PROVIDER NUMBERS

Medicare/Medicaid part B payment rules only allow for payment to the patient or to the patient's physician. In addition, the physician is not allowed to assign his or her right to such income to another party. There are two relevant exceptions to this assignment prohibition: Payment may be made to the employer of the provider of services if the employee is required, as a condition of employment, to pay over such amounts to the employer; and if the services are provided in a hospital, rural primary care hospital, or other facility, payment may be made to the facility in which the service was provided if the facility has a contractual agreement with the provider of services and that agreement requires the facility to submit the bill for such service.

If an IDS acquires a physician practice (including accounts receivable), the assignment of Medicare and Medicaid accounts receivable by the physician to the IDS might constitute a violation of the assignment prohibition. In addition, if physicians are contractually established as independent contractors of the IDS, the IDS may have difficulty receiving the Medicare or Medicaid receivables for the performance of services. Practically speaking, most physicians are employed by the IDS, and this problem does not arise. If the problem exists, however, the IDS may contract with the physician for everything except Medicaid services, and the physician's Medicaid provider number might be used to bill and collect all revenues for Medicaid patients. The total amount paid by the IDS to the physician would be net of any Medicaid receipts received by the physician.

ANTITRUST LAW

There are two types of risks that potentially arise from the development of an IDS: the risk from developing the IDS (i.e., monopoly and other risks associated with consolidating a hospital and a physician practice), and the risk arising from the ongoing operations of the IDS (i.e., tying arrangements and other illegal activities conducted by the IDS).

In 1996 a major legal development involving antitrust law occurred. Under pressure from the American Medical Association, the Department of Justice and the Federal Trade commission have revised their guidelines for the development of physician networks. Several commentators believe that these guidelines may also be used in the development of hospital–physician networks. Overall, the new guidelines allow providers to establish networks to negotiate and enter into payer contracts even if there is not the direct financial integration that arises from capitated payments. The guidelines make clear that the government will look at other forms of integration, such as the development of withhold accounts, quality assurance programs, and other measures that indicate that the providers are working together to provide a better product to the market, in applying a "rule of reason" assessment as to the legality of a provider network or IDS. This legal development does not mean that competing providers can simply establish prices together, but it does provide significant leeway for providers to join forces and market their services as a collective unit. This legal development may slow the trend of providers merging with each other and rejuvenate an increasing trend of providers remaining legally separate but joint venturing their efforts in PHOs, individual practice associations, or other loosely affiliated networks.

With respect to the development of an IDS, the parties should carefully examine Section 7 of the Clayton Act, which prohibits mergers and acquisitions that have the potential to restrain competition in the market unreasonably. If the development of an IDS creates a monopoly power or even market dominance with respect to any particular service (e.g., outpatient surgery or other services), the IDS arrangement might be challenged. Nonetheless, the parties should review the most recent developments in the Marshfield Clinic case and assess whether the facts of that case are applicable to their own particular IDS.[8] In addition, the parties should review the enforcement policy statements issued by the Department of Justice and the Federal Trade Commission on 27 September 1994 to assess the risk of government action against the proposed IDS.[9]

In assessing whether the development of an IDS presents risk, the parties should first determine whether the formation creates too much market power for the IDS and its participants. Critical to this analysis is the definition of the market, which can be summarized as the area in which consumers will freely move to receive similar services. This is a highly factual determination. If physicians who join the IDS previously competed with each other and, through the merger of their practices into the IDS, effectively eliminated competition among themselves, the risk of an antitrust challenge increases as the percentage of physicians who otherwise would have competed with each other (absent the IDS) increases.

If the IDS has an exclusive relationship with a significant number of physicians so that no other hospital can contract with a sufficient number of physicians to develop a competing IDS product, the monopolist IDS may be subject to a successful challenge. Presently, exclusive dealing arrangements can tie up to 35 percent of total physicians in a particular specialty in the market without raising significant antitrust concerns.

Another issue is that the IDS may not participate in an agreement among competitors by which it refuses to deal with other competitors (or causes others not to deal with those competitors). Such group boycotts generally are illegal if they foreclose excluded competitors from something that those competitors need to compete effectively in the market. A fourth issue is that the IDS should not condition its sale of a service (such as hospital services) in which the IDS enjoys market power upon the payer's agreeing to purchase another service offered by the IDS (such as physician services). Finally, the parties should be careful not to engage in any price-fixing activities before they form the IDS and should not engage in any price-fixing activities with independent physicians after they form the IDS.

Although it is not common in the IDS setting, the parties should determine whether they need to file a Hart-Scott-Rodino notification. This premerger notification must be filed if the parties merge, if one party acquires the assets or stock of the other parties, or if new legal entities are established to operate the IDS and if all three of the following conditions are met:

1. The IDS or at least one participant is engaged in or affects commerce.
2. The transaction (merger of the parties or acquisition) involves the acquisition of assets or voting securities, the acquired firm has total assets of $10 million or more, and the acquiring firm has annual net sales or total assets of $100 million or more; or the acquired firm has total assets or annual net sales of $100 million or more; and the acquiring firm has total assets or annual net sales of $10 million or more.
3. If the transaction results in the acquiring party obtaining 15 percent or more of the voting securities or assets of the acquired party, or the acquiring party obtains voting securities or assets of the acquired party that in aggregate exceed $15 million, the third condition is met.

At the time of this writing, the filing fee is $45,000 for the premerger notification.

INDEPENDENT CONTRACTOR STATUS

The IDS must decide whether it will employ its physicians or contract with them as independent contractors. This decision will have several ramifications, including the IDS's liability for the actions of the physicians and the inclusion of physicians in the employee benefits plans of the IDS. In addition, this decision will determine whether the IDS issues a W-2 or 1099 form to the physicians.

Most often, this issue is resolved by law, not by the business decision of the parties. Even if the IDS enters into a contract with a physician as an independent contractor, the law may reclassify the physician as an employee of the IDS (and assess back taxes and penalties against the IDS). Thus it is important for a tax specialist to determine whether the physician should be treated as an employee or independent contractor for the purposes of tax reporting and for an employee benefits specialist to determine whether the physician must be offered employee benefits.

An employer must withhold payroll taxes from the wages that the employer pays to its employees.[10] These payroll taxes include federal income tax withholding, Federal Insurance Contribution Act (FICA) taxes, and Federal Unemployment Tax Act taxes. If a physician is not an employee (but is an independent contractor) of the employer, the employer is not fully responsible for these taxes. Thus employers prefer to classify workers as independent contractors, but the IRS prefers that workers be classified as employees (thereby ensuring collection of the taxes).

Recently, the IRS has given increased attention to the classification of individual service providers as independent contractors. The Comprehensive Audit Program conducted by the IRS has specifically targeted this issue as an area of focus (because the IRS might be able to collect revenues from the exempt organization if it finds that a worker has been misclassified as an independent contractor). Typically, the structure and documentation of the worker's arrangement will determine proper classification.

An employer–employee relationship generally exists if the employer has common law control over the worker. The IRS has established a list of 20 factors that are used to determine whether sufficient control exists to constitute an employer–employee relationship.[11] The 20 factors are weighed as part of a subjective balancing test. The Internal Revenue Manual states "Any single fact or small group of facts is not conclusive evidence of the presence or absence of control."[12] The 20 factors are listed in Exhibit 30–1. Taken together, the 20 factors are balanced on a case-by-case basis to determine whether a worker (or a class of workers) is an employee. When the 20 factors determine that an employer–employee relationship exists, it is immaterial to the IRS which label the parties attach to the relationship.[13]

The IRS has established audit guidelines that focus on specific factors for assessing whether physicians should be classified as independent contractors, including the following[14]:

- whether the physician has a private practice
- whether the hospital pays wages to the physician
- whether the hospital provides supplies and support staff to the physician
- whether the hospital bills and collects revenues for the physician
- whether the physician and hospital divide the physician's professional fees on a percentage basis
- whether the hospital regulates or otherwise has the right to control the physician
- whether the physician has specific hours to be on duty at the hospital
- whether the physician's uniform has the hospital's logo or name
- whether the hospital pays the physician's malpractice insurance premiums

Exhibit 30–1 IRS's 20 Factors Used in Determining Employer–Employee Relationship

1. *Instructions.* An employer may require an employee to follow instructions. An independent contractor may only be required to follow overall project specifications.
2. *Training.* An employer generally trains an employee as to its methodologies and practices. An independent contractor generally has his or her own style and does not require training.
3. *Integration.* When a person is so integrated into a business that the success or failure of the business depends a good deal on such person's performance, the worker is under the employer's control. An independent contractor is generally not necessary for the longevity of the employer.
4. *Services rendered personally.* Employees provide services personally. An independent contractor can generally assign a task; qualified people are fungible.
5. *Hiring, supervising, and paying assistants.* An employee generally works with other people who are also employees of the employer; an employee does not hire, fire, supervise, or pay assistants. Independent contractor, however, hire, supervise, and pay their own assistants.
6. *Continuing relationship.* The longer a relationship continues between an employer and a worker, the more likely it is that relationship is an employer–employee relationship. This may include services that recur frequently, even if at irregular intervals (e.g., either on call by the employer or whenever the work is available).
7. *Set hours of work.* The more formal and rigid a worker's hours, the more control the employer has over the worker. An independent contractor generally works on his or her own schedule and only has specified overall project or task deadlines.
8. *Full time required.* When a worker works substantially full time for an employer and does not work for any other employers, the employer has control over the worker's time. An independent contractor usually works for several employers at the same time. An employee may also have more than one employer, however.
9. *Doing work on employer's premises.* Evidence of control over an employee exists when an employer can designate the place where work is to be done and has control over that environment.
10. *Order or sequence set.* If an employer retains the right to control the order or sequence of the work that is to be performed and the type of work does not naturally dictate the order or sequence, evidence of control over the worker exists.
11. *Oral or written reports.* The more often a worker reports to an employer, the more likely it is that the employer controls the worker. It is acceptable for an independent contractor to issue progress reports as phases of a project are completed, however.
12. *Payment by hour, week, or month.* An employee generally receives a set wage based upon a time period. On the other hand, an independent contractor receives payment based upon a project or straight commission. A contract may specify when payments are due. The independent contractor should invoice the employer for amounts due, however. The payments should not be made automatically.
13. *Payment of business and/or traveling expenses.* When an employer controls expenses, the employer also controls the worker's activities. Generally, independent contractors take care of their own incidental expenses.
14. *Furnishing of tools and materials.* The more tools and materials supplied by the employer, the more likely it is that the worker is an employee. The weight of this factor will depend on the occupation of the worker and the type of tools and materials supplied.
15. *Significant investment.* If a worker makes an investment in facilities or tools that are not normally invested in by employees, this factor will show a lack of control by the employer. Use of an employer's facilities generally indicates control by the employer. Facilities include premises and equipment, such as office furniture and machinery.
16. *Realization of profit or loss.* Employees have no opportunity to realize a gain or loss. Independent contractors, however, are business people who take risks expecting either to enhance their return or to suffer a loss.
17. *Working for more than one firm at a time.* When an individual works for more than one firm and performs de minimis services for each, it is likely that none of the firms will have control over the individual. Even if a person works for more than one employer, however, if enough control exists, the person could be considered to be an employee of more than one employer.
18. *Making services available to the general public.* The more a person offers services to the general public, the less likely it is that control will be found to exist. Indicia of making services available to the general public are advertising, business cards, stationery, telephone listings, holding a license, and the like.

continues

Exhibit 30–1 continued

19. *Right to discharge.* If a person can be discharged at will, then the person is an employee. The person who possesses the right to discharge is an employer. Independent contractors cannot be fired so long as they are in compliance with the contract.

20. *Right to terminate.* Independent contractors cannot quit; employees can terminate at will. Therefore, to be an independent contractor there must be a legal obligation to complete the contract.

The audit guidelines instruct IRS agents to pay particular attention to hospital-based specialists, such as radiologists, pathologists, and anesthesiologists. The IRS particularly believes that such physicians should be employees of the hospital for purposes of federal employment taxes (regardless of the state's corporate medicine doctrine).

The IRS has instituted a health care industry specialization program, pursuant to which it conducts coordinated audits of tax exempt health organizations. As part of this program, the IRS has developed a physician issue paper that sets forth the IRS's proposed position regarding the independent contractor/employee classification of hospital-based physicians. This paper still relies on the 20-factor test identified in Exhibit 30–1 but attempts to assign emphasis to certain of the 20 common law factors for the analysis of relationships with physicians. Its approach is to give less emphasis to factors that are common to all hospital–physician relationships, thereby making it easier to isolate the factors that are strong indicators of employee versus independent contractor status. The paper identifies several factors as important in classifying a physician as an employee of a hospital, including whether the hospital reserves the right to specify the physician's hours, whether the hospital is entitled to the physician's professional fees, and whether the hospital bears the risk and expenses associated with the physician's delivery of services (e.g., operating costs).

The paper also provides examples of when a hospital-based physician would be classified as an independent contractor, when a physician should be characterized as an employee of his or her own professional corporation, and when the physician must be recognized as having dual status (i.e., the physician is both an employee and an independent contractor of the same organization when he or she is acting in more than one capacity for that organization). It also states categorically that residents and interns are almost always common law employees of the hospital at which they are being trained.

Internal Revenue Code Section 530 precludes the IRS from challenging an employer for failure to withhold federal employment taxes with respect to certain independent contractor arrangements. An employer can avoid retroactive assessments of federal employment taxes caused by reclassification of workers from independent contractors to employees if each of the following three requirements is met:

1. The employer must have a reasonable basis for treating the worker as an independent contractor (it is not clear whether this reasonable basis must have existed before 31 December 1978). There are four safe harbors for meeting this requirement: reliance on a published IRS ruling or judicial precedent; reliance on the outcome of a prior audit by the IRS if the IRS reviewed workers who held similar positions as the position that is at issue; reliance on the long-standing recognized practice of a significant segment of the industry, even if the practice of treating the worker as an independent contractor is not uniform throughout the entire in-

dustry; or any other reasonable basis for not classifying a worker as an employee.[15]

2. The employer must not have treated the worker as an employee anytime after 1977. In particular, the employer should not have withheld federal income tax or FICA taxes from the worker's wages, must not have filed certain employment tax returns for the worker, and must not have treated any worker holding a similar position as an employee for any period after 31 December 1977.

3. The employer must have filed all appropriate federal tax returns in a manner that is timely and consistent with the worker not being treated as an employee (e.g., 1099 forms must have been filed properly.)

The IRS has published form SS-8, which may be used by a taxpayer to request that the IRS determine whether a person is an employee or an independent contractor. This form may be submitted either by an employer or an employee. It may not always be advisable to submit this form, however, because once an answer is received, the employer has no basis for treating a worker contrary to the IRS's determination.

If a worker is misclassified as an independent contractor and is later determined to be an employee, the employer is then liable for the employment taxes not previously paid plus interest and any penalties that may be imposed by the IRS. If an independent contractor is reclassified as an employee, the employer must review the tax-qualified pension and employee benefit plans for the years at issue. In situations where qualification was marginal, the reclassification of independent contractors may disqualify pension or benefit plans.

Failure to classify a worker properly as an employee and then having a nonfavorable redetermination can cause severe financial hardship to an enterprise and to the enterprise participants. Past payroll taxes and the associated penalties and interest can bankrupt many small enterprises. If the enterprise cannot pay the IRS's payroll tax assessment, the participants in the enterprise may be personally liable for the assessment, depending on the enterprise participant's role in the enterprise and/or the type of entity chosen for the enterprise. Last, if payroll taxes are assessed personally against an enterprise participant, the taxes may not be discharged in bankruptcy proceedings.

COVENANTS NOT TO COMPETE

In its first determination letters (e.g., the Friendly Hills determination letter), the IRS put certain restrictions on the covenants not to compete that an IDS may enforce against physicians. This created a controversy because it restricted the IDS from realizing the full benefit of its covenant not to compete and thereby prevented the IDS from realizing the full benefits of the amounts paid to physicians in exchange for the covenants not to compete (the IRS would counter that the IDS should have simply paid less for the covenant not to compete). In the 1996 guidelines and in recent determination letters, there appears to be a loosening of this attitude by the IRS. Presently, it is not clear whether the IRS has any restrictions upon covenants not to compete. Parties should negotiate a significant covenant not to compete between themselves and should wait for the IRS to make any modifications (and then argue with the IRS regarding those modifications before conceding the point).

CONCLUSION

The development of an IDS also involves an examination of numerous business issues (which are beyond the scope of this chapter but are addressed in part in Chapter 4). Most important, the parties should be careful that their cultural differences (e.g., physicians are independent and hospital administrators are committee oriented) are identified and addressed. Numerous miscellaneous legal issues (e.g., employee benefits law, labor law, tax identification numbers, certificate of need law, corporate/partnership law, financing law, state licensuring and corporate practice of medicine law, malpractice liability law, rate and review law, real property laws, recordkeeping laws, state antireferral laws, securities law, tax law and tax exemption law, insurance issues, intellectual property law, medical staff issues, and possibly environmental law) must be considered.

One should not expect an IDS to be developed overnight, but one also should not languish into the 18- to 24-month backwater of merger negotiations. Most important, the parties must recognize that, after the merger is done, the real work begins. They must decide how well they work together, and they should not try to integrate themselves operationally more than they are culturally capable of tolerating. Often, an IDS will simply allow the physician organization to operate separately from the hospital organization and will look for common areas where capital allocations improve the overall delivery of health care services to the community. The parties must commit themselves to some level of operational integration (including capital planning, strategic planning, payer contracting, etc.), or else they should question why they developed the IDS in the first place. Nonetheless, they should be careful not to integrate their operations excessively if such integration will cause undue burden or strains upon the parties.

Finally, the parties should be careful to address any political issues that arise from the formation of the IDS. Most importantly, reaction of independent physicians who are not part of the IDS can be a fatal factor if IDS leadership does not properly address those physicians' concerns. An IDS is not for everyone, and the parties should be careful before expending the time and money in developing an IDS to determine that the effort will generate appropriate benefits for themselves and their constituents.

Study Questions

1. Identify four common organizational structures and the differences between each.
2. What are the primary issues of developing an IDS under federal tax-exemption laws?
3. What anti-referral laws are most often implicated in the development of an IDS?
4. What are the major business issues that should be discussed in developing an IDS?

REFERENCES AND NOTES

1. 1996 CPE at pp. 390–391.
2. See 1996 CPE at p. 389 and 1995 CPE at p. 227. Some IRS officials have defended their 20 percent restriction based on the fact that physicians do not represent more than 20 percent of a community. Thus no more than 20 percent of a board or committee can comprise physicians if it is to be broadly representative of the community. This logic has not yet been extended to race, sex, or age (or other occupations), but one might wonder why not. Also, it should be noted that the IDS may create committees to consider the clinical or professional service aspects of the health care to be provided by the IDS and that these committees may contain unlimited physician representation.
3. 1996 CPE at p. 388.
4. See 1994 CPE at p. 227 for more information about the 20 percent safe harbor.
5. 1996 CPE at pp. 386–387.
6. 1996 CPE at p. 391.
7. T.A. Jacobs and P.G. Royalty, "Taxation of Managed Health Care Plans," in *The Managed Health Care Handbook*, 3d ed., ed. P.R. Kongstvedt (Gaithersburg, Md.: Aspen, 1996), 648–658.
8. *Blue Cross & Blue Shield United of Wisc. & Compcure Health Services Insur Corp. v. The Marshfield Clinic & Security Health Plan of Wisc., Inc.*, 881 F. Supp. 1309 (W.D. Wisc. 1994).
9. *Statements of Enforcement Policy and Analytical Principles Relating to Health Care and Antitrust.* U.S. De-

partment of Justice and Federal Trade Commission (September 27, 1994).

10. I.R.C. Section 3402.
11. Rev. Rul. 87-41, 1987-1 C.B. 296.
12. 2 *Internal Revenue Manual* (CCH) 8465 (1988).
13. Treas. Reg. Sections 31.3306(i)–1(d), 31.3121(d)–1(a)(3), and 31.3401(b)–1(e).
14. *IRS Audit Guidelines for Hospitals*, Manual Transmittal 7 (10) 69–38; *Exempt Organizations Guidelines Handbook* Section 331(1) (27 March 1992).
15. See Priv. Ltr. Rul. 8733004.

SUGGESTED READING

Peters, G.R. 1995. *Healthcare Integration: A Legal Manual for Constructing Integrated Organizations*. Washington, D.C.: National Health Lawyers Association.

National Health Lawyers Association. 1994. *Health Law Practice Guide*.

Health Law Center. 1995. *Managed Care Law Manual*. Gaithersburg, Md.: Aspen.

Epilogue

What Might the Future Hold?

Frederick B. Abbey, Garry Carneal, Peter D. Fox, Robert E. Hurley, Peter R. Kongstvedt, Jerry R. Peters, Craig Schub, Roger S. Taylor, and Carlos Zarabozo

As noted in the introduction to this book, the world of managed health care is highly volatile and ever-changing. These changes apply equally to managed care organizations (MCOs), providers, and the legislative and regulatory environment. Therefore, it is very likely that certain issues discussed in this book will have changed by the time of publication. That cannot be helped, but this epilogue is our effort at discussing some of the possible changes to come. This epilogue builds upon the relevant chapters that precede it in the book, and presents the opinions of the authors as of the Fall of 1996.

THE FEDERAL SECTOR

The federal sector continues to undergo significant pressures, both political and economic. While the federal sector encompasses many areas, this epilogue will examine only two: Medicaid and Medicare.

Medicaid

The future structure of Medicaid remains both a political battleground and a major unresolved public policy question. The battlelines fall out along both partisan lines and also among differing viewpoints about state-federal relations. While a significant breakthrough did occur in welfare reform in 1996 with block grants to states replacing the existing program, the Medicaid program continues to be jointly financed and administered by the states and federal government. Proposals to move to a block grant model for Medicaid have been stymied for the foreseeable future in large measure because of resistance to the loss of the individual entitlement to benefits this move would represent. In addition to this philosophical concern, serious practical obstacles arose around how to determine the allocation of funds among the states in a block grant arrangement.

Despite the continued lack of consensus on the ultimate shape of Medicaid, there are two key areas of certainty in future reform of the Medicaid program being crafted by Congress, the Clinton Administration, and the state governors. One of these is that future cost growth rates in Medicaid will have to be substantially below recent historical experience and possibly even below general inflation rates. The other area where the direction of change is certain is that states will get expanded flexibility in designing and managing their Medicaid programs, including, to varying degrees, determination of who is eligible, what services will be covered, and how providers will be paid. While this flexibility is not likely to come in the form of full block grants but in reduced federal requirements and a liberalized waiver-granting policy, the net effect will be the same—variation among states will grow as will their reliance on managed care.

The contributions of Craig Schub, Senior Vice President, Government Programs, PacifiCare Health Systems, Cypress, California, and Roger S. Taylor, President and CEO, Connecticut Health Enterprises, Monroe, Connecticut, are greatully acknowledged.

Rapid and pervasive conversion of Medicaid's delivery system to a managed care model seems assured. Shifting greater risk for financing cost growth in Medicaid to states will intensify their desires to transmit this risk on to prepaid managed care plans. While primary care case management models will be preferred in some low health maintenance organization (HMO) penetration states, these are likely to be interim arrangements until organized delivery systems evolve. Reduced federal financial participation will also lead states to try to reduce their own administrative costs and contracting with prepaid health plans allows them to off load many administrative functions, such as provider payment, to the plans. Elimination of payment mandates and relaxation of benefit requirements will allow states to exercise more discretion and flexibility in contracting and in how, and how much, they will pay for services. Likewise, federal strictures on marketing, enrollment, plan qualification, and selection (such as the 75/25 rule) may disappear or be liberalized to enable states to maneuver more freely in the managed care marketplace. Until such liberalization is forthcoming, states will move ahead, as they have in the past, by maneuvering and negotiating through the existing 1915b and 1115 waiver processes.

Perhaps the most critical area of uncertainty hanging over future Medicaid reform is whether states will be mandated to continue to cover all or some of the currently eligible beneficiaries in an expanded flexibility environment where the entitlement to benefits may be altered or eliminated. There seems to be general consensus that women and children (at least up to a specified maximum age) will retain a guarantee, as will people with disabilities. Both of these groups will be getting their services predominantly through prepaid managed care arrangements. Other current beneficiaries may continue to get some or all of their existing coverage, again through a growing transition to managed care models, including persons in long-term care.

There is considerable uncertainty surrounding the extension of mandatory managed care arrangements to Medicaid beneficiaries with disabilities, chronic illness, and other special needs. Progress in this area continues to be slow, difficult, and rife with controversy (Medicaid Managed Care: Serving the Disabled Challenges State Programs, GAO/HEHS-96-136. Washington, DC: US General Accounting Office) because of the complex constellation of issues that have to be addressed to satisfy beneficiaries, advocates, and providers. These issues include model development, benefit package design, rate setting, consumer protection, and quality improvement strategies. Many individuals qualify for both Medicaid and Medicare further complication coordination of services and coverage. This is clearly an area where carefully crafted partnerships between plans, providers, and purchasers are going to have to be devised if enrollment in managed care arrangements is ultimately to be required for everyone.

A final area where there is great uncertainty is whether states will avail themselves of opportunities to expand coverage for currently enrolled populations by perhaps providing them access to a reduced benefit package. Certainly, many of the current crop of 1115 waivers—which have been a kind of de facto block grant, in some cases—initially were committed to this goal. But recent experience suggests that this goal is proving elusive with several states with waivers in hand, unable to finance expansions or openly skeptical about the sustainability of these efforts in the face of reduced rates of financial support. A more plausible, and ominous, scenario is that states may be forced to reduce coverage for even traditionally eligible populations in the future, particularly if savings associated with the embrace of managed care are more modest than expected.

Medicare

It is highly likely that significant Medicare reform will occur during the life span of this book. Below is a brief description of some directions that reform could take.

Reduction in Budgeted Inflation Rate for Medicare

As currently funded and administered, the Medicare program will run out of money, even before the baby boom generation reaches 65 years of age. To preserve Medicare, the choices for Congress and the President are limited. They must either increase funding (taxes or the deficit), reduce benefits (including increasing cost sharing, reducing coverage, or modifying eligibility by, for example, raising eligibility age), and/or restructure the method of delivery.

Raising taxes or decreasing coverage for services are the least popular options, leaving restructuring of the delivery system and some manipulation of eligibility and cost sharing as the politically viable options for future savings. Indeed, it is to these options that both the President and Congress have turned.

In regard to the level of budgeted reduction in inflation, there is general agreement in Washington that one cannot balance the budget and avoid raising taxes without significantly reducing Medicare's 10% inflation rate. The congressional Republicans, through the Medicare Preservation Act of 1995, would have reduced inflation by $200 billion over the next seven years—the conservative Democrats proposed a $125 billion reduction. The President has tacitly supported the smaller reduction but would use different methods to get there. But everyone agrees the issue needs to be addressed.

Medicare Managed Care Payment Reform

Payment reform proposals include the establishment of a "floor" for average area per capita cost (AAPCC) payments in the range of $300 or more, with the intent of making current low-payment areas attractive to managed care organizations. The AAPCC would exclude medical education and disproportionate share payments to hospitals, but the Health Care Financing Administration (HCFA) would make medical education payments directly to teaching hospitals rendering services to Medicare risk HMO enrollees.

Some legislative proposals call for changing Medicare from a "defined benefit" program to a "defined contribution" or "voucher" program, by which Medicare beneficiaries would be provided with a "voucher" of a certain dollar value to purchase a Medicare health care plan. Health care plans would be able to charge amounts in excess of the voucher if the voucher payment level was insufficient to cover the cost of the Medicare benefit package; or health plans would be able to offer "rebates" on the voucher if the health plan's cost of providing the Medicare package was below the voucher level.

The Congressional Budget Office's (CBO's) recently released "Reducing the Deficit: Spending and Revenue Options" contains some additional suggestions related to Medicare HMOs and deficit reduction: reduction of payments to risk HMOs below 95 percent of the AAPCC (as direct program savings), and cash rebates as a means of increasing enrollment (on the assumption that Medicare managed care saves money—though the CBO report highlights the need for a health status adjuster).

Yearly payment changes for risk HMOs after a given base year likely will be at a specified rate (7% in one proposal while the CBO mentions the possibility of tying rate increases to "an external factor, such as the rate of growth of the overall economy"), with a minimum increase incorporated into law (2%). The Republican Congress proposal sets an administrative cap on annual inflation over a seven-year period, whereas the administration has suggested a number of separate mechanisms to gain its savings targets. The AAPCC might also become a blend of national and local area costs, with the share of each being split so that the local costs are the larger share (70/30, for example). These payment changes may be phased in over a certain period of time.

Current proposals would redistribute payments from areas of high managed care penetration to areas of low penetration. The proposal's objectives are to encourage MCOs to enter new markets and to encourage new types of MCOs. The estimated result of these proposals, according to the CBO, would be to increase national managed care penetration to about 22%. These are conservative estimates that do not take into account any behavioral changes due to changes in the enrollment process.

Expansion in Product Offerings to Medicare Eligibles

The success of private sector employees in controlling the rate of health care inflation has not gone unnoticed in Washington, D.C. The Medicare Preservation Act of 1995 borrows heavily from large employers' experience, offering Medicare recipients a choice of HMOs, point of service (POS) plans, preferred provider organizations (PPOs), and fee-for-service plans. As in the private sector, Medicare recipients would be responsible for choosing the plan that best meets their needs. If the plan they choose is more expensive, they would pay the difference. Figure 1 presents these choices schematically, and they are discussed below.

Both parties support this expansion of choice as a method to allow the market to restructure the delivery system, but the President and Congress have some key differences on what the options are and how they are paid. For example, the President has opposed the idea of allowing any plan to offer less than a full Medicare benefit. This has put him at odds with congressional Republicans who support the idea of a catastrophic coverage option (e.g., $6,000 deductible plan) combined with a Medicare savings account (MSA) in which the beneficiary deposits any savings in Medicare premium experienced by the government. The principal concern expressed by the Administration and others, is that favorable risk selection will result in the government contributing an inappropriately high sum to the MSA, thereby costing the government more.

Regarding provider-sponsored organizations, the Administration bill does permit direct Medicare risk contracting with provider-sponsored organizations (PSOs), sometimes called provider-sponsored networks (PSNs), which could be regulated on an interim basis by the federal government (pre-empting state jurisdiction over these entities), followed by a wider role of state regulators in regulating all Medicare managed care plans.

The proposals advanced to date would preempt State licensure requirements or otherwise enable PSOs to meet the licensure requirements through solvency standards tailored to the needs of the PSOs. There would be waiver provisions or modification of how members are counted for meeting the minimum enrollment and 50/50 requirements. Controversial issues that would have to be resolved are the extent to which there will be variant standards for these organizations, their status with respect to State versus Federal regulation (i.e., how much Congress will be willing to reduce states' rights to regulate the insurance options within their borders), and the issue of what kinds of organizations would qualify as PSOs (e.g., what is the nature of the affiliation among providers within the PSO). The other trend in PSOs appears to be that more states are enacting separate PSO legislation (New York, Georgia, in addition to Minnesota and Iowa), which would open the way for PSOs to contract with Medicare as competitive medical plans.

While it's not clear what will finally happen as it relates to MSAs and PSOs, the restructuring of Medicare necessary for inflation control and a balanced budget will require massive migration of beneficiaries into prepaid (capitated) HMOs, PPOs, and POS plans. It seems highly probable that the legislation needed to support this migration will occur sooner rather than later.

Increased Education of Beneficiaries and Coordination of Enrollment

Expanding the product offerings to Medicare beneficiaries creates both opportunities and threats. The opportunity of course, is that many seniors will be attracted to the better benefits, preventive care focus, and accountable delivery systems in managed care offerings; their positive experience and training will help create wide acceptance of managed care. The threat is

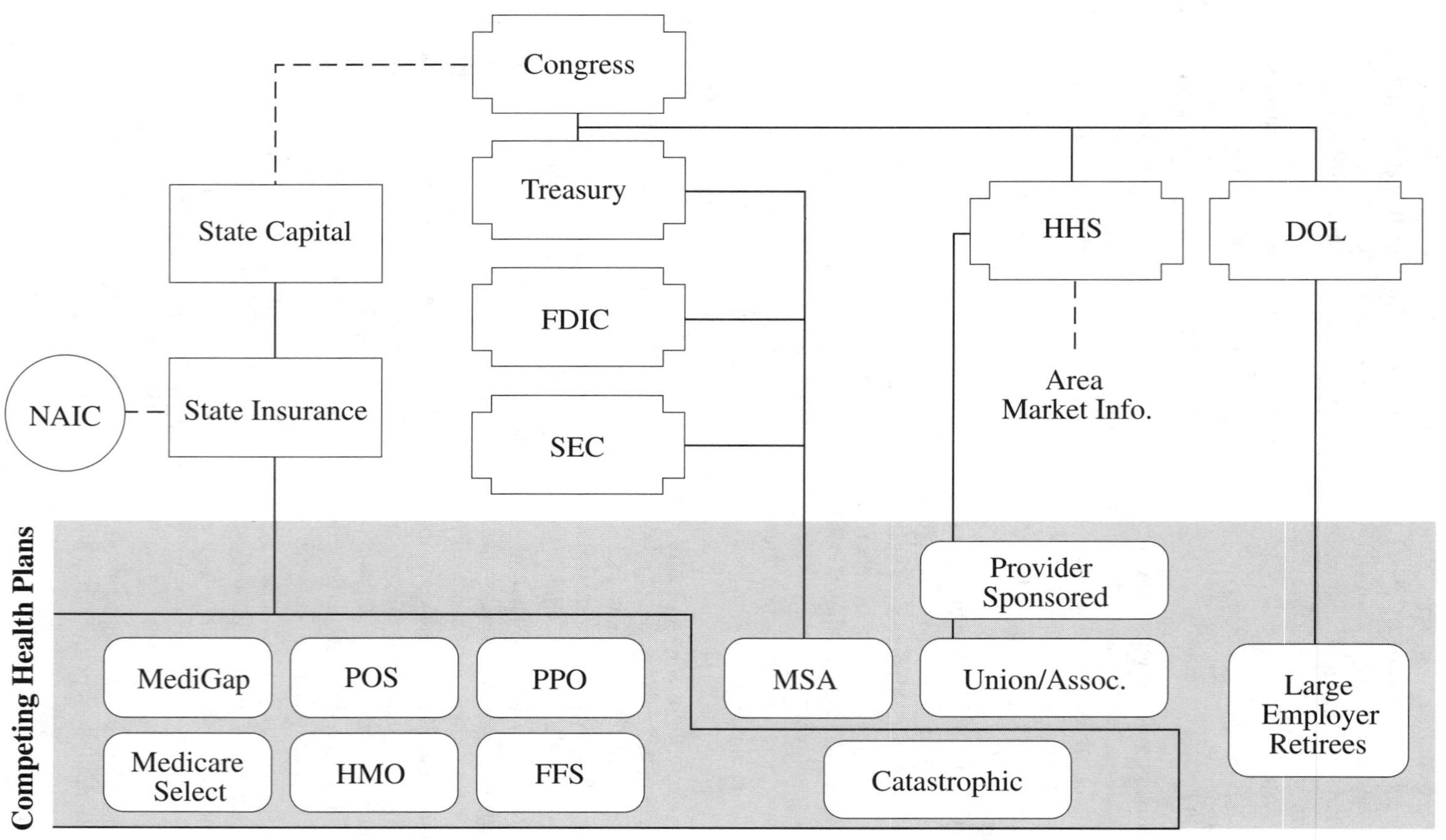

Figure 1 Medicare's Future: Oversight and Choices. *Source:* Courtesy of Analysis of Medicare Preservation Act, Ernst & Young LLP, 1995, Washington, D.C.

that seniors might be confused by the wide range of product offerings and either stay in traditional Medicare out of fear or confusion, or be swayed by slick and misleading advertising to join a plan that spends its entire budget on marketing and provides very poor service and benefits.

To ensure that Medicare beneficiaries understand the range of options and have a realistic and unbiased view of the advantages and disadvantages of each option, all parties agree that the government must support Medicare reform with a regular (annual) education effort. That effort would include a government-published spreadsheet of the Medicare Plus options available within each community. In addition, marketing material and member information must, in most plans, be approved by HCFA, and must conform to specified standards. Further, there would in all proposals be an appeals process to ensure members have the right to receive all services and benefits promised by the plan.

In an attempt to simplify the education and enrollment management process, both Congress and the Administration have proposed concentrating all education and decision making into an annual open enrollment period for all seniors. Using the employer group model, these proposals also require an annual lock-in; that is, once seniors elect a certain health plan option, they must stay in that plan until the next annual election period (with some exceptions). This is in contrast to the current system, which allows beneficiaries to change plans on a monthly basis. The goal of this lock-in approach is to support the annual enrollment cycle and to reduce the risk of adverse selection; that is, to reduce the chance that sicker Medicare recipients would move back into the less restrictive traditional Medicare during the year, leaving the Medicare Plus options with a healthier risk mix.

A number of employers offer Medicare retirees a Medicare risk HMO option. In many cases, employers are making Medicare risk the only option for Medicare-eligible retirees who want employer-sponsored Medicare coverage. There is a growing camp, however, that feel the group employer model doesn't apply to seniors. Medicare Risk HMOs and Medigap insurance have always been an individual insurance decision, with seniors able to elect in and out of the plan any month of the year. With less than 10 percent of seniors in managed care, and with seniors valuing the freedom of choice the way they do, this camp argues that an annual enrollment and lock-in will frighten seniors unfamiliar with managed care and retard the growth of Medicare Plus. Additionally, the annual lock-in limits the individual's ability to select the most qualified plan and protect themselves from being locked into a substandard system.

This camp proposes an annual education effort, and possibly even a single month when all plans are open for enrollment, but they would permit plans to continue monthly enrollment if they so choose. Likewise, this camp would allow seniors to change plans (possibly with some frequency limit) when they choose, although they have acknowledged that some form of lock-in may be less problematic in highly penetrated markets where seniors are more familiar with managed care options and delivery systems have developed adequate capacity and flexibility to manage the large annual shift in membership.

Whatever the actual model finally adopted, it's likely that marketing and general communication with Medicare beneficiaries will be more managed, as will the enrollment and disenrollment process.

Modification of the Rules for Operation and Expansion

For the budgeting goals of Medicare reform to occur, a large percentage of beneficiaries must shift into the premium-controlled Medicare Plus plans. As a result, most proposals make it easier for existing Medicare Plus participants (including Medicare Risk HMO) to expand to new markets. One common method is the elimination of the 50/50 requirement for experienced plans, so they no longer need at least 50 percent commercial enrollment in each new market, although at the time of this writing, there was some interest on the part of some members of Congress to retain it. Also common to most proposals is a decrease in administrative oversight of materials and processes already approved for other markets, and a time limit on how long HCFA can take to disapprove or approve submissions.

Finally, there is a large grab bag of proposals designed to ensure members' rights are preserved, quality of care is delivered, proper data is captured and reported, appeal and grievances are processed appropriately, and plans are operated in compliance with all established rules and regulations. As those supporting free market controls debate these details with those who only trust that which is tightly regulated and audited, it's too early to predict the level of new regulation that will ultimately control Medicare Plus operations. At a minimum, there will be requirements that protect patients' rights and general plan compliance with federal policy.

Many proponents of managed care see this last areas as the most subtly dangerous of the five areas of reform. While they feel they can debate and win on many elements of budgeting, product expansion, and beneficiary education, it is in the operating rules that they fear opponents of managed care could seed trouble. Under the popular banner of "patient protection" and "fairness to providers," legislation could pass that might threaten the very core of how HMOs work. In the future, under the banner of "administrative and quality oversight," managed care could be burdened with extensive and expensive processes and reporting requirements not expected from their less managed competitors. Fortunately, many in the Administration and Congress have educated themselves on these issues and are anxious not to overly restrict the marketplace. The level of anti-managed care sentiment in the media today, however, could increase the calls for regulatory control. As with all other elements of reform being debated, only time will tell.

SAFE HARBORS

The area of "safe harbors" from fraud and abuse regulations has been a murky one regarding managed care. On January 26, 1996, the Health and Human Services Inspector General issued a final rule clarifying and revising an interim rule it had published on November 5, 1992. The rule affects interactions between providers, health plans, and beneficiaries. The first safe harbor allows health plans to offer enrollees certain incentives such as waivers of deductible and coinsurance amounts. Two standards must be met for incentives offered to enrollees: The same incentive must be offered to all enrollees for all covered services, and a health plan may not claim the cost of the incentive as bad debt or shift the cost to Medicare or state health care programs.

The second safe harbor protects price reduction agreements between participating providers and health plans. These agreements must meet certain criteria in regard to length of contract (at least one year), the scope of covered services, reports to HCFA that state the amount a provider has been paid, and an understanding that the provider could not claim payment of the discounted amount from HCFA or state health care programs without specific authorization.

In addition to these new safe harbors, the existing safe harbor addressing waiver of beneficiary coinsurance and deductible amounts was amended to protect certain agreements entered into between hospitals and Medicare SELECT hospitals. The final rule reflects industry comments by expanding the definition of a health plan and narrowing the prohibition against cost shifting that had appeared in an interim rule. The definition of a health plan now includes physician hospital organizations, self-insured or ERISA plans, and organizations that act as intermediaries (such as PPOs) between participating health care providers and employers, union welfare funds, or insurance companies. An entity also must furnish or arrange for the provision of items or services in exchange for either a premium or fee to be considered a health plan. Cost shifting is now prohibited against the Medicare and state health care programs only, instead of all payers, as had been the case in the interim rule.

FEDERAL INSURANCE REFORM

In 1996, the Congress passed the Health Insurance Portability and Accountability Act, also known as the Kassebaum-Kennedy health insurance reform bill on August 21, and the President signed it. This bill contains numerous provisions, many of them technical, and the reader is urged to review this on their own. Key provisions of the act are portability of health insurance, guaranteed issue of health insurance (if certain conditions of prior coverage are met), mental health parity as regards life-time limits, mandatory minimum length of stay for obstetrics, the creation of a test of MSAs, and further fraud and abuse sanctions.

The significance of this bill is multifaceted. Congressional efforts to reform health care could either decrease the amount of uncompensated care delivered by providers or increase the price of insurance—with a corresponding surge in the ranks of the uninsured. Why such different outcome scenarios for a bill described as an incremental attempt to improve access the health insurance for individuals who lose their jobs or are moving between jobs? The bill's impact is highly dependent on characteristics of local health care markets. Also, some states wouldn't be affected by the bill because they already have portability laws that exceed the requirements in Kassebaum-Kennedy. As many as 32 states may receive exemptions from the bill's rules since the bill has safe harbor provisions that apply to states with guaranteed issue regulations or medical high-risk pools.

The impact of health insurance laws on providers is inextricably tied to their effect on premiums. Although Kassebaum-Kennedy would likely increase premiums if every other aspect of the health care market were held constant, the bill's effect may be masked by the overall trend of stable or slightly decreasing costs in the health care industry. Kassebaum-Kennedy also contains a long-term care provision that may assist providers who generate significant amounts of revenue from long-term care services. The provision provides tax deductibility for long-term care expenses including insurance premiums.

The following are market conditions that may increase the impact of the Kassebaum-Kennedy bill:

- large number of small employers
- highly mobile population
- low degree of portability of coverage allowed in existing state insurance laws
- local market cost of health insurance higher than the national average
- high percentage of self-pay patients
- high percentage of revenues from mental health services
- high percentage of revenues from long-term care services

STATE REGULATORY ISSUES

In the state arena, it is likely that several issues will continue to have a high level of activity in the next several years.

Regarding general licensing and regulatory issues, states will lobby Congress for more regulatory responsibility including Medicare and Medicaid programs. They will also continue actively licensing provider-sponsored managed care organizations (e.g., PSOs or PSNs) through existing enabling laws that currently apply to managed care organizations such as HMOs or preferred provider organizations.

State regulators also will be more active in authorizing and regulating HMO-sponsored POS products where the out-of-plan coverage is underwritten by the HMO (HMO enrollees in POS products should jump from 2.6 million in 1993 to an estimated 15 million in 1997). States will further regulate stop-loss coverage for health services; and update and expand their managed care laws through the adoption of risk-based capital standards for health plans, additional grievance procedures, and perhaps experimental treatment protocols—among other initiatives.

Anti-managed care legislation will continue to be introduced in record numbers. Figure 2 demonstrates the rise in a representative sample of anti-managed care bills introduced during the past four years—from approximately 100 proposals in 1993 to a projected 500 proposals in 1996. However, only a small percentage of proposed anti-managed care bills will be enacted in the states. For example in 1995, 63 any willing provider bills were introduced in 28 states, but only three bills in Texas and Arkansas were enacted. Moreover, 41 provider protection initiatives (so-called patient protection acts) were introduced in over 20 states, but only two limited bills in Maryland and Oregon were adopted. During the first three quarters of 1996, over 75 any-willing-provider proposals were introduced in 23 states; only one state, Kentucky, adopted a limited any-willing-provider requirement. This trend should continue in 1997.

Anti-managed care and other burdensome proposals that should receive a fair amount of state attention during the next several years include mandated benefits, direct access and freedom of choice requirements, any willing provider proposals, disclosure provisions, emergency room coverage mandates for non-emergency services, unitary drug pricing, and limits on physician compensation arrangements (e.g., capitation, withholds). In addition, maternity length of stay requirements were enacted in over 25 states in 1996; legislative activity on this issue is likely to dwindle because of the volume of legislation already considered at the state level and several federal initiatives under active consideration by the congress and administration.

Heading out a few years, the most popular private market reforms will be directed at the individual insurance market and the further refine-

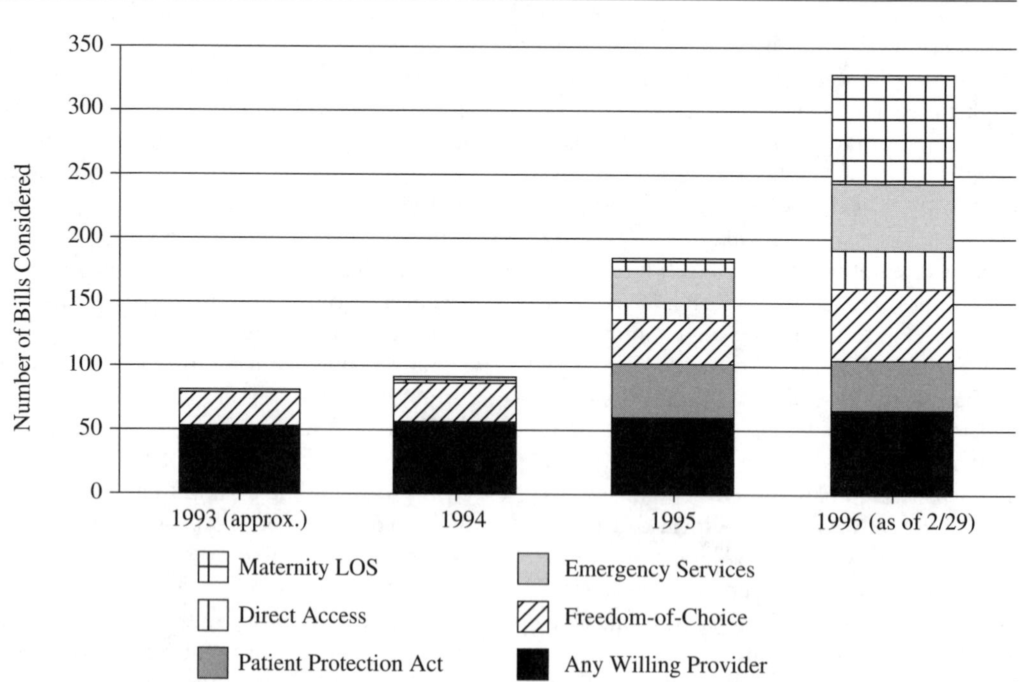

Figure 2 State Anti-Managed Care Legislation, 1993–1996. *Source:* Courtesy of the American Association of Health Plans, Washington, D.C.

ment of previously enacted reforms for small group coverage (e.g., employee groups under 50).

Furthermore, a new twist has been introduced to state-based insurance reforms. The federal government is extending its reach. The Health Insurance Portability and Accountability Act of 1996, also known as the Kassebaum/Kennedy bill, is designed to create more collaboration between several federal agencies and the states as regulations are drafted and implemented. For all states, some impact will be felt as federal portability provisions, long-term care requirements, fraud and abuse sanctions, and an MSA pilot project, among other provisions, are implemented. For some states who have aggressively adopted small group and individual reforms (e.g., community-rating requirements, limits on pre-existing conditions) in the past, the federal insurance reforms will have less of an effect. Under normal circumstances, one would speculate that new introductions of MSA enabling legislation (i.e., MSA deductibility from state taxes) would begin to drop because over half of the state already have adopted these proposals. However, the new federal pilot project may further increase the popularity of MSAs.

Other reform proposals that were popular during the past three to four years—such as purchasing alliances, employer mandates, play or pay proposals, single payor systems, and universal access requirements—will continue to drop in frequency in 1997.

LEGAL ISSUES AFFECTING INTEGRATED DELIVERY SYSTEMS

Although the Federal Budget Bill has not been enacted at the time of this writing, it includes several changes that may affect organizers of an integrated delivery system (IDS).

First, it is anticipated that the Stark law will be significantly revised to exclude compensation as a "financial interest." If this occurs, it will be simpler to establish compensation arrangements within an IDS, as well as compensation relationships with subcontracting physicians. An analysis would still need to be made of any such arrangement, however, under anti-kickback laws and tax-exempt status rules (if applicable).

The proposed legislation reportedly seeks to make it easier for the Office of Inspector General (OIG) to prosecute anti-kickback law violations. The primary legal change is for the word "willful" to be removed from the statute, thereby effectively overruling *Hanlester*.[1] It is not clear what practical effect this statutory revision will have on the development of an integrated delivery system, but the OIG may use it to challenge systems that it believes are disguised payments to lock in patient referrals to a hospital. A particular concern would be situations in which a hospital develops an IDS with a physician group using a competing hospital. If the physician group shifts all or most of its patients to the purchasing hospital after receiving a large acquisition payment from the hospital, the OIG may decide to challenge the arrangement.

The Internal Revenue Service (IRS) has recently been given new authority to impose "intermediate sanctions" against individuals in a tax-exempt organization who develop or approve arrangements that result in excessive private benefit or inurement for "insiders." Under this legislation, the IRS can hold responsible persons personally liable for allowing an improper transaction or arrangement with insiders to occur. The first critical issue in assessing risk under this law is determining the definition of who constitutes an "insider." Not all physicians are necessarily insiders. Instead one must make a factual determination of whether the physician exerts significant control over the exempt organization. In developing an IDS, one must be careful to assess the intermediate sanctions risk.

THE PROVIDER WORLD

The world of providers is continuing to consolidate. On the hospital side, hospitals are actively seeking partners or merger candidates. The number of not-for-profit hospitals being acquired by for-profit hospital companies continues to rise at a very rapid rate, especially in urban or highly competitive areas. Some even think that it is possible that in the next 10 years, there will be between 40 and 1,000 integrated delivery systems (IDSs) in the country, with each major statistical metropolitan area supporting between 3 and 7 such systems, and many of these systems will be part of larger national or regional chains.[2]

With the consolidation of institutional providers and the increase in enrollment in managed care among the Medicare population, Medicare payments to hospitals would be reduced to about 40 percent of expenditures by the year 2002, from about 50 percent today.

Physicians will likewise be compelled to organize into larger systems. These may be vertical alignments (e.g., becoming employed by hospitals) or they may be horizontal alignments (e.g., large single- or multi-specialty group practices). The trend of hospitals acquiring physician practices appears to be slowing down as many hospitals find that the acquired practices do not necessarily perform as expected (with a reduction in productivity occurring not infrequently), and not achieving critical mass of primary care physicians to be a fully functional delivery system. With a number of large, vertically aligned HMOs spinning off their medical groups and hospitals, it is possible that many of the vertically integrated health systems will ultimately spin off their physician practices as well, implying that many current integration activities are transitional in nature. Physician practice management companies will also play a role in the continued aggregation of physicians into larger organizations. While it is not clear how many of these new organizations will be stable, it is clear that they are a factor in some marketplaces.

The era of solo physicians or small groups will slowly come to a close. Existing practices of successful physicians will most probably be able to weather the changes until retirement, but physicians new to practice, burdened with debt and needing to meet target incomes, will find that joining groups or large organizations will be their most attractive options, while new solo physicians will find it increasingly hard to access revenue.

With the ascendancy of primary care as the focal point of many managed care systems, specialty physicians will continue to feel the pressures, at least in highly competitive markets. This may lead to more specialists migrating to less competitive markets, thereby creating a medical marketplace that in turn becomes more competitive. Specialists will also continue to form new types of organizations in hopes of being able to exert economically greater control and benefit. It is possible that specialty physicians will divide up into those who, through either large groups or by being part of organized systems, will prosper but work very hard, and those who will be economically squeezed.

One issue that is not at all clear is the degree that individual physicians will be reimbursed through capitation. In some mature markets such as Minneapolis, the degree of capitation is actually quite low, with salary and fee-for-service being strong forms of payment. Given the degree of margin inherent in capitation, it is possible that some HMOs as well as large self-funded employers, will be unwilling to cede that margin.

THE PAYER WORLD

Consolidation in MCOs will also continue. Although there are more newly licensed HMOs in 1996 than in previous years, the market concentration of the largest MCO companies remains formidable. Many of these new starts are reactive on the part of IDSs wanting to gain more control, while others are entrepreneurial in nature and have as their goal selling out to a larger firm. This market concentration will continue, especially in urban areas. It is also likely that large MCOs will be compelled to vigorously enter the public sector market in order to sustain growth.

The number of MCOs willing to contract with IDSs on a percent of premium basis will increase, barring a regulatory challenge to the practice (i.e., global capitation on a percent of premium basis may be considered too much risk transfer by some insurance departments). The number of joint ventures between payers and providers will also increase, but many will flounder. Those MCOs that rely primarily on driving ever lower unit prices from providers (e.g., ever lower fees or per diems) may provoke a backlash by IDSs to try to access the market through other channels (e.g., by obtaining their own license), an action that would become necessary if the MCO does not even pay the direct cost of care provided.

MEDICAL MANAGEMENT

Medical management continues to advance as well. Utilization levels found in certain parts of California are now being found in other parts of the nation as well. New techniques in medical management, described in this book and elsewhere, are slowly becoming more mainstream, replacing older models of utilization and quality management. Many mature MCOs desire to get out of the business of micromanaging medical care, and would prefer to delegate those activities to providers. As providers organize into systems of care and adopt advanced medical management techniques, this becomes ever more possible.

CONCLUSION

The pace of change in health care today can only accelerate in the near term. Whatever a MCO or IDS looks like today, it will not look that way in the years to come. Those legislative events occurring today will be modified in years to come. We will enter the millennium in a state of continual change. Some of that change will be painful and not necessarily positive; for example, if monetary resources become desperately low, then no amount of management will be able to create value from nothing. But most change will ultimately be beneficial, providing more efficient, higher quality medical care for less cost. As American medicine moves from a cottage industry to an organized system, we stand able to leverage new resources to continue forward progress.

REFERENCE AND NOTE

1. *Hanlester Network v. Shalala*, 95 Daily Journal D.A.R. 4286, 4290 (April 6, 1995). It should be noted that the *Hanlester* case is only binding in the Ninth Circuit. The government has decided not to appeal *Hanlester*, but will fight the issues anew in other circuits.
2. K.C. Nolan, 1995. Unpublished data, Ernst & Young, LLP, Washington, D.C.

Glossary of Terms and Acronyms

"Words are not as satisfactory as we should like them to be,
but, like our neighbours, we have got to live with
them and must make the best and
not the worst of them."

Samuel Butler
(1835–1902)
Samuel Butler's Notebooks (1951)

AAHP—American Association of Health Plans. The trade organization that represents all forms of MCOs. Created in 1996 by the merger of GHAA and AMCRA. Based in Washington, D.C., the AAHP has a heavy focus on lobbying, educational activities, and service to member plans.

AAPCC—Adjusted average per capita cost. The HCFA's best estimate of the amount of money it costs to care for Medicare recipients under fee-for-service Medicare in a given area. The AAPCC is made up of 142 different rate cells; 140 of them are factored for age, sex, Medicaid eligibility, institutional status, working aged, and whether a person has both part A and part B Medicare. The two remaining cells are for individuals with end-stage renal disease.

AAPPO—American Association of Preferred Provider Organizations. A trade organization for PPOs.

Accrete—The term used by the HCFA for the process of adding new Medicare enrollees to a plan. See also *delete*.

Accrual—The amount of money that is set aside to cover expenses. The accrual is the plan's best estimate of what those expenses are and (for medical expenses) is based on a combination of data from the authorization system, the claims system, the lag studies, and the plan's history.

ACG—Ambulatory care group. ACGs are a method of categorizing outpatient episodes. There are 51 mutually exclusive ACGs, which are based on resource use over time and are modified by principal diagnosis, age, and sex. See also *ADG* and *APG*.

ACR—Adjusted community rate. Used by HMOs and CMPs with Medicare risk contracts. A calculation of what premium the plan would charge for providing exactly the Medicare-covered benefits to a group account adjusted to allow for the greater intensity and frequency of utilization by Medicare recipients. The ACR includes the normal profit of a for-profit HMO or CMP. The ACR may be equal to or lower than the APR but can never exceed it. See also *APR*.

Actuarial assumptions—The assumptions that an actuary uses in calculating the expected costs and revenues of the plan. Examples include utilization rates, age and sex mix of enrollees, and cost of medical services.

ADG—Ambulatory diagnostic group. ADGs are a method of categorizing outpatient episodes. There are 34 possible ADGs. See *ACG* and *APG*.

Adverse selection—The problem of attracting members who are sicker than the general population (specifically, members who are sicker than was anticipated when the budget for medical costs was developed).

ALOS—See *LOS*.

AMCRA—American Managed Care and Review Association. A trade association that represented managed indemnity plans, PPOs, MCOs, and HMOs. Merged with GHAA in 1995 to become the AAHP in 1996. See also *AAHP*.

APG—Ambulatory patient group. A reimbursement methodology developed by 3M Health Information Systems for the HCFA. APGs are to outpatient procedures what DRGs are to inpatient days. APGs provide for a fixed reimbursement to an institution for outpatient procedures or visits and incorporate data regarding the reason for the visit and patient data. APGs prevent unbundling of ancillary services. See also *ACG* and *ADG*.

APR—Average payment rate. The amount of money that the HCFA could conceivably pay an HMO or CMP for services to Medicare recipients under a risk contract. The figure is derived from the AAPCC for the service area adjusted for the enrollment characteristics that the plan would expect to have. The payment to the plan, the ACR, can never be higher than the APR, but it may be less.

ASO—Administrative services only (sometimes referred to as an administrative services contract [ASC]). A contract between an insurance company and a self-funded plan where the insurance company performs administrative services only and does not assume any risk. Services usually include claims processing but may include other services, such as actuarial analysis, utilization review, and so forth. See also *ERISA*.

Assignment of benefits—The payment of medical benefits directly to a provider of care rather than to a member. Generally requires either a contract between the health plan and the provider or a written release from the subscriber to the provider allowing the provider to bill the health plan.

AWP (any willing provider)—This is a form of state law that requires an MCO to accept any provider willing to meet the terms and conditions in the MCO's contract, whether the MCO wants or needs that provider or not. Considered to be an expensive form of anti-managed care legislation.

AWP (average wholesale price)—Commonly used in pharmacy contracting, the AWP is generally determined through reference to a common source of information.

Balance billing—The practice of a provider billing a patient for all charges not paid for by the insurance plan, even if those charges are above the plan's UCR or are considered medically unnecessary. Managed care plans and service plans generally prohibit providers from balance billing except for allowed copays, coinsurance, and deductibles. Such prohibition against balance billing may even extend to the plan's failure to pay at all (e.g., because of bankruptcy).

Capitation—A set amount of money received or paid out; it is based on membership rather than on services delivered and usually is expressed in units of PMPM. May be varied by such factors as age and sex of the enrolled member.

Carve-out—Refers to a set of medical services that are carved out of the basic arrangement. In terms of plan benefits, may refer to a set of benefits that are carved out and contracted for separately; for example, mental health/substance abuse services may be separated from basic medical–surgical services. May also refer to carving out a set of services from a basic capitation rate with a provider (e.g., capitating for cardiac care but carving out cardiac surgery and paying case rates for that).

Case management—A method of managing the provision of health care to members with high-cost medical conditions. The goal is to coordinate the care to improve both continuity and quality of care and to lower costs. This generally is a dedicated function in the utilization management department. The official definition, according to the Certification of Insurance Rehabilitation Specialists Commission, is as follows: "Case management is a collaborative process which assesses, plans, implements, coordinates, monitors, and evaluates the options and services required to meet an individual's health needs, using communication and available resources to promote quality, cost-effective outcomes" and "occurs across a continuum of care, addressing ongoing individual needs" rather than being restricted to a single practice setting. When focused solely on high-cost inpatient cases, may be referred to as large case management or catastrophic case management.

Case mix—Refers to the mix of illness and severity of cases for a provider.

Certificate of coverage—Refers to the document that a plan must provide to a member to show evidence that the member has coverage and to give basic information about that coverage. Required under state regulations.

CHAMPUS—Civilian Health and Medical Program of the Uniformed Services. The federal program providing health care coverage to families of military personnel, military retirees, certain spouses and dependents of such personnel, and certain others.

Churning—The practice of a provider seeing a patient more often than is medically necessary, primarily to increase revenue through an increased number of services. Churning may also apply to any performance-based reimbursement system where there is a heavy emphasis on productivity (in other words, rewarding a provider for seeing a high volume of patients, whether through fee for service or through an appraisal system that pays a bonus for productivity).

CLM—Career-limiting move. A boneheaded mistake by a manager. What this book is designed to try to prevent.

Closed panel—A managed care plan that contracts with physicians on an exclusive basis for services and does not allow those physicians to see patients for another managed care organization. Examples include staff and group model HMOs. Could apply to a large private medical group that contracts with an HMO.

CMP—Competitive medical plan. A federal designation that allows a health plan to obtain eligibility to receive a Medicare risk contract without having to obtain qualification as an HMO. Requirements for eligibility are somewhat less restrictive than for an HMO.

COA—Certificate of authority. The state-issued operating license for an HMO.

COB—Coordination of benefits. An agreement that uses language developed by the National Association of Insurance Commissioners and prevents double payment for services when a subscriber has coverage from two or more sources. For example, a husband may have Blue Cross/Blue Shield through work, and the wife may have elected an HMO through her place of employment. The agreement gives the order for what organization has primary responsibility for payment and what organization has secondary responsibility for payment.

COBRA—Consolidated Omnibus Budget Reconciliation Act. A portion of this act requires employers to offer the opportunity for terminated employees to purchase continuation of health care coverage under the group's medical plan. Another portion eases a Medicare recipient's ability to disenroll from an HMO or CMP with a Medicare risk contract. See also *conversion*.

Coinsurance—A provision in a member's coverage that limits the amount of coverage by the plan to a certain percentage, commonly 80 percent. Any additional costs are paid by the member out of pocket.

Cold claim—A claim for medical services received by the plan for which no authorization has been received; i.e., it arrives "cold."

Commission—The money paid to a sales representative, broker, or other type of sales agent for selling the health plan. May be a flat amount of money or a percentage of the premium.

Community rating—The rating methodology required of federally qualified HMOs, HMOs under the laws of many states, and occasionally indemnity plans under certain circumstances. The HMO must obtain the same amount of money per member for all members in the plan. Community rating does allow for variability by allowing the HMO to factor in differences for age, sex, mix (average contract size), and industry factors; not all factors are necessarily allowed under state laws, however. Such techniques are referred to as community rating by class and adjusted community rating. See also *experience rating*.

CON—Certificate of need. The requirement that a health care organization obtain permission from an oversight agency before making changes. Generally applies only to facilities or facility-based services.

Concurrent review—Refers to utilization management that takes place during the provision of services. Almost exclusively applied to inpatient hospital stays.

Contract year—The 12-month period for which a contract for services is in force. Not necessarily tied to a calendar year.

Contributory plan—A group health plan in which the employees must contribute a certain amount toward the premium cost, with the employer paying the rest.

Conversion—The conversion of a member covered under a group master contract to coverage under an individual contract. This is offered to subscribers who lose their group coverage (e.g., through job loss, death of a working spouse, and so forth) and who are ineligible for coverage under another group contract. See also *COBRA*.

Copayment—That portion of a claim or medical expense that a member must pay out of pocket. Usually a fixed amount, such as $5 in many HMOs.

Corporate practice of medicine acts or statutes—State laws that prohibit a physician from working for a corporation; in other words, a physician can only work for himself or herself or another physician. Put another way, a corporation cannot practice medicine. Often created through the effort on the part of certain members of the medical community to prevent physicians from working directly for managed care plans or hospitals.

Cost sharing—Any form of coverage in which the member pays some portion of the cost of providing services. Usual forms of cost sharing include deductibles, coinsurance, and copayments.

Cost shifting—When a provider cannot cover the cost of providing services under the reimbursement received, the provider raises the prices to other payers to cover that portion of the cost.

CPT-4—*Current Procedural Terminology*, 4th edition. A set of five-digit codes that apply to medical services delivered. Frequently used for billing by professionals. See also *HCPCS*.

Credentialing—The most common use of the term refers to obtaining and reviewing the documentation of professional providers. Such documentation includes licensure, certifications, insurance, evidence of malpractice insurance, malpractice history, and so forth. Generally includes both reviewing information provided by the provider and verification that the information is correct and complete. A much less frequent use of the term applies to closed panels and medical groups and refers to obtaining hospital privileges and other privileges to practice medicine.

Custodial care—Care provided to an individual that is primarily the basic activities of living. May be medical or nonmedical, but the care is not meant to be curative or as a form of medical treatment, and it is often life long. Rarely covered by any form of group health insurance or HMO.

CVO—Credentialing verification organization. This is an independent organization that performs primary verification of a professional provider's credentials. The managed care organization may then rely on that verification rather than requiring the provider to provide credentials independently. This lowers the cost and "hassle" for credentialing. The NCQA has issued certification standards for CVOs. See also *NCQA*.

CWW—Clinic without walls. See *GPWW*.

Date of service—Refers to the date that medical services were rendered. Usually different from the date a claim is submitted.

DAW—Dispense as written. The instruction from a physician to a pharmacist to dispense a brand-name pharmaceutical rather than a generic substitution.

Days per thousand—A standard unit of measurement of utilization. Refers to an annualized use of the hospital or other institutional care. It is the number of hospital days that are used in a year for each thousand covered lives.

DCI—Duplicate coverage inquiry. A document used in COB when one plan contacts another to inquire about dual coverage of medical benefits.

Death spiral—An insurance term that refers to a vicious spiral of high premium rates and adverse selection, generally in a free-choice environment (typically, an insurance company or health plan in an account with multiple other plans, or a plan offering coverage to potential members who have alternative choices, such as through an association). One plan, often the indemnity plan competing with managed care plans, ends up having continually higher premium rates such that the only members who stay with the plan are those whose medical costs are so high (and who cannot change because of provider loyalty or benefits restrictions, such as preexisting conditions) that they far exceed any possible premium revenue. Called the death spiral because the losses from underwriting mount faster than the premiums can ever recover, and the account eventually terminates coverage, leaving the carrier in a permanent loss position.

Deductible—That portion of a subscriber's (or member's) health care expenses that must be paid out of pocket before any insurance coverage applies, commonly \$100 to \$300. Common in insurance plans and PPOs, uncommon in

HMOs. May apply only to the out-of-network portion of a point-of-service plan. May also apply only to one portion of the plan coverage (e.g., there may be a deductible for pharmacy services but not for anything else).

Delete—The term used by the HCFA for the process of removing Medicare enrollees from a plan. See also *accrete*.

Dependent—A member who is covered by virtue of a family relationship with the member who has the health plan coverage. For example, one person has health insurance or an HMO through work, and that individual's spouse and children, the dependents, also have coverage under that contract.

DHMO—Dental health maintenance organization. An HMO organized strictly to provide dental benefits.

Direct contracting—A term describing a provider or integrated health care delivery system contracting directly with employers rather than through an insurance company or managed care organization. A superficially attractive option that occasionally works when the employer is large enough. Not to be confused with direct contract model.

Direct contract model—A managed care health plan that contracts directly with private practice physicians in the community rather than through an intermediary, such as an IPA or a medical group. A common type of model in open panel HMOs.

Discharge planning—That part of utilization management that is concerned with arranging for care or medical needs to facilitate discharge from the hospital.

Disease management—The process of intensively managing a particular disease. This differs from large case management in that it goes well beyond a given case in the hospital or an acute exacerbation of a condition. Disease management encompasses all settings of care and places a heavy emphasis on prevention and maintenance. Similar to case management, but more focused on a defined set of diseases.

Disenrollment—The process of termination of coverage. Voluntary termination would include a member quitting because he or she simply wants out. Involuntary termination would include a member leaving the plan because of changing jobs. A rare and serious form of involuntary disenrollment is when the plan terminates a member's coverage against the member's will. This is usually only allowed (under state and federal laws) for gross offenses such as fraud, abuse, nonpayment of premium or copayments, or a demonstrated inability to comply with recommended treatment plans.

DME—Durable medical equipment. Medical equipment that is not disposable (i.e., is used repeatedly) and is only related to care for a medical condition. Examples include wheelchairs, home hospital beds, and so forth. An area of increasing expense, particularly in conjunction with case management.

Dread disease policy—A peculiar type of health insurance that only covers a specific and frightening type of illness, such as cancer. Uncommon.

DRG—Diagnosis-related group. A statistical system of classifying any inpatient stay into groups for the purposes of payment. DRGs may be primary or secondary; an outlier classification also exists. This is the form of reimbursement that the HCFA uses to pay hospitals for Medicare recipients. Also used by a few states for all payers and by many private health plans (usually non-HMO) for contracting purposes.

DSM-IV—*Diagnostic and Statistical Manual of Mental Disorders*, 4th edition. The manual used to provide a diagnostic coding system for mental and substance abuse disorders. Far different from ICD-9-CM. See also ICD-9-CM.

Dual choice—Sometimes referred to as Section 1310 or mandating. That portion of the federal HMO regulations that required any employer with 25 or more employees that resided in an HMO's service area, paid minimum wage, and offers health coverage to offered a federally qualified HMO as well. The HMO had to request it. This provision was "sunsetted" in 1995. Another definition, unrelated to the previous one, pertains to point of service. See also *POS*.

Dual option—The offering of both an HMO and a traditional insurance plan by one carrier.

Duplicate claims—When the same claim is submitted more than once, usually because payment has not been received quickly. Can lead to duplicate payments and incorrect data in the claims file.

DUR—Drug utilization review.

EAP—Employee assistance program. A program that a company puts into effect for its employees to provide them with help in dealing with personal problems, such as alcohol or drug abuse, mental health or stress issues, and so forth.

Effective date—The day that health plan coverage goes into effect or is modified.

Eligibility—When an individual is eligible for coverage under a plan. Also used to determine when an individual is no longer eligible for coverage (e.g., a dependent child reaches a certain age and is no longer eligible for coverage under his or her parent's health plan).

ELOS—See *LOS*.

Encounter—An outpatient or ambulatory visit by a member to a provider. Applies primarily to physician office visits but may encompass other types of encounters as well. In fee-for-service plans, an encounter also generates a claim. In capitated plans, the encounter is still the visit, but no claim is generated. See also *statistical claim*.

Enrollee—An individual enrolled in a managed health care plan. Usually applies to the subscriber or person who has the coverage in the first place rather than to their dependents, but the term is not always used that precisely.

EOB—Explanation of benefits (statement). A statement mailed to a member or covered insured explaining how and why a claim was or was not paid; the Medicare version is called an explanation of Medicare benefits, or EOMB. See also *ERISA*.

EPO—Exclusive provider organization. An EPO is similar to an HMO in that it often uses primary physicians as gatekeepers, often capitates providers, has a limited provider panel, and uses an authorization system. It is referred to as exclusive because the member must remain within the network to receive benefits. The main difference is that EPOs are generally regulated under insurance statutes rather than HMO regulations. Not allowed in many states that maintain that EPOs are really HMOs.

Equity model—A term applied to a form of for-profit vertically integrated health care delivery system in which the physicians are owners.

ERISA—Employee Retirement Income Security Act. One provision of this act allows self-funded plans to avoid paying premium taxes, complying with state-mandated benefits, or otherwise complying with state laws and regulations regarding insurance, even when insurance companies and managed care plans that stand risk for medical costs must do so. Another provision requires that plans and insurance companies provide an explanation of benefits statement to a member or covered insured in the event of a denial of a claim, explaining why the claim was denied and informing the individual of his or her rights of appeal. Numerous other provisions in ERISA are important for a managed care organization to know.

Evidence of insurability—The form that documents whether an individual is eligible for health plan coverage when the individual does not enroll through an open enrollment period. For example, if an employee wants to change health plans in the middle of a contract year, the new health plan may require evidence of insurability (often both a questionnaire and a medical examination) to ensure that it will not be accepting adverse risk.

Experience rating—The method of setting premium rates based on the actual health care costs of a group or groups.

Extracontractual benefits—Health care benefits beyond what the member's actual policy covers. These benefits are provided by a plan to reduce utilization. For example, a plan may not provide coverage for a hospital bed at home, but it is more cost effective for the plan to provide such a bed than to keep admitting a member to the hospital.

FAR—Federal acquisition regulations. The regulations applied to the federal government's acquisition of services, including health care services. See also *FEHBARS*.

Favored nations discount—A contractual agreement between a provider and a payer stating that the provider will automatically provide the payer the best discount it provides anyone else.

Federal qualification—Applies to HMOs and CMPs. It means that the HMO/CMP meets federal standards regarding benefits, financial solvency, rating methods, marketing, member services, health care delivery systems, and other standards. An HMO/CMP must apply for federal qualification and be examined by the OMC, including an on-site review. Federal qualification does place some restrictions on how a plan operates but also allows it to enter the Medicare and FEHBP markets in an expedited way. Federal qualification is voluntary and not required to enter the market.

Fee schedule—May also be referred to as fee maximums or a fee allowance schedule. A listing of the maximum fee that a health plan will pay for a certain service based on CPT billing codes.

FEHBARS—Federal Employee Health Benefit Acquisition Regulations. The regulations applied to OPM's purchase of health care benefits programs for federal employees.

FEHBP—Federal Employee Health Benefits Program. The program that provides health benefits to federal employees. See also *OPM*.

FFS—Fee for service. A patient sees a provider, and the provider bills the health plan or patient and gets paid based on that bill.

Flexible benefit plan—When an employer allows employees to choose a variety of options in benefits up to a certain total amount. The employee then can tailor his or her benefits package among health coverage, life insurance, child care, and so forth to optimize benefits for his or her particular needs.

Formulary—A listing of drugs that a physician may prescribe. The physician is requested or required to use only formulary drugs unless there is a valid medical reason to use a nonformulary drug.

Foundation—A not-for-profit form of integrated health care delivery system. The foundation model is usually formed in response to tax laws that affect not-for-profit hospitals or in response to state laws prohibiting the corporate practice of medicine. The foundation purchases both the tangible and intangible assets of a physician's practice, and the physicians then form a medical group that contracts with the foundation on an exclusive basis for services to patients seen through the foundation. See also *corporate practice of medicine acts or statutes*.

Foundation model—Refers to an integrated health care delivery system in which a not-for-profit foundation is responsible for providing the income to a medical group that is exclusive with the foundation. The foundation is usually, but not necessarily, associated with a not-for-profit hospital and is often found in states with corporate practice of medicine acts.

FPP—Faculty practice plan. A form of group practice organized around a teaching program. It may be a single group encompassing all the physicians providing services to patients at the teaching hospital and clinics, or it may be multiple groups drawn along specialty lines (e.g., psychiatry, cardiology, or surgery).

FTE—Full-time equivalent. The equivalent of one full-time employee. For example, two part-time employees are 0.5 FTE each, for a total of 1 FTE.

Full capitation—A loose term used to refer to a physician group or organization receiving capitation for all professional expenses, not just for the services it provides itself; does not include capitation for institutional services. The group is then responsible for subcapitating or otherwise reimbursing other physicians for services to its members. See *global capitation*.

Gatekeeper—An informal, although widely used, term that refers to a primary care case management model health plan. In this model, all care from providers other than the primary care physician, except for true emergencies, must be authorized by the primary care physician before rendered. This is a predominant feature of almost all HMOs.

Generic drug—A drug that is equivalent to a brand-name drug but usually less expensive. Most managed care organizations that provide drug benefits cover generic drugs but may require a member to pay the difference in cost between a generic drug and a brand-name drug or pay a higher copay, unless there is no generic equivalent.

GHAA—Group Health Association of America, now AAHP. A trade association that represented managed care with a focus on HMOs, both open and closed panel. Merged with AMCRA in 1995. See also *AAHP*.

Global capitation—A capitation payment that covers all medical expenses, including professional and institutional expenses. May not necessarily cover optional benefits (e.g., pharmacy). Sometimes called total capitation.

GPWW—Group practice without walls. A group practice in which the members of the group come together legally but continue to practice in private offices scattered throughout the service area. Sometimes called a clinic without walls (CWW).

Group—The members who are covered by virtue of receiving health plan coverage at a single company.

Group model HMO—An HMO that contracts with a medical group for the provision of health care services. The relationship between the HMO and the medical group is generally close, although there are wide variations in the relative independence of the group from the HMO. A form of closed panel health plan.

Group practice—The American Medical Association defines group practice as three or more physicians who deliver patient care, make joint use of equipment and personnel, and divide income by a prearranged formula.

HCFA—Health Care Financing Administration. The federal agency that oversees all aspects of health financing for Medicare and also oversees the Office of Managed Care.

HCFA-1500—A claims form used by professionals to bill for services. Required by Medicare and generally used by private insurance companies and managed care plans.

HCPCS—HCFA Common Procedural Coding System. A set of codes used by Medicare that describes services and procedures. HCPCS includes CPT codes but also has codes for services not included in CPT, such as DME and ambulance. Although HCPCS is nationally defined, there is provision for local use of certain codes.

HCPP—Health care prepayment plan. A form of cost contract between the HCFA and a medical group to provide professional services but does not cover Medicare Part A institutional services.

HEDIS—Healthplan Employer Data Information Set. Developed by the NCQA with considerable input from the employer community and the managed care community, HEDIS is an ever-evolving set of data reporting standards. HEDIS is designed to provide some standardization in performance reporting for financial, utilization, membership, and clinical data so that employers and others can compare performance among plans.

HMO—Health maintenance organization. The definition of an HMO has changed substantially. Originally, an HMO was defined as a prepaid organization that provided health care to voluntarily enrolled members in return for a preset amount of money on a PMPM basis. With the increase in self-insured businesses, or with financial arrangements that do not rely on prepayment, that definition is no longer accurate. Now the definition needs to encompass two possibilities: a licensed health plan (licensed as an HMO, that is) that places at least some of the providers at risk for medical expenses, and a health plan that utilizes designated (usually primary care) physicians as gatekeepers (although there are some HMOs that do not). Many in the field have given up and now use the looser term *MCO* because it avoids having to make difficult definitions such as this one.

IBNR—Incurred but not reported. The amount of money that the plan had better accrue for medical expenses that it knows nothing about yet. These are medical expenses that the authorization system has not captured and for which claims have not yet hit the door. Unexpected IBNRs have torpedoed more managed care plans than any other cause.

ICD-9-CM—*International Classification of Diseases*, 9th revision, clinical modification. The classification of disease by diagnosis codified into six-digit numbers. The ICD-10 will use alphanumeric codes and is scheduled for publication soon.

IDFN—See *IDS*.

IDFS—See *IDS*.

IDN—See *IDS*.

IDS—Integrated delivery system; also referred to as an integrated health care delivery system. Other acronyms that mean the same thing include IDN (integrated delivery network), IDFS (integrated delivery and financing system), and IDFN (integrated delivery and financing network). An IDS is a system of health care providers organized to span a broad range of health care services. Although there is no clear definition of an IDS, in its full flower an IDS should be able to access the market on a broad basis, optimize cost and clinical outcomes, accept and manage a full range of financial arrangements to provide a set of defined benefits to a defined population, align financial incentives of the participants (including physicians), and operate under a cohesive management structure. See also *IHO*, *IPA*, *PHO*, *MSO*, *equity model*, *staff model*, *foundation model*.

IHO—Integrated health care organization. An IDS that is predominantly owned by physicians. Not a common term at the time this edition was written.

IPA—Independent practice association. An organization that has a contract with a managed care plan to deliver services in return for a single capitation rate. The IPA in turn contracts with individual providers to provide the services either on a capitation basis or on a fee-for-service basis. The typical IPA encompasses all specialties, but an IPA can be solely for primary care, or it may be a single specialty. An IPA may also be the "PO" part of a PHO.

Joint Commission (formerly JCAHO)—Joint Commission for the Accreditation of Healthcare Organizations. A not-for-profit organization that performs accreditation reviews primarily on hospitals, other institutional facilities, and outpatient facilities. Most managed care plans require any hospital under contract to be accredited by the Joint Commission.

Lag study—A report that tells managers how old the claims are that are being processed and how much is paid out each month (both for that month and for any earlier months, by month) and compares these with the amount of money that was accrued for expenses each month. A powerful tool used to determine whether the plan's reserves are adequate to meet all expenses. Plans that fail to perform lag studies properly may find themselves staring into the abyss.

Line of business—A health plan (e.g., an HMO, EPO, or PPO) that is set up as a line of business within another, larger organization, usually an insurance company. This legally differentiates it from a freestanding company or a company set up as a subsidiary. It may also refer to a unique product type (e.g., Medicaid) within a health plan.

LOS/ELOS/ALOS—Length of stay/estimated length of stay/average length of stay.

Loss ratio—See *medical loss ratio*.

MAC—Maximum allowable charge (or cost). The maximum, although not the minimum, that a vendor may charge for something. This term is often used in pharmacy contracting; a related term, used in conjunction with professional fees, is *fee maximum*.

Managed health care—A regrettably nebulous term. At the very least, a system of health care delivery that tries to manage the cost of health care, the quality of that health care, and access to that care. Common denominators include a panel of contracted providers that is less than the entire universe of available providers, some type of limitations on benefits to subscribers who use noncontracted providers (unless authorized to do so), and some type of authorization system. Managed health care is actually a spectrum of systems, ranging from so-called managed indemnity through PPOs, POS plans, open panel HMOs, and closed panel HMOs. For a better definition, the reader is urged to read this book and formulate his or her own.

Mandated benefits—Benefits that a health plan is required to provide by law. This is generally used to refer to benefits above and beyond routine insurance type benefits, and it generally applies at the state level (where there is high variability from state to state). Common examples include in-vitro fertilization, defined days of inpatient mental health or substance abuse treatment, and other special condition treatments. Self-funded plans are exempt from mandated benefits under ERISA.

Master group contract—The actual contract between a health plan and a group that purchases coverage. The master group contract provides specific terms of coverage, rights, and responsibilities of both parties.

Maximum out-of-pocket cost—The largest amount of money a member will ever need to pay for covered services during a contract year. The maximum out-of-pocket cost includes deductibles and coinsurance. Once this limit is reached, the health plan pays for all services up to the maximum level of coverage. Applies mostly to non-HMO plans such as indemnity plans, PPOs, and POS plans.

MCE—Medical care evaluation. A component of a quality assurance program that looks at the process of medical care.

MCO—Managed care organization. A generic term applied to a managed care plan. Some people prefer it to the term *HMO* because it encompasses plans that do not conform exactly to the strict definition of an HMO (although that definition has itself loosened considerably). May also apply to a PPO, EPO, IDS, or OWA.

Medical loss ratio—The ratio between the cost to deliver medical care and the amount of money that was taken in by a plan. Insurance companies often have a medical loss ratio of 92 percent or more; tightly managed HMOs may have medical loss ratios of 75 percent to 85 percent, although the overhead (or administrative cost ratio) is concomitantly higher. The medical loss ratio is dependent on the amount of money brought in as well as on the cost of delivering care; thus, if the rates are too low, the ratio may be high even though the actual cost of delivering care is not really out of line.

Medical policy—Refers to the policies of a health plan regarding what will be paid for as medical benefits. Routine medical policy is linked to routine claims processing and may even be automated in the claims system; for example, the plan may only pay 50 percent of the fee of a second surgeon or may not pay for two surgical procedures done during one episode of anesthesia. This also refers to how a plan approaches payment policies for experimental or investigational care and payment for noncovered services in lieu of more expensive covered services.

Member—An individual covered under a managed care plan. May be either the subscriber or a dependent.

Member months—The total of all months for which each member was covered. For example, if a plan had 10,000 members in January and 12,000 members in February, the total member months for the year to date as of 1 March would be 22,000.

MeSH—Medical staff–hospital organization. An archaic term. See *PHO*.

MET—Multiple employer trust. See *MEWA*.

MEWA—Multiple employer welfare association. A group of employers who band together for purposes of purchasing group health insurance, often through a self-funded approach to avoid state mandates and insurance regulation. By virtue of ERISA, such entities are regulated little, if at all. Many MEWAs have enabled small employers to obtain cost-effective health coverage, but some MEWAs have not had the financial resources to withstand the risk of medical costs and have failed, leaving the members without insurance or recourse. In some states, MEWAs and METs are no longer legal.

MIS—Management information system (or service). The common term for the computer hardware and software that provides the support for managing the plan, or a department or group that administers and maintains such computer hardware and software.

Mixed model—A managed care plan that mixes two or more types of delivery systems. This has traditionally been used to describe an HMO that has both closed panel and open panel delivery systems.

MLP—Midlevel practitioner. Physician's assistants, clinical nurse practitioners, nurse midwives, and the like. Nonphysicians who deliver medical care, generally under the supervision of a physician but for less cost.

MSO—Management service organization. A form of integrated health delivery system. Sometimes similar to a service bureau, the MSO often actually purchases certain hard assets of a physician's practice and then provides services to that physician at fair market rates. MSOs are usually formed as a means to contract more effectively with managed care organizations, although their simple creation does not guarantee success. See also *service bureau*.

Multispecialty group—Just what it sounds like: a medical group made up of different specialty physicians. May or may not include primary care.

NAHMOR—National Association of HMO Regulators.

NAIC—National Association of Insurance Commissioners.

NCQA—National Committee on Quality Assurance. A not-for-profit organization that performs quality-oriented accreditation reviews of HMOs and similar types of managed care plans. The NCQA also accredits CVOs and develops HEDIS standards.

NDC—National drug code. The national classification system for identifying prescription drugs.

Network model HMO—A health plan that contracts with multiple physician groups to deliver health care to members. Generally limited to large single-specialty or multispecialty groups. Distinguished from group model plans that contract with a single medical group, IPAs that contract through an intermediary, and direct contract model plans that contract with individual physicians in the community.

Nonpar—Short for nonparticipating. Refers to a provider that does not have a contract with the health plan.

OBRA—Omnibus Budget Reconciliation Act. What Congress calls the many annual tax and budget reconciliation acts. Most of these acts contain language important to managed care, generally in the Medicare market segment.

OMC—Office of Managed Care. The latest name for the federal agency that oversees federal qualification and compliance for HMOs and eligibility for CMPs. Old names were HMOS (Health Maintenance Organization Service), OHMO (Office of Health Maintenance Organizations), OPHC (Office of Prepaid Health Care), and OPHCOO (Office of Prepaid Health Care Operations and Oversight). Once part of the Public Health Service, the OMC and most of its predecessors are now part of the HCFA. This agency could be reorganized yet again as this book is being written, so heaven only knows what its new acronym will be.

Open enrollment period—The period when an employee may change health plans; usually occurs once per year. A general rule is that most managed care plans will have around half their membership up for open enrollment in the fall for an effective date of 1 January. A special form of open enrollment is still law in some states. This yearly open enrollment requires an HMO to accept any individual applicant (i.e., one not coming in through an employer group) for coverage, regardless of health status. Such special open enrollments usually occur for 1 month each year. Many Blue Cross/Blue Shield plans have similar open enrollments for indemnity products.

Open panel HMO—A managed care plan that contracts (either directly or indirectly) with private physicians to deliver care in their own offices. Examples include direct contract HMOs and IPAs.

OPL—Other party liability. See *COB*.

OPM—Office of Personnel Management. The federal agency that administers FEHBP. This is the agency with which a managed care plan contracts to provide coverage for federal employees.

Outlier—Something that is well outside an expected range. May refer to a provider who is using medical resources at a much higher rate than his or her peers, or to a case in a hospital that is far more expensive than anticipated, or in fact to anything at all that is significantly more or less than expected.

OWA—Other weird arrangement. A general acronym that applies to any new and bizarre managed care plan that has thought up a new twist.

Package pricing—Also referred to as bundled pricing. An MCO pays an organization a single fee for all inpatient, outpatient, and professional expenses associated with a procedure, including preadmission and postdischarge care. Common procedures that use this form of pricing include cardiac bypass surgery and transplants.

Par provider—Shorthand term for participating provider (i.e., one who has signed an agreement with a plan to provide services). May apply to professional or institutional providers.

PAS norms—The common term for Professional Activity Study results of the Commission on Professional and Hospital Activities. Broken out by region; the western region has the lowest average LOS, so that it tends to be used most often to set an estimated LOS. Available as *LOS: Length of Stay by Diagnosis*, published by CPHA Publications, Ann Arbor, Michigan.

Pay and pursue—A term in OPL that refers to a plan paying for a benefit first, then pursuing another source of payment (e.g., from another plan). Also referred to as "pay and chase." See also *Pursue and pay*.

PCCM—Primary care case manager. This acronym is used in Medicaid managed care programs and refers to the state designating PCPs as case managers to function as gatekeepers, but reimbursing those PCPs using traditional Medicaid fee for service as well as paying them a nominal management fee, such as $2 to $5 PMPM.

PCP—Primary care physician. Generally applies to internists, pediatricians, family physicians, and general practitioners and occasionally to obstetrician/gynecologists.

Per diem reimbursement—Reimbursement of an institution, usually a hospital, based on a set rate per day rather than on charges. Per diem reimbursement can be varied by service (e.g., medical–surgical, obstetrics, mental health, and intensive care) or can be uniform regardless of intensity of services.

PHO—Physician–hospital organization. These are legal (or perhaps informal) organizations that bond hospitals and their attending medical staff. Frequently developed for the purpose of contracting with managed care plans. A PHO may be open to any member of the staff who applies, or it may be closed to staff members who fail to qualify (or who are part of an already overrepresented specialty).

PMG—Primary medical group. A group practice made up of primary care physicians, although some may have obstetrician/gynecologists as well.

PMPM—Per member per month. Specifically applies to a revenue or cost for each enrolled member each month.

PMPY— Per member per year. The same as PMPM, but based on a year.

POD—Pool of doctors. This refers to the plan grouping physicians into units smaller than the entire panel but larger than individual practices. Typical PODs have between 10 and 30 physicians. Often used for performance measurement and compensation. The POD is often not a real legal entity but rather a grouping. Not to be confused with the pod people from *Invasion of the Body Snatchers*.

POS—Point of service. A plan where members do not have to choose how to receive services until they need them. The most common use of the term applies to a plan that enrolls each member in both an HMO (or HMO-like) system and an indemnity plan. Occasionally referred to as an HMO swingout plan, an out-of-plan benefits rider to an HMO, or a primary care PPO. These plans provide a difference in benefits (e.g., 100 percent coverage rather than 70 percent) depending on whether the member chooses to use the plan (including its providers and in compliance with the authorization system) or to go outside the plan for services. Dual choice refers to an HMO-like plan with an indemnity plan, and triple choice refers to the addition of a PPO to the dual choice. An archaic but still valid definition applies to a simple PPO where members receive coverage at a greater level if they use preferred providers (albeit without a gatekeeper system) than if they choose not to do so.

PPA—Preferred provider arrangement. Same as a PPO but sometimes used to refer to a somewhat looser type of plan in which the payer (i.e., the employer) makes the arrangement rather than the providers. Archaic term.

PPM—Physician practice management company. An organization that manages physicians' practices and in most cases either owns the practices outright or has rights to purchase them in the future. PPMs concentrate only on physicians, not on hospitals, although some PPMs have also branched into joint ventures with hospitals and insurers. Many PPMs are publicly traded.

PPO—Preferred provider organization. A plan that contracts with independent providers at a discount for services. The panel is limited in size and usually has some type of utilization review system associated with it. A PPO may be risk bearing, like an insurance company, or non–risk bearing, like a physician-sponsored PPO that markets itself to insurance companies or self-insured companies via an access fee.

PPS—Prospective payment system. A generic term applied to a reimbursement system that pays prospectively rather than on the basis of charges. Generally it is used only to refer to hospital reimbursement and is applied only to DRGs, but it may encompass other methodologies as well.

Precertification—Also known as preadmission certification, preadmission review, and precert. The process of obtaining certification or authorization from the health plan for routine hospital admissions (inpatient or outpatient). Often involves appropriateness review against criteria and assignment of length of stay. Failure to obtain precertification often results in a financial penalty to either the provider or the subscriber.

Preexisting condition—A medical condition for which a member has received treatment during a specified period of time before becoming covered under a health plan. May have an effect on whether treatments for that condition will be covered under certain types of health plans.

Private inurement—What happens when a not-for-profit business operates in such a way as to provide more than incidental financial gain to a private individual; for example, if a not-for-profit hospital pays too much money for a physician's practice or fails to charge fair market rates for services provided to a physician. The IRS frowns heavily on this.

PRO—Peer review organization. An organization charged with reviewing quality and cost for Medicare. Established under TEFRA. Generally operates at the state level.

Prospective review—Reviewing the need for medical care before the care is rendered. See also *precertification.*

PSA—Professional services agreement. A contract between a physician or medical group and an IDS or MCO for the provision of medical services.

PSN—Provider-sponsored network; occasionally the acronym stands for provider–service network. Also referred to as a PSO (provider-sponsored organization). A network developed by providers, whether as a vertically integrated IDS with both physicians and hospitals or as a physician-only network. Formed for the purpose of direct contracting with employers and government agencies. A PSN may even end up being an HMO, but its origins are with sponsoring providers rather than nonproviders.

PSO—See *PSN.*

PTMPY—Per thousand members per year. A common way of reporting utilization. The most common example is hospital utilization, expressed as days per thousand members per year.

Pursue and pay—A term used in OPL that refers to a plan not paying for a benefit until alternate sources of payment (e.g., another plan) have been pursued. Also referred to as "chase and pay." See also *Pay and pursue*.

QA or QM—Quality assurance (older term) or quality management (newer term).

Rate—The amount of money that a group or individual must pay to the health plan for coverage. Usually a monthly fee. Rating refers to the health plan developing those rates.

RBRVS—Resource-based relative value scale. This is a relative value scale developed for the HCFA for use by Medicare. The RBRVS assigns relative values to each CPT code for services on the basis of the resources related to the procedure rather than simply on the basis of historical trends. The practical effect has been to lower reimbursement for procedural services (e.g., cardiac surgery) and to raise reimbursement for cognitive services (e.g., office visits).

Reinsurance—Insurance purchased by a health plan to protect it against extremely high-cost cases. See also *stop loss*.

Reserves—The amount of money that a health plan puts aside to cover health care costs. May apply to anticipated costs, such as IBNRs, or to money that the plan does not expect to have to use to pay for current medical claims but keeps as a cushion against future adverse health care costs.

Retrospective review—Reviewing health care costs after the care has been rendered. There are several forms of retrospective review. One form looks at individual claims for medical necessity, billing errors, or fraud. Another form looks at patterns of costs rather than individual cases.

Risk contract—Also known as a Medicare risk contract. A contract between an HMO or CMP and the HCFA to provide services to Medicare beneficiaries under which the health plan receives a fixed monthly payment for enrolled Medicare members and then must provide all services on an at-risk basis.

Risk management—Management activities aimed at lowering an organization's legal and financial exposures, especially to lawsuits.

SCP—Specialty care physician. A physician who is not a PCP.

Second opinion—An opinion obtained from another physician regarding the necessity for a treatment that has been recommended by another physician. May be required by some health plans for certain high-costs cases, such as cardiac surgery.

Self-insured or self-funded plan—A health plan where the risk for medical cost is assumed by the company rather than an insurance company or managed care plan. Under ERISA, self-funded plans are exempt from state laws and regulations, such as premium taxes and mandatory benefits. Self-funded plans often contract with insurance companies or third party administrators to administer the benefits. See also *ASO*.

Sentinel effect—The phenomenon that, when it is known that behavior is being observed, that behavior changes, often in the direction the observer is looking for. Applies to the fact that utilization management systems and profiling systems often lead to reductions in utilization before much intervention even takes place simply because the providers know that someone is watching.

Service area—The geographic area in which an HMO provides access to primary care. The service area is usually specifically designated by the regulators (state or federal), and the HMO is prohibited from marketing outside the service area. May be defined by county or by ZIP code. It is possible for an HMO to have more than one service area and for the service areas to be either contiguous (i.e., they actually border each other) or noncontiguous (i.e., there is a geographic gap between the service areas).

Service bureau—A weak form of integrated delivery system in which a hospital (or other organization) provides services to a physician's practice in return for a fair market price. May also try to negotiate with managed care plans, but generally is not considered an effective negotiating mechanism.

Service plan—A health insurance plan that has direct contracts with providers but is not necessarily a managed care plan. The archetypal service plans are Blue Cross/Blue Shield plans. The contract applies to direct billing of the plan by providers (rather than billing of the member), a provision for direct payment of the provider (rather than reimbursement of the member), a requirement that the provider accept the plan's determination of UCR and not balance bill the member in excess of that amount, and a range of other terms. May or may not address issues of utilization and quality.

Shadow pricing—The practice of setting premium rates at a level just below the competition's rates whether or not those rates can be justified. In other words, the premium rates could actually be lower, but to maximize profit the rates are raised to a level that will remain attractive but result in greater revenue. This practice is generally considered unethical and, in the case of community rating, possibly illegal.

SHMO—Social health maintenance organization. An HMO that goes beyond the medical care needs of its membership to include their social needs as well. A relatively rare form of HMO.

Shoe box effect—When an indemnity type benefits plan has a deductible, there may be beneficiaries who save up their receipts to file for reimbursement at a later time (i.e., they save them in a shoe box). Those receipts then get lost, or the beneficiary never sends them in, so that the insurance company never has to pay.

Single point of entry—A relatively new term that means that an individual uses the same system to access both group health medical benefits and benefits for work-related medical conditions.

SMG—Specialty medical group. A medical group made up predominantly of specialty physicians. May be a single-specialty group or a multispecialty group.

Specialty network manager—A term used to describe a single specialist (or perhaps a specialist organization) that accepts capitation to manage a single specialty. Specialty services are supplied by many different specialty physicians, but the network manager has the responsibility for managing access and cost and is at economic risk. A relatively uncommon model as this book is being written.

Staff model HMO—An HMO that employs providers directly, and those providers see members in the HMO's own facilities. A form of closed panel HMO. A different use of this term is sometimes applied to vertically integrated health care delivery systems that employ physicians but in which the system is not licensed as an HMO.

Statistical claim—Another term for an encounter when the data is entered by an MCO's claims department but no FFS payment is made. Occurs in a capitated environment.

Stop loss—A form of reinsurance that provides protection for medical expenses above a certain limit, generally on a year-by-year basis. This may apply to an entire health plan or to any single component. For example, the health plan may have stop-loss reinsurance for cases that exceed $100,000. After a case hits $100,000, the plan receives 80 percent of expenses in excess of $100,000 back from the reinsurance company for the rest of the year. Another example would be the plan providing a stop loss to participating physicians for referral expenses greater than $2,500. When a case exceeds that amount in a single year, the plan no longer deducts those costs from the physician's referral pool for the remainder of the year.

Subacute care facility—A health facility that is a step down from an acute care hospital. May be a nursing home or a facility that provides medical care but not surgical or emergency care.

Subrogation—The contractual right of a health plan to recover payments made to a member for health care costs after that member has received such payment for damages in a legal action.

Subscriber—The individual or member who has health plan coverage by virtue of being eligible on his or her own behalf rather than as a dependent.

Sutton's law—"Go where the money is!" Attributed to the Depression era bank robber Willy Sutton, who, when asked why he robbed banks, replied "That's where the money is." Sutton apparently denied ever having made that statement. In any event, it is a good law to use when determining what needs attention in a managed care plan.

TAT—Turnaround time. The amount of time it takes a health plan to process and pay a claim from the time it arrives.

TEFRA—Tax Equity and Fiscal Responsibility Act. One key provision of this act prohibits employers and health plans from requiring full-time employees between the ages of 65 and 69 to use Medicare rather than the group health plan. Another key provision codifies Medicare risk contracts for HMOs and CMPs.

Termination date—The day that health plan coverage is no longer in effect.

Time loss management—The application of managed care techniques to workers' compensation treatments for injuries or illnesses to reduce the amount of time lost on the job by the affected employee.

Total capitation—The term used when an organization receives capitation for all medical services, including institutional and professional. The more common term is global capitation.

TPA—Third party administrator. A firm that performs administrative functions (e.g., claims processing, membership, and the like) for a self-funded plan or a start-up managed care plan. See also *ASO*.

TPL—Third party liability. Also called OPL. See *COB*.

Triage—The origins of this term are grizzly: the process of sorting out wounded soldiers into those who need treatment immediately, those who can wait, and those who are too severely injured to try to save. In health plans, this refers to the process of sorting out requests for services by members into those who need to be seen right away, those who can wait a little while, and those whose problems can be handled with advice over the phone.

Triple option—The offering of an HMO, a PPO, and a traditional insurance plan by one carrier.

Twenty-four-hour care—An ill-defined term that essentially means that health care is provided 24 hours per day regardless of the financing mechanism. Applies primarily to the convergence of group health, workers' compensation, and industrial health all under managed care.

UB-92—The common claim form used by hospitals to bill for services. Some managed care plans demand greater detail than is available on the UB-92, requiring hospitals to send additional itemized bills.

UCR—Usual, customary, or reasonable. A method of profiling prevailing fees in an area and reimbursing providers on the basis of that profile. One common technology is to average all fees and choose the 80th or 90th percentile, although a plan may use other technologies to determine what is reasonable. Sometimes this term is used synonymously with a fee allowance schedule when that schedule is set relatively high.

Unbundling—The practice of a provider billing for multiple components of service that were previously included in a single fee. For example, if dressings and instruments were included in a fee for a minor procedure, the fee for the procedure remains the same, but there are now additional charges for the dressings and instruments.

Underwriting—In one definition, this refers to bearing the risk for something (e.g., a policy is underwritten by an insurance company). In another definition, this refers to the analysis of a group that is done to determine rates and benefits or to determine whether the group should be offered coverage at all. A related definition refers to health screening each individual applicant for insurance and refusing to provide coverage for preexisting conditions.

Upcoding—The practice of a provider billing for a procedure that pays better than the service actually performed. For example, an office visit that would normally be reimbursed at $45 is coded as one that is reimbursed at $53.

URAC—Utilization Review Accreditation Commission. A not-for-profit organization that performs reviews of external utilization review agencies (freestanding companies, utilization management departments of insurance companies, or utilization management departments of managed care plans). Its sole focus is managed indemnity plans and PPOs, not HMOs or similar types of plans. States often require certification by URAC for a utilization management organization to operate.

URO—Utilization review organization. A freestanding organization that does nothing but utilization review, usually on a remote basis using the telephone and paper correspondence. It may be independent or part of another company, such as an insurance company that sells utilization review services on a standalone basis.

Wholesale HMO—A term occasionally used when a licensed HMO does not market itself directly, but rather contracts with another licensed HMO and accepts capitation in return. This most commonly occurs when an IDS wants to accept global capitation from an HMO, and in turn capitate other providers, since many states will only allow an HMO to capitate providers. Therefore, the IDS obtains an HMO license, but does not go directly to market to the public, and thus does not disrupt existing relationships with other MCOs.

Workers' compensation—A form of social insurance provided through property–casualty insurers. Workers' compensation provides medical benefits and replacement of lost wages that result from injuries or illnesses that arise from the workplace; in turn, the employee cannot normally sue the employer unless true negligence exists. Workers' compensation has undergone dramatic increases in cost as group health has shifted into managed care, resulting in workers' compensation carriers adopting managed care approaches. Workers' compensation is often heavily regulated under state laws that are significantly different from those used for group health insurance and is often the subject of intense negotiation between management and organized labor. See also *time loss management and twenty-four-hour care*.

Wraparound plan—Commonly used to refer to insurance or health plan coverage for copays and deductibles that are not covered under a member's base plan. This is often used for Medicare.

Zero down—The practice of a medical group or provider system distributing all the capital surplus in a health plan or group to the members of the group rather than retaining any capital or reinvesting it in the group or plan.

Index

A

About the Editor

Peter R. Kongstvedt, MD, FACP, is a partner in the Washington, D.C. office of Ernst & Young LLP, where he plays a leadership role in the firm's managed care practice. He is responsible for both leading and assisting consulting engagements in managed care strategy and operations, as well as numerous other projects for the firm. He is a frequent lecturer and writer in managed health care, and functions in a thought leadership role.

Dr. Kongstvedt has extensive experience in managed care, particularly in the HMO industry. He has served as Chief Executive Officer of several large health maintenance organizations, as Chief Operating Officer of a large insurer and managed care company, as a regional officer of a large insurer, and many other operating positions in the managed health care industry. In addition, he has served on a number of state and national level health care policy and strategy committees and is the editor and principal author of prior and current editions of *The Managed Health Care Handbook*, now in its third edition, and its academic version, *The Essentials of Managed Health Care*, as well as contributing numerous articles and chapters in other books. He also serves on the editorial board of many publications in the field.

Dr. Kongstvedt is a board-certified internist, currently licensed in five states. He received his undergraduate and medical degrees from the University of Wisconsin. He is a fellow of the American College of Physicians and a member of a number of professional societies.